# GROWTH IN
# AGREEMENT III

# GROWTH IN AGREEMENT III

*International Dialogue*
*Texts and Agreed Statements,*
*1998 - 2005*

Edited by
Jeffrey Gros, FSC
Thomas F. Best
Lorelei F. Fuchs, SA

**WCC Publications, Geneva**
**William B. Eerdmans Publishing Company**
**Grand Rapids, Michigan / Cambridge, U.K.**

Faith and Order Paper No. 204

Published 2007
in Switzerland by
World Council of Churches
150 route de Ferney, P.O. Box 2100
1211 Geneva 2, Switzerland
www.oikoumene.org

and in the United States of America by
Wm. B. Eerdmans Publishing Co.
2140 Oak Industrial Drive N.E.,
Grand Rapids, Michigan 49505 /
P.O. Box 163, Cambridge CB3 9PU U.K.
www.eerdmans.com


11  10  09  08  07      5  4  3  2  1

WCC ISBN 978-2-8254-1511-5
Eerdmans ISBN 978-0-8028-6229-7

Cover design: Rob Lucas and Marie-Arnaud Snakkers

Printed in France

# Table of Contents

*International Anglican-Roman Catholic Commission for Unity and Mission*

**Part E**

XXI. WORLD COUNCIL OF CHURCHES

# Introduction

## The search for visible unity: complementary approaches

### The multilateral discussions: an essential framework

In their response to Christ's prayer that all might be one, the Christian churches have produced a rich array of agreements and common statements on the threshold of the third millennium. All the texts in this volume serve, in one way or another, the reconciliation of the churches on their pilgrimage towards deeper communion with Christ and with one another.

For those churches which see the full, visible unity of the church as a biblical mandate, the multilateral dialogues conducted under the auspices of World Council of Churches' Faith and Order commission have provided a comprehensive venue for discerning the nature and shape of the unity we seek. As early as 1961 the member churches of the World Council of Churches were able to say together:

> We believe that the unity which is both God's will and his gift to his church is being made visible as all in each place who are baptized into Jesus Christ and confess him as Lord and Saviour are brought by the Holy Spirit into one fully committed fellowship, holding the one apostolic faith, preaching the one gospel, breaking the one bread, joining in common prayer, and having a corporate life reaching out in witness and service to all and who at the same time are united with the whole Christian fellowship in all places and all ages in such wise that ministry and members are accepted by all, and that all can act and speak together as occasion requires for the task to which God calls his people. [1]

In subsequent assemblies of the World Council of Churches, its members have been able to speak more specifically about the nature of that unity: at Uppsala in 1968 the notion of catholicity was advanced as a quality which, in its fullness, would enable the church to be a prophetic sign of the kingdom; [2] at Nairobi in 1975 as a conciliar fellowship of local churches "which are themselves truly united in each place", and linked worldwide through conciliar forms of decision-making; [3] at Vancouver in 1983 in terms of a "eucharistic vision", marked also by agreement on the apostolic faith, a mutual recognition of baptism, eucharist and ministry, and some form of common ways of decision-making and teaching authoritatively; [4] and at Canberra in 1991 as a communion (*koinonia*) characterized by common confession of the apostolic faith, common sacramental life and mutually recognized and reconciled ministries, with bonds of common witness and service to the world. [5]

Since 1961 the Catholic Church has participated in these assemblies through sending observers, and since 1969 the commission has engaged as a full member in the life and work of the Faith and Order commission even as the commission has developed the statements later approved by the various assemblies. In this sense these expressions of the shape of visible unity embody the commitments of the Catholic Church as well as those of the Protestant, Anglican and Orthodox member churches of the World Council of Churches.

Included in this volume is another text in this series of assembly "unity statements". This text, "Called To Be the One Church", was adopted by WCC member churches at their assembly held in Porto Alegre, Brazil, in February 2006. It aims to clarify the present situation in our common quest for unity, and to encourage the churches to recommit themselves to the pilgrimage towards full visible unity.

8. All who have been baptized into Christ are united with Christ in his body: "Therefore we have been buried with him by *baptism* into death, so that, just as Christ was raised from the dead by the glory of the Father, so we too might walk in newness of life" (Rom. 6:4). In baptism, the Spirit confers Christ's holiness upon Christ's members. Baptism into union with Christ calls churches to be open and honest with one another, even when doing so is difficult: "But speaking the truth in love, we must grow up in every way into him who is the head, into Christ" (Eph. 4:15). Baptism bestows upon the churches both the freedom and the responsibility to journey towards common proclamation of the word, confession of the one faith, celebration of one eucharist, and full sharing in one ministry. There are some who do not observe the rite of baptism in water but share in the spiritual experience of life in Christ.[6]

9. Our common belonging to Christ through baptism in the name of the Father and of the Son and of the Holy Spirit enables and calls churches to walk together, even when they are in disagreement. We affirm that there is one baptism, just as there is one body and one Spirit, one hope of our calling, one Lord, one faith, one God and Father of us all (cf. Eph. 4:4-6). In God's grace, baptism manifests the reality that *we belong to one another*, even though some churches are not yet able to recognize others as church in the full sense of the word. We recall the words of the Toronto Statement, in which the member churches of the WCC affirm that "the membership of the church of Christ is more inclusive than the membership of their own church body. They seek, therefore, to enter into living contact with those outside their own ranks who confess the Lordship of Christ."[7]

15. Our churches *journey together* in conversation and common action, confident that the Risen Christ will continue to disclose himself as he did in the breaking of bread at Emmaus, and that he will unveil the deeper meaning of fellowship and communion (Luke 24:13-35). Noting the progress made in the ecumenical movement, we encourage our churches to continue on this arduous yet joyous path, trusting in God the Father, Son and Holy Spirit, whose grace transforms our struggles for unity into the fruits of communion.[8]

The Porto Alegre ecclesiology statement concludes with questions, directed to several areas of the faith and life of the churches, which are aimed at "testing" the degree of mutual recognition *actually experienced* among them today. The responses to these questions will provide a solid – and realistic – basis for further, more detailed work on issues which continue to be divisive. Multilateral study documents, such as the recent Faith and Order text *The Nature and Mission of the Church*,[9] will also be helpful in this process.

## *The bilateral discussions: an essential complement*

Concrete steps towards union, or towards relationships of "full communion", must be taken by the churches themselves. Thus the multilateral dialogues find their necessary complement in bilateral dialogues, focused discussions among pairs of churches or traditions. A rich harvest of such bilateral dialogues has provided the basis on which concrete steps towards full, visible communion can be taken. Most of the texts in this volume are of this bilateral character. For the most part they give the latest fruits of long-standing, continuing dialogues; historical introductions for these have been provided in the earlier volumes of this series, *Growth in Agreement*[10] and *Growth in Agreement II.*[11]

Such texts issue from Catholic, Protestant, Orthodox and Anglican churches which share a common quest for the visible unity of the Christian church, however understood. There are other traditions, springing mainly from the Reformation in the West, which have understood this unity rather in spiritual terms or have not seen the call for unity so clearly in their reading of scripture.

For many within these churches, however, there is a clear biblical mandate for reconciliation with fellow Christians and a clear evangelical need for common Christian witness in the world. Increasingly these churches and movements have begun to enter into dialogue with other Christians. Some of the texts from these dialogues are indeed "historic" and will be noted as such in the texts themselves, and in the historical section below. Texts from these conversations – not not oriented towards full communion, but outlining a basis for mutual understanding among divided Christians – are also included.

## The present collection

### *Types of texts*

Each of the texts in this collection is designed to serve a specific reconciling purpose. Some are authoritative common declarations between leaders or bodies authorized to speak authoritatively for their churches. These may be declarations of commitment and good will. Others witness to the resolution of doctrinal issues which have divided the two churches for centuries. Each text has been reproduced together with its introductory material and the list of participants, when available.

Most of the texts are the result of bilateral dialogues between two churches, and are offered as proposals to the churches for reconciling previously church-dividing issues. These texts carry weight in proportion to the quality of the theology developed within them through the care and scholarship of the drafters. They remain before the churches for reception and evaluation. Some texts are explorations aimed at increasing mutual understanding and dispelling historical misunderstandings and stereotypes. Still others are reports of experts from a variety of traditions and offer guidelines, theological proposals or common analyses which are being made available as resources to the churches and ecumenical groups.

The texts have been gathered into categories similar (but not identical) to those used in earlier volumes of the *Growth in Agreement* series.

- Part A includes dialogues and common declarations with Eastern and Oriental Orthodox participation.
- Part B includes dialogues, common declarations, and an ecumenical eucharistic guideline, with Roman Catholic participation.
- Part C includes dialogues between various Reformation churches.
- Part D includes reports from the Joint Working Group between the Roman Catholic Church and the World Council of Churches.
- Part E includes a text from World Council of Churches.

## Historical notes to particular texts

All the texts in Part A, and most of those in Part B, are continuations of dialogues which have been introduced in earlier volumes of this series.

Two texts in Part B (16 and 17), from the International Anglican-Roman Catholic Commission for Unity and Mission, are not the results of dialogues themselves but rather commitments of the two communions to begin acting together, to build on their dialogues and to increase their levels of lived communion in their local situations around the world.

Text 28 in Part B, on Assyrian and Chaldean Catholic sacramental sharing, is an important ecumenical contribution even though it is a statement of one church, the Catholic Church. This is because, based on common scholarship and dialogue, it resolves an issue which has endured for centuries, namely the Catholic evaluation of a particular and unique eucharistic text which does not explicitly include the words of institution.

The Catholic texts produced with the Mennonites (29) and with the World Evangelical Fellowship (30) represent beginnings of new stages of dialogue. The texts themselves provide historical notes as to the genesis, purpose and authority of these dialogues.

In Part C the three texts from Reformed dialogues are of distinct interest. The Adventists (31) are a worldwide communion of Christians who are often active in local ecumenical communities but do not yet have a long tradition of dialogue or ecumenical engagement. Therefore this text reflects an important beginning of dialogue, in this case with the Reformed churches.

In post-colonial Africa the relatively new African Instituted churches are important communities within the Christian family. Some of these churches are members of the World Council of Churches and others are not. However, this dialogue (texts 32 and 33) also begins a process of public conversation with the Reformed family of churches, a conversation which will become increasingly important as the ecumenical pilgrimage continues.

Two significant texts reflect Baptist involvement, 34 with the Anglicans and 36 with the Mennonites. Given the character of Baptist ecclesiology these are not oriented towards establishing full communion, but rather towards gaining mutual understanding. The Baptist-Anglican dialogue, a series of case studies, has a character especially appropriate to the focus on the local church. This long text has been excerpted here to provide the basic content of the dialogue without all the descriptive detail of the case studies.

The Pentecostal community is one of the largest in the world; it does not have a single ecclesiastical centre. Earlier volumes in this series have documented Pentecostal dialogues with Roman Catholics, but the text in this volume (38) is the first developed with Protestant churches, namely those represented in the World Alliance of Reformed Churches.

Three texts in Part C, and one in Part D, demonstrate both the progress of ecumenical reconciliation and the challenge of contextualizing the unity that we are seeking. The churches of the Reformation developed initially in national centres, eventually spreading by evangelization through the entire globe as did, in their own ways, the Catholic and Orthodox churches. The ecumenical movement has seen from early on that a united church will include "all in each place".[12] Therefore the "younger churches" of Asia, Africa and Latin America will develop – as did those of Europe, the Middle East and North America – their own theological character and ecclesial ethos, along with their own internal tensions and pathways towards reconciliation.

With the international success of some of the multilateral and bilateral dialogues, and with churches in different parts of the world moving into new relationships with one another, consultations have been necessary which focus on the distinct issues arising in particular regional and national contexts, and how the various contexts relate to one another.

Lutheran, Anglican, Reformed and Baptist Christian world communions have sponsored dialogues contributing particularly to this process of listening and coordination between the international and the regional and local church contexts, in all their variety. Texts from these dialogues are included here as numbers 34, 35 and 37 in Part C. The Joint Working Group between the Roman Catholic Church and the World Council of Churches has also provided a survey and comparative text, number 40 in Part D, which addresses in its own way the relation between international, regional and local engagement and dialogues. All these texts provide rich ecclesiological reflection, and provide the background for a new stage in the dialogue process.

Part E includes (43) the ecclesiology text from the World Council of Churches' ninth assembly in Porto Alegre, Brazil. Standing in the tradition of assembly unity statements, this text is a call to the churches to renew their commitment to the search for visible unity, and to continue their dialogue on issues which yet divide them. Adopting the text by full consensus WCC member churches committed themselves to respond, by the time of the next assembly, to a series of questions which probe the degree of effective mutual recognition among them.

## Conclusion

The texts gathered in this volume clearly demonstrate the impact of the common ecumenical journey. They show the influence of classic World Council of Churches Faith and Order texts such as "Scripture, Tradition and traditions"[13] and *Baptism, Eucharist and Ministry*,[14] as well as the later ecclesiology texts cited above. They show the fruitful interaction and mutual impact of the bilateral discussions among themselves. Thematically they show the centrality in ecumenical dialogue of the discussion on the doctrine of the church, and the use of a theology of communion/*koinonia* in taking forward the churches' journey towards unity in Christ.

We offer these texts as a documentation of the agreements and common statements made by the churches in recent years, and as an inspiration and resource for further work. May they contribute to the churches' quest to make the unity given them in Christ both visible and more effective in witness and service in the world.

*   *   *

We extend our thanks to Alan Falconer for his work in collecting many of the texts appearing in this volume, and to Joan Cambitsis for her careful and tireless work in preparing the texts for publication.

---

Analogous collections of agreed dialogue texts and common declarations exist in other languages:

Italian: *Enchiridion Oecumenicum: Documenti Del Dialogo Teologico Interconfessionale, 7, Dialoghi Internazionali 1995-2006*, eds Giovanni Cereti and James F. Puglisi, Bologna, Edizioni Dehoniane, 2006.

German: *Dokumente wachsender Übereinstimmung: Sämtliche Berichte und Konsenstexte interkonfessioneller Gespräche auf Weltebene*, Band III, 1990-2001, eds Harding Meyer, Damaskinos Papandreou, Hans Jörg Urban and Lukas Vischer, Paderborn, Bonifatius Druck Buch Verlag, and Frankfurt am Main, Otto Lembeck, 2003.

French: *Accords et dialogues oecuméniques, bilateraux/multilateraux, français/européens/internationaux*, eds André Birmelé and Jacques Terme, Paris, Les Bergers et les Mages, 1995.

Spanish: *Enchiridion Oecumenicum: Relaciones y Documentos de los Diálogos Interconfesionales de la Iglesia Católica y Otras Iglesias Cristianas y Declaraciones de sus Autoridades 1975/84-1991, Con Anexos de Diálogos Locales y Documentación complementaria des Diálogo Teológico Interconfesional*, 2, ed. Adolfo Gonzalez Montes, Salamanca, Centro de Estudios Orientales y Ecuménicos "Juan XXIII", Universidad Pontificia de Salamanca, 1993.

---

NOTES

[1] "Report of Section: Unity", *The New Delhi Report*, ed. W. A. Visser 't Hooft, London, SCM, 1962, §2, p.116.

[2] "The Holy Spirit and the Catholicity of the Church", in *The Uppsala Report*, ed. Norman Goodall, WCC, 1968, §§6-11, pp.11-15.

[3] "Report of Section II: What Unity Requires", in *Breaking Barriers, Nairobi 1975: Official Report, Fifth Assembly, World Council of Churches*, ed. David M. Paton, London, SPCK, and WCC, 1976, §3, p.60.

[4] "Taking Steps Towards Unity", in *Gathered for Life: Official Report, Sixth Assembly, World Council of Churches*, ed. David Gill, WCC, and Grand Rapids MI, Eerdmans, 1983, I.4, p.44 and II.5-9, p.45.

[5] "The Unity of the Church as Koinonia: Gift and Calling" [The "Canberra Statement"], in *Signs of the Spirit: Official Report, Seventh Assembly, World Council of Churches*, ed. Michael Kinnamon, WCC Publications, Grand Rapids MI, Eerdmans, 1991, 2.1, p.173.

6 Cf. "The Unity of the Church as Koinonia: Gift and Calling", in *Signs of the Spirit*, 3.2, p.174.

7 "Statement on 'The Church, the Churches and the World Council of Churches': The Ecclesiological Significance of the World Council of Churches" [The "Toronto Statement"], in W.A. Visser 't Hooft, *The Genesis and Formation of the World Council of Churches*, WCC, 1982, IV.3, p.117.

8 "Called To Be the One Church" [The Porto Alegre Ecclesiology Text], in *The Ecumenical Review*, vol. 58, nos. 1-2, Jan.-April 2006, pp.114-15,117.

9 Faith and Order Paper No. 198, WCC Publications, 2005, §5, p.10.

10 *Growth in Agreement: Reports and Agreed Statements of Ecumenical Conversations on a World Level*, Ecumenical Documents II, Faith and Order Paper no. 108, eds Harding Meyer and Lukas Vischer, New York/Ramsey, Paulist, and WCC, 1984, pp.1-11, 36, 40, 278, 390-91.

11 *Growth in Agreement II: Reports and Agreed Statements of Ecumenical Conversations on a World Level, 1982-1998*, Faith and Order Paper no. 187, eds Jeffrey Gros, FSC, Harding Meyer and William G. Rusch, WCC Publications and Grand Rapids MI, Eerdmans, 2000, pp.190,191-93,194-99 respectively.

12 The New Delhi WCC assembly unity statement, cf. endnote 1.

13 See the "Report from Section II", *The Fourth World Conference on Faith and Order: Montreal 1963*, eds P. C. Rodger and L. Vischer, Faith and Order Paper no. 42, London, SCM Press, pp.50-61.

14 Faith and Order Paper no. 111, WCC, 1982. Also published as "Baptism, Eucharist, Ministry: Report of the Faith and Order Commission, World Council of Churches, Lima, Peru, 1982", in *Growth in Agreement*, pp.465-503.

# Part A

# 1. To All Our Children, Protected by God
## A Synodal and Patriarchal Letter of the Holy See of Antioch

### Damascus, Syria, 12 November 1991

Beloved:

You must have heard of the continuous efforts for decades by our church with the sister Syrian Orthodox Church to foster a better knowledge and understanding of both churches, whether on the dogmatic or pastoral level. These attempts are nothing but a natural expression that the Orthodox churches, and especially those within the holy see of Antioch, are called to articulate the will of the Lord that all may be one, just as the Son is One with the Heavenly Father (John 10:30).

It is our duty and that of our brothers in the Syrian Orthodox Church to witness to Christ in our Eastern region where He was born, preached, suffered, was buried and rose from the dead, ascended into heaven, and sent down his holy and life-giving Spirit upon his holy apostles.

All the meetings, the fellowship, the oral and written declarations meant that we belong to one faith even though history had manifested our division more than the aspects of our unity.

All this has called upon our holy synod of Antioch to bear witness to the progress of our church in the see of Antioch towards unity that preserves for each church its authentic Oriental heritage whereby the one Antiochian church benefits from its sister church and is enriched in its traditions, literature and holy rituals.

Every endeavour and pursuit in the direction of the coming together of the two churches is based on the conviction that this orientation is from the Holy Spirit, and it will give the Eastern Orthodox image more light and radiance, that it has lacked for centuries before.

Having recognized the efforts done in the direction of unity between the two churches, and being convinced that this direction was inspired by the Holy Spirit and projects a radiant image of Eastern Christianity overshadowed during centuries, the holy synod of the church of Antioch saw the need to give a concrete expression of the close fellowship between the two churches, the Syrian Orthodox Church and the Eastern Orthodox, for the edification of their faithful.

Thus, the following decisions were taken:

1. We affirm the total and mutual respect of the spirituality, heritage and holy fathers of both churches. The integrity of both the Byzantine and Syriac liturgies is to be preserved.

2. The heritage of the fathers in both churches and their traditions as a whole should be integrated into Christian education curricula and theological studies. Exchanges of professors and students are to be enhanced.

3. Both churches shall refrain from accepting any faithful from one church into the membership of the other, irrespective of all motivations or reasons.

4. Meetings between the two churches, at the level of their synods, according to the will of the two churches, will be held whenever the need arises.

5. Every church will remain the reference and authority for its faithful, pertaining to matters of personal status (marriage, divorce, adoption, etc.).

6. If bishops of the two churches participate at a holy baptism or funeral service, the one belonging to the church of the baptized or deceased will preside. In case of a holy matrimony service, the bishop of the bridegroom's church will preside.

7. The above mentioned is not applicable to the concelebration in the divine liturgy.

8. What applies to bishops equally applies to the priests of both churches.

9. In localities where there is only one priest, from either church, he will celebrate services for the faithful of both churches, including the divine liturgy, pastoral duties and holy matrimony. He will keep an independent record for each church and transmit that of the sister church to its authorities.

10. If two priests of the two churches happen to be in a locality where there is only one church, they take turns in making use of its facilities.

11. If a bishop from one church and a priest from the sister church happen to concelebrate a service, the first will preside even when it is the priest's parish.

12. Ordinations into the holy orders are performed by the authorities of each church for its own members. It would be advisable to invite the faithful of the sister church to attend.

13. Godfathers, godmothers (in baptism) and witnesses in holy matrimony can be chosen from the members of the sister church.

14. Both churches will exchange visits and will cooperate in the various areas of social, cultural and educational work.

We ask God's help to continue strengthening our relations with the sister church, and with other churches, so that we all become one community under one Shepherd.

Patriarch Ignatios IV
of the Greek Antiochian Church

Patriarch Ignatius Zakka Iwas
of the Syrian Orthodox Church
of Antioch

# 2. Communiqué

## Joint Commission of the Theological Dialogue between the Orthodox Church and the Oriental Orthodox Churches

### Geneva, Switzerland, 1-6 November 1993

Following the mandate of their churches, the Joint Commission for the Dialogue between the Orthodox Church and the Oriental Orthodox Churches held their fourth meeting at the Orthodox Centre of the Ecumenical Patriarchate at Chambésy, Geneva, Switzerland, between 1-6 November 1993, to consider the procedure for the restoration of full communion.

The official representatives of the two Orthodox families of churches and their advisers met in an atmosphere of prayer and warm, cordial, Christian brotherly love. They experienced the gracious and generous hospitality of His Holiness Patriarch Bartholomaios I, through His Eminence Metropolitan Damaskinos of Switzerland, in the Orthodox Centre of the Ecumenical Patriarchate.

The 31 participants (see the list of participants) came from Albania, Austria, Cyprus, the Czech Republic, Egypt, Ethiopia, Finland, Greece, India, Lebanon, Poland, Romania, Russia, Switzerland, Syria, United Kingdom and USA.

The plenary meetings of the Joint Commission were co-chaired by His Eminence Metropolitan Damaskinos of Switzerland and His Eminence Metropolitan Bishoy of Damiette. His Eminence Metropolitan Damaskinos in his inaugural address explained the procedure which was to be followed and stressed that "the present meeting of the full Joint Theological Commission for the Dialogue between the Orthodox Church and the Oriental Orthodox Churches is of the utmost importance not only for evaluating correctly the truly historic theological work of our commission which has been already accomplished in our previous meetings, but also for facilitating the necessary ecclesiastical procedures for the restoration of full communion".

After the inaugural meeting each side met separately to consider papers prepared on the following subjects:

- What is the competent ecclesiastical authority from each side for the lifting of the anathemas and what are the presuppositions for the restoration of ecclesiastical communion?
- Which anathemas of which synods and persons could be lifted in accordance with the proposal of paragraph 10 of the second common statement?
- Which is the canonical procedure from each side for the lifting of the anathemas and the restoration of ecclesiastical communion?

- How could we understand and implement the restoration of ecclesiastical communion in the life of our church?
- Which are the canonical and liturgical consequences of full communion?

They produced two reports which were presented to the plenary meeting for clarifications and discussion on the third day of the proceedings. As a result of these discussions the Oriental Orthodox presented a document of response which opened the way for further discussions in the plenary. A drafting committee consisting of H.E. Metropolitan Bishoy of Damiette, H.E. Metropolitan Gregorios Yohanna Ibrahim of Aleppo, H.E. Archbishop Mesrob Krikorian from the Oriental Orthodox side and Professors Fr John Romanides, Fr George Dragas and Vlassios Phidas from the Orthodox side were appointed to prepare appropriate proposals to the two church families on lifting of anathemas from each side and restoring full communion among them.

The text of these proposals, unanimously agreed upon after discussion in plenary session, is as follows:

## Proposals for lifting of anathamas

1. In the light of our agreed statement on Christology at St Bishoy Monastery, 1989, and of our second agreed statement at Chambésy, 1990, the representatives of both church families agree that the lifting of anathemas and condemnations of the past can be consummated on the basis of their common acknowledgment of the fact that the councils and fathers previously anathematized or condemned are orthodox in their teachings. In the light of our four unofficial consultations (1964, 1967, 1970, 1971) and our three official meetings which followed on (1985, 1989, 1990), we have understood that both families have loyally maintained the authentic Orthodox christological doctrine, and the unbroken continuity of the apostolic tradition, though they may have used christological terms in different ways.

2. The lifting of the anathemas should be made unanimously and simultaneously by the heads of all the churches of both sides, through the signing of an appropriate ecclesiastical act, the content of which will include acknowledgment from each side that the other one is Orthodox in all respects.

3. The lifting of the anathemas should imply:
   a) that restoration of full communion for both sides is to be immediately implemented;
   b) that no past condemnation, synodical or personal, against each other is applicable any more;
   c) that a catalogue of diptychs of the heads of the churches should be agreed upon to be used liturgically.

4. At the same time the following practical steps should be taken:
   a) the joint sub-committee for pastoral issues should continue its very important task according to what had been agreed at the 1990 meeting of the joint commission;
   b) the co-chairmen of the joint commission should visit the heads of the churches with the view to offering fuller information on the outcome of the dialogue;
   c) a liturgical sub-committee should be appointed by both sides to examine the liturgical implications arising from the restoration of communion and to propose appropriate forms of concelebration;

d) matters relating to ecclesiastical jurisdiction should be left to be arranged by the respective authorities of the local churches according to common canonical and synodical principles;

e) the two co-chairmen of the joint commission with the two secretaries of the dialogue should make provisions for the production of appropriate literature explaining our common understanding of the Orthodox faith which has led us to overcome the divisions of the past, and also coordinating the work of the other sub-committees.

Damaskinos Papandreou  
Metropolitan of Switzerland  
Archbishop Dr Mesrob K. Krikorian

Metropolitan Bishoy of Damiette  
Prof. Vlassios Phidas

## Joint commission

### Oriental Orthodox churches

*Coptic Orthodox Church*  
Metropolitan Bishoy, Co-president  
Metropolitan of Damiette, General Secretary Holy Synod  
Bishop Serapion, Adviser  
Deacon Dr Emile Maher Ishak, Adviser, Professor at the Coptic Orthodox Theological College at Cairo  
Doctoral Cand. Joseph Moris Faltas, Assistant Co-secretary

*Syrian Orthodox Patriarchate of Antioch and All the East*  
Metropolitan Gregorios Yohanna Ibrahim of Aleppo

*Supreme Catholicosate of All Armenians, Etchmiadzin*  
Archbishop Dr Mesrob K. Krikorian, Co-secretary, Patriarchal Delegate for Central Europe and Sweden

*Catholicosate of Cilicia*  
Archbishop Aram Keshishian of Lebanon  
Archbishop Mesrob Ashdjian, Prelate of the Eastern Diocese of USA

*Malankara Orthodox Syrian Church of the East*  
Father K.M. George

*Ethiopian Orthodox Church*  
Archbishop Makarios of Axum and Tigray  
Megabe Beluy Yohannes Seife Seflassie

**Orthodox churches**

*Ecumenical Patriarchate*
Metropolitan Damaskinos Papandreou of Switzerland, Co-president
Metropolitan Chrysostomos Gerasimos Zaphiris of Peristerion, Adviser
Rev. Prof. George Dragas, Adviser, University of Durham
Prof. George Martselos, Adviser

*Greek Orthodox Patriarchate of Alexandria*
Metropolitan Petros Yakumelos of Aksum
Prof. Vlassios Phidas, Co-secretary

*Greek Orthodox Patriarchate of Antioch*
Metropolitan George Khodr of Mount Lebanon

*Russian Patriarchate*
Metropolitan Pitirim Necajev of Volokolamsk and Jurjev
Mr Nikolai Zabolotski

*Romanian Patriarchate*
Metropolitan Antonie Plamadeala of Transilvania

*Church of Cyprus*
Horepiskopos Barnabas Solomos of Salamis
Prof. Andreas Papavasiliou

*Church of Greece*
Metropolitan Meletios Kalamaras of Nikopolis and Preveza
Rev. Prof. John S. Romanides

*Church of Albania*
Rev. Jani Trebicka
Rev. Martin Ritsi

*Czechoslovakian Orthodox Church*
Rev. Protopr. Prof. Pavel Ales
Prof. Roman Juriga

*Finnish Orthodox Church*
Rev. Father Heikki Huttunen

# 3. Memorandum of Convergences
## Ecumenical Patriarchate and the Patriarchate of Ethiopia

### Addis Ababa, 21 January 1995

Following an invitation of His Holiness the Abuna Paul, Patriarch of Ethiopia, His All Holiness the Ecumenical Patriarch Bartholomew, accompanied by several metropolitans, visited the church of Ethiopia from 11 to 21 January 1995. In the course of his stay in Ethiopia, the delegation of the Ecumenical Patriarchate, under the presidency of His Holiness Bartholomew, visited monasteries and ancient churches in Addis Ababa, Bachir Dar, Lalibella, Gondar and Axoum. They were received courteously by their Excellencies Miles Zebawi, president of the republic, and Tamirat Laine, prime minister of the provisional government of Ethiopia. They also placed a wreath of flowers on the tomb of Emperor Haile-Selassie I, and the martyred Patriarch Theophilus, at the monument of the government dignitaries and emperor executed by the dictatorial regime of Mengistu.

The delegation was warmly received with fraternal sentiments that expressed the centuries-old relations of the two ancient churches, Constantinople and Ethiopia. In the course of their stay in Ethiopia the delegation of the Ecumenical Patriarchate carried on cordial discussions with the holy synod of the church of Ethiopia and an agreement on the following points was completed:

1. Concerning the decisions recently adopted by the dialogue commission between the two families of churches over their relationship, to make known and to advance the adoption and confirmation of the decisions mentioned above by the respective holy synods of our two churches.

2. Concerning the dogmatic questions and others which impede the relationship of the two churches, it was accepted that their study in depth and detail must be pursued until it is completed, having as the ultimate goal strengthening communion between these two churches.

3. Concerning the monastery of Deir Sultan in Jerusalem, His Holiness the Abuna Paul explained to the delegation of the Ecumenical Patriarchate how for thousands of years it was the property of the Patriarchate of Ethiopia and he underlined that, in contradiction to the ecumenical spirit, certain churches have tried again to sue for this historic, sacred and legitimate property.

4. The two parties decided to exchange high-level delegations on an annual basis.

5. The two parties decided to contribute to the protection of peace and, on the international level, to the harmony of the world.

|  |  |
|---|---|
| The Ecumenical Patriarch | Abuna Paul |
| Bartholomew | The Patriarch of Ethiopia |
| Archbishop of Constantinople |  |

# 4. Pastoral Agreement

## Coptic Orthodox Church and Greek Orthodox Patriarchate of Alexandria and All Africa

### Cairo, Egypt, 5 April 2001

Since the holy synods of both the Coptic Orthodox Church and the Greek Orthodox Patriarchate of Alexandria and All Africa have already accepted the outcome of the official dialogue on Christology between the Orthodox church and the Oriental Orthodox churches, including the two official agreements: the first on Christology signed in June 1989 in Egypt, and the second also on Christology and on the lifting of anathemas and restoration of full communion signed in Geneva 1990, in which it is stated that "In the light of our agreed statement on Christology..., we have now clearly understood that both families have always loyally maintained the same authentic Orthodox christological faith, and the unbroken continuity of apostolic tradition". It was agreed to have mutual recognition of the sacrament of baptism, based on what St Paul wrote, "one Lord, one faith, one baptism" (Eph. 4:5).

But since up until now we are waiting for the responses of the holy synods of some other churches in both families, the restoration of full communion is not yet reached between the two sides of the bilateral dialogue. And due to the pastoral consequences and implications caused by mixed Christian marriages between the members of the two Patriarchates of Alexandria, having the majority of their people living in the same countries, those marriages being difficult to perform in both churches at the same time or in concelebration. The result is that many sensitivities are created between the two families of the partners of such marriages. Those sensitivities which can extend even after the marriage and may affect the relation between the two communities of churches.

For those mentioned reasons, the holy synods of both Patriarchates have agreed to accept the sacrament of marriage which is conducted in either church, with the condition that it is conducted for two partners not belonging to the same Patriarchate of the other church from their origin. Both the bride and the groom should carry a valid certificate from his/her own Patriarchate that he/she has a permit of marriage and indicating the details of his/her marriage status up to date.

Each of the two Patriarchates shall also accept to perform all of its other sacraments to that new family of mixed Christian marriage.

It is agreed that the Patriarchate which shall perform the marriage shall be responsible for any marriage problems that may happen concerning this certain marriage, taking into consideration the unified marriage laws signed by the heads of churches in Egypt in the year 1999.

Each Patriarchate shall preserve its right not to give its sacraments to any persons whom she does not find fulfilling its canons according to the apostolic Tradition.

Petros VII
Pope and Patriarch of Alexandria
and All Africa

Shenouda III
Pope of Alexandria
and Patriarch of the See
of St Mark

# 5. Authority in and of the Church
## Lutheran-Orthodox Joint Commission

### Seventh Plenary, Sandbjerg, Denmark, 5-10 July 1993

## A. The ecumenical councils

1. The church's authority is grounded in God's saving revelation in Jesus Christ to which the scriptures of the Old and New Testaments and holy Tradition bear witness. Moreover the church as the body of Christ is empowered by the Holy Spirit. The joint commission in Allentown, 1985, stated,

> God's revelation in Jesus Christ is realized and actualized in the church and through the church as the body of Christ. The paschal and pentecostal mysteries instituted the church of the New Testament in which revelation is lived, proclaimed and transmitted. The Holy Spirit sustains the church's life and growth until the last day through the proclamation of the gospel in the fullness of the apostolic Tradition and its transmission from place to place and from generation to generation, not only by words but also by the whole life of the church. (§4)

2. The nature of the church's authority differs from worldly authority. Our Lord Jesus Christ said to his disciples,

> The kings of the Gentiles exercise lordship over them; and those in authority over them are called benefactors. But not so with you; rather let the greatest among you become as the youngest, and the leader as one who serves. For which is the greater, one who sits at table, or one who serves? But I am among you as one who serves. (Luke 22:25-27)

All authority in and of the church is rooted in the saving work of Christ who gave his life for us. Authority and soteriology are indivisible. Christ's authority, present in the church's mission (Matt. 28:18-20), is undergirded by the Paraclete who leads the faithful into all truth (John 14:26, 16:7-14) and through the apostles and their successors it is given to the whole church. Both Orthodox and Lutherans affirm that apostolic authority was exercised in the ecumenical councils of the church in which the bishops, through illumination and glorification brought about by the Holy Spirit, exercised responsibility. Ecumenical councils are a special gift of God to the church and are an authoritative inheritance through the ages. Through ecumenical councils the Holy Spirit has led the church to preserve and transmit the faith once delivered to the saints. They handed on the prophetic and apostolic truth, formulated it against heresies of their time and safeguarded the unity of the churches.

3. The seven ecumenical councils of the early church were assemblies of the bishops of the church from all parts of the Roman empire to clarify and express the apostolic faith. These councils are Nicea (325 AD), Constantinople I (381), Ephesus (431), Chalcedon (451), Constantinople II (553), Constantinople III (680/81) and Nicea II (787). Of the councils it was stated at Crete, 1987,

> The holy Tradition as ongoing action of the Holy Spirit in the church expresses itself in the church's whole life. The decisions of the ecumenical councils and local synods of the church, the teaching of the holy fathers and liturgical texts and rites are especially important and authoritative expressions of this manifold action of the Holy Spirit. (§8)

Ecumenical councils are the epitome of biblical theology and they summarize main themes of the holy Tradition. They are not merely of historical significance but are irreplaceable events for the church's life. Through them the apostolic faith and Tradition, brought about by the saving revelation of God in Christ, was confirmed by the consensus of the gathered representatives of the church led by the Holy Spirit.

4. The teachings of the ecumenical councils of the early church are normative for the faith and life of our churches today. The trinitarian and christological formulations of these councils are an indispensable guide for understanding God's saving work in Christ and are the foundation of all later dogmatic clarifications. The creed of Nicea/Constantinople is the best-known statement of faith from the ancient councils, and now that its original form is increasingly common in the West it is an ever more living bond between our churches. It shapes the language of prayers and blessings in our worship, and by its use the church has remained faithful to the revelation of the triune God.

5. The ecumenical councils did not only take decisions on doctrinal problems which threatened the integrity of God's revelation and the church's unity; they also issued "canones" (canons) for good order within the church. These "canones" establish a close relation between the faith once for all delivered to the saints and the necessity of ordering the church's life and structure. The "oroi" (doctrinal decrees) safeguard the teachings of the church concerning salvation; the "canones" order various aspects of the church's life. They are practical applications of the "oroi". The two belong together as aspects of the same reality. All the same, not all decisions on canonical matters have the same authority as the doctrinal decisions and their reception and use in the Orthodox and Lutheran churches differ.

6. The ecumenical councils were called together to deal with specific problems that had arisen in the churches. They were not an ongoing ecclesiastical institution regularly convoked but ad hoc gatherings which met only as occasion required. The ecumenical councils were charismatic events. The statements of the bishops illuminated by the Holy Spirit went through a process of reception in the years that followed. Reception has taken place in the whole range of the church's life, worship, catechesis and service even when those councils are not explicitly named. Reception also took place through subsequent theological discussions which clarified the meaning of the terms and expressions formulated at prior councils. A notable example is the theological discussion after Nicea which culminated in the decrees and creed of the first council of Constantinople in 381.

7. As Lutherans and Orthodox we affirm that the teachings of the ecumenical councils are authoritative for our churches. The ecumenical councils maintain the integrity of the teaching of the undivided church concerning the saving, illuminating/justifying and

glorifying acts of God and reject heresies which subvert the saving work of God in Christ. Orthodox and Lutherans, however, have different histories. Lutherans have received the Nicene-Constantinopolitan Creed with the addition of the filioque. The seventh ecumenical council, the second council of Nicea in 787, which rejected iconoclasm and restored the veneration of icons in the churches, was not part of the tradition received by the Reformation. Lutherans, however, rejected the iconoclasm of the 16th century, and affirmed the distinction between adoration due to the triune God alone and all other forms of veneration (CA 21). Through historical research this council has become better known. Nevertheless, it does not have the same significance for Lutherans as it does for the Orthodox. Yet, Lutherans and Orthodox are in agreement that the second council of Nicea confirms the christological teaching of the earlier councils and in setting forth the role of images (icons) in the lives of the faithful reaffirms the reality of the incarnation of the eternal Word of God, when it states,

> The more frequently Christ, Mary, the mother of God, and the saints are seen, the more are those who see them drawn to remember and long for those who serve as models, and to pay these icons the tribute of salutation and respectful veneration. Certainly this is not the full adoration in accordance with our faith, which is properly paid only to the divine nature, but it resembles that given to the figure of the honoured and life-giving cross, and also to the holy books of the gospels and to other sacred objects. (definition of the second council of Nicea)

8. Agreement on authority of the ecumenical councils requires us to discuss at future meetings the Orthodox and Lutheran understanding of salvation in light of these councils.

# 6. Authority in and of the Church
## Lutheran-Orthodox Joint Commission

Eighth Plenary, Limassol, Cyprus, 2-7 August 1995

## B. Understanding of salvation in the light of the ecumenical councils

(At the fifth joint commission meeting of the Lutheran-Orthodox dialogue in Bad Sege-berg, Germany, 1989, it was decided to continue the work of the dialogue under the new theme, "Authority in and of the Church". This theme, with special reference to the ecu-menical councils, was discussed and elaborated with an agreed statement at the seventh joint commission meeting in Sandbjerg, Denmark, 1993, and it was agreed that the "Understanding of Salvation in the Light of the Ecumenical Councils" be the theme of the eighth joint commission meeting in Limassol, Cyprus, 1995.)

*I. The mystery of God and formulations of dogma*

1. The triune God is the mystery "in whom we live and move and have our being" (Acts 17:28). This mystery, revealed in Jesus Christ through the outpouring of the Holy Spirit at Pentecost, is continuously lived and experienced in the church. The doctrinal formulations of the seven ecumenical councils are expressions of the continuity of the apostolic faith in the life of the church, and guides to the Christian life. These formula-tions enable the faithful rightly to worship, praise and witness to the glory of God.

2. The mystery of God should not be confused with formulations of doctrine in relation to the Holy Trinity and the incarnation. These doctrinal formulations are necessary point-ers on the narrow path, helping the faithful avoid heretical deviations and idolatry which identify theological speculation with the substance and essence of God and with the per-sons of the Holy Trinity. "It is impossible to express God and even more impossible to conceive him" (St Gregory the Theologian, *Oratio Theologica* 2.4).

3. Both the orthodoxy of our doctrine and the reality of our participation in the body of Christ are manifested and tested in an ecclesial life of love and prayer, a life of which it can truly be said in the words of St Paul, "It is no longer I who live but it is Christ who lives in me. And the life I now live in the flesh I live by faith in the Son of God, who loved me and gave himself for me" (Gal. 2:20).

4. As Lutherans and Orthodox we affirm that Christians, led by the Holy Spirit, grow through faith in the experience of God as a mystery, nurtured by the liturgical life of the

church, by the apostolic faith, by prayer, and by sharing in the fellowship of the local church (cf. Acts 2:42).

5a. We agree on the doctrine of God, the Holy Trinity, as formulated by the ecumenical councils of Nicea and Constantinople and on the doctrine of the person of Christ as formulated by the first four ecumenical councils. The fathers of the four councils rejected the Arian and Eunomian notion that the Logos, the Angel of the Great Counsel (Isa. 9:6 LXX) was created before the ages, and insisted that the Logos is *homoousios to Patri*. They also rejected the Nestorian notion that the One born of the Virgin Mary was not the Logos himself and that the Logos only dwelled in the One who was born of the Virgin Mary. In short, the fathers of these councils affirmed that he who was born of the Virgin Mary is God by nature and not just by the will of the Father, and that he became *homoousios* with us in his humanity. The union of the divine and human natures in the hypostasis of the Logos is, according to the council of Chalcedon, "without confusion, without change, without division, and without separation". The ecumenical councils which followed continued this teaching and applied it to new challenges to the faith. The fifth ecumenical council accepted as orthodox two theological terminologies in the confession of the one Lord Jesus Christ. The sixth ecumenical council affirmed the two natural wills and energies, with their natural properties, of the one person of the Logos incarnate. The seventh ecumenical council drew conclusions from the affirmation of the hypostatic union in Christ in order to confirm the veneration of icons.

5b. We agree in these fundamental teachings, confessing Jesus Christ, the Logos who for us and for our salvation (*soteria*) came down from heaven, was incarnate by the Holy Spirit of the Virgin Mary, and who for our sake was crucified, raised and exalted to the right hand of the Father; he will come again in glory to judge the living and the dead.

5c. We affirm that between Pentecost and the final parousia the Holy Spirit, the Lord and Giver of life, "whom I (Jesus Christ) will send to you from the Father, the Spirit of truth who proceeds from the Father" (John 15:26), calls, gathers, enlightens and glorifies believers in the body of Christ.

5d. We affirm that the saving work (oikonomia) of the triune God encompasses all of sinful humanity. "God in Christ was reconciling the world to himself", and through the ministry of reconciliation he challenges all people: "be reconciled to God" (2 Cor. 5:19-20).

5e. These are the dogmatic foundations of apostolic and orthodox teaching in the church about salvation.

## II. Justification and glorification as descriptions of salvation

6. The language with which the ecumenical councils and the fathers of the ancient church expressed and clarified the biblical witness on salvation is the privileged, unique and irreplaceable Christian language. According to their understanding, salvation in both the Old and New Testaments is our liberation from slavery to sin, the devil and death, and our participation in the life of Christ, who destroyed death by his death and gives life to those in the tomb. In this context justification (*dikaiosis*) is liberation from the dominion of the devil and the restoration of our communion with God. Those who are justified are glorified (Rom. 8:30) in the body of Christ, the church. By baptism and participation in the other mysteries (sacraments) of the church, the faithful are raised to a new life of

righteousness in Christ, together with all the prophets and saints of the Old and New Testaments. God gives them, in the Holy Spirit, the power to pass through purification and illumination of the heart and arrive "with all the saints" (Eph. 3:18) at glorification (Matt. 17:2; John 17:22; 2 Cor. 3:18; 2 Pet. 1:4). In this life, glorification may have various forms and be experienced for various durations, and in the next life will go from glory to glory without end.

7. The teaching of the ecumenical councils and the fathers – as also holy scripture – has to be transmitted from generation to generation in all human languages, for God wills that all human beings come to the knowledge of the truth (1 Tim. 2:4). In the New Testament the one mystery of salvation is expressed in different but essentially complementary terms such as sanctification, justification, redemption, adoption, liberation, glorification, etc. In interpreting the apostolic teaching on salvation, our two ecclesiastical traditions developed different emphases.

8. For the Orthodox church, salvation is a gratuitous gift of God offered in Jesus Christ to all human beings (1 Tim. 2:4; John 3:17), which they must both freely choose (Rev. 3:20) and work for (1 Cor. 3:13, 15:58; Phil. 2:12). According to St Paul, this is *synergeia* (1 Cor. 3:9; 2 Cor. 6:1). Once this gift of the divine grace is accepted by faith, Christ truly becomes the doctor of the souls and bodies of the faithful in the Holy Spirit, through the word of God and the mysteries of the church. He purifies their hearts (Ps. 50-51:10; Acts 15:9) and constantly renews their minds (Rom. 12:2; 2 Cor. 4:16), leading them from illumination/justification (2 Cor. 4:6) manifested by prayer in the heart (Rom. 8:26; Eph. 5:19, 6:18; Col. 3:16) and keeping of the commandments (1 John 3:22), to glorification (John 17:22; 1 Cor. 12:26). The Orthodox church does not hold that humanity inherited the guilt of the sin of Adam and Eve and is therefore worthy of eternal damnation, or that God chose from those thus guilty certain ones only to be saved without personal merit, or that Christ died on the cross only for them, or that Christ loves only those sinners who are destined for heaven, or that God had to be reconciled to humanity by Christ's crucifixion.

9. Lutherans understand the saving work which God accomplishes in Christ through the Holy Spirit primarily through the concept of "justification". For Lutherans, justification is God's gracious declaration of the forgiveness of sins for the sake of Jesus Christ, crucified and risen, and at the same time the free gift of new life in him. Through the liturgical life, preaching and sacraments of the church, the Holy Spirit enables us to have faith in the gospel – that is, in God's gracious promise of forgiveness and new life. This promise is received by faith alone (*sola fide*); this means that salvation is by Christ alone, and not by any human works or merits. In faith Christians entrust themselves entirely to God's grace in Christ for salvation. In this way they enter a new relationship with God, as St Paul says: "Since we are justified by faith we have peace with God through our Lord Jesus Christ" (Rom. 5:1). Justification is a real participation in Christ, true God and true human being. In the church, the believer by faith participates in Christ and all his gifts, and so has a share in the divine life. The presence of Christ in faith genuinely effects the righteousness of Christ in us, and leads believers to the sanctification of their lives. In this way, believers work out their salvation in fear and trembling, trusting that God in Christ is at work in them, both to will and to work for his good pleasure (Phil. 2:12-13).

10. Lutherans and Orthodox agree that the ecumenical councils of the early church are a specific gift of God to his church. The councils are an authoritative inheritance through

the ages because they keep prophetic and apostolic truth, and provide guidelines for the purification and illumination of the heart to glorification in Christ for the salvation and justification of humanity throughout the ages.

11. Lutherans and Orthodox still need to explore further their different concepts of salvation as purification, illumination and glorification, with the use of *synergeia*, which is the Orthodox teaching and tradition, and as justification and sanctification, with the use of *sola fide*, which is the Lutheran teaching and tradition.

# 7. Authority in and of the Church
## Lutheran-Orthodox Joint Commission

### Ninth Plenary, Sigtuna, Sweden, 31 July-8 August 1998

## C. Salvation: grace, justification and synergy

(The general theme of the Lutheran-Orthodox joint commission proposed already in 1989 in Bad Segeberg, Germany, and in 1991 in Moscow, Russia, was finally adopted in Sandbjerg, Denmark, in 1993: "Authority in and of the Church in the Light of the Ecumenical Councils". The eighth meeting of the Lutheran-Orthodox joint commission in Limassol, Cyprus, 1995, agreed at the end of their statement on the "Understanding of Salvation in the Light of the Ecumenical Councils", that Lutherans and Orthodox still needed to explore further their different concepts of *synergeia* in the Orthodox teaching and tradition, and *sola fide* in the Lutheran teaching and tradition. In response to this request the ninth plenary of the joint commission in Sigtuna agreed on the following statement.)

1. "God so loved the world that He gave his only begotten Son, so that everyone who believes in him may not perish but may have eternal life" (John 3:16). The Logos, the Son of God, in whom everything was created, is the light which enlightens everyone. The Logos revealed himself to Abraham, to the prophets of the Old Testament, and in the law given to Moses. In the last days "He became man for us and for our salvation" (Nicene-Constantinopolitan Creed 381) which He fulfilled through his life, death and resurrection, and through the gift of the Holy Spirit to the church at Pentecost. Salvation depends entirely upon the grace of the Holy Trinity, given to us and experienced through word and sacraments in the life of the church. The grace of God comes to humanity from the Father, through the Son, in the Holy Spirit. The Father creates, redeems and glorifies us through the Son, in the Spirit.

2. Lutherans and Orthodox teach that divine grace eternally flows out of God's love for his creation. It overcomes the sin of humanity to achieve God's plan for the fullness of time, which is "to gather up all things in [Christ], things in heaven and things on earth" (Eph. 1:10). Grace is not simply a reaction to human sin. Lutherans and Orthodox both teach that God invites humanity to full communion in him, still remaining true God beyond all human comprehension. Orthodox express this reality by the distinction between the divine essence, which is unapproachable (cf. Exod. 33:18-23; 1 Tim. 6:16) and the divine, uncreated energies, the multitude of divine grace in which God comes

down to us and in which we are called to participate. As St Basil the Great says, "We know our God from his energies, but we do not claim that we can draw near to his essence; for his energies come down to us, but his essence remains unapproachable" (*Epist.* 234.1). Lutherans in their terminology do not make use of the distinction between essence and energies, but they fully accept the belief that God's grace eternally flows to us from his very being because "God is love and who abides in love abides in God, and God in him" (1 John 4:16).

3. As St Paul teaches, the grace which saves us is centred in Christ (cf. Rom. 5). Grace presupposes the work of Christ both in the Old Testament (cf. 1 Cor. 10:2-4) and in the New Testament (cf. Rom. 3:24), and is given as the grace of our Lord Jesus Christ himself (cf. 2 Cor. 13:13). We receive the grace of Christ in the Holy Spirit, and without the Holy Spirit no one can believe in Christ (cf. 1 Cor. 12:3). The Holy Spirit, whom Christ sends from the Father, forms us in the divine likeness. The Holy Spirit calls human beings to faith in Christ through the gospel in the church, frees them from sin and death in holy baptism, enlightens them and bestows his gifts upon them. He sanctifies and sustains the baptized in true faith; He nourishes them by the flesh and blood of the Lord (cf. John 6:56) in the communion (koinonia) of Christ's body (cf. 1 Cor. 10:16-17). He thus leads them through many depths "from glory to glory" (2 Cor. 3:18).

4. Though human beings may feel dependence on God (cf. Acts 17:23,27), because of sin they can neither ask for, nor obtain, divine grace through their own powers. Grace is entirely God's gift, which God gives because God wants all human beings to be saved (cf. 1 Tim. 2:4). Faith is God's gift from its inception, since it is the Holy Spirit who, by divine grace, enlightens the human mind and strengthens the human will to turn to God. As stated by Cyril of Alexandria, "For it is unworkable for the soul of man to achieve any of the goods, namely, to control its own passions and to escape the mightiness of the sharp trap of the devil, unless he is fortified by the grace of the Holy Spirit and on this count he has Christ himself in his soul" (*Against Julian*, 3).

5. Both Lutherans and Orthodox teach that divine grace operates universally and that God freely grants grace to all human beings. God's saving grace does not operate by necessity or in an irresistible manner, since human beings can reject it. Regarding the way in which salvation is appropriated by the believers, Lutherans, by teaching that justification and salvation are by grace alone through faith (*sola gratia, sola fide*), stress the absolute priority of divine grace in salvation. When they speak about saving faith they do not think of the dead faith which even the demons have (cf. James 2:19), but the faith which Abraham showed and which was reckoned to him as righteousness (cf. Gen. 15:6; Rom. 4:3,9).

The Orthodox also affirm the absolute priority of divine grace. They underline that it is God's grace which enables our human will to conform to the divine will (cf. Phil. 2:13) in the steps of Jesus praying "not as I will but as You will" (Matt. 26:39), so that we may work out our salvation in fear and trembling (cf. Phil. 2:12). This is what the Orthodox mean by "synergy" (working together) of divine grace and the human will of the believer in the appropriation of the divine life in Christ. The understanding of synergy in salvation is helped by the fact that the human will in the one person of Christ was not abolished when the human nature was united in him with the divine nature, according to the christological decisions of the ecumenical councils.

While Lutherans do not use the concept of synergy, they recognize the personal responsibility of the human being in the acceptance or refusal of divine grace through faith, and in the growth of faith and obedience to God. Lutherans and Orthodox both understand good works as the fruits and manifestations of the believer's faith and not as a means of salvation.

6. Lutherans, together with the Orthodox, affirm that salvation is real participation by grace in the nature of God as St Peter writes, "that we may be partakers of the divine nature" (2 Pet. 1:4). That happens through our participation in the death and resurrection of the Lord in his body, in whom all the fullness of God dwells (cf. Col. 2:9). This is the way in which salvation is realized as purification, illumination and glorification, also referred to as deification (*theosis*).

This terminology has not been central in Lutheran tradition. Lutherans prefer to speak of the sanctification in the body of Christ who is himself present in the faith of the believers. Lutherans, together with the Orthodox, affirm the reality of the believers' participation in the divine life, in which they grow by the grace of God.

7. Lutherans and Orthodox affirm that on the cross Christ the incarnate Word, through whom God reconciled us to himself (cf. 2 Cor. 5:18-19), died for our sins (cf. 1 Cor. 15:3) and freed us for a new life by his resurrection (cf. Rom. 6:5), so that having crucified the passions of the flesh we may live in the freedom of the Spirit (cf. Gal. 5:24-25).

Lutherans, seeing that Christian life is a continuous struggle against sin and "flesh" (cf. Gal. 5:16-18), and being afflicted by this experience, do not look to their own good works, or their own failures, but look to Christ on the cross and his resurrection and trust in God's promise, the word of forgiveness in the church. Therefore Lutherans place specific emphasis on the forensic dimension of salvation. They stress that God forgives sin and imputes the righteousness of Christ to sinners through faith, and that we may therefore for salvation rely entirely upon the Father's mercy in Christ through the communion of the Holy Spirit (cf. 2 Cor. 13:13).

For the Orthodox, the redemptive work of Christ is received by the believer in the church, his body, to whom the promise of forgiveness of sins has been given by the Lord (cf. Matt. 18:18). In faith and humility, the believer puts his trust in the truth and power of the said promise, in the unsearchable riches of Christ's mercies (cf. Eph. 2:4, 3:8) and his boundless love for humankind (*philanthropia*) and in the prayers of the communion of saints (cf. Heb. 12:1,22-23) and the intercession of the most holy Theotokos (cf. John 2:3, 19:26-27). The struggle against passions (cf. 1 Cor. 9:24-27; Eph. 6:10-17) in the power of the Holy Spirit is a participation in the death and resurrection of Christ. It aims at the purification of the heart (cf. Matt. 5:8) and the illumination (cf. Matt. 5:14; 2 Cor. 4:6) leading to glorification (cf. John 17:22; 2 Cor. 3:18; 2 Pet. 1:4).

8. Lutherans and Orthodox believe that "the sufferings of the present time are not worthy of comparing with the glory about to be revealed in us" (Rom. 8:18). In salvation we become children of God by grace and "it has not yet been revealed what we shall be. But we know that when it is revealed, we shall be like him, for we shall see him as He is" (1 John 3:2). And we also know that "the earnest expectation of the creation eagerly waits for the revealing of the sons of God" (Rom. 8:19) and his daughters, and we know that "creation shall be delivered from the bondage of corruption into the glorious liberty of the children of God" (Rom. 8:21; cf. 1 Cor. 15:52-54).

Having thoroughly explored and discussed our respective understandings of salvation in relation to grace, justification and synergy, according to the mandate given to us in Limassol, we have noted during this ninth session of our dialogue the central points of agreement between Lutherans and Orthodox with differences in emphasis and terminology.

The joint commission expresses its strong affirmation of the continuation of the dialogue between the two traditions, and proposes a new general theme for the next period: "The Mystery of the Church," and as its first sub-theme: "Word and Sacraments (Mysteries) in the Life of the Church".

# 8. The Mystery of the Church: Word and Sacraments
## Lutheran-Orthodox Joint Commission

### Tenth Plenary, Damascus, Syria, 3-10 November 2000

## A. Word and sacraments (*mysteria*) in the life of the church

(The Lutheran-Orthodox joint commission has been officially working since 1981. Between 1985 and 1998 the commission has discussed the following topics: divine revelation, scripture and Tradition, the canon and the inspiration of the holy scripture, authority in and of the church in the light of the ecumenical councils. In the ninth meeting of the Lutheran-Orthodox joint commission in Sigtuna, Sweden, in 1998 an agreed statement "Salvation: Grace, Justification and Synergy" was adopted. This ended the treatment of the topic "Authority in and of the Church". A new general theme was proposed in Sigtuna: "The Mystery of the Church", with its first sub-theme as "Word and Sacraments *[Mysteria]* in the Life of the Church". The joint commission thus deepens the treatment of salvation by dealing with the issue of the Christian's life in the church. In 1998 it was affirmed that "salvation is real participation by grace in the nature of God as St Peter writes, 'that we may be partakers of the divine nature' [2 Pet. 1:4]. This takes place through our participation in the death and resurrection of the Lord in his body, in whom all the fullness of God dwells [cf. Col. 2:9]" [Sigtuna, §6]. This participation is the work of the Holy Spirit through word and sacraments in the life of the church. In accordance with this the joint commission agreed in Damascus, Syria, in 2000, to the following statement on word and sacraments *[Mysteria]* in the life of the church.)

1. The church as the body of Christ is the *mysterion* par excellence, in which the different *mysteria*/sacraments find their place and existence and through which the believers participate in the fruits of the entire redemptive work of Christ. God "has made known to us the mystery of his will according to his good pleasure that he set forth in Christ, as a plan for the fullness of time to gather up all things in him, things in heaven and things on earth" (Eph. 1:9-10). The apostle Paul also writes of this *mysterion*: "I am now rejoicing in my sufferings for your sake, and in my flesh I am completing what is lacking in Christ's afflictions for the sake of his body, that is, the church. I became its servant according to God's commission that was given to me for you, to make the word of God fully known, the mystery that has been hidden throughout the ages and generations but has now been revealed to his saints" (Col. 1:24-26).

2. We affirm this Pauline view of the church as *mysterion*. Within this view we understand the various sacraments/*mysteria* as means of salvation, i.e., as specific, divine,

saving acts of the church for the salvation of believers. We understand the *mysteria* in the sense that in them, and through them, Christ imparts his saving grace to believers in a real though ineffable way, in which we grasp the visible signs but perceive only by faith the divine grace given in and through them. This grace of the sacraments is a free gift of God in the Holy Spirit.

3. The *mysteria* of the church are grounded in the historical redemptive work of Christ, and as such they differ radically from Hellenistic, pagan and neo-pagan mysteries connected with magic. The word "mysteria" does not have the same meaning for the Orthodox tradition as the word sacrament. "Sacramentum" is the Latin translation of the Greek "mysterion" and it is from this Latin word that specific theological concepts have developed in the West. *Mysteria* refers to the ineffable action of the divine grace imparted in and through the specific acts performed in and by the church. Lutherans use the word "sacrament" in accordance with the Latin tradition in which these ineffable actions are the means of imparting the saving grace that the Father gives through the Son in the Holy Spirit to the church for the salvation of the world.

4. The expression "word of God" carries distinct but related meanings. With regard to the Holy Trinity it refers to the divine Logos. With regard to Christology and soteriology it means Jesus Christ, the incarnate divine Logos and Saviour. With regard to the sacraments it means the same incarnate and resurrected Christ as the subject of the *mysteria*/sacraments. Besides the reference to the divine Logos and his redemptive work in history, the expression "word of God" carries the meaning of the church's proclamation of Christ and witness to him (*kerygma*). The proclamation of the word of God thus brings about faith; people cannot believe unless the word is preached in the power of the Holy Spirit (cf. Rom. 10:14-18).

5. Affirming the Christocentric nature of the church, our traditions approach word and sacrament from that perspective. Both traditions connect sacramental theology with the divine grace outpouring from the sacrifice of Jesus Christ on the cross, remembering also the apostle Paul's exhortation "to present your bodies as a living sacrifice, holy and acceptable to God, which is your spiritual worship" (Rom. 12:1). By participation in the life of the church, believers grow in holiness, "to maturity, to the measure of the full stature of Christ" (Eph. 4:13).

6. Together we affirm that when the word of God is preached and taught, believers, under the guidance of the Holy Spirit, respond by confessing the faith of the church and entering its sacramental life. In this sense the preaching of the word of God precedes the sacraments, while the confession of faith exists as an essential element of the celebration of the sacraments (cf. Justin, I *Apology*, 66-67). St Irenaeus of Lyon writes that he who possesses in himself the rule of faith, which he has received through baptism, cannot deviate from the true faith (*Adv. Haer.*, I.9.4.) This is because the rule of faith is constantly confirmed in the sacrament of the divine eucharist. The interpenetration of the word of God and the sacraments finds an absolute expression in the eucharist. According to St Irenaeus, "our [the church's] teaching is in agreement with the eucharist, while the eucharist confirms the teaching" (*Adv. Haer.*, IV.18.5).

7. Lutherans and Orthodox converge in their teaching of the church as the body of Christ, i.e., as a divine and human reality. Of this theandric reality St Paul writes, "But as it is, God arranged the members in the body, each one of them, as he chose. If all were a single member, where would the body be? As it is, there are many members, yet one body…

Now you are the body of Christ and individually members of it" (1 Cor. 12:18-20,27). Being in communion with Christ and with one another through the power of the Holy Spirit, the church exists in history as the community of the faithful awaiting the second coming of its Lord at the end of time (Acts 3:20-21).

8.  With regard to the manifestation of the church in the divine economy, i.e., in the history of salvation, we affirm together that the proclamation of the gospel and the administration of the sacraments by the ordained ministry in the church are among the most important marks of the church. Both of our traditions teach that the visible and material elements of the sacraments, such as water, bread and wine, constitute concrete and unchangeable elements of the operations of the triune God in the history of salvation. Created things thus become, by the power of the Holy Spirit, the symbols of the sacrifice, cross and resurrection of Christ so that we may participate in the divine life. In this new life in Christ believers by grace partake in the communion/koinonia of the triune God who sets them free from sin and death and leads them to glorification and eternal life.

# 9. The Mystery of the Church: *Mysteria*/Sacraments

## Lutheran-Orthodox Joint Commission

### Eleventh Plenary, Oslo, Norway, 3-10 October 2002

### B. *Mysteria*/sacraments as means of salvation

(Meeting in Sigtuna, Sweden, in 1998, the Lutheran-Orthodox joint commission selected the theme of "The Mystery of the Church". In 2000 at its meeting in Damascus, Syria, the commission adopted an agreed statement entitled "The Mystery of the Church: Word and Sacraments *[Mysteria]* in the Life of the Church". In addition, the commission decided to examine next under the same theme the issue of "The Sacraments *[Mysteria]* as Means of Salvation". The following statement thus builds on the consensus previously discovered, not only on the topic of "Word and Sacraments *[Mysteria]* in the Life of the Church", but also that reflected even earlier in the dialogue, particularly in the 1998 statement "Salvation: Grace, Justification and Synergy". The present statement should be seen in the context of the commission's previous work which has affirmed both that "salvation is real participation by grace in the nature of God" [Sigtuna 1998.6] and that the sacraments/*mysteria* are "means of salvation, i.e., specific divine acts of the church for the salvation of believers" [Damascus 2000.2]. By means of the sacraments, "Christ imparts his saving grace to believers", for the "grace of the sacraments is a free gift of God in the Holy Spirit" [Damascus 2000.2]).

1. The *mysteria*/sacraments are founded on the incarnation, teaching, death and resurrection of Jesus Christ as witnessed in the holy scriptures. The sacraments of the church are the means by which Christ extends his saving work, which took place once and for all in the past, into the history of the church. These *mysteria* regenerate believers in the love of God the Father through the power of the Holy Spirit, and incorporate them into the body of Christ – the church – where they participate in the life of Christ. The sacraments are fruits of the salvific work of Christ. They are performed in the church, and grant specific gifts of grace for the salvation of the faithful and for building up the body of Christ.

2. Church and sacraments are inseparable: the church is manifested through the sacraments, and there are no sacraments without or outside the church. We agree that the church is in itself a *mysterion*, not in the sense that it should be taken as the source of the other sacraments, or as an additional sacrament alongside them, but in the sense that it is the body of Christ, its Lord, "the fullness of him who fills all in all" (Eph. 1:23).

3.  We also agree that those who perform the sacraments in the church do so *in persona Christi*. When the ordained servants of Christ carry out their sacramental ministries in the church, Christ himself acts as the true high priest and chief liturgist. The sacraments of the church are therefore the acts of Christ, in the power of the Holy Spirit, by means of which he baptizes, forgives sin, bestows life, and gives his own body and blood for the salvation of all believers. As St Ambrose says, in the consecration "the priest does not use his own words, but uses the words of Christ. Therefore the word of Christ effects this sacrament" (*De Sacramentis*, 4.14). The salvation given in the church is thus the work of the triune God, as St John Chrysostom says: "The Father and the Son and the Holy Spirit do everything, while the priest lends his tongue and offers his hand" (Commentary on the Gospel of St John, *PG* 59.472).

4.  The salvation imparted by means of the sacraments must be appropriated personally, by faith and life in Christ, through the Holy Spirit. Lutherans have expressed this point by saying that the sacraments are objectively valid by the word and command of Christ, while they depend for their efficacy on the believer's faithful reception. The language of "validity" and "efficacy" is not used by the Orthodox in this context. Lutherans and Orthodox, however, both seek to avoid two extremes, one of which would make the sacraments depend for their efficacy on the worthiness of the celebrant or administrator, the other of which would insist that the sacraments confer grace by the mere performance of an act. Thus we agree, for instance, that those who receive the body and blood of Christ in faith do so to their salvation, while whoever "eats the bread and drinks the cup of the Lord in an unworthy manner will be guilty of profaning the body and blood of the Lord" (1 Cor. 11:27).

5.  Lutherans and Orthodox teach that the sacraments are instituted by Jesus Christ, and revealed through the Holy Spirit in the church. With regard to the number of sacraments, for the Orthodox the following sacraments have been instituted by the Lord: baptism, chrismation, eucharist, penance, ordination, matrimony and holy unction (*euchelaion*). Besides these seven sacraments which are given for the salvation of believers, there are numerous other liturgical acts through which God blesses many aspects of the lives of the faithful as well as the whole creation. Lutherans do not insist on a specific number of sacraments, but generally employ a somewhat more restrictive concept of a sacrament, insisting that of the many ritual acts mentioned in the holy scriptures only two – baptism and the eucharist or Lord's supper – include both a command of Christ ("do this") and an accompanying promise of salvation. At the same time, there are elements in the Lutheran theological tradition which extend this concept of a sacrament beyond baptism and the eucharist, so that, for example, both penance and ordination may be regarded as sacraments (see *Apol.* XIII.). Lutherans and Orthodox agree that God has bound Christians for their salvation to the sacraments in the church, but that his sovereign freedom remains uncompromised by his fidelity to us in them.

6.  Orthodox and Lutherans, discussing the sacraments on a preliminary basis, agree to give emphasis to the sacraments of initiation of the ancient church, that is, baptism, chrismation and the eucharist. We also agree that baptism takes place with water, in the name of the Father, and the Son, and the Holy Spirit. It brings the forgiveness of sins, and is a participation in the death and resurrection of Christ which incorporates the believer into the body of Christ as a member of the church. For the Orthodox this incorporation is completed through chrismation, in which the baptized receive the gifts of the Holy Spirit.

For Lutherans, anointing with the Holy Spirit takes place within the rite of baptism itself, and finds its expression in the laying-on of hands after water baptism.

7. With regard to the holy eucharist, Lutherans and Orthodox converge in their insistence on the reality of the body and blood of Christ given and received in the eucharistic elements. In this respect, Orthodox speak of the change (*metabole*) in the elements of the eucharist such that after the invocation of the Holy Spirit (epiclesis) there is no longer "bread" and "wine" but the real body and blood of Christ. Lutherans traditionally say that the real body and blood of Christ are present "in, with and under" the bread and the wine. Lutherans and Orthodox agree that in holy communion we do not receive ordinary bread and ordinary wine, but the body and blood of Christ. As St Paul teaches, "The cup of blessing that we bless, is it not a sharing in the blood of Christ? The bread that we break, is it not a sharing in the body of Christ?" (1 Cor. 10:16).

# 10. The Mystery of the Church: Baptism and Chrismation

## Lutheran-Orthodox Joint Commission

### Twelfth Plenary, Duràu, Romania, 6-15 October 2004

#### C. Baptism and chrismation as sacraments of initiation into the church

(The Lutheran-Orthodox joint commission, meeting in Sigtuna, Sweden, in 1998, selected the topic "The Mystery of the Church" for the next round of conversations. The topic has been dealt with so far in three sub-topics: (a) "The Mystery of the Church: Word and Sacrament" [Damascus, Syria, 2000, §2]; (b) "The Sacraments *[Mysteria]* as Means of Salvation" [Oslo, Norway, 2002, §6]; (c)"Baptism and Chrismation as Sacraments of Initiation into the Church" [Duràu, Romania, 2004]. Thus, the Oslo statement builds on the consensus previously achieved on the topic "Word and Sacraments *[Mysteria]* in the Life of the Church". However, it also takes into account the earlier consensus, particularly that achieved in the 1998 statement "Salvation: Grace, Justification and Synergy". The commission's previous work has affirmed both that "salvation is a real participation by grace in the nature of God" [Sigtuna, 1998, §6] and that the sacraments/*mysteria* are "means of salvation, i.e., specific divine acts of the church for the salvation of believers" [Damascus, 2000, §2].)

The present statement builds on the agreement reached in Oslo "to give emphasis to the sacraments of initiation of the ancient church, that is, baptism, chrismation and the eucharist" (Oslo, 2002, §6). In Duràu we have explored areas of convergence and divergence in the process of Christian initiation focusing on the three events of death with Christ, resurrection with Christ, and the gift of the Holy Spirit.

Our method has been to compare our respective rites of initiation because we believe that they clearly express the teaching of our churches. The Orthodox rites of Christian initiation are found in the *Euchologion*, which are translated into the various liturgical languages. The English translation used here is from the *Service Book* of the Antiochian Orthodox Church in America (1987). The Lutheran rites of holy baptism are based on *The Baptismal Booklet (Taufbüchlein)*, which is an appendix to Luther's Small Catechism in the *Book of Concord* (The Confessions of the Evangelical Lutheran Church), edited by Kolb and Wengert (2000). The rite of holy baptism in the *Lutheran Book of Worship* (1978), published in North America and used widely by other Lutheran churches, includes elements retrieved from the ancient patristic tradition under the influence of the Lutheran liturgical renewal movement.

1. Lutherans and Orthodox agree that entry into the life of the one, holy, catholic and apostolic church is a gift given by God through the sacraments, which are enacted in the church. "Repent, and be baptized every one of you in the name of Jesus Christ so that your sins may be forgiven, and you will receive the gift of the Holy Spirit" (Acts 2:38). In both traditions the sacrament of baptism is administered with water in the name of the Father and of the Son and of the Holy Spirit (cf. Matt. 28:19). Therefore, salvation is the work of the triune God. In both traditions baptism is normally administered by an ordained minister: in Orthodox churches this is normally done by triple immersion, and in Lutheran churches normally by pouring water three times on the head. There is agreement between the two traditions that immersion is the most symbolically appropriate form of the administration of this sacrament. Lutherans and Orthodox also agree that in cases of emergency baptism may be administered by lay persons. Our churches agree that the sacrament of baptism is unrepeatable.

2. There are three basic components in the process of Christian initiation: death with Christ, resurrection with Christ, and the sealing with the Holy Spirit. For Orthodox, Christian initiation finds its fulfilment in the holy eucharist. Lutherans do not normally speak of the eucharist as a sacrament of initiation, but when an older child or adult is baptized, that person is immediately admitted to the eucharist.

3. In preparation for Christian initiation, Orthodox and Lutheran churches use their own rites of exorcism. In the Orthodox order of baptism the priest says, "O Lord… look upon your servant; prove him/her and search him/her and root out of him/her every operation of the devil. Rebuke the unclean spirits and expel them, and purify the works of your hands …" (*Service Book*, p.147). In the Lutheran *Baptismal Booklet* the minister says: "Depart from [name], you unclean spirit, and make way for the Holy Spirit" (*Book of Concord*, p.373).

4. Both Lutherans and Orthodox incorporate in their rite of initiation the renunciation of the devil and the confession of faith. The Orthodox priest asks the candidate for baptism, or the sponsor/godparent, the question, "Do you renounce Satan, and all his angels, and all his works, and all his service, and all his pride?" (*Service Book*, p.148). Similarly the Lutheran minister asks, "Do you renounce the devil?" (*Baptismal Booklet*, p.374). In the Orthodox rite this is immediately followed by a confession of Christ and the Nicene-Constantinopolitian Creed (325/381), while in the Lutheran rite the Apostles' Creed is used. Thus, in both traditions the faith of the candidate for baptism or that of the sponsors/godparents is expressed through the confession of the creed.

5. Although theological discourse may ascribe different effects to our participation in Christ's death and resurrection, they nevertheless form a unity in our liturgical rites and we will therefore treat them together in this document. Lutherans and Orthodox agree that our participation in Christ's death and resurrection bestows on us the following gifts: death of the old Adam (cf. Rom. 6:6), union with Christ (cf. Rom. 6:5), redemption, sanctification, purification of flesh and spirit (cf. 1 Cor. 6:11), deliverance from death and the devil, forgiveness of sins, victory over the power of sin (cf. Rom. 6), illumination of the soul (cf. Heb. 6:4), regeneration, new birth (cf. Titus 3:5), new life in Christ, adoption as God's children (cf. Rom. 8:16), renewal of the image of God (cf. Col. 3:10; Eph. 3:10), eternal life, and incorporation into Christ's body, the church.

6. The bestowal of these gifts is clearly attested in both the Lutheran and Orthodox rites of initiation. In the Lutheran order the minister addresses those present and explains the

meaning of baptism: "In holy baptism our gracious heavenly Father liberates us from sin and death by joining us to the death and resurrection of our Lord Jesus Christ. We are born children of the fallen humanity; in the water of baptism we are reborn children of God and inheritors of eternal life. By water and the Holy Spirit we are made members of the church which is the body of Christ" (*Lutheran Book of Worship*, p.121). The gifts are also highlighted in Luther's "Flood Prayer", which is reflected in most Lutheran rites: "... By the baptism of his own death and resurrection, your beloved Son has set us free from bondage to sin and death, and has opened the way to the joy and freedom of ever-lasting life. He made water a sign of the kingdom and of cleansing and rebirth... Pour out your Holy Spirit so that those who are here baptized may be given new life. Wash away the sin of all those who are cleansed by this water and bring them forth as inheritors of your glorious kingdom" (*Lutheran Book of Worship*, p.122).

7. In the Orthodox rite, the priest prays over the water of baptism, "... Master of all, show this water to be the water of redemption, the water of sanctification, the purification of flesh and spirit, the loosing of bonds, the remission of sins, the illumination of the soul, the laver of regeneration, the renewal of the spirit, the gift of adoption to sonship, the garment of incorruption, the fountain of life... You have bestowed on us from on high a new birth through water and the spirit. Wherefore, O Lord, manifest yourself in this water, and grant that he/she who is baptized in it may be transformed; that he/she may put away from him/her the old man, which is corrupt through the lust of the flesh, and that he/she may be clothed with the new man, and renewed after the image of him who created him/her; that being buried, after the pattern of your death, in baptism, he/she may, in like manner, be a partaker of your resurrection..." (*Service Book*, pp.155-56).

8. Orthodox and Lutherans agree that the third component of Christian initiation is the gift and seal of the Holy Spirit (2 Cor. 1:22; Eph. 4:30). In Lutheran rites, the gift of the Spirit is connected with the laying-on of hands and either a post-baptismal blessing or a prayer for the Spirit. After the minister pours water three times on the head of the candidate in the name of the Father, and of the Son, and of the Holy Spirit, the *Baptismal Booklet* continues with the prayer, "The almighty God and Father of our Lord Jesus Christ, who has given birth to you for a second time through water and the Holy Spirit and has forgiven you all your sins, strengthen you with his grace to eternal life" (*Baptismal Booklet*, p.375).

9. It is also customary in Lutheran churches for the minister to lay both hands on the head of the newly baptized and to pray for the Holy Spirit: "God, the Father of our Lord Jesus Christ, we give you thanks for freeing your sons and daughters from the power of sin and for raising them up to a new life through this holy sacrament. Pour your Holy Spirit upon [name]: the spirit of wisdom and understanding, the spirit of counsel and might, the spirit of knowledge and the fear of the Lord, the spirit of joy in your presence" (*Lutheran Book of Worship*, p.124). The *Handbook of the Lutheran Book of Worship* notes that "the laying-on of hands with the prayer for the gifts of the Holy Spirit signals a return to the liturgical fullness of the ancient church which was lost when confirmation became a separate rite" (p.31). According to the *Lutheran Book of Worship*, the minister may make the sign of the cross on the forehead of the newly baptized saying, "[Name], child of God, you have been sealed by the Holy Spirit and marked with the cross of Christ forever" (p.125). Lutheran churches that follow this rite have reclaimed the ritual action of chrismation and have clearly distinguished it as a distinct moment in the baptismal rite, though they do not define it theologically as a separate sacrament.

10. The gift of the Holy Spirit is more explicit in the Orthodox rite. Attending closely to patristic tradition, the Orthodox see a profound parallel between participation in the sacraments of the church and the historical unfolding of the economy of salvation as proceeding from the Father, through the Son, in the Holy Spirit. After the immersion, the priest anoints the newly baptized with holy chrism (myron) saying: "… compassionate King of all, grant also to him/her the seal of the gift of your holy, and almighty, and adorable Spirit …" (*Service Book*, p.159). Thus, as Jesus Christ received the gift of the Holy Spirit in his human nature, so all who follow him must, after the pattern of the gathered church at Pentecost, receive that same gift. The holy chrismation (the anointing of the baptized with the holy myron and prayer for their reception of the Holy Spirit) is the distinct but inseparable sacrament that imparts to the individual believer the church's own Pentecost. Endowed with the gift of the Spirit, believers are prepared and enabled to participate in the eucharist, the sacrament which effects their union with Christ, so that they truly become with him one body (*syssomos*) and one blood (*homaimos*). Accordingly, in the Orthodox tradition, all those who have been baptized and chrismated are immediately admitted to the eucharist, including infants. The Orthodox tradition places particular significance on the holy myron, which is prepared during the holy week every ten years from pure olive oil and over fifty other aromatic ingredients and symbolizes the ecclesial character of chrismation, which unites the newly baptized with the universal church through the Holy Spirit.

11. Orthodox and Lutherans, at their meeting in Duràu, 6-15 October 2004, found that the three components of Christian initiation are to a large extent included in each other's rites. These components find their fulfilment in the Christian's full participation in the life of Christ and his church through eating his body and drinking his blood in the holy eucharist. The topic for the meeting of the 13th Lutheran-Orthodox joint commission will be "The Mystery of the Church: D. The Holy Eucharist in the Life of the Church".

# 11. Common Declaration
## Archbishop George Carey and Catholicos Aram

### Canterbury, England, 8 June 1998

In response to the invitation of His Grace, the Most Reverend and Right Honourable Dr George Carey, the Archbishop of Canterbury, His Holiness Aram I, Catholicos of Cilicia and the moderator of the central and executive committees of the World Council of Churches, visited both London and Canterbury between 5 and 8 June 1998. At the end of this visit, and as a result of their deliberations, His Grace and His Holiness issued the following joint declaration:

Our encounter during these days has provided us with a wonderful opportunity to pray together as brothers joined in the love of our common Lord and Saviour Jesus Christ. We have remembered together the meetings of our predecessors and the long-standing relationship between the Armenian Catholicosate of Cilicia and the Anglican Communion. This time together has given us an opportunity to discuss, in the spirit of Christian love and fellowship, a number of issues and questions of common concern.

The Christian presence and witness in the Middle East has claimed our attention with its urgency to re-establish a comprehensive and lasting peace with justice in that region. The active participation of all the churches and faith communities of the Middle East is vital for the nation-building process in this region. We affirm the need to strengthen Christian-Muslim dialogue and to find ways of collaborating on ethical and social issues, and on matters relating to justice, peace and the establishment of human rights.

The unity of the church is needed if we are to give credible witness and effective service both in the Middle East and elsewhere in the world. To this end we pledge ourselves to give a new vitality and a more organized expression to the theological dialogue between the Anglican Communion and the family of the Oriental Orthodox churches within the context of the Anglican-Oriental Orthodox international forum.

Both our churches recognize the distinctive role that the World Council of Churches has as a privileged instrument of the ecumenical movement. It provides the place where the churches of the Anglican Communion and the Armenian Catholicosate of Cilicia join with others in seeking that visible unity of the church which is God's gift and our calling. The World Council of Churches also provides an appropriate space where we can address the many challenges before Christians in the world today.

We stand on the eve of many celebrations: the Lambeth Conference, the eighth assembly of the WCC, the 1700th anniversary of the founding of the Armenian Church in Armenia. These will provide important opportunities for reaffirming our commitment to visible unity and our work for justice, peace and the integrity of creation as we move into the next millennium.

As a result of our time together we reaffirm our commitment to a closer collaboration between the Anglican Communion and the Armenian Catholicosate of Cilicia, particularly in the areas of Christian education, theological formation and service. We commit ourselves to strengthening and expanding our ecumenical partnership in the years ahead. May the peace of you, Lord Jesus Christ, the love of God and the communion of the Holy Spirit sustain us and bring these commitments to fruition.

# 12. Agreed Statement on Christology

## Anglican-Oriental Orthodox International Commission

### Holy Etchmiadzin, Armenia, 5-10 November 2002

## Introduction

In 1990 the second forum of representatives of the Oriental Orthodox churches and the churches of Anglican Communion, meeting at the Monastery of St Bishoy in Wadi El Natroun, Egypt, was able to produce the following statement: "God, as revealed in the life, teaching, passion, death, resurrection and ascension of Jesus Christ, calls his people into union with himself. Living by the Holy Spirit, his own people have been given authority to proclaim this good news to all creation."

The forum was also able to suggest that an agreement on Christology between the Oriental Orthodox and the Anglican Communion was now possible, taking note of the detailed theological work done by representatives of the two families of Orthodoxy between 1964 and 1971, resulting in the agreed statement of 1989, the work done in the unofficial Pro Oriente conversations, and of the history of convergence in Christology between the churches of the Anglican Communion and the Oriental Orthodox churches. To this must now be added the agreed statement on Christology of the Reformed-Oriental Orthodox dialogue (Driebergen, Netherlands, 13 September 1994).

Our first meeting as the Anglican-Oriental Orthodox international commission, in Holy Etchmiadzin, Armenia, 5-10 November 2002, following the meeting of the preparatory committee in Midhurst, England, 27-30 July 2001, has taken forward this work. This has been done in a spirit of service of the Risen Christ and of the human race whom He came to save. Our work recognizes the presence of Christ with those who suffer in the tragic history of humanity. It expresses both the hope of a new humanity and the hope of glory wherein we will partake in Christ's holiness. With the will for unity-in-Christ within us it has been our privilege in this work of exploration and collaboration to handle the person of Christ Jesus (1 John 1:1) together.

After hearing the papers presented in our meeting and studying relevant documents we have been able to agree on the following statement:

## Agreed Statement on Christology

We confess that our Lord, God and Saviour Jesus Christ is the only-begotten Son of God who became incarnate and was made human in the fullness of time, for us and for our salvation. God the Son incarnate, perfect in his divinity and perfect in his humanity, consubstantial with the Father according to his divinity and consubstantial with us according to his humanity. For a union has been made of two natures. For this cause we confess one Christ, one Son and one Lord [based on the Formula of Re-union, AD 433].

Following the teaching of our common father St Cyril of Alexandria we can confess together that in the one incarnate nature of the Word of God two different natures continue to exist without separation, without division, without change and without confusion.

In accordance with this sense of the unconfused union, we confess the holy Virgin to be Theotokos, because God the Word became incarnate and was made man, and from the very conception united to himself that perfect humanity, without sin, which he took from her. As to the expressions concerning the Lord in the gospel and in the epistles, we are aware that theologians understand some in a general way as relating to one person, and others they distinguish, as relating to two natures, explaining those that befit the divine nature according to the divinity of Christ, and those of a humble sort according to his humanity [based on the formula of re-union, AD 433].

Concerning the four adverbs used to qualify the mystery of the hypostatic union: "without commingling" (or confusion) (*asyngchtos*), "without change" (*atreptos*), "without separation" (*achoristos*), and "without division" (*adiairetos*), those among us who speak of two natures in Christ are justified in doing so since they do not thereby deny their inseparable indivisible union: similarly, those among us who speak of one incarnate nature of the Word of God are justified in doing so since they do not thereby deny the continuing dynamic presence in Christ of the divine and the human, without change, without confusion. We recognize the limit of all theological language and the philosophical terminology of which it makes and has made use. We are unable to confine the mystery of God's utter self-giving in the incarnation of the divine Word in an ineffable, inexpressible and mysterious union of divinity and humanity, which we worship and adore.

Both sides agree in rejecting the teaching which separates or divides the human nature, both soul and body in Christ, from his divine nature, or reduces the union of the natures to the level of conjoining and limiting the union to the union of persons and thereby denying that the person of Jesus Christ is a single person of God the Word. "Jesus Christ is the same yesterday, today and forever" (Heb. 13:8 NRSV). Both sides also agree in rejecting the teaching which confuses the human nature in Christ with the divine nature so that the former is absorbed in the latter and thus ceases to exist. Consequently, we reject both the Nestorian and the Eutychian heresies.

In the Anglican tradition in the 16th century Richard Hooker witnesses to the continuing relevance of these concerns. In the fifth book of the *Laws of Ecclesiastical Polity*, section 5e, he emphasizes the necessary mystery of the person in Christ. "It is not man's ability either to express perfectly or to conceive the manner how [the incarnation] was brought to pass." "In Christ the verity of God and the complete substance of man were with full agreement established throughout the world, until the time of Nestorius." The church, Hooker contends, rightly repudiated any division in the person of Christ. "Christ is a Person both divine and human, howbeit not therefore two persons in one, neither both these in one sense, but a Person divine because he is personally the Son of God, human, because he hath really the nature of the children of men" (*Laws* 52.3).

"Whereupon it followeth against Nestorius, that no person was born of the Virgin but the Son of God, no person but the Son of God baptized, the Son of God condemned, the Son of God and no other person crucified; which one only point of Christian belief, the infinite worth of the Son of God, is the very ground of all things believed concerning life and salvation by that which Christ either did or suffered as man in our belief" (*Laws* 52.3). In the following consideration of the teaching of St Cyril, Hooker maintains both the importance of St Cyril's insistence on the unity of the Person of Christ while repudiating any Eutychian interpretation of that unity. Hooker quotes with approval Cyril's letter to Nestorius: "His two natures have knit themselves the one to the other, and are in that nearness as uncapable of confusion as of distraction. Their coherence hath not taken away the difference between them. Flesh is not become God but doth still continue flesh, although it be now the flesh of God" (q. *Laws* 53.2).

We agree that God the Word became incarnate by uniting to his divine uncreated nature with its natural will and energy, created human nature with its natural will and energy. The union of natures is natural, hypostatic, real and perfect. The natures are distinguished in our mind in thought alone. He who wills and acts is always the one hypostasis of the Logos incarnate with one personal will. In the Armenian tradition in the 12th century St Nerses the Graceful (Shenorhali) writes, "We do not think that the divine will opposes the human will and vice versa. We do not think either that the will of the one nature was different at different times, sometimes the will was divine, when He wanted to show his divine power, and sometimes it was human, when He wanted to show human humility."

The perfect union of divinity and of humanity in the incarnate Word is essential to the salvation of the human race. "For God so loved the world, that he gave his only Son, so that everyone who believes in him may not perish but may have eternal life" (John 3:16 NRSV). The Son of God emptied himself and became human, absolutely free from sin, in order to transform our sinful humanity to the image of his holiness. This is the gospel we are called to live and proclaim.

We also note the concerns of the Oriental Orthodox churches about the Christology of the Assyrian Church of the East as expressed in its official and unofficial dialogues with other churches. A particular concern of the Oriental Orthodox is that the Assyrians consider the persons and teachings of Diodore of Tarsus, Theodore of Mopsuestia and Nestorius as orthodox and thus venerate them in the liturgies of their church.

The Oriental Orthodox concerns were also addressed specifically to the report of the 1998 Lambeth Conference, which made reference to the consent made towards the Christology of the Assyrian Church, based on the Lambeth Conference of 1908 and 1920 reports and resolutions 08.63/64 and 20.21. We have noticed that the report of the Lambeth Conference of 1930 was not addressed in 1998. While the Eastern churches committee of the Church of England did preliminary christological work between 1908 and 1912 both in relation to the Oriental Orthodox churches and to the Assyrian Church, this work was never brought to an agreed statement on Christology. With reference to the Assyrian Church, the 1930 Lambeth Conference reported, "It has not been possible, owing to political and other conditions, to obtain the authoritative statement recommended in 1920 as to whether or not the present ecclesiastical authorities in the Assyrian Church adhere to the position of 1911." The Anglicans are therefore asking the Inter-Anglican Standing Commission on Ecumenical Relations (IASCER) to take into account these Oriental Orthodox theological reservations in any further christological work with the Assyrian Church of the East, which, in accordance with the Lambeth Conference resolution of 1998, will be in local and regional discussions. The result of any such discussions will have to be evaluated by the IASCER and any future Lambeth Conference, in the light of this christological agreement.

We submit this statement to the authorities of the Oriental Orthodox churches and the Anglican Communion for their consideration and action.


Rt Rev. Dr Geoffrey Rowell                    H. E. Metropolitan Bishoy
Anglican Co-chairman                          Oriental Orthodox Co-chairman

# 13. Report

## International Theological Dialogue between the Oriental Orthodox Family of Churches and the World Alliance of Reformed Churches 1993-2001

### Antelias, Lebanon, 23-28 January 2001

## I. Introduction

1. Impelled by the prayer of our Lord "that all may be one" (John 17:21) and helped by the Holy Spirit, we, the participants in the Oriental Orthodox-Reformed dialogue, seek to understand each other's traditions and grow together towards holistic Christian fellowship and visible unity.

Reformed churches and the Oriental Orthodox family of churches live side by side in several countries. However, decades of separate existence have caused them to drift apart, resulting in little or no relationship between the churches. In general, biases about each other have kept the contact between these two communions to a minimum in spite of the inherited Christian faith expressed in the Nicene Creed.

2. The Oriental Orthodox churches are living Christian communities in Egypt, Syria, Armenia, Lebanon, Ethiopia, India and Eritrea, and in lands of immigration. They are ancient apostolic traditional churches in the East which believe in the creed composed at the holy ecumenical council at Nicea in 325, and completed at the second holy ecumenical council at Constantinople in 381. They also follow the teaching of the third ecumenical council at Ephesus in 431. As such they believe in the Holy Trinity and in the divine incarnation of the Son of God.

3. They follow the teaching of St Cyril of Alexandria about one incarnate nature of the Word of God. They reject both the teaching of Nestorius and Eutyches. The one incarnate nature of Jesus Christ to them does not mean that the humanity of Jesus Christ was absorbed in his divinity and thus ceased to exist, but that they were united without separation and without change and continued to exist in the union.

4. During and after the council of Chalcedon in 451, the Oriental Orthodox churches formed a family of churches since they did not accept the condemnation at this council of their St Dioscorus, the successor of St Cyril of Alexandria, and due to difference in expressing the mystery of incarnation of the Son of God. Now the misunderstanding that happened during the council of Chalcedon is being removed and christological agreements are being reached among Chalcedonian and non-Chalcedonian churches.

5. The World Alliance of Reformed churches has been involved for about four decades in bilateral theological dialogues with several other world Christian communions.[1]

In 1992 the World Alliance of Reformed Churches evaluated the results of bilateral dialogues and reaffirmed the significance of such dialogues for the future relationship of Christian churches in the world.

6. The Oriental Orthodox family of churches have been in recent years in theological dialogue with the Eastern Orthodox family of churches, the Roman Catholic Church, the Lutheran and Anglican churches. The unofficial dialogue with the Eastern Orthodox started in 1964 and became official in 1985.

7. Informal conversations and contacts among the Reformed and Oriental Orthodox churches during earlier ecumenical gatherings eventually paved the way for officially organizing such dialogues between these two Christian communions. Unlike the Reformed churches, which have the World Alliance of Reformed Churches as a structure to promote international fellowship, the autocephalous Oriental Orthodox churches participating in this dialogue (namely, the Coptic Orthodox Church, the Syrian Orthodox Church of Antioch, the Armenian Apostolic Church [Catholicosate of All Armenians in Holy Etchmiadzin and Catholicosate of Cilicia in Antelias], the Ethiopian Orthodox Tewahedo Church and the Malankara Orthodox Syrian Church) do not have such a central structure, hence the decision to engage in conversations with the Reformed Christians had to be agreed to by each of the Oriental Orthodox churches. After an informal assurance that these churches were open to dialogue with the Reformed family, a formal letter of invitation was sent out by the general secretary of the World Alliance of Reformed Churches to the head of each of the churches in November 1991. In his letter the general secretary indicated that Reformed Christians were engaged in several other bilateral dialogues and that they were committed to work for Christian unity.

8. Such contacts and conversations led to a first meeting on 27 August 1992 among a group of authorized representatives of the Oriental Orthodox churches and representatives of the World Alliance of Reformed Churches at the Ecumenical Centre, Geneva, Switzerland, on the occasion of the central committee meeting of the World Council of Churches. This meeting was co-chaired by His Holiness Pope Shenouda III, Pope of Alexandria and Patriarch of the See of St Mark, and Dr Milan Opocensky, then general secretary of the World Alliance of Reformed Churches.

9. The representatives of both families were of the opinion that they and their respective churches were enthusiastic about the possibility of engaging in dialogue and were committed to pursuing it with all sincerity and prayer so that these two families could move towards greater Christian fellowship. An invitation graciously extended by His Holiness Pope Shenouda III to hold the first meeting at Anba Bishoy Monastery, Wadi-El-Natroun, Egypt, from 2 to 5 May 1993 was accepted, and the meeting was held accordingly.

10. Subsequent meetings were held at "Kerk en Wereld", Driebergen, The Netherlands, from 10 to 15 September 1994, at the invitation of the Netherlands Reformed Church; at the Sophia Centre, Orthodox Theological Seminary, Kottayam, India, from 10 to 15 January 1997, at the invitation of His Holiness the Catholicos Moran Mar Baselios Mar Thoma Matthews II of the Malankara Orthodox Syrian Church; at Union Theological Seminary and the Presbyterian School of Christian Education, Richmond, Virginia, USA, from 10 to 15 January 1998, at the invitation of the Presbyterian Church (USA) and UTS/PSCE; at St Ephrem Syrian Orthodox Seminary, Ma'arat Saydnaya, Syria, from 10 to 15 January 1999, at the invitation of His Holiness Moran Mar Ignatius Zakka I, Syrian Orthodox Patriarch of Antioch and All the East; at the Carberry Tower

conference centre, Musselburgh, Scotland, from 11 to 15 January 2000, at the invitation of the Church of Scotland; and at the Armenian Catholicosate of Cilicia, Antelias, Lebanon, from 23 to 28 January 2001, at the invitation of His Holiness Catholicos Aram I, where this report was presented and discussed and then submitted for consideration, as the result of the seven sessions of the dialogue, to the churches represented on both sides of the dialogue. During these conversations both families were informed and challenged in the process of mutual understanding and listening to each other.

11. The Oriental Orthodox churches, living in the Eastern tradition, and the Reformed churches, originating from the Western Latin tradition, have inherited different doctrinal approaches to the mystery of God, accompanied by differences and some misunderstandings of each other's positions. Therefore, the objective of the dialogue has been to create an atmosphere of openness and sincerity in order to facilitate our witness to the Lord Jesus Christ, in accordance with the apostolic faith in the face of contemporary realities. So the dialogue started by dealing with the understanding of scripture and Tradition in each other's churches. But such a search was connected to the mission and ministry of the church today. Needless to say, the progress has been slow, but also productive.

12. One of the highlights of these dialogues has been the adoption, at the session in Driebergen, The Netherlands, on 13 September 1994, of the agreed statement on Christology emerging from the biblical teaching and the patristic roots to which both the partners in dialogue owe their allegiance. This statement is reproduced below:

## II.  Agreed statement on Christology

INTRODUCTION

13. In our search for a common understanding of differences in Christology that have existed between us, we have thought it appropriate to focus upon the formula of re-union, AD 433. This formula represents an agreement reached by Antioch and Alexandria following the third ecumenical council in 431 and, as such, provides a common point of departure for both parties. We find the interpretations in this agreement to be in accord with the christological doctrines in both of our traditions.

AGREED STATEMENT

14. "We confess our Lord Jesus Christ, the only-begotten Son of God, perfect in divinity and perfect in humanity consisting of a rational soul and a body, begotten of the Father before the ages according to his divinity, the Same, in fullness of time, for us and for our salvation, born of the Virgin Mary, according to his humanity; the Same, consubstantial with the Father, according to his divinity. For a union had been made of two natures. For this cause we confess one Christ, one Son, one Lord.

15. "In accordance with this sense of the unconfused union, we confess the holy Virgin to be Theotokos, because God the Word became incarnate and was made human, and from the very conception united to himself the temple taken from her. As to the expressions concerning the Lord in the gospels and epistles, we are aware that theologians

understand some as common, as relating to one Person, and others they distinguish, as relating to two natures, explaining those that befit the divine nature according to the divinity of Christ, and those of a humble sort according to his humanity" [based on the formula of re-union, AD 433].

16. The four adverbs used to qualify the mystery of the hypostatic union belong to our common christological tradition: "without commingling" (or confusion) (*asyngchytos*), "without change" (*atreptos*), "without separation" (*achoristos*), and "without division" (*adiairetos*). Those among us who speak of two natures in Christ are justified in doing so since they do not thereby deny their inseparable, indivisible union; similarly, those among us who speak of one united divine-human nature in Christ are justified in doing so since they do not thereby deny the continuing dynamic presence in Christ of the divine and the human, without change, without confusion.

17. Both sides agree in rejecting the teaching which separates or divides the human nature, both soul and body in Christ, from his divine nature or reduces the union of the natures to the level of conjoining. Both sides also agree in rejecting the teaching which confuses the human nature in Christ with the divine nature so that the former is absorbed in the latter and thus ceases to exist.

18. The perfect union of divinity and of humanity in the incarnate Word is essential for the salvation of the human race. "For God so loved the world, that he gave his only Son, that whosoever believeth in him should not perish, but have everlasting life" (John 3:16 KJV).

CONCLUSION

19. In offering this statement, we recognize the mystery of God's act in Christ and seek to express that we have shared the same authentic christological faith in the one incarnate Lord.

20. We submit this statement to the authorities of the Oriental Orthodox churches and to the executive committee of the World Alliance of Reformed Churches for their consideration and action.

Signatures of co-chairmen on behalf of the representatives of the two church families:

His Grace Metropolitan Bishoy
General Secretary of the Holy Synod
of the Coptic Orthodox Church

Rev. Dr Milan Opocensky
General Secretary
of the World Alliance
of Reformed Churches

## III. Convergences and divergences on Tradition and holy scripture, theology, church and mission, priesthood/ministry and sacrament

21. The particularity of the various dialogue sessions has been retained in the presentation of the third part of this report. This third part is organized on the basis of the themes addressed during these sessions. Thirty papers were presented, commented upon, discussed and analyzed. Despite a variety of differences in the views of the two sides, areas of convergence have emerged.

III.1. TRADITION AND HOLY SCRIPTURE

22. The understanding of Tradition and holy scripture by the two families was extensively discussed during the first, second and third sessions of the dialogue.

*Oriental Orthodox view*

23. The Oriental Orthodox distinguish the Tradition of the entire church regarding matters of faith from local traditions of the various churches. They understand both Tradition and holy scripture as constituting one reality emerging from the continuing life of the church. Tradition must be essentially in agreement with the intention of holy scripture, and the authority of the fathers of the church is recognized from their acceptance by the church as a whole.

*Reformed view*

24. While the Reformed churches respect the position of the Oriental Orthodox churches, they affirm the normative character of holy scripture, which itself embodies the "Tradition", in the sense of what was received and handed down by the apostles (apostolic testimony). The Reformed churches affirm a critical distance of holy scripture in relation to "traditions", in the sense of teachings, practices, customs and interpretations of or alongside the one scriptural Tradition. Hence, the church must always examine and reform its traditions in the light of holy scripture.

*Areas of emerging convergence*

25. Both sides acknowledge the deep relationship between the early traditions (the total life) of the church, as guided by the Holy Spirit, and the emergence of holy scripture. The incarnate Word of God is both the source and the judge of the Tradition and the holy scripture of the church which bear witness to him.

26. Both sides agreed on the normative function of holy scripture for the life of the church. The Word incarnate makes use of human means, including human language and culture. So holy scripture and its correct interpretation, guided by Tradition, witnesses to the word of God in our different contexts.

## 27. Areas that need further clarification

- concepts of history and revelation, with special attention to the 18th and 19th century historical-critical Bible study in the Reformed understanding;
- methods of interpreting holy scripture and evaluating Tradition;
- how our historical contexts affect our understanding of holy scripture;
- the question of canonical books in our respective traditions;
- understanding of the holy scripture: its authority and its inspiration.

### III.2. THE ROLE OF THE THEOLOGIAN IN THE CHRISTIAN COMMUNITY

28. The role and function of theology and the theologian in the community was discussed at the third session. The two families affirm that:

- Almighty God's eternal divine essence cannot be comprehended. Human reason can approach God only when illumined by the Holy Spirit, through prayers and holy scripture.
- Theology is not only an act of thinking but should be practically related to life and to our salvation.
- A Christian theologian is one who is rooted in the faith community and nurtured by it.
- Theologians are called upon to express the beauty and splendour of the divine presence in their theological work. Story and poetry, music and iconography, art and architecture, rites and rituals have been used in various Christian traditions precisely to bring out this aesthetic dimension of theology.
- Our ultimate goal to reach a common theological understanding which is rooted in our Lord Jesus Christ is based on the holy scriptures, and is related to the needs and sufferings of humanity at large.

### III.3. THE NATURE OF THE CHURCH AND HER MISSION

29. The nature of the church and her mission were among the themes discussed in the first and the fourth sessions. The Oriental Orthodox and the Reformed participants prepared statements expressing their views regarding this topic.

### The Oriental Orthodox view

30. Regarding the church, the Oriental Orthodox affirm that the church is built on the foundation of the apostles and prophets, and Jesus Christ is the chief cornerstone. We believe in one, holy, catholic and apostolic church. Many names have been given to the church to describe her nature and mission. Some of these names are:

- the people of God (1 Pet. 2:9);
- the mother of the believers (Gal. 4:31);

- the body of Christ (1 Cor. 12:27);
- the new creation in Christ (2 Cor. 5:17);
- the bride of Christ (Rev. 19:7; Matt. 9:14-15);
- the dwelling place of Christ (Eph. 2:21);
- the house of faith and salvation (2 Pet. 3:20-21);
- the community of love and joy (1 John 3:14,16, 4:7,8);
- the communion of saints (Heb. 12:1);
- the temple of the Holy Spirit (2 Cor. 6:19);
- the church of the first-born (Heb. 12:23);
- the icon of heaven (Heb. 8:5-6).

31. Unity is a natural characteristic of the church which reflects her unity with the triune God: Father, Son and Holy Spirit. There is one body, one Spirit, one Lord, one faith and one baptism.

32. Unity in Christ harmonizes the diverse gifts of the Holy Spirit in our different contexts. The continuity of the church in Christ is maintained and guided by the Holy Spirit through the holy Tradition and the apostolic succession. The renewal of the church is a constant growth and joy in this new life.

33. Regarding mission, the Oriental Orthodox affirm that the church, as the living body of Christ, constantly called together and renewed by the Holy Spirit, worships the triune God on behalf of all God's creation. This is mission in its totality. The good news (gospel) of Jesus Christ crucified and risen is the heart of the worshipping community. The church announces the gospel of life in diverse ways, always respecting the norm of God's love and compassion for the world. Proclamation of the word of God is directed to bring about and foster the signs of the rule of God in human history. The good news of the redeeming sacrifice of Jesus Christ are proclaimed with the aim of bringing salvation to those who believe in him and are baptized in the name of the Holy Trinity. The church's prayer and pastoral care, struggle for justice and search for communion are all vital expressions of her participation in the mission of Jesus Christ, her Lord and Saviour. This redeeming mission calls upon members of the body of Christ to refrain from all forms of aggression and cultural domination in the name of Christ, and instead to encourage healing and forgiveness, justice and human dignity, peace and mutual respect among all the peoples on earth. Our freedom in Christ as children of God enjoins us to be compassionately open to all human initiatives for realizing God's will for the created world. The ultimate form of the church's mission is to carry the whole creation in all its brokenness and misery before the transforming presence of the triune God in a perpetual act of praise and thanksgiving.

*Reformed view*

34. According to the Reformed tradition the church is called together by Jesus Christ to be his body in the world through worship, service and witness. Together with believers through the ages, the Reformed confess that Jesus Christ is Lord, and in him is their hope and peace. United by the Spirit to the risen Christ, our participation in the mission of the triune God flows out in service and witness to the world. Confessing the Lordship of

Jesus Christ over the church and the whole world, we affirm that we are called not for our benefit alone but for mission and service in the ministry of reconciliation. In response to that call we participate in the mission of the triune God, through which God is at work redeeming and perfecting the whole of creation. As we grow into the likeness of the triune God, we are conscious that we are called to grow in fellowship with those who confess the name of Christ, and also to join and welcome those of other faiths and world-views who work in God's mission. In order to communicate the Christian faith, we have the task of translating the message in different cultural contexts, in ways which are both appropriate and authentic. This is an ongoing task which involves both teaching and lis-tening, a task done in obedience to Christ who draws everything together in him.

35. We are aware that we have sinned and fallen short of all that God calls us to do and to be. However, recognizing the power of God's forgiveness, and confident that God will reconcile all things in heaven and earth, we press on in hope towards the goal where every tear will be wiped from every eye and God will be all in all (Rev. 21:4; 1 Cor. 15:28).

*Areas of emerging convergence*

36. Both sides agree in acknowledging that the church has an existence that transcends any attempt to describe it in purely historical or sociological terms. Biblical teachings, and titles and images of the church contained therein, testify to the church's origin in the eternal purpose of God. Participating in the mission of Christ, the church announces the gospel of life for the healing and redemption of all humanity.

III.4. PRIESTHOOD/MINISTRY

37. The fifth session of the dialogue was devoted to discussion of priesthood/ministry. It included papers and discussion on the understanding of this topic as well as the iden-tification of points of agreement and disagreement on this matter.

*The Oriental Orthodox understanding*

38. The Oriental Orthodox churches understand priesthood to be one of the seven sacra-ments of the church. It is a divine order and calling instituted by the Lord Jesus Christ when He ordained his twelve apostles: "Then Jesus said to them again: Peace be with you! As the Father has sent Me, I also send you. And when He had said this, He breathed on them, and said to them, receive the Holy Spirit. If you forgive the sins of any, they are forgiven; if you retain the sins of any, they are retained" (John 20:21-23). Also, during the last supper the Lord Jesus Christ gave his body and blood to the apostles and ordered them "do this in remembrance of me" (1 Cor. 11:24). This divine command of celebrat-ing the holy eucharist with bread and wine links our priesthood to the priesthood of Melchizedek through Christ who is the High Priest forever after the order of Melchizedek (Heb. 6:20).

39. *Priesthood in the Old Testament*: The early patriarchs such as Noah, Abraham, Isaac and Jacob offered sacrifices as the priests of the Lord. Their priesthood was exercised in a clear way. This same priesthood of the Old Testament was developed in an organized way through the Mosaic priesthood. It begins with the divine orders revealed to Moses after which he organized the priesthood of Aaron. Aaron's descendents were chosen from among the male Levites to serve as priests.

40. *Priesthood in the New Testament*: In the New Testament priesthood was not cancelled but changed from the Levites' priesthood to the priesthood after the order of Melchizedek: "For when there is a change of the priesthood, there must be also a change of the law" (Heb. 7:12).

41. The Lord chose a special group of believers. He ordained them and called them his apostles (Luke 6:13; John 15:16). He entrusted to them the responsibility of leading his church. He appointed them to tend to his flock, leading them into the path of truth and salvation (Matt. 28:20). He gave them the power to hold and absolve sins (Matt. 18:18), and to administer the sacraments for the believers.

42. The apostles in turn gave these gifts to their successors, the bishops, by the laying-on of hands (Acts 20:28). They charged them to instruct and teach the faithful and to ordain presbyters and deacons: "For this reason I left you in Crete, that you should set in order the things that are lacking, and appoint elders in every city as I commanded you" (Titus 1:5) (see also 1 Tim. 6:2).

43. The apostles understood themselves to be priests and, as such, ministers of the sacraments of God: "To be a minister of Christ Jesus to the Gentiles with the priestly duty proclaiming the gospel of God, so that the Gentiles might become an offering acceptable to God, sanctified by the Holy Spirit" (Rom. 15:16).

44. The covenant of the New Testament is based on the sacrificial death of Jesus Christ on the cross, not as separate from the holy eucharist, but indeed shown and expressed in the holy eucharist. The Lord Jesus Christ said regarding the eucharistic cup, "This cup is the New Testament in my blood" (Luke 22:20 and 1 Cor. 11:25). St Paul also writes the following, "For as often as you eat this bread, and drink this cup, you do show the Lord's death till He comes" (1 Cor. 11:26).

45. If Jesus Christ is the High Priest after the order of Melchizedek, who used bread and wine for his offering, it follows necessarily that the priesthood of the New Testament is an office to celebrate the holy eucharist by offering bread and wine. This eucharistic offering is not a repetition of the sacrifice of the cross, but is the sacrifice of the cross present in the church everywhere and in all generations, beyond time and space limitations.

46. The Lord Jesus Christ commanded his apostles, "Go and make disciples of all nations, baptizing them in the name of the Father and of the Son and of the Holy Spirit" (Matt. 28:19). The apostles were able to ordain baptized believers as bishops, priests and deacons even out of Gentiles without being necessarily descendents of the people of Israel. This was prophetically mentioned in the Old Testament: " And they shall declare my glory among the Gentiles. And they shall bring all your brethren for an offering unto the Lord out of all nations… And I will also take of them for priests and Levites, says the Lord" (Isa. 66:19-21).

47. *Spiritual priesthood*: Any believer in Christ can offer up spiritual sacrifices to God. This applies to both Old Testament and New Testament, as is written, "Let my prayer be

set forth before You as incense; and the lifting-up of my hands as the evening sacrifice" (Ps. 141:2) and "By him, therefore, let us offer the sacrifice of praise to God continually, that is, the fruit of our lips, giving thanks to his name" (Heb. 13:15). But this does not mean that those who are offering spiritual sacrifices, like praying and praising the Lord and helping the poor, are official priests offering the eucharistic sacrifice and ministering in the church.

48. *A kingdom of priests*: It was equally mentioned in the Old Testament and the New Testament that the people of God are a kingdom of priests: "And you shall be unto me a kingdom of priests, and a holy nation" (Exod. 19:6) and, "But you are a chosen generation, a royal priesthood, a holy nation, a peculiar people" (1 Pet. 2:9). This does not imply at all that the whole people of God are officially priests serving the altar in the church.

49. In view of the last two points we can understand (1 Pet. 2:5): "You also, as living stones, are built into a spiritual house, a holy priesthood, to offer up spiritual sacrifices acceptable to God by Jesus Christ."

50. *Threefold priesthood*: While we acknowledge the spiritual priesthood of all believers in Christ, three ranks of priesthood – episcopos, presbyter and deacon – were instituted in the holy church through the power of the Holy Spirit (1 Tim. 3:5; Titus 1:5; Acts 6:5-6).

51. *The role of laity*: The participation and involvement of the faithful in the whole liturgical and sacramental life of the church is very important and this is always affirmed throughout the life and witness of the church.

52. *The dual role of the priesthood*: In offering the holy eucharist the priest acts as the representative of the whole creation. The priest represents the people of the church in front of God and represents God in front of the people and he performs his service by the power of the Holy Spirit.

53. *Laying-on of hands and apostolic succession*: Laying-on of hands was practised by the apostles for different purposes. It is not used only for ordination, but for many other purposes: for blessing the people as Jesus has done with the children (Matt. 19:13), for healing the sick (Mark 15:18), for confirmation (Acts 8:15-17) and for ordination (Acts 6:6, 13:3; 1 Tim. 4:14, 5:22).

54. The authority of laying-on of hands for ordination, consecration and confirmation was confined to the apostles so that Philip, the ordained deacon and preacher, after baptizing the people of Samaria, could not lay hands on them to grant them the gift of the Holy Spirit, and the church sent the Apostles St Peter and St John especially to Samaria to pray and lay hands upon the people in order to receive the Holy Spirit (Acts 6:5, 8:5,12,14-17). The apostles passed on the authority of laying-on of hands to some of the presbyters whom they have ordained by making them bishops who were able to ordain presbyters (1 Tim. 5:22; Titus 1:5).

55. This apostolic succession remained unbroken in the church as the Lord has promised: "You did not choose me, but I chose you and appointed you to go and bear fruit – fruit that will last" (John 15:16).

56. *Service of women in the church*: Women are honoured in the church and can become saints who are venerated at all levels. St Mary is the most venerated saint in the church, but she was not a priest serving the altar. They can serve as deaconesses without having a priestly order. They do not serve in the sanctuary or officiate at the sacraments of the

church, but they can help the bishop and the priest in many pastoral offices. Women can be prophets, but cannot be priests or teachers of the church.

57. The church is following the teachings of the holy scriptures which declare that the man is the head of the woman although they are equal in nature: "Now I want you to realize that the head of every man is Christ, and the head of the woman is man, and the head of Christ is God" (1 Cor. 11:3; see also Eph. 5:22,23,32). Also, the holy scriptures tell us that women are not allowed to teach men or have authority over them (1 Tim. 2:11,15; 1 Cor. 14:33,34-38). There were no women priests in the Old Testament, too. The icon of Christ and the church can be seen in the relation of man and woman in the church.

## *The Reformed understanding*

58. The Reformed understanding of ministry begins with the ministry of the whole people of God who, as the body of Christ, continue Christ's ministry to the world. This ministry, empowered by the Holy Spirit, follows the pattern of Christ's threefold ministry of prophet, priest and king through the proclamation of the faith, the practice of Christian love and the search for justice and peace in the world. This ministry is the privilege and responsibility of every believer by virtue of their baptism into Christ. In this context the Reformed tradition speaks of the "priesthood of all believers". In addition to the general priesthood of all believers the Reformed tradition also maintains a ministry of elders. Elders are chosen and appointed from the congregation to form a conciliar body that is responsible for spiritual discipline, the exercise of public worship and the governance of the life of the church.

59. The Reformed tradition also maintains a particular ministry of the word and sacrament. This ministry is bestowed on those who the church recognizes as being called and empowered by God to be set apart to this function. The minister of word and sacrament is an elder with a particular responsibility for teaching and the celebration of the sacraments. There is equality between teaching elders (ministers of word and sacrament) and the ruling elders. The ministry of word and sacrament is vital for the upbuilding of the church and the edification of God's people. The importance of this ministry can be demonstrated by reference to the traditional Reformed criteria for the recognition of a true church, namely a church exists wherever the word of God is faithfully preached and heard and the sacraments administered according to the word of God.[2]

60. Admittance to the ministry of word and sacrament follows the preparation of the candidate through a programme of theological training and examination by the church. Ordination to the ministry of word and sacrament requires the call of God's people and is administered by a prayer of invocation of the Holy Spirit and the laying-on of hands by elders of the church. In this unrepeatable act of ordination the ministry is formally entrusted to the ordinand and the ordinand vows to be faithful to God in their practice of ministry. Most Reformed churches ordain both women and men to the ministry of word and sacrament. On the basis of their one baptism and their participation in the priesthood of all believers women and men are called by the Holy Spirit to the ordained ministry.

61. The Reformed tradition regards the institutional expression of ministry as belonging to the bene esse of the life of the church rather than the esse. As such the precise organization and pattern of ministry is in principle revisable as the church responds, under the direction and guidance of the Holy Spirit and in faithfulness to the scriptures,

to changing historical circumstances. Generally speaking, member churches of the Reformed family do not have a personal episcopate. The exercise of *episcope* is vested in communal and conciliar bodies where ruling elders and teaching elders are represented on equal basis. The Reformed tradition believes itself to be in continuity with the faith of the apostles as evidenced by its proclamation of the gospel, its celebration of the sacraments, its acceptance of the creeds and its service to the world.

## 62. *Points of agreement*

- Both traditions acknowledge that the Lord Jesus Christ is the foundation of all ministry in the church.
- The celebrant of the sacraments in the church should be an ordained priest/minister who should have a special gift through the power of the Holy Spirit.
- Baptism and eucharist are accepted sacraments in each tradition in spite of the difference in understanding of the essence and implications of these sacraments. These differences require further discussion.
- Spiritual/universal priesthood (as distinct from official ordained priesthood in the Oriental Orthodox understanding) is granted to all who believe in Christ, including men and women.
- Conciliarity of the church and conciliar forms of government are expressed and practised in both traditions.

## *Points of disagreement*

### 63. *Oriental Orthodox view*

- The concept of priesthood in the Oriental Orthodox differs from the Reformed tradition. The Oriental Orthodox believe in a clear distinction between the official priesthood and the spiritual priesthood of all believers in Christ in both the Old Testament and the New Testament.
- The unbroken apostolic succession by the laying-on of hands is essential for the continuity of priestly ministry in the church.
- The bishop is the successor of the apostles. Only the bishop is entitled to perform ordination by the laying-on of hands.
- Three ranks of priesthood, namely bishop, priest and deacon, are clear and distinct in the Oriental Orthodox tradition from the beginning of the early church.
- In order that the Lord Jesus Christ should be believed as the High Priest after the order of Melchizedek, it follows necessarily that there should be also priests in the church offering the eucharist using bread and wine.
- The priestly offering of the eucharist makes the sacrifice of the cross present everywhere and in every generation beyond space and time limitations, and as such is not understood as a repetition of the sacrifice of the Lord on the cross.

• The following seven sacraments are recognized and practised in the life of the church: baptism, confirmation, repentance and confession, holy eucharist, matrimony, anointing the sick, and priesthood.
• The ordination of women to priestly ministry is unacceptable based on the teachings of the holy scriptures.

*Reformed view*

64. It is a common Reformed understanding that a uniform church order which is universally applicable in all times and all places cannot be found in the New Testament. The Reformed understanding of holy scripture does not necessarily suggest the practice of a hierarchical pattern of ministry. The Reformed churches assert that they are in continuity with the succession of apostolic faith. The uninterrupted episcopal succession does not in itself guarantee the pure proclamation of the gospel and the proper administration of the sacraments.

65. In relation to the ministry of word and sacrament, Reformed churches affirm that the ordained minister does not differ from any other believer except in function. The ordained minister does not possess a distinct character or "imprint". The ordained ministry belongs to the well-being of the church (bene esse). Since the priestly ministry has been fulfilled by Christ, a minister of a Reformed church does not perform any special priestly function. The Reformed tradition asserts that the power to ordain is not vested in an individual person or office but belongs communally to the church. The call of God, adequate ministerial formation and the invocation of the Holy Spirit are the indispensable prerequisites for ordination. The act of ordination does not simply depend on the "laying-on of hands".

66. Most Reformed churches do not agree that the ordained ministry is withheld from women. According to the Reformed understanding there are no biblical or theological reasons for denying ordination to women.

III.5. SACRAMENTS

67. The last two sessions of the Oriental Orthodox-Reformed dialogue discussed extensively the doctrine, number and practice of the sacraments in the two families. Variations and differences between the two traditions concerning the nature and number of the sacraments were openly expressed.

*Oriental Orthodox view*

68. The Oriental Orthodox family of churches believes in seven sacraments; namely, baptism, chrismation, repentance and confession, eucharist, priesthood, marriage (matrimony), and unction of the sick.

69. A sacrament performed by a canonically ordained priest in a concrete form of a special material is an unseen work of the Holy Spirit.

70. The role of the Holy Spirit in the sacraments is essential because the gifts of God are "from the Father through the Son by the Holy Spirit". (St Athanasius wrote, "The Father does all things through the Word in the Holy Spirit", First Letter to Serapion, ch. 28, "Concerning the Holy Spirit").[3]

71. The minister of the sacrament is the steward of God as is written by St Pau: "Let a man so consider us, as servants of Christ and stewards of the mysteries of God" (1 Cor. 4:1), "For a bishop must be blameless, as a steward of God" (Tit. 1:7).

72. In the Oriental Orthodox presentations, the role of the Holy Spirit in the seven sacraments was clarified based on the holy scripture. Therefore, the role of the Holy Spirit cannot be divided from the sacraments.

73. The sacraments of the church are experienced as a life that one lives inside the church and not as something that one just hears about. One tastes its efficacy and experiences its effect in his life, and the more he experiences such effect the more his belief in it increases.

*Reformed view*

74. The two sacraments administered by the Reformed churches, baptism and the eucharist, are always celebrated in the context of worship. A major difference between the two families is in the number of sacraments observed. Although the Reformed tradition does not recognize marriage, ordination, confirmation and confession and unction as sacraments, their importance as religious ordinances is not ignored. For example, our worship books contain several different orders of worship such as morning prayer, Sunday public worship (including confession and eucharist), baptism, wedding, memorial service, ordination, installation, healing and confirmation. These rich and varied liturgical practices show that we have these rites in common with the Oriental Orthodox family. From the perspective of our lay people or members, these ceremonies are very important.

75. For the Reformed family of churches, two of these practices are dominical sacraments, namely baptism and eucharist. Based on the teaching of Our Lord Jesus Christ (Matt. 26:26-28, 28:18-20), we regard them as means of grace made available by God to all people through the church. While affirming that baptism and the eucharist are essential, we do not limit God's grace to these means. God's power to save is in God's hands alone.

76. In which way are the aacraments means of salvation? We understand grace to be communicated by God, not in any automatic way. We do not believe there is anything mechanical about the process of God's salvation. In the final analysis, it is God's grace rather than human action and it is normally a lifelong commitment.

77. Word and sacrament are very closely linked in the Reformed tradition: "It is the efficacy of the word that is brought to light in a sacrament, for a sacrament is a proclamation of the gospel – different in form, but not in function, from the preaching of the word."[4]

78. Reformed liturgies were developed in the 16th century when the protestant Reformers, confronted with worship practices they considered unacceptable, went back to the original sources of scriptures and worship practices of the early church. Over the cen-

turies, there have been renewed attempts to reappropriate the biblical meaning of worship. Such changes are implemented by the highest synodal levels of our churches. They involve lengthy consultations with theological experts and church members.

79.  Reformed churches regarded the full participation of lay people as essential to both sacraments. The administration includes always lay and clergy participation. They are in fact corporate acts of the congregation. For instance, baptism liturgies commit parents and the congregation equally to the Christian nurture and development of a child. Lay people participate together with the ministers in the preparation for the sacraments. In the eucharist, this includes prayer, confession and proclamation.

*Emerging convergence*

80.  While differing on many points concerning the number and nature of the sacraments, both families affirm that the sacraments are the gracious gifts of God for nourishing and maintaining the life of the church and for strengthening her union with Christ.

## IV. Conclusion

81.  Our seven sessions of dialogue have been only the beginning of a process of acquaintance and mutual knowledge between two Christian traditions that have never officially engaged in dialogue with each other before. Centuries of separation and minimal or non-interaction on the ecclesiastical, theological and spiritual levels – but also on the cultural level – have made our dialogue both exciting and slow. Exciting, because we felt that we were breaking new ground by simply getting to know each other and how we understand and express our Christian and ecclesial identities. Slow, because we realized that we needed to catch up with each other on many levels and required much more time together to bear lasting fruit in our encounters. Nevertheless, the results we did achieve were quite significant and certainly historic, e.g., the agreement on Christology that resolved a centuries-old theological controversy. We realize that there are many areas of theological difference which still exist and need further dialogue.

82.  The Oriental Orthodox-Reformed dialogue has already given the opportunity to discuss issues of mutual concern. None can foresee the results clearly today. Any activity intending church unity is an answer to the call of Jesus Christ that churches exhibit Christian unity in order to bear witness to his mission in the world. Who knows how the Holy Spirit has led this dialogue in planting unity among the Reformed and the Oriental Orthodox families of churches in generations to come? Hope for Christian unity is both present and future. We pray that God may use us for the fulfilment of this hope.

83.  We submit this report to the authorities of the Oriental Orthodox churches and to the executive committee of the World Alliance of Reformed Churches for their consideration and action.

## Appendix I:  List of Papers Presented

*First session: Anba Bishoy Monastery, Wadi-El Natroun, Egypt, 2-5 May 1993*
Introduction to the Oriental Orthodox churches (Bishop Matta Roham Mar Eustathius)
The main characteristics of the Reformed churches (Dr Karel Blei)
Oriental Orthodox view of tradition and scripture (Pope Shenouda III)
A Reformed view on tradition and scripture (Dr Silke-Petra Bergjan)
The nature and the mission of the church: an Oriental Orthodox view (Dr Kondothra M. George)
The nature and the mission of the church: a Reformed view (Dr Samuel Habib)

*Second session: Driebergen, Netherlands, 10-15 September 1994*
Christological controversies of the fourth and fifth centuries (Dr George Sabra)
A survey of the recent bilateral agreements between the Oriental (non-Chalcedonian) Orthodox churches and the Eastern Orthodox church and other Christian communions (Metropolitan Bishoy)
The bilateral agreements between the Oriental Orthodox and the Eastern Orthodox: a Reformed response (Dr Silke-Petra Bergjan)
Tradition and its role in the Syrian Orthodox Church (Bishop Matta Roham Mar Eustathius)
Holy scripture and Tradition: a Reformed perspective (Dr Rebecca Weaver)
Holy scripture: its use and misuse from an Oriental Orthodox perspective (Dr Kondothra M. George)
The use and abuse of the scriptures in relation to mission, evangelism and proselytism from a Reformed perspective (Dr Peter McEnhill)

*Third session: Sophia Centre, Kottayam, India, 10-15 January 1997*
Theology and theologian: their function and authority in the Orthodox church (Dr Kondothra M. George)
The beauty and service of theology (Dr Milan Opocensky)
A brief history of the Reformed churches in India (Dr Franklyn J. Balasundaram)
Holy scripture: its authority and its inspiration (Dr Karel Blei)

*Fourth session: Richmond, Virginia, USA, 9-16 January 1998*
Mission: an Oriental Orthodox perspective (Dr M. Kondothra George)
The nature of the church from a Reformed perspective (Dr Christopher B. Kaiser)
Some key issues in contemporary mission debate (Dr H.S. Wilson)

*Fifth session: St Ephrem Syrian Orthodox Seminary, Ma'arat Saydnaya, Syria, 10-15 January 1999*
The understanding of ministry in the Reformed tradition (Dr Peter McEnhill)
Ministry in the Orthodox tradition (His Grace Archbishop Aphrem Karim Mar Cyril)
The link between priesthood and eucharist in the New Testament (Metropolitan Bishoy)

*Sixth session: Musselburgh, Scotland, 11-16 January 2000*
Introduction to the sacraments of the church (Metropolitan Bishoy)
The mystery/sacrament of baptism (Very Rev. Nareg Alemezian)
Introduction to the sacrament of holy liturgy/eucharist (Geevarghese Mar Coorilos)
An interrogation of the sacraments of baptism and eucharist (Dr J. Jayakiran Sebastian)
The Reformed understanding of the sacraments (Dr George Sabra)

*Seventh session: Catholicosate of Cilicia in Antelias, Beirut, Lebanon, 23-28 January 2001*

Introduction to the sacraments: an Oriental Orthodox perspective (Metropolitan Yohanna Ibrahim Mar Gregorios)

## Appendix II:  Participants

### 1.  Oriental Orthodox

*In the 1992 planning meeting*

Pope Shenouda III (Co-chair), Patriarch of Alexandria, Coptic Orthodox Church
Archbishop Aram Keshishian, Armenian Apostolic Church
Dr Kondothra M. George, Malankara Orthodox Syrian Church
Metropolitan Yohanna Ibrahim Mar Gregorios, Syrian Orthodox Church
Archbishop Timotheos, Ethiopian Orthodox Tewahedo Church

*In the dialogue sessions held between 1993 and 2001*

Pope Shenouda III (Co-chair), Patriarch of Alexandria, Coptic Orthodox Church [1993, 1994]
Metropolitan Bishoy (Co-chair from 1997), Coptic Orthodox Church [1993, 1994, 1997, 1999, 2000, 2001]
Very Rev. Father Nareg Alemezian, Armenian Apostolic Church [1999, 2000, 2001]
Bishop Vicken Aykazian, Armenian Apostolic Church [1993, 1997, 1998]
Bishop Dirayr Panossian, Armenian Apostolic Church [1997, 1998, 1999, 2000, 2001]
Bishop Moussa, Coptic Orthodox Church [1993, 1994, 1997]
Bishop Serapion, Coptic Orthodox Church [1993]
Bishop Youssef, Coptic Orthodox Church [1998]
Bishop Antony, Coptic Orthodox Church [2000]
Archbishop Abuna Kerlos, Ethiopian Orthodox Tewahedo Church [2000]
Rev. Seife Selassie Yohannes, Ethiopian Orthodox Tewahedo Church [1994, 2000]
Geevarghese Mar Coorilos, Malankara Orthodox Syrian Church [1993, 1994, 1997, 1998, 1999, 2000, 2001]

Dr Kondothra M. George, Malankara Orthodox Syrian Church [1993, 1994, 1997, 1998]
Metropolitan Philipos Mar Eusebius, Malankara Orthodox Syrian Church [invited 1997]
Mr P.C. Abraham, Malankara Orthodox Syrian Church [invited 1997]
Mrs P. Lukose, Malankara Orthodox Syrian Church [invited 1997]
Father John Mathews, Malankara Orthodox Syrian Church [invited 1997]
Father John Thomas, Malankara Orthodox Syrian Church [invited 1997]
Archbishop Yohanna Ibrahim Mar Gregorios, Syrian Orthodox Church [1998, 1999, 2000]
Archbishop Aphrem Karim Mar Cyril, Syrian Orthodox Church [1998, 1999, 2000]
Bishop Matta Roham Mar Eustathius, Syrian Orthodox Church [1993, 1994, 1999]


## 2. Reformed

*In the 1992 planning meeting*

Dr Milan Opocensky (Co-chair), Evangelical Church of Czech Brethren
Dr Silke-Petra Bergjan, Evangelical-Reformed Church, Germany

*WARC staff*

Dr H.S. Wilson, Church of South India

*In the dialogue sessions held between 1993 and 2001*

Dr Milan Opocensky (Co-chair), Evangelical Church of Czech Brethren [1993, 1994, 1997, 1998, 1999, 2000]
Dr Jana Opocenská, Evangelical Church of Czech Brethren [1993]
Dr Silke-Petra Bergjan, Evangelical-Reformed Church, Germany [1993, 1994, 1999, 2000]
Rev. Dr Karel Blei, Netherlands Reformed Church [1993, 1994, 1997]
Dr Samuel Habib, Synod of the Nile of the Evangelical Church, Egypt [1993]
Rev. Dr Abdel Masih Istafanous, Synod of the Nile of the Evangelical Church, Egypt [1993]
Dr Christopher Kaiser, Reformed Church in America [1994, 1997, 1998, 1999, 2000, co-chair 2001]
Dr Peter McEnhill, Church of Scotland, UK [1994, 1997, 1998, 1999, 2000, 2001]
Dr George Sabra, National Evangelical Synod of Syria and Lebanon [1993, 1994, 1998, 2000, 2001]
Dr J. Jayakiran Sebastian, Church of South India [1993, 1994, 1997, 1998, 2000, 2001]
Dr Eugene Turner, Presbyterian Church (USA) [1993, 1994, 1997, 1998, 1999, 2000, 2001]
Dr Harold Vogelaar, Reformed Church in America [1993]
Dr Rebecca Weaver, Presbyterian Church (USA) [1993, 1994, 1997, 1998, 1999]
Rev. Emile Zaki, Synod of the Nile of the Evangelical Church, Egypt [1997, 2000]
Dr H.S. Wilson [1999], Wartburg Theological Seminary, USA

*Consultant*
Dr Franklyn Balasundaram, Church of South India [1997]

*Visitors*
Rev. Dr C.S. Calian, Presbyterian Church (USA) [1998]
Rev. Dr Victor Makari, Presbyterian Church (USA) [1998]

*WARC staff*
Dr H.S. Wilson, Church of South India [1993, 1994, 1997, 1998]
Dr Odair Pedroso Mateus, Independent Presbyterian Church of Brazil [2000, 2001]

NOTES
[1] Roman Catholic-Reformed (since 1970), Lutheran-Reformed (since 1970), Baptist-Reformed (1973-77), Anglican-Reformed (1981-1984), Mennonite-Reformed (1984), Disciples of Christ-Reformed (1984), Prague consultations on the first, radical and second Reformations (since 1986), Methodist-Reformed (1987), Orthodox-Reformed (since 1988), Pentecostal-Reformed (1996-2000), African Instituted Churches-Reformed (since 1999), Adventist-Reformed (2001).
[2] The Augsburg Confession (1530) art. 7; the Geneva Confession (1536) art. 18; the First Helvetic Confession (1536) art. 14; the Confession of Faith Used in the English Congregation at Geneva (1556) art. 4; the French Confession (1559) art. XXVIII; the Scottish Confession (1560) ch. XVIII; the Belgic Confession (1561) art. 29; the Second Helvetic Confession (1566) ch. XVII.
[3] C.R.B. Shapland, *The Letters of Saint Athanasius Concerning the Holy Spirit*, London, Epworth, 1951, pp.134-35.
[4] Brian A. Gerrish, *Grace and Gratitude: The Eucharistic Theology of John Calvin*, Edinburgh, T & T Clark, 1998, p.108.

# Part B

# 14. The Gift of Authority
# (Authority in the Church III)

## Anglican-Roman Catholic International Commission

### Palazzola, Italy, 3 September 1998

### Preface by the co-chairmen

An earnest search for full visible unity between the Anglican Communion and the Roman Catholic Church was initiated over thirty years ago by the historic meeting in Rome of Archbishop Michael Ramsey and Pope Paul VI. The commission set up to prepare for the dialogue recognized, in its 1968 Malta report, that one of the "urgent and important tasks" would be to examine the question of authority. In a sense, this question is at the heart of our sad divisions.

When *The Final Report* of ARCIC was published in 1981 half of it was devoted to the dialogue about authority in the church, with two agreed statements and an elucidation. This was important groundwork, preparing the way for further convergence. The official responses, by the 1988 Lambeth Conference of the Anglican Communion and by the Catholic Church in 1991, encouraged the commission to carry forward the "remarkable progress" that had been made. Accordingly ARCIC now offers this further agreed statement, "The Gift of Authority".

A scriptural image is the key to this statement. In chapter one of his second letter to the Corinthians, Paul writes of God's "Yes" to humanity and our answering "Amen" to God, both given in Jesus Christ (cf. 2 Cor. 1:19-20). God's gift of authority to his church is at the service of God's "Yes" to his people and their "Amen".

The reader is invited to follow the path that led the commission to its conclusions. They are the fruit of five years of dialogue, of patient listening, study, and prayer together. The statement will, we hope, prompt further theological reflection; its conclusions present a challenge to our two churches, not least in regard to the crucial issue of universal primacy. Authority is about how the church teaches, acts and reaches doctrinal decisions in faithfulness to the gospel, so real agreement about authority cannot be theoretical. If this statement is to contribute to the reconciliation of the Anglican Communion and the Catholic Church and is accepted, it will require a response in life and in deed.

Much has happened over these years to deepen our awareness of each other as brothers and sisters in Christ. Yet our journey towards full, visible unity is proving longer than some expected and many hoped. We have encountered serious obstacles which make progress difficult. At such a stage, the persevering, painstaking work of dialogue is all the more vital. The present Archbishop of Canterbury, Dr George Carey, and Pope John Paul II stated very frankly the need for this work on authority when they met in 1996: "Without agreement in this area we shall not reach the full, visible unity to which we are both committed."

We pray that God will enable the commission's work to contribute to the end we all desire, the healing of our divisions so that together we may say a united "'Amen' to the glory of God" (2 Cor. 1:20).

+Cormac Murphy-O'Connor                     +Mark Santer

Palazzola, Feast of St Gregory the Great, 3 September 1998

**The status of the document**

The document published here is the work of the Anglican-Roman Catholic International Commission (ARCIC). It is a joint statement of the commission. The authorities who appointed the commission have allowed the statement to be published so that it may be widely discussed. It is not an authoritative declaration by the Roman Catholic Church or by the Anglican Communion, who will evaluate the document in order to take a position on it in due time.

Citations from scripture are from the New Revised Standard Version.

# THE GIFT OF AUTHORITY
## (AUTHORITY IN THE CHURCH III)

## I. Introduction

1. The dialogue between Anglicans and Roman Catholics has shown significant signs of progress on the question of authority in the church. This progress can already be seen in the convergence in understanding of authority achieved by previous ARCIC statements, notably:

- acknowledgment that the Spirit of the Risen Lord maintains the people of God in obedience to the Father's will: by this action of the Holy Spirit, the authority of the Lord is active in the church (cf. *The Final Report*, Authority in the Church, I.3);
- a recognition that because of their baptism and their participation in the *sensus fidelium* the laity play an integral part in decision-making in the church (cf. Authority in the Church: Elucidation, 4);

- the complementarity of primacy and conciliarity as elements of *episcope* within the church (cf. Authority in the Church, I.22);
- the need for a universal primacy exercised by the bishop of Rome as a sign and safeguard of unity within a re-united church (cf. Authority in the Church, II.9);
- the need for the universal primate to exercise his ministry in collegial association with the other bishops (cf. Authority in the Church, II.19);
- an understanding of universal primacy and conciliarity which complements and does not supplant the exercise of *episcope* in local churches (cf. Authority in the Church, I.21-23; Authority in the Church, II.19).

2. This convergence has been officially noted by the authorities of the Anglican Communion and the Roman Catholic Church. The Lambeth Conference, meeting in 1988, not only saw the ARCIC agreements on eucharistic doctrine and on ministry and ordination as consonant in substance with the faith of Anglicans (resolution 8:1) but affirmed that the agreed statements on authority in the church provided a basis for further dialogue (resolution 8:3). Similarly, the Holy See, in its official response of 1991, recognizing areas of agreement on questions of very great importance for the faith of the Roman Catholic Church, such as the eucharist and the church's ministry, noted the signs of convergence between our two communions on the question of authority in the church, indicating that this opened the way to further progress.

3. However, the authorities of our two communions have asked for further exploration of areas where, although there has been convergence, they believe that a necessary consensus has not yet been achieved. These areas include:

- the relationship between scripture, Tradition and the exercise of teaching authority;
- collegiality, conciliarity, and the role of laity in decision-making;
- the Petrine ministry of universal primacy in relation to scripture and Tradition.

Even though progress has been made, some serious difficulties have emerged on the way to unity. Issues concerning authority have been raised acutely for each of our communions. For example, debates and decisions about the ordination of women have led to questions about the sources and structures of authority and how they function for Anglicans and Roman Catholics.

4. In both communions the exploration of how authority should be exercised at different levels has been open to the perspectives of other churches on these issues. For example, the *Virginia Report* of the inter-Anglican theological and doctrinal commission (prepared for the Lambeth Conference of 1998) declares, "The long history of ecumenical involvement, both locally and internationally, has shown us that Anglican discernment and decision-making must take account of the insights into truth and the Spirit-led wisdom of our ecumenical partners. Moreover, any decisions we take must be offered for the discernment of the universal church" (*Virginia Report*, 6.37). Pope John Paul II also, in his encyclical letter *Ut Unum Sint*, invited leaders and theologians of other churches to engage with him in a fraternal dialogue on how the particular ministry of unity of the bishop of Rome might be exercised in a new situation (cf. *UUS* 95-96).

5. There is an extensive debate about the nature and exercise of authority both in the churches and in wider society. Anglicans and Roman Catholics want to witness, both to the churches and to the world, that authority rightly exercised is a gift of God to bring reconciliation and peace to humankind. The exercise of authority can be oppressive and

destructive. It may, indeed, often be so in human societies and even in churches when they uncritically adopt certain patterns of authority. The exercise of authority in the ministry of Jesus shows a different way. It is in conformity with the mind and example of Christ that the church is called to exercise authority (cf. Luke 22:24-27; John 13:14-15; Phil. 2:1-11). For the exercise of this authority the church is endowed by the Holy Spirit with a variety of gifts and ministries (cf. 1 Cor. 12:4-11; Eph. 4:11-12).

6. From the beginning of its work, ARCIC has considered questions of church teaching or practice in the context of our real but imperfect communion in Christ and the visible unity to which we are called. The commission has always sought to get behind opposed and entrenched positions to discover and develop our common inheritance. Building on the previous work of ARCIC, the commission offers a further statement on how the gift of authority, rightly exercised, enables the church to continue in obedience to the Holy Spirit, who keeps it faithful in the service of the gospel for the salvation of the world. We wish further to clarify how the exercise and acceptance of authority in the church is inseparable from the response of believers to the gospel, how it is related to the dynamic interaction of scripture and Tradition, and how it is expressed and experienced in the communion of the churches and the collegiality of their bishops. In the light of these insights we have come to a deepened understanding of a universal primacy which serves the unity of all the local churches.

## II. Authority in the church

*Jesus Christ: God's "Yes" to us and our "Amen" to God*

7. God is the author of life. By his Word and Spirit, in perfect freedom, God calls life into being. In spite of human sin, God in perfect faithfulness remains the author of the hope of new life for all. In Jesus Christ's work of redemption God renews his promise to his creation, for "God's purpose is to bring all people into communion with himself within a transformed creation" (ARCIC, *Church as Communion*, 16). The Spirit of God continues to work in creation and redemption to bring this purpose of reconciliation and unity to completion. The root of all true authority is thus the activity of the triune God, who authors life in all its fullness.

8. The authority of Jesus Christ is that of the "faithful witness", the "Amen" (cf. Rev. 1:5, 3:14) in whom all the promises of God find their "Yes". When Paul had to defend the authority of his teaching he did so by pointing to the trustworthy authority of God: "As surely as God is faithful, our word to you has not been Yes and No. For the Son of God, Jesus Christ, whom we preached among you... was not Yes and No; but in him it is always Yes. For all the promises of God find their Yes in him. That is why we utter the Amen through him, to the glory of God" (2 Cor. 1:18-20). Paul speaks of the "Yes" of God to us and the "Amen" of the church to God. In Jesus Christ, Son of God and born of a woman, the "Yes" of God to humanity and the "Amen" of humanity to God become a concrete human reality. This theme of God's "Yes" and humanity's "Amen" in Jesus Christ is the key to the exposition of authority in this statement.

9. In the life and ministry of Jesus, who came to do his Father's will (cf. Heb. 10:5-10) even unto death (cf. Phil. 2:8; John 10:18), God provided the perfect human "Amen" to his purpose of reconciliation. In his life, Jesus expressed his total dedication to the Father (cf. John 5:19). The way Jesus exercised authority in his earthly ministry was perceived

by his contemporaries as something new. It was recognized in his powerful teaching and in his healing and liberating word (cf. Matt. 7:28-29; Mark 1:22, 27). Most of all, his authority was demonstrated by his self-giving service in sacrificial love (cf. Mark 10:45). Jesus spoke and acted with authority because of his perfect communion with the Father. His authority came from the Father (cf. Matt. 11:27; John 14:10-12). It is to the Risen Lord that all authority is given in heaven and on earth (cf. Matt. 28:18). Jesus Christ now lives and reigns with the Father, in the unity of the Holy Spirit; he is the Head of his body, the church, and Lord of all creation (cf. Eph. 1:18-23).

10. The life-giving obedience of Jesus Christ calls forth through the Spirit our "Amen" to God the Father. In this "Amen" through Christ we glorify God, who gives the Spirit in our hearts as a pledge of his faithfulness (cf. 2 Cor. 1:20-22). We are called in Christ to witness to God's purpose (cf. Luke 24:46-49), a witness that may for us too include obedience to the point of death. In Christ obedience is not a burden (cf. 1 John 5:3). It springs from the liberation given by the Spirit of God. The divine "Yes" and our "Amen" are clearly seen in baptism, when in the company of the faithful we say "Amen" to God's work in Christ. By the Spirit, our "Amen" as believers is incorporated in the "Amen" of Christ, through whom, with whom, and in whom we worship the Father.

### The believer's "Amen" in the "Amen" of the local church

11. The gospel comes to people in a variety of ways: the witness and life of a parent or other Christian, the reading of the scriptures, participation in the liturgy, or some other spiritual experience. Acceptance of the gospel is also enacted in many ways: in being baptized, in renewal of commitment, in a decision to remain faithful, or in acts of self-giving to those in need. In these actions the person says, "Indeed, Jesus Christ is my God: he is for me salvation, the source of hope, the true face of the living God."

12. When a believer says "Amen" to Christ individually, a further dimension is always involved: an "Amen" to the faith of the Christian community. The person who receives baptism must come to know the full implication of participating in divine life within the body of Christ. The believer's "Amen" to Christ becomes yet more complete as that person receives all that the church, in faithfulness to the word of God, affirms to be the authentic content of divine revelation. In that way, the "Amen" said to what Christ is for each believer is incorporated within the "Amen" the church says to what Christ is for his body. Growing into this faith may be for some an experience of questioning and struggle. For all it is one in which the integrity of the believer's conscience has a vital part to play. The believer's "Amen" to Christ is so fundamental that individual Christians throughout their life are called to say "Amen" to all that the whole company of Christians receives and teaches as the authentic meaning of the gospel and the way to follow Christ.

13. Believers follow Christ in communion with other Christians in their local church (cf. Authority in the Church, I.8, where it is explained that "the unity of local communities under one bishop constitutes what is commonly meant in our two communions by 'a local church'"). In the local church they share Christian life, together finding guidance for the formation of their conscience and strength to face their difficulties. They are sustained by the means of grace which God provides for his people: the holy scriptures, expounded in preaching, catechesis and creeds; the sacraments; the service of the ordained ministry; the life of prayer and common worship; the witness of holy persons.

The believer is incorporated into an "Amen" of faith, older, deeper, broader, richer than the individual's "Amen" to the gospel. So the relation between the faith of the individual and the faith of the church is more complex than may sometimes appear. Every baptized person shares the rich experience of the church which, even when it struggles with contemporary questions, continues to proclaim what Christ is for his body. Each believer, by the grace of the Spirit, together with all believers of all times and all places, inherits this faith of the church in the communion of saints. Believers then live out a twofold "Amen" within the continuity of worship, teaching and practice of their local church. This local church is a eucharistic community. At the centre of its life is the celebration of the holy eucharist in which all believers hear and receive God's "Yes" in Christ to them. In the great thanksgiving, when the memorial of God's gift in the saving work of Christ crucified and risen is celebrated, the community is at one with all Christians of all the churches who, since the beginning and until the end, pronounce humanity's "Amen" to God – the "Amen" which the Apocalypse affirms is at the heart of the great liturgy of heaven (cf. Rev. 5:14, 7:12).

*Tradition and apostolicity: the local church's "Amen" in the communion of the churches*

14. The "Yes" of God commands and invites the "Amen" of believers. The revealed Word, to which the apostolic community originally bore witness, is received and communicated through the life of the whole Christian community. Tradition (*paradosis*) refers to this process. The gospel of Christ crucified and risen is continually handed on and received (cf. 1 Cor. 15:3) in the Christian churches. This tradition, or handing-on, of the gospel is the work of the Spirit, especially through the ministry of word and sacrament and in the common life of the people of God. Tradition is a dynamic process, communicating to each generation what was delivered once for all to the apostolic community. Tradition is far more than the transmission of true propositions concerning salvation. A minimalist understanding of Tradition that would limit it to a storehouse of doctrine and ecclesial decisions is insufficient. The church receives, and must hand on, all those elements that are constitutive of ecclesial communion: baptism, confession of the apostolic faith, celebration of the eucharist, leadership by an apostolic ministry (cf. *Church as Communion*, 15.43). In the economy (oikonomia) of God's love for humanity, the Word who became flesh and dwelt among us is at the centre of what was transmitted from the beginning and what will be transmitted until the end.

15. Tradition is a channel of the love of God, making it accessible in the church and in the world today. Through it, from one generation to another, and from one place to another, humanity shares communion in the Holy Trinity. By the process of tradition, the church ministers the grace of the Lord Jesus Christ and the koinonia of the Holy Spirit (cf. 2 Cor. 13:14). Therefore Tradition is integral to the economy of grace, love and communion. For those whose ears have not heard and eyes have not seen, the moment of receiving the saving gospel is an experience of enlightenment, forgiveness, healing, liberation. Those who participate in the communion of the gospel cannot refrain from transmitting it to others, even if this means martyrdom. Tradition is both a treasure to be received by the people of God and a gift to be shared with all humanity.

16. Apostolic Tradition is a gift of God which must be constantly received anew. By means of it, the Holy Spirit forms, maintains and sustains the communion of the local

churches from one generation to the next. The handing-on and reception of apostolic Tradition is an act of communion whereby the Spirit unites the local churches of our day with those that preceded them in the one apostolic faith. The process of Tradition entails the constant and perpetual reception and communication of the revealed Word of God in many varied circumstances and continually changing times. The church's "Amen" to apostolic Tradition is a fruit of the Spirit who constantly guides the disciples into all the truth; that is, into Christ who is the way, the truth and the life (cf. John 16:13, 14:6).

17. Tradition expresses the apostolicity of the church. What the apostles received and proclaimed is now found in the Tradition of the church where the word of God is preached and the sacraments of Christ celebrated in the power of the Holy Spirit. The churches today are committed to receiving the one living apostolic Tradition, to ordering their life according to it, and to transmitting it in such a way that the Christ who comes in glory will find the people of God confessing and living the faith once for all entrusted to the saints (cf. Jude 3).

18. Tradition makes the witness of the apostolic community present in the church today through its corporate memory. Through the proclamation of the word and the celebration of the sacraments the Holy Spirit opens the hearts of believers and manifests the Risen Lord to them. The Spirit, active in the once for all events of the ministry of Jesus, continues to teach the church, bringing to remembrance what Christ did and said, making present the fruits of his redemptive work and the foretaste of the kingdom (cf. John 2:22, 14:26). The purpose of Tradition is fulfilled when, through the Spirit, the word is received and lived out in faith and hope. The witness of proclamation, sacraments and life in communion is at one and the same time the content of Tradition and its result. Thus memory bears fruit in the faithful life of believers within the communion of their local church.

*The holy scriptures: the "Yes" of God and the "Amen" of God's people*

19. Within Tradition the scriptures occupy a unique and normative place and belong to what has been given once for all. As the written witness to God's "Yes" they require the church constantly to measure its teaching, preaching and action against them. "Since the scriptures are the uniquely inspired witness to divine revelation, the church's expression of that revelation must be tested by its consonance with scripture" (Authority in the Church: Elucidation, 2). Through the scriptures God's revelation is made present and transmitted in the life of the church. The "Yes" of God is recognized in and through the "Amen" of the church which receives the authentic revelation of God. By receiving certain texts as true witnesses to divine revelation, the church identified its holy scriptures. It regards this corpus alone as the inspired word of God written and, as such, uniquely authoritative.

20. The scriptures bring together diverse streams of Jewish and Christian traditions. These traditions reveal the way God's word has been received, interpreted and passed on in specific contexts according to the needs, the culture and the circumstances of the people of God. They contain God's revelation of his salvific design, which was realized in Jesus Christ and experienced in the earliest Christian communities. In these communities God's "Yes" was received in a new way. Within the New Testament we can see

how the scriptures of the First Testament were both received as revelation of the one true God and also reinterpreted and re-received as revelation of his final word in Christ.

21. All the writers of the New Testament were influenced by the experience of their own local communities. What they transmitted, with their own skill and theological insights, records those elements of the gospel which the churches of their time and in their various situations kept in their memory. Paul's teaching about the body of Christ, for instance, owes much to the problems and divisions of the local church in Corinth. When Paul speaks about "our authority which the Lord gave for building you up and not for destroying you" (2 Cor. 10:8), he does so in the context of his turbulent relationship with the church of Corinth. Even in the central affirmations of our faith there is often a clear echo of the concrete and sometimes dramatic situation of a local church or of a group of local churches, to which we are indebted for the faithful transmission of apostolic Tradition. The emphasis in the Johannine literature on the presence of the Lord in the flesh of a human body that could be seen and touched both before and after the resurrection (cf. John 20:27; 1 John 4:2) is linked to the conflict in the Johannine communities on this issue. It is through the struggle of particular communities at particular times to discern God's word for them that we have in scripture an authoritative record of the apostolic Tradition which is to be passed from one generation to another and from one church to another, and to which the faithful say "Amen".

22. The formation of the canon of the scriptures was an integral part of the process of Tradition. The church's recognition of these scriptures as canonical, after a long period of critical discernment, was at the same time an act of obedience and of authority. It was an act of obedience in that the church discerned and received God's life-giving "Yes" through the scriptures, accepting them as the norm of faith. It was an act of authority in that the church, under the guidance of the Holy Spirit, received and handed on these texts, declaring that they were inspired and that others were not to be included in the canon.

23. The meaning of the revealed gospel of God is fully understood only within the church. God's revelation has been entrusted to a community. The church cannot properly be described as an aggregate of individual believers, nor can its faith be considered the sum of the beliefs held by individuals. Believers are together the people of faith because they are incorporated by baptism into a community which receives the canonical scriptures as the authentic word of God; they receive faith within this community. The faith of the community precedes the faith of the individual. So, though one person's journey of faith may begin with individual reading of scripture, it cannot remain there. Individualistic interpretation of the scriptures is not attuned to the reading of the text within the life of the church and is incompatible with the nature of the authority of the revealed Word of God (cf. 2 Pet. 1:20-21). Word of God and church of God cannot be put asunder.

*Reception and re-reception: the church's "Amen" to the word of God*

24. Throughout the centuries, the church receives and acknowledges as a gracious gift from God all that it recognizes as a true expression of the Tradition which has been once for all delivered to the apostles. This reception is at one and the same time an act of faithfulness and of freedom. The church must continue faithful so that the Christ who comes in glory will recognize in the church the community He founded; it must continue to be

free to receive the apostolic Tradition in new ways according to the situations by which it is confronted. The church has the responsibility to hand on the whole apostolic Tradition, even though there may be parts which it finds hard to integrate in its life and worship. It may be that what was of great significance for an earlier generation will again be important in the future, though its importance is not clear in the present.

25. Within the church the memory of the people of God may be affected or even distorted by human finitude and sin. Even though promised the assistance of the Holy Spirit, the churches from time to time lose sight of aspects of the apostolic Tradition, failing to discern the full vision of the kingdom of God in the light of which we seek to follow Christ. The churches suffer when some element of ecclesial communion has been forgotten, neglected or abused. Fresh recourse to Tradition in a new situation is the means by which God's revelation in Christ is recalled. This is assisted by the insights of biblical scholars and theologians and the wisdom of holy persons. Thus, there may be a rediscovery of elements that were neglected and a fresh remembrance of the promises of God, leading to renewal of the church's "Amen". There may also be a sifting of what has been received because some of the formulations of the Tradition are seen to be inadequate or even misleading in a new context. This whole process may be termed re-reception.

## Catholicity: the "Amen" of the whole church

26. There are two dimensions to communion in the apostolic Tradition: diachronic and synchronic. The process of tradition clearly entails the transmission of the gospel from one generation to another (diachronic). If the church is to remain united in the truth, it must also entail the communion of the churches in all places in that one gospel (synchronic). Both are necessary for the catholicity of the church. Christ promises that the Holy Spirit will keep the essential and saving truth in the memory of the church, empowering it for mission (cf. John 14:26, 15:26-27). This truth has to be transmitted and received anew by the faithful in all ages and in all places throughout the world, in response to the diversity and complexity of human experience. There is no part of humanity, no race, no social condition, no generation, for whom this salvation, communicated in the handing on of the word of God, is not intended (cf. *Church as Communion*, 34).

27. In the rich diversity of human life, encounter with the living Tradition produces a variety of expressions of the gospel. Where diverse expressions are faithful to the Word revealed in Jesus Christ and transmitted by the apostolic community, the churches in which they are found are truly in communion. Indeed, this diversity of traditions is the practical manifestation of catholicity and confirms rather than contradicts the vigour of Tradition. As God has created diversity among humans, so the church's fidelity and identity require not uniformity of expression and formulation at all levels in all situations, but rather catholic diversity within the unity of communion. This richness of traditions is a vital resource for a reconciled humanity. "Human beings were created by God in his love with such diversity in order that they might participate in that love by sharing with one another both what they have and what they are, thus enriching each other in their mutual communion" (*Church as Communion*, 35).

28. The people of God as a whole is the bearer of the living Tradition. In changing situations producing fresh challenges to the gospel, the discernment, actualization and communication of the word of God is the responsibility of the whole people of God. The

Holy Spirit works through all members of the community, using the gifts he gives to each for the good of all. Theologians in particular serve the communion of the whole church by exploring whether and how new insights should be integrated into the ongoing stream of Tradition. In each community there is an exchange, a mutual give-and-take, in which bishops, clergy and lay people receive from as well as give to others within the whole body.

29. In every Christian who is seeking to be faithful to Christ and is fully incorporated into the life of the church, there is a *sensus fidei*. This *sensus fidei* may be described as an active capacity for spiritual discernment, an intuition that is formed by worshipping and living in communion as a faithful member of the church. When this capacity is exercised in concert by the body of the faithful we may speak of the exercise of the *sensus fidelium* (cf. Authority in the Church: Elucidation, 3-4). The exercise of the *sensus fidei* by each member of the church contributes to the formation of the *sensus fidelium* through which the church as a whole remains faithful to Christ. By the *sensus fidelium*, the whole body contributes to, receives from and treasures the ministry of those within the community who exercise *episcope*, watching over the living memory of the church (cf. Authority in the Church, I.5-6). In diverse ways the "Amen" of the individual believer is thus incorporated within the "Amen" of the whole church.

30. Those who exercise *episcope* in the body of Christ must not be separated from the "symphony" of the whole people of God in which they have their part to play. They need to be alert to the *sensus fidelium*, in which they share, if they are to be made aware when something is needed for the well-being and mission of the community, or when some element of the Tradition needs to be received in a fresh way. The charism and function of *episcope* are specifically connected to the ministry of memory, which constantly renews the church in hope. Through such ministry the Holy Spirit keeps alive in the church the memory of what God did and revealed, and the hope of what God will do to bring all things into unity in Christ. In this way, not only from generation to generation, but also from place to place, the one faith is communicated and lived out. This is the ministry exercised by the bishop, and by ordained persons under the bishop's care, as they proclaim the word, minister the sacraments, and take their part in administering discipline for the common good. The bishops, the clergy and the other faithful must all recognize and receive what is mediated from God through each other. Thus the *sensus fidelium* of the people of God and the ministry of memory exist together in reciprocal relationship.

31. Anglicans and Roman Catholics can agree in principle on all of the above, but need to make a deliberate effort to retrieve this shared understanding. When Christian communities are in real but imperfect communion they are called to recognize in each other elements of the apostolic Tradition which they may have rejected, forgotten or not yet fully understood. Consequently, they have to receive or reappropriate these elements, and reconsider the ways in which they have separately interpreted the scriptures. Their life in Christ is enriched when they give to, and receive from, each other. They grow in understanding and experience of their catholicity as the *sensus fidelium* and the ministry of memory interact in the communion of believers. In this economy of giving and receiving within real but imperfect communion, they move closer to an undivided sharing in Christ's one "Amen" to the glory of God.

## III. The exercise of authority in the church

*Proclaiming the gospel: the exercise of authority for mission and unity*

32. The authority which Jesus bestowed on his disciples was, above all, the authority for mission, to preach and to heal (cf. Luke 9:1-2, 10:1). The Risen Christ empowered them to spread the gospel to the whole world (cf. Matt. 28:18-20). In the early church, the preaching of the word of God in the power of the Spirit was seen as the defining characteristic of apostolic authority (cf. 1 Cor. 1:17, 2:4-5). In the proclamation of Christ crucified, the "Yes" of God to humanity is made a present reality and all are invited to respond with their "Amen". Thus, the exercise of ministerial authority within the church, not least by those entrusted with the ministry of *episcope*, has a radically missionary dimension. Authority is exercised within the church for the sake of those outside it, that the gospel may be proclaimed "in power and in the Holy Spirit and with full conviction" (1 Thess. 1:5). This authority enables the whole church to embody the gospel and become the missionary and prophetic servant of the Lord.

33. Jesus prayed to the Father that his followers might be one "so that the world may know that you have sent me and have loved them even as you have loved me" (John 17:23). When Christians do not agree about the gospel itself, the preaching of it in power is impaired. When they are not one in faith they cannot be one in life, and so cannot demonstrate fully that they are faithful to the will of God, which is the reconciliation through Christ of all things to the Father (cf. Col. 1:20). As long as the church does not live as the community of reconciliation God calls it to be, it cannot adequately preach this gospel or credibly proclaim God's plan to gather his scattered people into unity under Christ as Lord and Saviour (cf. John 11:52). Only when all believers are united in the common celebration of the eucharist (cf. *Church as Communion*, 24) will the God whose purpose it is to bring all things into unity in Christ (cf. Eph. 1:10) be truly glorified by the people of God. The challenge and responsibility for those with authority within the church is so to exercise their ministry that they promote the unity of the whole church in faith and life in a way that enriches rather than diminishes the legitimate diversity of local churches.

*Synodality: the exercise of authority in communion*

34. In each local church all the faithful are called to walk together in Christ. The term synodality (derived from syn-hodos meaning "common way") indicates the manner in which believers and churches are held together in communion as they do this. It expresses their vocation as people of the Way (cf. Acts 9:2) to live, work and journey together in Christ who is the Way (cf. John 14:6). They, like their predecessors, follow Jesus on the way (cf. Mark 10:52) until He comes again.

35. Within the communion of local churches the Spirit is at work to shape each church through the grace of reconciliation and communion in Christ. It is only through the activity of the Spirit that the local church can be faithful to the "Amen" of Christ and can be sent into the world to draw all people to participate in this "Amen". Through this presence of the Spirit the local church is maintained in the Tradition. It receives and shares the fullness of the apostolic faith and the means of grace. The Spirit confirms the local church in the truth in such a way that its life embodies the saving truth revealed in Christ. From generation to generation the authority of the living Word should be made present

in the local church through all aspects of its life in the world. The way in which authority is exercised in the structures and corporate life of the church must be conformed to the mind of Christ (cf. Phil. 2:5).

36. The Spirit of Christ endows each bishop with the pastoral authority needed for the effective exercise of *episcope* within a local church. This authority necessarily includes responsibility for making and implementing the decisions that are required to fulfill the office of a bishop for the sake of koinonia. Its binding nature is implicit in the bishop's task of teaching the faith through the proclamation and explanation of the word of God, of providing for the celebration of the sacraments, and of maintaining the church in holiness and truth. Decisions taken by the bishop in performing this task have an authority which the faithful have a duty to receive and accept (cf. Authority in the Church, II.17). By their *sensus fidei* the faithful are able in conscience both to recognize God at work in the bishop's exercise of authority, and also to respond to it as believers. This is what motivates their obedience, an obedience of freedom and not slavery. The jurisdiction of bishops is one consequence of the call they have received to lead their churches in an authentic "Amen"; it is not arbitrary power given to one person over the freedom of others. Within the working of the *sensus fidelium* there is a complementary relationship between the bishop and the rest of the community. In the local church the eucharist is the fundamental expression of the walking together (synodality) of the people of God. In prayerful dialogue, the president leads the people to make their "Amen" to the eucharistic prayer. In unity of faith with their local bishop, their "Amen" is a living memorial of the Lord's great "Amen" to the will of the Father.

37. The mutual interdependence of all the churches is integral to the reality of the church as God wills it to be. No local church that participates in the living Tradition can regard itself as self-sufficient. Forms of synodality, then, are needed to manifest the communion of the local churches and to sustain each of them in fidelity to the gospel. The ministry of the bishop is crucial, for this ministry serves communion within and among local churches. Their communion with each other is expressed through the incorporation of each bishop into a college of bishops. Bishops are, both personally and collegially, at the service of communion and are concerned for synodality in all its expressions. These expressions have included a wide variety of organs, instruments and institutions, notably synods or councils, local, provincial, worldwide, ecumenical. The maintenance of communion requires that at every level there is a capacity to take decisions appropriate to that level. When those decisions raise serious questions for the wider communion of churches, synodality must find a wider expression.

38. In both our communions, the bishops meet together collegially, not as individuals but as those who have authority within and for the synodal life of the local churches. Consulting the faithful is an aspect of episcopal oversight. Each bishop is both a voice for the local church and one through whom the local church learns from other churches. When bishops take counsel together they seek both to discern and to articulate the *sensus fidelium* as it is present in the local church and in the wider communion of churches. Their role is magisterial: that is, in this communion of the churches, they are to determine what is to be taught as faithful to the apostolic Tradition. Roman Catholics and Anglicans share this understanding of synodality, but express it in different ways.

39. In the Church of England at the time of the English Reformation the tradition of synodality was expressed through the use both of synods (of bishops and clergy) and of

parliament (including bishops and lay people) for the settlement of liturgy, doctrine and church order. The authority of general councils was also recognized. In the Anglican Communion, new forms of synods came into being during the 19th century and the role of the laity in decision-making has increased since that time. Although bishops, clergy and lay persons consult with each other and legislate together, the responsibility of the bishops remains distinct and crucial. In every part of the Anglican Communion, the bishops bear a unique responsibility of oversight. For example, a diocesan synod can be called only by the bishop, and its decisions can stand only with the bishop's consent. At provincial or national levels, houses of bishops exercise a distinctive and unique ministry in relation to matters of doctrine, worship and moral life. Further, though Anglican synods largely use parliamentary procedures, their nature is eucharistic. This is why the bishop as president of the eucharist appropriately presides at the diocesan synod, which assembles to bring God's redemptive work into the present through the life and activity of the local church. Furthermore, each bishop has not only the *episcope* of the local church but participates in the care of all the churches. This is exercised within each province of the Anglican Communion with the help of organs such as houses of bishops and the provincial and general synods. In the Anglican Communion as a whole the primates meeting, the Anglican Consultative Council, the Lambeth Conference and the archbishop of Canterbury serve as instruments of synodality.

40. In the Roman Catholic Church the tradition of synodality has not ceased. After the Reformation, synods of bishops and clergy continued to be held from time to time in different dioceses and regions, and on the universal level three councils have been held. By the turn of the 20th century specific meetings of bishops and episcopal conferences emerged as means of consultation to enable local churches of a given region to face together the demands of their mission and to deal with new pastoral situations. Since the Second Vatican Council these have become a regular structure in nations and regions. In a decision which received the support of the bishops at that council, Pope Paul VI instituted the synod of bishops to deal with issues concerning the church's mission throughout the world. The ancient custom of *ad limina* visits to the tombs of the apostles Peter and Paul and to the bishop of Rome has been renewed by their visiting not singly but in regional groups. The more recent custom of visits by the bishop of Rome to local churches has attempted to foster a deeper sense of their belonging to the communion of churches, and to help them be more aware of the situation of others. All these synodal institutions provide the possibility of a growing awareness by both local bishops and the bishop of Rome of ways of working together in a stronger communion. Complementing this collegial synodality, a growth in synodality at the local level is promoting the active participation of lay persons in the life and mission of the local church.

*Perseverance in the truth: the exercise of authority in teaching*

41. In every age Christians have said "Amen" to Christ's promise that the Spirit will guide his church into all truth. The New Testament frequently echoes this promise by referring to the boldness, assurance and certainty to which Christians can lay claim (cf. Luke 1:4; 1 Thess. 2:2; Eph. 3:2; Heb. 11:1). In their concern to make the gospel accessible to all who are open to receive it, those charged with the ministry of memory and teaching have accepted new and hitherto unfamiliar expressions of faith. Some of these

formulations have initially generated doubt and disagreement about their fidelity to the apostolic Tradition. In the process of testing such formulations, the church has moved cautiously, but with confidence in the promise of Christ that it will persevere and be maintained in the truth (cf. Matt. 16:18; John 16:13). This is what is meant by the indefectibility of the church (cf. Authority in the Church, I,18; Authority in the Church, II,23).

42.  In its continuing life, the church seeks and receives the guidance from the Holy Spirit that keeps its teaching faithful to apostolic Tradition. Within the whole body, the college of bishops is to exercise the ministry of memory to this end. They are to discern and give teaching which may be trusted because it expresses the truth of God surely. In some situations, there will be an urgent need to test new formulations of faith. In specific circumstances, those with this ministry of oversight (*episcope*), assisted by the Holy Spirit, may together come to a judgment which, being faithful to scripture and consistent with apostolic Tradition, is preserved from error. By such a judgment, which is a renewed expression of God's one "Yes" in Jesus Christ, the church is maintained in the truth so that it may continue to offer its "Amen" to the glory of God. This is what is meant when it is affirmed that the church may teach infallibly (see Authority in the Church, II. 24-28,32). Such infallible teaching is at the service of the church's indefectibility.

43.  The exercise of teaching authority in the church, especially in situations of challenge, requires the participation, in their distinctive ways, of the whole body of believers, not only those charged with the ministry of memory. In this participation the *sensus fidelium* is at work. Since it is the faithfulness of the whole people of God which is at stake, reception of teaching is integral to the process. Doctrinal definitions are received as authoritative in virtue of the divine truth they proclaim as well as because of the specific office of the person or persons who proclaim them within the *sensus fidei* of the whole people of God. When the people of God respond by faith and say "Amen" to authoritative teaching, it is because they recognize that this teaching expresses the apostolic faith and operates within the authority and truth of Christ, the Head of the church. The truth and authority of its Head is the source of infallible teaching in the body of Christ. God's "Yes" revealed in Christ is the standard by which such authoritative teaching is judged. Such teaching is to be welcomed by the people of God as a gift of the Holy Spirit to maintain the church in the truth of Christ, our "Amen" to God.

44.  The duty of maintaining the church in the truth is one of the essential functions of the episcopal college. It has the power to exercise this ministry because it is bound in succession to the apostles, who were the body authorized and sent by Christ to preach the gospel to all the nations. The authenticity of the teaching of individual bishops is evident when this teaching is in solidarity with that of the whole episcopal college. The exercise of this teaching authority requires that what it teaches be faithful to holy scripture and consistent with apostolic Tradition. This is expressed by the teaching of the Second Vatican Council, "This teaching office is not above the word of God, but serves it" (*DV*, 10).

*Primacy: the exercise of authority in collegiality and conciliarity*

45.  In the course of history the synodality of the church has been served through conciliar, collegial and primatial authority. Forms of primacy exist in both the Anglican Communion and in the churches in communion with the bishop of Rome. Among the

latter, the offices of metropolitan archbishop or patriarch of an Eastern Catholic church are primatial in nature. Each Anglican province has its primate and the primates meeting serves the whole communion. The archbishop of Canterbury exercises a primatial ministry in the whole Anglican Communion.

46. ARCIC has already recognized that the "pattern of complementary primatial and conciliar aspects of *episcope* serving the koinonia of the churches needs to be realized at the universal level" (Authority in the Church, I.23). The exigencies of church life call for a specific exercise of *episcope* at the service of the whole church. In the pattern found in the New Testament one of the twelve is chosen by Jesus Christ to strengthen the others so that they will remain faithful to their mission and in harmony with each other (see the discussion of the Petrine texts in Authority in the Church, II.2-5). Augustine of Hippo expressed well the relationship among Peter, the other apostles and the whole church, when he said,

> After all, it is not just one man that received these keys, but the church in its unity. So this is the reason for Peter's acknowledged pre-eminence, that he stood for the church's universality and unity, when he was told, To you I am entrusting, what has in fact been entrusted to all. I mean to show you that it is the church which has received the keys of the kingdom of heaven. Listen to what the Lord says in another place to all his apostles: Receive the Holy Spirit; and straight away, whose sins you forgive, they will be forgiven them; whose sins you retain, they will be retained (John 20:22-23). This refers to the keys, about which is said, whatever you bind on earth shall be bound in heaven (Matt. 16:19). But that was said to Peter... Peter at that time stood for the universal church. (Sermon 295, On the Feast of the Martyrdom of the Apostles Peter and Paul)

ARCIC has also previously explored the transmission of the primatial ministry exercised by the bishop of Rome (see Authority in the Church, II.6-9). Historically, the bishop of Rome has exercised such a ministry either for the benefit of the whole church, as when Leo contributed to the council of Chalcedon, or for the benefit of a local church, as when Gregory the Great supported Augustine of Canterbury's mission and ordering of the English church. This gift has been welcomed and the ministry of these bishops of Rome continues to be celebrated liturgically by Anglicans as well as Roman Catholics.

47. Within his wider ministry, the bishop of Rome offers a specific ministry concerning the discernment of truth, as an expression of universal primacy. This particular service has been the source of difficulties and misunderstandings among the churches. Every solemn definition pronounced from the chair of Peter in the church of Peter and Paul may, however, express only the faith of the church. Any such definition is pronounced within the college of those who exercise *episcope* and not outside that college. Such authoritative teaching is a particular exercise of the calling and responsibility of the body of bishops to teach and affirm the faith. When the faith is articulated in this way, the bishop of Rome proclaims the faith of the local churches. It is thus the wholly reliable teaching of the whole church that is operative in the judgment of the universal primate. In solemnly formulating such teaching, the universal primate must discern and declare, with the assured assistance and guidance of the Holy Spirit, in fidelity to scripture and Tradition, the authentic faith of the whole church, that is, the faith proclaimed from the beginning. It is this faith, the faith of all the baptized in communion, and this only, that each bishop utters with the body of bishops in council. It is this faith which the bishop of Rome in certain circumstances has a duty to discern and make explicit. This form of

authoritative teaching has no stronger guarantee from the Spirit than have the solemn definitions of ecumenical councils. The reception of the primacy of the bishop of Rome entails the recognition of this specific ministry of the universal primate. We believe that this is a gift to be received by all the churches.

48. The ministers God gives the church to sustain her life are marked by fragility:

> Therefore, since it is by God's mercy that we are engaged in this ministry, we do not lose heart... but we have this treasure in clay jars, so that it may be made clear that this extraordinary power belongs to God and does not come from us (2 Cor. 4:1,7).

It is clear that only by the grace of God does the exercise of authority in the communion of the church bear the marks of Christ's own authority. This authority is exercised by fragile Christians for the sake of other fragile Christians. This is no less true of the ministry of Peter:

> "Simon, Simon, behold Satan demanded to have you, that he might sift you like wheat, but I have prayed for you that your faith may not fail; and when you have turned again, strengthen your brethren" (Luke 22:31-32; cf. John 21:15-19).

Pope John Paul II makes this clear in *Ut Unum Sint*:

> I carry out this duty with the profound conviction that I am obeying the Lord, and with a clear sense of my own human frailty. Indeed, if Christ himself gave Peter this special mission in the church and exhorted him to strengthen his brethren, he also made clear to him his human weakness and his special need of conversion. (*UUS*, 4)

Human weakness and sin do not only affect individual ministers: they can distort the human structuring of authority (cf. Matt. 23). Therefore, loyal criticism and reforms are sometimes needed, following the example of Paul (cf. Gal. 2:11-14). The consciousness of human frailty in the exercise of authority ensures that Christian ministers remain open to criticism and renewal and above all to exercising authority according to the example and mind of Christ.

### *Discipline: the exercise of authority and the freedom of conscience*

49. The exercise of authority in the church is to be recognized and accepted as an instrument of the Spirit of God for the healing of humanity. The exercise of authority must always respect conscience, because the divine work of salvation affirms human freedom. In freely accepting the way of salvation offered through baptism, the Christian disciple also freely takes on the discipline of being a member of the body of Christ. Because the church of God is recognized as the community where the divine means of salvation are at work, the demands of discipleship for the well-being of the entire Christian community cannot be refused. There is also a discipline required in the exercise of authority. Those called to such a ministry must themselves submit to the discipline of Christ, observe the requirements of collegiality and the common good, and duly respect the consciences of those they are called to serve.

*The church's "Amen" to God's "Yes" in the gospel*

50.  We have come to a shared understanding of authority by seeing it, in faith, as a manifestation of God's "Yes" to his creation, calling forth the "Amen" of his creatures. God is the source of authority, and the proper exercise of authority is always ordered towards the common good and the good of the person. In a broken world, and to a divided church, God's "Yes" in Jesus Christ brings the reality of reconciliation, the call to discipleship, and a foretaste of humanity's final goal when through the Spirit all in Christ utter their "Amen" to the glory of God. The "Yes" of God, embodied in Christ, is received in the proclamation and Tradition of the gospel, in the sacramental life of the church and in the ways that *episcope* is exercised. When the churches, through their exercise of authority, display the healing and reconciling power of the gospel, then the wider world is offered a vision of what God intends for all creation. The aim of the exercise of authority and of its reception is to enable the church to say "Amen" to God's "Yes" in the gospel.

## IV.  Agreement in the exercise of authority: steps towards visible unity

51.  We submit to our respective authorities this agreed statement on authority in the church. We believe that if this statement about the nature of authority and the manner of its exercise is accepted and acted upon, this issue will no longer be a cause for continued breach of communion between our two churches. Accordingly, we set out below some of the features of this agreement, recent significant developments in each of our communions, and some issues which they still have to face. As we move towards full ecclesial communion, we suggest ways in which our existing communion, albeit imperfect, may be made more visible through the exercise of a renewed collegiality among the bishops and a renewed exercise and reception of universal primacy.

*Advances in agreement*

52.  The commission is of the view that we have deepened and extended our agreement on:

- how the authority of Christ is present and active in the church when the proclamation of God's "Yes" calls forth the "Amen" of all believers (§§7-18);
- the dynamic interdependence of scripture and apostolic Tradition and the normative place of scripture within Tradition (§§19-23);
- the necessity of constant reception of scripture and Tradition, and of re-reception in particular circumstances (§§24-26);
- how the exercise of authority is at the service of personal faith within the life of the church (§§23,29,49);
- the role of the whole people of God, within which, as teachers of the faith, the bishops have a distinctive voice in forming and expressing the mind of the church (§§29-30);
- synodality and its implications for the communion of the whole people of God and of all the local churches as together they seek to follow Christ who is the Way (§§34-40);

- the essential cooperation of the ministry of *episcope* and the *sensus fidei* of the whole church in the reception of the word of God (§§29,36,43);
- the possibility, in certain circumstances, of the church teaching infallibly at the service of the church's indefectibility (§§41-44);
- a universal primacy, exercised collegially in the context of synodality, as integral to *episcope* at the service of universal communion; such a primacy having always been associated with the bishop and see of Rome (§§46-48);
- how the ministry of the bishop of Rome assists the ministry of the whole episcopal body in the context of synodality, promoting the communion of the local churches in their life in Christ and the proclamation of the gospel (§§46-48);
- how the bishop of Rome offers a specific ministry concerning the discernment of truth (§47).

*Significant developments in both communions*

53. The Lambeth Conference of 1988 recognized a need to reflect on how the Anglican Communion makes authoritative decisions. At the international level, Anglican instruments of synodality have considerable authority to influence and support provinces, yet none of these instruments has power to over-rule a provincial decision, even if it threatens the unity of the communion. Accordingly, the Lambeth Conference of 1998, in the light of the *Virginia Report* of the inter-Anglican theological and doctrinal commission, resolved to strengthen these instruments in various ways, particularly the role of the archbishop of Canterbury and of the primates meeting. The conference also requested the primates meeting to initiate a study in each province "on whether effective communion, at all levels, does not require appropriate instruments, with due safeguards, not only for legislation, but also for oversight... as well as on the issue of a universal ministry in the service of Christian unity" (res. III.8.h). Alongside the autonomy of provinces, Anglicans are coming to see that interdependence among local churches and among provinces is also necessary for fostering communion.

54. The Roman Catholic Church, especially since the Second Vatican Council, has been gradually developing synodal structures for sustaining koinonia more effectively. The developing role of national and regional episcopal conferences and the regular holding of general assemblies of the synod of bishops demonstrate this evolution. There has also been renewal in the exercise of synodality at the local level, although this varies from place to place. Canonical legislation now requires lay men and women, persons in the religious life, deacons and priests to play a part in parochial and diocesan pastoral councils, diocesan synods and a variety of other bodies, whenever these are convened.

55. In the Anglican Communion there is a reaching towards universal structures which promote koinonia, and in the Roman Catholic church a strengthening of local and intermediate structures. In our view these developments reflect a shared and growing awareness that authority in the church needs to be properly exercised at all levels. Even so there are still issues to be faced by Anglicans and Roman Catholics on important aspects of the exercise of authority in the service of koinonia. The commission poses some questions frankly but in the conviction that we need the support of one another in responding to them. We believe that in the dynamic and fluid situation in which they are

posed, seeking to answer them must go together with developing further steps towards a shared exercise of authority.

## Issues facing Anglicans

56. We have seen that instruments for oversight and decision-making are necessary at all levels to support communion. With this in view the Anglican Communion is exploring the development of structures of authority among its provinces. Is the communion also open to the acceptance of instruments of oversight which would allow decisions to be reached that, in certain circumstances, would bind the whole church? When major new questions arise which, in fidelity to scripture and Tradition, require a united response, will these structures assist Anglicans to participate in the *sensus fidelium* with all Christians? To what extent does unilateral action by provinces or dioceses in matters concerning the whole church, even after consultation has taken place, weaken koinonia? Anglicans have shown themselves to be willing to tolerate anomalies for the sake of maintaining communion. Yet this has led to the impairment of communion manifesting itself at the eucharist, in the exercise of *episcope* and in the interchangeability of ministry. What consequences flow from this? Above all, how will Anglicans address the question of universal primacy as it is emerging from their life together and from ecumenical dialogue?

## Issues facing Roman Catholics

57. The Second Vatican Council has reminded Roman Catholics of how the gifts of God are present in all the people of God. It has also taught the collegiality of the episcopate in its communion with the bishop of Rome, head of the college. However, is there at all levels effective participation of clergy as well as lay people in emerging synodal bodies? Has the teaching of the Second Vatican Council regarding the collegiality of bishops been implemented sufficiently? Do the actions of bishops reflect sufficient awareness of the extent of the authority they receive through ordination for governing the local church? Has enough provision been made to ensure consultation between the bishop of Rome and the local churches prior to the making of important decisions affecting either a local church or the whole church? How is the variety of theological opinion taken into account when such decisions are made? In supporting the bishop of Rome in his work of promoting communion among the churches, do the structures and procedures of the Roman Curia adequately respect the exercise of *episcope* at other levels? Above all, how will the Roman Catholic Church address the question of universal primacy as it emerges from "the patient and fraternal dialogue" about the exercise of the office of the bishop of Rome to which John Paul II has invited "church leaders and their theologians"?

## Renewed collegiality: making visible our existing communion

58. Anglicans and Roman Catholics are already facing these issues but their resolution may well take some time. However, there is no turning back in our journey towards full ecclesial communion. In the light of our agreement the commission believes our two

communions should make more visible the koinonia we already have. Theological dialogue must continue at all levels in the churches, but is not of itself sufficient. For the sake of koinonia and a united Christian witness to the world, Anglican and Roman Catholic bishops should find ways of cooperating and developing relationships of mutual accountability in their exercise of oversight. At this new stage we have not only to do together whatever we can, but also to be together all that our existing koinonia allows.

59. Such cooperation in the exercise of *episcope* would involve bishops meeting regularly together at regional and local levels and the participation of bishops from one communion in the international meetings of bishops of the other. Serious consideration could also be given to the association of Anglican bishops with Roman Catholic bishops in their *ad limina* visits to Rome. Wherever possible, bishops should take the opportunity of teaching and acting together in matters of faith and morals. They should also witness together in the public sphere on issues affecting the common good. Specific practical aspects of sharing *episcope* will emerge from local initiatives.

### Universal primacy: a gift to be shared

60. The commission's work has resulted in sufficient agreement on universal primacy as a gift to be shared, for us to propose that such a primacy could be offered and received even before our churches are in full communion. Both Roman Catholics and Anglicans look to this ministry being exercised in collegiality and synodality – a ministry of *servus servorum Dei* (Gregory the Great, cited in *Ut Unum Sint*, 88). We envisage a primacy that will even now help to uphold the legitimate diversity of traditions, strengthening and safeguarding them in fidelity to the gospel. It will encourage the churches in their mission. This sort of primacy will already assist the church on earth to be the authentic catholic koinonia in which unity does not curtail diversity, and diversity does not endanger but enhances unity. It will be an effective sign for all Christians as to how this gift of God builds up that unity for which Christ prayed.

61. Such a universal primate will exercise leadership in the world and also in both communions, addressing them in a prophetic way. He will promote the common good in ways that are not constrained by sectional interests, and offer a continuing and distinctive teaching ministry, particularly in addressing difficult theological and moral issues. A universal primacy of this style will welcome and protect theological enquiry and other forms of the search for truth, so that their results may enrich and strengthen both human wisdom and the church's faith. Such a universal primacy might gather the churches in various ways for consultation and discussion.

62. An experience of universal primacy of this kind would confirm two particular conclusions we have reached:
- that Anglicans be open to and desire a recovery and re-reception under certain clear conditions of the exercise of universal primacy by the bishop of Rome;
- that Roman Catholics be open to and desire a re-reception of the exercise of primacy by the bishop of Rome and the offering of such a ministry to the whole church of God.

63. When the real yet imperfect communion between us is made more visible, the web of unity which is woven from communion with God and reconciliation with each other

is extended and strengthened. Thus the "Amen" which Anglicans and Roman Catholics say to the one Lord comes closer to being an "Amen" said together by the one holy people witnessing to God's salvation and reconciling love in a broken world.

## Members of the commission

*Anglican members*

Rt Rev. Mark Santer, Bishop of Birmingham, UK (*co-chairman*)

Rt Rev. John Baycroft, Bishop of Ottawa, Canada

Dr E. Rozanne Elder, Professor of History, University of Western Michigan, USA

Rev. Prof. Jaci Maraschin, Professor of Theology, Ecumenical Institute, São Paulo, Brazil

Rev. Canon Richard Marsh, Archbishop of Canterbury's Secretary for Ecumenical Affairs, London, UK (from 1996)

Rev. Dr John Muddiman, Fellow and Tutor in Theology, Mansfield College, University of Oxford, UK

Rt Rev. Michael Nazir-Ali, Bishop of Rochester, UK

Rev. Dr Nicholas Sagovsky, Research Fellow, University of Newcastle, UK

Rev. Dr Charles Sherlock, Senior Lecturer, Trinity College Theological School, Parkville, Australia

Rev. Dr Donald Anderson, Director of Ecumenical Relations and Studies, Anglican Communion Office, London, UK (1994-96)

Rev. Canon David Hamid, Director of Ecumenical Affairs and Relations, Anglican Communion Office, London, UK (from 1996)

Rev. Canon Stephen Platten, Archbishop of Canterbury's Secretary for Ecumenical Affairs, London, UK (until 1994)

*Roman Catholic members*

Rt Rev. Cormac Murphy-O'Connor, Bishop of Arundel and Brighton, UK (*co-chairman*)

Sister Sara Butler MSBT, Assistant Professor of Systematic Theology, University of St Mary of the Lake, Mundelein, Illinois, USA

Rev. Peter Cross, Professor of Systematic Theology, Catholic Theological College, Clayton, Australia

Rev. Dr Adelbert Denaux, Professor, Faculty of Theology, Catholic University, Leuven, Belgium

Rt Rev. Pierre Duprey, Titular Bishop of Thibaris, Secretary, Pontifical Council for Promoting Christian Unity, Vatican City

Most Rev. Patrick A. Kelly, Archbishop of Liverpool, UK (from 1996)

Rt Rev. Monsignor William Steele, Episcopal Vicar for Mission and Unity, Diocese of Leeds, UK (1994-95)

Rev. Jean M.R. Tillard OP, Professor, Dominican Faculty of Theology, Ottawa, Canada

Rev. Liam Walsh OP, Professor of Dogmatic Theology, University of Fribourg, Switzerland
Rev. Timothy Galligan, staff member, Pontifical Council for Promoting Christian Unity, Vatican City

*World Council of Churches observer*
Prof. Dr Michael Root, Trinity Lutheran Seminary, Columbus, Ohio, USA (from 1995)
Rev. Dr Günther Gassmann, Director, Faith and Order Commission, WCC, Geneva, Switzerland (until 1994)

# 15. Mary: Grace and Hope in Christ
# The Seattle Statement

## Seattle, USA, 2 February 2004

### Preface by the co-chairmen

In the continuing journey towards full communion, the Roman Catholic Church and the churches of the Anglican Communion have for many years prayerfully considered a number of questions concerning the faith we share and the way we articulate it in the life and worship of our two households of faith. We have submitted agreed statements to the Holy See and to the Anglican Communion for comment, further clarification if necessary, and conjoint acceptance as congruent with the faith of Anglicans and Roman Catholics.

In framing this agreed statement, we have drawn on the scriptures and the common tradition which predates the Reformation and the Counter-Reformation. As in previous Anglican-Roman Catholic International Commission (ARCIC) documents, we have attempted to use language that reflects what we hold in common and transcends the controversies of the past. At the same time, in this statement we have had to face squarely dogmatic definitions which are integral to the faith of Roman Catholics but largely foreign to the faith of Anglicans. The members of ARCIC, over time, have sought to embrace one another's ways of doing theology and have considered together the historical context in which certain doctrines developed. In so doing, we have learned to receive anew our own traditions, illumined and deepened by the understanding of and appreciation for each other's tradition.

Our agreed statement concerning the Blessed Virgin Mary as pattern of grace and hope is a powerful reflection of our efforts to seek out what we hold in common and celebrates important aspects of our common heritage. Mary, the mother of our Lord Jesus Christ, stands before us as an exemplar of faithful obedience, and her "be it to me according to your word" is the grace-filled response each of us is called to make to God, both personally and communally, as the church, the body of Christ. It is as figure of the church, her arms uplifted in prayer and praise, her hands open in receptivity and availability to the outpouring of the Holy Spirit, that we are one with Mary as she magnifies the Lord. "Surely", Mary declares in her song recorded in the gospel of Luke, "from this day all generations will call me blessed."

Our two traditions share many of the same feasts associated with Mary. From our experience we have found that it is in the realm of worship that we realize our deepest convergence as we give thanks to God for the Mother of the Lord who is one with us in that vast community of love and prayer we call the communion of saints.

+ Alexander J. Brunett             + Peter F. Carnley
Seattle, Feast of the Presentation

2 February 2004

THE STATUS OF THE DOCUMENT

The document published here is the work of the Anglican-Roman Catholic International Commission (ARCIC). It is a joint statement of the commission. The authorities who appointed the commission have allowed the statement to be published so that it may be widely discussed. It is not an authoritative declaration by the Roman Catholic Church or by the Anglican Communion, who will study and evaluate the document in due course.

# MARY: GRACE AND HOPE IN CHRIST

## Introduction

1. In honouring Mary as Mother of the Lord, all generations of Anglicans and Roman Catholics have echoed the greeting of Elizabeth: "Blessed are you among women, and blessed is the fruit of your womb" (Luke 1:42). The Anglican-Roman Catholic International Commission now offers this agreed statement on the place of Mary in the life and doctrine of the church in the hope that it expresses our common faith about the one who, of all believers, is closest to our Lord and Saviour Jesus Christ. We do so at the request of our two communions, in response to questions set before us. A special consultation of Anglican and Roman Catholic bishops, meeting under the leadership of the Archbishop of Canterbury, Dr George Carey, and Cardinal Edward I Cassidy, president of the Pontifical Council for Promoting Christian Unity, at Mississauga, Canada, in 2000, specifically asked ARCIC for "a study of Mary in the life and doctrine of the church". This request recalls the observation of the *Malta Report* (1968) that "real or apparent differences between us come to the surface in such matters as… the Mariological definitions" promulgated in 1854 and 1950. More recently, in *Ut Unum Sint* (1995), Pope John Paul II identified as one area in need of fuller study by all Christian traditions before a true consensus of faith can be achieved "the Virgin Mary, as Mother of God and icon of the church, the spiritual Mother who intercedes for Christ's disciples and for all humanity" (§79).

2. ARCIC has addressed this topic once before. *Authority in the Church* II (1981) already records a significant degree of agreement:

> We agree that there can be but one mediator between God and man, Jesus Christ, and reject any interpretation of the role of Mary which obscures this affirmation. We agree in recognizing that Christian understanding of Mary is inseparably linked with the doctrines of Christ and the church. We agree in recognizing the grace and unique vocation of Mary, Mother of God Incarnate (Theotokos), in observing her festivals, and in according her honour in the communion of saints. We agree that she was prepared by divine grace to be the mother of our Redeemer, by whom she herself was redeemed and received into glory. We further agree in recognizing in Mary a model of holiness, obedience and faith for all Christians. We accept that it is possible to regard her as a prophetic figure of the church of God before as well as after the incarnation. (§30)

The same document, however, points out remaining differences:

> The dogmas of the immaculate conception and the assumption raise a special problem for those Anglicans who do not consider that the precise definitions given by these dogmas are sufficiently supported by scripture. For many Anglicans the teaching authority of the bishop of Rome, independent of a council, is not recommended by the fact that through it these Marian doctrines were proclaimed as dogmas binding on all the faithful. Anglicans would also ask whether, in any future union between our two churches, they would be required to subscribe to such dogmatic statements. (§30)

These reservations in particular were noted in the official response of the Holy See to *The Final Report* (1991, §13). Having taken these shared beliefs and these questions as the starting-point for our reflection, we are now able to affirm further significant agreement on the place of Mary in the life and doctrine of the church.

3. The present document proposes a fuller statement of our shared belief concerning the Blessed Virgin Mary and so provides the context for a common appreciation of the content of the Marian dogmas. We also take up differences of practice, including the explicit invocation of Mary. This new study of Mary has benefited from our previous study of reception in *The Gift of Authority* (1999). There we concluded that, when the church receives and acknowledges what it recognizes as a true expression of the Tradition once for all delivered to the apostles, this reception is an act both of faithfulness and of freedom. The freedom to respond in fresh ways in the face of new challenges is what enables the church to be faithful to the Tradition which it carries forward. At other times, some element of the apostolic Tradition may be forgotten, neglected or abused. In such situations, fresh recourse to scripture and Tradition recalls God's revelation in Christ: we call this process re-reception (cf. *Gift*, 24-25). Progress in ecumenical dialogue and understanding suggests that we now have an opportunity to re-receive together the tradition of Mary's place in God's revelation.

4. Since its inception ARCIC has sought to get behind opposed or entrenched positions to discover and develop our common inheritance of faith (cf. *Authority*, I 25). Following *The Common Declaration* in 1966 of Pope Paul VI and the Archbishop of Canterbury, Dr Michael Ramsey, we have continued our "serious dialogue… founded on the gospels and on the ancient common traditions". We have asked to what extent doctrine or devotion concerning Mary belongs to a legitimate "reception" of the apostolic Tradition, in

accordance with the scriptures. This Tradition has at its core the proclamation of the trinitarian "economy of salvation", grounding the life and faith of the church in the divine communion of Father, Son and Spirit. We have sought to understand Mary's person and role in the history of salvation and the life of the church in the light of a theology of divine grace and hope. Such a theology is deeply rooted in the enduring experience of Christian worship and devotion.

5. God's grace calls for and enables human response (cf. *Salvation and the Church*, 1987, 9). This is seen in the gospel account of the annunciation, where the angel's message evokes the response of Mary. The incarnation and all that it entailed, including the passion, death and resurrection of Christ and the birth of the church, came about by way of Mary's freely uttered fiat – "let it be done to me according to your word" (Luke 1:38). We recognize in the event of the incarnation God's gracious "Yes" to humanity as a whole. This reminds us once more of the apostle's words in 2 Corinthians 1:18-20 (*Gift*, 8ff.): all God's promises find their "Yes" in the Son of God, Jesus Christ. In this context, Mary's fiat can be seen as the supreme instance of a believer's "Amen" in response to the "Yes" of God. Christian disciples respond to the same "Yes" with their own "Amen". They thus know themselves to be children together of the one heavenly Father, born of the Spirit as brothers and sisters of Jesus Christ, drawn into the communion of love of the blessed Trinity. Mary epitomizes such participation in the life of God. Her response was not made without profound questioning, and it issued in a life of joy intermingled with sorrow, taking her even to the foot of her son's cross. When Christians join in Mary's "Amen" to the "Yes" of God in Christ, they commit themselves to an obedient response to the word of God, which leads to a life of prayer and service. Like Mary, they not only magnify the Lord with their lips: they commit themselves to serve God's justice with their lives (cf. Luke 1:46-55).

## A. Mary according to the scriptures

6. We remain convinced that the holy scriptures, as the word of God written, bear normative witness to God's plan of salvation, so it is to them that this statement first turns. Indeed, it is impossible to be faithful to scripture and not to take Mary seriously. We recognize, however, that for some centuries Anglicans and Roman Catholics have interpreted the scriptures while divided from one another. In reflecting together on the scriptures' testimony concerning Mary, we have discovered more than just a few tantalizing glimpses into the life of a great saint. We have found ourselves meditating with wonder and gratitude on the whole sweep of salvation history: creation, election, the incarnation, passion, and resurrection of Christ, the gift of the Spirit in the church, and the final vision of eternal life for all God's people in the new creation.

7. In the following paragraphs, our use of scripture seeks to draw upon the whole Tradition of the church, in which rich and varied readings have been employed. In the New Testament, the Old Testament is commonly interpreted typologically:[1] events and images are understood with specific reference to Christ. This approach is further developed by the fathers and by medieval preachers and authors. The Reformers stressed the clarity and sufficiency of scripture, and called for a return to the centrality of the gospel message. Historical-critical approaches attempted to discern the meaning intended by the

biblical authors, and to account for texts' origins. Each of these readings has its limitations, and may give rise to exaggerations or imbalances: typology can become extravagant, Reformation emphases reductionist, and critical methods overly historicist. More recent approaches to scripture point to the range of possible readings of a text, notably its narrative, rhetorical and sociological dimensions. In this statement, we seek to integrate what is valuable from each of these approaches, as both correcting and contributing to our use of scripture. Further, we recognize that no reading of a text is neutral, but each is shaped by the context and interest of its readers. Our reading has taken place within the context of our dialogue in Christ, for the sake of that communion which is his will. It is thus an ecclesial and ecumenical reading, seeking to consider each passage about Mary in the context of the New Testament as a whole, against the background of the Old, and in the light of Tradition.

*The witness of scripture: a trajectory of grace and hope*

8. The Old Testament bears witness to God's creation of men and women in the divine image, and God's loving call to covenant relationship with himself. Even when they disobeyed, God did not abandon human beings to sin and the power of death. Again and again God offered a covenant of grace. God made a covenant with Noah that never again would "all flesh" be destroyed by the waters of a flood. The Lord made a covenant with Abraham that, through him, all the families of the earth might be blessed. Through Moses he made a covenant with Israel that, obedient to his word, they might be a holy nation and a priestly people. The prophets repeatedly summoned the people to turn back from disobedience to the gracious God of the covenant, to receive God's word and let it bear fruit in their lives. They looked forward to a renewal of the covenant in which there would be perfect obedience and perfect self-giving: "This is the covenant which I will make with the house of Israel after those days, says the Lord: I will put my law within them, and I will write it upon their hearts; and I will be their God, and they shall be my people" (Jer. 31:33). In the prophecy of Ezekiel, this hope is spoken of not only in terms of washing and cleansing, but also of the gift of the Spirit (Ezek. 36:25-28).

9. The covenant between the Lord and his people is several times described as a love affair between God and Israel, the virgin daughter of Zion, bride and mother: "I gave you my solemn oath and entered into a covenant with you, declares the Sovereign Lord, and you became mine" (Ezek. 16:8; cf. Isa. 54:1 and Gal. 4:27). Even in punishing faithlessness, God remains forever faithful, promising to restore the covenant relationship and to draw together the scattered people (Hosea 1-2; Jer. 2:2, 31:3; Isa. 62:4-5). Nuptial imagery is also used within the New Testament to describe the relationship between Christ and the church (Eph. 5:21-33; Rev. 21:9). In parallel to the prophetic image of Israel as the bride of the Lord, the Solomonic literature of the Old Testament characterizes holy wisdom as the handmaid of the Lord (Prov. 8.22f; cf. Wis. 7:22-26), similarly emphasizing the theme of responsiveness and creative activity. In the New Testament these prophetic and wisdom motifs are combined (Luke 11:49) and fulfilled in the coming of Christ.

10. The scriptures also speak of the calling by God of particular persons, such as David, Elijah, Jeremiah and Isaiah, so that within the people of God certain special tasks may be performed. They bear witness to the gift of the Spirit or the presence of God enabling

them to accomplish God's will and purpose. There are also profound reflections on what it is to be known and called by God from the very beginning of one's existence (Ps. 139:13-16; Jer. 1:1-5). This sense of wonder at the prevenient grace of God is similarly attested in the New Testament, especially in the writings of Paul, when he speaks of those who are "called according to God's purpose", affirming that those whom God "foreknew, he also predestined to be conformed to the image of his Son... And those whom he predestined he also called; and those whom he called he also justified; and those whom he justified he also glorified" (Rom. 8:28-30; cf. 2 Tim. 1:9). The preparation by God for a prophetic task is exemplified in the words spoken by the angel to Zechariah before the birth of John the Baptist: "He will be filled with the Holy Spirit, even from his mother's womb" (Luke 1:15; cf. Judg. 13:3-5).

11. Following through the trajectory of the grace of God and the hope for a perfect human response which we have traced in the preceding paragraphs, Christians have, in line with the New Testament writers, seen its culmination in the obedience of Christ. Within this christological context, they have discerned a similar pattern in the one who would receive the word in her heart and in her body, be overshadowed by the Spirit and give birth to the Son of God. The New Testament speaks not only of God's preparation for the birth of the Son, but also of God's election, calling and sanctification of a Jewish woman in the line of those holy women, such as Sarah and Hannah, whose sons fulfilled the purposes of God for his people. Paul speaks of the Son of God being born "in the fullness of time" and "born of a woman, born under the Law" (Gal. 4:4). The birth of Mary's son is the fulfilment of God's will for Israel, and Mary's part in that fulfilment is that of free and unqualified consent in utter self-giving and trust: "Behold I am the handmaid of the Lord; let it be done to me according to your word" (Luke 1:38; cf. Ps. 123:2).

*Mary in Matthew's birth narrative*

12. While various parts of the New Testament refer to the birth of Christ, only two gospels, Matthew and Luke, each from its own perspective, narrate the story of his birth and refer specifically to Mary. Matthew entitles his book "the Genesis of Jesus Christ" (1:1), echoing the way the Bible begins (Gen. 1:1). In the genealogy (1:1-18) he traces the genesis of Jesus back through the Exile to David and ultimately to Abraham. He notes the unlikely role played in the providential ordering of Israel's salvation history by four women, each of whom stretches the boundaries of the covenant. This emphasis on continuity with the old is counter-balanced in the following account of Jesus' birth by an emphasis on the new (cf. 9:17), a type of re-creation by the Holy Spirit, revealing new possibilities of salvation from sin (1:21) and of the presence of "God with us" (1:23). Matthew stretches the boundaries further in holding together Jesus' Davidic descent through the legal fatherhood of Joseph, and his birth from the Virgin according to Isaiah's prophecy: "Behold a virgin shall conceive and bear a son" (Isa. 7:14 LXX).

13. In Matthew's account, Mary is mentioned in conjunction with her son in such phrases as "Mary his mother" or "the child and his mother" (2:11,13,20,21). Amid all the political intrigue, murder and displacement of this tale, one quiet moment of reverence has captured the Christian imagination: the Magi, whose profession it is to know when the time has come, kneel in homage to the infant King with his royal mother (2:2, 11). Matthew emphasizes the continuity of Jesus Christ with Israel's messianic

expectation and the newness that comes with the birth of the Saviour. Descent from David by whatever route, and birth at the ancestral royal city, disclose the first. The virginal conception discloses the second.

### Mary in Luke's birth narrative

14. In Luke's infancy narrative, Mary is prominent from the beginning. She is the link between John the Baptist and Jesus, whose miraculous births are laid out in deliberate parallel. She receives the angel's message and responds in humble obedience (1:38). She travels on her own from Galilee to Judea to visit Elizabeth (1:40) and in her song proclaims the eschatological reversal which will be at the heart of her son's proclamation of the kingdom of God. Mary is the one who in recollection looks beneath the surface of events (2:19,51) and represents the inwardness of faith and suffering (2:35). She speaks on Joseph's behalf in the scene at the temple and, although chided for her initial incomprehension, continues to grow in understanding (2:48-51).

15. Within the Lucan narrative, two particular scenes invite reflection on the place of Mary in the life of the church: the annunciation and the visit to Elizabeth. These passages emphasize that Mary is in a unique way the recipient of God's election and grace. The annunciation story recapitulates several incidents in the Old Testament, notably the births of Isaac (Gen. 18:10-14), Samson (Judg. 13:2-5) and Samuel (1 Sam. 1:1-20). The angel's greeting also evokes the passages in Isaiah (66:7-11), Zechariah (9:9) and Zephaniah (3:14-17) that call on the "Daughter of Zion", i.e., Israel awaiting with joy the arrival of her Lord. The choice of "overshadow" *(episkiasei)* to describe the action of the Holy Spirit in the virginal conception (Luke 1:35) echoes the cherubim overshadowing the Ark of the Covenant (Exod. 25:20), the presence of God overshadowing the tabernacle (Exod. 40:35), and the brooding of the Spirit over the waters at the creation (Gen. 1:2). At the Visitation, Mary's song (Magnificat) mirrors the song of Hannah (1 Sam. 2:1-10), broadening its scope so that Mary becomes the one who speaks for all the poor and oppressed who long for God's reign of justice to be established. Just as in Elizabeth's salutation the mother receives a blessing of her own, distinct from that of her child (1:42), so also in the Magnificat Mary predicts that "all generations will call me blessed" (1:48). This text provides the scriptural basis for an appropriate devotion to Mary, though never in separation from her role as mother of the Messiah.

16. In the annunciation story, the angel calls Mary the Lord's "favoured one" (Greek *kecharitomene*, a perfect participle meaning "one who has been and remains endowed with grace") in a way that implies a prior sanctification by divine grace with a view to her calling. The angel's announcement connects Jesus' being "holy" and "Son of God" with his conception by the Holy Spirit (1:35). The virginal conception then points to the divine Sonship of the Saviour who will be born of Mary. The infant not yet born is described by Elizabeth as the Lord: "And why is this granted to me that the mother of my Lord should come to me?" (1:43). The trinitarian pattern of divine action in these scenes is striking: the incarnation of the Son is initiated by the Father's election of the Blessed Virgin and is mediated by the Holy Spirit. Equally striking is Mary's fiat, her "Amen" given in faith and freedom to God's powerful word communicated by the angel (1:38).

17.  In Luke's account of the birth of Jesus, the praise offered to God by the shepherds parallels the Magi's adoration of the infant in Matthew's account. Again, this is the scene that constitutes the still centre at the heart of the birth story: "They found Mary and Joseph and the baby lying in a manger" (Luke 2:16). In accordance with the law of Moses, the baby is circumcised and presented in the Temple. On this occasion, Simeon has a special word of prophecy for the mother of the Christ-child, that "a sword will pierce your soul" (Luke 2:34-35). From this point on Mary's pilgrimage of faith leads to the foot of the cross.

*The virginal conception*

18.  The divine initiative in human history is proclaimed in the good news of the virginal conception through the action of the Holy Spirit (Matt. 1:20-23; Luke 1:34-35). The virginal conception may appear in the first place as an absence, i.e. the absence of a human father. It is in reality, however, a sign of the presence and work of the Spirit. Belief in the virginal conception is an early Christian tradition adopted and developed independently by Matthew and Luke.[2] For Christian believers, it is an eloquent sign of the divine Sonship of Christ and of new life through the Spirit. The virginal conception also points to the new birth of every Christian, as an adopted child of God. Each is "born again (from above) by water and the Spirit" (John 3:3-5). Seen in this light, the virginal conception, far from being an isolated miracle, is a powerful expression of what the church believes about her Lord, and about our salvation.

*Mary and the true family of Jesus*

19.  After these birth stories, it comes as something of a surprise to read the episode, narrated in all three synoptic gospels, which addresses the question of Jesus' true family. Mark tells us that Jesus' "mother and his brothers" (Mark 3:31) come and stand outside, wanting to speak to him.[3] Jesus in response distances himself from his natural family: he speaks instead of those gathered around him, his "eschatological family", that is to say, "whoever does the will of God" (3:35). For Mark, Jesus' natural family, including his own mother, seems at this stage to lack understanding of the true nature of his mission. But that will be the case also with his disciples (e.g. 8:33-35, 9:30-33, 10:35-40). Mark indicates that growth in understanding is inevitably slow and painful, and that genuine faith in Christ is not reached until the encounter with the cross and the empty tomb.

20.  In Luke, the stark contrast between the attitude towards Jesus of his natural and eschatological family is avoided (Luke 8:19-21). In a later scene (11:27-28) the woman in the crowd who utters a blessing on his mother, "Blessed is the womb that bore you and the breasts that you sucked", is corrected: "Blessed rather are those who hear the word of God and keep it." But that form of blessing, as Luke sees it, definitely includes Mary who, from the beginning of his account, was ready to let everything in her life happen according to God's word (1:38).

21.  In his second book, the Acts of the Apostles, Luke notes that between the ascension of the Risen Lord and the feast of Pentecost the apostles were gathered in Jerusalem "together with the women and Mary the mother of Jesus, and with his brothers" (Acts 1:14). Mary, who was receptive to the working of God's Spirit at the birth of the Messiah

(Luke 1:35-38), is here part of the community of disciples waiting in prayer for the out-pouring of the Spirit at the birth of the church.

### Mary in John's gospel

22. Mary is not mentioned explicitly in the prologue of John's gospel. However, something of the significance of her role in salvation history may be discerned by placing her in the context of the considered theological truths that the evangelist articulates in unfolding the good news of the incarnation. The theological emphasis on the divine initiative, that in the narratives of Matthew and Luke is expressed in the story of Jesus' birth, is paralleled in the prologue of John by an emphasis on the predestining will and grace of God by which all those who are brought to new birth are said to be born "not of blood, nor of the will of the flesh, nor of the will of man, but of God" (1:13). These are words that could be applied to the birth of Jesus himself.

23. At two important moments of Jesus' public life, the beginning (the wedding at Cana) and the end (the cross), John notes the presence of Jesus' mother. Each is an hour of need: the first on the surface rather trivial, but at a deeper level a symbolic anticipation of the second. John gives a prominent position in his gospel to the wedding at Cana (2:1-12), calling it the beginning *(archē)* of the signs of Jesus. The account emphasizes the new wine which Jesus brings, symbolizing the eschatological marriage feast of God with his people and the messianic banquet of the kingdom. The story primarily conveys a christological message: Jesus reveals his messianic glory to his disciples and they believe in him (2:11).

24. The presence of the "mother of Jesus" is mentioned at the beginning of the story: she has a distinctive role in the unfolding of the narrative. Mary seems to have been invited and be present in her own right, not with "Jesus and his disciples" (2:1-2); Jesus is initially seen as present as part of his mother's family. In the dialogue between them when the wine runs out, Jesus seems at first to refuse Mary's implied request, but in the end he accedes to it. This reading of the narrative, however, leaves room for a deeper symbolic reading of the event. In Mary's words "they have no wine", John ascribes to her the expression not so much of a deficiency in the wedding arrangements, as of the longing for salvation of the whole covenant people, who have water for purification but lack the joyful wine of the messianic kingdom. In his answer, Jesus begins by calling into question his former relationship with his mother ("What is there between you and me?"), implying that a change has to take place. He does not address Mary as "mother", but as "woman" (cf. John 19:26). Jesus no longer sees his relation to Mary as simply one of earthly kinship.

25. Mary's response, to instruct the servants to "do whatever he tells you" (2:5), is unexpected; she is not in charge of the feast (cf. 2:8). Her initial role as the mother of Jesus has radically changed. She herself is now seen as a believer within the messianic community. From this moment on, she commits herself totally to the Messiah and his word. A new relationship results, indicated by the change in the order of the main characters at the end of the story: "After this he went down to Capernaum, with his mother and his brothers and his disciples" (2:12). The Cana narrative opens by placing Jesus within the family of Mary, his mother; from now on, Mary is part of the "company of Jesus", his

disciple. Our reading of this passage reflects the church's understanding of the role of Mary: to help the disciples come to her son, Jesus Christ, and to "do whatever he tells you".

26. John's second mention of the presence of Mary occurs at the decisive hour of Jesus' messianic mission, his crucifixion (19:25-27). Standing with other disciples at the cross, Mary shares in the suffering of Jesus, who in his last moments addresses a special word to her: "Woman, behold your son", and to the beloved disciple: "Behold your mother." We cannot but be touched that, even in his dying moments, Jesus is concerned for the welfare of his mother, showing his filial affection. This surface reading again invites a symbolic and ecclesial reading of John's rich narrative. These last commands of Jesus before he dies reveal an understanding beyond their primary reference to Mary and "the beloved disciple" as individuals. The reciprocal roles of the "woman" and the "disciple" are related to the identity of the church. Elsewhere in John, the beloved disciple is presented as the model disciple of Jesus, the one closest to him who never deserted him, the object of Jesus' love, and the ever-faithful witness (13:25, 19:26, 20:1-10, 21:20-25). Understood in terms of discipleship, Jesus' dying words give Mary a motherly role in the church and encourage the community of disciples to embrace her as a spiritual mother.

27. A corporate understanding of "woman" also calls the church constantly to behold Christ crucified, and calls each disciple to care for the church as mother. Implicit here perhaps is a Mary-Eve typology: just as the first "woman" was taken from Adam's "rib" (Gen. 2:22, *pleura* LXX) and became the mother of all the living (Gen. 3:20), so the "woman" Mary is, on a spiritual level, the mother of all who gain true life from the water and blood that flow from the side (Greek *pleura*, literally "rib") of Christ (19:34) and from the Spirit that is breathed out from his triumphant sacrifice (19:30, 20:22, cf. 1 John 5:8). In such symbolic and corporate readings, images for the church, Mary and discipleship interact with one another. Mary is seen as the personification of Israel, now giving birth to the Christian community (cf. Isa. 54:1, 66:7-8), just as she had given birth earlier to the Messiah (cf. Isa. 7:14). When John's account of Mary at the beginning and end of Jesus' ministry is viewed in this light, it is difficult to speak of the church without thinking of Mary, the Mother of the Lord, as its archetype and first realization.

## *The woman in Revelation 12*

28. In highly symbolic language, full of scriptural imagery, the seer of Revelation describes the vision of a sign in heaven involving a woman, a dragon, and the woman's child. The narrative of Revelation 12 serves to assure the reader of the ultimate victory of God's faithful ones in times of persecution and eschatological struggle. In the course of history, the symbol of the woman has led to a variety of interpretations. Most scholars accept that the primary meaning of the woman is corporate: the people of God, whether Israel, the church of Christ, or both. Moreover, the narrative style of the author suggests that the "full picture" of the woman is attained only at the end of the book when the church of Christ becomes the triumphant New Jerusalem (Rev. 21:1-3). The actual troubles of the author's community are placed in the frame of history as a whole, which is the scene of the ongoing struggle between the faithful and their enemies, between good and evil, between God and Satan. The imagery of the offspring reminds us of the struggle in Genesis 3:15 between the serpent and the woman, between the serpent's seed and the woman's seed.[4]

29. Given this primary ecclesial interpretation of Revelation 12, is it still possible to find in it a secondary reference to Mary? The text does not explicitly identify the woman with Mary. It refers to the woman as the mother of the "male child who is to rule all the nations with a rod of iron", a citation from Psalm 2 elsewhere in the New Testament applied to the Messiah as well as to the faithful people of God (cf. Heb. 1:5, 5:5; Acts 13:33 with Rev. 2:27). In view of this, some Patristic writers came to think of the mother of Jesus when reading this chapter.[5] Given the place of the book of Revelation within the canon of scripture, in which the different biblical images intertwine, the possibility arose of a more explicit interpretation, both individual and corporate, of Revelation 12, illuminating the place of Mary and the church in the eschatological victory of the Messiah.

*Scriptural reflection*

30. The scriptural witness summons all believers in every generation to call Mary "blessed"; this Jewish woman of humble status, this daughter of Israel living in hope of justice for the poor, whom God has graced and chosen to become the virgin mother of his Son through the overshadowing of the Holy Spirit. We are to bless her as the "handmaid of the Lord" who gave her unqualified assent to the fulfilment of God's saving plan, as the mother who pondered all things in her heart, as the refugee seeking asylum in a foreign land, as the mother pierced by the innocent suffering of her own child, and as the woman to whom Jesus entrusted his friends. We are at one with her and the apostles, as they pray for the outpouring of the Spirit upon the nascent church, the eschatological family of Christ. And we may even glimpse in her the final destiny of God's people to share in her son's victory over the powers of evil and death.

## B.  Mary in the Christian Tradition

*Christ and Mary in the ancient common Tradition*

31. In the early church, reflection on Mary served to interpret and safeguard the apostolic Tradition centred on Jesus Christ. Patristic testimony to Mary as "God-bearer" (Theotokos) emerged from reflection on scripture and the celebration of Christian feasts, but its development was due chiefly to the early christological controversies. In the crucible of these controversies of the first five centuries, and their resolution in successive ecumenical councils, reflection on Mary's role in the incarnation was integral to the articulation of orthodox faith in Jesus Christ, true God and true man.

32. In defence of Christ's true humanity, and against Docetism, the early church emphasized Jesus' birth from Mary. He did not just "appear" to be human; he did not descend from heaven in a "heavenly body", nor when he was born did he simply "pass through" his mother. Rather, Mary gave birth to her son of her own substance. For Ignatius of Antioch (†c.110) and Tertullian (†c.200), Jesus is fully human, because "truly born" of Mary. In the words of the Nicene-Constantinopolitan Creed (381), "he was incarnate of the Holy Spirit and the Virgin Mary, and was made man". The definition of Chalcedon (451), reaffirming this creed, attests that Christ is "consubstantial with the Father according to the divinity and consubstantial with us according to the humanity". The Athanasian

Creed confesses yet more concretely that he is "man, of the substance of his Mother". This Anglicans and Roman Catholics together affirm.

33. In defence of his true divinity, the early church emphasized Mary's virginal conception of Jesus Christ. According to the Fathers, his conception by the Holy Spirit testifies to Christ's divine origin and divine identity. The One born of Mary is the eternal Son of God. Eastern and Western Fathers – such as Justin (†c.150), Irenaeus (†c.202), Athanasius (†373), and Ambrose (†397) – expounded this New Testament teaching in terms of Genesis 3 (Mary is the antitype of "virgin Eve") and Isaiah 7:14 (she fulfils the prophet's vision and gives birth to "God with us"). They appealed to the virginal conception to defend both the Lord's divinity and Mary's honour. As the Apostles' Creed confesses: Jesus Christ was "conceived by the Holy Spirit and born of the Virgin Mary". This Anglicans and Roman Catholics together affirm.

34. Mary's title Theotokos was formally invoked to safeguard the orthodox doctrine of the unity of Christ's person. This title had been in use in churches under the influence of Alexandria at least from the time of the Arian controversy. Since Jesus Christ is "true God from true God", as the council of Nicea (325) declared, these churches concluded that his mother, Mary, can rightly be called the "God-bearer". Churches under the influence of Antioch, however, conscious of the threat Apollinarianism posed to belief in the full humanity of Christ, did not immediately adopt this title. The debate between Cyril of Alexandria (†444) and Nestorius (†455), patriarch of Constantinople, who was formed in the Antiochene school, revealed that the real issue in the question of Mary's title was the unity of Christ's person. The ensuing council of Ephesus (431) used Theotokos (literally "God-bearer"; in Latin, *Deipara*) to affirm the oneness of Christ's person by identifying Mary as the Mother of God the Word incarnate.[6] The rule of faith on this matter takes more precise expression in the definition of Chalcedon: "One and the same Son… was begotten from the Father before the ages as to the divinity and in the latter days for us and our salvation was born as to the humanity from Mary the Virgin Theotokos." In receiving the council of Ephesus and the definition of Chalcedon, Anglicans and Roman Catholics together confess Mary as Theotokos.

*The celebration of Mary in the ancient common traditions*

35. In the early centuries, communion in Christ included a strong sense of the living presence of the saints as an integral part of the spiritual experience of the churches (Heb. 12:1,22-24; Rev. 6:9-11, 7, 8:3-4). Within the "cloud of witnesses", the Lord's mother came to be seen to have a special place. Themes developed from scripture and in devotional reflection reveal a deep awareness of Mary's role in the redemption of humanity. Such themes include Mary as Eve's counterpart and as a type of the church. The response of Christian people, reflecting on these themes, found devotional expression in both private and public prayer.

36. Exegetes delighted in drawing feminine imagery from the scriptures to contemplate the significance both of the church and Mary. Fathers as early as Justin Martyr (†c.150) and Irenaeus (†c.202), reflecting on texts like Genesis 3 and Luke 1:26-38, developed, alongside the antithesis of Adam/New Adam, that of Eve/New Eve. Just as Eve is associated with Adam in bringing about our defeat, so Mary is associated with her Son in the conquest of the ancient enemy (cf. Gen. 3:15, vide supra note 4): "virgin" Eve's

disobedience results in death; the virgin Mary's obedience opens the way to salvation. The New Eve shares in the New Adam's victory over sin and death.

37. The fathers presented Mary the Virgin Mother as a model of holiness for consecrated virgins, and increasingly taught that she had remained "Ever-Virgin".[7] In their reflection, virginity was understood not only as physical integrity, but as an interior disposition of openness, obedience, and single-hearted fidelity to Christ which models Christian discipleship and issues in spiritual fruitfulness.

38. In this patristic understanding, Mary's virginity was closely related to her sanctity. Although some early exegetes thought that Mary was not wholly without sin,[8] Augustine (†430) witnessed to contemporary reluctance to speak of any sin in her.

> We must except the holy Virgin Mary, concerning whom I wish to raise no question when it touches the subject of sins, out of honour to the Lord; for from him we know what abundance of grace for overcoming sin in every particular was conferred on her who had the merit to conceive and bear him who undoubtedly had no sin. (*De natura et gratia*, 36.42).

Other fathers from West and East, appealing to the angelic salutation (Luke 1:28) and Mary's response (Luke 1:38), support the view that Mary was filled with grace from her origin in anticipation of her unique vocation as Mother of the Lord. By the 5th century they hail her as a new creation: blameless, spotless, "holy in body and soul" (Theodotus of Ancyra, *Homily* 6,11: †before 446). By the 6th century, the title *panaghia* ("all-holy") can be found in the East.

39. Following the christological debates at the councils of Ephesus and Chalcedon, devotion to Mary flourished. When the patriarch of Antioch refused Mary the title of Theotokos, Emperor Leo I (457-474) commanded the patriarch of Constantinople to insert this title into the eucharistic prayer throughout the East. By the 6th century, commemoration of Mary as "God-bearer" had become universal in the eucharistic prayers of East and West (with the exception of the Assyrian Church of the East). Texts and images celebrating Mary's holiness were multiplied in liturgical poetry and songs, such as the Akathist, a hymn probably written soon after Chalcedon and still sung in the Eastern church. A tradition of praying with and praising Mary was thus gradually established. This has been associated since the 4th century, especially in the East, with asking for her protection.[9]

40. After the council of Ephesus, churches began to be dedicated to Mary and feasts in her honour began to be celebrated on particular days in these churches. Prompted by popular piety and gradually adopted by local churches, feasts celebrating Mary's conception (8/9 December), birth (8 September), presentation (21 November), and dormition (15 August) mirrored the liturgical commemorations of events in the life of the Lord. They drew both on the canonical scriptures and also on apocryphal accounts of Mary's early life and her "falling asleep". A feast of the conception of Mary can be dated in the East to the late 7th century, and was introduced into the Western church through southern England in the early 11th century. It drew on popular devotion expressed in the 2nd century Proto-evangelium of James, and paralleled the dominical feast of the annunciation and the existing feast of the conception of John the Baptist. The feast of Mary's "falling asleep" dates from the end of the 6th century, but was influenced by legendary narratives of the end of Mary's life already widely in circulation. In the West, the most influential of them are the *Transitus Mariae*. In the East the feast was known as the

"dormition", which implied her death but did not exclude her being taken into heaven. In the West the term used was "assumption", which emphasized her being taken into heaven but did not exclude the possibility of her dying. Belief in her assumption was grounded in the promise of the resurrection of the dead and the recognition of Mary's dignity as Theotokos and "Ever Virgin", coupled with the conviction that she who had borne Life should be associated to her Son's victory over death, and with the glorification of his body, the church.

*The growth of Marian doctrine and devotion in the Middle Ages*

41. The spread of these feasts of Mary gave rise to homilies in which preachers delved into the scriptures, searching for types and motifs to illuminate the Virgin's place in the economy of salvation. During the high Middle Ages a growing emphasis on the humanity of Christ was matched by attention to the exemplary virtues of Mary. Bernard, for example, articulates this emphasis in his homilies. Meditation on the lives of both Christ and Mary became increasingly popular, and gave rise to the development of such devotional practices as the rosary. The paintings, sculptures and stained glass of the high and late Middle Ages lent to this devotion immediacy and colour.

42. During these centuries there were some major shifts of emphasis in theological reflection about Mary. Theologians of the high Middle Ages developed patristic reflection on Mary as a "type" of the church, and also as the New Eve, in a way that associated her ever more closely with Christ in the continuing work of redemption. The centre of attention of believers shifted from Mary as representing the faithful church, and so also redeemed humanity, to Mary as dispensing Christ's graces to the faithful. Scholastic theologians in the West developed an increasingly elaborate body of doctrine about Mary in her own right. Much of this doctrine grew out of speculation about the holiness and sanctification of Mary. Questions about this were influenced not only by the scholastic theology of grace and original sin, but also by presuppositions concerning procreation and the relation between soul and body. For example, if she were sanctified in the womb of her mother, more perfectly even than John the Baptist and Jeremiah, some theologians thought that the precise moment of her sanctification had to be determined according to the current understanding of when the "rational soul" was infused into the body. Theological developments in the Western doctrine of grace and sin raised other questions: how could Mary be free of all sin, including original sin, without jeopardizing the role of Christ as universal Saviour? Speculative reflection led to intense discussions about how Christ's redeeming grace may have preserved Mary from original sin. The measured theology of Mary's sanctification found in the *Summa Theologiae* of Thomas Aquinas, and the subtle reasoning of Duns Scotus about Mary, were deployed in extended controversy over whether Mary was immaculate from the first moment of her conception.

43. In the late Middle Ages, scholastic theology grew increasingly apart from spirituality. Less and less rooted in scriptural exegesis, theologians relied on logical probability to establish their positions, and Nominalists speculated on what could be done by the absolute power and will of God. Spirituality, no longer in creative tension with theology, emphasized affectivity and personal experience. In popular religion, Mary came widely to be viewed as an intermediary between God and humanity, and even as a worker of miracles with powers that verged on the divine. This popular piety in due course influ-

enced the theological opinions of those who had grown up with it, and who subsequently elaborated a theological rationale for the florid Marian devotion of the late Middle Ages.


*From the Reformation to the present day*

44. One powerful impulse for Reformation in the early 16th century was a widespread reaction against devotional practices which approached Mary as a mediatrix alongside Christ, or sometimes even in his place. Such exaggerated devotions, in part inspired by presentations of Christ as inaccessible Judge as well as Redeemer, were sharply criticized by Erasmus and Thomas More and decisively rejected by the Reformers. Together with a radical re-reception of scripture as the fundamental touchstone of divine revelation, there was a re-reception by the Reformers of the belief that Jesus Christ is the only mediator between God and humanity. This entailed a rejection of real and perceived abuses surrounding devotion to Mary. It led also to the loss of some positive aspects of devotion and the diminution of her place in the life of the church.

45. In this context, the English Reformers continued to receive the doctrine of the ancient church concerning Mary. Their positive teaching about Mary concentrated on her role in the incarnation: it is summed up in their acceptance of her as the Theotokos, because this was seen to be both scriptural and in accord with ancient common tradition. Following the traditions of the early church and other Reformers like Martin Luther, the English Reformers such as Latimer (*Works*, 2:105), Cranmer (*Works*, 2:60; 2:88) and Jewel (*Works*, 3:440-441) accepted that Mary was "Ever Virgin". Following Augustine, they showed a reticence about affirming that Mary was a sinner. Their chief concern was to emphasize the unique sinlessness of Christ, and the need of all humankind, including Mary, for a Saviour (cf. Luke 1:47). Articles IX and XV affirmed the universality of human sinfulness. They neither affirmed nor denied the possibility of Mary having been preserved by grace from participation in this general human condition. It is notable that the *Book of Common Prayer* in the Christmas collect and preface refers to Mary as "a pure virgin".

46. From 1561, the calendar of the Church of England (which was reproduced in the 1662 BCP) contained five feasts associated with Mary: conception of Mary, nativity of Mary, annunciation, visitation, and purification/presentation. There was, however, no longer a feast of the assumption (15 August): not only was it understood to lack scriptural warrant, but was also seen as exalting Mary at the expense of Christ. Anglican liturgy, as expressed in the successive *Books of Common Prayer* (1549, 1552, 1559, 1662) when it mentions Mary, gives prominence to her role as the "pure Virgin" from whose "substance" the Son took human nature (cf. Article II). In spite of the diminution of devotion to Mary in the 16th century, reverence for her endured in the continued use of the Magnificat in evening prayer, and the unchanged dedication of ancient churches and lady chapels. In the 17th century writers such as Lancelot Andrewes, Jeremy Taylor and Thomas Ken reappropriated from patristic tradition a fuller appreciation of the place of Mary in the prayers of the believer and of the church. For example, Andrewes in his *Preces Privatae* borrowed from Eastern liturgies when he showed a warmth of Marian devotion "commemorating the all holy, immaculate, more than blessed mother of God and ever-virgin Mary". This reappropriation can be traced into the next century, and into the Oxford Movement of the 19th century.

47.  In the Roman Catholic Church, the continued growth of Marian doctrine and devotion, while moderated by the reforming decrees of the council of Trent (1545-63), also suffered the distorting influence of Protestant-Catholic polemics. To be Roman Catholic came to be identified by an emphasis on devotion to Mary. The depth and popularity of Marian spirituality in the 19th and the first half of the 20th centuries contributed to the definitions of the dogmas of the immaculate conception (1854) and the assumption (1950). On the other hand, the pervasiveness of this spirituality began to give rise to criticism both within and beyond the Roman Catholic Church and initiated a process of re-reception. This re-reception was evident in the Second Vatican Council which, consonant with the contemporary biblical, patristic and liturgical renewals, and with concern for ecumenical sensitivities, chose not to draft a separate document on Mary, but to integrate doctrine about her into the Constitution on the Church, *Lumen Gentium* (1964) – more specifically, into its final section describing the eschatological pilgrimage of the church (ch. VIII). The council intended "to explain carefully both the role of the Blessed Virgin in the mystery of the Word Incarnate and of the mystical body, as well as the duties of the redeemed human race towards the God-bearer, mother of Christ and mother of humanity, especially of the faithful" (art. 54). *Lumen Gentium* concludes by calling Mary a sign of hope and comfort for God's pilgrim people (art. 68-69). The fathers of the council consciously sought to resist exaggerations by returning to patristic emphases and placing Marian doctrine and devotion in its proper christological and ecclesial context.

48.  Soon after the council, faced by an unanticipated decline in devotion to Mary, Pope Paul VI published an apostolic exhortation, *Marialis Cultus* (1974), to remove doubts about the council's intentions and to foster appropriate Marian devotion. His review of the place of Mary in the revised Roman rite showed that she has not been "demoted" by the liturgical renewal, but that devotion to her is properly located within the christological focus of the church's public prayer. He reflected on Mary as "a model of the spiritual attitudes with which the church celebrates and lives the divine mysteries" (art. 16). She is the model for the whole church, but also a "teacher of the spiritual life for individual Christians" (art. 21). According to Paul VI, the authentic renewal of Marian devotion must be integrated with the doctrines of God, Christ and the church. Devotion to Mary must be in accordance with the scriptures and the liturgy of the church; it must be sensitive to the concerns of other Christians and it must affirm the full dignity of women in public and private life. The pope also issued cautions to those who err either by exaggeration or neglect. Finally, he commended the recitation of the angelus and the rosary as traditional devotions which are compatible with these norms. In 2002, Pope John Paul II reinforced the christological focus of the rosary by proposing five "mysteries of Light" from the gospels' account of Christ's public ministry between his baptism and passion. "The rosary," he states, "though clearly Marian in character, is at heart a Christocentric prayer" (*Rosarium Virginis Mariae*, 1).

49.  Mary has a new prominence in Anglican worship through the liturgical renewals of the 20th century. In most Anglican prayer books, Mary is again mentioned by name in the eucharistic prayers. Further, 15 August has come to be widely celebrated as a principal feast in honour of Mary with scripture readings, collect and proper preface. Other feasts associated with Mary have also been renewed, and liturgical resources offered for use on these festivals. Given the definitive role of authorized liturgical texts and practices in Anglican formularies, such developments are highly significant.

50. The above developments show that in recent decades a re-reception of the place of Mary in corporate worship has been taking place across the Anglican Communion. At the same time, in *Lumen Gentium* (ch. VIII) and the exhortation *Marialis Cultus* the Roman Catholic Church has attempted to set devotion to Mary within the context of the teaching of scripture and the ancient common tradition. This constitutes, for the Roman Catholic Church, a re-reception of teaching about Mary. Revision of the calendars and lectionaries used in our communions, especially the liturgical provision associated with feasts of Mary, gives evidence of a shared process of re-receiving the scriptural testimony to her place in the faith and life of the church. Growing ecumenical exchange has contributed to the process of re-reception in both communions.

51. The scriptures lead us together to praise and bless Mary as the handmaid of the Lord, who was providentially prepared by divine grace to be the mother of our Redeemer. Her unqualified assent to the fulfilment of God's saving plan can be seen as the supreme instance of a believer's "Amen" in response to the "Yes" of God. She stands as a model of holiness, obedience and faith for all Christians. As one who received the Word in her heart and in her body, and brought it forth into the world, Mary belongs in the prophetic tradition. We are agreed in our belief in the Blessed Virgin Mary as Theotokos. Our two communions are both heirs to a rich tradition which recognizes Mary as ever virgin, and sees her as the new Eve and as a type of the church. We join in praying and praising with Mary whom all generations have called blessed, in observing her festivals and according her honour in the communion of the saints, and are agreed that Mary and the saints pray for the whole church (see below in section D). In all of this, we see Mary as inseparably linked with Christ and the church. Within this broad consideration of the role of Mary, we now focus on the theology of hope and grace.

## C. Mary within the pattern of grace and hope

52. Participation in the glory of God, through the mediation of the Son, in the power of the Spirit is the gospel hope (cf. 2 Cor. 3:18, 4:4-6). The church already enjoys this hope and destiny through the Holy Spirit, who is the "pledge" of our inheritance in Christ (Eph. 1:14; 2 Cor. 5:5). For Paul especially, what it means to be fully human can only be understood rightly when it is viewed in the light of what we are to become in Christ, the "last Adam", as opposed to what we had become in the old Adam (1 Cor. 15:42-49; cf. Rom. 5:12-21). This eschatological perspective sees Christian life in terms of the vision of the exalted Christ leading believers to cast off sins that entangle (Heb. 12:1-2) and to participate in his purity and love, made available through his atoning sacrifice (1 John 3:3, 4:10). We thus view the economy of grace from its fulfilment in Christ "back" into history, rather than "forward" from its beginning in fallen creation towards the future in Christ. This perspective offers fresh light in which to consider the place of Mary.

53. The hope of the church is based upon the testimony it has received about the present glory of Christ. The church proclaims that Christ was not only raised bodily from the tomb, but was exalted to the right hand of the Father, to share in the Father's glory (1 Tim. 3:16; 1 Pet. 1:21). Insofar as believers are united with Christ in baptism and share in Christ's sufferings (Rom. 6:1-6), they participate through the Spirit in his glory, and

are raised up with him in anticipation of the final revelation (cf. Rom. 8:17; Eph. 2:6; Col. 3:1). It is the destiny of the church and of its members, the "saints" chosen in Christ "before the foundation of the world", to be "holy and blameless" and to share in the glory of Christ (Eph. 1:3-5, 5:27). Paul speaks as it were from the future retrospectively, when he says, "Those whom God predestined he also called; those whom he called he also justified; and those whom he justified he also glorified" (Rom. 8:30). In the succeeding chapters of Romans, Paul explicates this many-faceted drama of God's election in Christ, keeping in view its end: the inclusion of the Gentiles, so that "all Israel shall be saved" (Rom. 11:26).

*Mary in the economy of grace*

54. Within this biblical framework we have considered afresh the distinctive place of the Virgin Mary in the economy of grace, as the one who bore Christ, the elect of God. The word of God delivered by Gabriel addresses her as already "graced", inviting her to respond in faith and freedom to God's call (Luke 1:28,38,45). The Spirit is operative within her in the conception of the Saviour, and this "blessed among women" is inspired to sing "all generations will call me blessed" (Luke 1:42,48). Viewed eschatologically, Mary thus embodies the "elect Israel" of whom Paul speaks – glorified, justified, called, predestined. This is the pattern of grace and hope which we see at work in the life of Mary, who holds a distinctive place in the common destiny of the church as the one who bore in her own flesh "the Lord of glory". Mary is marked out from the beginning as the one chosen, called and graced by God through the Holy Spirit for the task that lay ahead of her.

55. The scriptures tell us of barren women who were gifted by God with children – Rachel, Manoah's wife, Hannah (Gen. 30:1-24; Judg. 13; 1 Sam. 1), and those past child-bearing – Sarah (Gen. 18:9-15, 21:1-7), and most notably Mary's cousin, Elizabeth (Luke 1:7,24). These women highlight the singular role of Mary, who was neither barren nor past child-bearing age, but a fruitful virgin: in her womb the Spirit brought about the conception of Jesus. The scriptures also speak of God's care for all human beings, even before their coming to birth (Ps. 139:13-18), and recount the action of God's grace preceding the specific calling of particular persons, even from their conception (cf. Jer. 1:5; Luke 1:15; Gal. 1:15). With the early church, we see in Mary's acceptance of the divine will the fruit of her prior preparation, signified in Gabriel's affirmation of her as "graced". We can thus see that God was at work in Mary from her earliest beginnings, preparing her for the unique vocation of bearing in her own flesh the new Adam, "in whom all things in heaven and earth hold together" (Col. 1:17). Of Mary, both personally and as a representative figure, we can say she is "God's workmanship, created in Christ Jesus for good works which God prepared beforehand" (Eph. 2:10).

56. Mary, a pure virgin, bore God incarnate in her womb. Her bodily intimacy with her son was all of a piece with her faithful following of him, and her maternal participation in his victorious self-giving (Luke 2:35). All this is clearly testified in scripture, as we have seen. There is no direct testimony in scripture concerning the end of Mary's life. However, certain passages give instances of those who follow God's purposes faithfully being drawn into God's presence. Moreover, these passages offer hints or partial analogies that may throw light on the mystery of Mary's entry into glory. For instance, the

biblical pattern of anticipated eschatology appears in the account of Stephen, the first martyr (Acts 7:54-60). At the moment of his death, which conforms to that of his Lord, he sees "the glory of God, and Jesus" the "Son of Man" not seated in judgment, but "standing at the right hand of God" to welcome his faithful servant. Similarly, the penitent thief who calls on the crucified Christ is accorded the special promise of being with Christ immediately in paradise (Luke 23:43). God's faithful servant Elijah is taken up by a whirlwind into heaven (2 Kings 2:11), and of Enoch it is written, "he was attested as having pleased God" as a man of faith, and was therefore "taken up so that he should not see death; and he was not found because God had taken him" (Heb. 11:5; cf. Gen. 5:24). Within such a pattern of anticipated eschatology, Mary can also be seen as the faithful disciple fully present with God in Christ. In this way, she is a sign of hope for all humanity.

57. The pattern of hope and grace already foreshadowed in Mary will be fulfilled in the new creation in Christ when all the redeemed will participate in the full glory of the Lord (cf. 2 Cor. 3:18). Christian experience of communion with God in this present life is a sign and foretaste of divine grace and glory, a hope shared with the whole of creation (Rom. 8:18-23). The individual believer and the church find their consummation in the new Jerusalem, the holy bride of Christ (cf. Rev. 21:2; Eph. 5:27). When Christians from East and West through the generations have pondered God's work in Mary, they have discerned in faith (cf. *Gift*, 29) that it is fitting that the Lord gathered her wholly to himself: in Christ, she is already a new creation in whom "the old has passed away and the new has come" (2 Cor. 5:17). Viewed from such an eschatological perspective, Mary may be seen both as a type of the church, and as a disciple with a special place in the economy of salvation.

*The papal definitions*

58. Thus far we have outlined our common faith concerning the place of Mary in the divine purpose. Roman Catholic Christians, however, are bound to believe the teaching defined by Pope Pius XII in 1950: "that the Immaculate Mother of God, the ever-Virgin Mary, having completed the course of her earthly life, was assumed body and soul into heavenly glory". We note that the dogma does not adopt a particular position as to how Mary's life ended, [10] nor does it use about her the language of death and resurrection, but celebrates the action of God in her. Thus, given the understanding we have reached concerning the place of Mary in the economy of hope and grace, we can affirm together the teaching that God has taken the Blessed Virgin Mary in the fullness of her person into his glory as consonant with scripture and that it can, indeed, only be understood in the light of scripture. Roman Catholics can recognize that this teaching about Mary is contained in the dogma. While the calling and destiny of all the redeemed is their glorification in Christ, Mary, as Theotokos, holds the pre-eminent place within the communion of saints and embodies the destiny of the church.

59. Roman Catholics are also bound to believe that "the most blessed Virgin Mary was, from the first moment of her conception, by a singular grace and privilege of Almighty God and in view of the merits of Christ Jesus the Saviour of the human race, preserved immune from all stain of original sin" (*Dogma of the Immaculate Conception of Mary,*

defined by Pope Pius IX, 1854). [11] The definition teaches that Mary, like all other human beings, has need of Christ as her Saviour and Redeemer (cf. *LG*, 53; *CCC*, 491). The negative notion of "sinlessness" runs the risk of obscuring the fullness of Christ's saving work. It is not so much that Mary lacks something which other human beings "have", namely sin, but that the glorious grace of God filled her life from the beginning. [12] The holiness which is our end in Christ (cf. 1 John 3:2-3) was seen, by unmerited grace, in Mary, who is the prototype of the hope of grace for humankind as a whole. According to the New Testament, being "graced" has the connotation of being freed from sin through Christ's blood (Eph. 1:6-7). The scriptures point to the efficacy of Christ's atoning sacrifice even for those who preceded him in time (cf. 1 Pet. 3:19; John 8:56; 1 Cor. 10:4). Here again the eschatological perspective illuminates our understanding of Mary's person and calling. In view of her vocation to be the mother of the Holy One (Luke 1:35), we can affirm together that Christ's redeeming work reached "back" in Mary to the depths of her being, and to her earliest beginnings. This is not contrary to the teaching of scripture, and can only be understood in the light of scripture. Roman Catholics can recognize in this what is affirmed by the dogma – namely "preserved from all stain of original sin" and "from the first moment of her conception".

60. We have agreed together that the teaching about Mary in the two definitions of 1854 and 1950, understood within the biblical pattern of the economy of grace and hope outlined here, can be said to be consonant with the teaching of the scriptures and the ancient common traditions. However, in Roman Catholic understanding as expressed in these two definitions, the proclamation of any teaching as dogma implies that the teaching in question is affirmed to be "revealed by God" and therefore to be believed "firmly and constantly" by all the faithful (i.e. it is *de fide*). The problem which the dogmas may present for Anglicans can be put in terms of article VI:

> Holy scripture containeth all things necessary to salvation: so that whatsoever is not read therein, nor may be proved thereby, is not to be required of any man, that it should be believed as an article of the faith, or be thought requisite or necessary to salvation.

We agree that nothing can be required to be believed as an article of faith unless it is revealed by God. The question arises for Anglicans, however, as to whether these doctrines concerning Mary are revealed by God in a way which must be held by believers as a matter of faith.

61. The particular circumstances and precise formulations of the 1854 and 1950 definitions have created problems not only for Anglicans but also for other Christians. The formulations of these doctrines and some objections to them are situated within the thought-forms of their time. In particular, the phrases "revealed by God" (1854) and "divinely revealed" (1950) used in the dogmas reflect the theology of revelation that was dominant in the Roman Catholic Church at the time that the definitions were made, and which found authoritative expression in the constitution *Dei Filius* of the First Vatican Council. They have to be understood today in the light of the way this teaching was refined by the Second Vatican Council in its constitution *Dei Verbum*, particularly in regard to the central role of scripture in the reception and transmission of revelation. When the Roman Catholic Church affirms that a truth is "revealed by God", there is no suggestion of new revelation. Rather, the definitions are understood to bear witness to what has been

revealed from the beginning. The scriptures bear normative witness to such revelation (cf. *Gift*, 19). This revelation is received by the community of believers and transmitted in time and place through the scriptures and through the preaching, liturgy, spirituality, life and teaching of the church, that draw upon the scriptures. In *The Gift of Authority* the commission sought to explicate a method by which such authoritative teaching could arise, the key point being that it needs to be in conformity with scripture, which remains a primary concern for Anglicans and Roman Catholics alike.

62. Anglicans have also questioned whether these doctrines must be held by believers as a matter of faith in view of the fact that the bishop of Rome defined these doctrines "independent of a council" (cf. *Authority*, II.30). In response, Roman Catholics have pointed to the *sensus fidelium*, the liturgical tradition throughout the local churches, and the active support of the Roman Catholic bishops (cf. *Gift*, 29-30): these were the elements through which these doctrines were recognized as belonging to the faith of the church, and therefore able to be defined (cf. *Gift*, 47). For Roman Catholics, it belongs to the office of the bishop of Rome that he should be able, under strictly limited conditions, to make such a definition (cf. *Pastor Aeternus* [1870]; *DS*, 3069-3070). The definitions of 1854 and 1950 were not made in response to controversy, but gave voice to the consensus of faith among believers in communion with the bishop of Rome. They were reaffirmed by the Second Vatican Council. For Anglicans, it would be the consent of an ecumenical council which, teaching according to the scriptures, most securely demonstrates that the necessary conditions for a teaching to be de fide had been met. Where this is the case, as with the definition of the Theotokos, both Roman Catholics and Anglicans would agree that the witness of the church is firmly and constantly to be believed by all the faithful (cf. 1 John 1:1-3).

63. Anglicans have asked whether it would be a condition of the future restoration of full communion that they should be required to accept the definitions of 1854 and 1950. Roman Catholics find it hard to envisage a restoration of communion in which acceptance of certain doctrines would be requisite for some and not for others. In addressing these issues, we have been mindful that "one consequence of our separation has been a tendency for Anglicans and Roman Catholics alike to exaggerate the importance of the Marian dogmas in themselves at the expense of the other truths more closely related to the foundation of the Christian faith" (*Authority*, II.30). Anglicans and Roman Catholics agree that the doctrines of the assumption and the immaculate conception of Mary must be understood in the light of the more central truth of her identity as Theotokos, which itself depends on faith in the incarnation. We recognize that, following the Second Vatican Council and the teaching of recent popes, the christological and ecclesiological context for the church's doctrine concerning Mary is being re-received within the Roman Catholic Church. We now suggest that the adoption of an eschatological perspective may deepen our shared understanding of the place of Mary in the economy of grace, and the tradition of the church concerning Mary which both our communions receive. Our hope is that the Roman Catholic Church and the Anglican Communion will recognize a common faith in the agreement concerning Mary which we here offer. Such a re-reception would mean the Marian teaching and devotion within our respective communities, including differences of emphasis, would be seen to be authentic expressions of Christian belief. [13] Any such re-reception would have to take place within the context of a mutual re-reception of an effective teaching authority in the church, such as that set out in *The Gift of Authority*.

## D. Mary in the life of the churches

64. "All the promises of God find their 'Yes' in Christ: that is why we offer the 'Amen' through him, to the glory of God" (2 Cor. 1:20). God's "Yes" in Christ takes a distinctive and demanding form as it is addressed to Mary. The profound mystery of "Christ in you, the hope of glory" (Col. 1:27) has a unique meaning for her. It enables her to speak the "Amen" in which, through the Spirit's overshadowing, God's "Yes" of new creation is inaugurated. As we have seen, this fiat of Mary was distinctive, in its openness to God's word, and in the path to the foot of the cross and beyond on which the Spirit led her. The scriptures portray Mary as growing in her relationship with Christ: his sharing of her natural family (Luke 2:39) was transcended in her sharing of his eschatological family, those upon whom the Spirit is poured out (Acts 1:14, 2:1-4). Mary's "Amen" to God's "Yes" in Christ to her is thus both unique and a model for every disciple and for the life of the church.

65. One outcome of our study has been awareness of differences in the ways in which the example of Mary living out the grace of God has been appropriated into the devotional lives of our traditions. Whilst both traditions have recognized her special place in the communion of saints, different emphases have marked the way we have experienced her ministry. Anglicans have tended to begin from reflection on the scriptural example of Mary as an inspiration and model for discipleship. Roman Catholics have given prominence to the ongoing ministry of Mary in the economy of grace and the communion of saints. Mary points people to Christ, commending them to him and helping them to share his life. Neither of these general characterizations do full justice to the richness and diversity of either tradition, and the 20th century witnessed a particular growth in convergence as many Anglicans were drawn into a more active devotion to Mary, and Roman Catholics discovered afresh the scriptural roots of such devotion. We together agree that in understanding Mary as the fullest human example of the life of grace, we are called to reflect on the lessons of her life recorded in scripture and to join with her as one indeed not dead, but truly alive in Christ. In doing so we walk together as pilgrims in communion with Mary, Christ's foremost disciple, and all those whose participation in the new creation encourages us to be faithful to our calling (cf. 2 Cor. 5:17,19).

66. Aware of the distinctive place of Mary in the history of salvation, Christians have given her a special place in their liturgical and private prayer, praising God for what he has done in and through her. In singing the Magnificat, they praise God with her; in the eucharist, they pray with her as they do with all God's people, integrating their prayers in the great communion of saints. They recognize Mary's place in "the prayer of all the saints" that is being uttered before the throne of God in the heavenly liturgy (Rev. 8:3-4). All these ways of including Mary in praise and prayer belong to our common heritage, as does our acknowledgment of her unique status as Theotokos, which gives her a distinctive place within the communion of saints.

*Intercession and mediation in the communion of saints*

67. The practice of believers asking Mary to intercede for them with her son grew rapidly following her being declared Theotokos at the council of Ephesus. The most common form today of such intercession is the "Hail Mary". This form conflates the greetings of Gabriel and Elizabeth to her (Luke 1:28,42). It was widely used from the

5th century, without the closing phrase, "pray for us sinners now and at the hour of our death", which was first added in the 15th century, and included in the Roman breviary by Pius V in 1568. The English Reformers criticized this invocation and similar forms of prayer, because they believed that it threatened the unique mediation of Jesus Christ. Confronted with exaggerated devotion, stemming from excessive exaltation of Mary's role and powers alongside Christ's, they rejected the "Romish doctrine of... the invocation of saints" as "grounded upon no warranty of scripture, but rather repugnant to the word of God" (art. XXII). The council of Trent affirmed that seeking the saints' assistance to obtain favours from God is "good and useful": such requests are made "through his Son our Lord Jesus Christ, who is our sole Redeemer and Saviour" (*DS*, 1821). The Second Vatican Council endorsed the continued practice of believers asking Mary to pray for them, emphasizing that "Mary's maternal role towards the human race in no way obscures or diminishes the unique mediation of Christ, but rather shows its power... in no way does it hinder the direct union of believers with Christ, but rather fosters it" (*LG*, 60). Therefore the Roman Catholic Church continues to promote devotion to Mary, while reproving those who either exaggerate or minimize Mary's role (*Marialis Cultus*, 31). With this background in mind, we seek a theologically grounded way to draw more closely together in the life of prayer in communion with Christ and his saints.

68. The scriptures teach that "there is one mediator between God and humankind, Christ Jesus, himself human, who gave himself as a ransom for all" (1 Tim. 2:5,6). As noted earlier, on the basis of this teaching "we reject any interpretation of the role of Mary which obscures this affirmation" (*Authority*, II.30). It is also true, however, that all ministries of the church, especially those of word and sacrament, mediate the grace of God through human beings. These ministries do not compete with the unique mediation of Christ, but rather serve it and have their source within it. In particular, the prayer of the church does not stand alongside or in place of the intercession of Christ, but is made through him, our Advocate and Mediator (cf. Rom. 8:34; Heb. 7:25, 12:24; 1 John 2:1). It finds both its possibility and practice in and through the Holy Spirit, the other Advocate sent according to Christ's promise (cf. John 14:16-17). Hence asking our brothers and sisters, on earth and in heaven, to pray for us, does not contest the unique mediatory work of Christ, but is rather a means by which, in and through the Spirit, its power may be displayed.

69. In our praying as Christians we address our petitions to God our heavenly Father, in and through Jesus Christ, as the Holy Spirit moves and enables us. All such invocation takes place within the communion which is God's being and gift. In the life of prayer we invoke the name of Christ in solidarity with the whole church, assisted by the prayers of brothers and sisters of every time and place. As ARCIC has expressed it previously, "The believer's pilgrimage of faith is lived out with the mutual support of all the people of God. In Christ all the faithful, both living and departed, are bound together in a communion of prayer" (*Salvation and the Church*, 22). In the experience of this communion of prayer believers are aware of their continued fellowship with their sisters and brothers who have "fallen asleep", the "great cloud of witnesses" who surround us as we run the race of faith. For some, this intuition means sensing their friends' presence; for some it may mean pondering the issues of life with those who have gone before them in faith. Such intuitive experience affirms our solidarity in Christ with Christians of every time and place, not least with the woman through whom he became "like us in all things except sin" (Heb. 4:15).

70. The scriptures invite Christians to ask their brothers and sisters to pray for them, in and through Christ (cf. James 5:13-15). Those who are now "with Christ", untrammelled by sin, share the unceasing prayer and praise which characterizes the life of heaven (e.g. Rev. 5:9-14, 7:9-12, 8:3-4). In the light of these testimonies, many Christians have found that requests for assistance in prayer can rightly and effectively be made to those members of the communion of saints distinguished by their holy living (cf. James 5:16-18). It is in this sense that we affirm that asking the saints to pray for us is not to be excluded as unscriptural, though it is not directly taught by the scriptures to be a required element of life in Christ. Further, we agree that the way such assistance is sought must not obscure believers' direct access to God our heavenly Father, who delights to give good gifts to his children (Matt. 7:11). When, in the Spirit and through Christ, believers address their prayers to God, they are assisted by the prayers of other believers, especially of those who are truly alive in Christ and freed from sin. We note that liturgical forms of prayer are addressed to God: they do not address prayer "to" the saints, but rather ask them to "pray for us". However, in this and other instances, any concept of invocation which blurs the trinitarian economy of grace and hope is to be rejected, as not consonant with scripture or the ancient common traditions.

*The distinctive ministry of Mary*

71. Among all the saints, Mary takes her place as Theotokos: alive in Christ, she abides with the one she bore, still "highly favoured" in the communion of grace and hope, the exemplar of redeemed humanity, an icon of the church. Consequently she is believed to exercise a distinctive ministry of assisting others through her active prayer. Many Christians reading the Cana account continue to hear Mary instruct them, "Do whatever he tells you", and are confident that she draws the attention of her son to their needs: "they have no wine" (John 2:1-12). Many experience a sense of empathy and solidarity with Mary, especially at key points when the account of her life echoes theirs, for example the acceptance of vocation, the scandal of her pregnancy, the improvised surroundings of her labour, giving birth, and fleeing as a refugee. Portrayals of Mary standing at the foot of the cross, and the traditional portrayal of her receiving the crucified body of Jesus (the *Pietà*), evoke the particular suffering of a mother at the death of her child. Anglicans and Roman Catholics alike are drawn to the mother of Christ, as a figure of tenderness and compassion.

72. The motherly role of Mary, first affirmed in the gospel accounts of her relationship to Jesus, has been developed in a variety of ways. Christian believers acknowledge Mary to be the mother of God incarnate. As they ponder our Saviour's dying word to the beloved disciple, "behold your mother" (John 19:27), they may hear an invitation to hold Mary dear as "mother of the faithful": she will care for them as she cared for her son in his hour of need. Hearing Eve called "the mother of all living" (Gen. 3:20), they may come to see Mary as mother of the new humanity, active in her ministry of pointing all people to Christ, seeking the welfare of all the living. We are agreed that, while caution is needed in the use of such imagery, it is fitting to apply it to Mary, as a way of honouring her distinctive relationship to her son, and the efficacy in her of his redeeming work.

73. Many Christians find that giving devotional expression to their appreciation for this ministry of Mary enriches their worship of God. Authentic popular devotion to Mary, which by its nature displays a wide individual, regional and cultural diversity, is to be respected. The crowds gathering at some places where Mary is believed to have appeared suggest that such apparitions are an important part of this devotion and provide spiritual comfort. There is need for careful discernment in assessing the spiritual value of any alleged apparition. This has been emphasized in a recent Roman Catholic commentary.

> Private revelation can be a genuine help in understanding the gospel and living it better at a particular moment in time; therefore it should not be disregarded. It is a help which is offered, but which one is not obliged to use... The criterion for the truth and value of a private revelation is therefore its orientation to Christ himself. When it leads us away from him, when it becomes independent of him or even presents itself as another and better plan of salvation, more important than the gospel, then it certainly does not come from the Holy Spirit. (Congregation for the Doctrine of the Faith, *Theological Commentary on the Message of Fatima*, 26 June 2000)

We are agreed that, within the constraints set down in this teaching to ensure that the honour paid to Christ remains pre-eminent, such private devotion is acceptable, though never required of believers.

74. When Mary was first acknowledged as mother of the Lord by Elizabeth, she responded by praising God and proclaiming his justice for the poor in her Magnificat (Luke 1:46-55). In Mary's response we can see an attitude of poverty towards God that reflects the divine commitment and preference for the poor. In her powerlessness she is exalted by God's favour. Although the witness of her obedience and acceptance of God's will has sometimes been used to encourage passivity and impose servitude on women, it is rightly seen as a radical commitment to God who has mercy on his servant, lifts up the lowly and brings down the mighty. Issues of justice for women and the empowerment of the oppressed have arisen from daily reflection on Mary's remarkable song. Inspired by her words, communities of women and men in various cultures have committed themselves to work with the poor and the excluded. Only when joy is joined with justice and peace do we rightly share in the economy of hope and grace which Mary proclaims and embodies.

75. Affirming together unambiguously Christ's unique mediation, which bears fruit in the life of the church, we do not consider the practice of asking Mary and the saints to pray for us as communion-dividing. Since obstacles of the past have been removed by clarification of doctrine, by liturgical reform and practical norms in keeping with it, we believe that there is no continuing theological reason for ecclesial division on these matters.

# Conclusion

76. Our study, which opens with a careful ecclesial and ecumenical reading of the scriptures, in the light of the ancient common traditions, has illuminated in a new way the place of Mary in the economy of hope and grace. We together reaffirm the agreements reached previously by ARCIC, in *Authority in the Church*, II.30:

- that any interpretation of the role of Mary must not obscure the unique mediation of Christ;

- that any consideration of Mary must be linked with the doctrines of Christ and the church;

- that we recognize the Blessed Virgin Mary as the Theotokos, the mother of God incarnate, and so observe her festivals and accord her honour among the saints;

- that Mary was prepared by grace to be the mother of our Redeemer, by whom she herself was redeemed and received into glory;

- that we recognize Mary as a model of holiness, faith and obedience for all Christians;

- that Mary can be seen as a prophetic figure of the church.

We believe that the present statement significantly deepens and extends these agreements, setting them within a comprehensive study of doctrine and devotion associated with Mary.

77. We are convinced that any attempt to come to a reconciled understanding of these matters must begin by listening to God's word in the scriptures. Therefore our common statement commences with a careful exploration of the rich New Testament witness to Mary, in the light of overall themes and patterns in the scriptures as a whole.

- This study has led us to the conclusion that it is impossible to be faithful to scripture without giving due attention to the person of Mary (§§6-30).

- In recalling together the ancient common traditions, we have discerned afresh the central importance of the Theotokos in the christological controversies, and the fathers' use of biblical images to interpret and celebrate Mary's place in the plan of salvation (§§31-40).

- We have reviewed the growth of devotion to Mary in the medieval centuries, and the theological controversies associated with them. We have seen how some excesses in late medieval devotion, and reactions against them by the Reformers, contributed to the breach of communion between us, following which attitudes towards Mary took divergent paths (§§41-46).

- We have also noted evidence of subsequent developments in both our communions, which opened the way for a re-reception of the place of Mary in the faith and life of the church (§§47-51).

- This growing convergence has also allowed us to approach in a fresh way the questions about Mary which our two communions have set before us. In doing so, we have framed our work within the pattern of grace and hope which we discover in scripture – "predestined… called… justified… glorified" (Rom. 8:30) (§§52-57).

*Advances in agreement*

78. As a result of our study, the commission offers the following agreements, which we believe significantly advance our consensus regarding Mary. We affirm together:

– the teaching that God has taken the Blessed Virgin Mary in the fullness of her person into his glory as consonant with scripture, and only to be understood in the light of scripture (§58);

– that in view of her vocation to be the mother of the Holy One, Christ's redeeming work reached "back" in Mary to the depths of her being and to her earliest beginnings (§59);

– that the teaching about Mary in the two definitions of the assumption and the immaculate conception, understood within the biblical pattern of the economy of hope and grace, can be said to be consonant with the teaching of the scriptures and the ancient common traditions (§60);

– that this agreement, when accepted by our two communions, would place the questions about authority which arise from the two definitions of 1854 and 1950 in a new ecumenical context (§§61-63);

– that Mary has a continuing ministry which serves the ministry of Christ, our unique mediator, that Mary and the saints pray for the whole church and that the practice of asking Mary and the saints to pray for us is not communion-dividing (§§64-75).

79. We agree that doctrines and devotions which are contrary to scripture cannot be said to be revealed by God nor to be the teaching of the church. We agree that doctrine and devotion which focuses on Mary, including claims to "private revelations", must be moderated by carefully expressed norms which ensure the unique and central place of Jesus Christ in the life of the church, and that Christ alone, together with the Father and the Holy Spirit, is to be worshipped in the church.

80. Our statement has sought not to clear away all possible problems, but to deepen our common understanding to the point where remaining diversities of devotional practice may be received as the varied work of the Spirit amongst all the people of God. We believe that the agreement we have here outlined is itself the product of a re-reception by Anglicans and Roman Catholics of doctrine about Mary and that it points to the possibility of further reconciliation, in which issues concerning doctrine and devotion to Mary need no longer be seen as communion-dividing, or an obstacle in a new stage of our growth into visible koinonia. This agreed statement is now offered to our respective authorities. It may also in itself prove a valuable study of the teaching of the scriptures and the ancient common traditions about the Blessed Virgin Mary, the Mother of God incarnate. Our hope is that, as we share in the one Spirit by which Mary was prepared and sanctified for her unique vocation, we may together participate with her and all the saints in the unending praise of God.

**Members of the commission**

*Anglican members*

Most Rev. Frank Griswold, Presiding Bishop of the Episcopal Church (USA) (co-chair until 2003)

Most Rev. Peter Carnley, Archbishop of Perth and Primate of the Anglican Church of Australia (co-chair from 2003)

Rt Rev. John Baycroft, Retired Bishop of Ottawa, Canada

Dr E. Rozanne Elder, Professor of History, University of Western Michigan, USA

Rev. Professor Jaci Maraschin, Professor of Theology, Ecumenical Institute, Sao Paulo, Brazil

Rev. Dr John Muddiman, University Lecturer in New Testament in the University of Oxford, Mansfield College, Oxford, UK

Rt Rev. Dr Michael Nazir-Ali, Bishop of Rochester, UK

Rev. Canon Dr Nicholas Sagovsky, Canon Theologian of Westminster Abbey, London, UK

Rev. Canon Dr Charles Sherlock, Registrar and Director of Ministry Studies of the Melbourne College of Divinity, Australia

Secretary:

Rev. Canon David Hamid, Director of Ecumenical Affairs and Studies, Anglican Communion Office, London, UK (until 2002)

Rev. Canon Gregory K. Cameron, Director of Ecumenical Affairs and Studies, Anglican Communion Office, London, UK (from 2002)

Archbishop of Canterbury's Observer:

Rev. Canon Dr Richard Marsh, Archbishop of Canterbury's Secretary for Ecumenical Affairs, London, UK (until 1999)

Rev. Dr Herman Browne, Archbishop of Canterbury's Assistant Secretary for Ecumenical and Anglican Communion Affairs (from 2000-2001)

Rev. Canon Jonathan Gough, Archbishop of Canterbury's Secretary for Ecumenism, London, UK (from 2002)

*Roman Catholic members*

Rt Rev. Cormac Murphy-O'Connor, Bishop of Arundel and Brighton, UK (co-chair until 2000)

Most Rev. Alexander Brunett, Archbishop of Seattle, USA (co-chair from 2000)

Sister Sara Butler, MSBT, Professor of Dogmatic Theology, St Joseph's Seminary, Yonkers, New York, USA

Rev. Dr Peter Cross, Professor of Systematic Theology, Catholic Theological College, Clayton, Australia

Rev. Dr Adelbert Denaux, Professor, Faculty of Theology, Catholic University, Leuven, Belgium

Rt Rev. Brian Farrell, LC, Secretary, Pontifical Council for Promoting Christian Unity, Vatican City (from 2003)

Rt Rev. Walter Kasper, Secretary, Pontifical Council for Promoting Christian Unity, Vatican City (1999-2000)

Rt Rev. Malcolm McMahon, OP, Bishop of Nottingham, UK (from 2001)

Rev. Prof. Charles Morerod, OP, Dean of the Faculty of Philosophy, Pontificia Università San Tommaso d'Aquino, Rome, Italy (from 2002)

Rt Rev. Marc Ouellet, PSS, Secretary, Pontifical Council for Promoting Christian Unity,Vatican City (2001-2002)

Rev. Jean Tillard, OP, Professor, Dominican Faculty of Theology, Ottawa, Canada (until 2000, deceased)

Rev. Professor Liam Walsh, OP, Professor Emeritus, Faculty of Theology, University of Fribourg, Switzerland.

Secretary:
Rev. Monsignor Timothy Galligan, Staff Member, Pontifical Council for Promoting Christian Unity, Vatican City (until 2001)

Rev. Canon Donald Bolen, Staff Member, Pontifical Council for Promoting Christian Unity, Vatican City (from 2001)

Consultant:
Dom Emmanuel Lanne, OSB, Monastery of Chevetogne, Belgium (from 2001)

*World Council of Churches observer*

Rev. Dr Michael Kinnamon, Dean, Lexington Theological Seminary, Kentucky, USA (until 2001)

*Administrative staff*

Mrs Christine Codner, Anglican Communion Office, London, UK

Ms Giovanna Ramon, Pontifical Council for Promoting Christian Unity, Vatican City

NOTES

1   By typology we mean a reading which accepts that certain things in scripture (persons, places and events) foreshadow or illuminate other things, or reflect patterns of faith in imaginative ways (e.g. Adam is a type of Christ: Rom. 5:14; Isa. 7:14 points towards the virgin birth of Jesus: Matt. 1:23). This typological sense was considered to be a meaning that goes beyond the literal sense. This approach assumes the unity and consistency of the divine revelation.

2   Given its strongly Jewish matrix in both Matthean and Lucan versions, an appeal to analogies with pagan mythology or to an exaltation of virginity over the married state to explain the origin of the tradition is implausible. Nor is the idea of virginal conception likely to derive from an over-literal reading of the Greek text of Isaiah 7:14 (LXX), for that is not the way the idea is introduced in the Lucan account. Moreover, the suggestion that it originated as an answer to the accusation of illegitimacy levelled at Jesus is unlikely,

as that accusation could equally have arisen because it was known that there was something unusual about Jesus' birth (cf. Mark 6:3; John 8:41) and because of the church's claim about his virginal conception.

3   Although the word "brother" usually denotes a blood brother, the Greek *adelphos*, like the Hebrew *'ah*, can have a broader meaning of kinsman, or relative (e.g. Gen. 29:12 LXX) or step-brother (e.g. Mark 6:17f.). Relatives who are not siblings could be included in this use of the term at Mark 3:31. Mary did have an extended family: her sister is referred to at John 19:25 and her kinswoman Elizabeth at Luke 1:36. In the early church different explanations of the references to the "brothers" of Jesus were given, whether as step-brothers or cousins.

4   The Hebrew text of Genesis 3:15 speaks about enmity between the serpent and the woman, and between the offspring of both. The personal pronoun (*hu'*) in the words addressed to the serpent, "He will strike at your head," is masculine. In the Greek translation used by the early church (LXX), however, the personal pronoun *autos* (he) cannot refer to the offspring (neuter: *to sperma*), but must refer to a masculine individual who could then be the Messiah, born of a woman. The Vulgate (mis)translates the clause as *ipsa conteret caput tuum* ("she will strike at your head"). This feminine pronoun supported a reading of this passage as referring to Mary which has become traditional in the Latin church. The Neo-Vulgate (1986), however, returns to the neuter *ipsum*, which refers to *semen illius: Inimicitias ponam inter te et mulierem et semen tuum et semen illius; ipsum conteret caput tuum, et tu conteres calcaneum eius.*

5   Cf. Epiphanius of Salamis (†402), *Panarion* 78.11; Quodvultdeus (†454) *Sermones de Symbolo* III, I.4-6; Oecumenius (†c.550) *Commentarius in Apocalypsin* 6.

6   The council solemnly approved the content of the Second Letter of Cyril to Nestorius: "It was not that an ordinary man was born first of the holy Virgin, on whom afterwards the Word descended; what we say is that: being united with the flesh from the womb, the Word has undergone birth in the flesh... therefore the holy fathers had the courage to call the Holy Virgin *Theotokos*" (*DS*, 251).

7   The Tome of Leo, which was decisive for the outcome of the council of Chalcedon (451), states that Christ "was conceived by the Holy Spirit in the womb of the Virgin Mother, who gave him birth without losing her virginity, as she conceived him without losing her virginity" (*DS*, 291). Similarly Athanasius speaks in *De Virginitate* (*Le Muséon* 42:244.248) of "Mary, who... remained a virgin to the end [as a model for] all to come after her" Cf. John Chrysostom (†407) *Homily on Matthew* 5,3. The first ecumenical council to use the term *Aeiparthenos (semper virgo)* was the second council of Constantinople (553). This designation is already implicit in the classical Western formulation of Mary's *virginitas* as *ante partum, in partu, post partum*. This tradition appears consistently in the Western church from Ambrose onward. As Augustine wrote, "She conceived him as a virgin, she gave birth as a virgin, she remained a virgin" (*Sermo* 51.18; cf. *Sermo* 196.1).

8   Thus Irenaeus criticizes her for "excessive haste" at Cana, "'seeking to push her son into performing a miracle before his hour had come" (*Adv. Haer.*, III.16.7); Origen speaks of her wavering in faith at the cross, "so she too would have some sin for which Christ died" (*Hom. in Lc*, 17,6). Suggestions like these are found in the writings of Tertullian, Ambrose and John Chrysostom.

9   Witness the invocation of Mary in the early text known traditionally as *Sub tuum praesidium* (Cf. O. Stegemüller, *Sub tuum praesidium. Bemerkungen zur ältesten Überlieferung*, in: *ZKTh* 74 [1952], pp.76-82 [77]. This text (with two changes) is used to this day in the Greek liturgical tradition; versions of this prayer also occur in the Ambrosian, Roman, Byzantine and Coptic liturgies. A familiar English version is: "We fly to thy protection, O holy Mother of God; despise not our petitions in our necessities but deliver us from all dangers, O ever glorious and blessed Virgin."

10   The reference in the dogma to Mary being assumed "body and soul" has caused difficulty for some, on historical and philosophical grounds. The dogma leaves open, however, the question as to what the absence of her mortal remains means in historical terms. Likewise, "assumed body and soul" is not intended to privilege a particular anthropology. More positively, "assumed body and soul" can be seen to have christological and ecclesiological implications. Mary as "God-bearer" is intimately, indeed bodily, related to Christ: his own bodily glorification now embraces hers. And, since Mary bore his body of flesh, she is intimately related to the church, Christ's body. In brief, the formulation of the dogma responds to theological rather than historical or philosophical questions in relation to Mary.

11   The definition addressed an old controversy about the timing of the sanctification of Mary, in affirming that this took place at the very first moment of her conception.

12   The assertion of Paul at Romans 3:23 – "all have sinned and fall short of the glory of God" – might appear to allow for no exceptions, not even for Mary. However, it is important to note the rhetorical-apologetic context of the general argument of Romans 1-3, which is concerned to show the equal sinfulness of Jews and Gentiles (3:9). Romans 3:23 has a quite specific purpose in context which is unrelated to the issue of the "sinlessness" or otherwise of Mary.

[13] In such circumstances, the explicit acceptance of the precise wording of the definitions of 1854 and 1950 might not be required of believers who were not in communion with Rome when they were defined. Conversely, Anglicans would have to accept that the definitions are a legitimate expression of Catholic faith, and are to be respected as such, even if these formulations were not employed by them. There are instances in ecumenical agreement in which what one partner has defined as de fide can be expressed by another partner in a different way, as for example in the *Common Declaration between the Roman Catholic Church and the Assyrian Church of the East concerning the Definition of Chalcedon* or the *Joint Declaration on the Doctrine of Justification between the Roman Catholic Church and the Lutheran World Federation.*

# 16. Communion in Mission
## Mississauga Meeting

### Mississauga, Canada, May 2000

1. This meeting of Anglican and Roman Catholic bishops from 13 countries, convened by His Eminence Edward Cardinal Cassidy and His Grace Archbishop George Carey, gathered at Mississauga, near Toronto, Canada, 14-20 May 2000. Our meeting was grounded in prayer and marked by a profound atmosphere of friendship and spiritual communion. We began on Good Shepherd Sunday, conscious of our common vocation as shepherds of the Good Shepherd, with a responsibility to lead God's people forward in active hope towards that unity in truth and holiness which our Lord wills for his church.

2. We came together to address the imperative for Christian reconciliation and healing, in a broken and divided world. We were also conscious of the fact that Christian people around the world are celebrating two thousand years since the birth of Jesus Christ. In this year of great jubilee, in which the churches are acting cooperatively for the remission of unpayable third-world debt, we are aware of the need to leave behind all past deficits with which our churches have themselves been burdened, so as to enter the new millennium renewed in deepening unity and peace.

3. At this meeting we have naturally focused on the special relationship between the Roman Catholic Church and the Anglican Communion as expressed in the Decree on Ecumenism of the Second Vatican Council. We also recognized the progress which has been made in our relations with other Christians and we recommit ourselves to the ecumenical endeavour with all Christian churches.

4. As day by day we prayed together and meditated on scripture in the chapel of Queen of Apostles Renewal Centre, we realized afresh both the degree of spiritual communion we already share in the richness of our common liturgical inheritance, but also the pain of our inability to share together fully in the eucharist. As we listened to experiences from the different regions we were struck by the extent of interchurch collaboration, particularly common action for social justice and joint pastoral care in which Anglican and Roman Catholic clergy and lay people are involved. We noted with concern some of the problems our disunity causes to the mission of the church, and recognized the opportunities for shared endeavour presented to us in the service of our fragmented world. As we reviewed the results of the Anglican-Roman Catholic International Commission (ARCIC), we came to appreciate the very impressive degree of agreement in faith that

already exists. This alerted us to the serious obligation to intensify the process of reception of those agreements at the local level.

5. There is one specific point that has been driven home to us during the meeting. Over the last thirty years we have become familiar with the concept of "degrees of communion". Despite our acknowledged differences, we have regularly affirmed that we share in the fundamental communion of a common faith and a common baptism. This degree of communion holds within it the promise of the full visible communion to which God is calling us. Our experience at Toronto encourages us to believe that we have reached a very significant new place on our journey. We feel compelled to affirm that our communion together is no longer to be viewed in minimal terms. We have been able to discern that it is not just formally established by our common baptism into Christ, but is even now a rich and life-giving, multifaceted communion.

6. We have come to a clear sense that we have moved much closer to the goal of full visible communion than we had at first dared to believe. A sense of mutual interdependence in the body of Christ has been reached, in which the churches of the Anglican Communion and the Roman Catholic Church are able to bring shared gifts to their joint mission in the world.

7. We appreciate that there are as yet unresolved differences and challenges which affect both communions. These have to do with such matters as: the understanding of authority in the church, including the way it is exercised, and the precise nature of the future role of the universal primate; Anglican orders; the ordination of women; moral and ethical questions. Though interchurch families can be signs of unity and hope, one pressing concern has to do with addressing the need to provide joint pastoral care for them. Sometimes those in interchurch families experience great pain particularly in the area of eucharistic life.

8. However, we believe these challenges are not to be compared with all that we hold in common. The communion constituted by what we already share has within it an inner dynamic which, animated by the Holy Spirit, impels us forward towards the overcoming of these differences. Indeed, we have become conscious that we have embraced what may be described, not only as a new era of friendship and cooperation, but as a new stage of "evangelical koinonia". By this we mean a communion of joint commitment to our common mission in the world (John 17:23).

9. The marks of this new stage of communion in mission are: our trinitarian faith grounded in the scriptures and set forth in the catholic creeds; the centrality of Christ, his death and resurrection, and commitment to his mission in the church; faith in the final destiny of human life; common traditions in liturgy and spirituality; the monastic life; preferential commitment to the poor and marginalized; convergence on the eucharist, ministry, authority, salvation, moral principles, and the church as communion, as expressed in agreed statements of ARCIC; episcopacy, particularly the role of the bishop as symbol and promoter of unity; and the respective roles of clergy and laity.

10. We believe that now is the appropriate time for the authorities of our two communions to recognize and endorse this new stage through the signing of a joint declaration of agreement. This agreement would set out: our shared goal of visible unity; an acknowledgment of the consensus in faith that we have reached, and a fresh commitment to share together in common life and witness. Our two communions would be invited to celebrate this agreement around the world.

11. As our meeting proceeded we became increasingly aware that as bishops we ourselves have a responsibility to guide, promote and energize the ongoing work of unity in our churches. We commit ourselves wholeheartedly to this task. Our action plan is appended to this statement.

12. The first recommendation of our action plan is that a joint unity commission be established. This commission will oversee the preparation of the joint declaration of agreement, and promote and monitor the reception of ARCIC agreements, as well as facilitate the development of strategies for translating the degree of spiritual communion that has been achieved into visible and practical outcomes.

13. It is important to be clear that this new stage on our journey is but a step on the way to full and visible unity. Our vision of full and visible unity is of a eucharistic communion of churches: confessing the one faith and demonstrating by their harmonious diversity the richness of faith; unanimous in the application of the principles governing moral life; served by ministries that the grace of ordination unites together in an episcopal body, grafted on to the company of the apostles, and which is at the service of the authority that Christ exercises over his body. The ministry of oversight has both collegial and primatial dimensions and is open always to the community's participation in the discernment of God's will. This eucharistic communion on earth is a participation in the larger communion which includes the saints and martyrs, and all those who have fallen asleep in Christ through the ages.

14. However, the shape of full visible unity is beyond our capacity to put into words. "God will always surprise us", as we were reminded in a meditation shared with us: "God cannot be understood through our human system or correspond to our positive or negative predictions for the future… In our ecumenical efforts we should keep in mind that one day we will rub our eyes and be surprised by the new things that God has achieved in his church."

# 17. Action Plan to Implement Communion in Mission

## Mississauga, Canada, 19 May 2000

### A. Joint Unity Commission

*Membership*

The membership of the commission to be predominantly bishops, to be appointed by the Pontifical Council for Promoting Christian Unity (PCPCU) and the Anglican Communion office.

*Accountability*

The Joint Unity Commission will report to the Pontifical Council for Promoting Christian Unity and the Inter-Anglican Standing Commission on Ecumenical Relations.

*Mandate*

The mandate of the commission will include the following functions:
- to prioritize the ongoing work;
- to oversee the preparation of a joint declaration of agreement and to plan the signing and celebration of the same;
- to promote and monitor the formal response and reception of the agreed statements of the Anglican-Roman Catholic International Commission (ARCIC);
- to promote the coherence of other bilateral dialogues that Anglicans and Roman Catholics are involved in;
- to examine the range of possible ways, within current canon law provisions, to deal generously and pastorally with situations of interchurch marriages involving Anglicans and Roman Catholics;
- to explore ways of communicating the results of the Toronto meeting to provinces and episcopal conferences not represented;
- to commission the production of resources (Bible studies, videos, CD-ROMs, etc.) to assist in making the work of ARCIC known throughout the churches;

- to encourage Anglican provinces and Roman Catholic episcopal conferences to set up national Anglican-Roman Catholic (ARC) dialogue groups where they do not exist;
- to invite one or two national ARCs to study the implications of our common baptism for the roles of men and women in the church, the results of which to be shared at all levels of the churches;
- to promote cooperation locally on clergy formation, education, and other pastoral matters;
- to promote collegiality through:
  - encouraging episcopal participation in each others' meetings at the international, national and local levels;
  - encouraging a joint meeting of bishops at the level of provinces and episcopal conferences within two years;
  - examining ways of ensuring formal consultation prior to one church making decisions on matters of faith and morals which would affect the other church, keeping in view the agreed statements of ARCIC;
  - planning for a future review consultation of bishops within five years.

## B. Follow-up by pairs of bishops

The pairs of bishops from 13 countries present at this meeting will endeavour:
- to report back to the bishops of the province episcopal conference within six months;
- to share the results of this meeting with the clergy and laity at the national and local church level.

## C. Anglican-Roman Catholic International Commission

ARCIC is invited to consider the following possible agenda items:
- the drafting of a document to link all the agreed statements produced by ARCIC, which would be a coherent summary of the work thus far: the papers produced for this meeting may form the basis of this work;
- a study of the place of Mary in the life and doctrine of the church.

ARCIC is urged to consider commissioning a volume of the agreed statements produced since *The Final Report* which would include introductory essays and selections of relevant responses to the texts.

## D. Annual informal talks

The annual informal talks is a meeting of staff of the PCPCU, the Anglican Communion Office, Lambeth Palace, the Anglican centre in Rome and the ARCIC co-chairmen. The next meeting in November will consider how the joint unity commission and ARCIC will relate to each other.

## E.  The Pontifical Council for Promoting Christian Unity and the Anglican Communion office

Staff from these offices will explore the publication in book form of appropriate papers, presentations, sermons, the liturgy "Celebration of Common Baptism", and other documents from this Anglican-Roman Catholic bishops meeting.

## Toronto meeting name list

*Anglican participants*

Archbishop of Canterbury: Most Rev. and Rt Honourable George L. Carey

Aotearoa, New Zealand and Polynesia: Rt Rev. John Paterson, Presiding Bishop and Primate

Australia: Most Rev. Peter Carnley, Primate and Archbishop of Perth

Brazil: Most Rev. Glauco Soares de Lima, Primate of Brazil and Bishop of São Paulo

Canada: Most Rev. Michael Peers, Primate of the Anglican Church of Canada

England: Rt Rev. John Hind, Bishop of Gibraltar in Europe

India: Rt Rev. Peter Sugandhar, Bishop of Medak, Church of South India

Ireland: Rt Rev. Dr Samuel Poyntz, Formerly Bishop of Connor

Nigeria: Rt Rev. Joseph A.Omyajowo, Bishop of Ijebu

Papua New Guinea: Most Rev. James A.Young, Primate and Bishop of Aipo Rongo

Southern Africa: Rt Rev. Davod Beetge, Bishop of The Highveld

Uganda: Rt Rev. Evans Mukasa Kisekka, Bishop of Luweero

USA: Rt Rev. Edwin F. Gulick Jr, Bishop of Kentucky

West Indies: Most Rev. Drexel Gomez, Primate and Bishop of Nassau and the Bahamas

*Catholic participants*

President, Pontifical Council for Promoting Christian Unity: His Eminence Edward Idris Cardinal Cassidy

Australia: Archbishop John Bathersby, Archbishop of Brisbane, Chair, Bishops Committee for Ecumenical and Interfaith Relations

Brazil: Bishop Antonio Celso de Queioz, Bishop of Cantanduva, Formerly Secretary General, Brazilian Bishops Conference

Canada: Bishop Gerald Wiesner, OMI, Bishop of Prince George, President, Canadian Bishops Conference

England: Archbishop Cormac Murphy-O'Connor, Archbishop of Westminster, Chairman, Bishops Conference Department for Mission and Unity, Formerly Co-Chairman, ARCIC

India (Latin rite): Archbishop Henry D'Souza, Archbishop of Calcutta, President of Conference of Catholic Bishops of India, Latin Rite

Ireland: Bishop Anthony Farouhar, Auxiliary Bishop of Down and Connor, Chair, Bishops Commission for Ecumenism

New Zealand: Bishop John Cunneen, Bishop of Christchurch, New Zealand, Bishops Conference Deputy for Ecumenism

Nigeria: Bishop Lucius Ugorji, Bishop of Umuahia

Papua New Guinea: Bishop Desmond Moore, MSC, Bishop of Alotau-Sideia, Chairman, Bishops Commission for Ecumenism, Co-Chair PNG ARC dialogue

Southern Africa: Archbishop George Daniel, Archbishop of Pretoria, Vice-Chairman, Bishops Department of Ecumenism

Uganda: Bishop Paul Kalandu, Bishop of Fort Portal, President, Ugandan Bishops Conference

USA: Archbishop William J. Levada, Archbishop of San Francisco, Chairman-Designate, ARC-USA

West Indies: Archbishop Samuel Carter, SJ, Formerly Archbishop of Kingston

*Others attending*

Archbishop Alexander Brunett, Roman Catholic co-chairman of ARCIC

Bishop Frank Griswold, Anglican co-chairman of ARCIC

Bishop Walter Kasper, Secretary of the Pontifical Council for Promoting Christian Unity

Canon John Peterson, Secretary General of the Anglican Consultative Council

*Guest speaker Wednesday morning*

Father Jean-Marie Tillard, OP

*The staff team*

*Process facilitators*

Dr Mary Tanner (Anglican)

Dr Donna Geernaert, SC (Catholic)

*Theological consultants*

Bishop John Baycroft (Anglican)

Rev. Peter Cross (Catholic)

*Co-secretaries*

Canon David Hamid (Anglican)

Monsignor Timothy Galligan (Catholic)

Archbishop of Canterbury's Secretary for Ecumenical Affairs: Canon Richard Marsh

*Secretarial assistants for the meeting*

Mrs Christine Codner, Anglican Communion office
Fr Francis Kodiyan, MCBS, Pontifical Council for Promoting Christian Unity
Secretarial assistant for the Archbishop of Canterbury:
Mrs Gill Harris-Hogarth, Lambeth Palace

# 18.  Receiving and Handing on the Faith:
# The Mission and Responsibility of the Church

## Disciples-Roman Catholic Dialogue

### Bose, Italy, 22 May 2002

## 1. Introduction

1.1.  From the beginning of the Disciples-Roman Catholic dialogue in 1977 the goal was to enable all Christians to be together in the visible unity of the one church of God. In the report of the first phase, the commission accepted "as a basic principle of ecumenism that there can be only one church of God (*unica ecclesia*) and that this church already exists"; furthermore it stated, "We see ourselves as having a communion *in via*... Now we have the task of giving external expression to the communion *in via*" (*Apostolicity and Catholicity*, p.11). This was reaffirmed in the report of the second phase: "Disciples and Roman Catholics continued their dialogue in order to discover the degree of communion they already share. Their goal is to be together, growing in this communion and fostering it" (*The Church as Communion in Christ*, §9). After restating some of the agreements about the vision of unity in the first report, the second report continued, "The goal of this statement of convergence is to elucidate a shared vision of the church" (*The Church as Communion in Christ*, §§19-20). As we report on this third phase of dialogue, we reaffirm these convictions about our goal.

1.2.  This report is a theological reflection. But it arises out of regular meetings each year in which we prayed and studied the Bible together, met with members of local congregations, and studied and discussed together the similarities and differences that characterize our two communities.[1] This sharing locally and internationally is a vital part of the "spiritual ecumenism" referred to in the first report.

1.3.  Both the previous reports referred to the relationship of the individual and the church. *Apostolicity and Catholicity* noted that "each Christian's faith is inseparable from the life of the community. Personal faith is an appropriation of the church's faith and depends on it for authenticity as well as for nurture" (p.9). *The Church as Communion in Christ* stated that "the inner dynamism of the gift of faith – the power of the Holy Spirit which draws believers into spiritual unity – sustains the interaction of the faith of the individual and the faith of the community" (§40). From this starting-point, we reflected on how the faith is handed on from one generation to another through history; and came to see that the proclamation of the good news provided a crucial context for understanding the whole process of receiving and handing on the faith.

1.4. Disciples and Roman Catholics share a commitment to the gospel of Jesus Christ; they place a similar emphasis on the church as communion, and on the sacraments of baptism and eucharist. They share some common beliefs about the nature of the church; yet there are also some differences, which reveal themselves in different structures. Perhaps the major query from a Roman Catholic perspective is how Disciples, with an apparent lack of structure and credal formulations, have handed on the gospel. For Disciples, on the other hand, the main question is whether the more elaborate hierarchical structure of the Roman Catholic Church, with an apparent emphasis on uniformity, gives people sufficient freedom of conscience in their response to the gospel.

1.5. Both Disciples and Roman Catholics acknowledge that in the New Testament the community of believers is primary, and that the identity of individuals is defined by their membership in the community, not vice versa. This understanding, which has been traditional for Roman Catholics, finds its own expression among Disciples. Throughout Disciples history there has also been a concern to identify with that which was believed always, everywhere and by everybody (to use a phrase of St Vincent of Lérins). The common-sense philosophy characteristic of the early Disciples leader, Alexander Campbell, depended on an appeal to that which the community as a whole could accept. This community is the context in and through which the Christian message is received and lived out.

1.6. The conviction that it is necessary for every Christian to come to a personal confession of faith (which has sometimes been regarded as representing an individualistic emphasis) does not in any way deny the logical and chronological priority of the faith of the whole Christian community of believers. Rather than arguing at length about the relative importance of the individual and the church, the commission affirms that a believer's "Yes" to Christ incorporates that person into the "Yes" of faith spoken by the church throughout the ages (cf. 2 Cor. 1:20).

1.7. This report therefore begins with a discussion of the word of God, proclaimed and received (section 2), and continues with a discussion of how the church in history holds to the faith (section 3). It then considers the question of the relation between the teaching office of the church and Christian freedom (section 4), and concludes by considering the mission of the whole church in handing on the faith (section 5). We offer this report hoping to remove mutual misunderstandings, to diminish the differences which still separate us and to renew the vital link between the mission and unity of the church.

## 2. The word of God, proclaimed and received

*The missionary nature of the church*

2.1. The Christian faith announces that God has reached out to humanity decisively in the incarnation. Jesus Christ is the living Word, the mediator and fullness of revelation. New Testament writers express, in a variety of ways, the truth that God wills to gather all humanity into the community that shares in the communion between the Father and Son in the Spirit (cf. Eph. 1:9-10; Col. 1:19-20; 1 John 1:3). The Holy Spirit, sent to make real the work of Christ in mysterious ways which are not all revealed, is thus the agent of mission. The church is gathered by God to carry on the work of the twofold mission of the Son and the Holy Spirit. Thus, the church is essentially a missionary community, a community of those sent into the world to proclaim the offer of God's gifts to all persons.

2.2. In living out its missionary identity the church proclaims the word of God and invites persons to be converted and become part of the communion of believers. Only there can the full meaning of the gospel be known. Our two communions are convinced that, in all the church says and does, its call to proclaim salvation is accompanied by the presence of the Holy Spirit empowering the church to discern that which is necessary for salvation.

*Hearing the word of God*

2.3. One way in which the Holy Spirit has assisted the church in its call to proclaim salvation to all is in the writing and identification of the books that came to be in the Bible. The books of the Bible had human authors to be sure; nevertheless, God is heard speaking through these books. We agree that we hear the word of God through the Bible when it is used in celebrating the sacraments, in preaching, in teaching the faith and in personal devotional activities.

2.4. Members of each communion participate in a living tradition of scriptural interpretation and prayer, which they pass on to others. The shaping of distinctive common ways of understanding and sharing the scriptural text links each Christian and each generation of Christians with those who have preceded them. It is through the reading and interpretation of the scriptures in the congregational life of each communion that the word of God is made real in both praise of God and Christian discipleship. Thus, the gospel message leads necessarily to life in community, which in turn helps to shape the understanding of the message for subsequent generations (cf. *The Church as Communion in Christ*, §§13-14,21-23). Both Disciples of Christ and Roman Catholics affirm that the Holy Spirit guides the church, which because of this guidance will not finally fail in its task of proclaiming the gospel. Our ultimate confidence is in God's promise to bring about the divine purpose for all.

2.5. Disciples of Christ and Roman Catholics agree on the necessary link between the word and the sacraments. The word of God has its own efficacy: and its saving power is experienced most fully when the word is received together with the sacraments, especially the eucharist. The fullness of the good news is received in the gift of communion with God and with each other, a communion beginning through baptism and incorporation into the body of Christ and extending throughout one's life. In both the Roman Catholic Church and the Disciples of Christ the sacraments make real the communion the gospel announces (cf. *Apostolicity and Catholicity*, pp.9,12). The sacraments are by their nature integral to the life and being of the church. They bring a new believer into the community, creating a link between the believer and all other Christians in every time and place. Thus each believer receives the living Tradition, becomes part of it, and participates in passing it on.

## 3. Holding to the faith: the church in history

3.1. As they waited in expectation for the return of the Lord, Christians wanted to remain faithful to him while they celebrated his presence in word and sacrament. The church has always recognized the need to hold on to the memory of the apostolic community about what God has done in Christ. Both Disciples and Roman Catholics recognize that the canon of the scriptures, councils of the church, and creeds confessing the faith were developed as instruments to do this, under the promised guidance of the Holy Spirit (John 14:26) (cf. *The Church as Communion in Christ*, §36). In our dialogue we have also come to appreciate more deeply the process the church used in discerning these instruments of faithfulness; this process of discernment continues whenever the church seeks to confess the gospel with courage in the face of new situations and challenges. Through our discussions on the formation of the canon, on councils and the declaration of the faith, and on the process of discerning the gospel in every age, we have enriched our understanding of the ways that the church holds on to the faith throughout history.

*Formation of the canon*

3.2. Why did Christians develop a canon of the books they came to regard as their scriptures? The reason can be stated simply: Christians wanted to hold on to the same faith preached by the apostolic community. In the face of controversies about the content of the faith, the churches in the East and the West began to list the venerable books, which they considered as the genuine documents of God's revelation, containing the substance of the apostolic faith and expressing the will of God for Christian life. In this diverse group of books the church recognized the authentic word of God in its written form inspired by the Holy Spirit.

3.3. The early churches included those begun by the apostles; but in addition churches were considered "apostolic" in which the apostles preached or to which they wrote letters. Some books not written by apostles were included in the early lists making up the canon because they too came from the apostolic era, they were sometimes read aloud during liturgical celebrations, and they were in agreement with the apostolic Tradition. The canon also enabled those churches with no direct personal link to the apostles to have the assurance that they too proclaimed the apostolic faith in communion with the apostolic churches. The books which constitute our New Testament are those in which, from apostolic times, guided by the Holy Spirit, the local churches in communion with one another had come to recognize the apostolic faith.

3.4. The way in which sayings and deeds of Jesus were transmitted helps us to understand concretely what the authority of the canon means. The deeds and words of Jesus were known and "received"[2] in the communities of believers from the teaching and preaching of the apostolic witnesses to the Christ-event. But not all these deeds and words were included in the written gospels; and not all the written gospels, but only four, were judged to have a reliably apostolic origin and "received" in the official canon.

3.5. The making of a list of books to serve as a canon does not imply that the truth concerning God and the norms for the guidance of Christian life are to be searched for only in these documents. But if Christians want to hold on to their faith, to preach authentic Christian doctrine, to live according to authentic evangelical norms, they must look at these documents and conform their words and deeds to these teachings. The intention of the canon is to indicate where the heart of Christian faith is authentically to be found, because the church is sure that in the documents listed – after centuries of testing – the "memory" of the church of God has been faithfully preserved and transmitted since earliest times.

3.6. Moreover, the church believes that the books which comprise the canon belong to the work of the Holy Spirit in history which keeps the church indefectibly attached to the revelation disclosed in the history of the people of God and ultimately given in Christ Jesus. Thus setting the canon was at the same time an act of obedience and of authority. In obedience to the Holy Spirit the church discerned which books contained the authentic apostolic witness, and acted with authority to set these books as its norm.

3.7. By holding together the Old Testament and the New Testament in this canon of inspired books, the church shows its recognition of the links between the books inherited from the Jewish community and the books recording the church's memory about Christ Jesus. And by holding together the rich but limited variety of books within the New Testament itself, the church manifests that the diversity found there is compatible with the koinonia of all the faithful in "one faith, one Lord, one baptism" (Eph. 4:5). The canon is therefore a symbol of unity in the diversity of the church's life; it is also part of the givenness of that life.

3.8. The formation of the canon was a process of ecclesial discernment which lasted many years and involved many aspects of the life of the church. Today Roman Catholics and Disciples recognize the significance of this process and the criteria which, at least implicitly, functioned to determine which books were to be included or not to be included in the canon. These criteria included apostolicity, conformity with the gospel of salvation in Jesus Christ, and use during liturgical celebrations. But these interlocking criteria did not function in isolation during the church's discernment process.

3.9. Although official lists were authorized by local churches as early as the 2nd century, only in 1442 did the canon enter a conciliar decree when the council of Florence listed the books of the canon within its statement on union with the Copts. While this was quite a long time after the canon-making process of the early church, the centre or heart of the canon had not been questioned. Disagreements between the Reformers and the council of Trent about the canon of scripture concerned only the somewhat imprecise edges of the canon of the Old Testament.[3] The differences between Roman Catholics and Disciples on the number of books in the Old Testament need not be church-dividing.

3.10. There is a close relationship between the canon of the scriptures and the unity of the church. Because it is held in common by Christians, the Bible holds Christians together with one another as they read and proclaim the same word of God received from the church of the apostles. The diversity of the Bible also helps to explain why the same word of God has led to different emphases among different Christian communities. The canon of the scriptures determines and supports the faith of both of our communions, so Roman Catholics and Disciples again and again recognize each other as brothers and sisters in Christ.

*Councils and the declaration of the faith*

3.11. Disciples and Roman Catholics share the desire to hold on to the emphasis on church unity which characterized the patristic period of the church's history. For Roman Catholics the patristic writers are witnesses to the Tradition who have a special authority because their foundational insights on the central trinitarian, christological and sacramental teachings have been received by the church, notably through the great councils.

Disciples for their part have received the major teachings of the patristic period without necessarily always using its texts explicitly. However most Disciples theologians turn less readily to the patristic writers, the councils and creeds, than do Roman Catholics.

3.12.  Roman Catholics and Disciples agree in recognizing the theological definitions of the first seven ecumenical councils as part of the common history of the church. In these councils the church responded to new controversies about the content of its faith and sought to hold on to the authentic teaching received from the apostles.

3.13.  We discovered that we share more agreement about these seven early councils than previously recognized. Disciples and Roman Catholics together recognize the first seven councils as authentic gatherings of the church able to speak in the name of the whole church for four main reasons:

a)  The councils articulated and defined the mystery of the triune God manifested in history, revealed through Christ Jesus, which the church has to proclaim "until he comes again".

b)  The councils were conscious that Christ is in their midst because they were gathered in his name. In their teachings received by the church they always remained "under the gospel": the Holy Spirit was at work in the community to maintain it in an authentic communion with what Christ did and taught despite the sometimes questionable tactics of some participants.

c)  In their decisions the councils respected and preserved the diversity of traditions present in the scriptures. As the councils of Nicea and Chalcedon themselves demonstrate, councils wished only to be at the service of the scriptures. Conciliar definitions were not intended as substitutes for the language of the New Testament authors; they clarified and made explicit the main affirmations of the scriptures.

d)  The councils gathered the bishops, who were seen as succeeding to the apostolic community. As leaders of their communities presiding at the eucharist, they were considered to embody their local churches and as such were able to speak for them in the process of clarifying or defining the faith. Subsequent to the councils, the bishops were responsible for interpreting the councils' decisions to their churches. All local churches were drawn into the decisions of the councils through reception afterwards.

3.14.  Roman Catholics believe that their life continues to be shaped by the work of the seven ecumenical councils celebrated and received by the Eastern and Western churches together. The Roman Catholic Church is assured that some of its provincial councils and its general councils assembled since the separation between the West and East and the Reformation divisions are providential instruments the Spirit of God uses to keep the people of God faithful to the gospel. Moreover the Roman Catholic Church claims that, when the college of bishops meets in an ecumenical council which is confirmed or at least recognized as such by the bishop of Rome, it is able to define doctrine as divinely revealed, to be accepted with the obedience of faith.

3.15.  The situation is not the same for the communities of the Disciples. Certainly Disciples recognize that their life continues to be shaped by many of the declarations and decisions of the councils – the seven ecumenical councils and some of the Western general councils – celebrated before the Reformation. The Disciples tradition has never held the theological positions condemned by the early ecumenical councils. Disciples hold that the conciliar christological and trinitarian definitions belong to the providential oikonomia (ordering) by which the church of God is kept within the path of the gospel and preserved from grave distortions in its confession of Christ Jesus, the Saviour. To the extent that they have accepted the decisions of those councils, Disciples have acknowledged their authority.

3.16. The first generation of Disciples leaders was critical of the way in which confessions of faith were used as tests of fellowship, particularly at the communion table. The main targets of their criticism were the Reformation and post-Reformation confessions such as the Westminster Confession and the Secession Testimony,[4] rather than the Apostles' or Nicene Creeds. The motto "No creed but Christ" was not intended to exclude the use of creeds for the purpose of teaching the faith. Disciples, however, have preferred to use New Testament confessions of faith; they emphasize the dependence of the conciliar creeds on the New Testament.

3.17. Today both Disciples and Roman Catholics draw on the central teachings of the first seven councils when judging new ideas or practices proposed in our churches. These conciliar teachings define the boundaries within which to search for faithful interpretations of the gospel. For example, a wide diversity of theological understandings of Christ can be used in preaching and teaching, but an understanding of Christ in opposition to the teaching of Nicea or Chalcedon is not acceptable. At the same time, affirming the teachings of these councils does not imply affirmation of their world-view or conceptual structure. Both Roman Catholics and Disciples recognize that no statement exhausts the mystery of God to which it points and that attempts to express in human language the mystery of God's saving work for humanity are open to restatement. A distinction may be drawn between the language in which conciliar definitions are expressed and the reality to which they bear witness. It may be necessary to restate that reality in different terms in later ages, but such restatement will always be faithful to the truth originally intended, and not contradict it. In fact, the councils demonstrate that sometimes the church finds such restatement necessary precisely in order to remain in continuity with the faith it has received.

3.18. The ecumenical commitment of the Second Vatican Council acts today as an invitation to Disciples to explore together with Roman Catholics what more may be received from the heritage of the councils. Ecumenical dialogue has become one of the most important channels for the diffusion and reception of conciliar teaching, and because of such dialogue Disciples are more ready than in the past to use the Nicene Creed in the celebration of the eucharist as Roman Catholics do. In fact, today some Disciples congregations are in a process of "re-reception" of the doctrinal formulations of the early councils. Yet ultimately the full reception of the work of councils will be unself-conscious, reflected in the everyday teaching and worship of the church.

3.19. The history of councils reveals God's guidance, but human sinfulness and frailty can be seen there as well. Sometimes councils failed to overcome divisions. Despite this, the history of the conciliar process itself gives our churches a record of a series of solutions to problems threatening the church's unity in faith. The heritage of the councils shows that a common faith can be maintained along with a diversity of theological interpretations. Disciples and Roman Catholics can take hope from the struggle for unity in this conciliar heritage.

*Discerning the gospel in every age*

3.20. As the commission discovered many unexpected agreements about the canon of the scriptures, ecumenical councils and the declaration of the faith, we also discovered agreements about the process by which they came to be received into the life and teaching of the church. In fact, this process of discerning the gospel is central to the life of the church because of what God has done "for us and our salvation" (Nicene Creed).

3.21. Christians believe that God has acted within, indeed has entered, history in Jesus Christ. Living in Christ, the church is both an eschatological and an historical reality. The church belongs to the reality of salvation and to the oikonomia (ordering) revealed in the incarnation of the Son of God, who became flesh in an authentic and concrete humanity marked by its historical and cultural context.

3.22. The discernment of the meaning of the revealed truth and of the imperatives of Christ's will for his people takes place in this historical situation. It cannot be detached from the contingencies of human dependence in regard to history. Time provides the opportunity for the church to sift authentic from inauthentic developments in its tradition.

3.23. The discernment and reception of the word of Truth are the fruit of the presence in all the faithful of the *sensus fidei* (the sense of the faith). It belongs to their Christian being. The Spirit gives to all the baptized believers this *sensus fidei*, together with a diversity of charisms. Among these are the gifts attached to the functions of exercising *episcope* (oversight), of teaching, of searching the meaning of the revealed Word through study and research. (The process of authoritative teaching is discussed further in §§4.9-4.16.)

3.24. This meaning is not discerned by the mere addition of individual insights. It is the result of the communion of all these diverse charisms expressing the mind of the entire body of Christ, through a process of mutual reception. To be authentic, ecclesial agreement in matters of faith will include ordained ministers with responsibility for teaching in the church, scholars working within the community of faith, and the body of the faithful who receive and celebrate this consensus in their worship and witness.

3.25. Disciples and Roman Catholics agree that the church must always be sensitive to contemporary questions and to diversity of cultures when discerning authentic developments in its understanding of the gospel. Elements harmful to the gospel must be distinguished from the insights necessary for its effective proclamation in that time and place. In every changing circumstance of its history the church stands under the judgment of God.

3.26. In many cases an immediate discernment is impossible because the community as such has to be involved in the complex dynamism of reception. Disciples and Roman Catholics both recognize the importance of the way in which the gospel has been received and handed on from generation to generation for an authentic understanding of scripture. They recognize a process of development in the understanding of doctrine in the church which can be traced through history. Reception plays a crucial part in this ongoing process. Disciples and Roman Catholics are not unanimous on the ways in which reception is achieved, but they agree on its necessity.

## 4. Receiving the faith: the individual in the community

4.1. Receiving the faith from previous generations is an important and complex process. Through the life and teaching of the church each generation seeks to work out the meaning and implications of obedience to the word of God in that time and place. Here there is a difference of emphasis between Disciples and Roman Catholics on the relative weight given to individual discernment and conscience, on the one hand, and to the communal mind of the church on the other. In *The Church as Communion in Christ*, we wrote, "Roman Catholics are convinced that, although they must decide for themselves, they cannot decide by themselves. Disciples, on the other hand, are convinced that, although they cannot decide by themselves, they must decide for themselves" (§16). This section explores this difference further. Nevertheless both Disciples and Roman Catholics agree that obedience to the word of God has priority.

*Conscience, freedom and being in Christ*

4.2.  The mission of the church is to proclaim the word of God. As it does so, the church respects the freedom of every human being created "in the image and likeness of God" (cf. Gen. 1:26-27). Both Roman Catholics and Disciples agree that the church affirms each person's freedom; but the church also has a responsibility to help its members make informed decisions, not to misuse the freedom that is God's gift, but use it for following God's will.

4.3.  Consideration of Christian freedom necessarily involves examination of the role of the conscience in matters of belief. For people need to be convinced about the teaching they receive. The words of St Paul come to mind, "The faith that you have, have as your own conviction before God" (Rom. 14:22).

4.4.  What is the role of conscience in matters of belief? Disciples of Christ and Roman Catholics agree that what we call human conscience is rightly described by the classical image of a voice of God, present in the heart of every human being. This is shown by St Paul's discussion of the position of Gentiles in relation to the Mosaic law when he writes, "They show that what the law requires is written on their hearts, to which their own conscience bears witness" (Rom. 2:15). Conscience may also be seen as a spiritual perception of what conforms with the dignity of the "image of God" and what has to be done according to this dignity. This first level of conscience is the work of God and, although sin can cloud conscience, it cannot destroy it.

4.5.  The church has a truth to teach which its members cannot discover only by themselves: it has been revealed in the person and work of Jesus Christ and kept in the memory which is guarded by the community of believers. In order to say a free human "Yes" to the gospel Christians need to know to whom and to what they are called to say "Yes". Indeed they will remain free to say "Yes" or "No". It is their responsibility to form a conscience which is open to what God is saying. Nothing can oblige them to act against their perception of the will of God. Family, school, friends and the culture all play a part in influencing human decisions. Because the church has received from God the mission to teach the gospel, it has a duty to help its members to make the faith of the church their own in order to inform their conscience. This is therefore the second level of Christian conscience – to make a reasoned response to the revelation of God in Jesus Christ.

4.6.  Sometimes in the history of the church individuals or groups, acting in obedience to the word of God as they discerned it, have disagreed with the prevailing teaching or practice. Disciples and Roman Catholics respond to this situation differently. Disciples came into existence because their leaders were unwilling to accept the restrictions which Presbyterians placed on access to the Lord's table. This memory has shaped their attitude towards the issue of disagreement with prevailing views. The nature of the history of the Roman Catholic Church means that it has no similar dominant memory; it also places a strong emphasis on the value of unity. Further work and reflection is needed on these differences. Nevertheless Disciples and Roman Catholics agree that certain groups in the history of the church have made an important and prophetic witness which has not immediately been recognized.

4.7. If men and women want to be in harmony with God, they have to hear and obey the voice of their conscience, informed and enlightened by the word of God, assisted by the gifts of the Holy Spirit and prudent advice, and guided by the teaching of the church. Christians respond to the gospel as the first disciples responded to the call of Christ; but like those first disciples they discover the truth of the words of Jesus, "You did not choose me but I chose you" (John 15:16). In so doing they are led to the peace and happiness of the kingdom for which they are created and redeemed.

4.8. The commission's discussion has been important in dispelling old stereotypes, such as the idea that the Roman Catholic Church has no place for freedom of conscience, or the idea that Disciples place no limits on the freedom of conscience. Both communions teach the place of the freedom of conscience and both see limits to its exercise within the community. This leads to two important agreements. Disciples and Roman Catholics both recognize that commitment to the gospel should be freely made. They also recognize that living the Christian life is a continuous process of receiving and living by the teaching handed on in the church and making personal decisions which are themselves shaped by life in communion with other believers.

*Teaching with authority*

4.9. Both Disciples of Christ and Roman Catholics agree that the faithful and truthful expression of the gospel is inherently persuasive, because its authority comes from God. Members of both communions also agree that the discernment of the authentic meaning of the revealed word belongs to the whole community, and that some members from within the community are called and empowered by the Spirit to teach the word of God. These are the pastors. *The Church as Communion in Christ* stated that "the ordained ministry is specifically given the charism for discerning, declaring and fostering what lies in the authentic memory of the church" (§45). The ordained ministers have a specific mission to teach the teaching church; and their teaching role is primary among their pastoral duties. Beyond that, Roman Catholics and Disciples would locate and describe the exercise of ministerial authority in different ways.

4.10. For Roman Catholics the discernment of the authentic meaning of the revealed word is expressed especially in the charism of ordained ministry. The unity of the ordained ministry is found in the communion of the bishop with all the other bishops, a unity sustained by the bishop of Rome. In this way the authority to teach is linked intimately with all the churches in the communion of the apostolic Tradition. In the sacrament of holy orders bishops are charged to "preach the gospel faithfully and constantly…, keeping in its authenticity and its integrity the deposit of faith according to the tradition always and everywhere transmitted since the apostles." Moreover, their service of the faith extends from their preaching and pastoral care to the celebration of the sacraments, culminating in the eucharist.

4.11. For Disciples this teaching is the function of theologically educated, ordained ministers. These are faithful persons, possessing the qualifications required to hand on the apostolic records of Christ's teachings, and to teach correctly what they contain. Alexander Campbell stated that "it is indeed the Holy Spirit and not the congregations, which creates bishops and deacons. The Spirit gives the qualifications both natural and acquired" (*The Christian System*, p.185). The office of what the first generation of Disciples called bishops (although the title was afterwards abandoned) or elders is specifically related to teaching and oversight within a particular local congregation. This office developed differently in different countries.[5] Local ministers do not teach alone but in consultation with their colleagues. They use teaching materials prepared regionally, nationally or internationally, often in collaboration with other churches.

4.12. In the Roman Catholic Church the bishops in communion with the bishop of Rome are responsible for the ordinary teaching of the church. The purpose of such teaching is not only to inform the faithful, but also to form their consciences so that they may take responsible decisions, confident that they are acting in accordance with the will of God. The special charism of the bishop is to keep the church in his care in communion with the whole church. Thus individual bishops are sometimes necessarily cautious in responding to new expressions of the faith. The Roman Catholic Church has a clearly identified teaching office which especially in contemporary times has articulated, with due regard for consultation, an increasingly large number of positions on new challenges or questions. Part of Roman Catholic life includes understanding these explanations of current magisterial teaching and also understanding the different levels of authority with which they are taught. Thus for Roman Catholics the authenticity of the faith is assured when bishops teach in communion with the bishop of Rome and the other bishops.

4.13. Among Disciples the teaching of the church is in the hands of ministers of local congregations, and the whole community is encouraged to read and study the scriptures daily. Following the confession of Christ celebrated in baptism, members are nurtured by regular church attendance and participation in the Lord's supper. Disciples expect ordained ministers to teach a common faith, taking account of the ecumenical consensus shared by other churches with whom they are in fellowship. Those persons with regional oversight also seek to keep their congregations in communion with the whole Disciple fellowship and they are responsible for exercising a prudent approach to the teaching of new ideas. But Disciples are more reluctant than Roman Catholics to provide official teaching on a wide range of matters. They often do not seek to articulate an official position when a question is under debate, preferring at times to leave the question open until time, debate and continuation in eucharistic fellowship lead to a consensus. This is an important difference in teaching practice. Beyond that, church members have a significant measure of freedom and personal responsibility to work out their own pattern of discipleship according to their conscience.

4.14. Among both Disciples and Roman Catholics teaching takes place within a set of limits or boundaries accepted by the community. However, there are differences of emphasis. Roman Catholics have emphasized that individuals cannot ignore the faith which the church has received through the Holy Spirit when proposing a new understanding of some point. Since the community of faith precedes the individual, anyone proposing new understandings of Christian teaching must be prepared to accept the community's discernment of those understandings. This communal discernment, in which the teaching office has a special role, acts as a discipline within which the theologian must work. Gradually a new consensus may emerge. The Disciples' process encourages continued conversation as the church seeks to identify those expressions of the faith that best show a clear relationship to the faith witnessed in the New Testament. When responding to people whose views or practice of the faith seem outside the common norms, the process is primarily pastoral.

4.15. In both communions, especially when crucial doctrinal and pastoral issues are at stake, it is the authority of the pastors, guided by the Holy Spirit, which is the instrument of God to keep the community in the right direction. It is their responsibility to show how their teaching is in communion with the faith of previous generations. Nevertheless bishops and pastors have not only to be aware of the needs of the community but also to weigh the various insights of the people and to "receive" those insights that are an authentic expression of the *sensus fidei* (sense of the faith) of the whole church of God. Their pastoral charism implies what the Catholic tradition designates as "pastoral prudence" enabling them to take into consideration inseparably the authentic evangelical truth and the concrete situation of their flock within the whole people of God. Disciples have used the term "common sense", that is, the sense common to the believing community. This prudence and common sense oblige the pastors to teach always within the common faith of all the Christian communities, with which they are in communion.

4.16. For both Roman Catholics and Disciples the authority of the church's teaching derives from a combination of elements: the truths of revelation, the theological arguments based upon them to guide human thought and behaviour, the position and experience of those responsible for teaching, and reception by the whole church. However, the relative weight attached to the elements differs between Roman Catholics and Disciples. Thus the claims made for the authority of the church in matters of conscience differ in our two communities. In the Roman Catholic Church those with episcopal or primatial oversight, who hold the apostolic teaching office conferred by ordination, can at times make decisions binding on the conscience of Roman Catholics. For Disciples ultimate oversight rests with a general assembly or conference (comprising both ministers and other church members), but their decisions do not bind the conscience of individual members. The commission needs to reflect further on whether these different emphases can be held together within the one body of Christ.

## 5. Handing on the faith: the mission of the whole church

*Equipping the faithful for evangelization*

5.1. Christ gave the whole church the commission to transmit, teach and nurture the faith. Through baptism all members of the body of Christ become partakers in the dignity and mission of Christ – prophet, priest and king. Hence they are called continually to receive and understand rightly the word of God. Furthermore, as the commission stated in *The Church as Communion in Christ*, the members of the church, because they are bound into a communion with the Father and with one another, "are called to live in such a way that, in spite of their failures and their weakness, this communion becomes visible and is constantly in search of a more perfect realization" (§47).

5.2.  Being bound together in a common mission undergirds our joint understanding that no teaching of the faith can ever be a completely solitary task. Teaching the faith occurs in many contexts: the loving mother or father showing a child how to pray, Sunday school teachers and catechists struggling to respond to the questions posed by young people and adults, university and seminary professors instructing future ministers and lay leaders, Roman Catholic bishops exercising their office as teachers of the faith, Disciples leaders with regional oversight guiding congregations through a church controversy, and many more. All these experiences of teaching and learning deepen and strengthen the ecclesial communion we have in Christ. This vision of the whole church's commission is crucial for our two communions.

5.3.  Faith is normally taught to the younger generation in the family, especially through the charisms God bestows on faithful parents. It is their responsibility to give a child the first experiences of love and constancy of care. These experiences can help that child see himself or herself as a child of God. When parents explicitly teach Christian truth to their children and when they help them to be formed in virtue, they are working to form in them a Christian conscience. But they do this also through the examples they themselves offer of their own visible struggle to live lives that are faithful to the gospel and by presenting to their children opportunities to learn about other witnesses to faithful Christian living. Catholics and Disciples agree in considering that the function of parents is rooted in the grace of God. The Catholic Church emphasizes that this grace is a particular gift of the sacrament of matrimony, and accordingly is integral to the sacramental life of the church.

5.4.  In Catholic and Disciple congregations, systematic initiation and education in the essential matters of faith (catechesis) plays an important role, through Sunday schools and catechetical programmes. For the Roman Catholic Church a very important part is played by church schools, which have often been founded and staffed by religious orders or congregations with the official approval of the bishops or of the See of Rome. *The Catechism of the Catholic Church*, an authoritative exposition of the one apostolic Tradition and a sure norm for teaching the faith, is used by local episcopal conferences in ways adapted to the local situation, but always in conformity with the common teaching of all the local churches in communion with the See of Rome. The discipline of the sacrament of penance and of participation in the eucharistic liturgy, following the course of the Christian liturgical year, with the example of Mary and the saints constantly presented, is also a major occasion of catechetical instruction in the context of prayer. Pastoral preparation for baptisms, marriage and death is another. The responsibility for catechesis shared by all the baptized is exercised by the bishops in a way unique to their office. Among Disciples the regular pattern of worship, including the weekly celebration of the Lord's supper and preaching, provides opportunity for spiritual growth and instruction. As well as preaching, ministers teach Sunday school classes and prepare candidates for baptism. Adult church school classes and women's and young people's fellowships form competent persons able to nurture Christian faith. In different ways, both our traditions enable individuals to explore the implications of Christian discipleship for themselves and to share their experience with others.

5.5.  In both our communions, professors, theologians and scholars in universities, seminaries and elsewhere are involved not only in the search for the right understanding of the sources of the faith or the history of their transmission, but also in teaching the teachers. An important contribution can also be made to the life of the faithful by spiritual writers.

5.6. The essential test for the church's teaching is its faithfulness to the gospel. Teaching the faith is more than communicating the content of a catechism or a book on Bible history and doctrine. It is inseparable from the witness of a faithful life and authentic devotion to God and the church. Here the authority comes from the baptismal and eucharistic grace at work in the lives of Christians, especially those whose faithfulness captures the imagination of the community. Conversion to Christ is a lifelong process, and in the church Christians are challenged repeatedly to receive the fullness of the gospel.

5.7. The church itself is also called continually to receive the fullness of the gospel. This is normally the fruit of a long process of interaction within the community. However, there may be occasions when an immediate decision needs to be taken for the sake of the gospel. Such was the decision of the early church to admit Gentile Christians without requiring them to conform to the whole Jewish law; in more recent centuries the decision of certain Christians to oppose slavery without waiting for a church consensus might be a similar example. The discernment process can be enhanced as the voices of other Christian communities and the insights of ecumenical work are taken into account. The teaching and living in the gospel of one communion may bring to mind an aspect of Christian faith or practice which others have neglected, and are therefore called to "receive". The implications of this for our understanding of communion require further patient discussion.

*Evangelization by word and witness*

5.8. In Jesus Christ the truth of God has come into the world in an historically unsurpassable and definitive way. The news of this is liberating and life-giving, yet also demanding; it is simultaneously gift and call. The good news calls for faith in the one who died and was raised by God to new life; it calls for repentance and a radical transformation of life. This proclamation of the good news is what is meant by evangelism or evangelization. The church is by nature a missionary community, a community of those who are sent by God into the world to share in the proclamation of the good news (Mark 16:15-16). Its proclamation of the gospel through preaching and the celebration of the sacraments requires intentional commitment to the task of evangelization. The message must be communicated in words to those who have never heard it, to those who have heard it but are no longer active in the life of the church, and to those who continue to shape their lives in and through the church.

5.9. Speaking and telling are not the only ways to evangelize. The witness of holy lives, strengthened by the eucharist, is also integral to the mission of the church. God's good news can be expressed in sacrificial lives and acts of mercy, before any word is spoken. Authentic witness to the gospel takes place through lives of faithfulness to God sustained by prayer, self-denial and acts of love.

5.10. Evangelization, which brings persons into life-giving communion with God and with others, requires both persuasive words and the effective expression of the new life being offered. Those who are led to profess the gospel will also show lives truly turned from concern for self to love of neighbour. Such love today will issue in witness to the cause of justice. When the Christian Church (Disciples of Christ) in the USA and Canada approved new principles for its division of overseas ministries in 1981, it stated that, "Evangelism is incomplete unless deed matches proclamation. In fact, in some contexts the deed is the only possible proclamation." Pope John Paul II stated that,

> Through the gospel message, the church offers a force for liberation which promotes development precisely because it leads to conversion of heart and ways of thinking, fosters the recognition of each person's dignity, encourages solidarity, commitment and service of one's neighbour, and gives everyone a place in God's plan, which is the building of his kingdom of peace and justice, beginning already in this life. (*RM*, §59)

Disciples and Roman Catholics therefore agree that the church must be a community with structures which facilitate evangelization and one which is a credible witness to the gospel it proclaims.

5.11. All Christians are called to the work of evangelization, although some take on special roles. Parents and teachers hand on the faith to children; religious orders devoted to evangelization emerge; missionary societies encourage and support the work; Christian schools, youth movements and lay adult organizations appear on the scene to do specific tasks. Through all of these efforts, the work of evangelization is strengthened. Ordained ministers have the special responsibility to lead and build up the community. Furthermore, the teaching office supports the work of evangelization by serving the church's unity in faith and life. Thus the church is extended by the establishment of new local churches of those committed to the cause of evangelization. When all work together, the church witnesses to the fact that the gospel is not only a dream, that with the grace of the Spirit it is possible to live according to the word of God.

5.12. Evangelization and the unity of the church go together. The concern to link evangelization and the unity of the church is a particular characteristic of Disciples of Christ and of Roman Catholics. The Decree on Ecumenism of the Second Vatican Council states that the division among Christians "is clearly contrary to Christ's will. It is a scandal to the world and damages the sacred cause of preaching the gospel to every creature" (§1). Pope John Paul II, in *Ut Unum Sint*, said that, "However true it is that the church, by the prompting of the Holy Spirit and with the promise of indefectibility, has preached and still preaches the gospel to all nations, it is also true that she must face the difficulties which derive from the lack of unity" (§98). Both Thomas and Alexander Campbell and Barton Stone, as well as later Disciples teachers, expressed in various ways the importance of Christians being united as they take up the task of evangelization. Stone, for example, wrote that Christian unity was "indispensable to the conversion of the world" (*Christian Messenger*, 1836). Thus we agree that the disunity of the church undermines the proclamation of the gospel.

5.13. The church invites people into communion with God and each other, but because of its divisions it fails to manifest that communion fully. All believers gathered at the eucharistic celebration are sent out into the world to proclaim Christ, but we cannot celebrate the eucharist together. That proclamation is therefore weakened. In this dialogue, we have increasingly come to recognize that the structures and instruments for the visible unity of the church of God are part of the necessary obedience to the command of Christ who said, "Go... and make disciples of all nations" (Matt. 28:19).

## 6. Future work

6.1. During this phase the commission has taken up only one of the tasks set out in *The Church as Communion in Christ*, namely exploring the nature of the rule of faith in a changing history. The other tasks – exploring issues related to the understanding of the eucharist, the structure of the church gathered around it, and the primacy of the bishop of Rome – remain. As we have grown to understand each other better, we have also become aware that we often do and say the same things but for different reasons. There is a need to investigate whether there is mutual recognition of the legitimacy of different ways of arriving at the same practices or the same conclusions. We also sometimes do different things to achieve the same purpose, and there is a corresponding need to reflect upon the legitimacy of that.

6.2. Because of the centrality of the eucharist in each of our traditions, we believe that the time may now be appropriate to return to that topic. Therefore we propose that there should be a further phase of our dialogue, and that its focus should be the presence of Christ in the church, with special reference to the eucharist. In *The Church as Communion in Christ* we said,

> Even if we agree on the signification and function of the eucharist, we feel that we still have to discuss our traditional teaching and practice concerning the presence of the Lord in the celebration of the supper, its sacrificial nature, the role of the ordained minister and the role of the community. This is important, given the emphasis that both Disciples and Roman Catholics put on the weekly celebration of the Lord's supper and its link with the visible unity of Christians. (§53a)

6.3. This third phase has seen some significant changes of membership in our dialogue. The Most Rev. Samuel E. Carter, SJ (former Roman Catholic co-chairperson) and the Rev. Dr Kilian McDonnell, OSB, have retired from the commission. We have also lost by death the Rev. Dr J.M.R. Tillard, OP, a founding member of the commission. We place on record our debt to them for the contributions they made to our work.

## Participants

*Disciples of Christ*

Rev. Dr Paul A. Crow, Jr, Indianapolis, Indiana, USA (co-chairperson)
Dr M. Eugene Boring, Fort Worth, Texas, USA
Rev. Dr Bevis Byfield, Kingston, Jamaica
Dr H. Jackson Forstman, Nashville, Tennessee, USA
Dr Nadia Lahutsky, Fort Worth, Texas, USA
Rev. Dr William Tabbernee, Tulsa, Oklahoma, USA
Rev. Dr David M. Thompson, Cambridge, England
Rev. Dr Robert K. Welsh, Indianapolis, Indiana, USA (co-secretary, 1999-2002)

*Roman Catholics*
Most Rev. Samuel E. Carter, SJ, Kingston, Jamaica (co-chairperson, 1993-95)
Most Rev. Daniel M. Buechlein, OSB, Indianapolis, Indiana, USA (co-chairperson, 1996-2002)
Most Rev. Basil Meeking, Chicago, USA
Monsignor Michael Jackson, Hove, England
Rev. Dr Kilian McDonnell, OSB, Collegeville, Minnesota, USA (1993-98)
Monsignor Dr John P. Meier, Notre Dame, Indiana, USA
Monsignor John Mutiso-Mbinda, Vatican City (co-secretary)
Dr Margaret O'Gara, Toronto, Canada
Rev. Dr J.M.R. Tillard, OP, Ottawa, Canada (1993-2000)
Rev. Robert D. Turner, Helena, Montana, USA (consultant, 2000-2002)

NOTES

1   For this third stage of our discussions, the dialogue met ten times: in Rome, Italy (1993); Indianapolis, Indiana (1994); Bose, Italy (1995); Bethany, West Virginia (1996); Venice, Italy (1997); Aibonito, Puerto Rico (1998); St Meinrad, Indiana (1999); Halifax, Nova Scotia (2000); Rome, Italy (2001); and Bose, Italy (2002).

2   The word "receive" is used here (and later) in its theological sense to refer to the appropriation by the whole church of the apostolic faith.

3   For many centuries Jews in different countries used slightly different collections of books as their scriptures, depending on whether the language was Greek or Hebrew. These differences were debated in the 16th century among Renaissance Catholic humanists and eventually in the Reformation disputes. In 1546 the council of Trent rejected Luther's view that the Jewish canon of Old Testament books should be decisive and repeated the list used by the council of Florence. Roman Catholics affirm the decree of the council of Trent where the canon consists of 46 Old Testament and 27 New Testament books. Disciples, following the Reformers, have a canon of 39 Old Testament and 27 New Testament books. Because the Reformation churches did not receive Trent's decree on the canon but followed Luther's view, the Disciples inherited the canon used by the Reformers with seven fewer books in the Old Testament than in Trent's list. The seven books in question are sometimes called by Roman Catholics "deuterocanonical". These books are today sometimes found in Protestant Bibles grouped together under the heading of the Old Testament Apocrypha.

4   The Westminster Confession (1646) was adopted by the Church of Scotland as its confession of faith in 1647, and subsequently became the standard confession in the English-speaking Presbyterian world. The Secession Testimony was a statement by those Presbyterians who seceded from the Church of Scotland in 1733 and was part of the doctrinal heritage in which Thomas and Alexander Campbell were reared in Ireland.

5   In some, such as the United Kingdom, it was emphasized that there should be a plurality of elders in each congregation, the minister being regarded as one of them; in others, such as the United States, the minister of the local congregation became the chief pastor. More recently, ministers have begun to exercise oversight of a number of local congregations in a given area. The way in which this has happened has varied, but some form of regional *episcope* exists in the United States, Canada, Australia, Congo, North India, Jamaica and the United Kingdom.

# 19. Speaking the Truth in Love: Teaching Authority among Catholics and Methodists

## Joint Commission between the Roman Catholic Church and the World Methodist Council, Brighton Report (2001)

Brighton, England, 2001

### Preface

During the past five years the joint commission between the Roman Catholic Church and the World Methodist Council has studied the exercise of teaching authority within and by the church. In doing so, it has taken further the understanding recorded in previous statements of the joint commission, *The Word of Life* (1996) and, before that, *The Apostolic Tradition* (1991). The themes of the Holy Spirit and the church, studied in previous phases of this dialogue, have now led to the more precise question of how the faith which comes from the apostles is transmitted from generation to generation in such a way that all the faithful continue to adhere to the revelation that has come in Christ Jesus. The teaching ministry in the church is a particular means for this transmission and for ensuring faithfulness not only in believing but also in what is believed. This latest statement contributes one more piece to a mosaic which has been slowly developed, illustrating the various interlocking elements which, through the power of the Holy Spirit, contribute to the life of the church as a faithful bearer of the revelation of Jesus Christ to succeeding generations.

A word may be helpful about the general structure of the present report, which deviates a little from the pattern customary in bilateral dialogues. The introduction indicates the biblical dynamic which energized the work of the commission during this quinquennium. Then the bulk of the document consists of two parts that differ from each other in nature. The first part states in systematic form what the commission believes it possible for Catholics and Methodists to agree on in the matter of authoritative teaching, noting along the way such divergences as remain and some questions which each side would wish to put to the other. The second part describes the current understandings and practices internal to Methodism and Catholicism respectively, though in a style intended to be more readily intelligible by the partner and by others. Ideally, the reader approaching the report with little knowledge of one or both partners will read this second, descriptive part of the report first and will then return to it in order to see what achievements and challenges the first, systematic part of the report represents. The general conclusion of the report, in fact, synthesizes the recognizable commonalities between Catholicism and Methodism and formulates the outstanding differences in terms of work still to be done.

Experiencing both continuity and changes in membership from previous rounds, the joint commission has enjoyed excellent working relationships and once more developed the mutual trust that comes from devotion to a common Lord and to a common goal, namely, the attainment between our churches of "full communion in faith, mission and sacramental life". We have thought together, written together, prayed together, and reverently attended each other's eucharistic gatherings.

The present document is the work of a joint commission whose members are officially appointed by the Pontifical Council for Promoting Christian Unity and by the World Methodist Council. We respectfully offer this report to our sponsors and ask for their evaluation of it.

+ Michael Putney
Bishop of Townsville
Catholic Co-chairman

Geoffrey Wainwright
Professor of Christian Theology
Duke University
Methodist Co-chairman

November 2000

**The status of this document**

The report published here is the work of the joint commission for dialogue between the Roman Catholic Church and the World Methodist Council. It is a statement from the commission. The authorities who appointed the commission have allowed the report to be published so that it may be widely discussed. It is not an authoritative declaration by the Roman Catholic Church or by the World Methodist Council, who will evaluate the document in order to take a position on it in due time.

*Ephesians 4:1-16 (NRSV)*
I therefore, the prisoner in the Lord,
beg you to lead a life worthy of the calling
to which you have been called,
with all humility and gentleness, with patience,
bearing with one another in love,
making every effort to maintain
the unity of the Spirit in the bond of peace.
There is one body and one Spirit,
just as you were called to the one hope of your calling,
one Lord, one faith, one baptism,
one God and Father of all,
who is above all and through all and in all.
But each of us was given grace
according to the measure of Christ's gift.
Therefore it is said,
"When he ascended on high he made captivity itself a captive;
he gave gifts to his people."
(When it says, "He ascended," what does it mean

but that he had also descended into the lower parts of the earth?
He who descended is the same one
who ascended far above all the heavens,
so that he might fill all things.)
The gifts he gave were that some would be apostles, some prophets,
some evangelists, some pastors, and teachers,
to equip the saints for the work of ministry,
for building up the body of Christ,
until all of us come to the unity of the faith
and of the knowledge of the Son of God,
to maturity, to the measure of the full stature of Christ.
We must no longer be children,
tossed to and fro and blown about by every wind of doctrine,
by people's trickery, by their craftiness in deceitful scheming.
But speaking the truth in love, we must grow up in every way
into him who is the Head,
into Christ, from whom the whole body,
joined and knit together by every ligament
with which it is equipped,
as each part is working properly,
promotes the body's growth in building itself up in love.

## Introduction

1. The Letter to the Ephesians celebrates the working out of the gracious divine purpose finally to bring all things together under the sovereignty of Jesus Christ, to the praise and glory of God the Father. The word of truth, which is the gospel of salvation, is now being preached, and those who receive it in faith are included in Christ and already made to sit with him in the heavenly places. As long as the consummation is awaited, however, the apostle finds it necessary to exhort the believers to hold fast to what has been given them by the Holy Spirit in anticipation of the End. What was apostolically recommended to the Ephesian Christians under the threat of disunity may be pertinent to later generations seeking to remedy the divisions which have in fact regrettably occurred. Expectantly, the joint commission turned in particular to the fourth chapter of the Letter to the Ephesians for scriptural guidance in its effort to resolve differences between Methodists and Catholics over the matter of teaching authority in the church.

2. According to Ephesians 4:4-6, the unity of the Christian community is founded on the sevenfold unity that is recognized within the church and upon which it depends for its existence. The church as the body of Christ is a unity in diversity that is enlivened by one Spirit, responding to the one hope and submitting to the one Lord and Head, Jesus Christ, through the faith that is celebrated in the one rite of baptism to the glory of the One God and Father of all. Thus the major topics of Christian doctrine appear as features of a living organism of beliefs. Correspondingly, the opening chapter of the commission's report articulates the basic trinitarian and christological faith shared by Catholics and Methodists, that is grounded in the scriptures, confessed together in the ecumenical

creeds, embodied in the respective liturgies of the churches, and proclaimed to the world as the gospel of its salvation.

3. In the second chapter of its present report, the commission attends especially to the Holy Spirit as the agent of unity (Eph. 4:3) and thereby highlights the pneumatological dimension that has marked its work from the 1981 report onwards. Now the church is viewed as God's prophetic community, anointed with the Spirit of truth. Sealed by the Holy Spirit, the church is preserved in one and the same truth in such a way that all Christians can actively respond to the vocation of bearing witness to the gospel which brings to humankind the hope of salvation.

4. The common vocation of Christians by no means excludes a diversity of compatible gifts and functions in the church. Ephesians 4:7-11 in fact details a variety of charisms bestowed on the church by the exalted Christ for the establishment of particular ministries to build up the body and equip all God's people for mission in the world. The Epistle's list comprises chiefly offices having to do with the proclamation and teaching of the word. Correspondingly, the commission's report next includes a chapter in which Methodists and Catholics try to develop a common understanding on the historically controversial questions concerning the manners and modes by which, in ever changing circumstances, accurate discernment of the truth of the gospel is attained and its authoritative proclamation accomplished.

5. Ephesians 4:12-14 states that the purpose of the teaching offices is to promote that "unity in faith and in the knowledge of the Son of God" which indicates maturity in the life of believers. Such maturity is revealed by certainty and stability with respect to matters of belief, and by the ability to distinguish between right and wrong teachings. Agreement in the truth of the gospel is a fundamental component in the stated aim of the dialogue between Catholics and Methodists: "full communion in faith, mission and sacramental life".[1]

6. "Speaking the truth in love" (Eph. 4:15) is the title of the commission's report: it captures both the spirit in which the dialogue has proceeded and the result that is hoped for from it. The apostle urges believers to rid themselves of all bitterness, wrath, anger, wrangling, slander and malice (4:31) and to cultivate rather the virtues of humility, gentleness and patience (4:2). Because Christ incarnates the love and truth of God, love is integral to truth, and truth to love. The continuing pursuit of both in tandem should strengthen the credibility of common Christian witness to the loving purpose of God, who in the Word and the Spirit gave and still gives himself to humankind. This is the truth of the gospel.

## PART ONE

### I. The church as communion in love and truth

*Object and source of teaching*

7. "Because God so loved the world, he sent his Son and the Holy Spirit to draw us into communion with himself. This sharing in God's life, which resulted from the mission of the Son and the Holy Spirit, found expression in a visible koinonia [communion, community] of Christ's disciples, the church."[2] This description indicates both the central content or object of the church's teaching and the ultimate source of the authority to teach. Since the central object of teaching is God revealed in Jesus Christ, who is also the ultimate source of authority, Christian doctrine is inseparably christological and trinitarian. Catholics and Methodists are able to make the following statements jointly, subject to the qualifications indicated along the way.

*Christology*

8. Given the way in which, according to the scriptures, God has entered human history, the church's doctrine is centred on Christ. It flows from the identification of Jesus of Nazareth as the Saviour expected by Israel, the people of God whose story is told in the Bible. The life, ministry, death and resurrection of Jesus, and the ensuing proclamation of the Lordship of the Risen Christ were the central topic of teaching for the first generations of Christian believers, as is shown in the New Testament. They must remain so for all subsequent generations in the church. Whenever we speak about Jesus Christ in our teaching, we follow the patristic councils in identifying him as the Second Person of the Trinity who has taken flesh.

*Trinity*

9. In a perspective that aims at the ultimate reality which stands beyond and within all that is visible, the core of Christian doctrine is that the Godhead is three Persons who are distinct from one another, yet in such a way that the divine being is perfectly present in each. The one and only God who was proclaimed and manifested in the Old Testament is revealed in the New as the Father of our Lord Jesus Christ; Jesus is known as the Father's eternal Son, his creative Word who has now been made flesh; and their eternal Spirit is manifest as the one who spoke through the prophets, inspired the scriptures, and is experienced as the divine presence acting in human life and throughout the universe.

*The works of God*

10. While seeing all God's acts as engaging all three Persons of the Trinity, Christian reflection guided by the scriptures has connected the works of God with specific divine Persons. Thus the creating act is appropriated to the Father, the redemption of Adam's

race to Christ the New Adam, the guidance of the church and the sanctification of believers to the Holy Spirit. The faithful are taught to read, not only the "book of scripture" as the inspired record of divine revelation, but also in its light the "book of nature", which shows traces of the creative power and presents images and analogies of the divine Persons, and the "book of the soul", the highest creaturely image of God on earth (*imago Dei*), that has been damaged by sin but restored in Christ. In this way Christians are led to contemplate the Godhead as the ultimate agent and the loving and compassionate providence that supports all things in being, and they look for God's direction in their life.

### The creeds

11. The Christian church professes the Apostles' and the Nicene-Constantinopolitan Creeds, which are christological and trinitarian. They name the Father, the Son and the Holy Spirit, and they place the life, death and resurrection of the Word incarnate at the centre of the articles of faith. The creeds embody the biblical teaching about God and Christ. Their confession is incorporated in the church's liturgies, notably the Apostles' Creed in the baptismal rite of Christian initiation and the Nicene Creed in the worship of the assembly. The creeds also function as a rule of faith (*regula fidei*), normative for conciliar and other official teaching.

### Marks of the church

12. The Creed of Nicea-Constantinople calls the church one, holy, catholic and apostolic. The church which Jesus founded is the gathered communion (koinonia) of all believers in Christ. It knows itself to be the redeemed people of God, the renewed Israel. It is by the same token one and holy. As the universal communion of the faithful "from the righteous Abel to the last of the elect", the church is catholic, destined to embrace all of redeemed humanity. Because it was chiefly through the apostles of Jesus – the Twelve and St Paul and other missionaries – that the Gentiles were grafted into the stem of Israel (cf. Rom. 11) by the preaching of the word, the church is apostolic.

### The church as communion

13. The church is designated in holy scripture by many images and metaphors which throw light on the church as a communion.[3] The biblical image of the church as body of Christ has been favoured for several reasons. It was emphasized by St Paul (cf. 1 Cor. 10:14-17, 12:12-30; Rom. 12:4-6), and it is closely related to the eucharistic body of Christ and to the image of the church as bride of God. Set at the heart of the Christian liturgy and piety, the eucharist as communion with Christ substantiates the doctrine of the church as communion. The image of the church as bride of God renews the perspective of Israel as divine bride and anticipates the church's eschatological fulfilment.

14. That the church is a communion is indisputably rooted in the design of God, the Trinity, in whom unity and the plurality of three inseparably imply each other. This character of the church is grounded in the creation itself, since humankind is, by the Creator's will, at the same time one and diverse. As communion, the church relates all believers to God and to one another, on the model and by the grace of the three Persons who are One

Eternal Being. The communion of the faithful in time and in space exists in the word of God and is united by the bond of the Spirit. It is a communion in the holy things that are the sacraments of grace, and primarily in baptism and in the eucharist.

15. The biblical images of the church converge on one point: the church issues from the self-communication of God, who in the incarnation comes to participate in the life of humankind and gives them a share in his own triune life. It thereby understands itself to be the domain of the Spirit, in keeping with the formula of the early baptismal creeds: "I believe… in the Holy Spirit in the holy church…" While the internal presence and the testimony of the Spirit in the hearts of Christians remain invisible, the whole life of the community lies publicly under the word of God for guidance and for judgment; and it is destined to give glory to God the Father.

## Primacy of the word

16. The word has primacy in the church. The eternal Logos, through the incarnation, brought God's final revelation to humankind and became the Redeemer of the world and the Lord of the church. The eternal Word made flesh is the ultimate norm of all the church's life and doctrine, orienting all that is done and taught in the church towards the praise and worship of God the Father, by the grace and power of the Holy Spirit. At the last day those who live in Christ will be raised into his kingdom, which "will have no end".

## Scripture

17. The word is present in the proclamation of the gospel and in the initiation, education and formation of believers. In proclamation and instruction the written word in the scriptures has primacy over all later formulations of divine revelation. It provides a permanent standard of belief, which is all the more necessary as missionary preaching of the gospel in new nations and times requires that the message be communicated in fresh ways to the various cultures of the world. It is the point of reference for the normative decisions that have to be taken when debates and diverging interpretations of doctrine threaten the right formulation and the correct transmission of the gospel.

## Tradition

18. The word is present in Tradition as the communication of the gospel to new generations of believers. Tradition is "the history of that continuing environment of grace in and by which all Christians live", it finds its "focal expression" in scripture,[4] and it will always be faithful to the biblical message. Since they preserve the proclamation of the news of salvation by the prophets and apostles, the scriptures are at the same time the model and the heart of the Tradition. In this Tradition, by which the word is transmitted from age to age, the word is read, proclaimed, explained and celebrated. The Tradition acquires normative value as its fidelity to the biblical norm and to the eternal Word is recognized. "Scripture was written within Tradition, yet scripture is normative for Tradition. The one is only intelligible in terms of the other."[5] That there is a harmony between scripture, Tradition, and the Christian life of faith and worship is part of the self-understanding of the church and integral to the manner in which the church, in the Holy Spirit, transmits itself from generation to generation. There is a growing convergence

between Methodists and Catholics on what Pope John Paul II has called "the relationship between sacred scripture, as the highest authority in matters of faith, and sacred Tradition, as indispensable to the interpretation of the word of God".[6]

## Maintained in the truth

19. In the history of the church it became urgent to decide between divergent traditions and conflicting interpretations of the gospel. A ministry serving such decision-making was present in apostolic times (cf. Acts 15) and given a particular shape in the early centuries, when at the local level pastoral care was entrusted to a college of presbyters under the presidency of a bishop, with the bishops themselves forming a college at the universal level, in which the Roman See presided "in charity" (*en agapé*).[7] Bishops in the Catholic Church continue to fulfill this ministry as they preside over a particular church (diocese), which they administer, and lead in faith, worship and witness. When gathered together in council, and when in their local churches they are seen to teach the same doctrines, they exercise a magisterial responsibility on behalf of the universal church. In their own historical circumstances, John Wesley and the Methodists were aware of a similar responsibility when they developed a pattern whereby the supervision of teaching is exercised by the Conference and by the superintendent ministers acting in its name.

20. The truth of the gospel and the doctrines that express it cannot be faithfully preserved without the assistance of the Spirit. Catholics and Methodists have been eager to invoke the Spirit and they trust in his unfailing grace. In the Catholic Church this concern for truth and fidelity has found a focus in a "charism of unfailing truth and faith" that is given to the bishops for the sake of the universal church.[8] This gift takes various forms, as when the ordinary teaching of all bishops is seen to be unanimous, or when, as occasionally though rarely happens, a doctrine is proclaimed "infallibly" by a council or by the bishop of Rome in the conditions that were determined by the First Vatican Council for definitions *ex cathedra*. By virtue of this "charism of unfailing truth and faith" the gospel is proclaimed indefectibly in spite of the sins and shortcomings of the church's members and leaders. A living witness to this faith has been given over the centuries by saints and scholars as well as ordinary believers, some of whom are honoured as "doctors of the church".

21. In their own concern for the truth of the gospel, Methodists have found assurance in the guidance of the Spirit that has been manifest in godly individuals like John Wesley himself, in such providential events as the Reformation, and in gatherings like the early councils and the Methodist Conferences. As they exercise their teaching office, these Conferences formulate doctrinal statements as needed, but do not ascribe to them guaranteed freedom from error. Methodists understand themselves to be under an obligation to accept as authoritative what can clearly be shown to be in agreement with the scriptures.

## Teaching the truth

22. Both Methodists and Catholics accept the scriptures, the creeds and the doctrinal decrees of the early ecumenical councils. In the Catholic Church further development of doctrine has occurred through other conciliar decrees and constitutions, and through pronouncements made by synods of bishops and by the bishop of Rome and the offices that

assist him in his care of all the churches. In Methodism the holy scriptures are believed to contain all things necessary to salvation. At the same time, Methodists' reading of the scriptures is guided by the early creeds and councils and certain standard texts, such as the sermons of John Wesley, his notes on the New Testament, and the articles of religion. The Methodist Conferences have the task of interpreting doctrine. Both Methodists and Catholics hold that all doctrine must remain under the word of God, against which the value of its content should be tested.

23. "Since the heart of the gospel and the core of the faith is the love of God revealed in redemption, then all our credal statements must derive from faith in Christ who is our salvation and the foundation of our faith."[9] For Catholics and Methodists there is an order among the doctrines of the faith based upon their relationship to this core. The Decree on Ecumenism of the Second Vatican Council speaks of a "hierarchy of truths",[10] and John Wesley of an "analogy of faith" or a "grand scheme of doctrine".[11] Methodists and Catholics also distinguish between doctrines and theological opinions, though they sometimes differ on which teachings belong to each category.

24. An essential moment in the process of Tradition is the reception of doctrine by the people of God. As this joint commission has said, "One criterion by which new developments in Christian teaching or living may be judged consonant with the gospel is their long-term reception by the wider church."[12] In Catholic teaching, the agreement of the faithful is not a condition of truth, but the church's assent cannot fail to be given,[13] not only to the gospel daily preached and explained, but also to doctrinal definitions destined to ensure its integrity. There develops a mutual trust and a common recognition that the Holy Spirit is at work at all levels of the community. Nonetheless perfection of language is not guaranteed by the "charism of unfailing truth and faith". In Methodist practice, Conferences hold the final authority in the interpretation of doctrine within the framework of their doctrinal standards. Methodists expect that Conference teaching firmly rooted in the normative sources of doctrine will be accepted. Refinement and reformation of teaching is part of an ongoing process through Conferences. When the teaching of a particular meeting of Conference is seen by the church to need better formulation, the next session of Conference is expected to carry out that task. We both agree that the church stands in need of constant renewal in its teaching as in its life.

*Theology*

25. Assent to the gospel is entirely due to divine grace, and the ensuing faith engages the entirety of the persons who believe. It then becomes the starting-point of reflection about the gospel, as it is appropriated in diverse cultures. As the reception of doctrine takes place within the cultures of those who believe, it gives rise to a variety of orientations which eventually build up different theological systems. The ministry of theologians is to seek proper answers to the implicit or explicit questions asked about the Christian faith, to relate faith and culture in intellectually coherent ways, to explore the depths of doctrine, to organize the insights of the saints in satisfying syntheses, to educate the members of the church in the contemplation of the divine mysteries, and to assist church leaders, both locally and when gathered in conciliar assembly, to formulate and preach the gospel in fidelity to the word of God written and transmitted. Thus theologians and church leaders are together called both to serve the unity of Christian faith and to pro-

mote the legitimate diversity in theology, liturgy and law that illustrates the life and ethos of specific communities and enriches the church's catholicity.

## The rule of prayer

26.  The faith of the Christian koinonia is expressed in its worship. As the Wesleyan hymn puts it, the Lord's supper is a privileged occasion for the church to be realized as the body of Christ:

> Jesus, we thus obey
> Thy last and kindest word;
> Here, in thine own appointed way,
> We come to meet thee, Lord. [14]

There the correlation between the sacramental body and the ecclesial body appears both necessary and indissoluble. In the liturgical assembly, the gospel is preached, the sacraments are celebrated, the faithful are one in prayer, blessings are shared, spiritual gifts exchanged, insights communicated, pains and sufferings softened by compassion, hopes placed in common. As they go from worship into the world, the faithful are one not only in faith and belief, but also in love; the "rule of prayer", the faith that they have sung, remains with them as their rule of belief and their rule of life; and privileged connections grow from this, through mutual encouragement and emulation, in distinctive spiritualities and ways of discipleship, in religious societies following a common rule and devoted to a common purpose of prayer and good works, and in many forms of witness (apostolate, evangelism) that are needed in contemporary society.

## The church as mission

27.  As at the moment of the ascension, the church is still sent today by the Saviour to "make disciples of all nations" (Matt. 28:19). Through the Word made flesh the apostles and other disciples received this mission from God, for which they were empowered by the Holy Spirit at Pentecost. From the apostles the mission has been handed on to the entire body of the church; and the Spirit, who acts as "the soul of the church", has been received by the faithful, confirming their baptism, making Christ present to them, leading them home to the Father. As they hear the gospel preached, Christians realize that mission is not the exclusive calling of a few but of the entire community and of its members, lay and ordained, according to their gifts and abilities. All should live by the gospel everywhere and at all times, in their homes and at their places of work and of leisure, so that the whole Christian church may truly be seen as sent by God to humankind. Indeed, Jesus promised that if the disciples love one another the world will believe that they are his disciples (cf. John 13:35). To bring the gospel effectively to all creatures the church depends on divine grace. Moreover, it is aware of its own inner contradiction when fulfilment of its mission is hampered by sin, lack of vision, disagreements, discouragement or fear. God's grace will be given, for the Holy Spirit is ever at work, enabling the church and the faithful to pursue their God-given callings.

*The ecumenical imperative*

28. The ultimate aim of mission is to serve God's saving purpose for all of humankind. Just as the church longs for the oneness of its members in love and prays for it in the liturgy, so it waits in hope for spiritual gifts that will lead it to a higher level of holiness, a more evident fullness of catholicity, and a greater fidelity in apostolicity. This striving after perfection in the God-given marks of the church implies an ecumenical imperative. All Christian churches should pray and work towards an eventual restoration of organic unity. Visionary Methodists from John R. Mott onwards have been among the pioneers of the modern ecumenical movement, and Methodist churches have wholeheartedly committed themselves to the recovery of the full visible unity of Christians. Likewise the Second Vatican Council committed the Catholic Church irrevocably to the same goal, a commitment which was reiterated with passion by Pope John Paul II in his encyclical letter *Ut Unum Sint* (1995). Catholics and Methodists have thus begun to enjoy a "union in affection" on their way to that "entire external union" [15] for which Wesley in his time hardly dared to hope.

## II. God's prophetic community

*Anointed with the Spirit of truth*

29. Methodists and Roman Catholics are united in the hope that the Holy Spirit will lead all believers to the truth, gathering them together into communion with Christ who is in person "the Way, the Truth and the Life" (John 14:6). The Second Vatican Council re-emphasized Catholic teaching on the place of the Holy Spirit at the heart of the life, worship and mission of Christ's church:

> The Spirit dwells in the church and in the hearts of the faithful as in a temple (cf. 1 Cor. 3:16, 6:19), and he prays in them and bears witness to their adoption as children (cf. Gal. 4:6; Rom. 8:15-16,26). He leads the church into all truth (cf. John 16:13), and he makes it one in fellowship and ministry, instructing and directing it through a diversity of gifts both hierarchical and charismatic, and he adorns it with his fruits (cf. Eph. 4:11-12; 1 Cor. 12:4; Gal. 5:22). Through the power of the gospel he rejuvenates the church, continually renewing it and leading it to perfect union with its spouse. [16]

The Wesleys affirmed the same truth:

> Head of thy church, whose Spirit fills
> And flows through every faithful soul,
> Unites in mystic love, and seals
> Them one, and sanctifies the whole: ...
> Pour out the promised gift on all,
> Answer the universal "Come!" [17]

This link between Spirit and church has always been essential to the life of the church; in the 3rd century, for instance, those being baptized in Rome were asked: "Do you believe in the Holy Spirit in the holy church?" [18] This has particular implications for the discernment of truth among the followers of Jesus. It is the whole church which is endowed with the Spirit of truth, and it is the whole church, in different ways and through different gifts, that the Spirit leads into all truth. Discerning the truth and discerning the will of God belong to the whole people of God, lay and ordained together, under the leadership of the Holy Spirit.

### Anointed in the truth

30. In the Old Testament, God spoke through individual prophets, each inspired by his Spirit. Through the prophet Joel, God promised the day of the Lord when he would pour out his Spirit on all humanity:

Then afterwards:

> I will pour out my spirit on all flesh;
> your sons and your daughters shall prophesy,
> your old men shall dream dreams,
> and your young men shall see visions.
> Even on the male and female slaves,
> in those days, I will pour out my spirit. (Joel 2:28-29)

31. Peter understands the extraordinary events of the day of Pentecost as the fulfilment of Joel's prophecy (cf. Acts 2:14-21). The new community of believers in the Risen Christ, his church, is anointed with the outpouring of the Spirit of truth promised by Jesus (cf. John 14:16f., 15:26, 16:13). While there are still particular individuals within that church who have special gifts of prophecy (cf. Acts 11:27, 15:32 and 21:10-11), the whole community is prophetic, just as the whole community is royal and priestly (cf. 1 Pet. 2:9f.). This is because the church is the body of Christ, so intimately united with him by the Spirit that believers can speak of themselves as being "in Christ". Jesus is the master who teaches the people with authority (cf. Mark 1:22,27; Luke 10:25). He is the anointed one, recognized as the long-expected prophet, sent by God the Father after a long line of prophets (cf. Matt. 21:11; Luke 7:16; John 6:14, 7:40). By our incorporation into Christ through water and the Holy Spirit, we are united to Christ, the "great prophet", and share in his prophetic role.

32. This commission has already affirmed this understanding in previous documents: "The Spirit guides the development of the church. In every age, as the Paraclete, he reminds us of all that Jesus said, leads us into all truth, and enables us to bear witness to salvation in Christ."[19] Maintaining God's people in the truth is "the loving work of the Spirit in the church".[20] The Spirit is seen as "the invisible thread running through the work of the church in the world, enabling our minds to hear and receive the word, enlightening them to understand the word, and giving us tongues to speak the word".[21] It is because the faithful are "in Christ and with Christ" that "they receive the Spirit and are in the Spirit".[22] This Spirit provides in the church "abundant gifts of perception and understanding".[23] Under the leading power of God's love, "the discernment of God's will is the task of the whole people of God".[24] Because of this powerful presence of the Spirit of truth, "the proclaiming community itself becomes a living gospel for all to hear".[25]

33. Further aspects of this mutual understanding have been expressed in our respective dialogues with the Anglican Communion. The Holy Spirit keeps the church under the Lordship of Christ, who never abandons his people, despite the all-too-obvious human

weaknesses of its members. The church's mission to proclaim and safeguard the gospel involves the whole people of God, lay people as well as ordained ministers:

> The people of God as a whole is the bearer of the living Tradition. In changing situations producing fresh challenges to the gospel, the discernment, actualization and communication of the word of God is the responsibility of the whole people of God. The Holy Spirit works through all members of the community, using the gifts he gives to each for the good of all. [26]

Some, however, "may rediscover or perceive more clearly than others certain aspects of saving truth". [27] We need, therefore, to "create the necessary conditions to foster a prepared and committed laity and clergy, both being necessary for the life and mission of a faithful church". [28]

34. The role of the lay faithful as essential witnesses to the gospel is affirmed in each of our churches. "All Christians are called to minister wherever Christ would have them serve and witness in deeds and words that heal and free." [29] Christ continues to carry out his prophetic task not only through ordained ministers "but also through the laity whom he constitutes his witnesses and equips with an understanding of the faith and a grace of speech (cf. Acts 2:17-18; Rev. 19:10), precisely so that the power of the gospel may shine forth in the daily life of family and society". [30]

35. Several key points emerge. It is the Holy Spirit who empowers the whole people of God in the work of witness and mission. The whole body of believers, lay and ordained together, is called to the task of proclamation of the gospel. It is the whole church which remains rooted in a communion of faith and life with the apostles themselves, faithful to their teaching and mission.

*Abiding in the truth*

36. Because Christ's faithful are incorporated into him through baptism, they share in Christ's priestly, prophetic and royal office, together as a community of faith and individually each in their own way. "All the faithful share in understanding and handing on revealed truth. They have received the anointing of the Holy Spirit, who instructs them and guides them into all truth." [31] The "theological task is both individual and communal" and "requires the participation of all... because the mission of the church is to be carried out by everyone who is called to discipleship". [32]

37. The church's "abiding in the truth" is the fruit of the powerful and manifold presence of the Holy Spirit in and among those who believe in Jesus Christ. A God-given sense or instinct is aroused and sustained in each believer by the Spirit of truth. This gift is an aspect of the gift of faith. It makes it possible for believers to recognize and respond to the word of God, to discern truth from falsehood in matters of faith and morals, to gain deeper insights into what they believe and to apply that belief to daily life. The Spirit, however, does not guarantee each person's exercise of this "insight into the faith" (*sensus fidei*). Individuals and groups can fall away from the truth and from holiness of life; the pilgrim church today is, as it always has been, a community of saints and sinners. Each person's "I believe" should participate fully in the communal "we believe" of Christ's church: "Faith is always personal but never private, for faith incorporates the believing individual into the community of faith." [33] It is the corporate belief of the whole people of God that is protected from error by the abiding presence of the Holy Spirit. The "faith-

ful" are those who, ideally, are full of God's gift of faith, a faith which is the faith of Christ's church, his body anointed with the Spirit of truth.

38. In its 1978 statement on authority, the then English Roman Catholic-Methodist committee affirmed that Methodists and Catholics "agree that Jesus promised to the church his presence and protection until the end of the age; to it he promised the Spirit of truth always; against it the powers of hell will never prevail".[34] Catholics and Methodists teach that absolute authority belongs properly only to God who has revealed himself supremely in the Word incarnate, Jesus Christ. We affirm together that this revelation is communicated to us by witnesses who, by God's call and gift, share in the divine authority. Their witness is found above all in the apostolic preaching, scripture and various organs of the continuing church.[35]

### Preserved in the truth

39. Methodists and Catholics believe that the Spirit preserves in Christ's church the revelation given for our salvation, although we are not yet completely agreed on what doctrines are essential. Both acknowledge the scriptures as their primary and permanent norm, to be interpreted authoritatively by the living voice of Tradition. Together we also affirm both the human frailty and the God-given indefectibility of Christ's church. The treasure of the mystery of Christ is held in the earthen vessel of the daily life of the pilgrim church, a community always in need of purification and reform.

40. Methodists emphasize that because human beings as creatures and sinners are fallible, "human witnesses may never in principle be exempt from the possibility of error, and the authority of the witness is to that extent always open to question". Methodists trust, however, that

> God always keeps witnesses sufficiently faithful to himself for saving knowledge of himself to be available. As they seek the truth of God, and his will for them in particular situations, Methodists believe that they are led by the Holy Spirit.[36]

41. Catholics emphasize that in order to preserve his church in the purity of the apostolic faith, Christ shares his own gift of infallibility with his community, so that it adheres unfailingly to this faith and hands on from generation to generation what has been "handed down from the apostles".[37] It is the whole community of believers, united with Christ by the Spirit, which is the recipient of the charism of infallibility (protection from error). When the community is united in belief "from the bishops to the last of the faithful", its faith cannot be in error.[38] Both the First and Second Vatican Councils taught that when the bishops together with the pope at their head, or the pope as successor of St Peter and head of the college of bishops, authoritatively define a doctrine of faith, it is the church's own charism of infallibility which is at work in them in a special way.[39] All such protection from error is totally the gift of God to his church, the Spirit of truth being strong amid the weakness of believers. Its purpose is to ensure the church's faithful service of proclaiming the good news of Jesus Christ to all the world.

42. Catholics and Methodists believe that God alone is the absolute truth. All members of the church on earth are fallible creatures and sinners in need of the mercy of God. The church is totally dependent on the active presence of the Holy Spirit in every aspect of its life and teaching.

*Co-workgroups in the truth*

43. The whole community of faith has been sealed with the gift of the Holy Spirit. It is the same Spirit who both awakens each believer's "insight into the faith" and who guides and guards the official teachers of the church. Taking account of the communal sense of all the faithful is integral to the process of authoritative discernment of the truth: this participation is something much richer than a mere opinion poll or referendum on matters of faith. All believers together are "co-workers with the truth" (3 John 8), with a co-responsibility for discerning and proclaiming the truth of the gospel, always under the leading power of the Spirit of truth. Authoritative discernment and proclamation can never be understood properly in isolation from the anointing by the Spirit of all the baptized, individually and together.

44. "Abiding in the truth" is a dynamic process led by the Spirit. Every believer has a part to play, listening to and reflecting on the word of God spoken afresh to each generation. The graced insights of individuals and groups of Christians can enrich the pilgrim church in its deeper penetration into the truth of the gospel:

> This tradition which comes from the apostles progresses in the church under the assistance of the Holy Spirit. There is growth in understanding of what is passed on, both the words and the realities they signify. This comes about through contemplation and study by believers, who "ponder these things in their hearts" (cf. Luke 2:19,51); through the intimate understanding of spiritual things which they experience; and through the preaching of those who, succeeding in the office of bishop, receive the sure charism of truth.[40]

Put more poetically,

> Come, Holy Ghost, our hearts inspire,
> Let us thine influence prove;
> Source of the old prophetic fire,
> Fountain of life and love.
> God through himself we then shall know,
> If thou within us shine;
> And sound, with all thy saints below,
> The depths of love divine.[41]

45. Because of the anointing of the whole community of faith with the Spirit of truth, every Christian shares in Christ's role as prophet and teacher, totally dependent upon him and needing to listen to his word of life. There should be no conflict within the prophetic people of God between the role of the laity and that of ordained ministers, for "in the church there is diversity in ministry, but unity in mission".[42] The diverse gifts bestowed by the Spirit serve the building up of the body of Christ "until all of us come to the unity of the faith and of the knowledge of the Son of God, to maturity, to the measure of the full stature of Christ" (Eph. 4:13). The Roman Catholic and Methodist perspectives on this are presented in this Commission's last document, *The Word of Life*:

> Wesley knew that, in the mind and the heart of the deeply convinced Christian believer, the Holy Spirit is ever at work, bonding the exercise of particular spiritual gifts into unity with the exercise of complementary gifts in all the other members of the body of Christ, the church. (§57)

In the perspective of Vatican II, this action of the Spirit brings about an interdependence in communion between the spiritual instinct of the whole body of the faithful and those who are empowered to make normative acts of discernment of what is, or is not, faithful to the Christian tradition. (§58)

*Called by the truth*

46. The interaction between the Spirit-led community and the Spirit-filled individual begins at baptism, when the gathered community, making present the body of Christ, invokes the Holy Spirit on the one to be baptized:

> Pour out your Holy Spirit
> that the one to be baptized in this water
> may die to sin,
> be raised with Christ,
> and be born to new life in the family of your church.[43]

Similarly when Catholics are confirmed and Methodists received into full membership, the prayer of the community is that the candidate may be confirmed by the Holy Spirit and may continue as God's servant for ever. Thus all the faithful have received the anointing of the Holy Spirit, and are constantly renewed by that Spirit in partaking together in the eucharist, as "the body of Christ and the community of the Holy Spirit".[44] The Holy Spirit is also invoked in a particular way on those who are discerned to have been called for the task of ordained ministry.

47. All the faithful are called and anointed by the Spirit to proclaim the gospel. This proclamation will always require a clear and unequivocal proclamation of our faith that "Jesus is Lord". The church's faith, its "abiding in the truth", is expressed in words but also proclaimed by witness in deeds (cf. 1 Pet. 2:12). Through wordless witness, Christians can "stir up irresistible questions in the hearts of those who see how they live".[45] This radiant witness is a silent, powerful and effective proclamation of the good news, inspired and made possible by the Spirit of truth. "Abiding in the truth" includes not only "speaking the truth in love" but also "doing the truth in love" (Eph. 4:15).

## III. Means of grace, servants of Christ and his church

48. Methodists and Roman Catholics affirm that the whole community of believers is called together by God our Father, placed under the Lordship of the Risen Christ, united with Christ as his body, and has the Holy Spirit as the source of its unity of life, worship and witness. In the Father's purpose for the church, each and every believer is to participate in the mission of the Son and the Holy Spirit, bringing God's outgoing, all-embracing and transforming love to all humanity. The church is "a community both of worship and of mission".[46] It is a community of faith called to preach and proclaim to the world the gospel of Jesus Christ, "good news of a great joy which will come to all the people" (Luke 2:10). Catholics and Methodists are firmly united in the passionate conviction that the gospel is offered to all.[47] The work of spreading the gospel is impaired if believers

are not truly one in the gospel of Christ, united in love and in truth. Our connection and communion with one another serve our growth towards holiness and our sharing in God's mission. Growth in unity is the work of the Holy Spirit, who leads believers into all love and all truth. As this joint commission affirmed in 1981, "To maintain God's people in the truth is the loving work of the Spirit in the church."[48] Methodists and Catholics agree that Jesus promised his presence and protection to the church until the end of time. He continues to endow his church with the Spirit of truth and holiness. God's faithfulness means that the powers of evil will never prevail against the church, as it engages in its mission for the salvation of the world (cf. Matt. 16:18).

## Servants and agents of God

49.  Christ's church is totally dependent on the free gift of God's grace for every aspect of its life and work. Apart from Christ we can do nothing (cf. John 15:5). Methodists and Catholics agree, however, that God works through people as servants, signs and instruments of his presence and action. Although God is not limited to such ways of working, we joyfully affirm together that God freely chooses to work through the service of human communities and individuals, empowered by his grace. The whole church is called to be a channel of God's grace to the world; within the church individuals and institutions become agents of the Lord and thus servants of their brothers and sisters. Such ministries are a gift of God to his church.

## Unity in diversity

50.  There has always been a wide variety of service in the church, carried out by lay people and ordained ministers in partnership. The diverse gifts in the body of Christ are complementary, and serve together the church's communion and connection in love and in truth. Ephesians 4:11 bears witness to the ministry of apostles, prophets, evangelists, pastors and teachers. Romans 12:7-8 refers to ministry, teaching, exhorting and leading, all as gifts. First Corinthians 12 makes clear that the gifts of the Holy Spirit are integrated and to be exercised in harmony. The New Testament repeatedly emphasizes that their purpose is to serve the whole body of Christ, enabling the community of believers to fulfill the mission in and for the world given to it by Christ.

51.  The ministry of oversight (*episcope*) is of key importance among these forms of service. Pastoral oversight has always included authoritative teaching and preaching, for unity in love and unity in truth belong together. Methodists and Catholics affirm together the place within the community of believers of authoritative servants of communion and connection in love and in truth, authorized agents of discerning and proclaiming the truth of the gospel. In the early church, the ministry of pastoral and doctrinal oversight was primarily exercised by bishops. In the Catholic communion, the college of bishops united with the pope exercises supreme oversight. Among Methodists, it is Conference which exercises oversight, with full authority within the church for the formulation and interpretation of doctrine. Within or alongside such structures of servant leadership, there have always been charismatic individuals whose personal ministry has been vital for the life of Christ's church. John Wesley himself stands out as such a person. Catholics and

Methodists affirm together that God chooses to use such individuals as well as visible structures to touch the lives of his people.

## Means of grace

52. "The Word was made flesh, and lived among us" (John 1:14). God's Son entered human history as one of us, taking upon himself human life and suffering. After the pattern of the incarnation, God continues to make visible the Invisible, and calls men and women to be signs and channels of the divine presence. A key point of agreement between Methodists and Roman Catholics is the need for graced, free and active participation in God's saving work.

> In the calling of disciples and the giving of the Holy Spirit, God committed himself to working with his people (2 Cor. 1:5-7, 6:1). The first Christians knew that they were called to participate in God's mission and to proclaim God's reign as Jesus had done (Luke 10:9,11; John 20:20-3). The church's calling remains the same.[49]

This is true not only of God's working through the church for the salvation of all humanity, but also within the community of the church. God chooses to work with, through and in various ministers and their ministries. Believers become God's co-workers (cf. 1 Cor. 3:9), they working with God and God working in them (cf. 2 Cor. 6:1). In all of this they rely on the primacy of God's grace over all human limitations and weaknesses, and on the invisible, active and powerful presence of the Holy Spirit who blows where he wills.

53. Methodists and Roman Catholics agree that God uses means of grace which are trustworthy channels. In this context, the joint commission has recognized the need to explore together more deeply the meaning of "sacrament". Its earlier report, *Towards a Statement on the Church*, began to do so, specifically with reference to baptism and eucharist. Sacraments are "outward signs of inward grace consisting of actions and words by which God encounters his people".[50]

Those actions of the church which we call sacraments are effective signs of grace because they are not merely human acts. By the power of the Holy Spirit they bring into our lives the life-giving action and even the self-giving of Christ himself. It is Christ's action that is embodied and made manifest in the church's actions which, responded to in faith, amount to a real encounter with the risen Jesus.[51]

Also, at the end of *The Apostolic Tradition*, reflecting on ordained ministry, the commission pointed to the need for "deeper common reflection on the nature of sacrament".[52]

54. In *The Word of Life* the discussion of the sacramental life begins with Christ himself as the "primary sacrament", "both the sign of our salvation and the instrument by which it is achieved". As incorporated into Christ, "the church may analogously be thought of in a sacramental way".[53] *Towards a Statement on the Church* already described the church as "enabled to serve as sign, sacrament and harbinger of the kingdom of God in the time between the times" and also affirmed that "Christ works through his church".[54]

The mystery of the Word made flesh and the sacramental mystery of the eucharist point towards a view of the church based upon the sacramental idea, i.e. the church takes its shape from the incarnation from which it originated and the eucharistic action by which its life is constantly being renewed.[55]

The church's mission is "none other than a sharing in the continuing mission of the Son and the Holy Spirit expressing the Father's love for all humankind"; "such participation in the mission of Christ is possible only because of the outpouring of the Holy Spirit".[56]

55. The sacraments are seen as particular instances of the revelation of the divine mystery. They "flow from the sacramental nature of God's self-communication to us in Christ. They are specific ways in which, by the power of the Holy Spirit, the Risen Jesus makes his saving presence and action effective in our midst."[57] Christ addressed himself in signs, in actions and in words to those who came to him in faith: "After Christ's passion, death and resurrection, the Saviour continues his words and actions among us by means of sacramental signs."[58] Roman Catholics understand seven rites, including ordination, as sacraments in the full sense of the word, although they consider baptism and the eucharist as foundational. Methodists affirm the full sacramental nature only of baptism and eucharist (as directly instituted by Christ), but they consider other practices also as "means of grace".[59]

56. Catholics too distinguish "sacraments" from other means of grace. A sacrament is a guaranteed means of grace, rooted in God's covenant to be with his people. Christ freely commits himself to be powerfully present through these signs, although we grow in holiness only as we respond with faith active in love. Christ covenants himself to work in these particular ways so that all may benefit from his faithful love. Catholics understand this commitment by the Risen Lord to be present in the sacraments as a practical outworking of his promise to be with his church until the end of time (cf. Matt. 28:20). Confidence in Christ's presence and action in the sacraments is grounded in God's faithfulness to the people he has chosen. Catholics believe that God also uses other rites and forms of ministry as means of grace even if they do not regard them as sacraments.

57. In this context Catholics distinguish sacraments from "sacramentals". In the strict sense, sacramentals are signs, instituted by the church and rooted in the baptismal priesthood of all believers. They always include a prayer, often accompanied by a gesture such as the laying-on of hands, the sign of the cross or sprinkling with holy water. Sacramentals do not confer the grace of the Holy Spirit in the same way as sacraments, but by the church's prayer they are intended to help prepare believers to receive and cooperate with God's free gift of grace. Sacramentals include blessings of people and things. Certain blessings consecrate people to God in a special way, or reserve objects and places for sacred use. "Every baptized person is called to be 'a blessing', and to bless."[60]

58. While Methodists affirm only baptism and the Lord's supper as sacraments directly instituted by Christ, they affirm other practices of the Christian life as "instituted means of grace". John Wesley described such means as "ordinary channels"[61] through which God conveys grace. He then used passages from scripture to show that Christ commanded that all Christians use these means and thereby promised grace to be given through them. Such "instituted" means include prayer, studying the scriptures, fasting and works of mercy. By "works of mercy" is meant doing good to our neighbour in both body and soul through such actions as feeding the hungry, clothing the naked, visiting prisoners, instructing and exhorting those seeking God. Thus, along with baptism and the Lord's supper, all of these are instituted means of grace.

59. Methodists also recognize that other practices can be effectual channels of God's grace if they are faithful to scripture and a meeting with Christ is experienced. John Wesley taught that we can trust that God's grace is regularly found in such places. They are thus "prudential means of grace". Celebrating the faith in hymnody and Christian conference are two such practices that have characterized Methodist ecclesial life since its beginning. By "Christian conference", Methodists understand not only the Conferences in which clergy and laity discern the will of God and make decisions about doctrine and discipline, but also other occasions when they gather for personal discernment and to watch over one another in love. Thus, class meetings, Sunday schools, and youth fellowship groups are all examples of prudential means of grace, which are not binding on all Christians everywhere at all times. A faithful community may or may not find them to be effective channels at particular times and places. Further, new means of grace may be discovered for new contexts as the church lives in faithful obedience to the Spirit.

60. In effect, Methodists treat ordination, prayer for healing, declaring the forgiveness of sins, marriage and confirmation as prudential means of grace that have a special status within this larger category. They are not sacraments like baptism and the Lord's supper, yet they have a sacramental quality. They are distinct from other prudential means in that they are grounded in the practices of the apostolic church as attested in scripture. Thus they are properly given liturgical expression in the life of the gathered community of faith. There may be value in exploring further any similarity between the Catholic categories of sacraments and sacramentals, and Wesley's categories of instituted and prudential means of grace.

61. Methodists and Catholics find significant convergence of understanding about the means of grace. We agree that God has promised to be with his church until the end of the age (cf. Matt. 28:20), and that all of the means of grace, whether sacraments or sacramentals, instituted means or prudential means, are channels of God's faithfulness to his promise. Methodists and Catholics affirm that baptism, confirmation and ordination are unrepeatable acts whereby God's grace is conveyed to the recipient in special ways. However, some of our remaining differences centre on whether and how a means of grace may be guaranteed or trustworthy. Catholics ask Methodists how and by what criteria they verify that a particular means is a trustworthy channel of God's grace. Methodists ask Catholics whether the idea of the guaranteed quality of a sacrament takes full account of the weakness, limitations and sinfulness of the human beings called to be agents of God's grace. We need to explore further together our understanding of the guarantee or trustworthiness of God's working through the means of grace in his church. This has an important bearing on our understanding of how God works through ordained ministers in their authoritative discernment and proclamation of the truth of the gospel.

*The call to serve*

62. All Christians, together and individually, are called to serve Christ in the world to the glory of God. This is the setting for understanding the particular roles of bodies such as the Methodist Conference or the college of Catholic bishops. Each is understood as a means of grace within a community of faith which is itself the agent of Christ's saving work in the world. All who minister, ordained and lay, serve a community whose mem-

bers are called to recognize and serve Christ in others. Ministers of Christ meet their Lord in those they serve.

### Ordained ministry

63. Methodists and Roman Catholics agree that by ordination a person is irrevocably called and set apart by God for special service in the community of believers, but this does not involve being separated from that community. It is a special calling within the general calling given to all. This dialogue has often returned to the question of what ordination does. There is much that can be affirmed together. By ordination a person becomes a minister of word and sacrament in the church of Christ. At the heart of all pastoral service by the ordained lies a ministry of oversight for the sake of the connection and communion of the church (cf. 1 Pet. 5:2,4).

64. The joint commission's first report outlined key areas of agreement on ordained ministry. After declaring that "the minister participates in Christ's ministry, acts in Christ's name", the document goes on to speak of the importance of the Holy Spirit in "calling people into the ministry", the "connectional" character of the ministry, the paramount authority of Christ himself in the church. Another significant area of agreement for the continuing dialogue was "the understanding of the ministry as, in some mysterious way, an extension of the incarnational and sacramental principle when human beings (as ministers), through their souls and bodies, become, by the power of the Holy Spirit, agents of Christ for bringing God into the lives and conditions of men" and women.[62] The commission's next report again understood ordained ministry as "the ministry of Christ himself, whose representative the minister is".[63] Increasingly, both Catholics and Methodists understand the ordained minister to represent both Christ and the Christian community. According to that report, Roman Catholics and Methodists also agree that "by ordination a new and permanent relationship with Christ and his church is established":[64] this is the foundation of our common belief that ordination is irrevocable and unrepeatable. In *The Apostolic Tradition* the commission stated that within the community of God's people, an authentic minister "communicates Christ to persons":[65] "as an instrument in God's hands, the ordained minister imparts the word of God to God's people, both by speech and by the sacraments of the church".[66] The report went on, however, to admit that there are remaining differences over the sacramental nature of ordination.[67]

65. Catholics understand ordination as a sacrament singling out men within the church to be living signs and instruments of the continuing pastoral oversight and leadership of Christ himself. It occurs through episcopal laying-on of hands and prayer. Both bishop and presbyter are regarded as "a sacramental representation"[68] of Christ as head to his body, of Christ as shepherd to his flock, of Christ as high priest to his priestly people, of Christ the only teacher to his community of faith. Through the ministry of bishops and presbyters in particular, the living presence of Christ as head of his body and pastor of his people is made visible in the midst of the church. This understanding is the sacramental foundation for Catholic doctrine on the teaching authority of the college of bishops. The first task of bishops, especially when together as the college of bishops, is to proclaim the gospel in its integrity to all. For Catholics, this ministry of authoritative preaching is intimately linked with the ministry of governance and the central liturgical ministry of presiding at the eucharist. All true ministry is pastoral at heart, serving to

draw all people deeper into the mystery of Christ the Shepherd, who gave his life in sacrificial love.

66. Methodists understand ordination as a gift from God to the church. In it men and women who are called by God to this form of ministry are accepted by the Conference after examination. "They are then ordained by prayer and the imposition of hands by the bishop, or the president of the Conference, and given the tasks of declaring the gospel, celebrating the sacraments and caring pastorally for Christ's flock."[69] While Methodists do not understand ordination as a sacrament, it is a liturgical action involving the community's prayer for the gift of the Holy Spirit appropriate to the particular form of ministry. Because this is a life-long and sacred commission, ordination is never repeated. It is understood as entry into a covenant relationship with all other ministers in the service of Christ. Thus, while ordination is a liturgical action, it is normally accompanied closely by the reception of the ordinand into connection with the Conference. Those Methodist churches which set apart or consecrate some ministers as bishops do not consider this a further ordination.

67. Catholics and Methodists hold several aspects of their understandings of ordination in common. Both churches set apart ministers for the church of Jesus Christ. Both churches understand this rite as a means of God's grace whereby the minister is introduced into a covenant relationship of permanent service in Christ's church. This specific form of leadership is always a service both to God and to God's people. It involves administering the sacraments, preaching and teaching the word, and sharing in the ordering of the church's life.

68. We joyfully affirm together that the ministries and institutions of our two communions are means of grace by which the Risen Christ in person leads, guides, teaches and sanctifies his church on its pilgrim path. Such an affirmation can be made only within a community of faith, relying on God's promise and grace: "All ministry continues to depend entirely upon God's grace for its exercise. The God who calls crowns his call with gifts for ministry."[70] Catholics ask Methodists whether they might not use sacramental language, such as has been used of the church itself, of ordained ministry in the church, and of its authoritative discernment of the truth of the gospel. Methodists ask Catholics why, given human weakness and fallibility, they understand ordained ministry not only as a sign but also as a guarantee of the active presence of Christ by the power of the Holy Spirit, especially in particular acts of authoritative discernment and proclamation. These questions lie at the heart of ecumenical dialogue between our two communions.

*The ministry of preaching and teaching*

69. Jesus was recognized as the rabbi or master, who stood out from other teachers because he spoke with authority (cf. Mark 1:22,27; Luke 5:5, 8:24). At the centre of Christ's ministry was the proclamation and teaching of the gospel. Soon after his baptism, Jesus began to proclaim the good news of the reign of God (cf. Mark 1:14). He taught crowds by the seashore, seeking to convey to them the nature of God's reign. In his acts of healing and other deeds of compassion, there was often a message for both recipient and audience. He constantly invited people to believe in him and to recognize that the reign of God was at hand.

70. Led by the Holy Spirit, the whole church, lay people and ordained ministers together, shares Christ's ministry of witnessing to the truth of God's good news. Christ told his followers, "You will receive power when the Holy Spirit has come upon you; and you will be my witnesses in Jerusalem, in all Judaea and Samaria, and to the ends of the earth" (Acts 1:8). Preaching and teaching in this broad sense belong to the mission of all Christians as members of the church called by Christ to make disciples of all nations (cf. Matt. 28:19). Christ's church is a community of interpreters and proclaimers. Both lay people and ordained ministers have complementary gifts of discerning the truth of the gospel and of interpreting how it should best be expressed in a particular cultural setting. Both have the gift and responsibility of witnessing by word and deed to all human beings, that they might be saved and given power to become children of God (cf. John 1:12, 3:16).

*Apostolic oversight*

71. Methodists and Catholics agree that the ministry of the apostles was essential to the proclamation and spread of the good news during the first century. It is clear from the New Testament that different functions and offices were also recognized early in the church as gifts from God, "to equip the saints for the work of ministry, for building up the body of Christ" (Eph. 4:12). Scholars find the historical record diverse, noting that episcopacy as an office developed gradually in a variety of places. Roman Catholic teaching emphasizes that there is nevertheless a collegial succession from the apostles to the bishops. There is agreement between Catholics and Methodists that the ministry of *episcope* (oversight) was always exercised in the church:

> From apostolic times, certain ordained persons have been entrusted with the particular tasks of superintendency. [71]

> During the 2nd and 3rd centuries, a threefold pattern of bishop, presbyter and deacon became established as the pattern of ordained ministry throughout the church. [72]

Both Roman Catholics and Methodists have retained something of that threefold pattern, with (1) bishops or superintendents, (2) elders, presbyters or priests, and (3) deacons.

72. In the early church, bishops became the normal celebrants and preachers for their local churches. Pastoral need, however, led to the development of the pattern of presbyters becoming the leaders of smaller communities, always in communion of faith with their bishop. Preaching and teaching were integral to the ministry of oversight in the early church, as they are today: "Central to the exercise of *episcope* is the task of maintaining unity in the Truth." [73]

73. There was no clear delineation between preaching and teaching in the early church. Preaching often involved the interaction of preacher and congregation, and was integrally related to the rest of the liturgy, particularly the sacraments of baptism and eucharist. It was also a form of basic Christian education. The practice of the early church challenges the harmful separation often practised today with regard to preaching and the eucharistic liturgy on a Sunday. The ministry of the word and the celebration of the sacrament belong together as two means in which the grace of our Lord Jesus Christ is given to God's people.

*Primary means of teaching and discernment*

74. The ministry of oversight (*episcope*) has been exercised among Methodists in two main ways. Firstly, fundamental to Methodism is the Conference, understood as the exercise of corporate *episcope* for the service of the church. In all Methodist churches, it is the Conference that authoritatively discerns the truth of the gospel for the church. Even where Methodism has adopted either life-long or term episcopacy, the Conference remains the instrument through which all matters of faith are discerned and then proclaimed in official teaching: "Conference is the final authority within the church with regard to its doctrines and all questions concerning the interpretation of its doctrines."[74] Conference exercises authority over preachers, and handles matters of discipline. Secondly, for all Methodist churches, a special ministry of oversight or superintendency is exercised by individuals set apart for either a specific term or a life-time of service to God in that office; some of these churches have "superintendents", others have "bishops". The Methodist Church in Great Britain has expressed its willingness to receive the historic episcopate into its life and ministry as and when it is required for the unity of Christians.

75. Roman Catholics readily concur with the description of the teaching role of bishops given in the United Methodist *Book of Discipline*: "To guard, transmit, teach and proclaim, corporately and individually, the apostolic faith as it is expressed in scripture and tradition, and, as they are led and endowed by the Holy Spirit, to interpret that faith evangelically and prophetically."[75] For Catholics, authoritative discernment of truth and faithful teaching are entrusted to the college of bishops united with the pope, which is understood to be endowed by the Holy Spirit with the gift of discernment. The catholicity of the church in both space and time means that the substance of the church's teaching must be the same in all places and all times. Hence, in their role as guardians of the church's unity the bishops seek to ensure that the same faith is being proclaimed now as was discerned by the church in earlier centuries and that the same faith is being taught in all parts of the world today. Nevertheless, important differences in expression and emphasis occur as the gospel is lived and proclaimed in various cultures at various times. Authoritative discernment by bishops does not take place in isolation. They must listen not only to scripture and Tradition, but also to the whole church community. Catholics understand the gift of apostolicity, including the discernment of divine truth, as belonging to the whole church: this is served and guaranteed by the apostolic ministry of the bishops.

76. Both Methodists and Roman Catholics have a strong sense of the corporate nature of the ministry of oversight. This reflects their common emphasis on the connection or communion of local communities of faith with one another in their Christian life, worship and mission. For each Methodist church, Conference exercises a form of corporate *episcope*. For Catholics, it is the college of bishops united with the bishop of Rome that exercises such a corporate *episcope*. The unity of local Catholic communities with one another is constituted and served by their communion with their bishop in a diocese, and the unity of their bishops by communion with the bishop of Rome. Methodists and Catholics affirm together that true Christian faith and discipleship always involve unity with one another in truth and in love. This understanding of the gospel is reflected in our ecclesial structures, which seek to serve the unity of the whole church. Although growth into perfect holiness and love under God's grace is always something deeply personal, it is never private. Both our churches make room for individual ministers who play

special roles of leadership and inspiration within the community, but these are always bound together in collegial responsibility for the faith and mission of believers.

*Participation of the laity in authoritative teaching*

77. Catholics and Methodists both understand that the whole church must be involved in discernment and teaching. Lay people and ordained ministers share this responsibility, but in different ways. Methodists affirm with Catholics that ordination establishes the minister in a new and permanent relationship with the Risen Christ. Hence, both churches understand that while the gift of discernment belongs to the whole church, ordained ministers in the due exercise of their office play a special role. Within local congregations and geographic areas (dioceses, districts, annual conferences) ordained ministers take a leading role in the functions of worship, preaching and teaching. However, there are many lay people, such as local preachers, trained theologians, catechists, Bible study leaders and Sunday school teachers, who also have a calling to teach in the church. Moreover, a vital part is played by people of holy life who teach by their example though they may hold no formal office.

78. There remain differences between Methodists and Roman Catholics concerning what part lay people have in the process of authoritative discernment and proclamation of the gospel. Catholics locate the authoritative determination of teaching in the college of bishops with the bishop of Rome at its head. Methodists locate that same authority in Conference, where lay people sit in significant numbers, with full rights of participation and decision-making.

79. Methodists understand that teaching authority is a gift to the whole church, and suggest that excluding presbyters and lay people from the place of final decision-making denies them the exercise of that gift, thereby weakening the church's ability to discern the faithful interpretation of God's word for a particular time and place. By having representatives of the whole church present in the decision-making body they can hope to hear the variety of perspectives and understandings needed to ensure the catholicity of the church. Lay people do actively participate and contribute in different ways in many areas of the structures of the Roman Catholic Church, for example in pastoral councils, diocesan synods, and meetings of the synod of bishops in Rome. However, Methodists ask Catholics why lay people could not be more formally involved in decision-making bodies, even when authoritative discernment and teaching is concerned, sharing responsibility in some way with the bishops who nevertheless retain their special ministry of authoritative teaching.

80. Catholics understand that the episcopal teaching function is exercised as a service to the whole church. Bishops lead communities of faith which are themselves bearers of the truth of the gospel. They authoritatively discern and proclaim the faith given to the whole people of God. The task of authoritatively ensuring catholicity and apostolicity is entrusted to the college of bishops. Methodists do have an ordained ministry, and a superintendency that has teaching functions. However, Catholics ask Methodists why, in their understanding and practice of the Conference, they do not more formally distinguish the role of ordained ministers, especially bishops and superintendents, particularly where authoritative discernment and teaching are concerned.

*Already agreed*

81. Both Roman Catholics and Methodists affirm that in calling people to be agents in discerning what is truly the gospel, God is using them as means of grace, trustworthy channels. All forms of ministry are communal and collegial. They seek to preserve and strengthen the whole community of faith in truth and in love, in worship and in mission. In both churches, oversight is exercised in a way which includes pastoral care and authoritative preaching and teaching. Methodists and Catholics can rejoice that the Holy Spirit uses the ministries and structures of both churches as means of grace to lead people into the truth of the gospel of Christ. The authority which Jesus bestows is "the authority for mission", and

> the exercise of ministerial authority within the church, not least by those entrusted with the ministry of *episcope*, has a radically missionary dimension… This authority enables the whole church to embody the gospel and to become the missionary and prophetic servant of the Lord.[76]

*For further exploration*

82. Christ has promised his presence and his Spirit to the church, but the implications of this for a fuller understanding of ordained ministry and of authoritative teaching need further exploration together. A significant point of divergence is the idea of a guaranteed or "covenanted" means of grace, and the grounding this gives to the Roman Catholic understanding of the teaching authority of the college of bishops united with the pope. Methodists wonder whether a doctrine of a guaranteed indefectibility of teaching takes full account of human frailty and sinfulness, although Catholics and Methodists agree that God uses mere earthen vessels as his agents, working through human weaknesses and imperfections to proclaim his word. Catholics wonder how, without such a "covenanted" understanding, Methodists can be sure that their preaching and teaching is truly that of Christ and his church. Methodists consider that they can indeed be sure with regard to essentials, but Catholics and Methodists do not yet agree what all those essentials are. Nor is there complete agreement about the participation of lay people in the church's decision-making, especially with regard to authoritative discernment and proclamation of the gospel. Methodists and Catholics are fully agreed, however, that the teaching of the church must always be tested against scripture and Tradition.

*Teaching authority: God's gift to the church*

83. Methodists and Catholics agree that teaching authority rightly exercised is a gift of God to his church, through which Christ exercises the headship of his body by the power of the Holy Spirit.[77] The gospel challenges Christians to reconsider what is meant by "authority", and to exercise it always in the likeness of Christ who came "not to be served, but to serve, and to give his life as a ransom for many" (Mark 10:45). "The heart of Christian ministry is Christ's ministry of outreaching love."[78] This is especially true of any ministry of authoritative leadership among Christians. John Wesley's use of the phrase "watching over one another in love"[79] challenges all individual ministers and collegial bodies, especially those exercising the ministry of oversight. The ministry of

authority should always seek the growth of those over whom it is exercised. Sadly, it has not always been exercised in this way, and all ministers will always be in need of reformation and renewal.

> It is clear that only by the grace of God does the exercise of authority in the communion of the church bear the marks of Christ's own authority. This authority is exercised by fragile Christians for the sake of other fragile Christians. [80]

84. Methodists and Catholics are committed to holiness in living, to faithfulness in teaching, and to participation in God's mission to the world. Our ministries, both individual and collegial, are means of grace which the Spirit of Christ uses as he wills to keep the church one, holy, catholic and apostolic in its life, faith and mission. In our human frailty, we trust together in Christ's promise to keep the church faithful to himself. As Charles Wesley's hymn reminds us, "Fortified by power divine, the church can never fail." [81]

## PART TWO

85. Part One of this report has explored both common understandings and distinct interpretations of the "means of grace" in Christ's church, especially regarding authoritative discernment and proclamation of the truth of the gospel. In this second part, Methodists and Catholics present in more detail how they respectively do this and why. These accounts are offered primarily to enable each tradition better to understand the other. Although these practices are distinctive there are many points of convergence between them.

## I. Methodist understanding and practice

*Historical perspectives*

86. For Methodists, their agents of discernment are shaped by the historical origins of the movement in 18th-century England. They inherited the basic doctrines and structures of the Christian church as mediated through the English Reformation of the 16th century. They believe that John Wesley and the people called Methodist were raised up by God in a particular situation for a particular task, that is, "to reform the nation, particularly the church, and to spread scriptural holiness over the land". [82] Doctrinally, the early Methodists held to the teaching of the Church of England. Wesley emphasized the Anglican doctrinal formularies specifically the thirty-nine Articles of Religion, the Homilies, and especially the *Book of Common Prayer*. For the Anglicans of his day, it was the *Book*

*of Common Prayer* that was the continuing vehicle of Reformation faith in the weekly and daily life of the parishes. Wesley remained true to this expression of the faith throughout his ministry. In addition, Wesley brought to bear his reading of the early church fathers.

87. From the point of view of organization, Methodists believe the Holy Spirit was actively guiding the development of the Methodist movement. Most features of Methodist practice were not planned in advance but discovered as a providential means for accomplishing the mission. "Methodism came down from heaven, as it was wanted, piece by piece", cried one of the preachers in 1836 with exuberant but pardonable exaggeration.[83] Charles Wesley saw clear parallels with the Exodus story:

> Captain of Israel's host, and guide
> of all who seek the land above...
> By thine unerring Spirit led,
> we shall not in the desert stray;
> we shall not full direction need,
> nor miss our providential way;
> as far from danger as from fear,
> while love, almighty love, is near.[84]

88. The early Methodists understood their movement as a revival of genuine Christianity. They sought to bring the truth of the gospel once again to the minds of the people, and share the life-changing love of God with those who did not know it in their hearts. For them, the truth of the gospel was the message of God's love for all and God's demand that people love God and neighbour in return. Theirs was a prophetic ministry, proclaiming salvation, both individual and social, to their contemporaries.

89. Given the situation in 18th-century England, certain themes needed to be highlighted. In particular, Wesley focused most of his preaching and teaching on the doctrines dealing most directly with salvation: original sin, justification and sanctification. He saw here the "general tenor of scripture" which he understood to be the "analogy of faith", that is, the sense of the whole message of scripture which serves as the key for interpreting individual passages. In view of the relatively low level of spiritual life in England at his time and the difficulties that the church had in reaching new areas of population, this focus on soteriology was the best way in which to accomplish the mission which had been set before him. However, Wesley saw his societies as existing within the Church of England. His Anglican inheritance, including his acceptance of the ancient creeds and his study of patristic sources, joined him to the Church catholic. Several times he indicated that Methodism was nothing new; rather it was "the old religion, the religion of the Bible, the religion of the primitive church, the religion of the Church of England".[85] In his publications he sought to teach his preachers and indeed all of the Methodist people what the whole of the Christian faith had to offer. The fifty volumes of his Christian library include authors from the early church, later Catholicism, the Reformation, Puritan Dissenters and the Anglican Divines. The hymns of his brother, Charles Wesley, were a powerful vehicle for teaching the Christian faith to the common people.

90. The goal was to spread scriptural holiness, and this mission led to the recruitment of lay and ordained preachers. Often in the face of official opposition and popular scorn,

they travelled widely, preaching the gospel to the disinherited, gathering people into societies and exercising pastoral oversight of them. The preachers met in Conference for the first time in 1744 for the purpose of guiding the revival. There were precedents in the Church of England. For example, other privately organized societies were developing which governed their work through meetings of their leaders, and at the most official level, the constitution of the Church of England allowed for convocations. Thus, a conciliar approach to discern the will of God for their movement appeared to them as the most appropriate way to proceed.

91. For early Methodists, the Conference exemplified the social character of Christianity. It had several functions. First, it determined the practical doctrine of the Methodist preachers ("what to teach"). Second, it was a place of education and encouragement ("how to teach"). Third, it supervised the mission of the church and the deployment of ministers ("what to do"). [86] Fourth, it was an occasion for holding the preachers accountable for what they preached and how they lived. While it is true that Wesley had final control of the decisions of Conference, he was influenced by the conferring. For both Britain and Ireland, a decision was made in 1784 that the Conference would exist after Wesley's death. A legal deed was executed providing for the corporate continuation of Methodism. In effect, the Conference was regarded as "the living Wesley". Thus, the functions of determining doctrine, exercising discipline, and stationing the preachers for the sake of mission were all lodged in the Conference.

92. The American situation was somewhat different. In light of the political independence and the great need for pastoral care, Wesley took steps to provide for American Methodism a liturgy, an ordained ministry and a general superintendency. The last was received by the Americans on condition that the Conference of preachers would elect superintendents, soon called bishops, in the Methodist Episcopal church. While the Conference exercised the authority for doctrinal decisions, the bishops were its leaders and had sole authority in stationing the preachers.

93. From 1816, the bishops had responsibility for supervising the course of study, an educational programme for the preachers. The bishops themselves were itinerant, as they said in their notes to the 1798 *Book of Discipline*: "Our grand plan, in all its parts, leads to an itinerant ministry. Our bishops are travelling bishops. All the different orders which compose our conferences are employed in the travelling line. Every thing is kept moving as far as possible." [87] In many ways, they exercised informal teaching authority. Francis Asbury and Thomas Coke functioned as teachers of the church through their preaching and their editing of the *Doctrines and Discipline*. Nevertheless, the final authority in doctrinal matters rested with what became the General Conference. In 1830 a group of Methodist laity and clergy formed the Methodist Protestant church, and for the first time added an equal number of lay persons to the membership of the Conference. Other branches added a significant lay representation at later dates, and the practice is now universal.

*Conference*

94. Wesley reckoned "Christian conference" among the prudential means of grace, found to be trustworthy channels used by God to help shape the lives of God's people. The Methodist Conference is a gathering of lay and ministerial leaders for worship, dis-

cernment of God's will, and deciding how best to follow faithfully the Spirit's leading. Bringing together the diversities of the people of God – whether of race, gender, nationality, theological opinion or moral judgment – they seek to "speak the truth in love" to each other as they discern the truth of the gospel for their age and place. As the Spirit directs, they seek to proclaim that truth apostolically and prophetically to the whole world in the name of God.

95. Historically, the inclusion of lay persons in Conference was part of a wider cultural trend which held that ultimate authority under God was given to the entire community. In the political sphere, this trend gave the right to vote to the adult population of many countries. Theologically, Methodists regard all Christians as a ministerial and priestly people. Various gifts of authority – whether in doctrinal, financial, disciplinary or organizational matters – are given to both ordained and lay. This is the theological foundation for including both in Conference.

96. Today, a Methodist Conference is the organizing centre of ecclesial life and has at least six functions:

- It is the gathering point and chief instrument of connection. There is a family feeling of reunion when Conference meets.

- It exercises corporate *episcope* and oversees the whole life of the church, including doctrine and discipline for the sake of mission.

- It has final authority over doctrine. Methodist Conferences have always accepted the scriptures as the supreme rule of faith and practice, and have been guided in their reading of them by Wesley's *Sermons and Explanatory Notes Upon the New Testament*. In understanding these authorities, the Conference is the final interpreter.

- It exercises its authority also by approving service books and hymn books to communicate doctrinal matters to the people. Through these the faith is taught and maintained by the local congregations.

- It provides for the orderly transmission of ministry by authorizing ordination. Even where there are bishops, the decision to ordain is the prerogative of the Conference. Ordination takes place during the Conference by prayer and the laying-on of hands, invoking the Holy Spirit.

- It elects its bishops and presidents. For most Methodist churches they serve for a limited term. Some churches elect their bishops (who serve as presidents of their annual Conferences) for life.

*Developments within contemporary Methodism*

97. In some parts of Methodism that historically have not had bishops, those exercising oversight, such as district chairpersons, are sometimes being given the title "bishop". Some Methodist churches have formally stated that their bishops should exercise a teaching office, with responsibility

> to guard, transmit, teach and proclaim, corporately and individually, the apostolic faith as it is expressed in scripture and Tradition, and as they are led and endowed by the Spirit, to interpret that faith evangelically and prophetically. [88]

98. Originating in the Oecumenical Methodist Conference of 1881, the World Methodist Council has been developing closer ties and a stronger teaching function for the world-wide family of Methodist churches. It is developing structures for consultation, teaching, and common action for mission. Its recent publication of Wesleyan *Essentials of Christian Faith* (1996) and its role in ecumenical dialogues have strengthened its function in these areas. Also, wherever Conference is held for an entire church, official representatives from other Methodist churches are invited. In addition, official letters are exchanged and other relationships between Conferences are developing. Regional associations of bishops from different Methodist churches have been formed to further common witness. During the 19th century the Methodists split into many different denominations. The 20th century has seen a trend towards unity both through different churches merging and through closer ties of cooperation between existing churches. As a rule where Methodists have entered into United churches, such churches have become members of the World Methodist Council and by their commitment to Christian unity have made a significant contribution to World Methodism. Given the growth of Methodism in Asia, Africa and Latin America, its churches are becoming increasingly diverse and yet simultaneously more unified.

## II. Catholic understanding and practice

99. The Catholic Church is a communion of Eastern and Latin churches, in each of which the church of Christ is truly present.[89] Invisible communion with Christ is experienced in the church's visible communion in love and truth. The church is united in a way that is enriched by and transcends geographical and cultural diversity. It stands in living communion with the church of the past while at the same time looking to the church of the future. Its communion through time extends back to the apostles themselves (cf. Rev. 21:14), who remain the foundations of the church in its life and mission, and who continue now to guide it. Christ himself leads the church through Peter and the other apostles, and through those who share and continue their ministry today, the pope and the rest of the college of bishops.

100. Catholic unity involves holding in common all the doctrines of the church. There is room in this Catholic unity for diversity of theological insight and expression, plurality of liturgical rites and canonical discipline. It allows for debate and discussion, but not for disunity in matters of faith. There have been times in the history of the Catholic Church when the tension between unity in truth and diversity of perspectives has not always been healthy and harmonious.

### Bishops

101. Among various ministries and charisms exercised in the church from earliest times, the primary service from the beginning is that of the bishop. Catholics understand the college of bishops as continuing the care of the apostles for all the churches. Bishops, assisted by presbyters and deacons, are called to lead into holiness, serving the church's unity with Christ by word and sacrament. The Second Vatican Council taught that the fullness of the sacrament of orders is given by ordination to the episcopate. At the heart

of the bishop's ministry is pastoral service of the unity of the church in love and in truth. To be effective instruments in this service, bishops must have the authority necessary to ensure the unity so essential to the church's life and mission.

102. As unity in love and unity in truth belong together, so do pastoral leadership and teaching authority, both focused above all in the celebration of the eucharist. Apostolic communities need people to proclaim the gospel with authority, themselves under the authority of Christ himself. There is "an interdependence in communion between the spiritual instinct of the whole body of the faithful and those who are empowered to make normative acts of discernment of what is, or is not, faithful to the Christian tradition".[90] This is the specific teaching role of the bishops in the church: "The task of authentic interpretation of God's word in scripture and Tradition has been entrusted only to the church's living teaching office, whose authority is exercised in the name of Jesus Christ."[91]

103. The church's teaching office (magisterium) is not above God's word, but serves the word. It teaches only what has been received. As teachers, bishops should first listen to the word, then ponder it in their hearts, with awe before the mystery of divine revelation, and then put it forward in purity.[92]

104. Bishops are members of the faithful entrusted with a special service in the name of Christ. The church is a community under the authority of the Risen Lord. It is Christ who is the overseer of the church, exercising an invisible *episcope* over its faith and life, its worship and mission (cf. 1 Pet. 2:25).

105. Catholics understand the invisible leadership of Christ as pastor and teacher to be exercised in many ways, especially through the college of bishops. Bishops are signs and instruments of Christ as head and shepherd of his church, and so share in the authority by which Christ himself builds up, teaches and sanctifies his body. This understanding of the ministry of bishops is essential to a Catholic presentation of their teaching authority, exercised in Christ's name but always as a service to the communion of the churches in love and in truth.

106. Pre-eminent among the duties of a bishop is the proclamation of the gospel.[93] Bishops serve as heralds of the faith and teachers who share in Christ's gift of authority. Christ himself wills to work through them to preserve the church unfailingly in the truth. There are many ways in which a bishop may teach with authority: in pastoral letters to his diocese; at diocesan gatherings; through involvement in national and international commissions and assemblies; through homilies in his cathedral or parishes; in celebrating the eucharist which is the source of the "holy communion" of the churches in Christ. The bishop is the teacher of the local church and, with his brother bishops, of the universal church. He proclaims with authority a faith already lived in the church he serves. With love he both listens to and speaks to the church which is led by the Spirit of truth. The teaching of any individual bishop in itself is not guaranteed to be preserved from error by the Holy Spirit, and there have been and can be bishops whose teaching and way of life are contrary to the gospel entrusted to them. A bishop's teaching is always more fruitful when he speaks the truth in love, bearing witness to that truth not only by his words but also by a life of holiness.

107. The authority of a bishop as chief pastor and teacher of a diocese is both territorial and personal. As territorial it extends to all the baptized in the diocese. As personal it implies particular care for priests and deacons, especially those of his diocesan clergy,

and for the religious communities located in the diocese. In both instances the exercise of episcopal responsibility requires frequent consultation with priests and people. Each diocese is mandated to develop consultative structures. On the one hand, priests and deacons authorized by a bishop share in the liturgical, teaching and pastoral ministry, and priests must be consulted by means of a presbyteral council. On the other hand, lay people also collaborate with bishops and priests in liturgical, teaching and pastoral ministry and they are consulted in many ways, especially through parish councils, pastoral councils, and diocesan synods. Lay people have specific responsibilities in catechetics, education and communication, in ecumenical and inter-religious dialogue, and in the missionary outreach of the church. In these and many other ways, they contribute to the teaching ministry of the church.

108.  By its very nature as a service to the communion of the church, the ministry of the bishop is properly exercised in communion with his fellow bishops. The bishop can only teach and lead in an authoritative way if he is united in communion of mind and heart with the bishops across the world and through the ages. The catholic unity of bishops with the faith of the church from the apostles is expressed through ordination in apostolic succession: the college of bishops today, in continuity with the college of apostles, receives new members through prayer and the laying-on of hands. One way in which this is signified is the requirement that under ordinary circumstances at least three bishops must be involved in the ordination of another bishop. The catholic unity of bishops with the universal church today is expressed in and served by their living communion with the bishop of Rome. United with him, the bishops together are the supreme authority in the church. Their service of teaching with authority is exercised above all at an ecumenical council. They can also teach in other gatherings (e.g., the synod of bishops, episcopal conferences and synods of Eastern Catholic churches) and each teaches in his own diocese.

109.  When bishops exercise their supreme teaching authority, the Holy Spirit guides and protects their discerning and proclaiming of the truth of the gospel. Those who are successors of the apostles have received from the Lord the spiritual gift of authoritatively proclaiming the true faith. This is a gift (charism) from the Lord, and like all charismata (cf. 1 Cor. 12-13) must be exercised in love. The sure charism of truth is given to all the bishops in apostolic succession, not so as to reveal new doctrines but to ensure the faithfulness of the church to the word of God.

110.  At an ecumenical council, the bishops, in communion with the bishop of Rome, may solemnly proclaim by a definitive act a doctrine pertaining to faith or morals. Catholics believe that when they do so, the bishops are preserved from error by the Holy Spirit, so that "the whole flock of Christ is preserved and progresses in unity of faith".[94] This preservation from error is what is meant by the "infallibility" of their proclamation of doctrine. In definitions of doctrine the truth of faith is unfailing, but that does not imply that the manner in which they are formulated, promulgated or presented could not be improved. In a living tradition, there is always room for further theological reflection and exploration of doctrine. This is part of the process of reception of the teaching and its appropriation in the faith-life of the community. A doctrine can only be defined if it coheres with other doctrines. Such statements do not add to the truth of the gospel, but serve to clarify the church's developing understanding of it, and help to discern what is and is not in conformity with the apostolic Tradition. Definitions of doctrine are intended to light the pilgrim path of faith and make it secure. Bishops also teach the truth of the

gospel infallibly whenever, even though dispersed throughout the world, they are in agreement in authoritatively teaching a matter of faith to be definitively held, while maintaining their communion among themselves and with the bishop of Rome.

## The bishop of Rome

111. As each local church (diocese) has a focus for its unity in love and in truth, so also do the local churches of the world in the communion of the universal church.[95] The local church of Rome has a primacy in love among the churches, and its bishop is the visible head of the college of bishops.

112. Catholics find a biblical basis for this service of primacy exercised by the bishop of Rome in Jesus' words to Simon Peter, "You are Peter, and on this rock I will build my church" (Matt. 16:19), read in the light of the last instructions to Peter, "Feed my lambs... feed my sheep... follow me" (John 21:15,17,22). The prolongation of the Petrine primacy in the Roman primacy is supported by the commissioning of Peter to strengthen his brothers (cf. Luke 22:32). Catholics recognize that the special position and role of the local church of Rome, and the distinctive ministry of its bishop, developed gradually in the early church, and the manner of its exercise continues to evolve. The joint commission has explored this in some depth in its report *Towards a Statement on the Church*.[96]

113. The pope's ministry to all his brother bishops and their churches is a pastoral service of the universal church's unity in love and truth. He is "the first servant of unity".[97] In order that this ministry may be effective, the jurisdiction of the bishop of Rome is "universal", "ordinary" and "immediate". His primatial authority is "universal" because it is at the service of the communion of all the churches. It is "ordinary" in that it belongs to him in virtue of his office, rather than as delegated by others. It is "immediate" in order to enable him, when necessary for the good of the universal church, and in faithfulness to the gospel, to act anywhere in order to preserve the church's unity in truth and in love. This authority is truly episcopal. As a fellow bishop, with a ministry of headship among them and for them, the pope serves the unity of the bishops that they in turn may serve the unity of their churches. The pope serves from within the college of bishops, as servant of the servants of God. As confirmed by the First Vatican Council and by Pope Pius IX, the primacy of the Roman pontiff is there not to undermine the bishops but to support and sustain them in their ministry as vicars of Christ.[98]

114. This universal primacy of the pope is a primacy of love, and his teaching authority is a central dimension of that primacy. The universal church can remain united in love only if it is united in faith. In service of the catholicity and apostolicity of the church's faith, and of the bishops' collegial responsibility for authentic discernment and proclamation of that faith, the pope is understood to be given, when needed, the charism of infallibly proclaiming true doctrine. When he makes a definition in this way, he is pronouncing judgment not as a private person but as the head of the college of bishops and chief pastor and teacher of the church, in whom the charism of the infallibility of the church itself is individually present.[99]

115. Catholics believe that St Peter's role of serving the unity of the community of faith "must continue in the church so that under her sole Head, who is Jesus Christ, she may be visibly present in the world as the communion of all his disciples".[100] Because of his

special ministry within the Catholic Church, the bishop of Rome also has a particular duty to foster the unity in faith and love of all Christians.

116. To say that the bishops in union with the pope teach and shepherd in the name of Christ is not to claim divine authority for all they say and do. Like Peter and the other apostles, the bishop of Rome and his fellow bishops are aware of their human weakness and their special need for continuing transformation of heart and life. The faithful exercise of their ministry in the church derives from grace and depends totally upon grace, just as the whole church is "founded upon the infinite power of grace".[101]

*Conclusion*

117. Both Methodists and Catholics trust the unfailing presence and grace of the Holy Spirit to preserve them in faithfulness and to protect the truth of the gospel they preach and teach. The Catholic Church recognizes this presence of the Spirit especially in the charism of unfailing truth and faith which is given to bishops in the church. The exercise of the ministry of teaching by bishops takes many forms and includes the special ministry of the bishop of Rome in proclaiming the faith of all the bishops and of the whole church. Methodists recognize the guidance of the Holy Spirit in Methodist Conferences though they do not ascribe to them a guaranteed freedom from error. At the same time, they accept their teaching as authoritative when it is clearly shown to be in agreement with the scriptures. Conference is the final authority for the interpretation of doctrine.

118. Both Catholics and Methodists recognize that it is the whole church which abides in the truth because of the presence of the Holy Spirit in the community of believers. Both recognize that all believers have a gift for recognizing, discerning and responding to the truth of the gospel, and so play a part in the formulation and interpretation of the church's faith. Most fundamentally, both Methodists and Catholics believe that it is the Spirit who preserves within the church the truth of the gospel proclaimed by Christ and the apostles, though there is not complete agreement on what constitute the essential components of that gospel.

119. The corporate belief of Christ's faithful must be taken into consideration by those who teach authoritatively within the church. Their ministry can never be exercised in isolation from the faith of the whole church. Methodists and Catholics, however, differ in the ways in which this collaboration occurs. Both recognize the role of the laity in the development of the faith through living it, preaching and teaching it, and meditating upon it. In Methodism lay people participate as members of Conference in the authoritative determination of the precise content of the church's faith. The Catholic Church, on the other hand, maintains that the authoritative determination of the precise content of the church's faith is properly the ministry of bishops. The reasons why Methodists and Catholics interpret differently the roles of the laity and of ordained ministers, particularly in regard to authoritative teaching, is a matter warranting further exploration.[102]

120. One reason for this variation in practice is a different interpretation of the effect of the rite of ordination, which is linked to the Catholic understanding of the sacramentality of that rite. Moreover, there is a further fundamental difference in the understanding

of the degree to which one can attribute a guaranteed reliability to any human instrumentality exercising a ministry of teaching within the church, even given the continuing presence of the Holy Spirit. The relationship between ordination, authoritative teaching and the sure guidance of the Holy Spirit remains a topic for further discussion between Methodists and Catholics.[103]

121.   At the same time, while this report acknowledges obvious differences in ministerial structure for authoritative teaching and in theological interpretation of the reliability of these ministerial structures, there remains a common fundamental belief in the presence of the Holy Spirit and the use by the Holy Spirit of recognized bodies for teaching authoritatively to ensure the truth of the gospel which is believed by both Methodists and Catholics. Moreover, the differing language used to describe the experience of authoritative teaching does not negate the fact that both, in practice, depend upon the sure guidance of the Holy Spirit for this ministry of authoritative teaching. The experience of ordinary Methodists and Catholics and their confidence in their respective understandings of the apostolic faith indicate that these perspectives may be much closer than the differing language might sometimes indicate.

122.   As Methodists and Catholics seek to move together towards full unity in love and in truth, they are committed here and now to "speak the truth in love" to each other and to all the people of the world.

## Participants in the dialogue

*Catholics*

Right Rev. Michael Putney, Bishop of Townsville, Australia (co-chairman)
Rev. Monsignor Timothy Galligan, Vatican City (co-secretary)
Most Rev. Alexander Brunett, Archbishop of Seattle, WA, USA
Sister Mary Charles-Murray, Oxford, England
Rev. Canon Michael Evans, Tunbridge Wells, England
Rev. Prof. Francis Frost, Ars, France
Rev. Prof. George Tavard, Boston, MA, USA
Most Rev. Peter Turkson, Archbishop of Cape Coast, Ghana

*Methodists*

Rev. Prof. Geoffrey Wainwright, Duke University, Durham, NC, USA (co-chairman)
Rev. Dr Joe Hale, World Methodist Council, Lake Junaluska, NC, USA (co-secretary)
Bishop Daniel C. Arichea Jr, Baguio City, Philippines
Bishop Mvume Dandala, Braamfontein, South Africa
Dr Scott J. Jones, Southern Methodist University, Dallas, TX, USA
Mrs Gillian Kingston, Dublin, Ireland
Bishop Richard C. Looney, Macon, GA, USA
Rev. Dr John Newton, Bristol, England

NOTES

1   Joint commission for dialogue between the Roman Catholic Church and the World Methodist Council (WMC-RC), *Towards a Statement on the Church*, 1986, 20.

2   *Idem*, §1.

3   The church is described in the Second Vatican Council's *LG* §6 as the sheepfold, the cultivated field, house, and family of God, the temple of the Spirit, the Holy City, the New Jerusalem, and the bride of God. In *LG* §7 it is especially emphasized that the church is the body of Christ. In trinitarian vein, the British Methodist Conference statement "Called to Love and Praise" (1999) speaks of the church as "the new people of God, the body of Christ, a communion in the Holy Spirit, a sacrament or sign of Christ's continuing presence in the world" (2.1.1). Many Christians, reflecting on the church as the bride of God which nurtures the faithful, see it as their mother. As John Wesley said, "In some sense [the church] is the mother of us all, who have been brought up therein" ("Reasons against Separation from the Church of England", *The Works of John Wesley*, Jackson ed., 13:230).

4   *The Book of Discipline of the United Methodist Church* (BOD), Nashville TN, United Methodist Publ. House, 1996, 77.

5   WMC-RC, *The Apostolic Tradition*, 1991, §21.

6   WWS, §79.

7   Ignatius of Antioch, *Letter to the Romans*, Introduction, no. 10.

8   Cf. First Vatican Council, Dogmatic Constitution on the Church of Christ, *Pastor Aeternus*, ch. IV, DS 3071; *DV* §8.

9   *The Apostolic Tradition*, §36.

10   *UR*, §11.

11   J. Wesley, Explanatory Notes upon the New Testament, Rom. 12:6.

12   WMC-RC, *The Word of Life*, 1996, §59.

13   Cf. *LG*, §25.

14   Hymns and Psalms, no. 614.

15   J. Wesley, "Catholic Spirit", §4, *The Works of John Wesley*, bicentennial ed., 2:82.

16   *LG*, §4.

17   Hymns and Psalms, no. 316.

18   Cf. Hippolytus, *Apostolic Tradition*, 21.

19   WMC-RC, "Towards an Agreed Statement on the Holy Spirit", 1981, §21.

20   *Idem*, §34.

21   *The Apostolic Tradition*, §52; cf. §31.

22   *Idem*, §27.

23   *Idem*, §37.

24   *The Word of Life*, §63.

25   *Idem*, §75.

26   ARCIC, *The Gift of Authority*, 1998, §28.

27   ARCIC, *Authority in the Church I*, 1976, §18.

28   Anglican-Methodist International Commission (AMIC), "Sharing in the Apostolic Communion", 1996, §59.

29   *BOD*, §105.

30   *LG*, §35.

31   *CCC*, §91.

32   *BOD*, §63.

33   *The Word of Life*, §113; cf. ARCIC, *The Gift of Authority*, §§11-13,23,29.

34   Authority Statement of the English Roman Catholic-Methodist Committee, 1978, §4.

35   *Idem*, §28.

36   *Idem*, §28.

37   *The Roman Missal*, Roman Canon.

38   *LG*, §12 quoting St Augustine.

39   Cf. *LG*, §25.

40   *DV*, §8.

[41] Hymns and Psalms, no. 469.

[42] *AA*, §2.

[43] Methodist Church of Great Britain, *The Methodist Worship Book*, 79.

[44] *The Word of Life*, §96.

[45] *EN*, §21.

[46] British Methodist Conference Statement, "Called to Love and Praise", 1999, 1.4.1.

[47] *Idem*, 4.2.1.

[48] Report of the joint commission, 1981, §34.

[49] "Called to Love and Praise", 2.1.7.

[50] *Towards a Statement on the Church*, §13.

[51] *Idem*, §16.

[52] *The Apostolic Tradition*, §89.

[53] *The Word of Life*, §§95-96.

[54] *Towards a Statement on the Church*, §§8,9.

[55] *Idem*, §10.

[56] *The Word of Life*, §§73,75.

[57] *Idem*, §98.

[58] *Idem*, §98.

[59] Cf. *idem*, §§100-107.

[60] *CCC*, §1669.

[61] "The Means of Grace", §II.1, *The Works of John Wesley*, bicentennial ed., 1:381.

[62] Report of the joint commission, 1971, §§89,90,94,108,92.

[63] "Growth in Understanding", 1976, §79.

[64] *Idem*, §98.

[65] *The Apostolic Tradition*, §83.

[66] *Idem*, §84.

[67] Cf. *idem*, §§88-91,94.

[68] Pope John Paul II, Post-Synodal Exhortation on Priestly Formation, *Pastores Dabo Vobis*, 1992, §15; cf. *CCC*, §§1548,1549.

[69] *The Apostolic Tradition*, §82.

[70] *Idem*, §84.

[71] *BOD*, §401.

[72] Baptism, Eucharist and Ministry, WCC, 1982, Ministry, §19.

[73] *The Apostolic Tradition*, §93.

[74] South African Methodists' *Book of Discipline*, §1.18 (cf. §§5.1, 5.4.3) 10th ed., 2000.

[75] *BOD*, §414.3.

[76] *The Gift of Authority*, §32.

[77] Cf. *idem*, §5.

[78] *BOD*, §104.

[79] "The Nature, Design and General Rules of the United Society", *The Works of John Wesley*, bicentennial ed., 9:69.

[80] *The Gift of Authority*, §48.

[81] Hymns and Psalms, no. 438.

[82] "Large Minutes", *The Works of John Wesley*, Jackson ed., 8:299.

[83] Gordon Rupp, *Thomas Jackson: Methodist Patriarch*, 1954, 41.

[84] Hymns and Psalms, no. 62.

[85] "On Laying the Foundation of the New Chapel", §11.1, *The Works of John Wesley*, bicentennial ed., 3:585.

[86] Cf. "Minutes, 1744", *The Works of John Wesley*, Jackson ed., 8:275.

[87] Francis Asbury and Thomas Coke, notes in *The Doctrines and Disciplines of the Methodist Episcopal Church*, 10th ed., Philadelphia, 1798, 42.

[88] *BOD*, §414.3.

89   Cf. *LG*, §26.

90   *The Word of Life*, §58; cf. 86.

91   *DV*, §10.

92   Cf. *DV*, §10.

93   Cf. *LG*, §25.

94   *LG*, §25.

95   *LG*, §18.

96   *Towards a Statement on the Church*, §§39-73.

97   *UUS*, §94; cf. §88.

98   Cf. First Vatican Council, *Pastor Aeternus*; *LG*, §27.

99   Cf. *LG*, §25.

100   *UUS*, §97.

101   *UUS*, §91.

102   See above, §§78-79.

103   See above, §68.

# 20. Joint Declaration

## Pope John Paul II and Patriarch Teoctist

### Bucharest, May 1999

On Saturday, 8 May, at the patriarchal palace in Bucharest, Pope John Paul II and Patriarch Teoctist signed a joint declaration on the urgent need for peace in the Balkans. Here is a translation of their statement, which was written in French:

While we are gathered together in brotherhood and charity, whose source lies in the risen Christ, "the Way, the Truth and the Life" (cf. John 14:6) for all humanity, our affectionate thoughts turn to our brothers and sisters in the Federal Republic of Yugoslavia, who are overwhelmed by so much hardship and suffering.

Fathers and servants of our communities, united with all those whose mission is to proclaim to today's world the One who "has called us to live in peace" (1 Cor. 7:15), and especially united with the pastors of our churches in the Balkans, we wish:

- to express our human and spiritual solidarity with all those who, driven from their homes and land and separated from their loved ones, are undergoing the cruel reality of emigration, as well as with the victims of the deadly bombings and all people prevented from living in tranquillity and peace;

- to appeal in God's name to all those who in one way or another are responsible for the current tragedy, that they will have the courage to return to dialogue and find the right conditions for achieving a just and lasting peace that will permit the displaced persons to return to their homes;

- to end the sufferings of all who live in the Federal Republic of Yugoslavia, Serbs, Albanians and people of other nationalities, and to lay the foundations for a new social harmony among all the peoples of the Federation;

- to encourage the international community and its institutions to use all their legal resources to help the parties in conflict resolve their differences in accordance with the conventions in force, especially those regarding respect for the basic rights of the person and cooperation between sovereign states;

- to support all humanitarian organizations, especially those of Christian inspiration, which are involved in relieving the suffering of the present time, while insisting that nothing be allowed to hinder their efforts to help all who are suffering great hardships, regardless of nationality, language or religion;

– lastly, to appeal to Christians of all denominations to be concretely committed and united in a unanimous and ceaseless prayer for peace and understanding between peoples, entrusting these intentions to the Blessed Virgin so that she will intercede with her Son "who is our peace" (Eph. 2:14).

In the name of God, Father of all mankind, we insistently ask the parties involved in the conflict to lay down their arms once and for all, and we vigorously urge them to make prophetic gestures so that a new art of living in the Balkans, marked by respect for all, by brotherhood and by social harmony can grow in this beloved land. This will be a powerful sign in the world's eyes and will show that the territory of the Federal Republic of Yugoslavia, together with all Europe, can become a place of peace, freedom and harmony for everyone who lives there.

# 21. Common Declaration

## Pope John Paul II and Patriarch Teoctist

### Vatican City, 12 October 2002

"The glory which you have given me I have given to them, that they may be one even as we are one, I in them and you in me, that they may become perfectly one, so that the world may know that you have sent me and have loved them even as you have loved me" (John 17:22-23).

In the deep joy of being together again in the city of Rome, close to the tombs of the holy apostles Peter and Paul, we exchange the kiss of peace under the gaze of the One who watches over his church and guides our steps; and we meditate anew on these words, which the evangelist John transmitted to us and which constitute Christ's heartfelt prayer on the eve of his passion.

1. Our meeting takes place in continuity with the embrace we exchanged in Bucharest in May 1999, while still resounding in our hearts is the moving appeal "*Unitate, unitate!* Unity, unity!*", that a great crowd of faithful spontaneously raised on that occasion when they saw us. This appeal is the echo of our Lord's prayer that "they may all be one" (John 17:21).

Today's meeting reinforces our dedication to pray and to work to achieve the full and visible unity of all the disciples of Christ. Our aim and our ardent desire is full communion, which is not absorption but communion in truth and love. It is an irreversible journey for which there is no alternative: it is the path of the church.

2. Still marked by the sad historical period during which people denied the name and Lordship of the Redeemer, even today Christian communities in Romania often have difficulty in surmounting the negative effects those years have had on the practice of fraternity and sharing, and on the quest for communion. Our meeting must be taken as an example: brothers must meet to be reconciled, to reflect together, to find the means to achieve mutual understanding, to expound and to explain each other's differences. We therefore urge those who are called to live side by side in the same land of Romania, to find solutions of justice and charity. By means of a sincere dialogue, we must overcome the conflicts, misunderstandings and suspicions coming from the past so that in this decisive period of their history Christians in Romania can be witnesses of peace and reconciliation.

3. Our relations must reflect the real and profound communion in Christ that already exists between us, even if it is not yet full. In fact, we recognize with joy that we possess

together the tradition of the undivided church centred on the mystery of the eucharist, to which the saints we have in common in our calendars bear witness. Moreover, the many witnesses of the faith who showed their fidelity to Christ in the times of oppression and persecution in the last century are a seed of hope in our present difficulties.

In order to promote the quest for full communion, even with the doctrinal differences that still remain, it is appropriate to find concrete means by setting up regular consultations, with the conviction that no difficult situation is destined to remain beyond redress, and that thanks to the attitude of listening and dialogue and the regular exchange of information, satisfactory solutions can be found to straighten out points of friction and reach equitable solutions for concrete problems.

We should reinforce this process so that the full truth of the faith becomes a common patrimony, shared by both sides, that can give birth to a truly peaceful conviviality, rooted in and founded in charity.

We know well how to behave to establish the orientations that must guide the work of evangelization so necessary after the sombre period of state atheism. We agree to recognize the religious and cultural traditions of each people, and religious freedom as well.

Evangelization cannot be based on a spirit of competition, but on reciprocal respect and cooperation which recognize the freedom of each person to live according to his own convictions in respect for his religious belonging.

4. In the development of our contacts, starting with the pan-Orthodox conferences and the Second Vatican Council, we have been the witnesses of a promising reconciliation between East and West, based on prayer and on a dialogue of charity and of truth, which has had many moments of profound communion. This is why we look with concern at the current difficulties that beset the joint international commission for theological dialogue between the Catholic Church and the Orthodox Church and, on the occasion of our meeting, we desire to express the hope that no initiative will be neglected that can reactivate the theological dialogue and relaunch the activity of the commission. We have the duty to do so, for theological dialogue makes stronger the affirmation of our shared will for communion over against the present situation of division.

5. The church is not a reality closed in on herself: she is sent to the world and she is open to the world. The new possibilities that are being created in an already united Europe that is in the process of extending its frontiers to associate the peoples and cultures of the Central and Eastern parts of the continent, are a challenge that the Christians of East and West must face together. The more the latter are united in their witness to the one Lord, the more they will contribute to giving voice, consistency and space to the Christian soul of Europe, to respect for life, to the dignity and the fundamental rights of the human person, to justice and to solidarity, to peace, to reconciliation, to the values of the family and to the protection of creation. Europe in its entirety needs the cultural richness forged by Christianity.

The Orthodox church of Romania, the centre of contacts and exchanges between the fruitful Slav and Byzantine traditions of the East, and the church of Rome who in her Latin element evokes the Western voice of the one church of Christ, must contribute together to a task that belongs to the third millennium. In accord with the traditional beautiful expression, the particular churches like to call one another "sister churches".

To be open to this dimension means collaborating to restore to Europe its deepest ethos and its truly human face.

With these perspectives and these dispositions, together we entrust ourselves to the Lord, imploring him to make us worthy of building the body of Christ, "until we all attain to the unity of the faith and of the knowledge of the Son of God, to mature manhood, to the measure of the stature of the fullness of Christ" (Eph. 4:13).

Vatican, 12 October 2002

# 22. Common Declaration

## Pope John Paul II and His Beatitude Christodoulos, Archbishop of Athens and All Greece

### Before the Bema of St Paul, the Apostle to the Nations
### Athens, Greece, 4 May 2001

We, Pope John Paul II, Bishop of Rome, and Christodoulos, Archbishop of Athens and All Greece, standing before the bema of the Areopagus, from which Saint Paul, the great apostle to the nations, "called to be an apostle, set apart for the gospel of God" (Rom. 1:1), preached to the Athenians the one true God, Father, Son and Holy Spirit, and called them unto faith and repentance, do hereby declare:

1. We give thanks to the Lord for our meeting and communication with one another, here in the illustrious city of Athens, the primatial see of the apostolic Orthodox Church of Greece.

2. We repeat with one voice and one heart the words of the apostle to the nations: "I appeal to you, brethren, by the name of our Lord Jesus Christ, that all of you agree and that there be no schisms among you, but that you be united in the same mind and the same judgment"(1 Cor. 1:10). We pray that the whole Christian world will heed this exhortation, so that peace may come unto "all those who in every place call on the name of our Lord Jesus Christ" (1 Cor. 1:2). We condemn all recourse to violence, proselytism and fanaticism in the name of religion. We especially maintain that relations between Christians, in all their manifestations, should be characterized by honesty, prudence and knowledge of the matters in question.

3. We observe that man's social and scientific evolution has not been accompanied by a deeper delving into the meaning and value of life, which in every instance is a gift of God, nor by an analogous appreciation of man's unique dignity, as being created according to the Creator's image and likeness. Moreover, economic and technological development does not belong equally to all mankind but belongs only to a very small portion of it. Furthermore, the improvement of living standards has not brought about the opening of men's hearts to their neighbours who suffer hunger and are naked. We are called to work together for the prevailing of justice, for the relief of the needy and for the ministry unto those who suffer, ever keeping in mind the words of St Paul: "the kingdom of God does not mean food and drink but righteousness and peace and joy in the Holy Spirit" (Rom. 14:17).

4. We are anguished to see that wars, massacres, torture and martyrdom constitute a terrible daily reality for millions of our brothers. We commit ourselves to struggle for the

prevailing of peace throughout the whole world, for the respect of life and human dignity, and for solidarity towards all who are in need. We are pleased to add our voice to the many voices around the world which have expressed the hope that, on the occasion of the Olympic Games to be held in Greece in 2004, the ancient Greek tradition of the Olympic truce will be revived, according to which all wars had to stop, and terrorism and violence had to cease.

5. We follow carefully and with unease what is referred to as globalization. We hope that it will bear good fruit. However, we wish to point out that its fruits will be harmful if what could be termed the "globalization of brotherhood" in Christ is not achieved in all sincerity and efficacy.

6. We rejoice at the success and progress of the European Union. The union of the European world in one civil entity, without her people losing their national self-awareness, traditions and identity, has been the vision of its pioneers. However, the emerging tendency to transform certain European countries into secular states without any reference to religion constitutes a retraction and a denial of their spiritual legacy. We are called to intensify our efforts so that the unification of Europe may be accomplished. We shall do everything in our power, so that the Christian roots of Europe and its Christian soul may be preserved inviolate.

With this common statement, we, Pope John Paul II, Bishop of Rome, and Christodoulos, Archbishop of Athens and All Greece, wish that "our God and Father and our Lord Jesus direct our way, so that we may increase and abound in love towards one another and towards all men and establish the hearts of all unblamable in holiness before our God and Father, at the coming of the Lord Jesus with all his saints" (cf. 1 Thess. 3:11-13). Amen.

Athens, at the Areopagus, 4 May 2001

# 23. Common Declaration on Environmental Ethics
## Pope John Paul II and Ecumenical Patriarch Bartholomew I

### Rome-Venice, Italy, 10 June 2002

We are gathered here today in the spirit of peace for the good of all human beings and for the care of creation. At this moment in history, at the beginning of the third millennium, we are saddened to see the daily suffering of a great number of people from violence, starvation, poverty and disease. We are also concerned about the negative consequences for humanity and for all creation resulting from the degradation of some basic natural resources such as water, air and land, brought about by an economic and technological progress which does not recognize and take into account its limits.

Almighty God envisioned a world of beauty and harmony, and He created it, making every part an expression of his freedom, wisdom and love (cf. Gen. 1:1-25).

At the centre of the whole of creation, He placed us, human beings, with our inalienable human dignity. Although we share many features with the rest of the living beings, Almighty God went further with us and gave us an immortal soul, the source of self-awareness and freedom, endowments that make us in his image and likeness (cf. Gen. 1:26-31, 2:7). Marked with that resemblance, we have been placed by God in the world in order to cooperate with him in realizing more and more fully the divine purpose for creation.

At the beginning of history, man and woman sinned by disobeying God and rejecting his design for creation. Among the results of this first sin was the destruction of the original harmony of creation. If we examine carefully the social and environmental crisis which the world community is facing, we must conclude that we are still betraying the mandate God has given us: to be stewards called to collaborate with God in watching over creation in holiness and wisdom.

God has not abandoned the world. It is his will that his design and our hope for it will be realized through our cooperation in restoring its original harmony. In our own time we are witnessing a growth of an ecological awareness which needs to be encouraged, so that it will lead to practical programmes and initiatives. An awareness of the relationship between God and humankind brings a fuller sense of the importance of the relationship between human beings and the natural environment, which is God's creation and which God entrusted to us to guard with wisdom and love (cf. Gen. 1:28).

Respect for creation stems from respect for human life and dignity. It is on the basis of our recognition that the world is created by God that we can discern an objective moral order within which to articulate a code of environmental ethics. In this perspective, Christians and all other believers have a specific role to play in proclaiming moral values and in educating people in ecological awareness, which is none other than responsibility towards self, towards others, towards creation.

What is required is an act of repentance on our part and a renewed attempt to view ourselves, one another, and the world around us within the perspective of the divine design for creation. The problem is not simply economic and technological; it is moral and spiritual. A solution at the economic and technological level can be found only if we undergo, in the most radical way, an inner change of heart, which can lead to a change in life-style and of unsustainable patterns of consumption and production. A genuine conversion in Christ will enable us to change the way we think and act.

First, we must regain humility and recognize the limits of our powers and, most importantly, the limits of our knowledge and judgment. We have been making decisions, taking actions and assigning values that are leading us away from the world as it should be, away from the design of God for creation, away from all that is essential for a healthy planet and a healthy commonwealth of people. A new approach and a new culture are needed, based on the centrality of the human person within creation and inspired by environmentally ethical behaviour stemming from our triple relationship to God, to self and to creation. Such an ethics fosters interdependence and stresses the principles of universal solidarity, social justice and responsibility, in order to promote a true culture of life.

Second, we must frankly admit that humankind is entitled to something better than what we see around us. We and, much more, our children and future generations are entitled to a better world, a world free from degradation, violence and bloodshed, a world of generosity and love.

Third, aware of the value of prayer, we must implore God the Creator to enlighten people everywhere regarding the duty to respect and carefully guard creation.

We therefore invite all men and women of good will to ponder the importance of the following ethical goals:

1. To think of the world's children when we reflect on and evaluate our options for action.

2. To be open to study the true values based on the natural law that sustain every human culture.

3. To use science and technology in a full and constructive way, while recognizing that the findings of science have always to be evaluated in the light of the centrality of the human person, of the common good and of the inner purpose of creation. Science may help us to correct the mistakes of the past, in order to enhance the spiritual and material well-being of the present and future generations. It is love for our children that will show us the path that we must follow into the future.

4. To be humble regarding the idea of ownership and to be open to the demands of solidarity. Our mortality and our weakness of judgment together warn us not to take irreversible actions with what we choose to regard as our property during our brief stay on this earth. We have not been entrusted with unlimited power over creation, we are only stewards of the common heritage.

5. To acknowledge the diversity of situations and responsibilities in the work for a better world environment. We do not expect every person and every institution to assume

the same burden. Everyone has a part to play, but for the demands of justice and charity to be respected the most affluent societies must carry the greater burden, and from them is demanded a sacrifice greater than can be offered by the poor. Religions, governments and institutions are faced by many different situations; but on the basis of the principle of subsidiarity all of them can take on some tasks, some part of the shared effort.

6. To promote a peaceful approach to disagreement about how to live on this earth, about how to share it and use it, about what to change and what to leave unchanged. It is not our desire to evade controversy about the environment, for we trust in the capacity of human reason and the path of dialogue to reach agreement. We commit ourselves to respect the views of all who disagree with us, seeking solutions through open exchange, without resorting to oppression and domination.

It is not too late. God's world has incredible healing powers. Within a single generation, we could steer the earth towards our children's future. Let that generation start now, with God's help and blessing.

Rome-Venice, 10 June 2002

# 24. Common Declaration

## Pope John Paul II and Patriarch Bartholomew I

### Rome, 29 June 2004

"Be watchful, stand firm in your faith, be courageous, be strong. Let all that you do be done in love" (1 Cor. 16:13-14).

1. In the spirit of faith in Christ and the reciprocal love that unites us, we thank God for this gift of our new meeting that is taking place on the Feast of the Holy Apostles Peter and Paul and witnesses to our firm determination to continue on our way towards full communion with one another in Christ.

2. Many positive steps have marked our common journey, starting above all with the historical event that we are recalling today: the embrace of Pope Paul VI and Patriarch Athenagoras I on the Mount of Olives in Jerusalem, on 5 and 6 January 1964. We, their successors, are meeting today to commemorate fittingly before God that blessed encounter, now part of the history of the church, faithfully recalling it and its original intentions.

3. The embrace in Jerusalem of our respective predecessors of venerable memory visibly expressed a hope that dwells in all hearts, as the communiqué declared:

> With eyes turned to Christ, together with the Father, the Archetype and Author of unity and of peace, they pray God that this encounter may be the sign and prelude of things to come for the glory of God and the enlightenment of his faithful people. After so many centuries of silence, they have now met with the desire to do the Lord's will and to proclaim the ancient truth of his gospel, entrusted to the church.[1]

4. Unity and peace! The hope kindled by that historic encounter has lit up our journey in these last decades. Aware that the Christian world has suffered the tragedy of separation for centuries, our predecessors and we ourselves have persevered in the "dialogue of charity", our gaze turned to that blessed, shining day on which it will be possible to communicate with the same cup of the precious blood and the holy body of the Lord.[2] The many ecclesial events that have punctuated these past years have put on firm foundations the commitment to brotherly love: a love which, in learning from past lessons, may be ready to forgive, more inclined to believe in good than in evil and intent first and foremost on complying with the Divine Redeemer and in being attracted and transformed by him.[3]

5.  Let us thank the Lord for the exemplary gestures of reciprocal love, participation and sharing that he has granted us to make; among them, it is only right to recall the Pope's visit to the Ecumenical Patriarch Dimitrios in 1979, when the creation of the joint international commission for theological dialogue between the Catholic Church and all the Orthodox churches was announced at the Phanar, a further step to sustain the "dialogue of truth" with the "dialogue of charity"; Patriarch Dimitrios's visit to Rome in 1987; our meeting in Rome on the feast of Saints Peter and Paul in 1995, when we prayed in St Peter's, despite the painful separation during the celebration of the eucharistic liturgy, since we cannot yet drink from the same chalice of the Lord. Then, more recently, there was the meeting at Assisi for the Day of Prayer for Peace in the World, and the Common Declaration on Environmental Ethics for the Safeguard of Creation, signed on 10 June 2002.[4]

6.  Despite our firm determination to journey on towards full communion, it would have been unrealistic not to expect obstacles of various kinds: doctrinal, first of all, but also the result of conditioning by a troubled history. In addition, the new problems which have emerged from the radical changes that have occurred in political and social structures have not failed to make themselves felt in relations between the Christian churches. With the return to freedom of Christians in Central and Eastern Europe, old fears have also been reawakened, making dialogue difficult. Nonetheless, St Paul's exhortation to the Corinthians: let all things be done in charity, must always be vibrant within us and between us.

7.  The joint international commission for theological dialogue between the Catholic Church and all the Orthodox churches, created with so much hope, has marked our progress in recent years. It is still a suitable instrument for studying the ecclesiological and historical problems that are at the root of our difficulties, and for identifying hypothetical solutions to them. It is our duty to persevere in the important commitment to reopen the work as soon as possible. In examining the reciprocal initiatives of the offices of Rome and of Constantinople with this in view, we ask the Lord to sustain our determination, and to convince everyone of how essential it is to pursue the "dialogue of truth".

8.  Our meeting in Rome today also enables us to face certain problems and misunderstandings that have recently surfaced. The long experience of the "dialogue of charity" comes to our aid precisely in these circumstances, so that difficulties can be faced serenely without slowing or clouding our progress on the journey we have undertaken towards full communion in Christ.

9.  Before a world that is suffering every kind of division and imbalance, today's encounter is intended as a practical and forceful reminder of the importance for Christians and for the churches to coexist in peace and harmony, in order to witness in agreement to the message of the gospel in the most credible and convincing way possible.

10.  In the special context of Europe, moving in the direction of higher forms of integration and expansion towards the East of the continent, we thank the Lord for this positive development and express the hope that in this new situation, collaboration between Catholics and Orthodox may grow. There are so many challenges to face together in order to contribute to the good of society: to heal with love the scourge of terrorism, to instil a hope of peace, to help set aright the multitude of grievous conflicts; to restore to the European continent the awareness of its Christian roots; to build true dialogue with Islam, since indifference and reciprocal ignorance can only give rise to diffidence and

even hatred; to nourish an awareness of the sacred nature of human life; to work to ensure that science does not deny the divine spark that every human being receives with the gift of life; to collaborate so that our earth may not be disfigured and that creation may preserve the beauty with which it has been endowed by God; but above all, to proclaim the gospel message with fresh vigour, showing contemporary men and women how the gospel can help them rediscover themselves and to build a more human world.

11. Let us pray to the Lord to give peace to the church and to the world, and to imbue our journey towards full communion with the wisdom of his Spirit, *ut unum in Christo simus* [so that we may be one in Christ].

From the Vatican, 29 June 2004

NOTES

¹  Common Declaration of Pope Paul VI and Patriarch Athenagoras I, *Tomos Agapis*, Vatican-Phanar, 1971, n. 50, p.120.
²  Cf. Patriarch Athenagoras I, address to Pope Paul VI, 5 Jan. 1964, *ibid.*, n. 48, p.109.
³  Address of Pope Paul VI to Patriarch Athenagoras I, 6 Jan. 1964, *ibid.*, n. 49, p.117.
⁴  In the context of the fourth symposium on ecology: The Adriatic Sea: a Sea at Risk – Unity of Purpose.

# 25. Common Declaration
## Pope John Paul II and Catholicos Aram I Keshishian

### Rome, 25 January 1997

At the end of their meeting on Saturday, 25 January, Pope John Paul II and Catholicos Aram I Keshishian signed a common declaration. The Week of Prayer for Christian Unity "recalls the urgent need for full communion between Christians, for the sake of carrying out their essential mission which is first and foremost the witness to Christ who died and rose for humanity's salvation", they said in their joint statement, which was written in French. Here is a translation.

At the end of their official meeting, His Holiness Pope John Paul II and His Holiness Aram I, Catholicos of Cilicia, give thanks to God who has enabled them to deepen their spiritual brotherhood in Jesus Christ and their pastoral and evangelizing vocation in the world. It was a privileged occasion to pray and reflect together, to renew their commitment to and their joint efforts for Christian unity.

The meeting between the Catholicos of the Great House of Cilicia and the Pope of the Catholic Church marks an important stage in their relationship. These relations, which date to the beginning of Christianity in Armenia, took on particular importance in Cilicia from the 11th to the 14th centuries, and continued after the Catholicosate of Sis was exiled from its see and established in 1930 in Antelias, Lebanon.

Pope John Paul II and Catholicos Aram I rejoice at their meeting in the context of the Week of Prayer for Christian Unity. It recalls the urgent need for full communion between Christians, for the sake of carrying out their essential mission which is first and foremost the witness to Christ who died and rose for humanity's salvation. For two millenniums, unity of faith in Jesus Christ, God's gift, was maintained as essential, despite christological and ecclesiological controversies which were frequently based on historical, political, or socio-cultural factors. This communion of faith, already affirmed in recent decades by their predecessors during their meetings, was solemnly reaffirmed recently at the meeting of His Holiness John Paul II with His Holiness Catholicos Karekin I. Today the Bishop of Rome, Successor of Peter, and the Catholicos of Cilicia pray that their communion of faith in Jesus Christ may progress because of the blood of the martyrs and the fidelity of the fathers to the gospel and the apostolic Tradition, manifesting itself in the rich diversity of their respective ecclesial traditions. Such a community of faith must be concretely expressed in the life of the faithful and must lead us towards full communion.

Thus the two spiritual leaders stress the vital importance of sincere dialogue bearing on theological and pastoral areas, as well as on other dimensions of the life and witness of believers. The relations already existing are an experience that encourages direct and fruitful collaboration between them. Their Holinesses are firmly convinced that in this century, when Christian communities are more deeply engaged in ecumenical dialogue, a serious rapprochement supported by mutual respect and understanding is the only sound and reliable way to full communion.

The Catholic Church and the Catholicosate of Cilicia also have an immense field of constructive cooperation before them. The contemporary world, because of ideologies expressed in materialistic values and by reason of the harm done by injustice and violence, represents a real risk to the integrity and identity of the Christian faith. Now more than ever, Christ's church must, by her fidelity to the gospel, bring the world a message of hope and charity and become the ardent herald of gospel values; active collaboration must also be envisaged in the field of theological study and instruction, religious education, the evaluation of pastoral situations where common action is possible and the promotion of ethical values. Furthermore, we must try to face together various problems related to mission and to pastoral and spiritual commitment to the renewal of Christian life and the transformation of society. The Pope and the Catholicos urge their clergy and faithful to take an active part in these efforts, which must be made and organized at all levels, especially the local, where believers are together confronted with difficult situations. The Christian faith is also an incentive to work together more effectively to promote the dignity and rights of every human being, as well as the right of all peoples to see their legitimate aspirations and cultural identity recognized.

Today the Armenian church faces living conditions and challenges that are an invitation to give a more effective witness in Armenia, Nagorno-Karabakh and the diaspora. Dispersed throughout the world, this church's faithful live in circumstances where dialogue is indispensable for her life and witness.

In today's pluralistic society, marked by exchanges where cultures, religions and civilizations are permanently relating and interacting with one another, the churches must promote dialogue. The Middle East context offers a source of mutual enrichment and a common witness for Christians who, to a large extent, share with their Muslim compatriots the same history, the same socio-economic problems and the same political destiny. Moreover, the churches are convinced of the importance of dialogue with Muslims and this is one of the tasks where there is room for mutual agreement. Within this framework, moreover, dialogue does not remain intellectual and theoretical but has a concrete effect on elements of daily life.

In the Middle East, the active presence and dynamic witness of Christians is particularly important, for they are engaged together in the struggle for justice and peace. It is therefore indispensable that a new impetus be given to the spiritual and social mission of the churches in the countries of the Middle East, where the establishment of a just, total and lasting peace and an equitable and satisfactory solution to the problem of the holy city of Jerusalem are seen as priorities.

Lebanon, where the Catholic Church and the Catholicosate of Cilicia have a tangible historical presence, is the particular context in which they carry out their mission. The efforts of the Lebanese for reconciliation and reconstruction of their country must not disregard the moral and religious values that constitute the identity of the great Lebanese family itself. They must also work to fully restore their country's identity, while respecting its freedom and pluralism, its unity, its sovereignty and its specific vocation in this region and in the world!

At the close of the second Christian millennium and the approach of the 17th centenary of the Armenian church, His Holiness Pope John Paul II and His Holiness Aram I thank and glorify the Holy Trinity who gives the spiritual strength to adhere firmly to the imperatives of the apostolic faith and the pastoral mission. They exhort their clergy and faithful to work ardently for the love, reconciliation, justice and peace demanded by the gospel in anticipation of the coming of the kingdom of God.

Rome, 25 January 1997

# 26. Statement on the Synod of Diamper, AD 1599

## Joint International Commission for Dialogue between the Catholic Church and the Malankara Orthodox Church

### Kottayam, India, 29 October 1999

This year being the fourth centenary of the synod of Diamper (Udayamperur), which was held from 20 to 26 June 1599, we, the members of the joint international commission for dialogue between the Catholic Church and the Malankara Orthodox Church, consider it very opportune to share with our brothers and sisters of both the churches our findings on the nature and consequences of the synod of Diamper, with the firm hope of creating an increasing awareness of the urgent need of healing the bitter memories of the past which stand in the way of our reconciliation and mutual communion.

The undivided ancient apostolic church of the St Thomas Christians came into contact with the Portuguese in the 16th century. The Roman Catholic missionaries who accompanied them unjustly accused the St Thomas Christians of upholding Nestorianism. Through the Goan synods and through the seminary formation at Cranganore. Vaipinkotta, etc., there was a systematic attempt to conform the indigenous church to the Latin church.

The activities in connection with the synod of Diamper brought drastic changes in the ecclesiastical life of the St Thomas Christians. Westernization and Latinization were the main results of the activities of the missionaries and the colonial power. The church was forced to adopt several changes in the Latin direction. Consequently the identity and the heritage of the St Thomas Christians were severely distorted.

As is evident from the canons of the synod, under the direction of the missionaries, the liturgy was mutilated, the hierarchical relation with the Persian church was discontinued and substantial changes regarding the practices and tradition of the St Thomas Christians were introduced.

Despite certain positive aspects great damage was done to the ecclesial heritage of this local church by the synod. The saddest consequence of the synod was the loss of freedom and the division of the one apostolic ancient church in India into two, one section which later came to be known as the Syro-Malabar church and the other one as the Malankara Orthodox Church. This also led to further divisions and all sections of the St Thomas Christians are suffering from it.

This common reading of such a crucial historical event in the life of St Thomas Christians takes us a long way in our search for reconciliation and rediscovery of the identity of the churches of St Thomas tradition.

We are happy that some efforts have been initiated towards this. The setting up of this joint commission for dialogue is one. We have already studied and drawn up an agreed statement on Christology; details of an interim agreement on interchurch marriage are being pursued, steps have been taken for a more effective common witness, to mention only a few. So we look forward to the future with hope, assured of the desire of our faithful.

# 27. Common Declaration

## His Holiness John Paul II and His Holiness Karekin II

### Holy Etchmiadzin, Republic of Armenia, 27 September 2001

The celebration of the 1700th anniversary of the proclamation of Christianity as the religion of Armenia has brought us together, John Paul II, Bishop of Rome and Pastor of the Catholic Church, and Karekin II, the Supreme Patriarch and Catholicos of All Armenians, and we thank God for giving us this joyous opportunity to join again in common prayer, in praise of his all-holy name. Blessed be the Holy Trinity, Father, Son and Holy Spirit, now and for ever.

As we commemorate this wondrous event, we remember with reverence, gratitude and love the great confessor of our Lord Jesus Christ, St Gregory the Illuminator, as well as his collaborators and successors. They enlightened not only the people of Armenia but also others in the neighbouring countries of the Caucasus. Thanks to their witness, dedication and example, the Armenian people in A.D. 301 were bathed in the divine light and earnestly turned to Christ as the Truth, the Life, and the Way to salvation.

They worshipped God as their Father, professed Christ as their Lord, and invoked the Holy Spirit as their Sanctifier; they loved the apostolic universal church as their Mother. Christ's supreme commandment, to love God above all and our neighbour as ourselves, became a way of life for the Armenians of old. Endowed with great faith, they chose to bear witness to the Truth and accept death when necessary, in order to share eternal life. Martyrdom for the love of Christ thus became a great legacy of many generations of Armenians. The most valuable treasure that one generation could bequeath to the next was fidelity to the gospel so that, with the grace of the Holy Spirit, the young would become as resolute as their ancestors in bearing witness to the truth. The extermination of a million and a half Armenian Christians, in what is generally referred to as the first genocide of the 20th century, and the subsequent annihilation of thousands under the former totalitarian regime are tragedies that still live in the memory of the present-day generation. These innocents who were butchered in vain are not canonized, but many among them were certainly confessors and martyrs for the name of Christ. We pray for the repose of their souls, and urge the faithful never to lose sight of the meaning of their sacrifice. We thank God for the fact that Christianity in Armenia has survived the adversities of the past seventeen centuries, and that the Armenian church is now free to carry out her mission of proclaiming the good news in the modern Republic of Armenia and in many areas near and far where Armenian communities are present.

Armenia is again a free country, as in the early days of King Tiridates and St Gregory the Illuminator. Over the past ten years, the right of citizens in the burgeoning republic to worship and practise their religion in freedom has been recognized. In Armenia and in the diaspora, new Armenian institutions have been established, churches have been built, associations and schools have been founded. In all of this we acknowledge the loving hand of God. For he has made his miracles visible in the continuing history of a small nation, which has preserved its particular identity thanks to its Christian faith. Because of their faith and their church, the Armenian people have developed a unique Christian culture, which is indeed a most valuable contribution to the treasury of Christianity as a whole.

The example of Christian Armenia testifies that faith in Christ brings hope to every human situation, no matter how difficult. We pray that the saving light of Christian faith may shine on both the weak and the strong, on both the developed and developing nations of this world. Particularly today, the complexities and challenges of the international situation require a choice between good and evil, darkness and light, humanity and inhumanity, truth and falsehood. Present issues of law, politics, science and family life touch upon the very meaning of humanity and its vocation. They call today's Christians no less than the martyrs of other times to bear witness to the truth even at the risk of paying a high price.

This witness will be all the more convincing if all of Christ's disciples could profess together the one faith and heal the wounds of division among themselves. May the Holy Spirit guide Christians, and indeed all people of good will, on the path of reconciliation and brotherhood. Here at Holy Etchmiadzin we renew our solemn commitment to pray and work to hasten the day of communion among all the members of Christ's faithful flock, with true regard for our respective sacred traditions.

With God's help, we shall do nothing against love, but "surrounded by so great a cloud of witnesses, we shall lay aside every weight, and sin which clings so closely, and shall run with perseverance the race that is set before us" (cf. Heb. 12:1).

We urge our faithful to pray without ceasing that the Holy Spirit will fill us all, as he did the holy martyrs of every time and place, with the wisdom and courage to follow Christ, the Way, the Truth and the Life.


      His Holiness John Paul II                       His Holiness Karekin II


Holy Etchmiadzin, 27 September 2001

# 28. Guidelines for Admission to the Eucharist between the Chaldean Church and the Assyrian Church of the East

## Pontifical Council for Promoting Christian Unity

### Rome, 20 July 2001

Given the great distress of many Chaldean and Assyrian faithful, in their motherland and in the diaspora, impeding for many of them a normal sacramental life according to their own tradition, and in the ecumenical context of the bilateral dialogue between the Catholic Church and the Assyrian Church of the East, the request has been made to provide for admission to the eucharist between the Chaldean Church and the Assyrian Church of the East. This request has first been studied by the joint committee for theological dialogue between the Catholic Church and the Assyrian Church of the East. The present guidelines subsequently have been elaborated by the Pontifical Council for Promoting Christian Unity, in agreement with the Congregation for the Doctrine of the Faith and the Congregation for the Oriental Churches.

## 1. Pastoral necessity

The request for admission to the eucharist between the Chaldean Church and the Assyrian Church of the East is connected with the particular geographical and social situation in which their faithful are actually living. Due to various and sometimes dramatic circumstances, many Assyrian and Chaldean faithful left their motherlands and moved to the Middle East, Scandinavia, Western Europe, Australia and Northern America. As there cannot be a priest for every local community in such a widespread diaspora, numerous Chaldean and Assyrian faithful are confronted with a situation of pastoral necessity with regard to the administration of sacraments. Official documents of the Catholic Church provide special regulations for such situations, namely the Code of Canons of the Eastern Churches, can. 671, 2-3 and the *Directory for the Application of Principles and Norms of Ecumenism*, n. 123.

## 2. Ecumenical rapprochement

The request is also connected with the ongoing process of ecumenical rapprochement between the Catholic Church and the Assyrian Church of the East. With the "Common Christological Declaration", signed in 1994 by Pope John Paul II and Patriarch Mar Dinkha IV, the main dogmatic problem between the Catholic Church and the Assyrian

Church has been resolved. As a consequence, the ecumenical rapprochement between the Chaldean Church and the Assyrian Church of the East also entered a further phase of development. On 29 November 1996 Patriarch Mar Raphaël I Bidawid and Patriarch Mar Dinkha IV signed a list of common proposals with a view to the re-establishment of full ecclesial unity among both historical heirs of the ancient church of the East. On 15 August 1997 this programme was approved by their respective synods and confirmed in a "joint synodal decree". Supported by their respective synods, both patriarchs approved a further series of initiatives to foster the progressive restoration of their ecclesial unity. Both the Congregation for the Oriental Churches and the Pontifical Council for Promoting Christian Unity support this process.

### 3. The anaphora of Addai and Mari

The principal issue for the Catholic Church in agreeing to this request related to the question of the validity of the eucharist celebrated with the anaphora of Addai and Mari, one of the three anaphoras traditionally used by the Assyrian Church of the East. The anaphora of Addai and Mari is notable because, from time immemorial, it has been used without a recitation of the institution narrative. As the Catholic Church considers the words of the eucharistic institution a constitutive and therefore indispensable part of the anaphora or eucharistic prayer, a long and careful study was undertaken of the anaphora of Addai and Mari, from a historical, liturgical and theological perspective, at the end of which the Congregation for the Doctrine of the Faith on 17 January 2001 concluded that this anaphora can be considered valid. H.H. Pope John Paul II has approved this decision. This conclusion rests on three major arguments.

In the first place, the anaphora of Addai and Mari is one of the most ancient anaphoras, dating back to the time of the very early church; it was composed and used with the clear intention of celebrating the eucharist in full continuity with the last supper and according to the intention of the church; its validity was never officially contested, neither in the Christian East nor in the Christian West.

Second, the Catholic Church recognizes the Assyrian Church of the East as a true particular church, built upon orthodox faith and apostolic succession. The Assyrian Church of the East has also preserved full eucharistic faith in the presence of our Lord under the species of bread and wine and in the sacrificial character of the eucharist. In the Assyrian Church of the East, though not in full communion with the Catholic Church, are thus to be found "true sacraments, and above all, by apostolic succession, the priesthood and the eucharist" (*UR*, §15).

Finally, the words of eucharistic institution are indeed present in the anaphora of Addai and Mari, not in a coherent narrative way and *ad litteram*, but rather in a dispersed euchological way, that is, integrated in successive prayers of thanksgiving, praise and intercession.

### 4. Guidelines for admission to the eucharist

Considering the liturgical tradition of the Assyrian Church of the East, the doctrinal clarification regarding the validity of the anaphora of Addai and Mari, the contemporary context in which both Assyrian and Chaldean faithful are living, the appropriate regulations which are foreseen in official documents of the Catholic Church, and the process of rapprochement between the Chaldean Church and the Assyrian Church of the East, the following provision is made:

1. When necessity requires, Assyrian faithful are permitted to participate and to receive holy communion in a Chaldean celebration of the holy eucharist; in the same way, Chaldean faithful for whom it is physically or morally impossible to approach a Catholic minister are permitted to participate and to receive holy communion in an Assyrian celebration of the holy eucharist.

2. In both cases, Assyrian and Chaldean ministers celebrate the holy eucharist according to the liturgical prescriptions and customs of their own tradition.

3. When Chaldean faithful are participating in an Assyrian celebration of the holy eucharist, the Assyrian minister is warmly invited to insert the words of the institution in the anaphora of Addai and Mari, as allowed by the holy synod of the Assyrian Church of the East.

4. The above considerations on the use of the anaphora of Addai and Mari and the present guidelines for admission to the eucharist, are intended exclusively in relation to the eucharistic celebration and admission to the eucharist of the faithful from the Chaldean Church and the Assyrian Church of the East, in view of the pastoral necessity and ecumenical context mentioned above.

## ADMISSION TO THE EUCHARIST IN SITUATIONS OF PASTORAL NECESSITY

### PROVISION BETWEEN THE CHALDEAN CHURCH AND THE ASSYRIAN CHURCH OF THE EAST

The Pontifical Council for Promoting Christian Unity recently issued a document entitled "Guidelines for Admission to the Eucharist between the Assyrian Church of the East and the Chaldean Church". This document has been elaborated in agreement with the Congregation for the Doctrine of the Faith and the Congregation for the Oriental Churches. The purpose of the article at hand is to clarify the context, the content and the practical application of this provision.

## 1. The Chaldean Church and the Assyrian Church of the East

Since the very early times of Christian missionary activity, a flourishing local church developed in Mesopotamia or Persia. As this church was situated outside the eastern borders of the Roman empire, it became commonly called the "church of the East". In 1552, after a series of individual conversions of bishops or provisional unions, part of the "church of the East" entered into full communion with the apostolic see of Rome. Since then, the particular church in full communion with Rome has usually been called the "Chaldean Church", while the other particular church took the name of "Assyrian Church of the East". Both particular churches, however, still share the same theological, liturgical and spiritual tradition; they both celebrate the sacraments or sacred mysteries according to the East-Syriac tradition.

On 11 November 1994 Pope John Paul II and Mar Dinkha IV, Patriarch of the Assyrian Church of the East, signed a common christological declaration.[1] This declaration removed the main doctrinal obstacle between the Catholic Church and the Assyrian Church of the East. Both church leaders declared, "Whatever our christological divergences have been, we experience ourselves united in the confession of the same faith in the Son of God who became man so that we might become children of God by his grace. We wish from now on to witness together to this faith in the One who is the Way, the Truth and the Life, proclaiming it in appropriate ways to our contemporaries, so that the world may believe in the gospel of salvation." "Living by this faith and these sacraments, it follows as a consequence that the particular Catholic churches and the particular Assyrian churches can recognize each other as sister churches."

In their common christological declaration, Pope John Paul II and Patriarch Mar Dinkha IV also pledged themselves to do everything possible to dispel the obstacles of the past which still prevent the attainment of full communion between our churches, so that we can better respond to the Lord's call for the unity of his own, a unity which has of course to be expressed visibly. For this purpose they decided to establish a joint committee for theological dialogue between the Catholic Church and the Assyrian Church of the East. This joint committee started its regular activities in 1995; during its annual meetings, it mainly dealt with questions of sacramental theology, in view of a future "Common Statement on Sacramental Life". The common christological declaration also paved the way for a process of ecumenical rapprochement between the Chaldean Church and the Assyrian Church of the East. Since 1994 Mar Dinkha IV and Mar Raphael I Bidawid, Patriarch of the Chaldean Church, supported by their respective synods, approved several initiatives to foster the progressive re-establishment of ecclesial unity between their particular churches. This process is supported by both the Congregation for the Oriental Churches and the Pontifical Council for Promoting Christian Unity.

Nowadays, many Chaldean and Assyrian faithful are living in a widespread diaspora. Due to various and sometimes dramatic circumstances, they left their motherlands (Iraq, Iran, Turkey) and moved towards the West. The great majority of the Assyrian faithful now live in the Middle East, Scandinavia, Western Europe, Australia and North America; only a small minority remain in the motherlands. Although a majority of Chaldean faithful still live in Iraq, about one third of them moved to the Middle East, Europe and North America. Both the Chaldean and the Assyrian Church are thus confronted, in various parts of the world, with a similar pastoral necessity: namely that many faithful cannot receive the sacraments from a minister of their own church.

Given the great distress of many Chaldean and Assyrian faithful, in their motherlands as well as in the diaspora, impeding for many of them a normal sacramental life according to their own tradition, and in the ecumenical context of the bilateral dialogue between the Catholic Church and the Assyrian Church of the East, the request has been made of a pastoral arrangement for admission to the eucharist, when necessity requires, between the Assyrian Church of the East and the Chaldean Church.

## 2. The anaphora of Addai and Mari

The principal issue for the Catholic Church in agreeing to this request related to the question of the validity of the eucharist celebrated with the anaphora of Addai and Mari, one of the three anaphoras traditionally used by the Assyrian Church of the East.[2]

This particular anaphora must have originated in Mesopotamia, possibly in the region of Edessa. There is no hard evidence for the dating of its final redaction: some scholars situate it about the year 200, others in the beginning of the 3rd century, others in the course of the 3rd century. The Assyrian Church of the East highly respects this anaphora as an essential element of the apostolic heritage they received from Addai and Mari, whom they venerate as two of the 72 disciples of Christ and as the founding missionaries of their particular church. The anaphora of Addai and Mari, however, as reproduced in the oldest codices retrieved, as well as in the uninterrupted liturgical practice of the Assyrian Church of the East, does not contain a coherent institution narrative. For many years, scholars discussed which version of the anaphora of Addai and Mari might have been the original one. Some scholars argued that the original formula of the anaphora of Addai and Mari was longer and did contain an institution narrative. Other scholars are convinced that the anaphora of Addai and Mari did not contain a coherent institution narrative and that the short version is consequently the original one. Nowadays, most scholars argue that it is highly probable that the second hypothesis is the right one. Anyhow, this historical question cannot be resolved with absolute certainty, due to the scarcity or absence of contemporary sources. The validity of the eucharist celebrated with the anaphora of Addai and Mari, therefore, should not be based on historical but on doctrinal arguments.

The Catholic Church considers the words of the institution as a constitutive part of the anaphora or eucharistic prayer. The council of Florence stated, "The form of this sacrament are the words of the Saviour with which he effected this sacrament. A priest speaking in the person of Christ effects this sacrament. For, in virtue of those words, the substance of bread is changed into the body of Christ and the substance of wine into his blood" (DHn 1321). The same council of Florence also characterized the words of the institution as "the form of words *[forma verborum]* which the holy Roman Church has always been wont to use *[semper uti consuevit]* in the consecration of the Lord's body and blood" (DHn 1352), without prejudice to the possibility of some variation in their articulation by the church. Although not having any authority as to the substance of the sacraments, the church does have the power to determine their concrete shaping, regarding both their sacramental sign *(materia)* and their words of administration *(forma)* (cf. CICO, can. 669). Hence the doctrinal question about the validity of the anaphora of Addai and Mari, when used in its short version without a coherent institution narrative. Do the words of administration *(forma)* correspond to the conditions for validity, as requested by the Catholic Church? To answer this question, three major arguments have to be taken into due consideration.

In the first place, the anaphora of Addai and Mari is one of the most ancient eucharistic prayers, dating back to the time of the very early church and the first liturgical regulations. It was composed and used with the clear intention of celebrating the eucharist in full continuity with the last supper, in obedience to the command of the Lord, and according to the intention of the church. The absence of a coherent institution narrative represents, indeed, an exception in comparison with Byzantine and Roman traditions, as developed in the 4th and 5th century. This exception, however, may be due to its very early origin and to the later isolation of the Assyrian Church of the East. The validity of the anaphora of Addai and Mari, in fact, was never officially contested.

The Assyrian Church of the East also uses two other eucharistic anaphoras, which are some centuries more recent: the anaphora of Nestorius, reserved to five liturgical occasions, and the anaphora of Theodore of Mopsuestia, used from the beginning of the liturgical year till Palm Sunday, for approximately sixteen weeks. The anaphora of Addai and Mari, however, is used during the longest and most important period of the liturgical year, which goes from Palm Sunday till the end of the liturgical year and covers about two hundred days. Moreover, the use of these three anaphoras is not free, as in the Latin tradition, but prescribed by the liturgical calendar. In conscience of faith, the Assyrian Church of the East was always convinced to celebrate the eucharist validly and so to perform in its fullness what Jesus Christ asked his disciples to do. It expressed this conscience of faith, whether using the anaphora of Theodore of Mopsuestia, the anaphora of Nestorius or the anaphora of Addai and Mari, independent of the fact that only the first two anaphoras, of later origin, contain the institution narrative. It should be added that, for the period of the Catholic patriarchate under Patriarch Sulaka (1551-1662), no document exists to prove that the Church of Rome insisted on the insertion of an institution narrative into the anaphora of Addai and Mari.

The Assyrian Church of the East also practises the so-called sacrament or mystery *(Rasà)* of holy leaven. From time immemorial, the Assyrian tradition relates that from the bread Jesus took in his hands, which He blessed, broke and gave to his disciples, He gave two pieces to St John. Jesus asked St John to eat one piece and to carefully keep the other one. After Jesus' death, St John dipped that piece of bread into the blood that proceeded from Jesus' side. Hence the name of "holy leaven", given to this consecrated bread, dipped into the blood of Jesus. Until this day, holy leaven has been kept and renewed annually in the Assyrian Church of the East. The local bishop renews it every year on Holy Thursday, mixing a remainder of the old leaven within the new one. This is distributed to all parishes of his diocese, to be used during one year in each, bread specially prepared by the priest before the eucharist. No priest is allowed to celebrate eucharist using eucharistic bread without holy leaven. This tradition of the sacrament or mystery of holy leaven, which precedes the actual eucharistic celebration, is certainly to be seen as a visible sign of historic and symbolic continuity between the present eucharistic celebration and the institution of the eucharist by Jesus.

Second, the Catholic Church recognizes the Assyrian Church of the East as a true particular church, built upon orthodox faith and apostolic succession. The Assyrian Church of the East also preserved full eucharistic faith in the presence of our Lord under the species of bread and wine and in the sacrificial character of the eucharist. In the Assyrian Church of the East, though not in full communion with the Catholic Church, are thus to be found "true sacraments, and above all, by apostolic succession, the priesthood and the eucharist, whereby they are still joined to us in closest intimacy" (*UR*, §15).

Finally, it must be observed that the Eastern and Western eucharistic anaphoras, while expressing the same mystery, have different theological, ritual and linguistic traditions. The words of the eucharistic institution are indeed present in the anaphora of Addai and Mari, not in a coherent way and *ad litteram*, but rather in a dispersed euchological way, that is, integrated in prayers of thanksgiving, praise and intercession. All these elements constitute a "quasi-narrative" of the eucharistic institution. In the central part of the anaphora, together with the epiclesis, explicit references are made to the eucharistic body and blood of Jesus Christ ("O my Lord, in thy manifold and ineffable mercies, make a good and gracious remembrance for all the upright and just fathers who were pleasing before thee, in the commemoration of the body and blood of thy Christ, which we offer to thee upon the pure and holy altar, as thou hast taught us"), to the life-giving mystery of Jesus' passion, death and resurrection, which is actually commemorated and celebrated ("that all the inhabitants of the world may know thee... and we also, O my Lord, thy unworthy, frail and miserable servants who are gathered and stand before thee, and have received by tradition the example which is from thee, rejoicing and glorifying and exalting and commemorating and celebrating this great and awesome mystery of the passion and death and resurrection of our Lord Jesus Christ"), to the eucharistic offering for the forgiveness of the sins, to the eschatological dimension of the eucharistic celebration and to the Lord's command to "do this in memory of me" (And let thy Holy Spirit come, O my Lord, and rest upon this offering of thy servants, and bless it and sanctify it that it may be to us, O my Lord, for the pardon of sins, and for the forgiveness of shortcomings, and for the great hope of the resurrection from the dead, and for new life in the kingdom of heaven with all who have been pleasing before thee). So the words of the institution are not absent in the anaphora of Addai and Mari, but explicitly mentioned in a dispersed way, from the beginning to the end, in the most important passages of the anaphora. It is also clear that the passages cited above express the full conviction of commemorating the Lord's paschal mystery, in the strong sense of making it present; that is, the intention to carry out in practice precisely what Christ established by his words and actions in instituting the eucharist.

A long and careful study was undertaken of the anaphora of Addai and Mari, from a theological, liturgical and historical perspective, at the end of which the Congregation for the Doctrine of the Faith on 17 January 2001 concluded that this anaphora can be considered valid. Pope John Paul II subsequently approved this decision.

## 3. Pastoral provision

The Catholic Church provides special regulations for situations of pastoral necessity, such as those the Assyrian Church of the East and the Chaldean Church face today. The Code of Canons of the Eastern Churches, can. 671:2 and 3, states, "If necessity requires it or genuine spiritual advantage suggests it and provided that the danger of error or indifferentism is avoided, it is permitted for Catholic Christian faithful, for whom it is physically or morally impossible to approach a Catholic minister, to receive the sacraments of penance, the eucharist and anointing of the sick from non-Catholic ministers, in whose churches these sacraments are valid. Likewise Catholic ministers licitly administer the sacraments of penance, the eucharist and anointing of the sick to Christian faithful of Eastern churches, who do not have full communion with the Catholic Church, if they ask for them on their own and are properly disposed." The *Directory for the Application of Principles and Norms of Ecumenism*, n. 123 and 125, gives the same regulations.

This provision of the Eastern Catholic church law and the *Directory for the Application of Principles and Norms on Ecumenism* can henceforth be applied between the Chaldean

Church and the Assyrian Church of the East. When necessity requires, Assyrian faithful are permitted to receive holy communion in a Chaldean celebration of the holy eucharist; in the same way, Chaldean faithful for whom it is physically or morally impossible to approach a Catholic minister are permitted to receive holy communion in an Assyrian celebration of the holy eucharist. In both cases, Assyrian and Chaldean ministers should continue to celebrate the holy eucharist according to the liturgical prescriptions and customs of their own tradition, especially regarding the use of the anaphora (cf. CICO, can. 674, 2).

When Chaldean faithful are participating in an Assyrian celebration of the holy eucharist, the minister of the Assyrian Church is warmly invited to insert the words of the institution in the anaphora of Addai and Mari. This possibility already exists in the Assyrian Church of the East. Indeed, the holy synod of the Assyrian Church of the East, assembled in 1978 in Baghdad, offered ministers in the Assyrian Church the option of reciting the words of the institution in the anaphora of Addai and Mari. Although this option does not affect the validity of the anaphora of Addai and Mari, it might have a particular relevance from a liturgical as well as an ecumenical viewpoint. From a liturgical viewpoint, this might be an appropriate means to bring the present use of the anaphora of Addai and Mari into line with the general usage in every eucharistic prayer both in the Christian East and in the Christian West. From an ecumenical viewpoint, it might be an appropriate expression of fraternal respect for members of other churches who receive holy communion in the Assyrian Church of the East and who are used, according to the theological and canonical tradition of their proper church, to hear the recitation of the words of the institution in every eucharistic prayer.

It should be noted that the present considerations on the use of the anaphora of Addai and Mari and the guidelines for admission to the eucharist are exclusively concerned with the admission to the eucharist between the Assyrian Church of the East and the Chaldean Church. The anaphora of Addai and Mari pertains to the liturgical patrimony and ecclesial identity of the Assyrian Church of the East, since time immemorial, and should remain so. The Assyrian Church of the East cherished and respectfully transmitted this anaphora from age to age, avoiding any alteration or adaptation in its recitation, out of respect for its venerable origin, traditionally related to the apostolic period. Because each particular church celebrates the sacraments according to its own traditions, principles and norms, it would be liturgically improper to transfer particular elements of one liturgical tradition into another liturgical tradition. Liturgical traditions, indeed, are like languages, having their particular vocabulary and grammar; essential elements from one liturgical tradition cannot be transferred into another without taking from the particularity of the first and harming the coherence of the second.

## Conclusion

The present guidelines have been transmitted to both H.H. Mar Dinkha IV, Patriarch of the Assyrian Church of the East, and H.B. Mar Raphaël I Bidawid, Patriarch of the Chaldean Church. The promulgation of this provision between the Assyrian Church of the East and the Chaldean Church belongs to the competence of both particular churches and their respective authorities (cf. CICO, can. 670:1; 671:4,5). Taking into consideration concrete circumstances and conditions, they will have to establish particular procedures and provide appropriate pastoral means to implement it.

This provision for admission to the eucharist in situations of pastoral necessity is not to be equated with full eucharistic communion between the Chaldean Church and the Assyrian Church of the East. Although closely related to one another in matters of faith and sacramental life, both particular churches are not yet in full communion. They are still travelling, with hope and courage, towards that blessed day when full and visible communion will be attained and when it will be possible to celebrate together in peace the holy eucharist of the Lord. As Pope John Paul II wrote in his encyclical letter *Ut Unum Sint*,

> From this basic but partial unity it is now necessary to advance towards the visible unity which is required and sufficient and which is manifested in a real and concrete way, so that the churches may truly become a sign of that full communion in the one, holy, catholic and apostolic church which will be expressed in the common celebration of the eucharist. (*UUS*, §78)

NOTES
[1]  PCPCU, *Information Service*, 88, 1995/I, pp.2-3.
[2]  Cf A. Gelston, *The Eucharistic Prayer of Addai and Mari*, Oxford, Clarendon, 1992, pp.48-55.

# 29.  Called Together To Be Peace-makers

## Report of the International Dialogue between the Catholic Church and the Mennonite World Conference

### Assisi, Italy, 1998-2003

**Preface**

1.  In the spirit of friendship and reconciliation, a dialogue between Catholics and Mennonites took place over a five-year period, 1998-2003. The dialogue partners met five times in plenary session, a week at a time. At the first four sessions, at least two papers were presented by each delegation as the joint commission explored their respective understandings of key theological themes and of significant aspects of the history of the church. At the fifth session the partners worked together on a common report.

2.  This was a new process of reconciliation. The two dialogue partners had had no official dialogue previous to this, and therefore started afresh. Our purpose was to assist Mennonites and Catholics to overcome the consequences of almost five centuries of mutual isolation and hostility. We wanted to explore whether it is now possible to create a new atmosphere in which to meet each other. After all, despite all that may still divide us, the ultimate identity of both is rooted in Jesus Christ.

3.  This report is a synthesis of the five-year Catholic-Mennonite dialogue. The introduction describes the origins of the dialogue within the contemporary interchurch framework, including other bilateral dialogues in which Catholics and Mennonites have participated in recent decades. It identifies specific factors that led up to this particular dialogue. The introduction then states the purpose and scope of the dialogue, names the participants, and conveys something of the spirit in which the dialogue was conducted. It concludes by naming the locations at which each of the annual dialogue sessions took place, and states the themes that were discussed at each session.

4.  Three chapters follow the introduction. The first of these, "Considering History Together", summarizes the results of our common study of three crucial eras (and related events) of history that have shaped our respective traditions and have yielded distinctive interpretations. These are (1) the rupture of the 16th century, (2) the Constantinian era, and (3) the Middle Ages as such. The aim of our study was to re-read history together for the purpose of comparing and refining our interpretations. Chapter I reports on our agreed-upon evaluations as well as some differing perspectives on the historical eras and events that were selected and examined.

5. In the second chapter, "Considering Theology Together", we report on our common and differing understandings of the church, of baptism, of the eucharist or the Lord's supper, and of peace. In each case, we state the historic theological perspectives of the Catholic Church and of the Mennonite churches.[1] This is followed by a summary of our discussion on major convergences and divergences on each theme. Of particular significance is our theological study and comparison of our respective peace teachings. The Mennonites are one of the "Historic Peace Churches",[2] which means that the commitment to peace is essential to their self-definition. The Catholic Church takes the promotion of unity – and accordingly peace – as "belonging to the innermost nature of the church".[3] Is it possible, therefore, that these two communities can give witness together to the gospel which calls us to be peace-makers in today's often violent world?

6. Chapter III is entitled "Towards a Healing of Memories". In a sense, every interchurch dialogue in which the partners are seeking to overcome centuries of hostility or isolation is aimed at healing bitter memories that have made reconciliation between them difficult. The third chapter identifies four components that, we hope, can help to foster a healing of memories between Mennonites and Catholics.

7. The members of this dialogue offer this report, the results of our work, to the sponsoring bodies in the hope that it can be used by Mennonites and Catholics not only within their respective communities but also as they meet together, to promote reconciliation between them for the sake of the gospel.

## INTRODUCTION

### The origin of these conversations

8. Since the beginning of the 20th century, separated Christian communions have come into closer contact, seeking reconciliation with each other. Despite ongoing divisions, they have started to cooperate with one another to their mutual benefit and often to the benefit of the societies in which they give witness to the gospel. They have engaged in theological dialogue, exploring the reasons for their original divisions. In doing so, they have often discovered that, despite centuries of mutual isolation, they continue to share much of the Christian heritage which is rooted in the gospel. They have also been able to clarify serious differences that exist between and among them in regard to various aspects of the Christian faith. In short, in modern times we have witnessed the emergence of a movement of reconciliation among separated Christians, bringing with it new openness to one another and, on the part of many, a commitment to strive for the unity of the followers of Jesus Christ.

9. Many factors have contributed to this contemporary movement. Among them are conditions and changes in the modern world. For example, the destructive power of modern weapons in a nuclear age has challenged Christians everywhere to reflect on the question of peace in a totally new way – and even to do so together. But the basic inspiration for dialogue between separated Christians has been the realization that conflict between

them impedes the preaching of the gospel and damages their credibility. Indeed, conflict between Christians is a major obstacle to the mission given by Jesus Christ to his disciples. It is difficult to announce the good news of salvation "so that the world may believe" (John 17:21) if those bearing the good news have basic disagreements among themselves.

10.  Since the Second Vatican Council (1962-65), the Catholic Church has been engaged in a wide variety of ecumenical activities, including a number of international bilateral dialogues. There has been dialogue between the Catholic Church and the Orthodox Church, the Coptic Orthodox Church, the Malankara Orthodox Churches, the Assyrian Church of the East, the Anglican Communion, the Lutheran World Federation, the World Alliance of Reformed Churches, the World Methodist Council, the Baptist World Alliance, the Christian Church (Disciples of Christ), the Pentecostals, and the Evangelicals. There have been consultations with the World Evangelical Alliance and Seventh-day Adventists. Also, since 1968 Catholic theologians have participated as full voting members of the multilateral commission on Faith and Order of the World Council of Churches.

11.  Mennonite World Conference (MWC) has previously held international bilateral dialogues with the World Alliance of Reformed Churches and with the Baptist World Alliance. Also, together with the Lutheran World Federation and the World Alliance of Reformed Churches, MWC sponsors the multilateral dialogue on the "first, second and radical Reformations", also known as the "Prague consultations". MWC and the Lutheran World Federation have agreed to international conversation beginning in 2004. Mennonite World Conference member churches in France, in Germany, and in the United States have held bilateral dialogues with Lutheran churches in those countries.

12.  Though Mennonites and Catholics have lived in isolation or in tension for centuries, they too have had increasing contact with each other in recent times. On the international level, they have met each other consistently in a number of interchurch organizations. For example, representatives of the Mennonite World Conference and the Pontifical Council for Promoting Christian Unity (PCPCU) meet annually at the meeting of the Conference of Secretaries of Christian World Communions (CS/CWC), a forum which has for more than forty years brought together the general secretaries of world communions for informal contacts and discussion. There have been numerous other contacts on national and local levels.

13.  More recently some Catholics and Mennonites have begun to invite one another to meetings or events each has sponsored. On the international level, Pope John Paul II invited Christian world communions, including the Mennonite World Conference, to participate in the Assisi Day of Prayer for Peace, held in October 1986. The MWC executive secretary, Paul Kraybill, attended that meeting. The MWC invited the PCPCU to send an observer to its world assembly in Calcutta in January of 1997. Msgr John Mutiso Mbinda attended on behalf of the PCPCU and brought a message from its president, Edward Idris Cardinal Cassidy, in which the cardinal expressed the "sincere hope that there will be other contacts between the Mennonite World Conference and the Catholic Church". After the international Mennonite-Catholic dialogue began in 1998, MWC was among those Pope John Paul II invited to send representatives to events in Rome related to the jubilee year 2000. The Mennonite co-chairman of this dialogue, Dr Helmut Harder, attended a jubilee event at the Vatican in 1999 on the subject of inter-religious dialogue.

More recently, accepting the invitation of Pope John Paul II to leaders of Christian world communions, Dr Mesach Krisetya, president of the MWC, participated in the Assisi Day of Prayer for Peace, 24 January 2002. Moreover, to name one example from a national context, the National Conference of Catholic Bishops in the USA,[4] in the course of writing its pastoral statement on peace in 1993, sought the expertise of persons from outside the Catholic Church, including that of Mennonite theologian John H. Yoder.

14. The possibility and desirability of an international Catholic-Mennonite dialogue came into view in the context of informal contacts during meetings of the CS/CWC. The question was first raised in the early 1990s in a conversation between Dr Larry Miller, executive secretary of the MWC, Bishop Pierre Duprey, secretary of the PCPCU, and Msgr John A. Radano, also of the PCPCU. During ensuing annual CS/CWC meetings, Msgr Radano and Dr Miller continued to informally discuss the possibility of an international dialogue. Two particularly compelling reasons for dialogue were the awareness that contemporary historical studies point to medieval sources of spirituality which Catholics and Mennonites share, and the conviction that both believe peace to be at the heart of the gospel. There was also a sense that, as in other relationships between separated Christians, there is need for a healing of memories between Mennonites and Catholics. In 1997 the leaders of both communions responded positively to a proposal that a Mennonite-Catholic dialogue should take place on the international level. The dialogue, envisioned initially for a five-year period, began the following year, organized on the Catholic side by the PCPCU and on the Mennonite side by the MWC.

## Purpose, scope and participants

15. The general purpose of the dialogue was to learn to know one another better, to promote better understanding of the positions on Christian faith held by Catholics and Mennonites, and to contribute to the overcoming of prejudices that have long existed between them.

16. In light of this purpose, two tracks were followed during each of the annual meetings. A contemporary component explored the positions of each side on a selected key theological issue. A historical track examined the interpretation of each dialogue partner with reference to a particular historical event or historical development that caused or represented separation from one another in the course of the history of the church.

17. In order to implement the study of these two tracks, MWC and PCPCU called on papers from participants who brought historical or theological expertise and understanding to the events, the themes and the issues that affect relationships between Catholics and Mennonites.

18. Mennonite delegation members were Dr Helmut Harder (co-chairman, Canada), systematic theologian and co-editor of "A Confession of Faith in Mennonite Perspective"; Dr Neal Blough (USA/France), specialist in Anabaptist history and theology; Rev. Mario Higueros (Guatemala), head of the Central American Mennonite seminary with advanced theological studies at the Salamanca Pontifical University in Spain and numerous contacts with Catholics in Latin America; Rev. Andrea Lange (Germany), Mennonite pastor and teacher, especially on themes related to peace church theology and

practice; Dr Howard J. Loewen (USA), Mennonite Brethren theologian and expert in the confessional history of Anabaptist/Mennonites; Dr Nzash Lumeya (D.R. Congo/USA), missiologist and Old Testament specialist; and Dr Larry Miller (co-secretary, USA/France), New Testament scholar and Mennonite World Conference executive secretary. Dr Alan Kreider (USA), historian of the early church, joined the group for the annual session of the dialogue in the year 2000.

19. On the Catholic side, participants included the Most Rev. Joseph Martino (co-chairman, USA), a church historian and auxiliary bishop of Philadelphia, located in an area which includes many communities of the Anabaptist tradition; Rev. Dr James Puglisi, SA (USA/Italy), director of the Centro Pro Unione and specialist in liturgy and sacraments; Dr Peter Nissen (The Netherlands), church historian and authority on relations between Catholics and Anabaptists in the 16th century; Msgr John Mutiso Mbinda (Kenya/Vatican City), PCPCU staff member who participated in the 1997 MWC world assembly meeting in Calcutta and whose work brings him into regular contact with international Christian organizations where Mennonites participate at times; Dr Joan Patricia Back (UK/Italy), on the staff of Centro Uno, ecumenical secretariat of the Focolare Movement, whose communities around the world have contacts with many Christian groups, including Mennonites; Rev. Dr Andrew Christiansen, SJ (USA), an expert in social ethics whose work in matters of peace both on the academic and the practical levels have brought him into contact and conversation with Mennonite scholars; and Msgr Dr John A. Radano (co-secretary, USA/Vatican City), head of the Western Section of the PCPCU who has participated in various international dialogues.

20. The atmosphere in the meetings was most cordial. Each side presented its views on the theological issues as clearly and forcefully as possible, seeking to foster an honest and fruitful dialogue. As the conversation partners heard the other's views clearly stated, it was possible to begin to see which parts of the Christian heritage are held in common by both Mennonites and Catholics, and where they have strong differences. In presenting their respective views on history, dialogue members did not refrain from allowing one another to see clearly the criticism each communion has traditionally raised against the other. At the same time, dialogue participants did this with the kind of self-criticism that is needed if an authentic search for truth is to take place. The constant hope was that clarifications in both areas of study, historical and theological, might contribute to a healing of memories between Catholics and Mennonites.

21. Prayer sustained and accompanied the dialogue. Every day of each meeting began and ended with prayer and worship, led by members of the delegations. On Sundays, dialogue participants attended services in a Mennonite or a Catholic congregation, depending on which side was hosting the meeting that year. During the week, the host side arranged a field trip to sites associated with its tradition. These services and trips contributed to the dialogue by helping each partner to know the other better.

## Locations and themes of annual meetings

22. The first meeting took place in Strasbourg, France, 14-18 October 1998. Each delegation made presentations in response to the question "Who are we today?" A second set of papers helped to shed light on the reasons for reactions to each other in the 16th

century. At the second meeting, held in Venice, Italy, 12-18 October 1999, the discussion in the theological sessions focused on the way each communion understands the church today. The historical track explored the Anabaptist idea of the restitution of the early church, as well as the medieval roots of the Mennonite tradition of faith and spirituality. At the third meeting, 24-30 November 2000, held at the Thomashof, near Karlsruhe, Germany, the contemporary discussion turned to an area of possible cooperation between Mennonites and Catholics today, with the theme formulated as a question: "What is a peace church?" In the historical sessions, each presented an interpretation of the impact of the "Constantinian shift" on the church. In the fourth meeting, at Assisi, Italy, 27 November-3 December 2001, each delegation presented its views on baptism and the eucharist or Lord's supper. The historical part of that meeting focused on the view of each on the relationship between church and state in the Middle Ages. At the fifth meeting, 25-31 October 2002, in Akron, Pennsylvania, USA, members worked on the final report of the dialogue. Drafting meetings in March, May and June 2003 provided occasions to refine the report in preparation for its submission.

Note: A list of the papers presented at the dialogue sessions, together with their authors, appears as an appendix at the end of this report.

## I. CONSIDERING HISTORY TOGETHER

### A. Introduction: shared hermeneutics or re-reading of church history

23. A common re-reading of the history of the church has proved to be fruitful in recent interchurch dialogues.[5] The same is true for our dialogue. Mennonites and Catholics have lived through more than 475 years of separation. Over the centuries they developed separate views of the history of the Christian tradition. By studying history together, we discovered that our interpretations of the past were often incomplete and limited. Sharing our insights and our assessments of the past helped us gain a broader view of the history of the church.

24. First of all, we recognized that both our traditions have developed interpretations of aspects of church history that were influenced by negative images of the other, though in different ways and to different degrees. Reciprocal hostile images were fostered and continued to be present in our respective communities and in our representations of each other in history. Our relationship, or better the lack of it, began in a context of rupture and separation. Since then, from the 16th century to the present, theological polemics have persistently nourished negative images and narrow stereotypes of each other.

25. Secondly, both our traditions have had their selective ways of looking at history. Two examples readily come to mind: the interplay of church and state in the Middle Ages, and the use of violence by Christians. We sometimes restricted our views of the history of Christianity to those aspects that seemed to be most in agreement with the self-definition of our respective ecclesial communities. Our focus was often determined by specific perspectives of our traditions, which frequently led to a way of studying the past in

which the results of our research were already influenced by our ecclesiological start-
ing-points.

26. The experience of studying the history of the church together and of re-reading it in
an atmosphere of openness has been invaluable. It has helped us gain a broader view of
the history of the Christian tradition. We have been reminded that we share at least fifteen centuries of common Christian history. The early church and the church of the
Middle Ages were, and continue to be, the common ground for both our traditions. We
have also discovered that the subsequent centuries of separation have spelled a loss to
both of us. Re-reading the past together helps us to regain and restore certain aspects of
our ecclesial experience that we may have undervalued or even discounted due to centuries of separation and antagonism.

27. Our common re-reading of the history of the church will hopefully contribute to the
development of a common interpretation of the past. This can lead to a shared new
memory and understanding. In turn, a shared new memory can free us from the prison
of the past. On this basis both Catholics and Mennonites hear the challenge to become
architects of a future more in conformity with Christ's instructions when he said, "I give
you a new commandment, that you love one another. Just as I have loved you, you also
should love one another. By this everyone will know that you are my disciples, if you
have love for one another" (John 13:34-35). Given this commandment, Christians can
take responsibility for the past. They can name the errors in their history, repent of them,
and work to correct them. Mennonite theologian John Howard Yoder has written, "It is
a specific element in the Christian message that there is a remedy for a bad record. If the
element of repentance is not acted out in interfaith contact, we are not sharing the whole
gospel witness."[6]

28. Such acts of repentance contribute to the purification of memory, which was one of
the goals enunciated by Pope John Paul II during the great jubilee of the year 2000. The
purification of memory aims at liberating our personal and communal consciences from
all forms of resentment and violence that are the legacy of past faults. Jesus asks us, his
disciples, to prepare for this act of purification by seeking personal forgiveness as well
as extending forgiveness to others. This he did by teaching his disciples the Lord's prayer
whereby we implore, "Forgive us our trespasses as we forgive those who trespass against
us" (Matt. 6:12). The purification of one's own memory, individually and as church communities, is a first step towards the mutual healing of memories in our interchurch dialogues and in our relationships (cf. Ch. III).

29. To begin the process of the healing of memories requires rigorous historical analysis and renewed historical evaluation. It is no small task to enter into

> a historical-critical investigation that aims at using all of the information available, with a view
> to a reconstruction of the environment, of the ways of thinking, of the conditions and the living
> dynamic in which those events and those words were placed in order in such a way to ascer-
> tain the contents and the challenges that – precisely in their diversity – they propose to our
> present time.[7]

Proceeding carefully in this way, a common re-reading of history may help us in purifying our understanding of the past as a step towards healing the often-painful memories
of our respective communities.

## B. A profile of the religious situation of Western Europe on the eve of the Reformation

30. On the eve of the Reformation, Christian Europe entered a time of change, which marked the transition from the medieval to the early modern period.[8] Up to 1500, the church had been the focal point of unity and the dominant institution of European society. But at the dawn of the early modern period its authority was challenged by the growing power of the first modern states. They consolidated and centralized their political authority and sovereignty over particular geographical areas. They tried to strengthen their power over their subjects in many aspects of human life. For centuries, secular rulers considered themselves responsible for religion in their states. But now they had new means at their disposal to consolidate such authority. This sometimes brought them into conflict with the church, for instance in the area of ecclesiastical appointments, legal jurisdiction and taxes.

31. The rise of the early modern states led to a decline of the consciousness of Christian unity. The ideal of a unified Christendom (*christianitas*) that reached its climax in the period of the Crusades was crumbling. This process had been stimulated already by the events of the 14th and 15th centuries. At that time there was the so-called Babylonian captivity of the papacy (1309-77), when the residence of the popes was in Avignon (in present day south-eastern France). Then followed the so-called great Western schism (1378-1417), when the papal office was claimed by two or even three rival popes.

32. At the same time, a divided Europe was experiencing massive social and economic changes. The 16th century was a period of enormous population growth. Historians estimate that the European population grew from 55 million in 1450 to 100 million in 1650. This growth was of course prominent in the urban settlements, although the majority of the population still lived in rural areas. Population growth was also accompanied by economic expansion, which mainly benefited the urban middle classes. They became the main carriers of ecclesiastical developments in the 16th century, both in the Reformation and in the Catholic renewal. But at the same time economic expansion was accompanied by a growing gap between rich and poor, especially in the cities but also in rural areas. Social unrest and upheaval became a familiar phenomenon in urban society, as peasant rebellions were in rural villages. To some extent this social unrest also contributed to the soil for the radical Reformation.[9]

33. During this period, the cultural elite of Europe witnessed a process of intellectual and cultural renewal, identified by the words "Renaissance" and "Humanism". This process showed a variety of faces throughout Europe. For instance, in Italy it had a more "pagan" profile than in northern Europe, where "biblical humanists" such as Erasmus and Thomas More used humanist techniques to further piety and biblical studies. Meanwhile in France Humanism was mainly supported by a revival of legal thought. The core spirit of the Renaissance, which took its roots in Italy in the 14th century, is well expressed in the famous words of the historian Jacob Burkhardt as "the discovery of the world and of humankind". These words indicate a new appreciation for the world surrounding humanity. They also herald a new self-consciousness characterized by recognition of the unique value and character of the individual human person. Humanism can be considered as the main intellectual manifestation of the Renaissance. It developed the study of the ancient classical literature, both Latin and Greek. But it also fostered the desire to return to the roots of European civilization, back to the sources (*ad fontes*) and

to their values. Within Christianity, this led to an in-depth study of scripture in its original languages (Hebrew and Greek), of the church fathers, and of other sources of knowledge about the early church. It led as well to the exploration of other sources of knowledge about the early church. Humanism also entailed an educational programme, which mainly reached the expanding urban middle classes. It fostered their self-consciousness, preparing them to participate in government and administration and to take on certain responsibilities and duties in church life and in ecclesiastical organization.

34. On the eve of the Reformation, church life and piety were flourishing. For a long time both Catholic and Protestant church historians have described religious life at the end of the Middle Ages in terms of crisis and decline. But today the awareness is growing that these terms reflect a retrospective assessment of the situation of the Middle Ages that was determined by inadequate criteria. There is a growing tendency, both among Catholic and Protestant historians, to give a more positive evaluation of religious life around the year 1500. [10] Many consider this period now to be an age of religious vitality, a period of "booming" religiosity. They perceive the Reformation and the Catholic Reform not only as a reaction against late medieval religious life, but also and principally as the result and the fruit of this religious vitality. Certainly there were abuses among the clergy, among the hierarchy and the papacy, and among the friars. There were abuses in popular religion, in the ecclesiastical tax system, and in the system of pastoral care and administration. Absenteeism of parish priests and bishops and the accumulation of benefices were among the indicators of the problem.

35. Yet this was hardly the whole story. Religious life was at the same time characterized by a renewed emphasis on good preaching and on religious education, especially among the urban middle classes. There was a strong desire for a more profound faith. Translations of the Bible appeared in the major European vernacular languages and spread through the recently invented printing press. Religious books dominated the book market. The many confraternities that were founded on the eve of the Reformation propagated a lay spirituality. These confraternities served the social and religious needs of lay people by organizing processions and devotions, by offering prayer services and sermons, and by propagating vernacular devotional books. They also provided care and help for the sick and the dying, and for people caught in other kinds of hardships. Zealous lay movements like the so-called *Devotio Moderna* [11] as well as preachers and writers from several religious orders propagated a spirituality of discipleship and of the "imitation of Christ". Many of the religious orders themselves witnessed reform movements in the 15th century, which led to the formation of observant branches. These groups desired to observe their religious rule in the strict and original way in which their founder intended it to be followed.

36. The church in general also witnessed reform movements whose goal was to free the Christian community from worldliness. From simple believers to the highest church authorities, Christians were called to return to the simplicity of New Testament Christianity. These reforms, which affected people at every level of society and church, criticized the pomp of the church hierarchy, spoke against absenteeism among pastors, noted the lack of good and regular preaching, and called into question the eagerness of church leaders to purchase church offices. These late medieval reform movements envisioned ideals that a century or two later would become common in the Protestant Reformation, the radical Reformation, and the Catholic Reform as well.

37. Of course, a certain externalism and even materialism and superstition were also present in late medieval popular piety. These were in evidence especially in the many devotions, in processions and pilgrimages, and in the veneration of saints and relics. But at the same time the performance of these many forms of religious behaviour reflects a strong desire for salvation, for religious experience, and a zeal for the sacred. In the 16th century, the Protestant Reformation, the radical Reformation, as well as the Catholic Reform benefited significantly from these yearnings for a higher spirituality.

## C.  The rupture between Catholics and Anabaptists

ORIGINS

38.  The separation of the Anabaptists from the established church in the 16th century is to be understood in the larger context of the first manifestations of the Reformation. The respective Anabaptist groups had varied origins within diverse political, social and religious circumstances. [12] Anabaptist movements first originated within the Lutheran and Zwinglian reformations in southern Germany and Switzerland during the 1520s. In the 1530s, Anabaptist (Mennonite) movements in the Netherlands broke more directly with the Catholic Church. These ruptures had to do with understandings of baptism, ecclesiology, church-state relationships and social ethics. The latter included the rejection of violence, the rejection of oath-taking, and in some cases the rejection of private property. For all at that time, but especially for the leaders in church and state, this must have been a very confusing situation. There were diverse and sometimes conflicting currents within the Anabaptist movement and within the radical Reformation, for instance concerning the use of the sword. Nevertheless, all the Anabaptist movements, contrary to the main reformers such as Luther, Zwingli and Calvin, agreed on the conviction that, since infants are not able to make a conscious commitment to Christ, only adults can be baptized after having repented of their sins and having confessed their faith. Since Anabaptists did not consider infant baptism valid, those Christians who were baptized as infants needed to be baptized again as adults. Anabaptist groups shared other convictions with related streams of the radical Reformation. While the first Anabaptists often saw themselves in harmony with the ideals and theology of Luther and Zwingli, their rejection of infant baptism and other theological or ethical positions led both Protestants and Catholics to condemn them.

39.  These condemnations should also be understood in relation to the disasters of the Peasants War (1524-25) and the "kingdom of Münster" in Westphalia (1534-35). For Catholic rulers, the peasants movement was a clear sign of the subversive nature of Luther's break with Rome. To defend himself against such accusations, Luther (and other Reformers) blamed the Peasants War on people called "Enthusiasts" or "Anabaptists". It is difficult to sort out historically the origins of Anabaptism in the context of the popular movement commonly designated as the "Peasants War". The early years of the Reformation were quite fluid, and historians now recognize that movements or churches designated as "Lutheran", "Zwinglian" or "Anabaptist" were not always clearly recognizable or distinct from each other, especially up until the tragic events of 1524-25. Nevertheless, the radical experiment of the kingdom of Münster, where in 1534-35 the

so-called Melchiorites (followers of the Anabaptist lay preacher Melchior Hoffman) established a violent and dictatorial regime in order to bring about the "Day of the Lord", confirmed both Catholic and Protestant authorities in their fear of the Anabaptist movement as a serious threat to church and society. Whereas many Anabaptist groups were faithful to their principles of non-violence and pacifism, some groups nevertheless allowed the use of the sword in the establishment of the kingdom of God. [13] As a result, the term "Anabaptist", employed in both Catholic and Protestant polemics, came to connote rebellion and anarchy. Often it was deemed that Anabaptist groups who claimed to be non-violent were only so because they lacked power. Rulers thought that, if the occasion arose, violence would once again be used by Anabaptists.

40. Given the close relationship between church and state, the practice of rebaptizing those who were already baptized as infants had an extremely provocative effect in the 16th century. For the Catholic Church and the emerging Protestant churches, it could only be considered heretical. The practice of rebaptism had already been condemned in the early 5th century as reflected in Augustine's polemics against the Donatists, a separatist movement in North Africa, who rebaptized all recruits from the established church. [14] For the state, a law of Roman Emperors Honorius and Theodosius of 413 determined severe penalties for the practice of rebaptism. In 529, Emperor Justinian I, in reproducing the Theodosian edict in his revision of Roman law, specified the penalty as capital punishment. [15] On the basis of this ancient imperial law against the Donatists, the diet of Speyer in 1529 proclaimed the death penalty for all acts of "rebaptism".

IMAGES OF EACH OTHER

41. Mennonites and Catholics have harboured negative images of each other ever since the 16th century. Such negative images must of course be put into the context of early modern Catholic and Protestant polemical theology. Nevertheless, both Catholics and Protestants condemned and persecuted the Anabaptists, and the Anabaptists considered the Protestant Reformers to be as reprehensible as the Catholic Church they had left.

42. Anabaptists shared many of the common Reformation images of the Catholic Church. Along with other Protestant reformers, Anabaptists accused Catholics of works righteousness and of sacramental idolatry. They saw the Reformation as a prelude to the end of time, and viewed the pope as the antichrist. Anabaptists soon left the Reformation camp, criticizing both Catholics and Protestants for what they saw as very unhealthy relationships with political power. They considered the church to be fallen. This fall was associated with the Emperors Constantine and Theodosius and the fact that Christianity was officially proclaimed as the only religion of the Roman empire. They saw infant baptism as the culminating sign of a religion that forced people to be Christians independent of any faith commitment. In the eyes of the Anabaptists, such Christianity could not be ethically serious nor produce the fruits of discipleship. Persecution and execution of Anabaptists increased the level of polemics and fostered negative images. Anabaptists saw Catholic religion as being based on ceremonies, works, tradition and superstition. Priests were characterized as ignorant, lazy and evil. The *Martyrs' Mirror*, compiled by a Dutch Mennonite in the 17th century, tells the stories of many Anabaptist martyrs. It puts them in the context of the faithful church throughout the centuries. Through narra-

tive and engravings, this very important book for Mennonites portrays Catholics and Protestants as persecutors, torturers and executioners. As the centuries went on, Mennonites often lacked direct knowledge about the Catholic Church and her history, but they retained their earlier views.

43. For Catholics, Anabaptists represented the logical outcome of Protestant heresy and schism. When Luther left the Catholic Church, he rejected the only legitimate Christian authority of the time. This opened up the door to numerous and contradictory readings of scripture as well as to political subversion. Alongside traditional Catholic objections to "Protestantism", the rejection of infant baptism and the practice of rebaptizing dominated the early Catholic theological reaction against Anabaptism. Catholics saw Anabaptists as ignorant people whose theologians did not know Latin. For example, they charged that the Anabaptist theologian Dr Balthasar Hubmaier was an agitator, an enemy of government and an immoral person. For a long time, even into the 20th century, Catholic writers associated the most peaceful followers of Menno Simons with the radical Melchiorites of Münster. In fact, Catholic theologians had limited knowledge of the history of Anabaptism. They saw Anabaptists as restoring old heresies that had been condemned long ago. All this was complicated by the fact that, during the 16th century, Catholic theologians were writing against people whom the state, at the request of both Catholic and Protestant princes, had already condemned to death at the diet of Speyer (see §40 above), and who therefore lived outside the protection of the law.

AN ECCLESIOLOGY OF RESTITUTION

44. The question of the apostolic nature of the church created a major ecclesiological divide between Anabaptists and Catholics during the 16th century. From the early centuries on, Christians of both East and West had understood apostolic succession via the office of bishops as ensuring the transmission of the faith and therefore the transmission of the apostolic nature of the church throughout the ages. Sixteenth-century Anabaptists, on the contrary, rejected the idea of an apostolic continuity guaranteed by the institutional church. They began to speak of the "fall" of the church and described it as a sign of her unfaithfulness. This unfaithfulness implied the necessity of a restitution of the "apostolic" church. The Catholics and most of the magisterial Reformers considered infant baptism to be an apostolic tradition, practised from the beginning of the church. Anabaptists, on the contrary, saw the general acceptance of infant baptism, together with the close political ties between church and empire (Constantine and Theodosius), as the major signs of apostasy from the apostolic vision of the faithful church and therefore as evidence of the "fall". For the Anabaptists, correspondence with the New Testament writings on ethical and doctrinal issues became the test for measuring apostolic Christianity. Faithfulness was defined not as maintaining institutional continuity, but as restitution of the New Testament faith. In their view, the restoration and preservation of the apostolic church required them to break away from the institutional church of their day. Continuity was sought not through the succession of bishops, but rather through faithfulness to the apostolic witness of scripture and by identification with people and movements. For example, the Waldensians and the Franciscans were considered by the Anabaptists as faithful representatives of true Christianity throughout the course of their long history.[16]

45. One of the results of the division among Christians in the 16th and 17th centuries, given the approach to judicial matters and punishment at that time, was persecution and martyrdom.[17] Given the close relationship between religion and society, the establishment of the principle *cuius regio, eius religio* (the religion of the ruler is to be the established religion of a region or a state) at the peace of Augsburg in 1555 contributed to the already strongly negative sentiments between separated Christians. It introduced a type of society where one specific Christian confession (Catholic, Lutheran, and later Reformed) became the established religion of a given territory. This type of society, the so-called confessional state, was characterized by intolerance towards persons of other Christian confessions. Due to this specific and particular political situation, martyrdom became a common experience for Christians of all confessions, be it Catholic, Lutheran, Reformed, Anglican or Anabaptist.

46. Mennonites suffered greatly in this period, both in Protestant and in Catholic states. Many governments did not tolerate radical Reformation dissidents, including pacifist Anabaptists. According to recent estimations, approximately 5000 persons were executed for their religious beliefs in the course of the 16th century. Of these, between 2000 and 2500 were Anabaptist and Mennonite men and women, the majority of them in Catholic territories, who were convicted of heresy.[18] Anabaptists could hardly find any stable political haven in 16th-century Europe. In some countries the persecution of Mennonites would last for centuries. In some states they were discriminated against and subjected to social and political restrictions even into the 20th century, especially because of their principled attitude of conscientious objection.

47. For Anabaptists and Mennonites, discipleship indeed implied the openness to oppression, persecution and violent death. The danger of persecution and martyrdom became a part of the Mennonite identity. As the Mennonite scholar Cornelius Dyck has written, "The possibility of martyrdom had a radical impact on all who joined the group – on their priorities, status and self-consciousness."[19] Mennonites held their martyrs in highest regard. They sang of their faithful testimony and celebrated their memory by collecting their stories in martyrologies, such as *Het Offer des Heeren* (The sacrifice unto the Lord) and Thieleman Jans van Braght's *Martelaers Spiegel* (*Martyrs Mirror*), which is still read today within the global Mennonite church.

48. Catholics never suffered any persecution at the hands of Mennonites.[20] Nevertheless, in the consideration of the Anabaptist and Mennonite experience of martyrdom and persecution, it is important to note that, in their post-medieval history, Catholics have also known this experience. In some territories where the Reformed and Lutheran confession was established, and also in England after the establishment of the Church of England, Catholics were subject to persecution and to the death penalty. A number of them, especially priests, monks and nuns, were brutally martyred for their faith. Persecution of Catholics and violation of religious freedom continued in some countries for centuries. For a long while, the practice of the Catholic faith was not allowed publicly in England and in several Lutheran countries such as in Scandinavia and in the Dutch republic. Catholics were able to practise their faith openly in these countries only by the end of the 18th or the beginning of the 19th century. In some cases discrimination against the Catholics lasted into the 20th century. During those restrictive years, both Catholics and Mennonites in several countries were constrained to live a hidden life.

49. When conflict occurs within an institution and separation ensues, discourse easily takes on the nature of self-justification. As Mennonites and Catholics begin discussion after centuries of separate institutional existence, we need to be aware that we have developed significant aspects of our self-understandings and theologies in contexts where we have often tried to prove that we are right and they are wrong. We need tools of historical research that help us to see both what we have in common as well as to responsibly address the differences that separate us. Mennonites now have almost five centuries of accumulated history to deal with, along with a growing experience of integration into the established society. Catholics, on the other hand, increasingly find themselves in situations of disestablishment where they are faced with the same questions as Mennonites were facing as a minority church in an earlier era. These facts could help both traditions to be more open to the concerns of the other, and to look more carefully at the fifteen centuries of commonly shared history as well as the different paths each has taken since the 16th century. Our shared history of fifteen centuries, built upon the foundation of the patristic period, reminds us of the debt that Western Christianity owes to the East, as well as of the rich and varied theological, cultural, spiritual and artistic traditions that flourished in the Middle Ages.

50. Contemporary historical scholarship speaks of the "left wing of the Reformation" or of the "radical Reformation". Less polemical and less confessional historical perspectives demonstrate that there were many different theologies and approaches among the Reformation dissidents. Not only were there Anabaptists, Spiritualists and Rationalists among those called "Enthusiasts" or "Schwärmer". There were also different kinds of Anabaptists and Spiritualists. Present-day Mennonites find their origins in the nonviolent Anabaptist groups of Switzerland, southern Germany and the Netherlands. Both Catholic and Mennonite scholars now have become aware of the complicated situation of the 16th-century rupture within Christianity. They also acknowledge that the rupture between the Catholic Church and the Anabaptist groups should be studied and understood within the broader framework of the social, political and religious conflicts of the 16th century. The oppression and persecution of Anabaptists and Mennonites need to be perceived and evaluated within the framework of a society that resorted to violent "solutions" rather than to dialogue.

51. Further joint studies by Catholic and Mennonite historians would deepen our knowledge and awareness of the complexity of our histories. Catholics would do well to acquaint themselves with the history of the extreme diversity of the radical movements. This would help prevent continual historical misrepresentations of Mennonites. At the same time, Mennonites need to rethink how difficult it must have been in the 16th century to sort out the differences among those who had rejected both Rome and Luther. Those who now call themselves Mennonites came to a doctrinal understanding of nonviolence only after the Peasants War (1527 at Schleitheim in the case of the Swiss Anabaptists) and after Münster (1534-35 in the case of the Dutch Anabaptists).

52. The common experience of martyrdom and persecution could help both Catholics and Mennonites to reach a renewed understanding of the meaning of martyrdom in the painful division of the Christian church in the early modern period, given the close relationship between religion and society at that time. A common study of the history of 16th-century martyrdom and persecution can help Catholics to appreciate and esteem the

Mennonite experience of martyrdom and its impact on Mennonite spirituality and identity. Mennonites could benefit from a study of the Catholic Church's minority status in many countries since the Reformation period and from the knowledge that Catholics have also had the experience of being persecuted over the centuries.

## D. The Constantinian era

53. After having studied the 16th century together, it became clear to our dialogue group that further joint historical work was necessary on two other periods. In the Reformation period conflicting understandings of these periods of history were a major reason for separation. The following sections reflect our consideration of both the Constantinian era and the later medieval period.

A JOINT READING OF EVENTS AND CHANGES

54. By "Constantinian era", "change" and "shift", we refer to the important developments that took place from the beginning of the 4th century onward. Mennonites and other radical reformers often refer to these changes as the "Constantinian fall".[21] In 313, Roman Emperor Constantine issued the edict of Milan which allowed Christianity to exist without persecution alongside other religions. He also required all buildings, cemeteries, and other properties taken in earlier persecutions to be returned to the church. In 380, Emperor Theodosius I decreed Christianity as the official religion of the empire by raising the Nicene Creed to imperial law. At this point, religions other than Christianity no longer had legal status in the Roman empire, and they often became the objects of persecution. Due to these changes, the church developed from a suppressed church (*ecclesia pressa*) to a tolerated church (*ecclesia tolerata*), and then to a triumphant church (*ecclesia vincens*) within the Roman empire.[22]

55. In the 4th and 5th centuries, Christianity became a respected religion, with greater freedom to fulfill its mission in the world. Churches were built and worship took place without fear of persecution. The gospel was preached throughout the world with the intention of evangelizing culture and society under favourable political circumstances. But during the same period, civil rulers sometimes exercised authority over the church and often asserted the right to control ecclesiastical affairs. And, in some instances, though not without resistance from the church, they convened synods and councils and controlled various kinds of ecclesiastical appointments, especially those of the bishops in the main cities of the empire. The church accepted the favours and the benevolent treatment by the state. The power of the state was used to enforce Christian doctrines. To some extent Christians even accepted the use of violence, for instance in the defence of orthodoxy and in the struggle against paganism although some did resist this use of violence. In the ensuing centuries of the Middle Ages, this arrangement led in some cases to forced conversion of large numbers of people, to coercion in matters of faith, and to the application of the death penalty against "heretics".[23] Together we repudiate those aspects of the Constantinian era that were departures from some characteristic Christian practices and deviations from the gospel ethic. We acknowledge the church's failure when she justified the use of force in evangelism, sought to create and to maintain a unitary Christian society by coercive means, and persecuted religious minorities.

56. A common re-reading of the history of the early church by Mennonites and Catholics has been fostered by at least two recent developments. First of all, the social environment and societal position of both the Catholic Church and the Mennonite churches have changed. In many parts of the world Mennonite churches have left their position of isolation that was often imposed by others. Thus Mennonites are experiencing the challenges of taking up responsibilities within society. At the Second Vatican Council (1962-65), the Catholic Church (1) affirmed freedom of religion and conscience for all, (2) opposed coercion in matters of religion, and (3) sought from the state for itself and all communities of believers only freedom for individuals and for communities in matters of religion.[24] The Catholic Church thus renounced any desire to have a predominant position in society and to be recognized as a state church.[25] In the following decades, the Catholic Church strenuously defended the principle of religious freedom and of the separation of church and state. In his encyclical *Centesimus Annus* (1991), Pope John Paul II stated that religious freedom is the "source and synthesis" of other human rights. Secondly, the 1999 document "Memory and Reconciliation", published by the international theological commission, challenges us to study the history of the church, and to recognize the faults of the past, as a means of facilitating the reconciliation of memories and the healing of wounds.

57. Both our traditions regret certain aspects of the Constantinian era, but we also recognize that some developments of the 4th and 5th centuries had roots in the early history of the church, and were in legitimate continuity with it. Mennonites have a strong negative interpretation of the Constantinian change. Catholics have a strong sense of the continuity of the church during that period and through the ages. But both of us also recognize that past eras were very different from the present, and we also need to be careful about judging historical events according to contemporary standards.

AREAS OF FUTURE STUDY

58. We can agree that through a reading together of sources of the early church, we are discovering ways of overcoming some of the stereotypes that we have had of each other. The ressourcement (return to the sources) that the Catholic Church engaged in when preparing for the Second Vatican Council enriched Catholicism, and a parallel movement is beginning in contemporary Anabaptism.[26] With the use of early Christian sources we can affirm new ways of understanding the question of continuity and of renewal in history. We can both agree that the study of the Constantinian era is significant for us in that it raises important questions regarding the mission of the church to the world and its methods of evangelization.

59. Various aspects of post-Constantinian Christendom have different meanings in our respective traditions. Catholics would see matters such as the generalization of infant baptism, the evolution of the meaning of conversion, as well as Christian attitudes towards military service and oath-taking as examples of legitimate theological developments. Mennonites consider the same phenomena as unfortunate changes of earlier Christian practice and as unfaithfulness to the way of Jesus. Catholics understand the establishment of a Christian society during the Middle Ages, which attempted to bring all social, political and economic structures into harmony with the gospel, to have been a worthy goal. Mennonites remain opposed to the theological justification of such an

endeavour, and are critical of its results in practice. Mennonites also tend to identify and locate the continuity of the church during this period in people and in movements that were sometimes rejected as heretical by the Catholic Church. To be sure, they also see continuity in reform movements within the medieval church.

60. Mennonites can affirm the position on religious liberty that was adopted in the Second Vatican Council's Declaration on Religious Freedom (*DH*) in 1965. A key quote from the declaration reads as follows:

> This Vatican Council declares that the human person has a right to religious freedom. This freedom means that all men are to be immune from coercion on the part of individuals or of social groups or of any human power, in such wise that no one is to be forced to act in a manner contrary to his own beliefs, whether privately or publicly, whether alone or in association with others, within due limits (*DH* 2).

This quotation and the entire text reflects in many ways the position that was taken by 16th-century Anabaptists. Such Anabaptists as Balthasar Hubmaier[27] or Pilgram Marpeck[28] questioned the use of coercion in relation to religious pluralism and criticized the use of political means against those who believe differently or who have no religious beliefs at all. This same declaration signifies that the Catholic Church renounces the claim to be a "state" church in any and every context. Protestants are no longer addressed as heretics, but as separated sisters and brothers in Christ, even while there are continuing disagreements, and while visible unity has not yet been achieved. It was this Declaration as well as other important documents of the Second Vatican Council that contributed significantly to dialogues such as this one. In light of these changes, new possibilities for relating to one another are becoming possible.

61. Catholics affirm that the Declaration on Religious Freedom represents a development in doctrine that has strong foundations in scripture and Tradition.[29] The declaration states,

> In the life of the people of God, as it has made its pilgrim way through the vicissitudes of human history, there has at times appeared a way of acting that was hardly in accord with the spirit of the gospel, or even opposed to it. Nevertheless, the doctrine of the church that no one is to be coerced into faith has always stood firm.[30]

Mennonite readings of medieval history doubt such a claim. They state that major theologians, popes, ecumenical councils, emperors and kings justified persecution theologically. They supported the punishment of heretics by the state, and in some instances, from Theodosius onward, the church forced the "Christianization" of large numbers of people. The continuity of the tradition and the differing interpretations of the development of doctrine in this respect, as well as the different ways of evangelization, need further joint study. Nonetheless, the contemporary Catholic position on this question allows for significant progress in dialogue, and for mutual comprehension and collaboration.

62. Catholics and Mennonites have different interpretations of the historical development of the practice of infant baptism in Christianity. Catholics understand the baptism of children as a long-held tradition of the church in the East and in the West, going back to the first centuries of Christianity. They refer to the fact that liturgical documents, such as "The Apostolic Tradition" (ca. 220) and church fathers such as Origen and Cyprian of Carthage speak about infant baptism as an ancient and apostolic tradition. Mennonites, on the other hand, consider the introduction of the practice of infant baptism as a

later development and they see its generalization as the result of changes in the concept of conversion during the Constantinian era. The historical development of the practice of baptism in relation to the changing position of the Christian church in culture and society needs to be studied together more thoroughly by both Catholic and Mennonite scholars.

## E.  Towards a shared understanding of the Middle Ages

REVIEWING OUR RESPECTIVE IMAGES OF THE MIDDLE AGES

63.  In looking repeatedly at church history in the Middle Ages, both Catholic and Mennonite historians are becoming aware of the fact that their images of the medieval church may be one-sided, incomplete, and often biased. These images need careful revision and amplification in the light of modern scholarship. To Catholic historians it is becoming clear that the Middle Ages were not as deeply Christianized as the 19th century image of the "Catholic Middle Ages"' wanted to see them.[31] To Mennonite historians it is becoming clear that the Middle Ages were not as barbaric and decayed as their restitutionist view depicted them. The period between the early church and the Reformation era is considered now to be much more complex, varied, many-voiced and many-coloured than the denominational images of this period wanted us to believe.

64.  Therefore, for both our traditions, it is important to see the "other" Middle Ages, namely those aspects of the period that are often lacking in the image that is popular and widespread in our respective religious communities. For Catholics, besides the positive aspects of the Christian civilization of the Middle Ages, it is important to see the elements of violence, of conversion by force, of the links between the church and secular power, and of the dire effects of feudalism in medieval Christendom. For Mennonites, besides the negative aspects, it is important to see that Christian faith also served as a basis for criticizing secular powers and violence in the Middle Ages. Several reform movements, led by monasteries (for example, Cluny), but also by the popes (notably, the Gregorian reform), tried to free the church from secular influences and political dominance.[32] Unfortunately, they succeeded only to a very limited extent. Other movements, often led by monks and ascetics, but also by popes and bishops, tried to restrict the use of violence in medieval Christianity, and sought to protect the innocent, the weak and the defenceless. Again, their efforts were met with very limited success. Nevertheless, within the often-violent society of medieval Christendom there was an uninterrupted tradition of ecclesiastical peace movements.[33] All these movements and initiatives reminded the medieval church of her vocation and her mission: to proclaim the kingdom of God and to promote peace and justice. Their pursuit of the freedom of the church from secular domination was also a pursuit of the purity of the church. Similar concerns took shape in the Free churches of the 16th century.

MEDIEVAL TRADITIONS OF SPIRITUALITY AND DISCIPLESHIP
AND THE ROOTS OF ANABAPTIST-MENNONITE IDENTITY

65.  Moreover, the medieval church reveals an ongoing tradition of Christian spirituality, of discipleship (*Nachfolge*), and of the imitation of Christ. From the early monastic

tradition up to the mendicant friars of the high Middle Ages, and from the movements of itinerant preachers up to the houses of Sisters and Brethren of the Common Life, medieval Christians were in search of what the challenge of the gospel might mean for their way of living.[34] They tried to discover how their personal relationship with Jesus might change their lives. The concept of conversion gained a new and real meaning to them. They were not Christians merely out of habit or by birth.

66.  Both Catholic and Mennonite historians have recently made clear that at least a part of the spiritual roots of the Anabaptist-Mennonite tradition is to be found in this medieval tradition of discipleship.[35] Key concepts of the Anabaptist-Mennonite identity, such as yieldedness (*Gelassenheit*), discipleship (*Nachfolge*), repentance (*Bussfertigkeit*), and conversion were developed through the Middle Ages in all kinds of spiritual traditions. They are found in the Benedictine and the Franciscan tradition, in the tradition of German mysticism, and in that of the "Modern Devotion". Medieval and post-medieval Catholic spirituality, on the one hand, and Anabaptist and Mennonite spirituality, on the other, are essentially in harmony, with respect to their common objective: holy living in word and deed.

67.  Recent scholarship has also shown that the early Anabaptist-Mennonite tradition, as well as others such as the Lutheran tradition, used the same catechetical basis as did medieval Christianity. Both traditions considered the Lord's prayer, the Apostles' Creed and the ten commandments to express and represent the essence of Christian faith and doctrine. In this sense, early Anabaptist sources stood in a clearly identifiable medieval tradition. As their medieval predecessors had done, Anabaptist leaders considered these three texts to be essential elements of Christian knowledge. They accepted conventional catechetical presuppositions of the medieval tradition and used them as a prerequisite and a preparation for baptism.[36]

AREAS OF FUTURE STUDY

68.  Mennonites and Catholics share the need for a fuller appreciation of the variety of medieval Christianity. They are both engaged in (re-)discovering unknown aspects of their common past, the "other" Middle Ages. Nevertheless, they still have a differing appreciation of their common medieval background. Mennonites might tend to evaluate certain spiritual movements in the Middle Ages as rare exceptions that prove the rule, whereas Catholics might be inclined to consider them as the normal pattern of medieval Christianity. Mennonites and Catholics might reach a deeper understanding of their common background by reading and studying the history of medieval Christian spirituality together. Finally, further scholarly research is important in the field of the relationship between medieval traditions of discipleship and the early Anabaptist-Mennonite tradition. Can Anabaptist-Mennonite piety indeed be understood as a non-sacramental and communitarian transformation of medieval spirituality and asceticism?

## II. CONSIDERING THEOLOGY TOGETHER

69. In addition to the foregoing historical considerations, we presented the respective beliefs that Catholics and Mennonites hold on several common themes, and we sought to ascertain the extent to which our theological points of view converge and diverge. Our theological dialogue was motivated by the commonly acknowledged biblical mandate, which calls for believers in Christ to be one so that the world may believe in the unity of the Father and the Son (John 17:20-23), and for the church to pursue the goal of "speaking the truth in love" (Eph. 4:16) and "building itself up in love" (Eph. 4:17). In the course of five years of dialogue, we identified and discussed several theological topics: the nature of the church; our understandings of baptism; of the eucharist and the Lord's supper; and our theologies of peace. Our dialogue has been deep and wide-ranging, and yet we were not able in this brief period to cover all aspects of the chosen topics or to identify all the issues that require careful consideration. Nonetheless we believe that our mutual consideration of theological issues was significant. We hope that our method of engaging one another can provide a model for the future of dialogue together wherever Catholics and Mennonites engage one another around the world.

### A. The nature of the church

70. The decision to discuss the nature of the church came quite naturally. The Catholic-Mennonite dialogue is a conversation between officially nominated representatives of the Catholic Church and the Mennonite World Conference, which is the world communion of Mennonite related churches. Since appropriate dialogue begins with personal introductions, it seemed right that each of us should introduce ourselves in terms of our identity as church bodies. Fortunately, over the years both have given major attention to their respective understandings of the church. It also seemed right to us that if we were to dialogue fruitfully with each other, we should attempt to define the relationship between us in terms of the common ground we occupy as well as the theological issues that separate us. This could set the stage for drawing conclusions, and for dialogue at some future time on outstanding issues.

A CATHOLIC UNDERSTANDING OF THE CHURCH

71. For Catholics, "the church is in Christ like a sacrament or as a sign and instrument both of a very closely knit union with God and of the unity of the whole human race".[37] The church comprises both "a divine and a human element".[38] A variety of biblical images have been employed to express the reality of the church (for example, church as servant, as spouse, as community of the reconciled, as communion, and so forth).

72. From among this variety, three images in particular come to the fore. First, the church is understood to be the people of God, namely a people God planned to assemble in the holy church who would believe in Christ. "Already from the beginning of the world the foreshadowing of the church took place. It was prepared in a remarkable way

through the history of the people of Israel and by means of the Old Covenant."[39] The church is therefore seen to be in continuity with the chosen people who were assembled on Mount Sinai and received the law and were established by God as his holy people (Ex. 19). Nonetheless a new and culminating point in salvation history comes about with the saving death and resurrection of Christ and with the coming of the Holy Spirit at Pentecost. Those who follow Christ are, as stated in 1 Peter 2:9ff., "a chosen race, a royal priesthood, a holy nation, God's own people, in order that they may proclaim the mighty acts of him who called you out of darkness into his marvellous light. Once you were not a people, but now you are God's people." Thus the church is given the vocation of participating in God's plan for all peoples to bring the light of salvation which is Christ to the ends of the earth.

73. A second image associated with the church is that she is the body of Christ in and for the world. Perhaps the most profound expression of this reality is to be found in the Pauline use of the image of the body where the term *ekklesia* is realized in the eucharistic assembly, being the body of Christ for the world (1 Cor. 11). Once again there is a clear continuity with the idea of the universal mission of Israel carried out through the presence of Christians who belong to the body of Christ in the world. Paul reminds us that Christ reconciled the world to God, thereby bringing about a new creation whereby all who are in Christ are ambassadors for Christ, "since God is making his appeal through us... be reconciled to God" (2 Cor. 5:20).

74. A third image is that of the church as the temple of the Holy Spirit (cf. Eph. 2:19-22; 1 Cor. 3:16; Rom. 8:9; 1 Pet. 2:5; 1 John 2:27, 3:24). The church is seen as the temple of the Spirit because she is to be the place of perpetual worship of God. Filled with the Holy Spirit, the church renders continual praise and adoration of God. Christians through their baptism become living stones in the edifice of the Temple of the Holy Spirit. According to the Dogmatic Constitution on the Church,

> the church prays and likewise labours so that into the people of God, the body of the Lord and the temple of the Holy Spirit, may pass the fullness of the whole world, and that in Christ, the head of all things, all honour and glory may be rendered to the Creator, the Father of the universe.[40]

Just as the Trinity is one, in the diversity of persons, so too is the church one though many members. For Catholics this unity is expressed above all in the sacrament of the eucharist (1 Cor. 10:17), where the realization of the unity of the Spirit in the bond of peace is actualized. As is said in the letter to the Ephesians: "There is one body and one Spirit... but each has been given a grace according to the measure of Christ and... the gifts were given... to equip the saints for the work of ministry, for the building-up of the body of Christ, until all of us come to the unity of the faith and of the knowledge of the Son of God, to maturity, to the measure of full stature of Christ" (cf. Eph 4:4-13).

75. Catholics express the mystery of the church in terms of the inner relation that is found in the life of the Trinity, namely koinonia or communion. Communion with God is at the heart of our new relationship with God. This has been described as "peace or communion" and is the reconciliation of the world to God in Jesus Christ (2 Cor. 5:19).[41] This gift of peace/communion is given to us through the one unique mediator between God and humanity, Jesus Christ. This makes Jesus Christ the paradigm of communion. He is the cornerstone upon which rests the edifice of the church; he alone is the head of the

body and we the members. This edifice is constructed as the "household of God, built upon the foundation of the apostles and prophets with Christ Jesus as the cornerstone" (Eph. 2:20).

76. One is truly incorporated into Christ and into the church through the sacrament of baptism, and fully integrated into the economy of salvation by receiving confirmation and eucharist.[42] Through these sacraments, new members are received into the body of Christ and assume co-responsibility for the life and mission of the church shared with their brothers and sisters.

77. Catholics likewise believe that the apostles, in showing their solicitude for that which they had received from the Lord, have chosen worthy men to carry on this task of transmitting the faithful witness of Christ down through the ages. Thus the apostolic continuity of the church is served by the apostolic succession of ministers whose task is to preach the word of God both "in season and out" (2 Tim 4:2), to teach with sound teaching and to preside over the building up of the body of Christ in love. The Dogmatic Constitution on Divine Revelation, *Dei Verbum*, states clearly the value of the revealed Word of God for believers when it says that "by divine revelation God wished to manifest and communicate both himself and the eternal decrees of his will concerning the salvation of mankind".[43] Vatican II further recognizes the role of the apostles in this transmission[44] and the role of the faithful people of God in the truthful transmission of the faith when it says that

> the whole body of the faithful who have an anointing that comes from the holy one (cf. 1 John 2:20, 27) cannot err in matters of belief. This characteristic is shown in the supernatural appreciation of the faith (*sensus fidei*) of the whole people, when "from bishops to the last faithful" they manifest a universal consent in matters of faith and morals.[45]

78. Furthermore, Catholics believe that sacred scripture and sacred Tradition make up a single deposit of the word of God. This single deposit has been entrusted to the church. The "task of giving an authentic interpretation of the word of God has been entrusted to the living teaching office of the church... Its authority in this matter is exercised in the name of Jesus Christ."[46] The "teaching office" (magisterium) is exercised by the bishops in communion with the bishop of Rome, the pope. Since the magisterium is not superior to the word of God,[47] the teaching office of the pope and bishops is at the service of the word of God and forms a unity with Tradition and scripture and teaches only that which has been handed down to it. In his encyclical on the Catholic Church's commitment to ecumenism, *Ut Unum Sint*, John Paul II identified this point as one of the five areas for further discussion:

> It is already possible to identify the areas in need of fuller study before a true consensus of faith can be achieved: (1) the relationship between sacred scripture, as the highest authority in matters of faith, and sacred Tradition, as indispensable to the interpretation of the word of God.[48]

79. The bishop of Rome has the office of ensuring the communion of all the churches and hence is the first servant of unity. This primacy is exercised on various levels, including vigilance over the handing down of the word, the celebration of the liturgy and the sacraments, the church's mission, discipline and the Christian life. He also has the duty and responsibility to speak in the name of all the pastors in communion with him. He

can also – under very specific conditions clearly laid down by the First Vatican Council – declare *ex cathedra* that a certain doctrine belongs to the deposit of faith. Furthermore,

> religious submission of mind and will must be shown in a special way to the authentic magisterium of the Roman pontiff, even when he is not speaking *ex cathedra*; that is, it must be shown in such a way that his supreme magisterium is acknowledged with reverence, the judgments made by him are sincerely adhered to, according to his manifest mind and will. [49]

By thus bearing witness to the truth, he serves unity. [50]

80. The church (the faithful and the ordained) therefore has the obligation to be a faithful witness of that which she has received in word (teaching/preaching) and deed (holy living). This is possible through the anointing that has been received by the Holy Spirit. (1 John 2:20f.) The church lives then under the word of God because she is sanctified in truth by that same word (cf. John 17:17), and being made holy she may then sanctify the world in truth. The Catholic Church confesses that the church is indeed holy because she is purified by her Lord and Saviour Jesus Christ, and she has been given the Holy Spirit, the Advocate, to plead the just cause of God before the nations. The followers of Jesus must conquer the spirit of this world with the Spirit of the beatitudes. This is the continuation of Jesus' mission to "prove the world wrong about sin and righteousness and judgment" (John 16:8ff.). This is possible only with the aid of the Holy Spirit, the Advocate.

81. When Catholics speak of the one church of God, they understand her to be realized "in and formed out of particular churches" [51] and that she is concretely real in the Catholic Church. [52] For the ecclesiology of Vatican II, the universal church is the body of particular churches from which (*in et ex quibus*) the one and only Catholic Church comes into being, [53] but the local churches also exist in and out of the one church, [54] shaped in its image. [55] The mutual relationship between the communion of particular churches and the one church, just described, means that the one church and the diversity of particular churches are simultaneous. They are interior to each other (perichoretic). Within this perichoresis the unity of the church has priority over the diversity of the local churches, and over all particular interests as is really very obvious in the New Testament (1 Cor. 1:10ff.). "For the Bible, the one church corresponds to the one God, the one Christ, the one Spirit, the one baptism (cf. Eph 4:5f.) and lives according to the model of the early community of Jerusalem (Acts 2:42)." [56]

82. A particular church is that portion of the people of God that is united around the bishop whose mission is to proclaim the gospel and to construct the church through the sacraments – in particular through baptism and the eucharist. [57] The communion of particular churches is presided over by the bishop of Rome, the successor of Peter to whom was entrusted the care for confirming and strengthening the faith of his brothers. Together with the bishops, the pope governs the Catholic Church in its mission to proclaim the good news of the kingdom of God and the gift of salvation in Jesus Christ that God offers freely to all of humanity.

83. In the past "catholicity" was understood to mean: extending over the whole world. While this aspect is true, there is a deeper meaning that indicates, in spite of the diversity of expression, there is the fullness of the faith, respect for the gifts of the Spirit in their diversity, communion with other apostolic churches and faithful representation to human cultures. [58] "Driven by the inner necessity of her own catholicity", the church's universal mission "strives ever to proclaim the gospel to all" and demands the particu-

larity of the churches. Hence the church is to speak all languages and embrace all cultures.[59] In addition the church is to imitate the incarnation of Christ who linked himself to certain social and cultural conditions of those human beings among whom he dwelt.[60] In this context catholicity of the church is a call to embrace all legitimate human particularities.[61] The catholicity of the church therefore consists in the recognition of the same apostolic faith that has been incarnated in diverse cultures and places throughout the world. In spite of the diversity of its expressions and practices in its celebration, the Catholic faith is understood to be the same faith contained in the scriptures, handed on by the apostles, and confessed in the creeds today.

A MENNONITE UNDERSTANDING OF THE CHURCH

84. In Anabaptist-Mennonite theology the church is understood as the community of faith endowed with the Spirit of God and shaped by its response to the grace of God in Christ. Three biblical images of the church are basic to a Mennonite perspective. First, the church is the new people of God.[62] While the concept of peoplehood indicates the continuity of the church with the people of faith of the Old Testament (Gal. 2:15-21), the initiative of God in Jesus Christ marks a new beginning. In Christ, God called "a chosen race, a royal priesthood, a holy nation, God's own people… out of darkness into his marvellous light" (1 Pet. 2:9). The life, death and resurrection of Christ established the good news that people of all races and classes and genders are invited through the grace of God to belong to the people of God (Gal. 3:28). The church, as a family or household of faith (Gal. 6:10; Eph. 2:19), adds to its characterization as people of God. Hospitality is a mark of the household of faith, as members of the household welcome all who join the family, care for one another, and together share their spiritual and material resources with those in need (James 2:14-17).

85. Secondly, the body of Christ is an important biblical image for an Anabaptist-Mennonite understanding of the church.[63] Reference to Christ in this figure points to the foundation (1 Cor. 3:11) and head (Col. 1:18) of the church. Members of the church are incorporated as a body into Christ. The image of the body has its background in the Hebrew concept of corporate personality. Corporate personality implies commitment to Christ as a body of believers (Rom. 12:15; Eph. 4:1-16), which in turn implies a commitment to one another as members of the church. Members of the body are called to be holy as Christ is holy: "The church, the body of Christ, is called to become ever more like Christ, its head, in its worship, ministry, witness, mutual love and care, and the ordering of its common life."[64]

86. A third image of the church, important for Anabaptist-Mennonites, is the community of the Holy Spirit.[65] A defining moment occurred when the risen Christ "breathed on [the disciples] and said to them, 'Receive the Holy Spirit. If you forgive the sins of any, they are forgiven them; if you retain the sins of any, they are retained'" (John 20:22-22). The endowment of the disciples with the Holy Spirit mandated his followers to become a forgiving community. A further step in the formation of the apostolic community took place when, after the outpouring of the Spirit at Pentecost, the first converts "devoted themselves to the apostles' teaching and koinonia (fellowship, community), to the breaking of bread and the prayers" (Acts 2:42). The early church understood itself as the "new Messianic community in which the main feature is the Holy Spirit's renewed presence

with God's people".[66] As such, the Spirit plays a crucial role in the functioning of the body of Christ, as the giver of spiritual gifts to its members (1 Cor. 12:4-11) and as the creator of the oneness of the body (1 Cor. 12:12ff.). Given the multi-faceted composition of the church, it is a formidable task for the community to maintain the unity of the Spirit in the bond of peace" (Eph. 4:3) The Spirit provides the power to vie for the church's oneness and to maintain its ethical focus on the "more excellent way" (1 Cor. 12:31; cf. 1 Cor. 13; 1 Pet. 1:2) of love.

87.  Besides these three images which follow the trinitarian formula, a Mennonite understanding of the church is illumined by various descriptions. The first of these is fellowship of believers. The Anabaptist movement established the idea that the church is comprised of all who, by their own free will, believe in Jesus Christ and obey the gospel. Submission to Christ implies mutual accountability to one another in congregational life (1 Cor 12:25; James 2:14-17; 1 John 3:16). This includes the task of reproving and forgiving as well as guiding and affirming one another in accordance with the biblical mandate to engage in "binding and loosing" on behalf of Christ (Matt. 16:19, 18:15-22; John 20:19-23).[67] Further, the Mennonite concept of the church requires the separation of church and state, with the clear understanding that the Christian's primary loyalty is to Jesus Christ. For example, in matters of warfare, allegiance to the Christ as Lord takes precedence over the demands of the state. Important to the original impetus of the Anabaptist movement was the idea of "a covenantal people" called out from among the nations to be a reconciling community internally[68] as well as "salt and light" in the world (Matt. 5:13-16). Mennonites depict themselves as being "in the world but not of the world" (John 17:15-17).

88.  Mennonites understand the church as a community of disciples. As was the case for New Testament believers, the acceptance of salvation made visible in baptism and in identification with the people of "the Way" (Acts 9:2), marks their resolute intention to be instructed in the way of Jesus of Nazareth, and to seek to follow the Master as his first disciples had done. Discipleship (*Nachfolge*) is integral to the Anabaptist-Mennonite understanding of faith, as exemplified in a quote from the Anabaptist Hans Denck (1526): "The medium is Christ whom no one can truly know unless he follow him in his life, and no one may follow him unless he has first known him."[69] Mennonite historians and theologians have identified discipleship as one of the most important legacies of the Anabaptist movement for the continuing Mennonite vision of the church and the vocation of its members. A recent confession of faith states, "The church is the new community of disciples sent into the world to proclaim the reign of God and to provide a foretaste of the church's glorious hope."[70]

89.  Mennonites understand the church as a people in mission. The Anabaptists took seriously Christ's commission to "be my witnesses… to the ends of the earth" (Acts 1:8).[71] Following a period of self-preservation in the 17th and 18th centuries, the latter 19th century brought with it a renewal of the missionary spirit. Today the church understands its very being as missional. That is, the call to proclaim the gospel and to be a sign of the kingdom of God characterizes the church and includes every member of it. Mission activity is carried out in a peaceful manner without coercion, and includes the ministries of evangelism, social service and advocacy for peace and justice among all people.

90.  The Mennonite church is a peace church. Peace is essential to the meaning and message of the gospel and thus to the church's self-understanding. The church submits to the

Prince of Peace, who calls for the way of peace, justice and non-resistance, and who exemplifies the way of non-violence and reconciliation among all people and for all God's creation. The peace church advocates the way of peace for all Christian churches. One important correlate of the church's identity as a peace church is the church's claim to be a "free" church. Mennonites believe that freedom is an essential gift of the Spirit to the church (2 Cor. 3:17). Church membership entails a free and voluntary act whereby the person makes a free and uncoerced commitment to faith. The separation of church and state along with the refusal to engage in violence against enemies is an implication of freedom of conscience and of the liberating power of the gospel.

91. Mennonites understand the church as a servant community. Jesus came to serve, and he taught his disciples the way of servanthood (Mark 10:43-45). In Anabaptist-Mennonite theology, the Sermon on the Mount (Matt. 5-7) is taken seriously as the operative ethical agenda for all who confess Christ as Saviour and Lord. The Spirit endows believers with varieties of gifts for building up the body of Christ and sharing its message in the world (1 Cor. 12). In the church some, both men and women, are called to serve in leadership ministries. These may include offices such as pastors, deacons and elders, as well as evangelists, missionaries, teachers and overseers. Patterns of leadership vary from place to place and from time to time as they already did in the apostolic church (Acts 6:1-6; Eph. 4:11; 1 Tim. 3:1-13). The "priesthood of all believers" is understood to encourage all believers as "priests" to lead a holy life and to give honour to God by serving one another in the church and in a needy world.

92. The church is a communion of saints. In Anabaptist-Mennonite thought, reference to "saints" includes all who believe in Jesus Christ and seek to follow him in holy living. The church in its particular setting shares the calling to sainthood "together with all those who in every place call on the name of our Lord Jesus Christ, both their Lord and ours" (1 Cor. 1:2; cf. also Rom. 15:26; 1 Cor. 14:33; Heb. 14:24; Rev. 22:21). The communion of saints includes the "cloud of witnesses" (Heb. 12:1) of the past who have endured faithfully to the end. Sainthood is not based on ethical merit, but is accorded those who have persevered to the end, "looking to Jesus the pioneer and perfecter of our faith" (Heb. 12:2). Anabaptists already claimed the depiction of the church as a fellowship of saints of "catholic" or "universal" nature in the early stages of the movement. The Anabaptist theologian, Balthasar Hubmaier, made this explicit in "A Christian Catechism" of 1526, where he wrote that "through this baptism for the forgiveness of sins the person, in open confession of his faith, makes his first entry and beginning in the holy, catholic, Christian church (outside of which there is no salvation)... and is at that time admitted and accepted into the community of the saints".[72]

Much later, in the 20th century, we find a similar standpoint as, for example, in the Mennonite Brethren confession of faith of 1902, which states,

> Although the members of [the Church of Jesus Christ] belong to all nations and ranks scattered here and there throughout the world and are divided in denominations, yet they all are one and among one another brethren and members and exist as one body in Christ their head, who is the Lord, Chief, Shepherd, Prophet, Priest and King of the church.[73]

CONVERGENCES

93. *Nature of the church.* Catholics and Mennonites agree on conceiving of the church as the people of God, the body of Christ, and the dwelling place of the Holy Spirit,

images that flow from the scriptures. Catholics and Mennonites agree that the church is called into being, is sustained and is guided by the triune God who nourishes her in "the grace of the Lord Jesus Christ, the love of God, and the communion of the Holy Spirit" (2 Cor. 13:13).

94. *Foundation of the church.* We agree that the church is "built upon the foundation of the apostles and prophets, with Christ Jesus himself as the cornerstone" (Eph. 2:20; cf. 1 Cor. 3:11). Catholics and Mennonites agree and teach that the faith of the church is founded on the authority of the scriptures, which bear witness to Jesus Christ, and is expressed in the early creeds of the church, such as the Apostles' Creed and the Nicene-Constantinopolitan Creed.[74] Both Catholics and Mennonites affirm the scriptures as the highest authority for the faith and life of the church.[75] Both affirm the inspiration of the Holy Spirit in the formation of the scriptures. Catholics speak of such divinely revealed realities as are contained and presented in sacred scripture as having been committed to writing under the inspiration of the Holy Spirit.[76] Mennonites speak similarly of the scripture as God's word written.[77]

95. *Incorporation into the body of Christ.* We agree that the invitation to be God's faithful people is offered to all in the name of Jesus Christ. Through baptism we become members of the church, the body of Christ.[78] The generous gifts of the Spirit, given to the community of faith, enable each member to grow in a life-long process of Christ-likeness. The eucharist and the Lord's supper respectively draw believers together in the church by nurturing their communion with the triune God and with one another.

96. *Mission of the church.* Mennonites and Catholics agree that mission is essential to the nature of the church. Empowered and equipped by the Holy Spirit, whose coming was promised by Jesus Christ, it is the mission of the church to bring the good news of salvation to all nations by proclaiming the gospel in word and in deed to the ends of the earth (cf. Isa. 2:1-4; Matt. 28:16-20; Eph. 4:11f.). The 1995 *Confession of Faith in a Mennonite Perspective* states: "We believe that the church is called to proclaim and to be a sign of the kingdom of God."[79] We also agree that the church's mission is carried out in the world through every follower of Jesus Christ, both leadership and laity.[80] A dimension of the mission of the church is realized when the church is present among people of all nations. Thereby the divinely destined unity of humanity as one people of faith is called into being from peoples of many tongues and nations (Eph. 4:4-6; Phil. 2:11).[81] Mission requires that Christians seek to become "one" for the sake of their witness to Jesus Christ and to the Father (John 17:20-21), and that they make "every effort to maintain the unity of the Spirit in the bond of peace" (Eph. 4:3).[82] It belongs to the mission of the church to present Jesus Christ to the world and to extend the work of Christ on earth.

97. *Visibility of the church.* We agree that the church is a visible community of believers originating in God's call to be a faithful people in time and place. The visible church was prefigured by the formation of the Old Testament people of God, and was renewed and expanded as the one new humanity, through the blood of Christ (Gen. 12:1-3; Eph. 2:13-15; 1 Pet. 2:9-10). Together we value the biblical image of the church as " the light of the world" and as "a city built on a hill" (Matt. 5:14). Accordingly, the visibility of the church is evidenced when, in word and deed, its members give public witness to faith in Christ.[83]

98. *Oneness of the church.* Together with other disciples of Christ, Catholics and Mennonites take seriously the scripture texts that call Christians to be one in Christ. We confess that our witness to the revelation of God in Christ is weakened when we live in disunity (John 17:20-23). Together we hear the call to "maintain the unity of the Spirit in the bond of peace" (Eph. 4:3). Together we ask: What does it mean for the churches to confess "one Lord, one faith, one baptism, one God and Father of all" (Eph. 4:5-6)? Together we pray the Lord's prayer, imploring God to increase his kingdom among us.

99. *Church as presence and promise of salvation.* Catholics and Mennonites agree that the church is a chosen sign of God's presence and promise of salvation for all creation. Catholics speak of this by affirming that the church is "the universal sacrament of salvation at once manifesting and actualizing the mystery of God's love for humanity".[84] Mennonites express the promissory character of the church by proclaiming that "in God's people the world's renewal has begun",[85] and that "the church is the new community of disciples sent into the world to proclaim the reign of God and to provide a foretaste of the church's glorious hope".[86] We agree that the church is still underway towards its heavenly goal, and we believe that God will sustain the faithful church unto the realization of its glorious hope.[87] Here and now the church manifests signs of its eschatological character and thus provides a foretaste of the glory yet to come.

100. *Ministry of the church.* We agree that ministry belongs to the whole church, and that there are varieties of gifts of ministry given for the good of all. We also agree that chosen leaders, ordained and lay,[88] are essentially servants of God's people, called "to equip the saints for the work of ministry, for building up the body of Christ" (Eph. 4:12).

101. *Holiness and discipleship.* Catholics and Mennonites have a common zeal for the Christian life of holiness, motivated by devotion to Jesus Christ and the word of God, and actualized in a spirituality of discipleship and obedience (Matt. 5-7; Rom. 12; Eph. 2:6-10).[89] The gift of faith freely received provides the motivation for Christian works offered to the world as thanksgiving for the abundant grace we have been given by God. The life of discipleship and holiness is referred to and expressed variously in terms of "following Christ" (*Nachfolge Christi*), "imitation of Christ" (*imitatio Christi*), Christ-likeness, and devotion to Christ.

102. *Education and formation.* Together we affirm the necessity of Christian formation by which individuals come to an understanding and acceptance of their faith and take responsibility for its implementation in life and witness (Phil. 2:12ff.). In Mennonite churches, Christian education is fostered in many ways: scripture reading, preaching, pre-baptismal instruction, Sunday school for all ages, marriage preparation, study groups, day schools for children and youth, discipleship programmes, Bible schools, college and seminary programmes, and voluntary service assignments at home and abroad. In Catholic communities, formation takes place in preparation for the sacraments of initiation (baptism, confirmation and eucharist) including the rite of Christian initiation for adults and pre-baptismal preparation for parents and sponsors, in homilies, in marriage preparation, in catechesis, adult education, college and seminary programmes, and for some in voluntary service programmes. Special formation is encouraged for the laity, and for those who become pastoral workers in the church.[90]

DIVERGENCES

103. *Church and the authority of Tradition.* Catholics and Mennonites differ in their understanding of the relationship of scripture and Tradition/tradition[91] and in their view of the authority of Tradition/tradition. Catholics speak of scripture and Tradition as forming one sacred deposit of the word of God, committed to the church.[92] Sacred Tradition, coming from the apostles, is the means by which the church comes to know the full canon of sacred scripture and understands the content of divine revelation. Tradition transmits in its entirety the Word of God entrusted to the apostles by Christ and the Holy Spirit. Sacred Tradition, sacred scripture and the teaching authority of the church, in accord with God's most wise design, are so linked and joined together that one cannot stand without the others, and that all together and each in its own way under the action of the one Holy Spirit contribute effectively to the salvation of souls.[93] Mennonites view tradition as the post-biblical development of Christian doctrine and practice. The church needs constantly to test and correct its doctrine and practice in the light of scripture itself. Tradition is valued, yet it can be altered or even reversed, since it is subject to the critique of scripture.

104. *Incorporation into the church.* Mennonites and Catholics differ in their understanding of who may be incorporated into the church, and by what means. For Catholics, "by the sacrament of baptism a person is truly incorporated into Christ and into his church and so is reborn to a sharing of the divine life. Baptism, therefore, constitutes the sacramental bond of unity existing among all who through it are reborn. Baptism, of itself, is the beginning, for it is directed towards the acquiring of fullness of life in Christ"[94] which takes place in the celebration of confirmation and the reception of the eucharist. The eucharist is the summit of initiation because it is through participation in Christ's eucharistic body that one is fully incorporated into the ecclesial body. The fact that infants cannot yet profess personal faith does not prevent the church from conferring baptism on them, since in reality it is by and in her own faith that the church baptizes them. For Mennonites, membership in the church follows upon adult baptism, while children are committed to the care of God and the grace of Christ until such a time as they freely request to be baptized and are received into church membership.

105. *Structure of the church.* For Catholics the visible church of Christ consists of particular churches united around their bishops in communion with one another and with the bishop of Rome as the successor of St Peter. For Mennonites, the primary manifestation of the church is the local congregation and the various grouping of congregations variously named conferences, church bodies, and/or denominations.

106. *Ministry, authority and leadership.* In the Anabaptist-Mennonite tradition, ministerial leaders, both men and women, are chosen and authorized by the congregation and/or by regional groups of congregations. In some Mennonite churches it is the practice to ordain leaders for life. In others, ordination is for a set period of time. Mennonites do not have a hierarchical priesthood. As "priests of God", all believers have access to God through faith.[95] While Catholics affirm the "common priesthood of the faithful",[96] they hold to a ministerial, hierarchical priesthood, differing from the former "not only in degree but also in essence",[97] that has roots in, and takes its authority from Christ's priesthood. With the outpouring of the Holy Spirit and the laying-on of hands, the sacrament of orders confers on bishops, priests and deacons gifts for the service of the church. Both laity and clergy share in the fundamental equality of the baptized in the one people

of God and in the one priesthood of Jesus Christ.[98] The differentiation of offices and roles within the Catholic Church reflects the variety of gifts given by one Spirit to the one body of Christ for the good of all (cf. 1 Cor. 12).[99]

AREAS OF FUTURE STUDY

107. *Church and Tradition.* Further discussion is needed on our respective understandings of the relationship between scripture as the highest authority in matters of faith, and Tradition/tradition as indispensable to the interpretation of the word of God.[100] It is recognized that the Catholic Church has a developed understanding of Tradition in God's revelation. While Mennonites may have an implicit understanding of the role of Tradition, little attention has been given to the role of Tradition relative to scripture and to the development of doctrine and ethics.

108. *Catholicity of the church.* We agree that further study and discussion is needed on the question of the definition and implications of our respective understandings of the catholicity and universality of the church. Mennonites believe that all who truly confess Christ as Lord, who are baptized, and follow him in life, are members of the church universal. For Catholics, catholicity properly means the fullness of the confession of faith, respect for the gifts of the Spirit in their diversity, communion with other churches, and witnessing in all human cultures to the mystery of Christ in fidelity to the apostolic Tradition.

109. *The church visible and invisible.* Agreement among us on the visibility of the church raises the question of the meaning of visible and invisible aspects of the church, suggested in such expressions as "cloud of witnesses" (Heb. 12:1) and "communion of saints" as stated in the Apostles' Creed.

110. *Ministry.* A comparative study of ministry, ordination, authority and leadership in our two traditions is needed.

## B. Sacraments and ordinances

111. Since differences of interpretation with respect to two traditional church practices, baptism and the mass, triggered the rupture between Anabaptists and Catholics in the 16th century, it seemed right to both Catholic and Mennonite members of the dialogue that we should present our respective current understandings of these practices, and upon that basis enter into a consideration of historic points of agreement and disagreement. Below is a synopsis of what we presented to each other, and of what we identified as convergences, divergences and areas for future study. As the discussion proceeded, we were challenged by words from Ephesians: "There is one body and one Spirit, just as you were called to the one hope of your calling, one Lord, one faith, one baptism, one God and Father of all, who is above all and through all and in all" (Eph. 4:4-6).

A CATHOLIC UNDERSTANDING OF SACRAMENTS

112. Sacrament is an important concept for Catholics. This concept has been expressed in many ways throughout the long history of the life of the church and especially with

two words: *mysterion* and *sacramentum*. *Mysterion* and *sacramentum* refer to the mysterious manner in which God has used the elements of his creation for his self-communication. The scriptures, especially the New Testament, reveal that for the Christian the place of fundamental encounter with God is Jesus Christ. Catholicism has traditionally understood that God's relationship to us is not to be understood solely in an individual way but also in a communal or corporate manner. This is basically a way of expressing the Pauline understanding of all having fallen in Adam and all having been raised (saved/justified) to new life in Christ (cf. Rom. 5:19; 2 Cor. 5:14f.; Acts 17:26ff.). Linked to the notion of corporate personality is that of the ecclesial dimension of the mysteries/sacraments, in that sacraments appear as the symbolic expression of the eschatological embodiment of God through the Spirit, first in Christ (the "source-sacrament") then in the church (the "fundamental-sacrament" of Christ). This dimension is important for the Catholic understanding of the sacraments since it is the church, as body of Christ, which is the fundamental sacrament of God's promise and deliverance of the kingdom.[101] Just as Christ is the sacrament of the encounter with God, so the church is the sacrament of encounter with Christ, and hence, ultimately, with God.

113. The Second Vatican Council speaks of the sacrament as a reality to be lived especially as the life of the Christian is linked to the paschal mystery:

> Thus, for well-disposed members of the faithful the liturgy of the sacraments... sanctifies almost every event of their lives with the divine grace which flows from the paschal mystery of the passion, death and resurrection of Christ. From this source all sacraments... draw their power. There is scarcely any proper use of material things, which cannot thus be directed towards sanctification of men and the praise of God.[102]

The whole sacramental system in the Catholic Church evolves from the understanding of the centrality of the paschal mystery. The paschal mystery is the place where God reveals and grants salvation in symbolic acts and words. The church in turn worships God through Christ, empowered by the Holy Spirit through the active participation of the faithful in word and symbolic action. Sacraments as the Council teaches are "sacraments of faith".[103] They are so in four ways: sacraments presuppose faith, nourish faith, fortify faith and express faith.

114. Vatican II offers four points of reference for sacraments which are important for their comprehension: (1) Sacraments are liturgical. As such they are located within the liturgy of the word[104] and within the action of the Spirit.[105] (2) Sacraments are linked to God, which means that they are the place of divine action. (3) They are linked to the church, since the church is where the sacraments are celebrated thanks to the priestly reality of the whole body[106] and because the church is edified by them. The sacraments are constitutive of the very reality of the church, and are seen as institutional elements building up the body of Christ.[107] (4) Lastly, sacraments are linked to the whole of Christian life, since there is a strong link between the sacramental celebration and the ethic of Christian living. Hence a link is made between the word of God proclaimed, the word of God celebrated and the word of God lived that engages each Christian in their daily life.

115. Baptism for Catholics is above all the sacrament of that faith by which, enlightened by the grace of the Holy Spirit, we respond to the gospel of Christ. Through baptism one is incorporated into the church and is built up in the Spirit into a house where God lives.

Baptism is the cleansing with water by the power of the living word that washes away every stain of sin and makes us sharers in God's own life. Those who are baptized are united to Christ in a life like his (Col. 2:12; cf. Rom. 6:4f.). Catholic teaching regarding baptism may be put in six points: (1) baptism is the beginning of the Christian life and the door to other sacraments; (2) it is the basis of the whole Christian life; (3) the principle effects of baptism are purification and new birth; (4) through baptism we become Christ's members and are incorporated into his church and made sharers in its mission; (5) confirmation that completes baptism deepens the baptismal identity and strengthens us for service; and (6) lastly, as true witnesses of Christ the confirmed are more strictly obligated to spread and defend the faith by word and deed. In addition, the Decree on Ecumenism of the Second Vatican Council adds, "Baptism, therefore, constitutes a sacramental bond of unity linking all who have been reborn by means of it."[108]

116. Both in the churches of the East and of the West, the baptizing of infants is considered a practice of *ancient Tradition*.[109] The oldest known ritual, describing at the start of the 3rd century the apostolic Tradition, contains the following rule: "First baptize the children. Those of them who can speak for themselves should do so. The parents or someone of their family should speak for the others."[110] The Catholic Church baptizes adults, infants and children. In each of these cases, faith is an important element. In the context of adults and children the individuals themselves make their profession of faith. In the context of infants the church has always understood that the one baptized is baptized into the faith of the church. It is the church that with her faith envelopes a child who cannot now make a personal confession of faith. At the basis of this reflection is the double solidarity found in the Pauline writings, namely the solidarity in Adam and the solidarity in Christ (Rom. 5). It is stated in the introduction to the rite of baptism of infants that

> to fulfill the true meaning of the sacrament, children must later be formed in the faith in which they have been baptized. The foundation of this formation will be the sacrament itself, which they have already received. Christian formation, which is their due, seeks to lead them gradually to learn God's plan in Christ, so that they may ultimately accept for themselves the faith in which they have been baptized.[111]

117. The eucharist is not simply one of the sacraments but it is the pre-eminent one. Vatican II states that the eucharist is the source and the summit of the whole life of the church.[112] Through the activity of the Holy Spirit, the atoning work of Jesus Christ is made universal and brings all things in heaven and on earth together under one head, Jesus Christ (Eph. 1:10). The sacramental basis of this koinonia or communion is the one baptism through which we are baptized in the one body of Christ (1 Cor. 12:12f.; cf. Rom. 12:4f.; Eph. 4:3f.) through baptism we are one in Christ (Gal. 3:26-28). The summit of this communion is found in the eucharist where the many become one through the participation in the one loaf and one cup (1 Cor. 10:16f.). Therefore the koinonia/communion in the one eucharistic bread is the source and sign of the koinonia/communion in the one body of the church. In the eucharist we are united to the heavenly liturgy and anticipate eternal life when God will be all in all. The eucharist, wherein Christ is really and substantially present, sacramentally represents the sacrifice of Christ made on the cross once and for all. It is a memorial of his passion, death and resurrection.[113] There is a richness in understandings of what the eucharist is for Catholics. By taking these together, we can have a fuller understanding of the meaning

of the eucharist. For example, the eucharist is understood as a meal that realizes and manifests the unity of the community; in addition this meal is understood in relationship to the unrepeatable death of Christ on the cross. In the eucharistic sacrifice, the whole of creation loved by God is presented to the Father through the death and resurrection of Christ. Through Christ the church can offer the sacrifice of praise in thanksgiving for all that God has made good, beautiful, and just in creation and in humanity. [114]

118. Even though the eucharistic celebration consists of several parts, it is conceived of as a single act of worship. The eucharistic table is the table of both the word of God and the body of the Lord. Vatican II taught that Christ is present in several ways in the celebration of the eucharist. First, in the presence of the minister who gathers the church in the name of the Lord and greets them in his Spirit; second, in the proclamation of the word; third, in the assembly gathered in God's name; and fourth, in a special way under the eucharistic elements. [115] The faithful are invited to share in the celebration of the liturgy in an active way by means of hymns, prayers and especially the reception of the eucharistic body and blood of the Risen Lord. The faithful commune at the table of the Lord by receiving both the eucharistic bread and the cup.

119. Lastly we can affirm that the church makes a link between what is celebrated and what is lived. Therefore as St Augustine taught, we are to become more fully that which we receive, namely the body of Christ. This means that as Paul taught in First Corinthians, we must live coherently the reality that we are (cf. 1 Cor. 11:17ff.), hence the link between the eucharist and justice, peace and reconciliation. Catholics are committed, because of this eucharistic reality, to become a living sign of Christ's peace and reconciliation for the world.

## A   Mennonite understanding of ordinances

120. The term ordinance is used instead of "sacrament" in Anabaptist-Mennonite theology. [116] To speak of baptism and the Lord's supper as ordinances emphasizes that the church began and continues these practices because Christ ordained (instituted) them (Matt. 26:26-29; 1 Cor. 11:23-26). Two ordinances are common to all Mennonite churches, namely baptism and the Lord's supper. A third, foot-washing, is practised by some (cf. John 13:3-17). [117] On another matter of terminology, Mennonites do not use the term "eucharist", but refer to the meal as the "Lord's supper", and sometimes as "holy communion". It has become common in theological and confessional writing to refer to the ordinances and to the elements of water, bread and wine, as symbols or signs. By this is meant that the ordinances and the elements point beyond themselves to their spiritual significance, and also, in the case of the Lord's supper, to its historic memory. This report will limit itself to the ordinances of baptism and the Lord's supper, since these were the focus of the Mennonite-Catholic dialogue.

### *Baptism*

121. In Anabaptist-Mennonite understanding, baptism derives its meaning from the biblical accounts of baptisms – the baptism of Jesus (Matt. 3:13-17; Mark 1:9-11; Luke 3:21-22; John 1:29-34) and of those baptized in Jesus' name (for example, Acts 2:41) – as well as biblical references to the meaning of baptism (for example, Rom. 6:3-4;

Col. 2:12; 1 John 5:7-8). Consideration of these texts leads to an understanding of water baptism as a sign that points to three inter-related dimensions of Christian initiation and formation:[118] (1) In baptism the individual bears witness before the congregation that he/she has repented of sin, has received the grace of God, and has been cleansed of all unrighteousness (Ezek. 36:25; Acts 2:38). Baptism is thus the sign of a good conscience before God and the church. (2) Water baptism signifies the outpouring of the Holy Spirit in the life of the Christian (Acts 2:17,33). Baptism is thus an acknowledgment on the part of the one being baptized, of the presence of the Spirit in his/her life of faith. (3) Baptism provides a public sign to the congregation of the person's desire to walk in the way of Christ. Such a walk is sometimes referred to in Anabaptist writings as "walking in the resurrection".[119]

122. The baptismal commitment to faith and faithfulness is not an individualistic action, as baptism and church membership are inseparable. The person is "baptized into one body" (1 Cor. 12:13), the body of Christ, the church. The baptismal candidate's affirmation of faith is an affirmation of the faith of the church, and an affirmation made in the context of the community of believers to which the baptized person is joined as a responsible member. The new church member declares a willingness to give and receive care and counsel and to participate in the church's life and mission. The individual relates to the trinitarian God in a deeply personal way, and also together in and with the community of believers where grace is experienced and faith is affirmed in and with the people of God.

123. Mennonite confessional statements as well as centuries of practice suggest that baptism is understood not only as a sign that points beyond the baptismal ritual to its historic and spiritual significance, but that in and through baptism the individual and the community of faith undergo effectual change. For example, the Dordrecht confession (1632) says that all penitent believers are to be baptized with water "to the burying of their sins, and thus to become incorporated into the communion of the saints".[120] Here participation in the baptismal act appears to effect the putting away of sins. A statement on baptism in the Ris confession (1766) speaks of baptism as a means of spiritual blessing, regeneration and renewal: "If Christian baptism is thus devoutly desired, administered, and received, we hold it in high esteem as a means of communicating and receiving spiritual blessing, nothing less than a washing of regeneration and renewing of the Holy Spirit."[121] More recent Mennonite confessional statements on baptism also reveal the expectation of transformation due to participation in the ordinance. The *Confession of Faith of the Mennonites in Canada* (1930) states:

> Baptism is an incorporation (*Einverleibung*) in Christ and his church and the covenant of a good conscience with God. It signifies the burial of our old life in the death of Christ and binds the baptized to unity with Christ in a new obedient life, to follow him in his footsteps and to do what he has commanded them to do.[122]

While there is the recognition in Mennonite theology and in Mennonite confessions that "something happens" in the very act of baptism, baptismal transformation in and through the ritual is conceivable only if and when it is verified in the faith and life of the individual undergoing baptism and of the baptizing community.

124. Mennonites practise adult baptism, sometimes referred to as "believers' baptism". Baptism is reserved for youth and adults who freely request it on the basis that they have

accepted Jesus Christ as their personal Saviour and Lord. This presupposes, on the part of the one being baptized, the ability to reason and to take personal accountability for faith, and to become a responsible participant in the life of the church. Baptism is administered "according to the command and doctrine of Christ, and the example and custom of the apostles". [123] The person is baptized with water in the name of the Father, the Son and the Holy Spirit. Mennonites understand baptism to include instruction in the word of God and in the way of discipleship (Matt. 28:19f.). The mode of baptism is either by effusion of water upon the individual (pouring or sprinkling) or by immersion of the person in water. [124]

### The Lord's supper

125.  The Mennonite church observes the Lord's supper in accordance with Jesus' institution of the supper and with the teachings of the New Testament concerning its meaning: (1) The Lord's supper is a meal of remembrance whereby participants thankfully recall that Jesus suffered, died, and was raised on behalf of all people, sacrificing his body and shedding his blood for the forgiveness of sins (Matt. 26:28; 1 Cor. 11:23-25). (2) The meal is a sign bearing witness to the new covenant established in and by the death and resurrection of Christ, and thus an invitation to participants to renew their covenant with Christ (Jer. 31:33-35; Mark 14:24; 1 Cor. 11:25). (3) The Lord's supper is a sign of the church's corporate sharing in the body and blood of Christ, recognition that the church is sustained by Christ, the bread of life, and thus an invitation for members of the church to be one (Luke 22:19f.; 1 Cor. 10:16f.). (4) The meal is a proclamation of the Lord's death, a joyous celebration of hope in his coming again, a foretaste of the heavenly banquet of the redeemed, and an occasion for hearing anew the call to serve the Lord in sacrificial living until his return (Luke 22:28-30; 1 Cor. 11:26).

126.  While throughout the Mennonite confessional tradition there runs a persistent emphasis on the Lord's supper as a memorial and a sign, Mennonite confessions of faith do not dismiss the effectual power of the ordinance to bring change to the participants and to the community of faith. The Schleitheim confession (1527) depicts the congregation of true believers as being "made one loaf together with all the children of God". [125] This suggests that in a spiritual sense the community becomes the loaf, the bread. Something of this power associated with the sharing of the bread itself is felt and known when brothers and sisters claim a spiritual closeness during the communion service, and when they leave the service "changed". In its statement on the Lord's supper, the Ris confession identifies the presence of this spiritual power when it states, "On the part of God and Christ [the Lord's supper] serves as a means to confirm and seal unto us in the most emphatic manner the great blessings comprehended in the gospel." [126] The *Confession of Faith in a Mennonite Perspective* (1995) states, "As we partake of the communion of the bread and the cup, the gathered body of believers shares in the body and blood of Christ and recognizes again that its life is sustained by Christ, the bread of life." [127] The key lies not in the elements as such, but in the context as a whole, including the communion of the gathered congregation, the prayerful aspiration of each individual, and the spiritual presence that is suggested and re-presented with the aid of appropriate symbols and liturgy. [128]

127.  The invitation to take part in the Lord's supper is open to all baptized believers who are in right fellowship with the Lord and with their congregation, and who by the grace

of God seek to live in accordance with the example and teachings of Christ. From the beginning of the Anabaptist-Mennonite movement, the unity of the body of believers was seen as a desired prerequisite for coming to the table of the Lord. [129] How can there be participation, it is asked, if there is not a striving for the unity of the one body of Christ? The emphasis upon preparing for the Lord's supper by ensuring that members are in "right" relationship with brothers and sisters in the church is a distinctive mark of the Mennonite practice of holy communion.

CONVERGENCES

128. The Catholic Church and the Mennonite Church agree that baptism and the Lord's supper have their origin and point of reference in Jesus Christ and in the teachings of scripture. Both regard the celebration of these sacraments/ordinances as extraordinary occasions of encounter with God's offer of grace revealed in Jesus Christ. They are important moments in the believers' commitment to the body of Christ and to the Christian way of life. Catholics and Mennonites see the sacraments/ordinances as acts of the church.

129. Mennonites and Catholics are agreed on the basic meaning and import of baptism as a dying and rising with Christ, so that "just as Christ was raised from the dead by the glory of the Father, so we too might walk in newness of life" (Rom 6:4). We both also emphasize that baptism signifies the outpouring of the Holy Spirit and the promised presence of the Holy Spirit in the life of the believer and the church.

130. Catholics and Mennonites agree that baptism is a public witness to the faith of the church, and the occasion for the incorporation of new believers into Christ and the church. Both hold that baptism is an unrepeatable act.

131. For Mennonites and Catholics a public profession of faith is required at the time of baptism. Mennonite churches baptize upon the candidate's own confession of faith. This is also the case in the Catholic rite of adult baptism. In the case of infant baptism in the Latin rite of the Catholic Church, it is the church, along with the parents and the godparents, that makes the profession of faith on behalf of the child. This profession becomes personal when the child is able to reason and to affirm the faith. This is done solemnly at confirmation. In the Eastern rite, all three sacraments are celebrated together and the sense of confirmation is the inserting of the candidate into the public witness of Christ and the reception of the grace proper to this public witness.

132. Mennonites and Catholics practise the rite of baptism as a public celebration in the congregation. Both practise baptism by effusion of water or immersion in water; and they baptize in the name of the Father, the Son and the Holy Spirit as Jesus instructed (cf. Matt. 28:19). In Mennonite churches, an ordained minister of the congregation administers baptism. In the Catholic Church, it is ordinarily a bishop, a priest or a deacon who administers baptism.

133. Mennonites and Catholics agree on significant aspects of the meaning of the Lord's supper or eucharist: (1) Both hold that the celebration of the eucharist/Lord's supper is rooted in God's marvellous gift of grace made available to all people by virtue of the suffering, death and resurrection of Jesus Christ. (2) We agree that the Lord's supper/eucharist recalls the suffering, the death and the resurrection of Christ. (3) We

agree that the meal provides an important occasion for the acknowledgment of our sinfulness and for receiving grace and forgiveness. (4) Both celebrate the eucharist/Lord's supper for the nourishing of Christian life; for the strengthening of the church's sense of mission; and for the conforming of our communities to the body of Christ in order to be ministers of reconciliation, peace and justice for the world (cf. 1 Cor. 11:17-32; 2 Cor. 5:16-21). (5) Both celebrate the Lord's supper/eucharist in the spirit of Christian hope, as a foretaste of the heavenly banquet anticipated in the coming kingdom of God.

134. Catholics and Mennonites agree that the Risen Christ is present at the celebration of the eucharist/Lord's supper. Christ is the one who invites to the meal; he is present in the faithful who are gathered in his name; and he is present in the proclaimed word.

DIVERGENCES

135. Both Mennonites and Catholics view sacraments and ordinances as outward signs instituted by Christ, but we have differing understandings of the power of signs. For Mennonites, ordinances as signs point to the salvific work of Christ and invite participation in the life of Christ. For Catholics, in addition to participating in the life of Christ, signs also communicate to those who receive them the grace proper to each sacrament.

136. The Catholic Church advocates both infant baptism and adult baptism, and accepts Mennonite baptism, which is done with water and in the name of the Trinity, as valid. In the Mennonite church, baptism is for those who understand its significance and who freely request it on the basis of their personally owned faith in Jesus Christ.

137. Mennonites and Catholics differ in part in their understanding of the role of a personal confession of faith as it pertains to baptism. Both agree to the necessity of the profession of faith. However, in the Catholic practice of infant baptism, a profession of faith is made on behalf of the child by the parents, the godparents, and the whole assembly. In the Mennonite churches, which do not practise infant baptism, it is required that a profession of faith and a baptismal commitment be made personally by the individual being baptized. In the Mennonite churches, the practice of making a profession of faith on behalf of a person being baptized, who does not at the moment of baptism realize the basic meaning and implications of his or her baptism, is not acceptable.

138. Catholics and Mennonites diverge in their understanding of how Christ is present in the eucharist or the Lord's supper. For Mennonites, the Lord's supper is primarily a sign or symbol that points to Jesus' suffering, death and resurrection, and that keeps this memory alive until his return. For Catholics, the eucharist is the source and the summit of the whole life of the church in which the sacrifice, made once and for all on the cross, is made really present under the species of the consecrated bread and wine, and presented to the Father as an act of thanksgiving and praise for the wonderful work of salvation offered to humanity.

139. Mennonites and Catholics diverge in their understanding of the presence of Christ at the eucharist/Lord's supper. The Anabaptists rejected the idea that there was a real bodily presence of Christ in the elements of bread and wine. Mennonites today view the elements as signs or symbols that recall the significance of the death of Christ for the forgiveness of sin and for the Christian's commitment to love and discipleship. In Catholic understanding, in the sacrament of the eucharist "the body and blood, together

with the soul and divinity, of our Lord Jesus Christ and, therefore, the whole Christ is truly, really, and substantially contained", [130] under the species of bread and wine which have been consecrated by an ordained bishop or presbyter.

140.  With respect to participation in the Lord's supper, most Mennonite churches extend an open invitation for all believers to partake, who are baptized, who are in good standing in their church, and who are in right relationship with the Lord and with one another. In Catholic understanding, the ecclesial dimension of the eucharist has consequences for the question of who may be admitted to the eucharistic communion, since the eucharist as the sacrament of unity presumes our being in full ecclesial communion. [131] Therefore the ecclesial dimension of the eucharist must be taken into consideration in the question of who is admitted to the eucharist.

AREAS OF FUTURE STUDY

141.  Discussion is needed concerning our divergent views on the role of the faith of the church as it bears on the status of infants and children. This would include a comparative study of the theology of sin and salvation, of the spiritual status of children, and of baptism.

142.  The question of recognizing or not recognizing one another's baptism requires further study.

143.  It is necessary to study, together, the history of the origin and development of the theology and practice of baptism for the purpose of ascertaining the origin of infant baptism, assessing the changes brought about with the Constantinian shift, the development of the doctrine of original sin, and other matters.

144.  It would be fruitful to have additional discussions of the relationship between the Catholic understanding of sacraments and the Mennonite understanding of ordinances, to further ascertain where additional significant convergences and divergences may lie.

## C.  Our commitment to peace

> Blessed are the peace-makers,
> for they shall be called the children of God. (Matt. 5:8)

145.  Through our dialogue, we have come to understand that Catholics and Mennonites share a common commitment to peace-making. That commitment is rooted in our communion with "the God of Peace" (Rom. 15:33) and in the church's response to Jesus' proclamation of "the gospel of peace" (Eph. 6:15). Christ has entrusted to us the ministry of reconciliation. As "ambassadors of Christ" (2 Cor. 5:20) we are called to be reconciled to God and to one another. Moved by the Spirit, we want to share with our brothers and sisters in faith, and with a wider world, our call to be instruments of God's peace.

146.  We present the results of our dialogue on the question of commitment to peace in four parts: (1) a survey of distinctive aspects of our respective views of peace-making and related Christian doctrines; (2) points of convergence; (3) points of divergence; and (4) issues requiring further exploration.

CATHOLIC PERSPECTIVES ON PEACE

147   *The church's social vision.* The primary way in which the church contributes to the reconciliation of the human family is the church's own universality [132] Understanding itself as "a sacrament of intimate union with God and of the unity of mankind", [133] the Catholic Church takes the promotion of unity, and accordingly peace, "as belonging to the innermost nature of the church". [134] For this reason it fosters solidarity among peoples, and calls peoples and nations to sacrifices of advantages of power and wealth for the sake of solidarity of the human family. [135] The eucharist, which strengthens the bonds of charity, nourishes such solidarity. The eucharist, in turn, is an expression of the charity which binds members of the community in Christ (1 Cor. 11:17-34). [136]

148.   The church views the human vocation as essentially communitarian, that is, all human relations are ordered to unity and love, an order of love confirmed by the life and teaching of Jesus and the Spirit-filled life of the church (cf. Luke 22:14-27; John 13:1-20, 15:1-17, 17:20-24). [137] This order of love is manifest in the lives of the faithful and in the community of the church, but is not restricted to them. In fact, by virtue of creation and redemption, it is found at all levels of human society.

149.   God created the human family for unity, and in Christ confirmed the law of love (Acts 17:26; Rom. 13:10). Accordingly, the church sees the growth of interdependence across the world, though not without problems due to sin, a force that can contribute to peace. [138] Thus, Pope John Paul II has written,

> The goal of peace, so desired by everyone, will certainly be achieved through the putting into effect of social and international justice, but also through the practice of virtues which favour togetherness, and which teach us to live in unity. [139]

150.   *The call to holiness.* All Christians share in God's call to holiness (1 Thess. 4:3; Eph. 1:4). [140] This is a sanctity "cultivated by all who under God's spirit and, obeying the Father's voice..., follow Christ, poor, humble and cross-bearing..." [141] As God's own people, living in the inauguration of the kingdom, we are to be "peace-makers" who "hunger and thirst for righteousness" (Matt. 5:6) and "are persecuted for righteousness' sake" (Matt. 5:11). We are to love one another, forgive one another, and live humbly in imitation of Jesus, who though he was "in the form of God... humbled himself becoming obedient unto death, even death on a cross" (cf. Phil. 2:6, 8). We are to be generous and forgiving with everyone, as God is generous with us (Luke 6:37f.). In a word, as disciples of Jesus, we are instructed to "Be perfect, therefore, as your heavenly Father is perfect" (Matt. 5:48).

151.   All the commandments, as St Paul teaches, are summed up in the saying, "Love your neighbour as yourself" (Rom. 13:9; cf. James 2:8; 1 John 4:11f.). For Catholics, love of neighbour takes special form in love and service of the poor and marginalized; indeed, in "a preferential option for the poor". The ministry of love to the neighbour is promoted through personal and corporate works of mercy, in organized charities, as well as in advocacy on behalf of justice, human rights and peace. Lay people, bishops and church agencies engage in such initiatives. [142] The love command likewise entails reverence and love for enemies (Matt. 5:43; 1 John 3:16). [143] Like our heavenly Father, who "makes the sun to rise on the evil and the good and sends rain on the righteous and the unrighteous" (Matt. 5:45), we are to love our enemies, bless them, pray for them, not retaliate, and share our possessions with those who would take things from us

(Luke 6:27-35). Furthermore, we must be prepared to establish just relations with them, for true peace is the fruit of justice, and "because justice is always fragile and imperfect, it must include and, as it were, be completed by the forgiveness which heals and rebuilds troubled human relations from their foundations".[144] Finally, in the midst of conflict, the Lord gives us his peace that we may have courage under persecution (John 16:33, 20:21).

152. Non-violence, in Catholic eyes, is both a Christian and a human virtue. For Christians, non-violence takes on special meaning in the suffering of Christ who was "led as a sheep to the slaughter" (Isa. 53:7; Acts 8:32). "Making up the sufferings lacking in Christ" (Col. 1:34), the non-violent witness of Christians contributes to the building up of peace in a way that force cannot, discerning the difference "between the cowardice which gives into evil and the violence which under the illusion of fighting evil, only makes it worse".[145] In the Catholic view, non-violence ought to be implemented in public policies and through public institutions as well as in personal and church practice.[146] Both in pastoral practice and through Vatican diplomacy, the church insists, in the face of conflict, that "peace is possible".[147] The church also attempts to nourish a culture of peace in civil society, and encourages the establishment of institutions for the practice of non-violence in public life.[148]

153. *Peace-making*. On the pastoral level, the Catholic theology of peace takes a positive stance. It focuses on resolving the causes of conflict and building the conditions for lasting peace. It entails four primary components: (1) promotion and protection of human rights, (2) advancing integral human development, (3) supporting international law and international organizations, and (4) building solidarity between peoples and nations.[149] This vision of peace is articulated in the whole body of contemporary Catholic social teaching beginning with Pope John XXIII's *Pacem in Terris* (Peace on Earth) forty years ago and continuing through Pope John Paul II's *Tertio Millennio Ineunte* (The Third Millennium) in 2000.[150]

154. The Catholic Church's work for peace is carried out in many ways. Since the Second Vatican Council, it has largely been carried out through a network of national and diocesan justice and peace commissions and through the Pontifical Council for Justice and Peace. Their work has been especially influential in the struggle for human rights in Asia, Latin America, and some parts of Africa. Catholic human-rights offices, like the Vicariate of Solidarity in Chile, Tutela Legal in El Salvador, Bartolomeo Casas in Mexico, the archdiocesan office in Guatemala City, and the Society of Saint Yves in Jerusalem have been models for active defence of the rights of the poor, of Indigenous people, and of those under occupation. Catholic relief and development agencies, especially Caritas Internationalis and the Caritas network, provide relief, development, refugee assistance and post-conflict reconstruction for divided societies. In many places, individual bishops have also played an important role in national conciliation efforts; and one, Bishop Felipe Ximenes Belo of East Timor, won the Nobel Peace Prize for his efforts.

155. The Holy See[151] exercises "a diplomacy of conscience" through the Vatican diplomatic corps and other special representatives. This diplomatic activity consists of advocacy on behalf of peace, human rights, development and humanitarian issues. It also contributes to international peace-making indirectly through initiatives of Catholic groups, like the Community of Sant'Egidio, and various bishops conferences. Above all, the pope exercises a unique ministry for peace through his teaching and public statements, in his

meetings with world figures, through his pilgrimages across the world, and through special events like the Assisi Days of Prayer and the great jubilee year 2000.

156. Since the Second Vatican Council, the church has sought to view war "with a whole new attitude".[152] In the encyclical letter, *Evangelium Vitae* (The Gospel of Life), Pope John Paul II identified war as part of the culture of death, and he found a positive sign of the times in "a new sensitivity ever more opposed to war as an instrument of the resolution of conflict between people, and increasingly oriented to finding effective but 'non-violent' means to counter the armed aggressor".[153]

157. The Catholic tradition today upholds both a strong presumption against the use of force and an obligation to resist the denial of rights and other grave public evils by active non-violence, if at all possible (cf. Rom. 12:14-21; 1 Thess. 5:14f.). All Catholics bear a general obligation to actively resist grave public evil.[154] Catholic teaching has increasingly endorsed the superiority of non-violent means and is suspect of the use of force in a culture of death.[155] Nonetheless, the Catholic tradition also continues to maintain the possibility of a limited use of force as a last resort (the just war), particularly when whole populations are at risk as in cases of genocide or ethnic cleansing.[156] As in the days before the US war against Iraq (2003), Pope John Paul II as well as Vatican officials and bishops conferences around the world have urged the international community to employ non-violent alternatives to the use of force. At the same time, they have employed just-war criteria to prevent war and to promote the limitation of force and to criticize both potential and actual uses of force by governments.

158. Just-war reasoning, however, is not a simple moral calculus. Following the notion of "right reason", valid application of the just-war criteria depends on possessing a virtuous character. Such virtues as moderation, restraint, and respect for life are intrinsic to sound application of just-war criteria, as are Christian virtues such as humility, gentleness, forgiveness and love of enemy. Accordingly, church teaching and application of the just-war criteria have grown more stringent in recent years, insisting that the function of the just-war tradition is to prevent and limit war, not just legitimate it.[157]

159. The just war today should be understood as part of a broad Catholic theology of peace applicable only to exceptional cases. War, as Pope John Paul II has said, "is never just another means that one can choose to employ for settling differences between nations".[158] The pope's overall assessment of the evils of war made at the end of the 1991 Gulf war remains valid today:

> No, never again war, which destroys the lives of innocent people, teaches how to kill, throws into upheaval even the lives of those who do the killing, and leaves behind a trail of resentment and hatred, thus making it all the more difficult to find a just solution of the very problems which provoked the war.[159]

160. *Religious freedom.* Jesus proclaimed the time "when true worshippers will worship the Father in spirit and in truth, for the Father seeks such as these to worship him (John 4:26)". Meek and humble of heart, Jesus "did not wish to be a political Messiah who would dominate by force but preferred to call himself the Son of Man who came to serve, and to give his life as 'a ransom for many'".[160] Today the Catholic Church repudiates the use of force in the name of the gospel and upholds freedom of conscience in matters of religion. In accord with Vatican II's Declaration on Religious Liberty (*DH*), Catholics affirm freedom of religion for all and repudiate the use of coercion in the

spread of the gospel. [161] The Catholic Church also repents of offences committed "in the name of truth" in past centuries by officials' use of the civil arm to suppress religious dissent, and she begs God's forgiveness for these violations. [162]

161. *History, eschatology and human achievement*. Catholics believe that human achievement of every sort, particularly the achievements of a political society that contributes to a greater measure of justice and peace in the world, prepares humanity "to share in the fullness which 'dwells in the Lord'". [163]

> For after we have obeyed the Lord, and in his Spirit have nurtured on earth the values of human dignity, brotherhood and freedom… we will find them again, but free of stain, burnished and transfigured. This will be so when Christ hands over to the Father a kingdom eternal and universal: "a kingdom of truth and life, of holiness and grace, of justice, love and peace". [164]

At the same time sin, which is always attempting to trap us and which jeopardizes our human achievements, is conquered and redeemed by the reconciliation accomplished by Christ (cf. Col. 1:20). [165]

MENNONITE PERSPECTIVES ON PEACE

162. *Christological basis of our peace commitment*. For the Mennonite church, peace has its basis in the love of God as revealed in creation, in God's story with his people, and in the life and message of Jesus Christ. The biblical word *shalom* expresses well-being, wholeness, and the harmony and rightness of relationships. Justice is the inseparable companion of peace, as the prophets testify: "and the effect of justice will be peace and the result of righteousness quietness and trust forever" (Isa. 32:17).

163. God's peaceable kingdom is expressed definitively in Jesus Christ, for "he is our peace, who has made us both [Gentile and Jew] one, and has broken down the dividing wall of hostility" (Eph. 2:14). In Christ we see that God's love is radical, loving even the enemy. The resurrection of Jesus Christ is the ultimate sign of the victory of the way of Jesus. Salvation and ethics are based on and permeated by this way of Jesus.

164. What is a peace church? A peace church is a church called to bear witness to the gospel of peace grounded in Jesus Christ. The peace church places this conviction at the centre of its faith and life, its teaching, worship, ministry and practice, calling Jesus Lord and following him in his non-resistant and non-violent way. A peace church is nothing other than the church, the body of Christ. Every church is called to be a peace church. [166]

165. The earliest Swiss Anabaptists, forerunners of the Mennonites, saw the necessity of separating the church from its allegiance to the state. Only in this way could they follow the non-violent way of Jesus and uphold their confession of Jesus as Lord, in accordance with the early Christians of the apostolic era. Their stance of non-resistance and conscientious objection to war was a choice of faith (Matt. 5:38-41). Within this frame of thinking, "just-war" considerations had no place, and the church must distance itself from the state. For this reason, a peace church says farewell to Constantinianism, the liaison of church and state. Even more, the church resists the captivity of the church in regard to her theological thinking. [167] For Mennonites, traditional Christology is often seen to have been weakened by "Constantinianism" with the result that the normative character of the teachings of Jesus is too often depreciated in ethics and ecclesiology. In

addition, theology too tightly tied to state structures has often formulated social ethics from a top-down perspective, looking to political leaders for articulation of what is possible rather than focusing on what Jesus taught his disciples and how that can concretely be lived out by the body of Christ in the world.

166. *Discipleship and peace-making.* The teachings and the example of Christ give orientation for our theology and teaching on peace. The concept of discipleship, of following Christ in life, is central for Mennonite theology. Mennonites insist that confessing Jesus Christ as Lord means that the humanity of Christ has ethical relevance. Though the decisions he made and the steps He took leading to his crucifixion must be interpreted in the context of his times, they reveal the love of God for his followers. [168] Christian love includes love of enemy, the message of forgiveness as a gift for everybody, the concern for those at the margins of society, and the call for a new community.

167. An ultimate theological challenge is to spell out the consequences of the cross for our teaching on peace and war. The atonement is the foundation of our peace with God and with one another. Reconciliation and non-violence belong to the heart of the gospel. Therefore an ethic of non-resistance, non-violence and active peace-making corresponds to our faith in God. God revealed his love for humanity in Jesus Christ, who was willing to die on the cross as a consequence of his message of the kingdom of God. Thus the cross is the sign of God's love of his enemies (Rom. 5:10f.). In the resurrection God confirms the way of Jesus and establishes new life. The conviction that "love is stronger than death" sustains Christians where their faith leads to suffering.

168. What kinds of attitudes and activities are the marks of a peace church? At the heart of its worship is the celebration of God's presence. Witnessing to the presence of God in this world, the church is a community of those being reconciled. In a "believer's church", reconciliation is reflected in all aspects of the church's life. Its discipline orients members to reconciliation and conflict resolution. In accordance with Matt. 18:15-22, it applies "binding and loosing" to biblical interpretation and ethical decisions. The disciples' witness to the kingdom of God includes non-violence, active peace-making, and the confrontation of injustice. Resistance to violence means not only refusing to take part in it, but also serving victims and confronting aggressors. The peace church seeks to love the enemy while at the same time confronting evil and oppression. It advocates justice for all. It expresses conscientious objection to war and conscientious participation in state and society.

169. Mennonites engage in peace groups in congregations, participate on peace committees on the national level, and promote international peace networks via Mennonite World Conference and Mennonite Central Committee. The conviction that peace has to be built in many steps has led Mennonites to foster voluntary service on different levels: as relief work and disaster service, as educational work and the promotion of human rights. Methods of conflict transformation and mediation have been worked out and improved. Christian peace-maker teams are an initiative of Mennonites and other Historic Peace churches to intervene in situations of armed conflict and protect threatened people by being present with them and putting themselves on the line.

170. Mennonites in all parts of the world grapple with peace issues and consider such a struggle to be a core practice of the church. For some, "non-resistance" would describe best their stance of faith in the sense of refusing to take part in war, shunning all forms of violence and even refusing service of any kind to government. For others, non-resist-

ance no longer characterizes their conviction; and a faith-based pacifism would be a more accurate term. In some places in the world, Mennonites are moving in their theology and praxis from "non-resistance" to active non-violence and to a position of just peace-making. [169] This includes the prophetic denunciation of violence through active criticism of government politics, as for example during the Balkan war.

171. Another dimension of peace understood biblically is protecting the integrity of creation. A life-style of simplicity and of responsible use of the world's limited resources has been a typical stance for Mennonites for a long time.

> As stewards of God's earth, we are called to care for the earth and to bring rest and renewal to the land and everything that lives on it. As stewards of money and possessions, we are to live simply, practise mutual aid within the church, uphold economic justice, and give generously and cheerfully. [170]

## CONVERGENCES

172. *Creation and peace.* Mennonites and Catholics can agree that God, "who from one man has created the whole human race and made them live all over the face of the earth" (Acts 17:26), has destined humanity for one and the same goal, namely, communion with God's own self. Likewise, created in the image and likeness of God, human beings are called to unity with one another, through reciprocal self-giving (cf. Gen. 1:26; John 17:21f.). [171] Redemption, moreover, has restored to creation the peace lost by sin (Gen. 9:1-17; Col. 1:19f.; Rev. 21:5). As God's new creation, Christians are called to live a new life in peace with one another and with all humankind (2 Cor. 13:11; Rom. 12:18).

173. We also agree that the biblical vision of peace as shalom entails protecting the integrity of creation (Gen. 1:26-31, 2:5-15, 9:7-17; Ps. 104). [172] The church is called to witness, in the spirit of stewardship, that people may live as caretakers and not exploiters of the earth.

174. *Christology and peace.* The peace witness of both Mennonites and Catholics is rooted in Jesus Christ "who is our peace, who has made us both one... making peace that he might reconcile us both to God in one body through the cross" (Eph. 2:14-16). We understand peace through the teachings, life and death of Jesus Christ. In his mission of reconciliation he remained faithful unto death on the cross, and his fidelity was confirmed in the resurrection. The cross is the sign of God's love of enemies. [173]

175. *Ecclesiology and peace.* The church is called to be a peace church, a peace-making church. This is based on a conviction that we hold in common. We hold that the church, founded by Christ, is called to be a living sign and an effective instrument of peace, overcoming every form of enmity and reconciling all peoples in the peace of Christ (Eph. 4:1-3). [174] We affirm that Christ, in his church, through baptism, overcomes the differences between peoples (Gal. 3:28). By virtue of their baptism into Christ, all Christians are called to be peace-makers. All forms of ethnic and inter-religious hatred and violence are incompatible with the gospel, and the church has a special role in overcoming ethnic and religious differences and in building international peace. [175] Furthermore, we agree that it is a tragedy when Christians kill one another.

176. Catholics and Mennonites share an appreciation of the church as different from simply human organizations, and together we stand for religious freedom and the inde-

pendence of the church. The freedom of the church from state intervention enables her to offer witness to the wider society. In virtue of their dignity as children of God, more-over, all men and women possess the right to freedom of religion and conscience. No one should be forced to act contrary to conscience, particularly in matters of religion.

177. *Peace and justice.* We affirm together that peace, in the sense of the biblical word shalom, consists of well being, wholeness, the harmony and rightness of relationships. As inheritors of this biblical tradition, we believe that justice, understood as right rela-tionships, is the inseparable companion of peace. As the prophets testify, "the effect of justice will be peace and the result of righteousness quietness and trust forever" (Isa. 32:17; cf. Ps. 85:10,13). [176]

178. We agree that the gospel's vision of peace includes active non-violence for the defence of human life and human rights, for the promotion of economic justice for the poor, and in the interest of fostering solidarity among peoples. Likewise, peace is the realization of the fundamental right to live a life in dignity, and so have access to all means to accomplish this: land, work, health and education. For this reason, the church is called to stand in solidarity with the poor and to be an advocate for the oppressed. A peace built on oppression is a false peace.

179. We hold the conviction in common that reconciliation, non-violence, and active peace-making belong to the heart of the gospel (Matt. 5:9; Rom. 12:14-21; Eph. 6:15). Christian peace-making embraces active non-violence in the resolution of conflict both in domestic disputes and in international ones, [177] and for resolving conflict situations. We believe that the availability of such practices to individual groups and governments reduces the temptation to turn to arms, even as a last resort.

180. *Discipleship and peace.* Both agree that discipleship, understood as following Christ in life in accordance with the teaching and example of Jesus, is basic to the Christian life. The earthly existence of Jesus is normative for human well-being (John 13:1-17; Phil. 2:1-11). [178] The decisions Jesus made and the steps he took leading to his crucifix-ion reveal the centrality of love, including love of enemy, in human life (Matt. 5:38-48). They also include the message of forgiveness as a gift for everybody, the concern for those at the margins of society, and the call for a new community. Love of neighbour is the fulfilment of the law, and love of our enemies is the perfection of love (Rom. 13:8; Matt. 5:43-48). [179]

181. Christian peace witness belongs integrally to our walk as followers of Christ and to the life of the church as " the household of God" and "a dwelling place of God in the Spirit" (Eph. 2:19,22). Christian communities have the responsibility to discern the signs of the times and to respond to developments and events with appropriate peace initia-tives based on the life and teaching of Jesus (Luke 19:41-44). [180] The Mennonite church tends to initiate its witness in and through the discerning congregation:

> Led by the Spirit, and beginning in the church, we witness to all people that violence is not the will of God... We give our ultimate loyalty to the God of grace and peace, who guides the church daily in overcoming evil with good, who empowers us to do justice, and who sustains us in the glorious hope of the peaceable reign of God. [181]

In the Catholic Church, peace initiatives come in many forms: from parishes, communi-ties of faith and religious movements, from justice and peace or human-rights commissions, from individual bishops and conferences of bishops, from the holy father and various offices of the Holy See.[182]

182. God revealed his love for humanity in Jesus Christ, who was willing to die on the cross as a consequence of his message of the kingdom of God. The cross is the sign of God's love of his enemies (Rom. 5:10f.). For both Catholics and Mennonites the ultimate personal and ecclesial challenge is to spell out the consequences of the cross for our teaching on peace and war. We acknowledge suffering as a possible consequence of our witness to the gospel of peace. We note with joy that we have a common appreciation for martyrs, "the great cloud of witnesses" (Heb. 12:1), who have given their lives in witness to truth.[183] Together we hold that "God's foolishness is wiser than human wisdom, and God's weakness is stronger than human strength" (1 Cor. 1:25).

183. Mennonites and Catholics live with the expectation that discipleship entails suffering. Jesus challenges us: "If any want to become my followers, let them deny themselves and take up their cross and follow me" (Mark 8:34). Love is stronger than death – this faith sustains Christians where their faith leads to suffering. Catholics affirm with Pope John Paul II:

> It is by uniting his own sufferings for the sake of truth and freedom to the sufferings of Christ on the cross that man is able to accomplish the miracle of peace and is in a position to discern the often narrow path between the cowardice which gives in to evil and the violence which, under the illusion of fighting evil, only makes it worse.[184]

Both Mennonites and Catholics take their inspiration from gospel texts such as Mark 10:35-45 and Luke 22:24-27, where Jesus invites his followers to offer up their lives as servants.

184. Both our communities endeavour to foster the peaceable virtues: forgiveness, love of enemies, respect for the life and dignity of others, restraint, gentleness, mercy, and the spirit of self-sacrifice. We also attempt to impart the spiritual resources for peace-making to our members. The mission of the church has an eschatological dimension. It anticipates the kingdom of God. The church lives in the tension between "already now" and "not yet". Already now the Messianic time has come. But the past age has not yet come to an end; its rules and values continue to exist. In this parallel existence of the old and the new the church has the decisive function: to foster peace and to incarnate the new order of the kingdom of God by helping its members to orient themselves according to the rules of the kingdom.

185. Mennonites and Catholics share the common conviction that worship and prayer belong to the core of Christian peace work. We celebrate what we have received from God. We cry out to God and we plead for peace. In prayer, we are renewed and by prayer we receive orientation. When we meet for ecumenical prayer services, we overcome existing divisions between us, and we experience communion with God and with one another in faith.

DIVERGENCES

186. *Church and society.* While Catholics and Mennonites regard political authority as part of the God-given moral order of the universe, they tend to diverge on the question

of participation in government. Catholics understand the social nature of humanity to be blessed by Christ's life and teaching. [185] Participation in government is honoured and encouraged as a contribution to the common good, and military service is respected. [186] At the same time, non-violent action, conscientious objection, and resistance to immoral orders are strongly endorsed. [187] Because of their long history of persecution and discrimination, Mennonites have tended to mistrust the state. They still tend to be critical of Christian involvement in government because of the use of violence involved and the possible corruption of power.

187. *Non-violence and just war*. Mennonites include non-violence as an essential component of discipleship in the sense that in principle they refuse to use violence in all situations. In situations of conflict, however, both Catholics and some Mennonites acknowledge that when all recourse to non-violent means has failed, the state or international authorities may use force in defence of the innocent. For Mennonites, however, Christians should not participate in this kind of action. [188] For Catholics, Christians ought to be committed "as far as possible, to live in peace with everyone" (Rom. 12:18) and to encourage their governments to resolve disputes peacefully, but Christians may take up arms under legitimate authority in exceptional circumstances for the defence of the innocent. Service in the military may be virtuous, but conscientious objection to military service is also respected. The just-war position provides tools for the prevention and limitation of conflict as well as for warranting force by political authorities. The principle of "right intention" requires that force be used only to restore the peace and to protect the innocent and not in a spirit of vengeance, a quest for domination, or out of other motives inconsistent with love of enemy.

188. Mennonites and Catholics have somewhat different views on non-resistance. Mennonites hold to non-resistance on principle without exception, while Catholics affirm non-resistance, but allow for exceptions. For Mennonites, non-resistance is part of the new way of Jesus (Matt. 5:38-41). There is an expectation that Christians are called to adhere to the principles of ethics implied in the "new way", and that through the power of the Holy Spirit and the encouraging support of the Christian community, it is possible to walk the way faithfully. For Catholics, non-resistance is "a counsel of perfection", and Catholics, as well as all people of goodwill, are required to resist grave public evil non-violently, if at all possible, but in exceptional circumstance by limited use of force exercised by public authorities. [189]

AREAS OF FUTURE STUDY

189. Many questions remain to be explored. Among these are the following: (1) What is the relationship of the different Christian peace positions to the apostolic faith? (2) What place do initiatives for conflict resolution and non-violent direct action have in a Catholic theology of peace? (3) What is the relation of human rights and justice to the non-violent resolution of conflict in contemporary Mennonite theology? (4) How can we meet the challenge of developing common theological perspectives on peace that reflect the diverse voices of men and women from different contexts worldwide? (5) What is the role of the church in promoting a culture of peace in civil society and establishing institutions for the practice of non-violence in public life? (6) What is the relationship between peace, peace witness, the call to Christian unity and the unity of the human

family? (7) How is ethical discernment – interpreting the signs of the times in regard to a unified and concerted Christian peace witness – carried out in Mennonite and Catholic communities on the local and global levels?

## III. TOWARDS A HEALING OF MEMORIES

190. Bitter memories have resulted from past conflicts and divisions between Christians and from the sufferings they have produced over ensuing centuries. Mutual hostility and negative images have persisted between separated Christians of the Catholic and Reformation traditions from the time of the divisions of the 16th century until today. It has therefore been the intention and hope from the beginning of this dialogue between Mennonites and Catholics that our conversations would contribute to a healing of memories.

191. The healing of memories involves several aspects. It requires a purification of memories so that both groups can share a picture of the past that is historically accurate. This calls for a spirit of repentance – a penitential spirit – on both sides for the harm that the conflicts have done to the body of Christ, to the proclamation of the gospel, and to one another. Healing the memories of divided Christians also entails the recognition that, despite conflict, and though still separated, they continue to hold in common much of the Christian faith. In this sense they remain linked to one another. Moreover a healing of memories involves the openness to move beyond the isolation of the past, and to consider concrete steps towards new relations. Together, these factors can contribute to reconciliation between divided Christians.

### A. The purification of memories

192. The healing of memories requires, first of all, a purification of memories. This involves facing those difficult events of the past that give rise to divergent interpretations of what happened and why. Past events and their circumstances need to be reconstructed as precisely as possible. We need to understand the mentalities, the conditions and the living dynamics in which these events took place. A purification of memory includes an effort to purge "from personal and collective conscience all forms of resentment or violence left by the inheritance of the past on the basis of a new and rigorous historical-theological judgment, which becomes the foundation for a renewed moral way of acting".[190] On this basis, both Catholics and Mennonites have the possibility of embarking on a sure and trustworthy way of thinking about and relating to each other that is in accordance with Christian love (cf. 1 Cor. 13).

193. Our effort to re-read church history together as Catholics and Mennonites (ch. I) helped us begin to reconcile our divergent memories of the past. We saw that "our relationship, or better the lack of it, began in a context of rupture and separation. Since then, from the 16th century to the present, theological polemics have persistently nourished

negative images and narrow stereotypes of each other." [191] Because of these dynamics, we have "sometimes restricted our views of the history of Christianity to those aspects that seemed to be most in agreement with the self-definition of our respective ecclesial communities". [192]

194. In our study of history we began to assess together, and in a fresh way, events or periods of history that Mennonites and Catholics have traditionally interpreted very differently from one another. For example, we have seen a more nuanced and complex picture of the Middle Ages, including the so-called "Constantinian era", than either side typically saw when explanations of those centuries were heavily influenced by post-Reformation polemics. In considering the era of the 16th-century Reformation, we saw that although there were serious abuses and problems within the Catholic Church at that time, there were also efforts to reform the church from within. Recent studies have indicated that Christian piety was flourishing in many ways on the eve of the Reformation and that it is too simplistic to describe the Christianity of that day as in a state of crisis or decline. Recent historical studies illustrating these factors call us to continue our study of that period, and to look for fresh evaluations of the circumstances that led to the separation of Christians at the time.

195. On the question of Christian witness to peace and non-violence based on the gospel, our study of history suggested points of reference that could open the door to mutual support and cooperative efforts between Catholics and Mennonites. For example, we observed that within the often-violent society of the Middle Ages there was, as part of the heritage of the Catholic Church, an uninterrupted tradition of ecclesiastical peace movements. [193] We saw also that even though some Anabaptist-related groups allowed the use of the sword in the establishment of the kingdom of God, many were faithful to principles of pacifism and non-violence from the beginning, and soon these positions were accepted doctrinally and held consistently by Anabaptists and Mennonites. [194] Purifying our memory on these points means that both Catholics and Mennonites need to continually struggle to maintain the gospel's perspective on questions of peace and non-violence. And both can find resources in the earlier history of the church to assist us in shaping a Christian witness to peace in today's violent world.

196. Briefly, we believe not only that reconciliation and purification of historical memories must continue in our communities, but also that this process may lead Catholics and Mennonites to new cooperation in witnessing to the gospel of peace.

197. On the Catholic side, statements of the Second Vatican Council reflect a purification of memory. Unlike in the past when others were blamed for ruptures that took place, the Council acknowledged the culpability of Catholics too. The Council made the admission with reference to past ruptures that "at times, men of both sides were to blame" [195] for what happened. Furthermore, in an open spirit inviting dialogue, the Council further acknowledged – and this reflects a Catholic attitude towards Mennonites today – that "one cannot impute the sin of separation to those who at present are born into these communities and are instilled therein with Christ's faith. The Catholic Church accepts them with respect and affection as brothers." [196] In a similar open spirit supporting dialogue, a recent statement of the executive committee of Mennonite World Conference has said, "We see Christian unity not as an option we might choose or as an outcome we could create, but as an urgent imperative to be obeyed." [197]

## B. A spirit of repentance, a penitential spirit

198. A healing of memories involves also a spirit of repentance, a penitential spirit. When Christians are divided and live with hostility towards one another, it is the proclamation of the gospel that often suffers. The integrity and power of the gospel is severely diminished in the mind of the hearer, when Christians witness to it in divergent and contradictory ways. Therefore, Christians separated from one another, including Catholics and Mennonites, have reason to ask God's forgiveness as well as forgiveness from each other. In doing so, they do not modify their convictions about the Christian faith. On the contrary, a penitential spirit can be another incentive to resolve, through dialogue, any theological divergences that prevent them from sharing together "the faith that was once for all entrusted to the saints" (Jude 1:3).

CATHOLIC DELEGATION STATEMENT

199. While a penitential spirit with respect to Christian divisions was reflected in the Second Vatican Council, the Catholic Church took a further step during the jubilee year 2000, on 12 March, the "Day of Pardon". In the Catholic tradition the holy year is a time of purification. Thus, "in order to reawaken consciences, enabling Christians to enter the third millennium with greater openness to God and his plan of love", [198] during the mass of the first Sunday of Lent, Pope John Paul II led the Catholic Church in a universal prayer including a confession of sins committed by members of the church during the past millennium, and a plea to God for forgiveness. He stated that, while "the church is holy because Christ is her head and her spouse [and] the Spirit is her life-giving soul…, [nonetheless] the children of the church know the experience of sin…. For this reason the church does not cease to implore God's forgiveness for the sins of her members." [199] Two of the seven categories of sins identified as having been committed during the previous millennium, and consequently confessed that day, were "sins which have harmed the unity of the church" and "sins committed in the service of truth". [200] At that Lenten mass, these categories of sins were presented in a generic way, without mentioning specific cases or situations.

200. During the ceremony, there was confession of "sins which have rent the unity of the body of Christ and wounded fraternal charity". On behalf of the Catholic Church, the pope beseeched God the Father that while "on the night before his passion, your Son prayed for the unity of those who believe in him…, [nonetheless] believers have opposed one another, becoming divided, and have mutually condemned one another and fought against one another". Therefore, he concluded, we "urgently implore your forgiveness and we beseech the gift of a repentant heart, so that all Christians, reconciled with you and with one another, will be able, in one body and in one spirit, to experience anew the joy of full communion". [201]

201. In regard to the "confession of sins committed in the service of truth", the introductory prayer asked that each one of us recognize "that even men of the church, in the name of faith and morals, have sometimes used methods not in keeping with the gospel in the solemn duty of defending the truth". The prayer then recited by the pope recalled that "in certain periods of history Christians have at times given in to intolerance and have not been faithful to the great commandment of love, sullying in this way the face

of the church, your spouse". He then prayed, "Have mercy on your sinful children and accept our resolve to seek and promote truth in the gentleness of charity, in the firm knowledge that truth can prevail only in virtue of truth itself." [202]

202. Catholics today are encouraged to look at the conflicts and divisions among Christians in general and, in the present context, at the conflicts between Mennonites and Catholics, in light of this call for repentance expressed during the "Day of Pardon". For their part, in the spirit of the "Day of Pardon", Catholics acknowledge that even the consideration of mitigating factors, such as cultural conditioning in previous centuries, which frequently converged to create assumptions which justified intolerance, "does not exonerate the church from the obligation to express profound regret for the weaknesses of so many of her sons and daughters". [203] Without compromising truth, Catholics in this dialogue can apply this spirit of repentance to the conflicts between Catholics and Mennonites in the 16th century, and can express a penitential spirit, asking forgiveness for any sins which were committed against Mennonites, asking God's mercy for that, and God's blessing for a new relationship with Mennonites today. We join our sentiments to those expressed by Walter Cardinal Kasper when he addressed the Mennonite World Conference representatives of the Catholic-Mennonite dialogue group on the occasion of their visit to Rome in November 2001:

> Is it not the case that we, Catholics and Mennonites, have mutually condemned one another? Each saw the other as deviating from the apostolic faith. Let us forgive and ask forgiveness. The authorities in centuries past often resolved problems in society by severe means, punishing with imprisonment or death those who were seen as undermining society. Especially, in the 16th century, the Anabaptists were among those who suffered greatly in this regard. I surely regret those instances when this took place in Catholic societies.

## MENNONITE DELEGATION STATEMENT

203. The statement of the executive committee of Mennonite World Conference, "God Calls Us to Christian Unity", invites a spirit of repentance on the part of the MWC community of churches in relations to other Christians, including Catholics. The statement says, in part,

> As Mennonites and Brethren in Christ, we give thanks to God for brothers and sisters of other traditions around the globe who accept the claims of scripture and seek to live as followers of our Lord. We confess that we have not done all we could to follow God's call to relate in love and mutual counsel to other brothers and sisters who confess the name of Jesus Christ as Lord and seek to follow him. We have seen peace-making and reconciliation as callings of all Christian disciples, but confess that we have not done all we could to overcome divisions within our circles and to work towards unity with other brothers and sisters. [204]

In regard to the 16th-century rupture, we recognize that as the Anabaptists sought to be faithful followers of Jesus Christ, they called into question the established churches and societies. We acknowledge that there were diverse and sometimes divergent currents within the Anabaptist movement. We believe that it was initially difficult for contemporaries to distinguish between the Anabaptists we claim as our spiritual forebears – those committed to biblical pacifism, ready to suffer martyrdom for the cause of Christ – and those who took the sword, thinking that they were doing God's will in preparing the way for the return of Jesus. We regret Anabaptist words and deeds that contributed to fracturing the body of Christ.

204. We confess also that in spite of a commitment to follow Jesus Christ in daily life, we and others in our family of faith have frequently failed to demonstrate love towards Catholics. Too often, from the 16th century to the present, we have thoughtlessly perpetuated hostile images and false stereotypes of Catholics and of the Catholic Church. For this, we express our regret and ask forgiveness.

COMMON STATEMENT

205. Together we, Catholic and Mennonite delegations, recognize and regret that 16th-century Christians, including Catholics and Anabaptists, were unable to resolve the problems of the church of that time in such way as to prevent divisions in the body of Christ that have lasted to the present day.

206. Together we acknowledge and regret that indifference, tension and hostility between Catholics and Mennonites exist in some places today, and this for a variety of historical or contemporary reasons. Together we reject the use of any physical coercion or verbal abuse in situations of disagreement and we call on all Christians to do likewise. We commit ourselves to self-examination, dialogue and interaction that manifest Jesus Christ's reconciling love, and we encourage our brothers and sisters everywhere to join us in this commitment.

## C. Ascertaining a shared Christian faith

207. Theological dialogue can contribute to healing of memories by assisting the dialogue partners to ascertain the degree to which they have continued to share the Christian faith despite centuries of separation. Mennonites and Catholics in this dialogue explained their own traditions to one another. This contributed to a deeper mutual understanding and to the discovery that we hold in common many basic aspects of the Christian faith and heritage. These shared elements, along with unresolved questions and disagreements, are outlined in chapter II.

208. Catholics and Mennonites are convinced that the first responsibility of a Christian is the praise of God and that all aspects of Christian life must be rooted in prayer. Therefore, in the course of the five years of this dialogue we started and ended each day with prayer together. Together we read and reflected on the scriptures and sang hymns. Each year we worshipped in each other's churches on Sunday in order to deepen mutual understanding of our traditions.

209. Among the important aspects of the Christian life that Catholics and Mennonites hold in common are faith in Jesus Christ as Lord and Saviour (fully divine and fully human), the trinitarian faith as expressed in the Apostles' Creed, and numerous perspectives on the church. There is also much that we can agree on concerning baptism and the Lord's supper as fundamental grace-filled celebrations of God's saving acts in Christ. We share a great deal in regard to the role of the church on matters of mission and evangelism, peace and justice, and life of discipleship. Moreover, Mennonites and Catholics both face the challenge of how to communicate the faith in an increasingly secular world, and both struggle with the complexities of the relationship between church and society.

210. While recognizing that we hold basic convictions of faith in common, we have also identified significant differences that continue to divide us and thus require further dialogue. Nonetheless, and although we are not in full unity with one another, the substantial amount of the apostolic faith which we realize today that we share allows us as members of the Catholic and Mennonite delegations to see one another as brothers and sisters in Christ. We hope that others may have similar experiences, and that these may contribute to a healing of memories.

## D. Improving our relationships

211. We believe that another fundamental part of the healing of memories is the call to foster new relationships. The significant elements of our common understanding of basic Christian faith ascertained in this dialogue may provide a sufficient theological foundation on which to build. Our experience of re-reading history conjointly suggests that looking together at those periods in which our conflicts initially took place may shed new light on the past and foster a climate for better relationships in the future. For centuries our communities lived with the memories generated from the conflicts of the 16th century and in isolation from one another. Can we not increase our efforts to create new relationships today so that future generations may look back to the 21st century with positive memories of a time in which Mennonites and Catholics began increasingly to serve Christ together?

212. Indeed, as the introduction to this report already suggested, the building of improved relationships is beginning as Mennonites and Catholics talk to one another. On the international level, this dialogue is an important sign that the Catholic Church and the Mennonite World Conference are willing, for the sake of Christ, to strive for mutual understanding and better relationships. We believe that one should not underestimate the importance of what it means for our two families of Christians, separated for centuries, to enter into conversation.

213. Locally as well, in several parts of the world, some Catholics and Mennonites already engaged with each other in theological dialogue and in practical cooperation. In various places collaboration between the Mennonite central committee and Caritas or Catholic Relief Services is taking place in humanitarian causes. We hear of Mennonites working with Catholics in the USA, in the Middle East and in India, to name but a few examples. And even though numerous local Catholic-Mennonite initiatives are unofficial and personal, they serve the wider church by helping to overcome false caricatures about and mutual prejudices of each other.

214. In light of this situation, the dialogue members encourage Mennonites and Catholics to engage each other in joint study and cooperative service. Areas of interaction could include a review of history textbooks on each side, participation in the Week of Prayer for Christian Unity, mutual engagement in missiological reflection, peace and justice initiatives, some programmes of faith formation among our respective members, and "get acquainted" visits between Catholic and Mennonite communities, locally and more widely.

## Conclusion

215.  After having worked with each other over these five years, we, Catholic and Mennonite members of this dialogue, want to testify together that our mutual love for Christ has united us and accompanied us in our discussions. Our dialogue has fortified the common conviction that it is possible to experience reconciliation and the healing of memories. Therefore we beseech God to bestow divine grace upon us for the healing of past relationships between Mennonites and Catholics, and we thank God for present commitments to reconciliation within the body of Christ. Together we pray that God may bless this new relationship between our two families of faith, and that the Holy Spirit may enlighten and enliven us in our common journey on the path forward.

NOTES

[1]   The word "church" is used in this report to reflect the self-understandings of the participating churches, without intending to resolve all the ecclesiological issues related to this term. Mennonites and Catholics do not share a common understanding of the church.

[2]   The term "Historic Peace churches", in use since about 1935, refers to Mennonites, Quakers (Society of Friends) and Church of the Brethren. For an orientation to the Historic Peace churches, see Donald Durnbaugh ed., *On Earth Peace: Discussions on War/Peace Issues between Friends, Mennonites, Brethren and European Churches 1935-1975*, Elgin, Brethren, 1978.

[3]   *GS*, 42.

[4]   Now called the United States Conference of Catholic Bishops.

[5]   Cf. the following samples from bilateral dialogues: (1) "Towards a Common Understanding of the Church: Reformed-Roman Catholic International Dialogue, Second Phase (1984-1990)", ch. 1, "Towards a Reconciliation of Memories", and ch. 3, "The Church We Confess and Our Divisions in History", *Information Service*, 74, 1990, III, pp.93-102,106-15; (2) The Joint Declaration on the Doctrine of Justification, signed by the Lutheran World Federation and the Catholic Church (1999), *Information Service*, 103, 2000, I-II, pp.3-6; (3) "Les entretiens luthéro-mennonites (1981-1984)", *Cahiers de Christ Seul*, no. 16, 1984; (4) *Bericht vom Dialog VELKD/Mennoniten: 1989 bis 1992*, Texte aus der VELKD, 53, Hannover, Lutherisches Kirchenamt der VELKD, 1993.

[6]   John Howard Yoder, "The Disavowal of Constantine: An Alternative Perspective on Interfaith Dialogue", in *The Royal Priesthood: Essays Ecclesiological and Ecumenical*, Grand Rapids MI, Eerdmans, 1994, pp.242-61, esp. p.251.

[7]   "Memory and Reconciliation: The Church and Faults of the Past", 4.1, International Theological Commission, Vatican City, Dec. 1999.

[8]   For §30 and following, cf. Thomas Brady Jr, Heiko A. Oberman and James D. Tracy eds, *Handbook of European History, 1400-1600: Late Middle Ages, Renaissance, and Reformation*, Leiden, Brill, 1994, 2 vols, reprinted Grand Rapids MI, 1996; John Bossy, *Christianity in the West, 1400-1700*, New York/Oxford, Oxford UP, 1985; John W. O'Malley ed., *Catholicism in Early Modern Europe*, St Louis, Center for Reformation Research, 1988; Robert Bireley, *The Refashioning of Catholicism, 1450-1700: A Reassessment of the Counter Reformation*, New York/London, Macmillan, 1999.

[9]   The term "radical Reformation" was introduced by the historian George Hunston Williams in his famous book of the same title, *The Radical Reformation*, 3rd ed., Kirksville, Sixteenth Century Journal Publishers, 1992. By "radical Reformation" we mean that 16th-century movement which rebelled not only against the Catholic Church at that time but also against the classical Reformers. It consisted of varied groups such as the leaders of the Great Peasants War (1524-25), the Anabaptists, the Spiritualists, Evangelical Rationalists, Unitarians and Schwenckfelders. Others label these groups as the "left wing of the Reformation".

[10]   For instance, see Bernd Moeller's famous article "Frömmigkeit in Deutschland um 1500", *Archiv für Reformationsgeschichte*, 56, 1965, pp.5-30, translated several times, for example, as "Piety in Germany around 1500", in Steven E. Ozment ed., *The Reformation in Medieval Perspective*, Chicago, Quadrangle, 1971, pp.50-75. See also Eamon Duffy, *The Stripping of the Altars: Traditional Religion in England 1400-1580*, New Haven/London, Yale UP, 1992.

[11]    *Devotio Moderna* or "Modern (= new, contemporary) Devotion" is the name of a movement of spiritual renewal that laid great emphasis on the inner life of the individual and on the imitation of Christ. It was inspired by the deacon Geert Grote (1340-84), and had its origins in the Low Countries, but during the 15th century it was spread all over Western Europe. See R.R. Post, *The Modern Devotion*, Leiden, Brill, 1968; G. Epinay-Burgard, *Gérard Grote (1340-1384) et les débuts de la dévotion moderne*, Wiesbaden, F. Steiner, 1970; John van Engen, *Devotio Moderna: Basic Writings*, New York, Paulist, 1988.

[12]    Cf. James M. Stayer, Werner O. Packull and Klaus Deppermann, "From Monogenesis to Polygenesis: The Historical Discussion of Anabaptist Origins", *Mennonite Quarterly Review*, 49, 1975, pp.83-122.

[13]    Cf. James M. Stayer, *Anabaptists and the Sword*, 2nd ed., Lawrence KS, Coronado, 1976.

[14]    Cf. William H.C. Frend, *The Donatist Church: A Movement of Protest in Roman North Africa*, Oxford, Clarendon, 1952.

[15]    Cf. Code of Justinian, book I, tit. 6, 2.

[16]    Extended efforts to describe this continuity can be found in *The Chronicle of the Hutterian Brethren*, translated and edited by the Hutterian Brethren, Rifton NY, Plough, 1987; and in Thieleman J. van Braght, *Bloody Theater or Martyrs' Mirror*, translated from the Dutch ed. of 1660 by Joseph Sohm, 5th English ed., Scottdale PA, Herald, 1950.

[17]    Brad S. Gregory, *Salvation at Stake: Christian Martyrdom in Early Modern Europe*, Cambridge MA, Harvard Univ., 1999, esp. ch. 6 on Anabaptists and martyrdom and ch. 7 on Roman Catholics and martyrdom.

[18]    James M. Stayer, "Numbers in Anabaptist Research", in C. Arnold Snyder ed., *Commoners and Community: Essays in Honour of Werner O. Packull*, Waterloo, Herald, 2002, pp.51-73, esp. pp.58-59. Anabaptist and Mennonite martyrs then constituted about 40-50 percent of all the religious martyrs of the 16th century.

[19]    Cornelius J. Dyck, "The Suffering Church in Anabaptism", *Mennonite Quarterly Review*, 59, 1985, p.5.

[20]    Cf. Gregory, *Salvation at Stake*, p.319. While there are no known instances of Mennonites persecuting or executing Catholics in the 16th or 17th centuries, Catholic soldiers may have been victims of the violence of the siege of Münster in Westphalia (1534-35). Whether or not this is an instance of Anabaptist persecution of Catholics is an unresolved question of our discussions. For Catholics, this incident raises the possibility of Catholic deaths at the hands of Anabaptists. For Mennonites, both the Schleitheim confession (1527) and Menno Simons' critiques during and after these events have founded a consistent Mennonite rejection, from that time until the present, of what happened at Münster and all efforts at theologically justifying such actions.

[21]    Cf. Walter Klaassen, "The Anabaptist Critique of Constantinian Christendom", *Mennonite Quarterly Review*, 55, 1981, pp.218-30.

[22]    Cf. Gerhard Ruhbach ed., *Die Kirche angesichts der Konstantinischen Wende*, Darmstadt,: Wissenschaftliche Buchgesellschaft, 1976; Robin Lane Fox, *Pagans and Christians*, New York, Knopf, 1987; Jochen Bleicken, *Constantin der Große und die Christen*, Munich, Oldenbourg,1992; Michael Grant, *Constantine the Great: The Man and his Times*, New York, Prentice Hall, 1994; T.G. Elliott, *The Christianity of Constantine the Great*, New York, Fordham UP, 1997.

[23]    Cf. Ramsey MacMullen, "Christianity Shaped through its Mission", in Alan Kreider ed., *The Origins of Christendom in the West*, Edinburgh, T&T Clark, 2001, pp.97-117; Gilbert Dagron, Pierre Riché and André Vauchez eds, *Évêques, moines et empereurs (610-1054)*, *Histoire du christianisme*, vol. 4, Paris, Desclée, 1993, p.637; Michel Rouche, *Clovis*, Paris, Fayard, 1996, p.143; W.R. Cannon, *Histoire du christianisme au Moyen Âge: de la chute de Rome à la chute de Constantinople*, Paris, Éditions Payot, 1961, p.8; Jacques le Goff and René Rémond eds, *Histoire de la France religieuse*, vol. 1, Paris, Seuil, 1988, p.179.

[24]    See *DH*, esp. 6-7, 12-13, also 2, 4, 9, and *GS* 41 and 42.

[25]    Cf. *GS* 76, which states, "The church, by reason of her role and competence, is not identified in any way with the political community nor bound to any political system... The church and the political community in their own fields are autonomous and independent from each other."

[26]    Alan Kreider, *The Change of Conversion and the Origin of Christendom*, Harrisburg, 1999; *idem, The Origins of Christendom*.

[27]    "But a Turk or heretic cannot be overcome by our own doing, neither by sword nor by fire, but alone with patience and supplication, whereby we patiently await divine judgment." Balthasar Hubmaier, "On Heretics and Those Who Burn Them", in H. Wayne Pipkin and John Howard Yoder eds, *Balthasar Hubmaier: Theologian of Anabaptism, Classics of the Radical Reformation*, 5, Scottdale, Herald, 1989, p.62.

[28]    "All external things including life and limb are subjected to external authority. But no one may coerce or compel true faith in Christ." Pilgram Marpeck, "Exposé of the Babylonian Whore", in Walter Klaassen, Werner Packull and John Rempel, *Later Writings of Pilgram Marpeck and his Circle*, vol. I, Kitchener, Pandora, 1999, p.27.

29  Cf. Walter Kasper, "The Theological Foundations of Human Rights", *The Jurist*, 50, 1990, p.153.

30  *DH* 12.

31  John Van Engen, "The Christian Middle Ages as an Historiographical Problem", *American Historical Review*, 91, 1986, pp.519-52.

32  Christopher M. Bellitto, *Renewing Christianity. A History of Church Reform from Day One to Vatican II*, New York, Paulist, 2001.

33  Ronald G. Musto, *The Catholic Peace Tradition*, Maryknoll NY, Orbis, 1986.

34  Bernard McGinn et al., *Christian Spirituality*, New York, Crossroad, 1985-89, 3 vols.

35  Kenneth Ronald Davis, *Anabaptism and Asceticism: A Study in Intellectual Origins*, Eugene, Wipf & Stock, 1998; C. Arnold Snyder, "The Monastic Origins of Swiss Anabaptist Sectarianism", *Mennonite Quarterly Review*, 57, 1983, pp.5-26; C. Arnold Snyder, *The Life and Thought of Michael Sattler*, Scottdale/Kitchener, Herald, 1984; Peter Nissen, "De Moderne Devotie en het Nederlands-Westfaalse Doperdom: op zoek naar relaties en invloeden", in P. Bange et al. eds, *De Doorwerking van de Moderne Devotie. Windesheim 1387-1987*, Hilversum, Verloren, 1988, pp.95-118; Dennis D. Martin, "Monks, Mendicants and Anabaptists: Michael Sattler and the Benedictines Reconsidered", *Mennonite Quarterly Review*, 60, 1986, pp.139-64; Dennis D. Martin, "Catholic Spirituality and Anabaptist and Mennonite Discipleship", *Mennonite Quarterly Review*, 62, 1988, pp.5-25.

36  Russell Snyder-Penner, "The Ten Commandments, the Lord's Prayer and the Apostles' Creed as Early Anabaptist Texts", *Mennonite Quarterly Review*, 68, 1994, pp.318-35.

37  *LG* 1.

38  *LG* 8.

39  *LG* 2.

40  *LG* 17. Cf. Rom. 12.

41  Cf. *AG* 3.

42  Cf. *UR* 22 and Directory 92.

43  *DV* 6.

44  Cf. *DV* 7.

45  *LG* 12.

46  *DV* 10.

47  Cf. *DV* 10.

48  The other points are: "(2) the eucharist, as the sacrament of the body and blood of Christ, an offering of praise to the Father, the sacrificial memorial and real presence of Christ and the sanctifying outpouring of the Holy Spirit; (3) ordination, as a sacrament, to the threefold ministry of the episcopate, presbyterate and deaconate; (4) the magisterium of the church, entrusted to the pope and the bishops in communion with him, understood as a responsibility and an authority exercised in the name of Christ for teaching and safeguarding the faith; (5) the Virgin Mary, as Mother of God and Icon of the church, the spiritual Mother who intercedes for Christ's disciples and for all humanity" (*UUS* 79).

49  *LG* 25.

50  Cf. *UUS* 94.2.

51  *LG* 23.1.

52  Cf. *LG* 8.

53  Cf. *LG* 23, 2; see also *CD* 11 and Congregation for the Doctrine of the Faith, in "Some Aspects of the Church Understood as Communion", *Communionis notio*, pp.7f.

54  Cf. *ibid.*, 9.

55  Cf. *LG* 23.

56  Walter Cardinal Kasper, "Present Situation and Future of the Ecumenical Movement", prolusio of the plenary meeting of the Pontifical Council for Promoting Christian Unity, *Information Service*, 109, 2002/I-II, p.18.

57  Cf. *CD* 11.

58  Cf. *LG* 13.3 and Directory 16.

59  Cf. *AG* 1, 4.

60  Cf. *AG* 10.

61  Cf. *AG* 22.

62  Cf. Harold S. Bender, *These Are My People: The New Testament Church*, Scottdale/Kitchener, Herald, 1962, pp.1ff.

63   Cf. *ibid.*, pp.23ff.

64   *Confession of Faith in a Mennonite Perspective*, 9, Scottdale/Waterloo, Herald, 1995, p.39.

65   Cf. Norman Kraus, *The Community of the Spirit*, Grand Rapids MI, Eerdmans, 1974; Bender, *These Are My People*, pp.42ff. Bender's terminology, "the holy community", is practically interchangeable with the image of the "community of the Holy Spirit".

66   Kraus, *The Community of the Spirit*, p.24.

67   Cf. John Howard Yoder, *Body Politics*, Nashville TN, Discipleship Resources, 1997, ch. 1.

68   Cf. F.H. Littell, *The Anabaptist View of the Church : A Study in the Origins of Sectarian Protestantism*, 2nd ed. revised and enlarged, Boston MA, Beacon/Starr King, 1958, pp.37ff.

69   Walter Klaassen ed., *Anabaptism in Outline*, Scottdale/Kitchener, Herald, 1981, p.87.

70   *Confession of Faith in a Mennonite Perspective*, 9, p.42.

71   Cf. R. Friedmann, *The Theology of Anabaptism*, Scottdale, Herald, 1973, pp.149ff.

72   Denis Janz, *Three Reformation Catechisms: Catholic, Anabaptist, Lutheran*, New York, Edwin Mellen, 1982, p.134.

73   Howard J. Loewen, *One Lord, One Church, One Hope, and One God: Mennonite Confessions of Faith*, Elkhart IN, Institute of Mennonite Studies, 1985, p.166.

74   Cf. *DV* 10-20; *Confession of Faith of the General Conference of Mennonite Brethren Churches*, 2, Winnipeg/Hillsboro, Kindred Productions, 1999; *Confession of Faith in a Mennonite Perspective*, 4, p.21. According to Rainer W. Burkart, secretary of the MWC Faith and Life Council, "statements of faith from the Mennonite and Brethren in Christ tradition often borrow language that can be found in the Apostles' and Nicene Creeds, and some view the Apostles' Creed as a foundational text for understanding the essentials of the faith. Many Mennonite and Brethren in Christ confessions follow the traditional credal order..." *Courier*, a quarterly publication of the Mennonite World Conference, 12, 4, 1997, p.3.

75   Although for Catholics this is never without relationship to "sacred Tradition as indispensable to the interpretation of the word of God", *UUS* 79.

76   Cf. *DV* 11.

77   For example, John C. Wenger, *God's Word Written*, Scottdale, Herald, 1966; *Confession of Faith in a Mennonite Perspective*, 4, p.42.

78   On the relationship between incorporation into the church and baptism, see §§76 and 115-16 for the Catholic position and §§92 and 121-24 for the Mennonite position.

79   *Confession of Faith in a Mennonite Perspective*, 4, p.28.

80   Cf. *LG* 17, 33; *AA* 2-4; Dordrecht Confession (1632), art. V, Loewen, *One Lord, One Church*, p.64.

81   Cf. *UR* 7.

82   *UR* 12.

83   Cf. Klaassen, *The Anabaptist Critique*, p.102.

84   *GS* 45.

85   Cf. Douglas Gwyn et al., *A Declaration on Peace*, Scottdale/Waterloo, Herald, 1991.

86   *Confession of Faith in a Mennonite Perspective*, 9, p.39.

87   Cf. *LG* 48-49.

88   For explanation of the difference between ordained and lay ministry in Catholic teaching, see §106.

89   Cf. Bender, "The Anabaptist Vision", 13-17; *LG* 39-42.

90   Cf. *AA* 28-32.

91   When Catholics capitalize Tradition they acknowledge the close bond that exists between sacred Tradition and sacred scripture as "forming one sacred deposit of the word of God" (*DV* 10) and not various human traditions that may develop in the course of the history of the church.

92   Cf. *DV* 10.

93   Cf. *DV* 7-10.

94   Directory, 91.

95   Cf. Marlin Miller, "Priesthood of all Believers", *Mennonite Encyclopedia*, vol. V, Scottdale/Waterloo, Herald, 1990, pp.721-22. For Mennonites, the Reformation's emphasis on the "priesthood of all believers" did not become a point of doctrine. The expression was used by some Anabaptists to support the New Testament's teaching that all believers corporately are a "kingdom of priests", a "royal priesthood".

96   *LG* 10.

97   *Ibid.*

98   Cf. *LG* 10, 34.

99   Cf. *LG* 12.

100  Cf. *UUS* 79.

101  Cf. *LG* 48; Phil, 2:12. In talking about the relationship of Israel to the church, *LG* 9 describes the sacramental nature of the church in this way: "Israel according to the flesh, which wandered as an exile in the desert, was already called the church of God (2 Esdr. 13:1; cf. Deut. 23:1ff.; Num. 20:4). So likewise the new Israel, which while living in this present age goes in search of a future and abiding city (Cf. Heb. 13:14), is called the church of Christ (cf. Matt. 16:18). For he has bought it for himself with his blood (cf. Acts 20:28), has filled it with his Spirit and provided it with those means which befit it as a visible and social union. God gathered together as one all those who in faith look upon Jesus as the author of salvation and the source of unity and peace, and established them as the church that for each and all it may be the visible sacrament of this saving unity."

102  *SC* 61.

103  *SC* 59; *LG* 40.1; *GS* 38.2.

104  Cf. *SC* 7.

105  Cf. *SC* 8.

106  Cf. *LG* 11.1.

107  Cf. *SC* 41.2.

108  *UR* 22. Directory, footnote 41.

109  Cf. Origen, *In Romanis*, V, 9: *PG* 14, 1047; cf. St Augustine, *De Genesi ad litteram*, X, 23, 39: *PL* 34, 426; *De peccatorum meritis et remissione et de baptismo parvulorum ad Marcellinum*, I, 26, 39: *PL* 44, 131. In fact, three passages of the Acts of the Apostles (16:15, 16:33, 18:81) speak of the baptism of a whole household or family. See also Irenaeus, *Adv. Haereses*, II, 22, 4: *PG* 7, 784; Harvey I, 330. Many inscriptions from as early as the 2nd century give little children the title of "children of God", a title given only to the baptized, or explicitly mention that they were baptized: cf., for example, *Corpus Inscriptionum Graecarum*, 9727, 9801, 9817; E. Diehl ed., *Inscriptiones Latinae Christianae Veteres*, Berlin, Weidmann, 1961, nos 1523 (3), 4429 A. For a comprehensive study of the question of the baptism of infants within the context of the rites of Christian initiation, see Maxwell E. Johnson, *The Rites of Christian Initiation: Their Evolution and Interpretation*, Collegeville MN, Liturgical Press, 1999.

110  Hippolytus of Rome, *Apostolic Tradition*, 21.

111  Rite of baptism for children, introduction. See also the instruction by the Congregation for the Doctrine of the Faith, *Pastoralis Actio* (20 Oct. 1980), 14, which states, "The fact that infants cannot yet profess personal faith does not prevent the church from conferring this sacrament on them, since in reality it is in her own faith that she baptizes them. This point of doctrine was clearly defined by St Augustine: 'When children are presented to be given spiritual grace', he wrote, 'it is not so much those holding them in their arms who present them – although, if these people are good Christians, they are included among those who present the children – as the whole company of saints and faithful Christians.... It is done by the whole of Mother Church which is in the saints, since it is as a whole that she gives birth to each and every one of them" (Epist. 98, 5: *PL* 33, 362; Cf. Sermo 176, 2, 2: *PL* 38, 950). This teaching is repeated by St Thomas Aquinas and all the theologians after him: the child who is baptized believes not on its own account, by a personal act, but through others, "through the church's faith communicated to it" (in *Summa Theologica*, IIIa, q. 69, a. 5, ad 3, cf. q. 68, a. 9, ad 3). This same teaching is also expressed in the new rite of baptism, when the celebrant asks the parents and godparents to profess the faith of the church, the faith in which the children are baptized (*Ordo baptismi parvulorum, Praenotanda*, 2: cf. 56).

112  Cf. *LG* 11.

113  The term memorial (*zikkaron* in Hebrew, *anamnesis* in Greek) is a technical term which is not merely the recollection of past events but the proclamation of the mighty works (*mirabilia Dei*) wrought by God for us (Ex. 13:3). In liturgical celebrations these events become in a certain way present and real.

114  Cf. *CCC* n. 1359.

115  Cf. *SC* 7.

116  Mennonites shied away from the use of the term "sacrament" because they feared what they called "sacramentalism", the temptation to attribute miraculous power to the ritual and its elements as such. Even then, the designation "sacrament" was used at times, as for example in art. 26 of the Ris confession (1766) which states, "That the Lord instituted this *sacrament* (italics added) with the intention that it is to be observed by his disciples in his church in all time, is plainly seen" (Loewen, *One Lord, One Church*, p.98).

117  A recent outline of Anabaptist ordinances adds "church discipline", although it is not commonly recognized as such. Church discipline replaced the sacrament of penance by following the New Testament pattern (Matt. 18:15-18) of offering the sinner an opportunity for repentance, forgiveness, and readmission

into the fellowship of the church. See C.A. Snyder, *From Anabaptist Seed*, Kitchener/Scottdale, Pandora/Herald, 1999, pp.28ff.

[118] Another way of outlining the meaning of baptism would be to follow an early scheme developed by the Anabaptists on the basis of 1 John 5:7-8, which is understood as a reference to a threefold outline: baptism of the Holy Spirit, baptism of water, and baptism of blood. Cf. "Confession of Faith According to the Holy Word of God" (ca 1600), 21, in van Braght, *Martyrs Mirror*, pp.396ff.

[119] H.S. Bender, "Walking in the Resurrection", *Mennonite Quarterly Review*, 35, April 1961, pp.11-25.

[120] *Dordrecht Confession*, art 7, Loewen, *One Lord, One Church*, p.65.

[121] Ris confession, art. 25, Loewen, *ibid.*, p.97.

[122] Loewen, *ibid.*, art. 9, p.306.

[123] *Dordrecht Confession*, art. 7, Loewen, *ibid.*, p.65.

[124] Cf. Ris confession, art. 25, Loewen, *ibid.*, pp.97f.

[125] Schleitheim confession, art. 3, Loewen, *ibid.*, p.80.

[126] Ris confession, art. 26, Loewen, *ibid.*, p.98.

[127] *Confession of Faith in a Mennonite Perspective*, 12, p.50.

[128] Cf. John D. Rempel, *The Lord's Supper in Anabaptism*, Scottdale/Waterloo, Herald, 1993. Rempel says that the Anabaptists "made the church as a community the agent of the breaking of bread. There is still a presider who symbolizes the community's order and authority. But it is the congregation that does the action. The Spirit is present in their action, transforming them so that they are reconstituted as the body of Christ. The life of the congregation, consecrated in its faith and love, consecrates the elements" (p.34).

[129] Cf. Schleitheim confession, 3, Loewen, *One Lord, One Church*, p.80.

[130] *CCC*, 1374 citing the council of Trent (1551), DS 1651.

[131] Communion with the local bishop and with the bishop of Rome is understood as a sign and service of the unity of the church.

[132] Cf. Acts 2; *LG* 1, 9, and esp. 13; *GS* 42.

[133] *LG* 1, 4, 9, 13.

[134] *GS* 42.

[135] Cf. *Sollicitudo Rei Socialis* 38-40, 45; *Centesimus Annus* 52.

[136] Cf. *SC* 9-10; *LG* 3, 7; *Sollicitudo Rei Socialis* 48.

[137] Cf. *GS* 24-25, 32.

[138] Cf. *LG* 1; GS 4, 6, 24-25; *Sollicitudo Rei Socialis* 45.

[139] *Sollicitudo Rei Socialis* 39. Cf. James 3:18.

[140] Cf. *LG* 39.

[141] *LG* 41.

[142] Cf. *GS* 43, 88-91; *Sollicitudo Rei Socialis* 42-43, 47; *Centesimus Annus* 58; Pope John Paul II, World Day of Peace Message, 1993, "If You Want Peace, Reach Out to the Poor". Cf. Matt. 25:41-36; Luke 14:15-24; James 2:1-7.

[143] Cf. *GS* 28; *Sollicitudo Rei Socialis* 40; *EN* 41.

[144] Pope John Paul II, "No Peace without Justice, No Justice without Forgiveness", World Day of Peace Message, 2000.

[145] *Centesimus Annus* 23, 25.

[146] Cf. *GS* 88-93; *Centesimus Annus* 52.

[147] Pope Paul VI, "Peace is Possible", World Day of Peace Message, 1973.

[148] Cf. *Centesimus Annus* 51-52.

[149] Cf. *GS* 44, 64-65, 83-90, 32.

[150] This constructive approach to peace (that is, Pope Paul VI: "If you want peace, work for justice") is a complement to the contemporary practice of Mennonites in conflict resolution, conflict transformation and technical peace-building. It also is supportive of broader conceptions of peace-building now being promoted in both Mennonite and Catholic circles.

[151] The Holy See is the title the Catholic Church employs in international affairs.

[152] *GS* 80.

[153] *Evangelium Vitae* 27; cf. 10-12, 39-41.

[154] Cf. *GS* 78.

[155] Cf. *Centesimus Annus*, 23, 25, 52.

156 Cf. *CCC* 2313; Pope John Paul II, "Address to the International Conference on Nutrition", 1992.

157 Cf. World Day of Peace Message, 2002; *Evangelium Vitae* 41; National Conference of Catholic Bishops, "Harvest of Justice Is Sown in Peace".

158 Pope John Paul II, "Address to the Diplomatic Corps", 12 Jan. 2003 (making reference to the conflict then developing between the United States and the United Kingdom with Iraq).

159 *Centesimus Annus* 52; *Evangelium Vitae* 10, 12.

160 *DH* 11. Cf. Luke 22:21-27; Mark 10:45.

161 Cf. *DH* 7.

162 Cf. Day of Pardon, §§200-202 below.

163 *Sollicitudo Rei Socialis* 31, 48.

164 *GS* 39.

165 *Sollicitudo Rei Socialis* 31.

166 Cf. Fernando Enns, *Friedenskirche in der Ökumene. Mennonitische Wurzeln einer Ethik der Gewaltfreiheit*, Göttingen, Vandenhoek & Ruprecht, 2003.

167 Cf. F. Enns, *Friedenskirche*, and John Howard Yoder, "Peace without Eschatology", in *The Royal Priesthood*.

168 Cf. John Howard Yoder, *The Politics of Jesus*, 2nd rev. ed., Grand Rapids MI, Eerdmans, 1994.

169 Cf. Glenn Stassen ed., *Just Peacemaking: Ten Practices for Abolishing War*, Cleveland OH, Pilgrim, 1998; Duane K. Friesen, *Christian Peacemaking and International Conflict: A Realist Pacifist Perspective*, Scottdale/Waterloo, Herald, 1986.

170 *Confession of Faith in a Mennonite Perspective*, 21. Cf. also H. S. Bender et al., "Simplicity", in *Mennonite Encyclopedia*, IV, pp.529-30.

171 For Catholics, the model for a vision of the union of humans with one another is based theologically on the union of the Trinity (cf. GS 24).

172 Cf. *Confession of Faith in a Mennonite Perspective*, 21. *Sollicitudo Rei Socialis* 26, 29-30, esp. 34; Pope John Paul II, "Peace with God, Peace with All Creation", World Day of Peace Message, 1990.

173 A quote from Menno Simons expresses the close theological bond in Christology between the peaceful nature of Jesus Christ and our lives: "Christ is everywhere represented to us as humble, meek, merciful, just, holy, wise, spiritual, long-suffering, patient, peaceable, lovely, obedient, and good, as the perfection of all things; for in him there is an upright nature. Behold, this is the image of God, of Christ as to the Spirit which we have as an example until we become like it in nature and reveal it by our walk" (Menno Simons, "The Spiritual Resurrection" [c. 1536], in J.C. Wenger ed., *The Complete Writings of Menno Simons*, Scottdale, Herald, 1956, pp.55f. Catholic teaching on the link between peace and the redemptive work of the Lord is best seen in *GS* 38: "Undergoing death itself for all of us sinners (cf. John 3:16; Rom. 5:8), he taught us by example that we too must shoulder that cross which the world and the flesh inflict upon those who search after peace and justice". See also *GS* 28 and 32.

174 Cf. *Confession of Faith in a Mennonite Perspective*, 22; *GS* 42 and 78.

175 Cf. Pope John Paul II, "To Build Peace, Respect Minorities", World Day of Peace Message, 1989; *GS* 42. A widely accepted Mennonite standpoint with respect to all conflict, including international conflict, is expressed in *A Declaration on Peace: In God's People the World's Renewal Has Begun*, co-authored by Douglas Gwyn, George Hunsinger, Eugene F. Roop and John Howard Yoder, Scottdale/Waterloo, Herald, 1991, which states in part, "The church's most effective witness and action against war... consists simply in the stand she takes in and through her members in the face of war. Unless the church, trusting the power of God in whose hand the destinies of the nations lie, is willing to 'fall into the ground and die', to renounce war absolutely, whatever sacrifice of freedoms, advantages, or possessions this might entail, even to the point of counselling a nation not to resist foreign conquest and occupation, she can give no prophetic message for the world of nations" (pp.74f.).

176 Cf. *Confession of Faith in a Mennonite Perspective*, 22; *Populorum Progressio* 76-80; *Centesimus Annus* 52.

177 Cf. *Confession of Faith in a Mennonite Perspective*, 22; *Centesimus Annus* 23.

178 Cf. *Confession of Faith in a Mennonite Perspective*, 17; *GS* 32.

179 Cf. *Confession of Faith in a Mennonite Perspective*, 22; *GS* 28.

180 Cf. *Octogesima Adveniens* 4.

181 *Confession of Faith in a Mennonite Perspective*, 22.

182 Cf. *GS* 89-90.

[183] For Mennonites, see *Martyrs Mirror*; for Catholics, in addition to the long liturgical tradition of commemorating martyrs and other witnesses to the faith in the course of the centuries, during the celebration of the great jubilee of the year 2000, there was an ecumenical commemoration of "recent witnesses and martyrs". See also Robert Royal, *The Catholic Martyrs of the Twentieth Century*, New York, Crossroads, 2000.

[184] *Centesimus Annus* 25.

[185] Cf. *GS* 32.

[186] Cf. *GS* 74, 79.

[187] Cf. *GS* 78-79.

[188] Cf. Schleitheim confession, 1527, VI., in Loewen, *One Lord, One Church*, pp.80f.

[189] Cf. *GS* 78; *Evangelium Vitae* 41; *CCC* 2267.

[190] Memory and Reconciliation, 5.1.

[191] § 24 above.

[192] § 25 above.

[193] Cf. §64 above.

[194] Cf. §39 above.

[195] *UR* 3.

[196] *Ibid.*

[197] "God Calls Us to Christian Unity", a statement adopted by the executive of Mennonite World Conference, Goshen IN, July 1998.

[198] Pope John Paul II, Angelus, 12 March 2000.

[199] *Ibid.*

[200] "Universal Prayer for Forgiveness", 12 March 2000, in *Information Service*, 103, 2000/I-II, p.56.

[201] *Ibid.*

[202] *Ibid.*

[203] *Tertio Millennio Adveniente*, 1994, 35.

[204] See footnote 197 above.

## Appendix A: Bibliography of Dialogue Papers and Their Authors

### Strasbourg, France, 14-18 October 1998

Howard John Loewen, "The Mennonite Tradition: An Interpretation"

James Puglisi, SA, "A Self-Description of Who We Are as Catholics Today"

Neal Blough, "Anabaptist Images of Roman Catholics during the Sixteenth Century"

Peter Nissen, "The Catholic Response to the Anabaptist Movement in the Sixteenth Century"

### Venice, Italy, 12-18 October 1999

Neal Blough, "The Anabaptist Idea of the Restitution of the Early Church"

Peter Nissen, "The Anabaptist/Mennonite Tradition of Faith and Spirituality and its Medieval Roots"

Helmut Harder, "A Contemporary Mennonite Theology of the Church"

James Puglisi, SA, "Towards a Common Understanding of the Church"

**Thomashof, Germany, 24-30 November 2000**

Peter Nissen, "The Impact of the Constantinian Shift on the Church: A Catholic Perspective"

Alan Kreider, "Conversion and Christendom: An Anabaptist Perspective"

Drew Christiansen, SJ, "What is a Peace Church? A Roman Catholic Perspective"

Mario Higueros, "Justice, the Inseparable Companion of Peace"

Andrea Lange, "What Is a Peace Church? An Answer from a Mennonite Perspective"

**Assisi, Italy, 27 November-3 December 2001**

Peter Nissen, "Church and Secular Power(s) in the Middle Ages"

Neal Blough, "From the Edict of Milan to Vatican II, via Theodosius, Clovis, Charlemagne and the Fourth Lateran Council or Why Some Mennonites Can't Quite Trust the 'Declaration on Religious Freedom'"

Helmut Harder, "What Anabaptist-Mennonite Confessions of Faith Say about Baptism and the Lord's Supper"

James F. Puglisi, SA, "Contemporary Theology of the Sacraments with Particular Attention to Christian Initiation (Baptism and Eucharist)"

# 30. Church, Evangelization and the Bonds of Koinonia

## A Report of the International Consultation
## between the Catholic Church and the World Evangelical Alliance

### Swanwick, UK, 1993-2002

## Preamble

We, the representatives of two Christian traditions deeply divided from each other historically, have been involved in a substantive consultation that we hope will lead to improved relations in the future. This experience for us has been momentous. We come from strong and vital Christian communities. The Catholic Church is the largest Christian communion in the world, with now over one billion members. The Evangelical movement, with its roots in the Reformation, is one of the most dynamic expressions of Christianity today, showing rapid growth in many parts of the world. The World Evangelical Alliance represents some 150 million from among more than 200 million Evangelical Christians. Yet in spite of exceptions over the centuries, from Zinzendorf and Wesley to Schaff and Congar, both traditions have long lived in isolation from one another. Our communities have been separated by different histories and theologies as well as by unhelpful stereotypes and mutual misunderstandings. This estrangement and misapprehension has occasioned hostility and conflicts that continue to divide the body of Christ in our own time.

In recent decades, however, a considerable number of Catholics and Evangelicals have been getting to know each other, and have discovered in the process how much they have in common. This change is due in part to situational factors: cultural and political changes in the second half of the 20th century, the growth of democracy in countries which formerly had repressive, authoritarian governments, the mixing of peoples and confessions in our increasingly diverse cultures, the discovery of common concerns in the area of ethics and in the struggle against secularism. In part, the changing relations between Evangelical and Catholic communities are due to internal developments, for example, in Catholicism, as a result of the Second Vatican Council and, among Evangelicals, the impact of the Lausanne Covenant. Finally, new attitudes were fostered by far-sighted individuals in both traditions, together with a significant number of initiatives designed to promote greater appreciation and understanding of each other. Billy Graham's ministry stands out here. Most importantly, there is a growing recognition in both our traditions that the spread of the gospel is hindered by our continuing divisions.

---

• Catholic Church and World Evangelical Alliance are the official names of the two co-sponsoring bodies. In using their official names, the co-sponsors of this consultation are not, in any way, claiming these characteristics, respectively, of "Catholic" or "Evangelical" exclusively for themselves.

As a result of these changes in our world and in our churches, many Catholics and Evangelicals have begun talking to and cooperating with each other, including praying together. In the process, they have not only become friends; they have begun to discover each other as brothers and sisters in the Lord. It might be helpful to note some of these formal initiatives, which are described extensively in the appendix.

The first international dialogue between Catholics and Evangelicals began with participants from both sides exploring the subject of mission from 1978 to 1984. This resulted in a 1985 report on their discussions. This international dialogue was sponsored, on the Catholic side, by the Secretariat for Promoting Christian Unity. Evangelical participants, like John Stott, while drawn from a number of churches and Christian organizations, were not official representatives of any international body.

The present consultations represent an important development in our relationship. For the first time these meetings were sponsored by international bodies on both sides: the World Evangelical Alliance and the Pontifical Council for Promoting Christian Unity. This initiative eventually resulted in formal consultations beginning in Venice in 1993, and continuing at Tantur, Jerusalem, in 1997, Williams Bay, Wisconsin, USA, in 1999, Mundelein, Illinois, USA, in 2001, and Swanwick, England, in 2002.

Initial meetings led us eventually to focus on two general areas: the church and her mission. As the discussion continued, it became clear that a common reflection on the biblical notion of koinonia would help us to clarify some convergences and differences between us on the church (part I). The focus on mission evolved into reflection on evangelization and the related issues of religious freedom, proselytism and common witness in light of koinonia (part II).

The purpose of these consultations has been to overcome misunderstandings, to seek better mutual understanding of each other's Christian life and heritage, and to promote better relations between Evangelicals and Catholics. This paper is a result of the first series of discussions and deals with a limited number of issues.

In these conversations, which were conducted in a very cordial and open atmosphere, each side has expressed clearly and candidly its own theological convictions and tradition, and listened as the other side did the same. Together they sought to discern whether there were convergences or even some agreements on theological issues over which Evangelicals and Catholics have long been divided, and also on what issues divisions clearly persist.

This consultation presents here the product of its work to the sponsoring bodies, with gratitude for the support they have given to this project.

We hope this study will be fruitful and serve the cause of the gospel and the glory of our Lord.

**The status of this report**

The report published here is the work of an international consultation between the Catholic Church and the World Evangelical Alliance. It is a study document produced by participants in this consultation. The authorities who appointed the participants have allowed the report to be published so that it may be widely discussed. It is not an authoritative declaration of either the Catholic Church or of the World Evangelical Alliance, who will both also evaluate the document.

# PART I

## CATHOLICS, EVANGELICALS AND KOINONIA

### A. The church as koinonia (fellowship, communion)

1. The use of koinonia brings an important biblical term to bear on ecclesiology, as it suggests those things that bind Christians together. Koinonia is undoubtedly "an early and important aspect of the church and its unity."[1] The biblical word koinonia can be translated in various ways: "fellowship", "belonging", "communion", "participation", "partnership", or "sharing in". Evangelicals often use the term "fellowship", while Catholics frequently use the term "communion".

1. NEW TESTAMENT "FELLOWSHIP"

2. In the Pauline writings, the term koinonia often refers to the relationship of Christians to one another, grounded in their relationship to the divine persons. Paul tells the Corinthian Christians, "You were called into the fellowship of his [God's] Son, Jesus Christ our Lord" (1 Cor. 1:9). He speaks of "the grace of the Lord Jesus Christ and the love of God and the fellowship of the Holy Spirit" (2 Cor. 13:14). Elsewhere he tells his readers that he received "the right hand of fellowship" from James, Cephas and John (Gal. 2:9). On another occasion he warns the Corinthians against having fellowship with unbelievers, asking the rhetorical question, "What fellowship has light with darkness?" (2 Cor. 6:14). Partnership appears to be the meaning in Philippians 1:5-7.

3. The term koinonia occurs also in Acts 2:42, where it again has the meaning of fellowship: "And they devoted themselves to the apostles' teaching and fellowship, and to the breaking of bread and the prayers." It is debatable exactly what type of fellowship Luke here has in mind, but it is evidently some kind of association among believers, received from Christ through solidarity with the apostles. It means the sharing of material goods in 2 Cor. 8:4, 9:13.

4. The Johannine writings reinforce this sense of koinonia as fellowship. The author of the first epistle speaks of proclaiming what he has seen "that you may have fellowship with us; and our fellowship is with the Father and with his Son Jesus Christ" (1 John 1:3). Again in verses 7-8 he refers to fellowship with the Son and among Christians themselves. The fellowship with God in Christ is evidently the basis for the fellowship with other believers, all members in the body of Christ. They are to be one as the Father and Son in the trinity are one (John 17:11,21).

2. VARIOUS EMPHASES IN NEW TESTAMENT INTERPRETATION

5. For both Evangelicals and Roman Catholics communion with Christ involves a transformative union whereby believers are "*koinonoi* of the divine nature and escape the corruption that is in the world by lust" (2 Pet. 1:4). Catholics tend to interpret koinonia in this passage to mean a participation in the divine life and "nature", while Evangelicals tend to interpret koinonia as covenant companionship, as it entails escaping moral corruption and the way of the world. According to many Eastern fathers of the church, the believer's participation in the life of Christ and the church leads to the process of the believer's divinization (*theosis, deificatio*). Evangelicals have reservations about the notion of *theosis*: the word is not found in the Bible and it suffers, they feel, from too much ambiguity. It appears to suggest that believers shall possess the essence of deity – a meaning which Catholic doctrine too denies. Evangelicals agree that the redemptive grace on the one hand restores the original godlikeness that was marred and defaced by human sin (Col. 3:10), and on the other hand that the Spirit transforms believers into the likeness of the Second Adam, "from glory to glory" (1 Cor. 15:48,49; 2 Cor. 3:18), a process that will reach completion only when Christ, the Lord and Saviour, comes from heaven (Phil 3:20-21; 1 Thess. 5:23-24).

6. Catholics believe that sacraments are Christ's instruments to effect the transformative union with the divine nature (1 Cor. 12:12-13, where they see water-baptism, and 10:16-17, eucharist). In passages such as these they hear other (Catholics would say deeper), more sacramental and participatory connotations in the word "koinonoi" than are expressed by the word "fellowship". Many Evangelicals consider the sacraments to be dominical means of grace or "ordinances" which are "visible words" that proclaim (*kataggellete*, 1 Cor. 11:26) or are signs and seals of the grace of union with Christ – grace to be received and enjoyed on the sole condition of personal faith.

3. PERSPECTIVES ON *COMMUNIO SANCTORUM*

7. While the earliest rendering of the term *communio sanctorum* in the Apostles' Creed has been translated as "communion of holy persons" (saints), this language has been translated as a reference to "holy things" (sacraments).[2] However, the doctrinal significance of *communio sanctorum* (*koinonia ton hagion*) was not relegated to one interpretation only. Later Western appropriation of the concept of divinization emphasized it as a participation in the eucharist. Evangelicals prefer to translate *communio sanctorum* as "the fellowship of holy persons" or "of saints", the "saints" being all those who truly belong to Jesus Christ by faith; they understand "communion" as the bond that binds all Christians in all generations.

8. Evangelicals, historically, have not given the same place to the sacraments nor connected sanctification so directly with them as Catholics have. They maintain the "forensic" (referring to the courts of law) meaning of justification, and tend to prefer the vocabulary of drama and law. The Bible, as they read it, is more favourable to categories such as covenant-breaking and covenant-renewal, condemnation and acquittal, enmity and reconciliation, than to the category of participation in being. But they do affirm with the apostle Paul that anyone who is in Christ is a "new creation" (2 Cor. 5:17; Gal. 6:15). The Holy Spirit effects a radical change, a new birth from above.

9. Catholics and Evangelicals anticipate perfect communion in the kingdom to be ushered in with the final coming of Jesus. In the light of this expectation, Catholics and Evangelicals should look to a deeper communion in this world, even if they disagree, between and among themselves, on the means by which this might be achieved, and on the extent to which it can be realized prior to the return of Christ. Since the biblical texts are authoritative for both Catholics and Evangelicals, they provide a solid foundation for our conversations. The growing familiarity with biblical categories on both sides, combined with recent reinterpretations of sacramental theology, suggests that koinonia continues to be a promising topic for further explorations in our conversations.

## B. Our respective understandings of the church and of other Christians

### 1. RECENT DEVELOPMENTS

10. In the Second Vatican Council, Catholics elaborated their distinctive understanding of the nature of the church and also their relationships to other Christians. Evangelicals also have explored this area in major conferences in recent decades on the topic of missions. It will be useful to describe the views in the two communities, before pointing out the implications for mutual understanding.

11. The Second Vatican Council marked a development in the ecclesiological self-understanding of the Catholic Church. Rather than positing a simple identity between the church of Christ and itself, *Lumen Gentium* teaches that "the church of Christ... subsists in the Catholic Church" (*LG* 8).[3] The Evangelical movement, on the other hand, received its characteristic modern shape from the influence of the 18th- and 19th-century revivals (preceded by Pietism and Puritanism): these revivals crossed denominational boundaries and relativized their importance. From the Roman Catholic side the recognition of the "others" as belonging to Christ takes the form of an emphasis on truly Christian elements and endowments in their communities; and from the Evangelical side, on the acknowledged presence of true believers indwelt by Christ's Spirit among Catholics.

### 2. CATHOLIC VIEWS

12. Vatican II in its Constitution on the Church (*Lumen Gentium*) speaks of the bonds between Catholics and other Christians in these terms:

> The unique church of Christ... constituted and organized in the world as a society, subsists in the Catholic Church, which is governed by the successor of Peter and by the bishops in union with that successor, although many elements of sanctification and of truth can be found outside her visible structure (*LG* 8).

> The church recognizes that in many ways she is linked with those who, being baptized, are honoured with the name of Christian, though they do not possess the faith in its entirety or do not preserve unity of communion with the successor of Peter. For there are many who honour sacred scripture, taking it as a norm of belief and of action, and who show a true religious zeal. They lovingly believe in God the Father Almighty and in Christ, Son of God and Saviour...

Likewise, we can say that in some real way they are joined with us in the Holy Spirit, for to them also He gives his gifts and graces, and is thereby operative among them with his sanctifying power. Some indeed He has strengthened to the extent of the shedding of their blood (*LG* 15).

13. In its Decree on Ecumenism (*UR*), Vatican II brings the concept of ecclesial elements into correlation with that of koinonia. The decree illustrates the Catholic perspective on full communion. The Holy Spirit, it affirms, "brings about that marvellous communion of the faithful and joins them together so intimately in Christ that he is the principle of the church's unity" (*UR* 2). The decree goes on to say that the Spirit brings about and perfects this wonderful union by means of the faithful preaching of the gospel, the administration of the sacraments, and the loving exercise of pastoral authority (cf. *UR* 2).

14. In the following paragraph the Decree on Ecumenism clarifies relationships with other communities and broaches the notion of "imperfect communion", which is so vital for contemporary interchurch relations. The decree states that some Christians have become separated from full communion with the Catholic Church but remain in a real, though imperfect, communion with it because "some, even very many, of the most significant elements or endowments which together go to build up and give life to the church herself can exist outside the visible boundaries of the Catholic Church: the written word of God; the life of grace, faith, hope and charity, along with other interior gifts of the Holy Spirit and visible elements" (*UR* 3).

15. In a later section of the Decree on Ecumenism the same notion of imperfect communion is applied specifically to Protestant communities. The Council here speaks of belief in the Holy Trinity, and of confession of Jesus Christ as God and Lord, and as sole Mediator between God and man (cf. *UR* 20). It then goes on to mention love and veneration for holy scripture, affirming that "the sacred utterances are precious instruments in the mighty hand of God for attaining that unity which the Saviour holds out to all men" (*UR* 21). Baptism properly conferred "constitutes a sacramental bond of unity linking all who have been reborn by means of it… But baptism, of itself, is only a beginning, a point of departure, for it is wholly directed towards the acquiring of fullness of life in Christ" (*UR* 22). Pope John Paul II reaffirms the teaching of Vatican II on the "many elements of sanctification and truth" in other Christian communities and on "the communion, albeit imperfect, which exists between them and the Catholic Church" (*UUS* 11).

16. All of these factors give concreteness to the use of the concept of koinonia by Roman Catholics. They make it clear that the ecclesial elements in question find expression in acts of faith, hope and charity. The degree of communion cannot be measured by outward and visible means alone because communion depends on the reality of life in the Spirit.

3. EVANGELICAL VIEWS

17. Evangelicals similarly emphasize that the most important bond is the life of the Spirit which flows from union with Christ. This bond is created when the gospel is received in faith and is foundational for the visible expression of the oneness or koinonia of all Christians. For Evangelicals the visibility of the church is subordinate to this primary truth. "The Gospel of Jesus Christ: An Evangelical Celebration" confesses:

All Christians are called to unity in love and unity in truth. As Evangelicals who derive our very name from the gospel, we celebrate this great good news of God's saving work in Jesus Christ as the true bond of Christian unity, whether among organized churches and denominations or in the many transdenominational cooperative enterprises of Christians together.

The Bible declares that all who truly trust in Christ and his gospel are sons and daughters of God through grace, and hence are our brothers and sisters in Christ.[4]

As the Lausanne Covenant of 1974 notes:

World evangelization requires the whole church to take the whole gospel to the whole world. The church is at the very centre of God's cosmic purpose and is his appointed means of spreading the gospel. But a church which preaches the cross must itself be marked by the cross. It becomes a stumbling block to evangelism when it betrays the gospel or lacks a living faith in God, a genuine love for people, or scrupulous honesty in all things including promotion and finance. The church is the community of God's people rather than an institution, and must not be identified with any particular culture, social or political system, or human ideology (John 17:18, 20:21; Matt. 28:19,20; Acts 1:8, 20:27; Eph. 1:9,10, 3:9-11; Gal. 6:14,17; 2 Cor. 6:3,4; 2 Tim. 2:19-20; Phil. 1:27) (Lausanne 6).

Evangelicals adhere to the Reformation doctrine of the "invisible church" (though with varying degrees of emphasis), without diminishing the importance of the visible church, as it is implied in the Amsterdam declaration:

The one, universal church is a transnational, transcultural, transdenominational and multi-ethnic family of the household of faith. In the widest sense, the church includes all the redeemed of all the ages, being the one body of Christ extended throughout time as well as space. Here in the world, the church becomes visible in all local congregations that meet to do together the things that according to scripture the church does (Amsterdam 9).

18. Evangelicals insist (as do Roman Catholics) that disciplinary and doctrinal criteria should be used for expressions in ecclesial life of the unity we have in Christ. "Church discipline, biblically based and under the direction of the Holy Spirit, is essential to the well-being and ministry of God's people."[5] In a world and in churches marred by human failure, church discipline may demand the curtailing of concrete forms of fellowship even in cases where offenders against the apostolic teaching are acknowledged as brothers or sisters (cf. 2 Thess. 3:14-15). This applies to deviations in all spheres of life, both in the confession of faith as well as in behaviour, which cannot be ultimately separated. Some Evangelicals hold that the concrete possibilities of fellowship depend on the degrees of agreement on the apostolic testimony as handed down in the New Testament.

19. The Manila Affirmations depict the resulting attitudes among Evangelicals today:

Our reference to "the whole church" is not a presumptuous claim that the universal church and the evangelical community are synonymous. For we recognize that there are many churches which are not part of the evangelical movement. Evangelical attitudes to the Roman Catholic and Orthodox churches differ widely. Some Evangelicals are praying, talking, studying scripture and working with these churches. Others are strongly opposed to any form of dialogue or cooperation with them. All are aware that serious theological differences between us remain. Where appropriate, and so long as biblical truth is not compromised, cooperation may be possible in such areas as Bible translation, the study of contemporary theological and ethical issues, social work and political action. We wish to make it clear, however, that common evangelism demands a common commitment to the biblical gospel (Manila 9).

### 4. WHAT OF THE CHURCH DO WE RECOGNIZE IN ONE ANOTHER?

20. We as Catholics and Evangelicals share sacred scripture[6] and belief in its inspiration by the Holy Spirit. We affirm the unique mediatorial role of Christ, his incarnation, his death and resurrection for our salvation. We affirm together our faith in the triune God, Father, Son and Holy Spirit. We are both able to pray the Lord's prayer and confess the Apostles' and Nicene Creeds.[7] We affirm the gospel call to conversion, to a disciplined life in the grace of Jesus Christ, and the ultimate promise of eternal reward. We recognize a Christian responsibility for service and the promotion of justice in the world. We share a common hope of Christ's return, as Judge and Redeemer, to consummate our salvation. We can commemorate together those who have witnessed by their blood to this common faith and now celebrate full communion before the face of our divine Saviour.

21. One of the results of interchurch cooperation and dialogue has been a greater appreciation by separated Christians of one another. (A gradual move towards a greater recognition of the ecclesial status of other Christian communities marks modern and contemporary developments.) For centuries, in ways heavily influenced by polemics and religious wars, the identification of and the incorporation into the true church were simplistically considered to be an all-or-nothing affair. One was either in the true church or in a false institution or a sect. Either one was a member in the full sense of the word, or one was outside of the church and deprived of all hope of salvation. Yet the awareness of spiritual complexity was not entirely repressed. The Roman Catholic Church maintained the validity of the baptism performed by heretics and also acknowledged a "baptism of desire". The 16th-century Reformers did not deny the presence of elements of the true church in Roman Catholicism. Though at times Luther spoke of the pope as anti-Christ, he recognized remnants of the church in the Roman communion. Calvin could write of his Roman Catholic opponents, "these muddlers will labour to no avail as they deck out their synagogue with the title church", yet he acknowledges traces (*vestigia*), remnants (*reliquias*), marks (*symbola*), and signs (*signa*) of the church under the papacy; churches in the Roman communion may be called churches "to the extent that the Lord wonderfully preserves in them a remnant of his people however woefully dispersed and scattered". And early proponents of religious toleration were found among the extremely diverse groups often referred to as the "radical Reformation". Though Anabaptists were painfully persecuted on all sides, Calvin exercised a nuanced judgment on their doctrine; later they benefited from the protection of such a prelate as the prince-bishop of Basel.

### 5. A COMMON CHALLENGE

22. In this section, we have come to recognize, with the help of God's Spirit, the koinonia with the life of the Trinity that both of our communities enjoy. We see it, therefore, as incumbent upon both of us to move from this singular condition of unity with

the life of the Trinity into an experienced unity with one another. To that end we need to take the actions which will move us from this rediscovery to forge the ecclesial bonds that will express this already bestowed unity. If God has not been dealing with us as if we were apart from him, why should we continue to live as if we were apart from one another.

## C. Some dimensions of the church

### 1. ORIGINS OF THE CHURCH

23. Evangelicals and Catholics both see in the Pentecost event the emergence of the church of the new covenant (Acts 2). The presence of persons from every nation at Pentecost represents the universal mission of the church. They agree that this church is built on the foundation of the prophet and apostles, with Christ as the cornerstone (Eph. 2:20). They recognize in the evangelizing mission of the apostles the founding of local churches. The communion of local churches in the New Testament was served by the ministry of the apostles and by the meeting of the council of Jerusalem (Acts 15). Support of one another, letters of recommendation, the collections for other churches, and mutual hospitality characterize this communion among churches. Evangelicals and Roman Catholics recognize the importance of subsequent developments in the life of the church, but give different weight and appreciation to these developments.

### 2. THE CHURCH LOCAL AND UNIVERSAL

*a) Evangelical and Catholic perspectives*

24. For Evangelicals today the "local church" designates the congregation in a particular place. For Catholics a "local" or "particular" church refers to a diocese, composed of a number of parishes, with a bishop at the centre, assisted by his presbyters and other ministers of pastoral service to the faithful for the sake of the gospel.

25. Catholics see the work of the Holy Spirit in a number of significant developments in the early church. These include the understanding of bishops as successors to the apostles; the emergence of the threefold ministry of bishop, priest and deacon; the clarification of the apostolic faith especially by ecumenical councils and the universal creeds; and the gradual acknowledgment of the effective leadership of the bishop of Rome within the whole church. Even from early times, the bishop of Rome had a prominent role in fostering the communion of local churches over which bishops presided, the initial expressions of a primacy that developed over the centuries. Since Vatican II there has been greater stress on the mutual relationship between the local churches and the church of Rome.

26. For their part, Evangelicals are overwhelmingly found in Protestant and Pentecostal churches, which have generally placed primary emphasis on local congregations: the place in which the word of God is proclaimed, the sacraments are administered, and God's people are gathered. Evangelicals live in a variety of church structures. Churches whose origin lies in the "magisterial" Reformation (e.g., Lutheran and Reformed) as well

as Anglicans and Methodists, have a strong sense of the universality of the church in time and space, but the way they function stresses the regional or national body and, for example, gives significance to regional or national synods. Nearly all other churches have espoused congregationalism which concentrates responsibility in the local community. This community is the concrete embodiment of the koinonia of the Spirit. It is the locus of spiritual life, mutual upbuilding through the diversity of gifts, and training for service in the world. The Free churches express solidarity through international agencies or alliances, denominational or interdenominational. Anabaptists in particular have had a strong tradition of community life; a vigilant discipline makes the assembly into a closely knit family of faith. Throughout history all these churches have had to fight divisive tendencies and, in the context of secularization, the destructive influences of individualism. The Lausanne Covenant candidly acknowledges, "We confess that our testimony has sometimes been marred by sinful individualism and needless duplication. We pledge ourselves to seek a deeper unity in truth, worship, holiness and mission" (Lausanne 7).

27. Whereas Catholic ecclesiology reserves certain sacramental functions to bishops who are understood to have received the fullness of the sacrament of orders, most Evangelical churches concentrate leadership more specifically in the ministry of the "pastor", whose role is considered to be that of the *episkopos/presbyteros* of New-Testament times (the pastor may be the "teaching elder" in association with the "ruling elders" of the church or parish, 1 Tim. 5:17). Other Evangelicals, even among a few free churches, have distinct ministries of oversight, but the difference is slight: the bishop or superintendent is charged with administrative tasks, but is not considered to have particular sacramental roles, a concept foreign to the Evangelical interpretation of ministry.

28. Global fellowship among Evangelicals is typically expressed by means of loose networks of worldwide associations (among which the WEA may lay claim to best-grounded representative legitimacy) and para-church organizations (such as the International Fellowship of Evangelical Students). These entities provide valuable channels of communication and tools for cooperation.

29. On the Catholic side, Vatican II re-emphasizes the key importance of the local church (diocese) as the place where the word is preached and the sacraments are administered. The church reveals herself most clearly when the people are gathered about the altar under the presidency of the bishop, with the assistance of the other clergy (cf. *SC* 41; and also *LG* 26). At every eucharist the unity of the whole church is indicated by the presider's expression of the union with the local bishop, other bishops, and especially the bishop of Rome as the centre of the whole communion.[8] The bishops in national and regional conferences are called upon to represent their particular churches. Catholics speak of the universal church, like the regional church, as a communion of particular churches under their respective bishops and in communion with the bishop of Rome. They recognize, however, that the church of Christ is not exclusively identified with the Catholic Church (cf. *LG* 8).

## b) Convergences and differences between Catholics and Evangelicals

30. While certainly not eliminating the differences with Evangelical Protestantism, these recent developments in Catholic ecclesiology facilitate mutual understanding. On the national and regional levels, Catholic episcopal conferences and synods of Oriental

Catholic churches are able to enter into conversations with national and regional Evangelical churches, alliances and organizations. Also, diocesan bishops are able to relate to the regional Evangelical officials as their counterparts, even if they are not bishops. There is a certain convergence with the renewed emphasis of Catholics on local church and of Evangelicals on worldwide fellowship.

31. Catholics speak of a reciprocity between the universal and the particular church, but they do not view the universal church as a federation of local churches. There is a sense in which Catholics can admit the priority of the local church since, in the words of Vatican II: "In and from such individual churches there comes into being the one and only Catholic Church" (*LG* 23). But to avoid misunderstanding, the Council also affirms that each particular church is "fashioned after the model of the universal church" (*ibid.*). The biblical evidence, as interpreted in Catholic theology, indicates that the church originated as a single community, into which people are incorporated by faith and baptism.[9]

32. Evangelicals understand the church to be called into being by the word (*creatura verbi*). The word is revealed in Christ, written in scripture, and received through hearing. The word calls forth faith and a community of faith in time and space, a visible church. But final judgment belongs to God as to believers and unbelievers within the visible church. God knows his own.

> Here in the world, the church becomes visible in all local congregations that meet to do together the things that according to scripture the church does. Christ is the head of the church. Everyone who is personally united to Christ by faith belongs to his body and by the Spirit is united with every other true believer in Jesus. (Amsterdam 9)

33. Evangelicals, like Catholics, recognize the value of worldwide fellowship, but because of different theological presuppositions and different interpretations of certain biblical passages, they have a different view of the relationship between the universal church and local churches. Evangelicals understand by "universal church" all those everywhere and in all ages who believe and trust in Christ for salvation. "All" includes believing Roman Catholics. Evangelicals have made use of Luther's distinction between the church invisible and the church visible. They affirm the universal church whose bond of unity, the Spirit of Christ, is invisible (Eph. 4:3-4); they stress incorporation by "faith alone", a faith by which all share in the gift of the Spirit (Gal. 3:2). Christ, however, also willed the founding of visible churches into which people are incorporated by (water) baptism. While primarily local, these congregations may seek federations and alliances as means to express the universal character of the church's nature and mission.

34. The visible structural and organizational manifestations of the church are shaped by particular historical situations, and can change. In the eyes of most Evangelicals the Bible provides no rigid pattern for organizing the church in every time and place. They find in the New Testament a considerable degree of variety in models of ministry and church order. In distinction from Catholic ecclesiology, Evangelicals thus affirm a variety of forms of church order, but these differences do not impede fellowship or membership in the invisible church.

35. Most Evangelicals agree that the universal church, not being a visible institution, is concretely expressed in the visible churches in particular times and places, and the translocal bonds they cultivate. They acknowledge that the correspondence between visible and invisible is not perfect. For example, "false brethren" may be found (Gal. 2:4)

who do not really belong (1 John 2:19). While the relationship between membership in the visible and invisible church, and baptism varies among Evangelicals, these differences do not hamper fellowship and collaboration. Visible communities have been endowed by Christ with institutions so that they may build themselves up and fulfill their mission in the world.

### 3. THE COMBINATION OF THE PERSONAL AND INSTITUTIONAL IN KOINONIA

*a) An ordered community of persons*

36. In the New Testament witness, Evangelicals and Catholics recognize an ordered community of persons, sharing a common faith and mission, given leadership, under Christ, by the apostles (1 Cor. 11-14; Rom. 12; Eph. 4). We recognize that there are differentiated ministries articulated in the epistles (1 Pet. 5; 1 Tim. 3; Titus), though we value them differently, and make different judgments as to their continuity in the contemporary church. However, we both affirm order and discipline as a framework of ecclesial communion (1 Cor. 14:33,40).

37. The idea of the church as communion has emerged from a return to a rich vein of biblical and patristic material. It has also been influenced by more personalist approaches in the modern world, against exaggerated forms of institutionalism and individualism. Sociologists have long distinguished between society and community. In early 20th-century ecclesiology this gave rise to a dualism between a church of law and a church of love. Pius XII, in his encyclical on the Mystical Body, taught that this opposition does not obtain in the church, which is both a mystical union and an organized society.[10]

*b) Catholic views*

38. Vatican II in its Constitution on the Church follows essentially the teaching of Pius XII on this matter. It describes the church as a single interlocking reality *(unam realitatem complexam, Lumen Gentium* 8), that is both visible and invisible, mystical and hierarchical. But for the Council the visible dimension serves the invisible dimension of the church. The church is divinely endowed with doctrines, sacraments and ministries for the purpose of bringing about and signifying a supernatural communion of life, love and truth among the members (cf. *LG* 14,18,20,21). The Council presents the church itself as a sacrament (*LG* 1).

39. Vatican II's move towards a more collegial ecclesiology shows a greater emphasis on the personal. Whereas Vatican I spoke of the pope as exercising jurisdiction over the other bishops of the Catholic communion, Vatican II clarifies this earlier teaching by saying that bishops must be in "hierarchical communion" with the pope in order to exercise their powers of teaching and shepherding their flocks (cf. *LG* 22; *CD* 5). The concept of "hierarchical communion" does not eliminate the juridical aspect but requires government through dialogue and consensus rather than command.

*c) Evangelical views*

40. In general, Evangelicals hold that the church is primarily a community of persons and only secondarily an institution. Abraham Kuyper, for instance, declares the church

"is not a salvific agency that would supply grace as medicine, not a mystical order that would magically act on lay people. She is nothing else than believing, confessing, persons."[11] The Lausanne Covenant of 1974 asserts, "The church is the community of God's people rather than an institution, and must not be identified with any particular culture, social or political system or human ideology" (Lausanne 6). However, most Evangelicals emphatically maintain the requirement of order and discipline and affirm the institutional dimension of church life.

*d)  Some mutual observations*

41.  Catholics and Evangelicals experience a convergence in the understanding of the way that order and discipline serve the koinonia of the church. Catholics have begun to re-emphasize the importance of the personal in understanding the church. Evangelicals show an increasing appreciation of visible expressions of unity in the life of the church beyond the bounds of their own denomination. Such a convergence in our understanding of biblical koinonia offers promise for a continuation of the dialogue.

## D.  Preparing for a different future

42.  There are, then, differences between the convictions of Catholics and Evangelicals. These differences, however, do not amount to simple opposition and have been fruitfully examined in our conversations. Our mutual understanding has opened avenues for further dialogue.

43.  As we complete these reflections we realize again the impact that our division has made on people that we serve. It is not possible to reverse history, but it is possible to prepare for a different future.

44.  We realize the need for a spirit of repentance before God because we have not made sufficient efforts to heal the divisions that are a scandal to the gospel. We pray that God grant us a spirit of metanoia. We need to continue to study and face issues which have separated us. We need to examine also the practices that uncritically continue the biases of the past.

45.  Could we not ask ourselves whether we sufficiently understand the levels of unity that we already share? For example, during the mass, when Catholics hear the words of the canon, "to strengthen in faith and love your pilgrim church on earth, your servant pope…, our bishop…, and all the bishops with the clergy and the entire people your Son has gained for you", do they understand that among those whom the "Son has gained" for the Father are the Christians from whom they are separated and with whom, since Christ also redeemed them, they share deep bonds of Christian life? And when Evangelicals intercede for the life, mission, and unity of "the church", do they genuinely understand this church to include Catholics?

46.  In a spirit of humility, we bring our concerns and our hopes to the Lord.

## PART II

## CATHOLICS, EVANGELICALS AND EVANGELIZATION IN LIGHT OF KOINONIA

47. We now turn to issues of evangelization, proselytism and religious freedom to explore them in the context of a theology of koinonia. In doing this we have learned from some of the insights of other dialogues on these issues and have built on them.

48. Evangelicals and Catholics agree that every Christian has the right and obligation to share and spread the faith. "It is contrary to the message of Christ, to the ways of God's grace and to the personal character of faith that any means be used which would reduce or impede the freedom of a person to make a basic Christian commitment" (*B* 34). Since evangelization is a focus of this section, we can now indicate briefly how Catholics and Evangelicals understand this responsibility.

### A. Our respective views on evangelization/evangelism

1. A CATHOLIC VIEW

49. Catholics view evangelization in the context of the one mission of the church. In this regard, "evangelization is a complex process involving many elements as, for example, a renewal of human nature, witness, public proclamation, wholehearted acceptance of, and entrance into, the community of the church, the adoption of the outward signs and of apostolic works" (*EN* 24).

50. "Evangelization will always contain, as the foundation, the centre and the apex of its whole dynamic power, this explicit declaration: In Jesus Christ... salvation is offered to every human person as the gift of the grace and mercy of God himself" (*EN* 27; cf. *RM* 44). It involves proclamation of this good news, aiming at Christian conversion of men and women (cf. *RM* 44-46). But it involves also efforts "to convert both the individual consciences of men and their collective consciences, all the attitudes in which they are engaged and, finally, their lives and the whole environment which surrounds them" (*EN* 18). Thus "evangelization is to be achieved... in depth, going to the very centre and roots of life. The gospel must impregnate the culture and the whole way of life of man..." (*EN* 20). Through inculturation the church makes the gospel incarnate in different cultures, "transmits to them her own values, at the same time taking the good elements that already exist in them and renewing them from within" (*RM* 52; cf. *EN* 20).

51. There is a diversity of activities in the church's one mission according to the different circumstances in which it is carried out. Looking at today's world from the viewpoint of evangelization, we can distinguish three situations. (a) People, groups and socio-cultural contexts in which Christ and his gospel are not known. In such a context Catholics speak of mission *ad gentes*. (b) Christian communities with adequate and solid ecclesial structures; they are fervent in their faith and in Christian living, in which participation in the sacraments is basic (cf. *EN* 47). In these communities the church carries out her

activities and pastoral care. (c) The intermediate situation, for example, in countries with ancient Christian roots, where entire groups of the baptized have lost a living sense of the faith. In this case what is needed is a new evangelization or a "re-evangelization". The boundaries between these three "are not clearly definable, and it is unthinkable to create barriers between them or to put them into water-tight compartments" (*RM* 34). There is a growing interdependence which exists between these various saving activities in the church.

## 2. AN EVANGELICAL VIEW

52. For Evangelicals, the heart and core of mission is proclamation. However, it is the core, not the totality of the church mission within the divine plan of redemption. The Lausanne Covenant refers to this comprehensive mission as "evangelization" (Lausanne, introduction) and places it within a trinitarian framework:

> We affirm our belief in the one eternal God, Creator (Isa. 40:28) and Lord of the world, Father, Son and Holy Spirit (Matt. 28:19), who governs all things according to the purpose of his will (Eph. 1:1). He has been sending forth a people for himself (Acts 15:14), and sending his people back into the world (John 17:18) to be his servants and witnesses, for the extension of his kingdom, the building up of Christ's body, and the glory of his name (Eph. 4:12). (Lausanne 1)

53. The Lausanne Covenant describes mission in its most inclusive sense as "Christian presence in the world" (Lausanne 4), which consists of "sacrificial service" and entails a "deep and costly penetration of the world", and a permeation of "non-Christian society" (Lausanne 6). Because followers of Christ are engaged in the mission of the triune God, who is "both the Creator and Judge of all", Christians "should share his concern for justice" (Gen. 18:25) and reconciliation throughout human society and for the liberation of men and women from every kind of oppression (Ps. 45:7; Isa. 1:17). Because all human beings are created in the image of God, "every person, regardless of race, religion, colour, culture, class, sex or age (Lev. 19:18; Luke 6:27,35), has an intrinsic dignity because of which he or she should be respected and served, not exploited" (James 3:9; Lausanne 5). When one is born again one is born into Christ's kingdom "and must seek not only to exhibit but also to spread its righteousness (Matt. 5:20; Matt. 6:33) in the midst of an unrighteous world" (*ibid*).

54. Although the mission of the triune God is as broad as "God's cosmic purpose" (Lausanne 6) and therefore calls God's people into this all-embracing mission, Evangelicals are particularly concerned to keep proclamation front and centre. Accordingly, the Lausanne Covenant circumscribes "evangelism itself" as "the proclamation of the historical, biblical Christ as Saviour (1 Cor. 1:23; 2 Cor. 4:5) and Lord, with a view to persuading people to come to him personally and to be reconciled to God" (2 Cor. 5:11,20; Lausanne 4). Moreover, Lausanne forcefully asserts the primacy of evangelism as proclamation: "In the church's mission of sacrificial service evangelism is primary." A subsequent World Evangelical Fellowship statement again stresses the crucial role of evangelism. Yet, the document does not treat evangelism "as a separate theme, because we see it as an integral part of our total Christian response to human need" (Matt. 28:18-21; Consultation on the Church in Response to Human Need, Wheaton, 1983, introduction). Clearly, the "great commission" is here seen as a call to holistic mission, with at its centre calling all people to believe in Jesus Christ.

## B. Old tensions in a new context of koinonia

55. It is our common belief that God has sent the Holy Spirit into the world to effect the reconciliation of the world to God. Those to whom the Spirit is sent participate in this mission of the Spirit. The heart of the mission of the Spirit is koinonia, a communion of persons in the communion of God, the Father, the Son and Holy Spirit.

56. The real koinonia we already share gives rise to our mutual concern to view conjointly the issues of religious freedom and proselytism that have divided us. We believe that the two issues of religious liberty and proselytism must not be treated as totally separable areas but must be firmly linked and considered jointly as related concerns, seen in the context of the meaning of evangelization and the possibility of common witness. Evangelical and Catholic Christians can now recognize that they share a real but imperfect communion with each other, and are able to take modest steps towards a more complete communion in Christ through the Holy Spirit. The inter-related components necessary for increasing koinonia are repentance, conversion and commitment, in which we commit ourselves to the convergence that has already begun in our life together.

57. The first component is repentance, a radical turning away from the habits of mind and heart that fall short of God's purposes and design. Those purposes are that there be a communion between persons and God, and between communities whose unity is authored by the Spirit. God intends that the church be the main instrument for the koinonia of all peoples in God. Therefore, the reconciliation of our Christian communities is urgent.

58. The second component for increasing koinonia is conversion in which by faith we turn to God in Christ and his saving message. Christian conversion itself is threefold: moral, intellectual and religious. In moral conversion we are freed by grace to value what God values and obey what God demands. In intellectual conversion we learn and embrace the truth. In religious conversion we come to abide in the love of God.

59. The third component that the Spirit enables is a turning to one another in our commitment to proclaim the gospel. Catholics and Evangelicals are striving to learn how to love one another in our efforts at evangelization. There are signs of convergence on how we are to participate in the mission of the Spirit in our sharing of the good news. Our two traditions have insights into the contents of this inexhaustible source. These insights need to be retained in the work of evangelization that we undertake respectively, so as to complement and affirm one another's efforts.

1. REPENTANCE: FROM WHAT ARE WE TURNING?

60. Catholics and Evangelicals are called to pray for grace as we come to a better understanding of the will of Christ, which our past relationships have not reflected (*P* 108). Our divisions in the past have led to conflicts in evangelization.

But, at Manila, 1989, Evangelicals exhorted one another,

> Evangelism and unity are closely related in the New Testament. Jesus prayed that his people's oneness might reflect his own oneness with the Father, in order that the world might believe in him, and Paul exhorted the Philippians to "contend as one person for the faith of the gospel". In contrast to this biblical vision, we are ashamed of the suspicions and rivalries, the

dogmatism over non-essentials, the power-struggles and empire-building which spoil our evangelistic witness. (Manila 9)

And Pope John Paul II, on behalf of Catholics, asked God's forgiveness for sins against unity with the following prayer:

> Merciful Father,
> on the night before his passion
> your Son prayed for the unity of those
> who believe in him:
> in disobedience to his will, however,
> believers have opposed one another, becoming divided,
> and have mutually condemned one another and
> fought against one another.
> We urgently implore your forgiveness
> and beseech the gift of a repentant heart,
> so that all Christians, reconciled with you and with one another,
> will be able, in one body and in one spirit,
> to experience anew the joy of full communion.
> We ask this through Christ our Lord. [12]

61. Concerning "proselytism", it should be pointed out that the understanding of the word has changed considerably in recent years in some circles. In the Bible the word proselyte was devoid of negative connotations. The term referred to someone apart from Israel who, by belief in Yahweh and acceptance of the law, became a member of the Jewish community. It carried the positive meaning of being a convert to Judaism (Ex. 12:48-49). Christianity took over this positive and unobjectionable meaning to describe a person who converted from paganism. Until the 20th century, mission work and proselytism were largely synonymous and without objectionable connotations (*B* 32,33). It is only in the 20th century that the term has come to be applied to winning members from each (*B* 33), as an illicit form of evangelism (*P* 90). At least, in some Evangelical circles proselytism is not a pejorative term; in Catholic and most ecumenical circles it is. The attempt to "win members from each other" (*B* 33) by unworthy means is negative and pejorative proselytism. Members of our communions have been guilty of proselytism in this negative sense. It should be avoided.

62. We affirm therefore "that the following things should be avoided: offers to temporal or material advantages... improper use of situations of distress... using political, social and economic pressure as a means of obtaining conversion ... casting unjust and uncharitable suspicion on other denominations; comparing the strengths and ideals of one community with the weakness and practices of another community" (*B* 36). This issue of seeking to win members from other churches has ecclesiologically and missiologically significant consequences, which require further exploration.

63. Unethical methods of evangelization must be sharply distinguished from the legitimate act of persuasively presenting the gospel. If a Christian, after hearing a responsible presentation of the gospel, freely chooses to join a different Christian community, it should not automatically be concluded that such a transfer is the result of proselytism (*P* 93,94).

64. Catholic-Evangelical relations have been troubled by the practice of seeking to evangelize people who are already members of a church, which causes misunderstanding and resentment, especially when Evangelicals seek to "convert" baptized Catholics away from the Roman Catholic Church. This is more than a verbal conflict about different uses of terms like conversion, Christian and church. Evangelicals speak of "nominal Christianity", referring to those who are Christians in name, but only marginally Christian in reality, even if they have been baptized. Nominal Christians are contrasted with converted believers, who can testify to a living union with Christ, whose confession is biblical and whose faith is active in love. This is a sharp distinction common among Evangelicals, who see nominal Christians as needing to be won to a personal relation with the Lord and Saviour. Evangelicals seek to evangelize nominal members of their own churches, as well as of others; they see this activity as an authentic concern for the gospel, and not as a reprehensible kind of "sheep-stealing" (*E* sec. iii). Catholics also speak of "evangelizing" such people, although they refer to them as "lapsed" or "inactive" rather than as "nominal", and still regard them as "Christian" since they are baptized believers. They are understandably offended whenever Evangelicals appear to regard all Roman Catholics as nominal Christians, or whenever they base their evangelism on a distorted view of Catholic teaching and practice.

65. We agree that a distinction must be made between one's estimate of the doctrines and practices of a church and the judgment that bears on an individual's spiritual condition, e.g. his or her relationship to Christ and to the church.

66. As to an individual's spiritual or religious condition, whether a person is nominal, lapsed, inactive or fallen away, a negative judgment is suspect of being intrusive unless the person to be evangelized is the source of that information. The spiritual condition of a person is always a mystery. Listening should be first, together with a benevolent presumption of charity, and in all cases we may share our perception and experience of the good news only in a totally respectful attitude towards those we seek to evangelize. This attitude should also be the case apart from evangelization in all attempts at persuading brothers and sisters in what we believe to be true.

67. Evangelicals and Catholics are challenged to repent of the practice of misrepresenting each other, either because of laziness in study, or unwillingness to listen, prejudice or unethical judgments (*E* i). We repent of the culpable ignorance that neglects readily accessible knowledge of the other's tradition (*P* 93). We are keenly aware of the command: "Thou shall not bear false witness against thy neighbour" (Ex. 20:16).

68. We repent of those forms of evangelization prompted by competition and personal prestige, and of efforts to make unjust or uncharitable reference to the beliefs or practices of other religious communities in order to win adherents (*E* I, p.91, *J* 19). We repent of the use of similar means for retaining adherents. We deplore competitive forms of evangelism that habitually pit ourselves against other Christians (*P* 93) (cf. *DH* 4,12; John Paul II, *Tertio Millennio Adveniente* 35). All forms of evangelization should witness to the glory of God.

69. We repent of unworthy forms of evangelization which aim at pressuring people to change their church affiliation in ways that dishonour the gospel, and by methods which compromise rather than enhance the freedom of the believer and the truth of the gospel (*B* 31).

70. Thus agreeing, we commit ourselves to seeking a "newness of attitudes" in our understanding of each other's intentions (cf. Eph. 4:23; *UR* 7).


## 2. CONVERSION: TO WHAT ARE WE TURNING?

### a) *Growing in koinonia*

71. The bonds of koinonia, which separated Christians already share, imply further responsibilities towards one another. Each must be concerned about the welfare and the integrity of the other. The bonds of koinonia imply that Christians in established churches protect the civil rights of the other Christians to free speech, press and assembly. At the same time, the bonds of koinonia imply that the other Christians respect the rights, integrity and history of Christians in established churches. Tensions can be reduced if Christians engaged in mission communicate with one another and seek to witness together as far as possible, rather than compete with one another.

72. Central to our understanding of religious conversion is our belief and experience that "the love of God has been poured out into our hearts through the Holy Spirit who has been given to us" (Rom. 5:5). "Everyone who believes that Jesus is the Christ has been born of God, and everyone who loves the parent loves the child" (1 John 5:1). Our failures in loving one another are the scandal that calls into question whether we have allowed this love to come into our hearts without obstruction. Since Evangelicals believe their church to be catholic, and Catholics believe their church to be evangelical, it would seem that our future task is to recognize better the aspects that each of us emphasizes in the others' view as well.

73. Evangelicals agree with Catholics that the goal of evangelization is koinonia with the triune God and one another. One enters into this koinonia through conversion to Christ by the Spirit within the proclaiming, caring community of faith which witnesses to the reign of God. Catholics agree with Evangelicals that all Christians of whatever communion can have a living personal relationship with Jesus as Lord and Saviour. On the basis of our real but imperfect communion we ask God to give us the grace to recommit ourselves to having a living personal relationship with Jesus as Lord and Saviour and deepening our relationship to one another.


### b) *Religious liberty*

74. We grow in koinonia when we support one another and acknowledge one another's freedom. Religious freedom is not only a civil right but one of the principles, together with that of mutual respect, that guide relationships among members of the body of Christ and, indeed, with the entire human family (*P* 99). We have been called to work together to promote freedom of conscience for all persons, and to defend civil guarantees for freedom of assembly, speech and press. Recognizing that we have often failed to respect these liberties in the past, Catholics and Evangelicals affirm the right of all persons to pursue that truth and to witness to that truth (*J* 15, *P* 104). We affirm the right of persons freely to adopt or change their religious community without duress. We deplore every attempt to impose beliefs or to manipulate others in the name of religion

(*J* 15, *P* 102). Evangelicals can concur with the position of the Second Vatican Council on religious freedom, namely that all "are to be immune from coercion on the part of individuals or of social groups and of any human power, in such wise that in matters religious no one is to be forced to act in a manner contrary to his own beliefs. Nor is anyone to be restrained from acting in accordance with his own beliefs, whether privately or publicly, whether alone or in association with others, within due limits" (*DH* 2; cf. *B* 40).

75. In the person of Pope John Paul II the Catholic Church has recognized and apologized for the violations of justice and charity for which its members have been responsible in the course of history.[13] Today it seeks to protect the religious liberty of all persons and their communities. At the same time, it is committed to spreading the message of the gospel to all without proselytism or reliance on the state.

76. While religious liberty has been a rallying point for Evangelicals from the earliest period, they have been called from their sectarianism to greater mutual respect and increased cooperation in mission by the catholic spirit of John Wesley, the revivals of the 19th century, and the challenges of world mission. Interdenominational, worldwide fellowship and cooperation in mission have been served by the Evangelical Alliance. The Alliance has always been concerned about religious liberty, indeed, as early as 1872 lobbying on behalf of oppressed Catholics in Japan.[14] According to the Manila Manifesto (1989):

> Christians earnestly desire freedom of religion for all people, not just freedom for Christianity. In predominantly Christian countries, Christians are at the forefront of those who demand freedom for religious minorities. In predominantly non-Christian countries, therefore, Christians are asking for themselves no more than they demand for others in similar circumstances. The freedom to "profess, practise and propagate" religion, as defined in the Universal Declaration of Human Rights, could and should surely be a reciprocally granted right (Manila 12.1).

We greatly regret any unworthy witness of which followers of Jesus may have been guilty (Manila 12.2).

77. Religious freedom is a right which flows from the very dignity of the person as known through the revealed Word of God: it is grounded in the creation of all human beings in the image and likeness of God (*P* 98). Civil authorities have an obligation to respect and to protect this right (cf. *DH* 2). For Catholics this view was formally adopted at Vatican II in the Declaration on Religious Freedom. Evangelicals at Lausanne 1974, Manila 1989 and Amsterdam 2000 affirmed a similar position.

78. Evangelicals and Roman Catholics differ somewhat in the theological and anthropological rationale for this position. Catholic social thought bases rights theory on natural law. It sees human rights as legitimate moral claims that are God-given; free moral agents have a corresponding responsibility to act in the light of those claims. Revelation is seen to complement this understanding of rights. In evangelical teaching, primacy belongs to the divine right over conscience, the Lord's immediate claim on each individual; human rights, then, are viewed not only in creational light but also against the backdrop of the human fall into sin. The history of sin makes the mandate for rights all the more important. God continues to pursue fallen creatures in the unfolding history of grace. Catholics and Evangelicals agree that human rights should be interpreted and exercised within the framework of scripture teaching and of rigorous moral reasoning. Due regard must be had for the needs of others, for duties towards other parties, and for the

common good (*P* 102, *DH* 7). Human rights language, also, must guard against being turned into narcissism, self-assertiveness and ideology.

### 3. TURNING TO ONE ANOTHER: THE CHALLENGE OF COMMON WITNESS

79. What remains as a hope and a challenge is the prospect of our common witness. We see the communities of faith, to which we belong, as set apart and anointed for mission. We are concerned about the growing secularization of the world and efforts to marginalize Christian values. It is urgent that our evangelization be ever more effective. Is it not also urgent that Christians witness together? In this sense the Second Vatican Council called Catholics to cooperate with other Christians in this way:

> To the extent that their beliefs are common, they can make before the nations a common profession of faith in God and in Jesus Christ. They can collaborate in social and in technical projects as well as in cultural and religious ones. Let them work together especially for the sake of Christ, their common Lord. Let his name be the bond that unites them! (AG 15)

The core of evangelization is the apostolic faith that is found in the word of God, the creeds, and is reflected in biblical interpretations and the doctrinal consensus of the patristic age. The possibility of Evangelicals and Catholics giving common witness lies in the fact that, despite their disagreements, they share much of the Christian faith. We rejoice, for example, that we can confess together the Apostles' Creed as a summary of biblical faith.

80. While acknowledging the divergences, which remain between us, we are discerning a convergence between our two communions regarding the need and possibilities of common witness:

The Amsterdam declaration 2000 urged Evangelicals "to pray and work for unity in truth among all true believers in Jesus and to cooperate as fully as possible in evangelism with other brothers and sisters in Christ so that the whole church may take the whole gospel to the whole world" (Amsterdam 14).

And Pope John Paul II asks, "How indeed can we proclaim the gospel of reconciliation without at the same time being committed to working for reconciliation between Christians?" (*UUS* 98).

Therefore, to the extent conscience and the clear recognition of agreement and disagreement allows, we commit ourselves to common witness.

81. We conclude this report by joining together in a spirit of humility, putting our work, with whatever strengths and limitations it may have, in the hands of God. Our hope is that these efforts will be for the praise and glory of Jesus Christ.

> Now to him who is able to do immeasurably more than all we ask or imagine, according to his power that is at work within us, to him be glory in the church and in Christ Jesus throughout all generations, for ever and ever! Amen. (Eph. 3:20-21)

# Appendix 1

## Evolution of this International Consultation: A Brief Overview

### 1. HISTORICAL BACKGROUND

Increasing contacts between Evangelicals and Catholics during the 1970s and 1980s provide a background for the international consultations between the World Evangelical Fellowship and the Catholic Church that have taken place since 1993.

Among these contacts, an international dialogue on mission between some Evangelicals and Roman Catholics took place between 1978 and 1984. On the Catholic side it was sponsored by the Vatican's Secretariat (after 1988, Pontifical Council) for Promoting Christian Unity. Evangelical participants included some prominent leaders such as John Stott, but the participants came on their own authority, without officially representing any Evangelical body. This dialogue led to an important report, published in 1985, the first in which Evangelicals and Catholics discussed together such themes as salvation, evangelization, religious liberty and proselytism.

Another important international arena in which Evangelical and Catholic leaders have encountered one another has been the annual meetings of the conference of secretaries of Christian world communions (CWCs). This conference, existing for more than forty years, includes the general secretaries or their equivalent, from a broad range of CWCs. The international director of the World Evangelical Fellowship and the secretary of the Pontifical Council for Promoting Christian Unity have been among the participants in this informal annual meeting.

The need for more direct relations was evident from a specific event which also led to the present WEF-Catholic conversations. This took place when two representatives of the Catholic Church, one of them from the Secretariat for Promoting Christian Unity, were invited as observers and brought greetings to the 1980 general assembly of WEF held in Hoddesdon, England. Their presence led to a heated debate, after which "the Italian Evangelical Alliance withdrew its membership and the Spanish Evangelical Alliance placed its participation in abeyance". The WEF Theological Commission responded by creating a 17-member ecumenical issues task force. It developed a statement that was published as *Roman Catholicism: A Contemporary Evangelical Perspective* (ed. Paul G. Schrotenboer, Grand Rapids, Baker, 1988) in which the details just mentioned are found (p.9).

The CWC meeting in Jerusalem in October 1988 provided an occasion for a private conversation on the book between, on the one hand, Rev. David Howard, international director of WEF, and Dr Paul Schrotenboer, general secretary of the Reformed Ecumenical Synod and chairman of the WEF Task Force, with, on the other hand, Rev. Pierre Duprey, secretary of the Pontifical Council for Promoting Christian Unity, and Msgr John Radano of the same Pontifical Council. They decided to hold a short meeting to discuss issues raised in the book. This meeting took place on the occasion of the CWC meeting in October 1990 in Budapest, Hungary. Two persons from each side – Dr Paul Schrotenboer and Dr George Vandervelde, for the WEF, and Msgr Kevin McDonald and Msgr John Radano, for the PCPCU – met for two full days to discuss the book. This discussion helped to pinpoint some of the differences between the two communions, but it was clear that more time was required to explore these issues. It was therefore proposed that a well prepared and longer consultation be arranged for a later date. Bishop Pierre Duprey invited the consultation to meet in Venice.

## 2. Brief overview of the meetings

Starting with the one held in Venice in October 1993, several international meetings have taken place. Their general aim has been to foster greater mutual understanding and better relations.

An initial assessment from the 1990 meeting ascertained that the important topics to discuss in Venice were scripture, Tradition (including the development of doctrine), and the nature of the church as communion. It became clear that the doctrine of justification, too, would have to be treated. Papers were prepared by Rev. Avery Dulles SJ ("Revelation as the Basis for Scripture and Tradition") with a response by Dr Henri Blocher, and by Dr George Vandervelde ("Justification between Scripture and Tradition"). The exploratory nature and delicacy of this encounter was reflected in the fact that no common statement or communique was published. Eventually the papers were published in 1997 in the *Evangelical Review of Theology*. The meeting confirmed the importance of the issues taken up for discussion but lifted up especially two issues that tend to divide Evangelicals and Catholics. Besides the nature of the church as communion, the other issue was the nature and practice of mission and evangelism.

These topics were taken up at the next consultation, held in October 1997 at the Tantur Ecumenical Institute in Jerusalem. Papers were given by Rev. Avery Dulles SJ ("The Church as One, Holy, Catholic and Apostolic"), Dr George Vandervelde ("Ecclesiology in the Breach: Evangelical Soundings"), Rev. Thomas Stransky CSP ("The Mission of the Church"), and Dr Samuel Escobar ("Missionary Dynamism in Search of Missiological Discernment"). Co-secretaries for this meeting were Dr Paul Schrotenboer and Rev. Timothy Galligan.

Increasing mutual confidence between the two partners was reflected in the fact that for the first time a communique about this meeting was published. The papers were published both in the *Evangelical Review of Theology* and in *One in Christ*, a Roman Catholic journal. Some months after this meeting we received the sad news of the death of Dr Paul Schrotenboer. His deep commitment to the process was reflected in the fact that as early as the Venice meeting, he participated despite the discomfort caused by the illness that was increasingly testing his strength. In 1997 he co-chaired the Tantur meeting, despite having had his leg amputated some months earlier. We give thanks to God for the firm witness of Dr Schrotenboer to overcoming misunderstanding and hostilities between Evangelicals and Catholics, which have persisted for so long.

The third meeting was held at Williams Bay, Wisconsin, USA, November 1999, at the invitation of the WEF. By this time it was agreed to proceed with these meetings on a regular basis. The Williams Bay session focused on the theme of the church as communion. Rev. Avery Dulles developed this theme on the Catholic side and Dr Henry Blocher on the Evangelical side. Rev. Thomas Stransky CSP presented a paper highlighting aspects of several reports dealing with "Religious Freedom, Common Witness and Proselytism". Daniel M. Carroll Rodas presented a paper on the same issues as they affect Roman Catholic-Evangelical relations in Latin America. Dr George Vandervelde and Msgr Timothy Galligan served the meeting as co-secretaries.

A new development in the conversations was marked by the request for the preparation of two collaboratively developed papers. Rev. Avery Dulles SJ and Prof. Henri Blocher were requested to prepare a unified summary on the convergences and differences on the church as koinonia. Dr Thomas Oden, Rev. Thomas Stransky CSP and Rev. John Haughey SJ were asked to prepare a paper on the themes of religious freedom, common witness and proselytism.

Besides the discussion of the papers, several important events took place during this Williams Bay meeting which helped to deepen our mutual understanding. The dialogue members together visited important Evangelical schools, including Wheaton College and Trinity Evangelical Divinity School. The participants met and had informal discussions with some of the faculty of both institutions. At Wheaton, they visited the Institute for the Study of American Evangelicals and had conversations with the director, and also visited the Billy Graham Museum, with its display of the history of Evangelicalism in the USA. At Trinity, they were welcomed at a reception by the academic dean, Dr Bingham Hunter, and addressed by Dr Kenneth Kantzer, a former president, after which they had the opportunity for informal discussions with the faculty. The members of the consultation also visited the seminary of the archdiocese of Chicago at Mundelein, where Cardinal Francis George, Archbishop of Chicago, hosted a dinner. Here the consultation team also met the local Catholic-Evangelical "common root" project. These various meetings and events gave the dialogue participants deeper insights into the life of their partner, and showed a broader view of Evangelical-Catholic contacts, all of which encouraged the dialogue in its important work.

Indicative of the growth of fellowship was the fact that the WEF accepted the invitation of Pope John Paul II, conveyed by the PCPCU, and extended also to many other churches and Christian world communions, to send a representative to the "Ecumenical Commemoration of Witnesses to the Faith in the Twentieth Century", held at the Colosseum in Rome on 7 May 2000, one of the ecumenical events of the jubilee year 2000. Dr George Vandervelde and Rev. Johan Candelin participated in this event on behalf of the WEF.

The fourth meeting took place at Mundelein, Illinois, USA, 18-23 February 2001. The evolution of this dialogue was reflected in the fact that for the first time it had before it an initial draft of a common text, namely, on the theme of koinonia, developed by Avery Dulles in cooperation with Henry Blocher (Rev. Dulles SJ was unable to attend this meeting because he was in Rome for his investiture as Cardinal by Pope John Paul II). Another text, prepared by Dr Thomas Oden, gathered representative aspects from previous dialogue documents on the themes of religious liberty and proselytism. This and a number of brief theses reflecting on this material, prepared by Rev. John Haughey SJ, were discussed as well.

A fifth meeting took place in Swanwick, England, 17-26 February 2002. Significant changes had taken place in both sponsoring bodies in the time between the previous meeting and this. The WEF's name was changed to World Evangelical Alliance (WEA), and it was in process of seeking new leadership. At the Pontifical Council for Promoting Christian Unity, changes in its leadership took place and a new president and secretary took office. Also, when Msgr Timothy Galligan, co-secretary of this consultation, completed his term of service to the PCPUC in 2001, Rev. Juan Usma Gómez was appointed to that responsibility on the Catholic side. Three new participants on the Evangelical side attended for the first time: Rev. Dr Rolf Hille, chairman of the theological commission of the WEA, Rev. Dr David Hilborn, theological adviser to the Evangelical Alliance UK, and Rev. Carlos Rodríguez Mansur, Fraternidad Teológica Latinoamericana in Brazil. While preparations for this meeting were slowed down because of these changes in both administrations, the consultation had before it at Swanwick an integrated draft of a proposed common report and aimed at bringing it to a completed form. The text achieved at the end of the week included two main parts. Part I focused on convergences between Catholics and Evangelicals on koinonia, and part II on the relationship of koinonia to evangelization.

It was agreed that the completed report would be presented to the sponsoring bodies requesting approval for its publication as a study text. The completion of this text brought a phase of conversations to a close. As they completed their work, the participants expressed the hope that this consultation between the World Evangelical Alliance and the Catholic Church would continue.

## Appendix 2

### List of Participants

*World Evangelical Alliance*                    *Catholic Church*


*Venice, Italy, 21-25 October 1993*

Dr Henri Blocher, France                        Bishop Jorge Mejía, Rome

Dr Pablo Perez, USA                             Rev. Karl Muller SVD, Germany

Dr Paul Schrotenboer, USA                       Rev. John Redford, England

Dr George Vandervelde, Canada                   Rev. Thomas Stransky CSP, Jerusalem

                                                Msgr. John Radano, Rome

                                                Rev. Timothy Galligan, Rome


*Jerusalem, 13-19 October 1997*

Dr Paul Schrotenboer, USA, Secretary            Rev. Timothy Galligan, Rome, Secretary

Dr Henri Blocher, France                        Rev. Frans Bouwen, M. Afr., Jerusalem

Dr Samuel Escobar, USA                          Msgr Joseph Dinh Duc Dao, Rome

Dr George Vandervelde, Canada                   Rev. Avery Dulles SJ, USA

Dr Stanley Mutunga, Kenya                       Sr Maria Ko FMA, Hong Kong/Rome

Dr Thomas Oden, USA

Dr Peter Kusmic, USA (unable to attend)

Msgr John Radano, Rome

Rev. Thomas Stransky CSP, Jerusalem

Rev. Juan Usma Gómez, Rome

*Williams Bay, WI, 7-13 November 1999*

Dr George Vandervelde, Canada, Secretary

Dr Henri Blocher, France

Dr Thomas Oden, USA

Dr M. Daniel Carroll Rodas, USA

Dr Tite Tienou, USA

Dr James Stamoolis, USA

Rev. Timothy Galligan, Rome, Secretary

Rev. Avery Dulles SJ, USA

Rev. John Haughey SJ, USA

Sr Maria Ko FMA, Hong Kong/Rome

Msgr John Radano, Rome

Rev. Thomas Stransky CSP, Jerusalem

Rev. Juan Usma Gómez, Rome

Br Jeffrey Gros FSC, USA

*Mundelein, IL, 18-23 February 2001*

Dr George Vandervelde, Canada, Secretary

Dr Henri Blocher, France

Dr Thomas Oden, USA

Prof. Lilia Solano, Colombia

Dr James Stamoolis, USA

Dr Daniel H. Williams, USA

Rev. Timothy Galligan, Rome, Secretary

Cardinal Avery Dulles SJ, USA (unable to attend)

Rev. John Haughey SJ, USA

Sr Maria Ko FMA, Hong Kong/Rome

Msgr John Radano, Rome

Rev. Juan Usma Gómez, Rome

Br Jeffrey Gros FSC, USA

Rev. Thomas Rausch SJ, USA

*Swanwick, UK, 17-26 February 2002*

Dr George Vandervelde, Canada, Secretary

Dr Henri Blocher, France

Dr Thomas Oden, USA

Dr Rolf Hille, Germany

Dr David Hilborn, UK

Rev. Carlos Rodríguez Mansur, Brasil

Dr James Stamoolis (unable to attend)

Dr Daniel H. Williams, USA (unable to attend)

Rev. Juan Usma Gómez, Rome, Secretary

Cardinal Avery Dulles SJ, USA (unable to attend)

Rev. John Haughey SJ, USA

Sr Maria Ko FMA, Hong Kong (unable to attend)

Msgr John Radano, Rome

Br Jeffrey Gros FSC, USA

Rev. Thomas Rausch SJ, USA

NOTES

1   John Reumann, "Koinonia in Scripture: Survey of Biblical Texts", Santiago, 62.

2   On the phrase "communio sanctorum" in the Apostles' Creed see J.N.D. Kelly, *Early Christian Creeds*, 3rd ed., New York, 1972, pp.389-90. This sacramental interpretation is favoured by Stephen Benko, *The Meaning of Communion of Saints*, Naperville IL, 1964, and Werner Elert, *Eucharist and Church Fellowship in the First Four Centuries*, St Louis, 1966, ch. 1 and excursuses 1, 2 and 3.

3   A list of abbreviations is found at the end of this volume.

4   "A Call to Evangelical Unity: 'The Gospel of Jesus Christ: An Evangelical Celebration'", *Christianity Today*, 43:7, 14 June 1999, pp.49-56.

5   "The Chicago Call: An Appeal to Evangelicals", 1977, GC I, 579.

6   We share the majority of biblical books, but the Catholic canon includes also the books Protestants call "The Apocrypha" and Catholics the "Deutero-canonical" books.

7   "Confessing the One Faith: An Evangelical Response by World Evangelical Fellowship Task Force on Ecumenical Issues", *Evangelical Review of Theology*, 18, 1994, pp.35-46.

8   This style of ecclesiology points to a vision of the universal church as a network of local churches in communion. According to the extraordinary assembly of the synod of bishops 1985, "The ecclesiology of communion is the central and fundamental idea of the Council's documents. Koinonia/communio, founded on the sacred scripture, has been held in great honour in the early church and in the Oriental churches to this day. Thus, much was done by the Second Vatican Council so that the church as communion might be more clearly understood and concretely incorporated into life" (*Relatio Finalis*, II, C, 1)

9   The Congregation of the Doctrine of the Faith in its letter to bishops on "Some Aspects of the Church Understood as Communion" emphasizes the priority of the universal over the particular church (Cf. *Origins*, 22, 25 June 1992, pp.108-12). In his presentation on *Lumen Gentium* at the International Meeting on the reception of Vatican II, 27 February 2000, Cardinal Ratzinger explained that the community of the 120 on whom the Holy Spirit descended (Acts 2:1-4) was a renewal of the community of the twelve, who had been commissioned to carry the gospel to the ends of the earth. This community was the New Israel. Cf. Joseph Ratzinger, "L'ecclesiologia della Costituzione Lumen Gentium", *Il Concilio Vaticano II, Recezione e attualità alla luce del Giubileo*, ed. Rino Fisichella, Milan, 2000, pp.66-81.

10  Pius XII, encyclical *Mystici Corporis Christi*, 79.

11  Abraham Kuyper, *Het Calvinisme*, Kampen, Kok, 1899, pp.53-54.

12  Cf. John Paul II, "Universal Prayer for Forgiveness, III. Confession of the sins which have harmed the unity of the body of Christ", during the liturgy of first Sunday of Lent, St Peter's Basilica, Vatican City, 12 March 2000. See PCPCU, Vatican City, *Information Service*, 103, 2000/I-II, p.56.

13  Cf. John Paul II, "Universal Prayer for Forgiveness, e) Confession of sins committed in actions against love, peace, the rights of peoples and respect for cultures and religions", Vatican City, 12 March 2000.

14  Cf. I. Randall and D. Hilborn, *One Body in Christ: The History and Significance of the Evangelical Alliance*, Carlisle, 2001, p.98.

Part C

# 31. Report

International Theological Dialogue between the Seventh-day Adventist Church and the World Alliance of Reformed Churches

Jongny sur Vevey, Switzerland, 1-7 April 2001

## I. Preamble

1. This document is a record of the dialogue between representatives of the General Conference of Seventh-day Adventists and the World Alliance of Reformed Churches held at Jongny sur Vevey, Switzerland, 1-7 April 2001. The theme of this dialogue was "The Church in the Setting of the Reformation Heritage: Its Mission in a World of Wide-spread Injustice and Ecological Destruction".

2. Over many years frequent contact has been made between representatives of the two bodies at annual meetings of secretaries of Christian world communions. In addition, an exploratory meeting between representatives of the two families was held in Geneva, 28-29 November 1999. The present dialogue arises from these contacts, and is inspired by a desire to increase mutual understanding, remove false stereotypes, and on the basis of many commonly held beliefs to address the question how we may jointly respond to the claims of justice and equity in a threatened, divided and broken world.

3. We see the present discussion as part of a wider programme of conversations in which each party has separately been engaged. On the Reformed side these include dialogues with classical Pentecostal churches and leaders, the Roman Catholic Church, the Organization of African Instituted Churches and the Oriental and Eastern Orthodox churches. On the Adventist side, while the conversations have been fewer and more recent, they have included discussions with the Lutherans, Orthodox and the World Evangelical Fellowship.

4. The churches of the Reformed tradition, while rooted in scripture, owe their more immediate origins to the Swiss/French wing of the Reformation. Their doctrines and polity were fashioned by a variety of theologians and, from the outset, were subject to development, not least in relation to the diverse socio-political environments into which they moved. The family comprises churches which espouse presbyterial or congregational church order, together with a number of united churches in which the two polities have been blended (in some cases with transconfessional ingredients as well). Through colonization and the modern missionary movement, the Reformed have spread to many parts of the world where they have adapted themselves in various ways to cultural and social contexts. The World Alliance of Reformed Churches (Presbyterian and Congregational), which represents some 75 million members and 214 churches in 106 countries,

was formed in 1970 as a result of the coming together of the World Presbyterian Alliance (1875) and the International Congregational Council (1891).

5. The Seventh-day Adventist Church is a scripture-based, Christ-centred church, which was organized in 1863. It emerged from the mid-century movement which looked for the imminent return of Christ. From a small beginning (3500 members when organized) the church has now spread to over 200 countries and has (in 2001) a baptized membership of more than 12 million, representing a total Adventist community of over 25 million people. The church is especially strong in some Latin American countries, Africa and the Far East. Adventists operate a school system of some 6000 institutions from primary to university levels, comprising one million students, as well as a large network of health institutions. It is also well known for its Adventist Development and Relief Agency (ADRA), and organized support for religious liberty.

6. From the above brief descriptions it will clearly be seen that the two communions represented in this dialogue embrace people of diverse cultural, linguistic and national origins. It should further be noted that the preponderance of their members now reside in Asia, Africa, Latin America and Australasia.

7. Every interchurch conversation has its own ethos and agenda, specific to the parties involved. Happily, Adventist-Reformed relations have not been blighted by anathemas, though they have been inhibited by misunderstandings. In this dialogue we sought to face and dispel some of these, and to articulate the common doctrinal ground on which we stand; and this with a view to proclaiming the eternal gospel in today's needy world.

## II. Common ground

8. The Adventists and the Reformed acknowledge as brothers and sisters all who confess Jesus Christ as Saviour and Lord. Among the many features we hold in common are the following:

- We accept the Bible as the rule of faith and practice, the supreme witness to God's saving grace in Christ.
- We believe in the triune God.
- We believe that God became truly human in Jesus Christ.
- We believe that through the life, death and resurrection of Jesus Christ, God reconciles the whole created order to himself. By the work of Christ, God's holiness is honoured and our sins forgiven.
- We believe that God calls all people to a new and better life.
- We believe that as followers of Jesus Christ we are called to proclaim the gospel of salvation to all people.
- We believe that Christ calls us to work to bring hope, healing and deliverance from spiritual and economic poverty.
- We believe we stand in the succession of those who, through the ages, have faithfully proclaimed the gospel of Christ.
- We believe that the Lord's supper is integral to the church's worship and witness.

- We acknowledge our debt to the Reformation with its biblical emphasis upon salvation by grace alone *(sola gratia)* through faith alone *(sola fide)* in Christ alone *(solus Christus)*.

- We welcome conversations with other Christian churches concerning doctrine and mission.

## III. Mutual misunderstandings and clarifications

9. Despite the considerable degree of common ground, the Reformed and the Adventists have frequently misunderstood one another and viewed each other with suspicion. The mutual clarifications specified below should help to clear the path to further Adventist-Reformed mutual reflection. What is clear is that both families have experienced a degree of doctrinal development as they have sought to bear witness to the gospel in ever-changing, diverse socio-intellectual environments.

ADVENTIST CLARIFICATIONS

10. Adventists have grown in their understanding and articulation of doctrine. Therefore, some expressions of their teachings found in earlier publications do not accurately represent their present positions. However, some criticisms levelled against them derive from misinformation and have never been true. In each of the following paragraphs, we express a frequently-asked question ("Q") followed by a brief Adventist reply ("A").

11. Q: Do Adventists set dates for the second coming of Jesus?

A: The Seventh-day Adventist Church was organized in 1863, and has never set such dates. It has officially and publicly rejected all such practices, as with attempts to attach significance to the year 2000. Occasionally, an Adventist preacher or writer may have set or implied dates for the second Advent, but they have acted without official endorsement or authority.

12. Q: Do Adventists believe in Christ's complete atonement on the cross?

A: Adventists believe that the death of Christ on the cross provided the once-for-all atonement for sins, all-sufficient in its efficacy. Their distinctive view of the high priestly ministry of Christ in the heavenly sanctuary teaches that he is applying the ongoing benefits of his atonement, not adding any value to it.

13. Q: Are Adventists legalists?

A: Adventists hold to the Reformation principle of grace alone, faith alone and Christ alone. They teach and preach that as saved people the Lord calls all Christians to holy living. This includes obedience to the ten commandments, with sabbath observance; however, they understand obedience to be the result, not the ground, of salvation.

14. Q: Do Adventists add to the canon of scripture?

A: Adventists believe that the biblical gift of prophecy was manifested in the life and ministry of Ellen G. White. They regard her writings highly as providing ongoing counsel, devotional material and biblical reflection. However, they hold firmly to the principle of *sola scriptura*, teaching that the Bible is the rule of faith and practice that tests all other writings, including those by Ellen White.

15. Q: Do Adventists believe that they are the only ones who will be saved?

A: No. Further, although they understand themselves to be given a particular mission, this is within the larger context of God's activity through many agencies. Their working policy states, "We recognize every agency that lifts up Christ before man as a part of the divine plan for the evangelisation of the world".

16. Q: Do Adventists neglect the social implications of the gospel?

A: Adventists have always been engaged in social betterment as part of their understanding of the gospel. They have been reluctant, however, to engage politically in challenging societal structures.

REFORMED CLARIFICATIONS

17. Understandably, the Adventists raised the question of predestination. In some cases the perplexity arises because "predestination" is mistakenly confused with "determinism". The biblical doctrine of predestination arises from Paul's grateful, retrospective confession that his standing before God was not of his own doing, but resulted from God's gracious, prior call. "Predestination" is thus a religious term which is not to be elided with "determinism" (as the latter term appears in, for example, moral philosophy, where Reformed participants may be found on both sides of the determinist-libertarian debate).

18. As to the perplexity caused by "double predestination", it must be admitted that this doctrine has given rise to a view of God as determining the eternal fate of individuals from the foundation of the world in accordance with his "inscrutable will", with some destined for heaven, others for hell. It should be remembered that Calvin and others did not place election to salvation on an equal footing with "preterition" ("passing by"). Subsequently, there was a hardening of this position whereby a relentless logic was ill-advisedly applied to a religious doctrine, to the extent that in some circles mission was inhibited because the free offer of the gospel was proscribed. Under the influence of the evangelical revival, further modifications were made, to the extent that some Reformed Christians can nowadays not only envisage a rapprochement with Arminians, but can happily live with them in united churches. There is thus a broad consensus to the effect that God's electing grace is not to be construed fatalistically, but in the context of God's undiscriminating love whereby all are called to salvation, to which call they may make their own, enabled, response.

19. It became clear to the participants in the Reformed-Methodist dialogue that the historic dispute over Calvinism and Arminianism need not be church-dividing. This conclusion resulted from the recognition that while Calvinists were seeking to honour God's sovereignty in salvation, Arminians were no less concerned to uphold human responsibility before God.

20. Adventists have queried the apparent relative lack of interest in eschatology (construed as the "doctrine of the last things") in Reformed theologies. While Reformed theologians have, down the centuries, written widely on this theme, it is true to say that on the whole they have not, traditionally, majored on it; nor has eschatology been central in

the piety of Reformed Christians. It may even be that distaste for more excitable millenarian claims has constituted an inhibiting factor in this connection. Nevertheless, eschatology is not to be played down – least of all in the present dialogue in which we are pondering our witness in relation to God's new heaven and earth.

21. Some Adventists challenge Reformed churches in certain regions to examine, and where necessary to adjust, the balance of gospel proclamation and socio-ethical witness, the latter being perceived as taking precedence over the former instead of being informed by it. While there are some grounds for this challenge (which have been shared for a long time by many Reformed churches), the Reformed respond by underlining their conviction that since salvation concerns the whole person, in the whole of society, the proclamation of the word cannot be divorced from the practical outworking of it in terms of the ideals of the kingdom of God.

## IV. Mission

22. As representatives of the Seventh-day Adventist Church and the World Alliance of Reformed Churches, we are called to bear witness to the gospel in a world characterized by a diverse set of opportunities, challenges and problems. Among the problems, we identify the following: social and economic injustices; ecological destruction; and racial, ethnic, gender and religious discrimination. We are deeply aware that we have contributed both directly and indirectly to these conditions. We believe the gospel compels us to respond imaginatively and creatively to these concerns both at a local and global level.

23. We recognize that often there is a real and serious danger that is created by our tendency to dogmatize our perceptions of what God would have us do and be in the world in terms of certain experiences or doctrinal positions. We realize the urgent need for our theologies to go beyond simplistic dichotomies of dividing human experience into secular and spiritual; soul and body; black and white; male and female; rich and poor.

24. These dualities often manifest themselves in setting one against the other or glorifying one at the cost of vilifying the other. For example, we have lived as though nature has to be exploited because it is material and temporal. This is the line of thought that has resulted in a sharp divide in the church's participation in justice and the mission of God in the world. The Adventist and the Reformed representatives concur that such divides are not justifiable, either on the basis of biblical faith or our traditions. We have found that the whole of life is a gift of God that is to be enjoyed and nurtured through faithful stewardship. Therefore, we reaffirm our commitment to joining with God and one another in the ministry of reconciliation.

25. Our approach to the following issues is grounded in our grateful response to the grace of God who creates us, redeems us, and calls us to stewardship. We seek to embrace God's mission in creative, redemptive and faithful obedience to our call to discipleship. We engage these matters not with the presumption that there can be simple resolution to the injustices that surround us, but with the deep desire to be in solidarity with the marginalized and hurting. We learn this commitment from the incarnation itself; God's very entrance into and solidarity with the human condition in the person of Jesus Christ.

S<small>OCIO-ECONOMIC INJUSTICE</small>

26.  We have become more aware of the socio-economic challenges that face many of our communities, particularly in the southern hemisphere. The global economy, dominated by multinational corporations and institutions that reinforce the indebtedness of developing nations to developed nations, exacerbates the economic and social hardship experienced by the majority of the inhabitants of the world. This phenomenon is manifest in the following tragedies, among others:

*Poverty:*

27.  We acknowledge the widespread poverty in the world, which is manifest in the lack of access to basic necessities (e.g., food, housing, water, clothing) needed for sustaining a dignified human existence. These consequences of poverty are so egregious that the church needs to become more assertive in confronting these injustices. As Adventists and members of the World Alliance, we acknowledge that we are not as proactive as we should be in addressing these concerns. We see an urgent need and invite our churches to work both individually and, wherever possible, together in alleviating and minimizing the effects of this malady.

*HIV/AIDS:*

28.  We painfully note the devastating effects of HIV/AIDS in all parts of the world, particularly in Asia and sub-Saharan Africa. This tidal wave of suffering and death, the loss of income, the burden of orphan care, the loss of hope, the desperation inflicting both individuals and communities, and the accompanying social stigma that threatens the dignity of the individual, make it difficult in many instances to deal realistically with the crisis.

29.  Compounding the difficulty are the self-serving financial policies and insensitivity of international pharmaceutical companies that prevent many in developing nations from gaining access and benefit from the available medications that would reduce human suffering and prolong life.

30.  There is need for our churches to address the disturbing issues related to this epidemic in their theological, ethical and pastoral dimensions, and this with a view to facilitating the whole church's pastoral care of the infected and the affected. This will include working to influence behavioural changes and responsible life-styles and grappling with the issue of how our two communions can cooperate in dealing with this issue as we proclaim the gospel.

*Violence:*

31.  The ugly head of violence rises everywhere – especially against women, children, and other vulnerable communities. Dictatorships, militarism, racism, industrialization that pushes people off their land, and racist violence against groups like the Dalit, blacks and Indigenous communities are responsible for a large share of the wave of ongoing

misery of countless multitudes. In addition, many structural adjustment programmes imposed on indebted developing countries have adverse effects upon human and peoples' rights. Such violence and discrimination brutalizes and dehumanizes people made in the image of God.

### ECOLOGICAL DESTRUCTION

32. In recent years there has been a global raising of consciousness to the ways in which human beings, particularly from affluent societies in the northern hemisphere, have contributed to the destruction of the environment. Manifestations of this destruction include reduction of valuable biomass (e.g., deforestation, over-harvesting of marine life, and overgrazing), compromises in maintaining eco-diversity balance (e.g., acid rain and use of fossil fuels), and global warming.

33. As Christian believers, we are called to respond to these crises by engaging in the work of healing and reconciliation. The doctrine of creation shapes our understanding of Christian mission in relation to environmental degradation. We view the world as God's good creation; a theatre of God's grace; a gift to be enjoyed and nurtured by God's creatures. Sabbath rest may well be a reminder both of God's providential care of the earth and our responsibility to serve as its creative stewards.

34. In light of the doctrine of creation, we exhort ourselves and other Christians to repent of the sinful ways we have exploited the environment and modify our behaviour accordingly. Positive practical steps that Christians can take on a local level to address these concerns include: recycling, conserving energy, buying ecologically friendly products, and supporting local conservation groups. Our discussions emphasized that Christians also need to think with global and systemic perspective about their mission. In agreement with a report submitted to the World Council of Churches central committee in 2001 (doc. PRII 3), we call Christians from industrialized countries to recognize that they carry "major moral responsibility for precipitating climate change and therefore must exercise leadership that results in real action to reduce the causes". In addition, we hold that Christians be aware of the relationship of multinational corporations to ecological destruction and refuse to condone business endeavours that benefit industrialized countries to the detriment of developing nations.

### PREJUDICES

35. We recognize that prejudices still persist in many of our societies, including faith-based communities. Wherever they exist, these prejudices constitute a denial of the gospel. In this section we focus on issues of religious freedom and gender which impinge on the holistic proclamation of the gospel.

### *Religious freedom:*

36. We recognize that religious freedom is a gift of God and a fundamental freedom that should be promoted and protected.

37. We are concerned by the increasing violations of religious freedom in several parts of the world leading to an increase of intolerance and conflict.

38. We encourage cooperation between our communions: (a) in defending and promoting religious freedom through international agencies, governments and churches; (b) in organizing conferences and symposia to discuss religious freedom issues; and (c) in sharing information and joining in common projects and prayers for those who are persecuted.

*Gender biases:*

39. Women experience discrimination, oppression and exploitation in many forms. We believe the church needs to continue combating gender discrimination. The doctrine of creation teaches that men and women are equally created in the image of God; in the household of faith we are all one in Christ. This theological affirmation needs to be supported by concrete action first in local contexts and then in networking with others from multiple contexts who are also advocates of women and women's concerns.

40. Women constitute a vital and dynamic force within the church. They keep the church active by their numerous contributions. But in many contexts they are excluded from leadership roles and decision-making bodies. The New Testament, by contrast, teaches that women are equal recipients of the gifts of the Holy Spirit and should therefore exercise leadership roles in the church's ministry. Reformed representatives emphasize that this includes the ordination of women to the ministry of word and sacrament, whilst admitting that the mere fact of the church's having this commitment does not imply that all gender-equality issues have been resolved. While it is true that, because of differences in biblical interpretation, Adventists do not at present ordain women to the ministerial office, women are occupying increasingly significant leadership roles, including service as local pastors.

41. In the course of our discussions we highlighted the need for: (a) ongoing interpretation of scriptures pertaining to gender equality; (b) raised consciousness of social evils including prostitution in relation to tourism, *sati* (an Indian term for widow-burning), dowry, female infanticide, female sterilization, job discrimination; and (c) increased understanding of the particular ways in which gender discrimination is manifest, depending on the particular context.

## V. Conclusion

42. We are happy to conclude that our conversation has been productive in a number of directions. We have affirmed the common doctrinal ground on which we stand, and we have specified some of the ways in which our teachings have developed over time. We have sought to dispel mutual misunderstandings concerning doctrine. We have eschewed the sectarian spirit, and have not questioned one another's status as Christians. Recognizing that the gospel of God's grace concerns the whole of life and the whole of society, we have turned our minds to some of the burning issues of the day. We invite our

constituencies to redouble their efforts to work for justice, the eradication of poverty, and the preservation and right stewardship of the created order.

43.  In many ways, this conversation was a learning process for both parties. The Adventists made clear their indebtedness to the historic creeds of the church, and to the Reformation heritage, while the Reformed were impressed by the considerable efforts made by Adventists in education, health, and the cause of religious freedom. It appeared that while the Adventists might do well to reflect further upon socio-political involvement grounded in the gospel, the Reformed might in some quarters question the relative weight they give to evangelism and social witness.

44.  In the course of our discussions, it became clear that there is scope for a greater degree of clarification on doctrinal and ethical issues than we have yet achieved. The following topics have emerged as candidates for future consideration, should the sponsoring bodies decide that further Reformed-Adventist dialogue should take place: the interpretation of the Bible; the sabbath; law and grace; eschatology; the concept of the "remnant"; the question of church discipline and holy living in relation to secularized societies; the relation of Ellen G. White's writings to the scriptures; the meaning and implications of "double predestination"; questions concerning worship and polity; the contributions of liberation theologies; and the meaning and significance of Christ's "high priestly ministry".

45.  We have every hope that, were such matters to be pursued, considerable convergence might be revealed. This would lead to increased mutual understanding and acknowledgment of our communions as authentic members of the one church of the Lord Jesus Christ.

## Appendix: Participants

*Reformed participants*

Prof. Dr Cynthia Rigby (Co-chair), Austin Presbyterian Theological Seminary

Prof. Dr Nalini Arles, United Theological College, Bangalore, India

Rev. Rupert Hambira, United Congregational Church of Southern Africa

Dr Arturo Piedra, San José, Costa Rica

Dr Alan Sell, United Theological College, Wales

Dr Setri Nyomi, World Alliance of Reformed Churches, Geneva, Switzerland

*WARC staff*

Ms Margaret Owen

Dr Odair Pedroso Mateus

*Seventh-day Adventist participants*

Dr Bert Beach (Co-chair), General Conference of Seventh-day Adventists, Silver Spring MD, USA

Dr Roy Adams, Associate Editor, *Adventist Review*

Dr Niels-Eric Andreasen, President, Andrews University, Berrien Springs MI, USA

Prof. John Baldwin, Andrews University, Berrien Springs MI, USA

Dr John Graz, Director, General Conference of SDA

Dr William Johnsson, Editor, *Adventist Review*

Prof. Hans La Rondelle, Sarasota FL, USA

Dr George Reid, Director, Biblical Research Institute, Silver Spring MD, USA

Dr Angel Rodriguez, Associate Director, Biblical Research Institute, Silver Spring MD, USA

*Apologies*

Dr Jean-Claude Verrechia, President, Saleve Adventist University, France

# 32. The Kigali Statement

Dialogue between the Organization of African Instituted
Churches and the World Alliance of Reformed Churches

Kigali, Rwanda, 13-19 October 1999

**Affirmations**

We have come together from two Christian families, the Reformed churches and the African Instituted churches, and rejoice in the spirit of unity, knowing that we share a common ministry. We meet in Kigali, Rwanda, and have been deeply moved by accounts of the 1994 killings in this nation and by our visits to some of the sites of genocide. We have been much encouraged by our Rwandan brothers and sisters as they seek reconciliation and the reconstruction of their country. Their example has been an inspiration to us as we ourselves seek to understand each other better and to overcome our own suspicions and spirit of disunity. We lament our past histories of division and hatred and resolve to continue to meet together in dialogue, seeking opportunities and means of common action.

We affirm a common faith:
- in the triune God;
- in the Lordship of Jesus Christ as God incarnate and crucified, who identifies with us in our suffering;
- in the Holy Spirit and his transforming power in our lives.

We affirm that the holy scriptures are for both of our families a yardstick for Christian faith and life, while recognizing that there may be differences in our interpretations. We affirm that African Christians have an identity that is both African and Christian, and that our faith calls us to witness and act in the social and political realities of our world. As representatives of the world church, and as leaders of churches in Africa, we confess the complicity of ourselves and our churches in the economic and political injustices that have impoverished and disempowered the people of this continent. We acknowledge that we have failed to speak prophetically when called to do so, and that we have shown a blatant disregard for the environment.

**Challenges and actions**

We have shared together our deep concerns about the present tragic situation of Africa, to which the following factors have contributed. We have agreed to do all we can as church leaders to assist our people to reconstruct our continent, and are committed to the following actions for ourselves, our churches and our people.

1. We are distressed by division and disunity in the church and society. We will use our pulpits and our churches to promote greater tolerance and understanding of different groups and persuasions, and to encourage a spirit of openness that will enable people to express themselves and accommodate diversity. As part of this process we will take steps to initiate dialogue at the local level between our two church families. We acknowledge a need to return to African models of reconciliation and of establishing and maintaining unity. As church members and leaders, we need to engage actively with society and its needs and problems in order to enable people to identify, prioritize, and find solutions to their own needs, and not just those of our churches.

2. For centuries the human and material resources of our continent have been exploited by others. Knowing that it is this exploitation that has increased poverty and unemployment in Africa, we have a duty to educate the members of our churches and local communities on the nature of the global and local processes involved. We will work with other churches and agencies to reduce our dependency on foreign models and solutions for these problems. In the face of widespread corruption and lack of accountability, we need to strengthen governance in our nations and institutions. We will therefore educate our people so as to form a strong and well-informed civil society. We will act to provide more information to the members of our churches, and train them to use this information in order to strengthen governance in our churches as well as in society. We will conduct programmes for sensitizing church and community members, through such means as the distribution of literature and through national and local forums, with the aim of empowering people to take initiatives themselves and to participate more actively in civil society.

3. We acknowledge that our own churches do not adequately model the democratic structures we are urging on the state. This is true of "family churches" among the AICs as well as of the more bureaucratic structures of the Reformed churches. We will be more courageous in confronting issues of corruption and misuse of power in government. The process of encouraging participation will also require some of us to change our attitudes as leaders, and to reduce our use of scripture or the Holy Spirit to enforce our decisions upon others. We will work to reduce attitudes and habits of dependency among our church members.

4. The Western models of development we are using in Africa are not sustainable. As a result, our environment has been exploited, spoilt and degraded, and our own societies have become polarized between rich and poor. We have accepted the dumping of toxic wastes. We will educate our churches and communities to take responsibility for protecting and improving the environment. This is something every member can share in, through such grassroots activities as tree-planting and the cleaning-up of our cities and villages.

5. As Christians we recognize the God-given dignity of human beings and the sacredness of life. In this regard, therefore, we oppose military regimes whose power is based on violence rather than the will of the people expressed through the ballot box . Working with the media, we will act to expose arms dealers and their customers, and we will cooperate with our partners in the North to advocate a shift from arms production to socially beneficial industries. We will continue to advocate against the ready supply of

illegal arms in our countries, and the lack of discipline and professionalism in our security forces, while recognizing that these problems are intimately related to our declining economies and increasing poverty. We will also encourage our governments and especially our own churches to continue to show hospitality to refugees, giving thanks for the self-sacrificing generosity in this area of many of our local congregations.

We will work to strengthen democratic values and institutions, and to research and develop models of democracy appropriate to African society, which can enable people of all ethnic groups and political and religious persuasions to participate in decision-making at all levels of church and state. We recognize that this will require a change in our own methods of working, away from concentration on seminars for leaders towards more exchange visits, in order to build relationships between people and communities across Africa, and to expose our members to other cultures and ways of working together.

6. We commit ourselves to promote the full participation of women at all levels in our church structures, and to work to expose oppressive tendencies and traditions, so that our churches can become exemplary models for the empowerment of women in the wider society.

7. Children are both the present and the future of our churches and societies. Yet they are exploited as child labour, as child soldiers, and as child prostitutes. Others are heads of families at a very young age or are forced to live and sleep on the streets. For their protection and better upbringing, we commit our churches to the task of sensitizing our members and communities about HIV/AIDS, unemployment, landlessness, Structural Adjustment Programmes and other issues which affect the lives of our children. We will advocate against all those practices which put children at risk, and we will train our own members in responsible parenthood.

8. Social forces in contemporary Africa threaten to destroy family life. We commit our churches to the promotion of family life education programmes. Education about changing attitudes to the care of the old, sensitization to HIV/AIDS, and education on the home care and support of people with AIDS, and on the importance of chastity before marriage and faithfulness in marriage should all be priorities in such programmes.

9. Extreme poverty contributes to rising levels of drug abuse and drug trafficking. This is true not only of the hard drugs but also of cannabis and of alcohol, in which the use of poisonous additives is of particular concern in some of our countries. As church leaders we will act to expose the trade, create awareness of the dangers of addiction, and support efforts to counteract its spread.

10. The process of globalization and the speeding-up of communications affects our continent in various ways. Because globalization is driven by market forces and is largely directed by transnational corporations which are beyond the control of national states, it threatens to destroy local values, traditions and self-reliance. This can be seen most clearly in the impact of the mass media on our people. To counter its ill-effects we need as church leaders to strengthen our sense of identity, and to encourage people to be proud of their roots in church and community. Furthermore, we need to sensitize our members and those of our communities to globalization and its effects, so that people can participate in the process, becoming agents of change themselves and not simply victims. Because globalization benefits those who have access to global networks, and is dependent on expensive technology, it threatens to marginalize the poor of Africa even further. Our churches must engage in research, and in networking with sympathetic partners in

order to be effective advocates against the ill-effects of globalization, and to prevent our people from being overwhelmed by processes which may otherwise be beyond their understanding or control.

11. In both our church families, we acknowledge a deficit in the area of contextualized theology. This deficit has contributed to the deep identity crisis felt by many of us as African Christians. The Reformed churches have much to learn here from the inculturation of the gospel in the AICs, but both our church families lack well-articulated and contextualized theologies for contemporary Africa. We will therefore work to encourage a writing culture in our churches, and to promote further reflection on the encounter between gospel and culture. An aspect of this encounter is the issue of polygamous marriages. We are agreed that the Christian ideal of marriage is faithful monogamy, but we recognize that some African churches need time to work out the theological and pastoral implications of this principle. We believe that churches should not be discriminated against on this and other pastoral issues which their leaders are seeking to handle with sensitivity among their members.

12. We are concerned about the spread of false teachings on our continent (including the so-called "prosperity gospel"), many of them coming from abroad. Our church members have become consumers of many different theologies which are not relevant to African realities. These have contributed to divisions in our churches, and to theological confusion. To counter this challenge, we commit our churches to encourage more study and teaching of the Bible, and to the promotion of theological education programmes which can reach all levels of church membership.

13. We acknowledge that our churches have often failed to obey the great commission, and have been preoccupied with maintaining already existing churches in areas where the gospel took root long ago. We commit ourselves to reach out to where the gospel has not yet been heard, and where churches have not yet been planted.

14. Many of our churches lack a strong financial base. As church leaders, we are called to increase the participation of our members in church activities, so that they become "owners" rather than "followers". We will encourage investment in church-owned income-generating projects. We will promote stronger biblical teaching on giving, stewardship, and accountability in our churches. We acknowledge that our behaviour and practice as leaders in this area has not always been above reproach, and we commit ourselves to greater transparency, integrity and accountability.

### Concrete actions

1. We have agreed to meet together again in 2000 at a venue to be arranged by the OAIC in consultation with the WARC.
2. We will distribute this statement to the member churches in Africa of our respective constituencies.
3. We will encourage our member churches to engage in dialogue and in work together at the local level, with feedback to our respective organizations.
4. We will invite representatives of our partners in this dialogue to attend significant meetings of our organizations and churches on the African continent.

# 33. The Final Report

## Dialogue between the African Independent or Instituted Churches and the World Alliance of Reformed Churches

### Mbagathi, Kenya, 9-14 February 2002

## 1. Introduction

*Dialogue between two Christian families*

This document is the record of a significant breakthrough in ecumenical dialogue. It is a report of a series of three meetings between the Reformed churches, represented by the World Alliance of Reformed Churches, Geneva, and the African Independent or Instituted churches (AICs), represented by the Organization of African Instituted Churches, Nairobi. To our knowledge, it is the first time the African Independent churches have been involved in a dialogue with another Christian world communion. During this process, members of churches that separated from churches of the Reformed family within living memory have been meeting with representatives of the churches from which they separated.

*The beginnings of the church in Africa*

According to tradition, the history of the church in Africa began with the preaching of the gospel to the Ethiopian eunuch, and with the arrival of the Evangelist St Mark in Alexandria in AD 42. St Mark was the founder of the Coptic Orthodox Church of Egypt, which formally separated from the other churches at the time of the council of Chalcedon, and has retained many of its traditions and original liturgy until the present day. The Copts took the gospel to the Nubians and Ethiopians, and beyond Africa, as far as Ireland. In other parts of North Africa, the Christian faith was planted and nourished by the Latin church. After the Muslim conquests of the 7th century, when much of the North African church was destroyed, and the Coptic church itself fell under hegemony of Muslim overlords, the Christian faith endured on the continent mainly in the Coptic and Ethiopian Orthodox churches. The next significant and enduring missionary expansion of the church was brought about by European and North American Protestant and Catholic missionaries of the 19th and 20th centuries. From the 1870s onwards, this missionary expansion became inextricably entwined with European colonial expansion and the "scramble for Africa". Thus, the gospel presented by European missionaries was not only heavily influenced by European culture (individualistic, materialist and capitalist) but became for the African convert a way of entry into the new colonial systems with their exploitative economies and racist assumptions. It was in this frequently highly oppressive context that the African Independent church movement was born.

## 2. African Independent or Instituted churches

*A new Christian phenomenon*

AICs are known by various names, of which African Independent and African Instituted churches are the most common. The term "instituted" was first used in the title of OAIC simply to obtain Kenyan government approval for its registration. Its use did not mean that AICs wanted to lose the older term "independent", and both terms are generally acceptable to the constituency.

Although AICs are now very widely spread in sub-Saharan Africa, originally they were focused in South Africa, Zimbabwe, Malawi, Kenya, the Congo basin, Nigeria, and along the West African coast between Côte d'Ivoire and Cameroon. Three factors led to the creation of a new form of Christian faith in these areas:
- the intensity of cultural conflict between the European colonizers and their associated missions, and the indigenous cultures;
- the degree of political and economic oppression in east and southern Africa, resulting in the seizure of lands and the displacement of African peoples;
- the extent of Christianization: AICs did not usually emerge until people had the Bible in their own mother tongues, and were able to challenge or "correct" mission church interpretations of the scriptures.

Thus AICs were born out of prophetic attempts by African peoples to interpret their oppressive situations, find meaning, create space for themselves, and often to fight for freedom.

From a sociological perspective, AICs can be seen as examples of the new religious movements (NRMs) which arose out of the impact of European culture and Christianity upon African cultures that were less powerful politically, militarily and economically. AICs stand at one end of a spectrum of NRMs which ranges from the movements very close to the African religious heritage at one end to fully Christian churches at the other. Other NRMs use the name "church" but are less than fully Christian, and may not even wish to be called Christian. Theologically, however, the term New Religious Movement does not do justice to the AICs. The OAIC constitution restricts membership to

> any African founded church which believes in Jesus Christ as Saviour, the Holy Trinity (the Father, the Son, and the Holy Spirit as one God) and Christian doctrine as founded in the holy Bible (Old Testament and New Testament).

The OAIC groups its members into three categories:
- *Nationalist churches* (also known as Ethiopian and African churches): These are churches that seceded from the mission churches during the colonial era (beginning in 1844 in South Africa and in 1891 in Nigeria) over issues of leadership and a desire that Africans should control the church and its teachings on cultural practices. They often saw the fight against colonialism as one of the legitimate goals of the church, and were influenced by the Marcus Garvey movement, which sought to unite

Africans of the continent and of the diaspora to work for the liberation of Africa and the dignity of African peoples. In liturgy and doctrine nationalist churches have retained much from the Western or historical churches. They often looked to Ethiopia as a symbol of African resistance to and independence from colonialism, and referred to Psalm 68:31 as a prophecy for themselves.

- *Spiritual churches* (also known as Zionist, Apostolic and Aladura churches): These churches (dating from 1910 onwards in southern Africa, and 1920 onwards in west and eastern Africa) are sometimes referred to as "prophet-healing" churches, because of the centrality of the charismatic gifts in their worship and ministry (prophecy, interpretation of dreams, healing and prayer for protection against evil). Their liturgies are more informal, and there is greater use of forms borrowed from African tradition. Especially in southern Africa, these churches look to Zion, as the symbol of a heaven.

- *African Pentecostal churches*: These are African-founded Pentecostal-style churches that have arisen since the mid-1960s. Though the stimulus to their foundation has frequently been the evangelistic missions and training conventions associated with Western Pentecostals (and as a result, there is some dispute whether these churches are fully African), a number of them (those that give a positive value to African culture) have found a home in the OAIC. There are tensions between these churches and the spiritual churches which relate more to styles of worship than to essential differences over doctrine.

### The Organization of African Instituted Churches

The Organization of African Instituted Churches was begun in Cairo in 1978, as a loose association of AICs, in order to express and to address their needs and concerns, among which theological education was the most urgent. At its second general assembly in Nairobi in 1982, a constitution was drawn up and the international headquarters were set up in Nairobi. The third general assembly, which took place in Limuru in August 1997, emphasized the empowerment of the seven OAIC regions. These are eastern Africa, southern Africa, Democratic Republic of Congo, Nigeria, Francophone West Africa, Anglophone West Africa and Madagascar. Some of these regions are composed of national chapters. The regions send three delegates to the general assembly, and their regional chairpersons form the OAIC executive committee, which appoints the general secretary, and through him oversees the running of the programmes. These programmes currently are: theological education by extension, participatory development, women's department, research and communication, and HIV/AIDS.

The total AIC constituency has been conservatively estimated at 60 million, and of this number some 15-20 million people are members of OAIC affiliated churches.

### 3. The Reformed churches

The Reformed family is the portion of Christian churches that recognize their most immediate origins primarily in the Swiss wing of the Reformation movement that culminated in the 16th century. Reformed churches share a set of doctrinal emphases – such as the sovereignty of God, the Lordship of Christ in the church and the world, and the affirmation of the scriptures of the Old and the New Testament as authority in matters of faith and church discipline – as well as adopting church orders known as Presbyterian (from the Greek word for "elder") or Congregational. There are more than 750 Christian churches that recognize themselves as part of the Reformed family. The World Alliance of Reformed Churches (WARC) in its current form is the result of the merger in 1970 between the World Presbyterian Alliance (founded in 1875) and the International Congregational Council (founded in 1891). The World Alliance of Reformed Churches represents some 75 million Reformed Christians, gathered in 215 churches in 106 countries.

Most African Reformed churches began in the 19th century missionary activities mainly from Western Europe. The only community that pre-dates this is the Dutch Reformed Church of South Africa which came with the migratory wave from the Netherlands a couple of centuries earlier. They then began spreading through southern Africa. Reformed churches (Presbyterian, Reformed, Congregational, Evangelical and United) can be found all over Africa (including Egypt). However, most of them are found in sub-Saharan Africa. Many of the 19th century-missionaries did not understand African culture and therefore condemned most elements of African culture as pagan – to be discarded. One needs to recall the fact that the 19th century was also the time when colonization was taking place and a good number of the missionary bodies enjoyed the protection of the colonial powers. Therefore, many indigenous Africans identified the missionaries with the colonial powers. One needs to credit these missionaries with a number of things. They brought with them the gospel, schools, hospitals and agricultural innovations. Many of them sacrificed their lives for the sake of the gospel. Today, the Reformed churches in Africa are increasingly living out the gospel within their cultural contexts and many of them are at the forefront of prophetic action in their nations.

## 4. Planning of the dialogue

At a preparatory meeting in Nairobi, 2-3 June 1998, the two families of churches defined the dialogue themes. These were:

*   *Unity:* The meeting expressed an over-riding concern for the lack of unity on the African continent, which threatens the survival of its peoples. These divisions are ethnic, denominational (with a proliferating number of new churches), and political, and had sometimes led to war and genocide. It was felt that in handling this issue, the theme of reconciliation would be more positive and productive.
*   *Gospel and culture*: Both Reformed churches and AICs are struggling to define their identity as Christians in Africa, both in relation to "culture" narrowly defined, and also in relation to the global and socio-political contexts in which our churches are set, and to which we are called to proclaim the gospel.
*   *Women:* The role of women in the church and church ministries is of great concern to both families of churches.

It was decided that the process could best be focused and guided under the overall theme of Christianity in the African context, and then broken down into three sub-headings, each of which would form the focus for a dialogue meeting:

- African Christian identity;
- reconciling identities – learning from and challenging each other;
- towards our common witness.

## 5. The nature of the process

Given the lack of formally articulated and published theologies among the AICs, the following tasks emerged as necessary if the dialogue was to succeed:

- Participants were challenged to develop a dialogue process concentrating initially on building trust, relationships and mutual respect as the necessary prerequisites for eliciting AIC and Reformed perceptions and accounts of their practices and beliefs.
- Participants were faced with bridging the gap between formal presentations of theology (a Reformed strength) and receiving testimony of first-hand experiences of faith, worship and life (the chief theological resource of the AICs).
- Participants uncovered the shared African roots of much grassroots Christian faith and practice among both Reformed and AIC participants, and were challenged to value these sources for theologizing appropriately, but not uncritically.

## 6. African Christian identity – Kigali, Rwanda, 13-19 October 1999

During the first meeting in Kigali, during which we were hosted by the Presbyterian Church of Rwanda, agreement on the practical challenges the African church faces formed the most significant part of our search for a common African Christian identity. AIC and Reformed participants reached substantial agreement on the crisis facing the African continent and its people, and the way in which the church was called to respond. As a prelude to this, a simple agreement was reached on our common faith.

## 7. Reconciling identities – Lagos, Nigeria, 4-7 March 2001

(Participants were hosted by the Eternal Sacred Order of the Cherubim and Seraphim, and by its sister churches in OAIC Nigeria. In this meeting, participants sought to address themselves to the two issues of the place and ministry of the Holy Spirit, and the role of education – both secular and theological – in the two families of churches. These were approached from the standpoint of the theme of the meeting, reconciling identities, which formed the subject of the two introductory papers from both families.)

The summary of the Lagos meeting appears in the following document:

### Lagos communiqué

*Addressing our common problems*

We, the representatives of two Christian families, the World Alliance of Reformed Churches (WARC) and the Organization of African Instituted Churches (OAIC), have met together in Lagos, Nigeria, as the guests of OAIC Nigeria. Our theme has been

"Reconciling Identities: Learning from and Challenging Each Other" (the prophetic role of the church, the free movement of the Holy Spirit).

We have heard from our Nigerian hosts the challenges they face as Christians as sharia law is enforced in certain states in this country, and we affirm a common desire to work towards relations with our Muslim brothers and sisters that will permit the full practice of both faiths. In this connection, we are agreed that killing people in the name of God is foreign to African tradition and can never be justified.

Building on our previous meetings in Nairobi, Kenya, in 1998, and Kigali, Rwanda, in 1999, we celebrate our continuing growth towards mutual understanding and unity in the Christian faith, and our common desire to address the continuing crisis on our continent. In this connection, we affirm the Kigali statement of 1999 as presenting an analysis that continues to be relevant of the problems and challenges facing Africa. We commend it again to our member churches, together with its recommendations for action. We note with regret the lack of response to the statement, and commit ourselves to ensure its wider circulation among our respective constituencies.

*Moving towards reconciliation of our identities*

In this meeting in Lagos we have further identified beliefs and standpoints that we share in common:

Both our families are committed to practising the Christian faith in its trinitarian fullness, although with different emphases.

Our continent has a profound spirituality and a belief in mysticism that is deeply rooted in our traditional cultures, and we share a commitment to developing and practising a Christian faith that addresses these spiritual realities. We acknowledge the long experience of the African Instituted churches (AICs), and the increasing involvement of the Reformed churches, in this ministry. In the difficult matter of discerning the spirits, we affirm two principles common to our families: that we test the spirits against the word of scripture, and that we do so in the context of the praying community (the local and universal church).

Our families show a common concern for providing appropriate education at all levels and for all members of our churches, an education that must have its roots in African culture and values. With regard to training our ministers and others who serve the church, we recognize the importance of:

– providing theological education in an ecumenical context;
– providing a theological education that will enable our ministers and workers to engage with social issues of the day, for example, with issues of governance and HIV/AIDS.

To this end, we commit ourselves to sharing resources, financial, intellectual and spiritual.

We celebrate the diversity of our peoples as God-given, and we recognize the right of every person to self-respect and human dignity. For this reason we affirm again the necessity of encouraging full participation in decision-making in church and society as we seek to empower our peoples to address the crises that surround them on this continent. As we engage with the fullness of African diversity, we do so from an understanding of our identity as open and inclusive. We draw from the model of the incarnation a willingness to take risks in order to achieve a new identity character-ized by integration and the harmonization of differences. It is in this spirit that we are committed to our continuing dialogue. As we move towards unity in the church we seek the unity of humankind.

*Moving ahead*: We have agreed to meet again for the final consultation of this pres-ent dialogue in Nairobi in 2002, in order to decide concrete steps that we can take together as part of our common witness on this continent. As a preliminary step we will address the gaps in our conversations (e.g., the interpretation of the Bible, the role of the sacraments, and the ministry of women).

Signed:

Rev. Dr André Karamaga
Vice President WARC
Co-chair of the dialogue

Rev. Dr Setri Nyomi
General secretary-WARC

Lagos, Nigeria, 7 March 2001

His Eminence Baba Aladura Dr
G.I.M. Outbu
International Chairman of OAIC
Co-chair of the dialogue

Most Rev. Njeru Wambugu
General secretary-OAIC

## 8. The testimony of Nairobi, 2002: Moving towards common witness

(The third meeting was held in Nairobi, and participants were hosted by the Presbyter-ian Church of East Africa. Members of the dialogue worshipped in churches of both families.)

*Hermeneutics*

We are agreed in both our families that scripture is central to the life and work of the church. The scriptures can only be properly interpreted within the hermeneutic commu-nity, which is not just local or oral, but denominational, ecumenical and global. AICs have particularly emphasized hermeneutical dialogue with the local community of the faithful, in which the congregation responds to the preachers with hymns and interjec-tions which strengthen the preacher and push the argument a stage further. Indeed, both Reformed and AIC traditions emphasize the importance of music and hymns in the hermeneutic process. The Reformed hermeneutic in addition has particularly emphasized the global and intergenerational community of biblical commentaries, and written theologies.

We recognize and celebrate certain especially African emphases in the hermeneutic process. Among these are a commitment to oral tradition and an interpretation which builds on and relates to the shared stories, proverbs, and memories of the community; an emphasis on God's word to the community rather than just to the individual; an understanding that all in life is sacred (with no division between sacred and secular); and a deep reliance on the role of and assistance from the Holy Spirit. Both families of churches agree that our hermeneutic must address itself both to the local situation and, at the same time, be aware of and be responsible to the global hermeneutic community. A closed hermeneutic community cannot in the long run remain faithful to the gospel.

*Sacraments*

We agree that the sacraments of baptism and the eucharist are grounded in scripture and are commended to the church for its spiritual growth. Baptism signifies the entrance of the believer into the community of faith, and his/her engrafting into the body of Christ. In communion, the faithful are fed with Christ himself. The experience of receiving Christ in the sacraments is made possible by the powerful and mysterious action of the Holy Spirit.

Some of the AICs have affirmed as many as seven sacraments: baptism, chrismation (confirmation), eucharist, marriage, confession, ordination and holy unction (anointing of the sick). Other AICs are non-sacramental in tradition, although they would say that they celebrate the sacraments spiritually. Some of them believe that, as the bread and wine are set aside as food for God's people, so God's holy people are themselves set aside as God's sacrament and gift to the world.

*The role of women in the church*

Both communities acknowledge and celebrate the gifts of the Holy Spirit to both women and men. We acknowledge that for cultural and historical reasons, women have not been allowed to develop and share these gifts adequately in the service of the wider Christian community. In many parts of Africa issues of purity and impurity deeply influence and limit the role of women in the church. This affects both the Reformed and the African Independent church families. Also, structural inequalities within the church often limit women's ministries. Sometimes these inequalities are seen in segregated and subordinate structures, often mistakenly called "parallel structures", of women's ministries or women's departments. Although these women's ministries and departments can and do play a significant role in the lives of women and men, and can help in raising their awareness, we are agreed that women must not be limited to these ministries. The church must remove restrictions on the ministries of women, and the lack of women's participation in the higher decision-making structures. It must find ways of dealing with its procedures (such as holding meetings only in the evenings), which effectively prevent women from playing a full role. It must also seek to understand, to challenge, and to motivate communities and congregations to change those of their traditions and perceptions which prevent them from welcoming an integrated model of equal partnership in ministry of women and men.

## 9. The way forward

We recognize that some of the AICs separated historically from member churches of the WARC, in a process of polarization in which the positions of the two sides became deeply entrenched. We acknowledge that ill-feelings and bitterness continue to exist between some of our members to the present day. We recommend that in the countries where this is the case leaders of the churches concerned meet to discuss the reconciliation of memories, and to consider how best to come together again in mutual repentance, in order to strengthen our common witness to the one Christ. In other situations, although bitter historical memories may not be present, prejudice and the lack of a spirit of common fellowship in the ministry may be present. Sometimes this prejudice is characterized by attitudes of rejection of the other based on false conceptions such as "lacking education", "backward", "lacking the Holy Spirit", "colonial churches". We commit ourselves to working much more strongly for mutual understanding and ecumenism, and we urge the leaders of the churches in our respective communities to work and act together to remove the misconceptions and prejudice, to build trust and share fully in joint Christian witness. In the crises that affect our continent, for the survival of our own people, we cannot afford disunity.

We recognize the dangers of training AIC students at colleges of the other Christian world communions and denominations, because they can easily be lost from the AICs to the denomination of the college. In this context, there is a need to explore how Reformed church theological institutions can be used for the training of AIC students, and how these institutions can be made more hospitable to AIC students, in order to build them up in their ministry in their own churches rather than purely in the context of the Reformed ministry. In this context, also, we consider that, initially, support should be given to the OAIC theological education by extension programme, and its attempts to revise its curriculum, and to obtain proper academic accreditation for its courses. In association with the Conference of African Theological Institutions (CATI), the Reformed churches in Africa, should consider encouraging some of their lecturers to cooperate in the process. Further, and as a long-term goal, we recognize the need for an increased number of further degree-level theological institutions run by and for AICs.

As a dialogue, we endorse the aspirations of the AIC community to come up with their own written theological material. We consider that an appropriate first step would be for AIC theologians to discuss the theological issues and logistics required in a continental-level workshop, and we commit ourselves in our various capacities to exploring how this can be made possible.

In view of the great measure of progress we have achieved in this dialogue at the international level, we urge our member churches over the next three years to engage in a process of dialogue between our two families at national levels. We will collect and record the progress made, and report back to our respective organizations, with the possibility of resuming the dialogue at international level at another date.

# 34. Conversations around the World

## International Conversations between the Anglican Communion and the Baptist World Alliance

### McClean, Virginia, USA, 2000-2005

### 1. Introduction: a new way of talking together

When two worldwide Christian communions are given the opportunity, and the responsibility, of spending five years in talking together in meetings on an international level, then a historic moment has been reached. Between 2000 and 2005, the Anglican Communion and the Baptist World Alliance have engaged in officially authorized "international conversations". Unlike other ecumenical conversations, the purpose of these has not been to work towards any scheme for structural unity; neither of the two commissioning bodies had this in mind, and nor did their member churches. But this has still been a deeply serious – as well as joyous – enterprise. The intention has been to deepen mutual understanding, in personal and theological terms, and by this means to lay the ground for more effective ways for Baptists and Anglicans around the globe to confess their faith together and to share together in the mission of God. Theology, life and action have always been linked in the discussions of the participants. This has been a purpose in which it has been worth investing time, travel, and hard and sometimes painful thinking.

To flesh out this intention, an initial meeting between staff of the two communions in McLean, Virginia, in March 2000 set out the following objectives for the international conversations:

1) to enable Anglicans and Baptists to learn from each other and to deepen understanding of relationships between our two communions in the light of their histories;

2) to share with each other how we understand the Christian faith and to work towards a common confession of the apostolic faith;

3) to identify issues of doctrine and the nature of the church to be explored further in possible future conversations;

4) to look for ways to cooperate in mission and community activities, and to increase our fellowship and common witness to the gospel.

While not being formal conversations on the way to visible unity, these conversations have thus broken through some usual ecumenical patterns in being more than "getting to know you" exercises. This has been possible because there are already practical partnerships in worship and mission between Baptists and Anglicans in many parts of the world, a situation to which the stories told later in this report amply bear witness.

Following an invitation received from a Baptist World Alliance general council meeting, the Lambeth Conference of 1988 first mandated for Anglicans a dialogue between the Anglican Communion and the Baptist World Alliance. Through the next decade the leadership of the Baptist World Alliance continued to ask that the resolution be acted upon, and in response the Lambeth conference in 1998 passed the following resolution IV.15:

> This conference recommends as a priority the implementation of resolution 10(3) of Lambeth 1988, by developing, in partnership with the Baptist World Alliance, coordinated regional and local discussions leading to the establishment of a continuing forum between Anglicans and Baptists at the world level. [1]

It was part of the objectives proposed in 2000 to "identify" doctrinal and ecclesiological issues, aiming for eventual elucidation of key theological areas "in possible future conversations". From the Anglican side at least, as expressed in the recommendation of the Lambeth conference for a "continuing forum", it was assumed that these conversations might be the first of two or more further rounds. Perhaps it seemed that not much could be expected in terms of theological conclusions at the end of the first quinquennium. While the present report is certainly not meant to be a definitive doctrinal document for either of the communions, the account of the conversations does in fact represent in some detail the theological positions of Anglicans and Baptists on many issues at the turn of the millennium – an important historic moment that represents a milestone of sorts in the ongoing story of Christianity in the modern world. Those participating in the conversations in different regions of the world clearly wanted, for their part, to make a careful exploration of the major theological issues confronting their two denominations. Without exceeding the remit given to them, the staff of the two communions and the co-chairmen felt it was appropriate to refer to the discussions not just as an "international forum" but as "international conversations".

Responding to this, the report offers not only a description of the views offered, no mere record of the conversations, but some theological reflection upon central themes. The report attempts to make some serious comment on points of sameness and divergence in areas of faith and life, and perhaps more progress has been achieved than was at first anticipated. The core committee responsible for the report has thus come to feel, through this experience, that the best way forward at this stage in Anglican-Baptist relations is not to move into further rounds of talks in the immediate future, but rather for a period to invite response to what has come to light through these conversations. We hope that this report will be received and widely read among the theologians and churches in the various regions of the world which have shaped it, and that their responses will lay the foundation for any future conversations that it might seem right to hold. We believe that this fulfils the recommendation of Lambeth to establish a "continuing forum", in a way that reflects the diversity and the distribution of both our communions.

This hope relates to another aspect of the conversations that we feel has "broken the mould" of ecumenical processes. Conversations between Christian churches usually take the form of appointing a fairly large representative group of participants who all meet together on a number of occasions; they might travel to different locations in the world to deal in turn with selected issues, and might well take the opportunity in doing so of taking soundings from the local communities. The officers of the Anglican Communion and the Baptist World Alliance, however, decided early on to make a much more thorough-going attempt at contextualizing the conversations in different cultures. The majority of the participants in the conversations would be appointed from churches in each of the six regions where the meetings were being held, while a small "continuation committee" would attend all the meetings, facilitate the discussion and be responsible for the final drafting of the report. This committee has consisted of only three members from each communion, together with a staff member from the Baptist World Alliance and the Anglican Communion. Each regional meeting has included up to twelve representatives from the locality, about half Anglican and Baptist.

This method has allowed church leaders, theologians and church historians from each region to be engaged in the process, and to bring their own context and experience to bear on the subjects being discussed. The eight themes into which the report has been divided have themselves emerged from the regional meetings, with some being proposed from the first meeting, and others being added along the way through a kind of "rolling report". Each regional group was informed of the deliberations of previous ones, but it was made clear that no fixed agenda was being imposed from the rounds that had already been held, so that new concerns and insights were genuinely able to emerge from each new context. In this way, voices have been listened to in turn from Europe (in Norwich, UK), Asia (in Yangon, Myanmar/Burma), Africa (in Nairobi, Kenya), the Southern Cone (in Santiago, Chile), the Caribbean (in Nassau, Bahamas) and North America (in Wolfville, Nova Scotia, Canada). The draft final report was then sent out to all participants from the different regions, for general comment and for specific assurance that they had been properly heard. We are truly grateful for the commitment and contribution of all those who have shared in this process. [*Growth in Agreement III* does not reproduce these regional stories in this reprint of the report.]

The members of the continuation committee, Anglicans and Baptists, are unanimous that this different way of handling ecumenical conversations has enriched the discussions. It has meant that each theological issue addressed can be understood from the vantage point of the whole international family of both communions. It has enabled far more people to be directly involved in the venture, has provided the opportunity for a greater diversity of representation than would normally be possible, and should mean that the reception of the report will be more widespread because more people have an interest in promoting the results of discussions in which they have been involved. Moreover, each meeting has seemed spontaneously to encourage a unique fellowship between the representatives of each communion in a way that might not always have been anticipated. There have been new opportunities for Anglicans and Baptists to worship together, and also to share in the Lord's supper. This truly heartening aspect of the process has, then, been more than just social courteousness. It indicates on its own a positive future for ways in which the two communions might anticipate further labours together for the sake of the salvation of the world which is the Lord's.

As co-chairmen, we believe we should offer a brief word of explanation about why the report does not refer to two recent events which have had a large impact on each of the communions in which they have happened. The continuation committee, towards the end of its work, was aware of the disruption that had been caused within the unity of the Anglican Communion by the consecration of an Episcopalian bishop in New Hampshire, USA, who lives in a committed homosexual relationship. At the same time, it was aware of the proposal from the largest Baptist convention in the world, the Southern Baptist Convention, to relinquish its membership in the Baptist World Alliance. The continuation committee felt that it should not address either issue in the final report for a number of reasons. First, both issues arose right at the end of the conversations in the regions (which were concluded in 2003), and there had been no opportunity for them to be discussed in any of the regional meetings. Given the method of this report as described above, it would have been contrary to the whole process of reflecting on church life in context for the continuation committee to have introduced a new topic altogether, for which they had no mandate from the regional groups with which they had been working. Second, with regard to the ordination of the Episcopalian bishop, the continuation committee noted that the reaction from provinces within the Anglican Communion made clear that this was a highly contested and local matter, and could not be regarded as reflecting the agreed teaching, doctrine or attitude of the family of Anglican churches throughout the world. It therefore did not affect the issues actually dealt with in the report, which arose out of four hundred years of history together, and the theological and practical interactions between Anglicans and Baptists during that period. Neither would it have been useful, in the task of mutual understanding, to have debated the reasons why Southern Baptists had withdrawn from the world fellowship of Baptists. Third, it was thought inappropriate in a report of this kind for one world communion to make pronouncements on the internal affairs of the other, when the issues are not those which lie between Anglicans and Baptists, but are issues being dealt with by the respective communions themselves.

Reports often carry recommendations. The continuation committee felt that the nature of these "international conversations", breaking the usual patterns, meant that recommendations to the two commissioning bodies would not be in place. However, the members of the committee felt that deep challenges had emerged for both communions that needed to be faced for the sake of the gospel. On the one hand, the report of the conversations shows how close – sometimes surprisingly close – the two communions are to each other in fundamental theological issues, and how great the potential is for further partnership in practical projects in the post-colonial, post-modern (and in the West, post-Christian) world in which we all live. While differences remain, especially on the issues of baptism and episcopacy, it can be seen from the report that the participants in the conversations regarded these not as hopeless barriers of division, but as signs of Christian devotion and faithfulness which were rooted in the experiences of history and which had been properly kept alive in the hearts of believers through the generations. On the other hand, if we are, as the objectives express it, to "look for ways to cooperate in mission and community activities, and to increase our fellowship and common witness to the gospel", then we need to look for even greater convergences in doctrine and practice. The questions which have been attached to the report in place of recommendations are intended to help both our communions to do this. The continuation committee has some confidence that these questions will be taken no less seriously than formal recommendations, and it is on this note of lively hope that it ends its task.

Paul S. Fiddes, Co-chairman (Baptist)     Bruce Matthews, Co-chairman (Anglican)

# PART ONE: THE REPORT

## 2. The two world communions

THE ANGLICAN COMMUNION

The Anglican Communion is the name adopted by a family of some 44 churches[2] across the globe. These are comprised of 34 "provinces" (national or regional churches), four "united churches", and six "extra-provincial jurisdictions".

The communion traces its origins back to the original Christian churches of the British Isles; these were founded in the 2nd or 3rd centuries by unknown missionaries to the Celtic peoples, and also in the 7th century amongst the Saxon peoples by the mission from Pope Gregory headed by St Augustine of Canterbury.

At the time of the Reformation, these churches renounced the jurisdiction of the bishop of Rome in order to undertake a process of reform in life and doctrine, aided initially by a king of England who had his own reasons for such a breach. The attempt to impose a new doctrinal and ecclesial unity on the peoples of Britain and Ireland failed in the course of the 17th century, leading to the establishment of a Presbyterian Church of Scotland and limited freedoms of dissent in the other kingdoms of the British Isles; it was within this framework that Baptist, Congregationalist and English and Welsh Presbyterian churches emerged. The Church of England remained the majority church in England and Wales, together with a separate Anglican Church of Ireland,[3] and a Scottish Episcopal Church. The essential character of these churches lay, as expressed in the motto which the Scottish Episcopal Church has retained to this day, in the assertion of "evangelical truth and apostolic order".

For many years Anglican and Baptists co-existed, and increasing British exploration, colonization and merchant activity provided the opportunity for Anglican and Baptist missions to carry the Christian gospel to every continent, although Anglican churches abroad effectively operated as overseas branches of the Church of England.

The first big crisis in the external ordering of Anglican life came with the American Revolution when, faced with intransigence and constitutional difficulties in England, American Anglicans resorted to the Scottish Episcopal Church to provide them with an independent episcopate. The 18th and 19th centuries saw the developing "naturalization" of Anglicanism in different societies across the globe, together with a renewal and rediscovery of, in turn, both its evangelical and catholic spirituality.

In the course of the 19th century, disputes in South Africa about biblical criticism and the nature of authority led in 1867 to the creation of the *Lambeth Conference* as a means by which Anglican bishops across the globe could consult with one another on matters of import affecting the whole; another impulse was the realization that new ways must be found to express the global nature of Anglicanism. In parallel with a process of decolonization in the British empire, a recognition of the autonomy of Anglican churches operating in "the dominions", and eventually other former colonies, led to the creation of separate *provinces of the Anglican Communion*. The phrase "communion" was adopted to mark the essentially spiritual nature of the bond which holds the churches together, but one which implies a unity of doctrine and discipline which is centred historically on the Thirty-Nine Articles of 1571 and the 1662 *Book of Common Prayer* and the accompanying ordinal.

The 20th century saw the growth of the communion, not only in organization but also in successful mission. In 1900, there were estimated, by the standards of the time, to be 31 million Anglicans; by 1968, this had become 59 million. Today it is estimated that there may be around 78 million Anglicans, although it is difficult to ascertain numbers with exactitude in situations of huge mission activity and there is the added difficulty of determining a universally agreed statistical basis. A core of thirteen provinces in 1930 had grown into 31 provinces and autonomous churches by 1978; growth has continued to the numbers of the present day. Provinces vary in size between large African churches with 15-18 million members through to smaller churches ("extra-provincial jurisdictions", which do not sustain a provincial structure) of between five to ten thousand.

The last century also saw the growth of diversity in Anglican theology and practice, but the communion has remained defined largely by geography (national or regional churches) rather than by theological bias. This diversity has led to increasing tensions, so that the communion has generated "instruments of unity" to stand beside the archbishop of Canterbury as the communion's focal points; these instruments are the Lambeth Conference (established 1867), the Anglican Consultative Council (established 1968) and the primates meetings (established 1978). Other churches have been adopted into the communion, in Iberia and in South Asia. In the latter region much of Anglicanism has blended with Protestant denominations to form "United churches", which have retained episcopal government, and which are fully members of the Anglican Communion.

As the Anglican Communion enters the 21st century, it continues to grow. It has been said that the average Anglican is "black, female, married with three children and under the age of thirty". But the challenge of diversity grows as well. Theologically, the communion is highly diverse, and has learned in recent years to become truly global. One church has become 44, and very recent tensions concerning sexual ethics have threatened to divide its historic unity. However, there remains a distinctive witness to a Christianity at once both evangelical and catholic, conservative and liberal, in which different traditions can find an almost contradictory expression within a single fellowship.

## THE BAPTIST WORLD ALLIANCE

Baptists are a missionary people. Since their beginnings 400 years ago, they have spread the good news of Jesus Christ throughout the world, together with their particular way of living out the Christian faith. Baptists brought significant leadership to the modern missionary movement, especially through the pioneering work of William Carey in India, Adoniram Judson in Myanmar, George Lisle in Jamaica, Johann Gerhard Oncken in continental Europe, Alfred Saker in Cameroon, William Buck Bagby in Brazil and George Grenfell in the Democratic Republic of Congo. Today Baptists are strongly represented in the United States, India, Nigeria, Democratic Republic of Congo, Brazil, Korea, Myanmar, Tanzania and Kenya. Indeed, very few countries can be found that do not have Baptist churches and people. Many Baptist unions and conventions that have been recipients of cross-cultural missionaries, generally from the Western world, are today sending out their own committed disciples to engage in cross-cultural service.

Some Baptists trace their earliest origins, at least indirectly, to the 16th-century Anabaptists in Switzerland, Germany, Austria and Holland. However, the more common view

among Baptist historians is that "general Baptists" arose out of English Puritan Separatists, when John Smyth formed a church practising believers' baptism out of a
congregation of English exiles in Amsterdam in 1609; a portion of this church, with
Thomas Helwys as its minister, returned to England forming the first Baptist congregation on English soil in Spitalsfield, London, in 1611. The "Particular Baptists" emerged
somewhat later, in about 1630, from Calvinistic independent groups in England.

From those troubled and humble beginnings in England, Baptists have grown to become
a major Protestant denomination that worships and serves God through Jesus Christ
around the world. Baptists affirm and adhere to the apostolic Christian faith including
such doctrines as the Trinity and the deity and humanity of Jesus Christ. At the same
time, guided as they believe by the Spirit of God in obedience to the word of God, Baptists are strongly committed to a church membership consisting of those who can profess faith for themselves, believers' baptism (normally by immersion), congregational
polity and religious liberty for all human beings.

In 1905, Baptists from the United Kingdom and North America were instrumental in
bringing into being a world fellowship of Baptist believers to which they gave the name
"Baptist World Alliance" (BWA). The initial meeting was held in London and representatives of 23 nations attended.

One hundred years later, the membership of the BWA has grown to the extent that the
statistical report at the end of 2004 (after the withdrawal of the Southern Baptist Convention in the USA) showed that there were about 31.5 million baptized believers in over
140,000 congregations around the globe. As these statistics refer only to people who have
been baptized as believers and received into church membership, and not the children of
Baptists, nor the many loyal attendees of Baptist congregations who for various reasons
elect not to be baptized, the family of Baptists related to the BWA is assumed to be at
least 80 million strong.

The evolution of the BWA from a body formed by European and North American Baptists to a world body that is truly representative of all its people can be seen in a number
of ways. For example, the present and former presidents of the BWA are from Asia
(Korea) and from Latin America (Brazil), respectively. Its sixteen vice-presidents are
drawn from all over the world and its executive staff comprises nationals of the United
States, Australia, England, Trinidad and Liberia. Each of the six regions of the BWA has
a regional secretary appointed by and from within the region. The BWA offices are
located in Falls Church, Virginia, USA, and the general secretary/treasurer is the executive officer of the BWA.

The BWA is the body that, in various ways represents Baptists internationally. It seeks
to address human needs through the division of Baptist world aid, to address issues of
justice and human rights, religious freedom and racism through the office of the BWA
general secretary, and to encourage Baptists in their ministries of mission, evangelism
and discipleship through the division of education and evangelism. Various Baptist leaders are well-known outside their own denomination for their global contributions: recent
examples include Dr Martin Luther King Jr, Dr Billy Graham and President Jimmy
Carter.

The BWA convenes international conferences on theological education, mission strategy, and worship and spirituality. It is uniquely positioned to provide opportunities for
fellowship among its member bodies and their people. Every five years it calls together

ordained ministers and other congregational leaders and church members from all its member bodies for a great international gathering featuring worship, instruction, sharing and fellowship. More recent congresses have been convened in Buenos Aires (1995) and Melbourne (2000) and the centenary congress is scheduled for July 2005 in Birmingham, UK.

As a further expression of its desire for Christian fellowship and to obey the prayer of Jesus for the unity or oneness of his disciples, as well as to clarify differences, the BWA has, during the last quarter-century, entered into international theological conversations with other world Christian communions. These have included the World Alliance of Reformed Churches, the Lutheran World Federation, the Roman Catholic Council for Promoting Christian Unity and the Mennonite World Conference. There have been "pre-conversations" with the holy synod of the Ecumenical Patriarchate in Istanbul. All these have been a prelude to the important international conversations that have taken place with the Anglican Communion between 2000 and 2005.

## 3. Themes of the conversations

INTRODUCTION

1. The content of this account has been shaped by the objectives which motivated the conversations, and by the method which has been employed in holding them. The dominant mood of the account is thus descriptive, with the aim of increasing mutual understanding between Baptists and Anglicans. A major aim is to map the way that Baptists and Anglicans relate and work together at present throughout the world. Against this background, it is hoped to clarify convergences and divergences between the two world communions, to identify the convictions that are held in common and to face openly the differences that remain. Since the conversations have been held in six regional phases – Europe (Norwich, UK), Asia (Yangon, Myanmar/Burma), Africa (Nairobi, Kenya), the Southern Cone (Santiago, Chile), the Caribbean (Nassau, the Bahamas) and North America (Wolfville, Novia Scotia, Canada) – the report appeals to the evidence produced from the regional groups on each topic under review, making reference both to written papers and to the oral contribution of participants in the round-table discussions. In this way, the reader of the report may gain a glimpse of the shape which is taken by Christian faith and life in different parts of the world today, as well as in different expressions of the Christian church. However, the content has not been *arranged* in a regional or geographical way. Themes which have emerged from the conversations have been chosen as the structure for the material, and this in turn has allowed for theological reflection throughout the account.

2. This element of theological reflection means that this account is more than descriptive. From time to time suggestions are made about ways in which further agreement might be possible between the two communions, though these suggestions are not presented formally as proposals. In a later part of the report, moreover, each section of this account is supplemented by questions addressed to Anglicans or Baptists, or to both. The continuation committee which has been responsible for the compiling of the report hopes that these questions will provoke reaction and further thought.

THE IMPORTANCE OF CONTINUITY: OR, WHAT IS THE STORY OF THE CHURCH
IN WHICH WE LIVE?

*Continuity in the English church*

3. As Anglicans and Baptists met, they found that the natural place to begin was not with
a comparison of beliefs and views, but with a telling of the story of their life over the
years as Christian churches. This was not just anecdotal, but theological. How had they
been a continuing manifestation of the people of God over the generations? How were
they an enduring part of the body of Christ in space and time? In the European phase,
meeting on the site of the medieval cathedral in Norwich and sharing in its worship, the
Anglican sense of continuity with the earlier church in the Western world was strong. As
one participant (from the evangelical wing of the Church of England) put it, "The Church
of England is the Catholic Church in this country… it is simply the ongoing tradition of
the Christian faith, having undergone some pruning and reappropriation of apostolicity
thanks to the Reformers."[4] As another Anglican contributor put it, "The Church of England is… the national church of the English people… what happened in the 16th century
was not the initiation of a new church, but precisely the reformation of an existing one."[5]
Anglicans trace this continuity with the earlier church through liturgy, spirituality, creeds
and ministry. The last element takes the form of the "historic episcopate", which in current understanding should not, however, be simply equated with "apostolic succession".
There is now widespread agreement between Christian churches that succession from
the apostles belongs to the whole community which lives by the faith of the gospel. A
succession of ordination through a historic line of bishops offers, for Anglicans, a God-
given *sign* of standing in continuity with the apostolic Tradition, even if this is not
regarded as a literally unbroken chain.

4. Mindful of its continuity with the earlier English church, the Church of England (as
the first participant quoted above observed), "has tried hard not to be a denomination,
[but rather] to exist as the church of the people of England for the people of England".
This is an attractive portrayal of a church that simply wants to serve the people, and it is
offered with an intention of humility. It does, however, produce some problems for those
who are not Anglicans, and especially for Baptists who are also children of the European
Reformation. It was pointed out at Norwich that English Baptists affirm that they are,
like the Church of England, part of the one, holy, catholic [i.e. universal] and apostolic
church which has experienced some "pruning" and reforming. In their beginnings as
Separatists in the early years of the 17th century they believed that they were stepping
into the continuity of covenant partnership between God and his church in England, and
since then they have understood themselves to have been serving English society as an
alternative stream of faith and witness alongside that of the church established by law.
They too try to be churches "for the people of England". Even if Baptists are regarded
by Anglicans as lacking an important *sign* of continuity in not having a "historic episcopate", it should not be forgotten that a kind of continuity nevertheless exists.

*Continuity through the English church*

5. So far this seems, however, to be a very English debate and a very English story. What
happens when it is transferred onto the world stage? What happens to the issue of con-

tinuity when the context is that of the Baptist World Alliance and the Anglican Communion worldwide, with all their diverse participants and different cultures? The meeting in Myanmar (Burma) provided one opportunity for testing this out, from the perspective of Asian Christianity. The presentation of the representatives from the Anglican Church of the Province of Myanmar began:

> We Anglicans in Myanmar trace our root back to the early church of the apostolic age… we also trace our identity to the reformation of the Church of England… up to the time of reformation the Church in England existed as part of the Western church union under the pope of Rome.[6]

This is, on the face of it, a story held in common with the Church of England. That is, Myanmar Anglicans trace their heritage as being that of the earliest church, developing into the Catholic Church in the West, and then being reformed and continuing in the form of the Church of England. A little later in their document, the Myanmar Anglicans explain that they regard the reformed Western church as having continued in three streams – "the *Lutheran* in Germany and Scandinavia, the *Calvinists* in Switzerland, Scotland and Holland, and *Anglican* in England".[7] Because of the colonial role of Great Britain and associated missionary activity, they stand in the third stream. They are indebted, through the circumstances of history, to the Church of England for providing them with a form of "Reformed Catholicism", so that they can stand in the heritage of the one catholic or universal church which has passed through the purging fires of reformation. A paper by an Anglican representative from the Province of Hong Kong Sheng Kung Hui showed an even stronger view of continuity with the Western church as mediated through British life, beginning thus:

> The Anglican Communion originated from early centuries when Celtic Christians began their work in England, Scotland, Ireland and Wales…[8]

Similarly, Anglican participants in the Latin American conversations traced their heritage back to the earliest centuries of Christian life in England, regarding the Anglican Church as "historic, reformed and biblical"; they affirmed their identity as "Catholic and Protestant", taking their part in a story which began long before the Reformation in England, but which is still indebted to renewal at the time of the Reformation.[9]

*Continuity with the New Testament church*

6.  What of Baptists in the world outside Britain? For them, the "English question" seems much less relevant. Some Baptists in Europe will want to point out that there are not just *three* streams of the reformed Western church as identified above – there is a fourth stream of the continuing catholic church, that of Christian communities which experienced a more "radical reformation", separating the church from the civil power, stressing the covenant privileges of the local congregation, gathered under the rule of Christ, and abandoning the existing system of oversight through bishops. Churches which still survive in this stream of Christianity carry names such as Mennonite, Baptist and Congregationalist. But many (perhaps most) Baptists beyond Europe have little interest in recalling this kind of story. This is partly because some of them trace their immediate origins to missionary work from the United States at a later period. But more signifi-

cantly, they believe themselves to stand in continuity with the apostolic Tradition on the grounds that the form of their congregational life *directly* reflects the situation of the earliest church, without worrying about the intervening years. The representatives of the Myanmar Baptists, for instance, presented their "Baptist heritage" by speaking of Baptist beliefs which are rooted in the Bible, especially the baptism of believers, and which express "what it mean to live biblically as one in Jesus Christ in spite of our ethnic consciousness". [10] A Baptist contributor in the North American round similarly noted the sense among Baptists that they have a "continuity in the gospel with the churches of the apostles"; for Baptists it is when they "are faithful to gospel imperatives and primitive church order" that they feel they are maintaining continuity with the church that has gone before them. [11]

*Other kinds of continuity in community*

7. There are, however, modes of continuity among Baptists which come close to the regard for the role of tradition in Anglicanism. Baptists in Europe, for example, will certainly think in the first place of a life which is continuous with that of the earliest communities as reflected in the pages of the New Testament; but many also have an interest in the heritage of a particular congregation, as recorded in its church minute book, and in stories of individual heroes of faith from the past. There is an urgent need to establish this latter tradition in some parts of Eastern Europe today, such as Russia, Bulgaria and Georgia, where Baptist faith is perceived by some as being associated with recently imported "foreign cults", and Baptists may be accused of not being true citizens of their country; here it is important to show that Baptist life is truly part of the culture of the society. There is also a form of continuity through organizations and institutions, especially in Britain and North America; voluntary societies for mission, education, Bible publishing and social reforms provide a continuing identity through the years with which congregations will align themselves. Particularly evident in the North American experience is "a subtle form of continuity through identification with a particular theological college or seminary". [12]

8. It seems important to Baptists outside Britain to recall the long tradition among Baptists of striving for religious liberty and freedom of conscience generally, a struggle which began in England at the beginning of the 17th century. [13] One Baptist participant in the Latin American round of conversations, from Brazil, affirmed that "we defend the identity which makes us know whence we came, who we are and where we go", [14] locating the beginning of this path in the English Reformation and in English Puritanism. But the period of the church's story between the New Testament and the Reformation seems to be of less interest to Baptists. One exception is in the rare places where Baptists now subscribe to so-called "Landmarkism" or "Successionism", which postulates an unbroken succession (a "kingdom") of local congregations of a Baptist type since the first century. Once a highly influential theory among Southern Baptists in the USA, this has now largely lost its fascination. But owing to the influence of the first Southern Baptist missionaries to Brazil the theory is still prevalent in that country, and though rejected by most Baptist scholars there, as elsewhere, [15] it has had an inhibiting and even disastrous effect on interchurch cooperation.

*A twofold continuity*

9. In short, both Baptists and Anglicans have a twofold sense of continuity – directly with the church of the New Testament (scripture), and with the story of the catholic church through the ages (tradition), but the emphasis differs in the two communions. Anglicanism, with an identity marked by the threefold sources of scripture, reason and tradition certainly gives priority to scripture, and it was pointed out in the Caribbean that a hallmark of Anglican worship is the frequency with which scripture is read;[16] but the tradition of the church, together with the employment of reason within a particular culture, is explicitly allowed its place in interpretation of scripture.[17] Baptists tend to concentrate their claims to the first kind of continuity, amounting even to a sense of direct engagement in the life of the New Testament church, and to underplay the second. Baptists, however, often fail to notice how dependent they are on formulations of doctrine made in the period of the church fathers, and how they also make place for the roles of reason and experience, a phenomenon which is given further attention later in this report.

*Continuity and ancestors in the faith*

10. In the round of conversations in Kenya the double story of the church took on a new form, shaped by the African honouring of the ancestor as a still "living" member of the community. In the first place, this applies to the story of the church through the ages. There is a strong sense of connection in both communions with the former preachers and martyrs of the faith in Africa in relatively modern times, whether European missionaries, freed slaves from the USA and the Caribbean or African converts. As in other regional conversations, Anglicans tend to have a clearer sense than Baptists of the "ancestors in the faith" before the coming of either Anglican or Baptist missions to their country, but both are anxious to recall and celebrate African saints of all ages and all denominations, as a vital part of the present community of faith. Baptists in Africa thus seem to have a stronger sense of tradition than Baptists in either Europe or Asia. In the second place there is continuity with the world of the scriptures. Both communions have a vivid awareness of direct continuity with the communities of faith of ancient Israel and the earliest Christian church. The world-view of the Bible is felt to be close to the African one, and many of its presuppositions about the way that God relates to the world seem to be familiar. As one Baptist participant (from Ghana) put it, there is a "redemptive dialogue between the biblical and African world-view" and "by reading the Bible in my own mother-tongue I get affirmation of my own cultural values". The people of Israel and the early disciples are thus recognized as "ancestors" through a line of descent which is simply African. This line of ancestry is supported by the early connections between North Africa/Egypt and figures in both Jewish and Christian heritage (Moses, Tertullian, Cyprian, Augustine), but there is a direct sense of the "African" roots in the biblical story beyond actual historical connections. As an Anglican participant from Ghana expressed it, "I walk back to the Bible in two ways – through the missionaries and through traditional religion." The same participant drew attention to the work of African women theologians in reflecting creatively on the African woman's life with God in the context of African culture.[18] A Baptist participant from Zimbabwe remarked that "in the matter of continuity, we have often ignored the richness of traditional African spiritual culture. We need to understand that we are embedded in African insights."[19] Some of those pres-

ent in the conversations would like to have had opportunity to explore more thoroughly the question of which areas in traditional African culture and religion are felt to be helpful to Christian discipleship, and why. Participants from the West thought that they needed to be helped in understanding this particular Christian world-view.

11. Respect for "ancestors in the faith" accounts for the continuing sense of affection towards the missionary agencies (for example, the Church Missionary Society, the United Society for the Propagation of the Gospel, the Baptist Missionary Society and the International Mission Board of the Southern Baptist Convention) among African churches. This seems to colour the Anglican valuing of connection with Canterbury, although there is also a sense of having inherited a "sacramental" tradition of priesthood and eucharist from the Anglican position in the Reformation. But, at the same time, there is considerable criticism of the present relation between the Western mission agencies and Western churches on the one hand, and African churches on the other. For all the new language of partnership, African churches feel they are treated as the "junior partner", and that the situation will not change as long as there is economic inequality.

*Continuity in a post-colonial world*

12. The question, raised in Africa, of finding identity in the situation of post-colonialism took on an even more obvious form in the Caribbean. The Anglican view of continuity there paid due attention to inheritance from the Christian church in the West. But at least a slight distancing from the Church in England was apparent. Quoting the formula that the Province of the West Indies maintains the faith, doctrine, sacraments and discipline of the one, holy, catholic and apostolic church, "*according as* the Church of England has received the same", presentations laid stress on debt to the tradition and episcopacy of the Western church in general,[20] and to the importance of the prayer book in holding together the many strands of Anglican identity. Although one of the Anglican participants in the Latin American round of conversations had stated that "Anglicanism can no longer be defined by the Church of England", in the West Indies there was an even stronger sense of unease in being identified with what had been the established church of the oppressors in the period of slavery, as well as the church of the colonial masters for some time afterwards. One telling example given was the need today to adapt civil family law for the culture of the Caribbean, rather than simply to reproduce the received English concept of "the nuclear family" which is still reflected in the view of the family within the Anglican Province of the West Indies.[21] For all that, however, there was admitted to be a perception that to be "Anglican" is to be more "Anglicized" (and middle class) than is true among Baptists.[22] There was a readiness for Anglicans to give credit to the Baptists and other non-conformist groups for being the earliest to provide pastoral care and education to the slave population and "labouring classes", though there was also recollection of Anglican involvement in the amelioration of the conditions of the slaves from 1823 onwards.[23]

13. Pleas for a programme of contextualization in a post-colonial era came from both the Anglican and Baptist representatives, but there was a particular stress here from Baptists from Jamaica. They made the emphatic statement that such a programme is not an option for the interpreters of the gospel in the Caribbean, and that the plurality of Caribbean theologies, matching the diversity of cultures, must be marked by the theme

of liberation. [24] Contextualization, it was affirmed, involves facing up to the facts of history – including the experience of slavery and oppression – without shame. Jamaican Baptist representatives, though having generally good memories of the Baptist Missionary Society and the involvement of its missionaries in working for emancipation of slaves, refused to speak of being "influenced" by English Baptists, insisting on their own Jamaican and Caribbean identity. However, there was perceived to be a danger of "religious re-colonization" in parts of the West Indies, and especially a new dependency of Baptist churches in the Bahamas on Baptist conventions in the USA. [25] The challenge for both Anglicans and Baptists is, then, how to foster a new identity in a post-colonial situation. For Anglicans this takes the form of seeking emancipation from an unsuitable English frame of mind while remaining conscious of the English origins of their orders of ministry and liturgy, and of the position of Canterbury as the senior see within a collegiate episcopacy. Baptists are less burdened by issues of succession, but perhaps more open to the dangers of becoming dependent on a powerful and wealthy neighbour in the present. It should be added that in Latin America there were also signs of a new dependency among Anglicans, with the comment that – due to extreme poverty among the people – there would be economic reliance for at least the next half-century on the Episcopal Church of the USA.

14. Participants in the conversations in the African and Caribbean rounds – both Anglican and Baptist – showed the strongest evidence of efforts towards contextualization of theology among all the regions visited. However, in the Asian round one Anglican participant from Korea urged the need to "pay attention to the Asian spirit" and "to listen to Asian people's desires and prayers". This has to a degree been carefully nurtured in some Asian Anglican dioceses (for example in Kurunegala, Sri Lanka), and the process of the indigenization of worship and liturgy continues to evolve in interesting and fruitful ways.

*Continuity and culture*

15. Conversations in North America brought to mind that this region offers the example of an earlier "post-colonial experience" for both Baptists and Anglicans. It also offers an instance of the way that a powerful culture (the "American way") can shape the form that continuity takes. Several participants drew attention to the phrase of Martin Marty, "the Baptistification of America", [26] as a phenomenon applying to all Christian churches, namely the belief that individual church members should have substantial input into everything in the life of the church. Perhaps uniquely, Anglicans and Baptists had common roots in ecclesiastical polity in the colonial situation, since pre-revolutionary Anglicanism was effectively without bishops (though nominally under the jurisdiction of the bishop of London) and essentially congregational, [27] with strong contribution from lay members through the "vestry" principle of government. As one Anglican participant put it, "The home country steadfastly refused to provide leadership, so Anglicans in their new local situation were forced to do their own thing." Baptists and Anglicans, for all their differences, also had a common experience of winning independence from a colonial situation, and were shaped by an individualism which was partly fostered by Enlightenment ideology and partly by the necessary self-sufficiency of the frontier situation. One Anglican contributor stressed the desire of American Anglicans to stand in the continuity of liturgy, spirituality and ministry from the English church (bishops were finally consecrated for North America in 1786-87), while at the same time "these elements were

adapted to the political, religious and social circumstances of the new country".[28] Other Anglican participants put this "adaptation" more strongly, even regarding it as a determination to establish an Anglican identity which was distinct from that of the Church of England.

16.  The development of Baptist life in the United States was perhaps even more strongly marked by individualism. Continuity with an ecclesiology based on the rule of Christ, as inherited from English Baptist life, was not entirely lost, but came to be absorbed into the cultural values of the new America. As one Baptist contributor reflected,

> In this heady environment of freedom and self-sufficiency, fortified by advances in technology and wealth, the Baptists were successful in establishing self-governing congregations. Local Baptists practised a form of democratic government which correlated to a great extent with the forms of government common in the American hinterland.[29]

The original understanding of the church as a christologically governed congregation was submerged in a new ecclesiastical functionalism, and in an emphasis on the total spiritual "competency" of the individual without relation to the community of faith.[30] Reflecting on similarities between the Anglican and Baptist stories in North America and on the undoubted achievement of both groups in communicating the gospel message within their culture, participants reflected that both have achieved a kind of "establishment status" in a situation where there is no legally established church; the question was thus raised as to how the churches might more effectively make room for those who have no established place in society.

17.  The contemporary culture, often called "post-modern", presents a challenge of a different kind to Anglicans and Baptists alike. How is it possible to maintain a continuity of the faith in a situation of relativism, where fixed values of all kinds are regarded as cultural constructions, and in which there is less confidence about the power of the individual self to create a world in which these values are respected? Participants in the North American conversations observed that there was a danger of a search for a merely human security. One contributor noted that North American Anglicans and Baptists seem curiously to have adopted the less adventurous features of each other's positions. On the one hand, Anglicans have recently tended to resort to the kind of use of scripture of which Baptists have (often wrongly) been accused – namely, the treatment of the text as a rational system of instructions without sufficient relation of scripture to the revelation of God in Christ. On the other hand, some Baptists have recently required ministers and teachers to subscribe to written statements of doctrinal beliefs as a condition of employment; while this is intended to clarify doctrinal truth, the result can be to use a creed or confession as an instrument of exclusion.[31] There was general agreement among participants that there was a need to recapture the risks of faith – trust in Christ and trust in each others' good faith before Christ.

CONFESSING THE FAITH

*The assumption of a common faith*

18.  A Baptist representative from Australia at Yangon remarked that "Baptists have always insisted that they share the fundamental beliefs of the many branches of the

worldwide Christian church. They become uneasy about references to "Baptist doctrine" or "Baptist theology". [32] A Brazilian Baptist in Santiago rejected the very concept of "Baptist doctrines": there are, he affirmed, only Christian and biblical *doctrines*, while there are Baptist principles and practices. [33] Perhaps this is why the regional meetings devoted little time to the second stated aim of the conversations, "to share with each other our understanding of the faith and to work towards a common confession of the apostolic faith". This may well have been assumed to be common ground. However, in every round of conversations, and most forcibly in Latin America, the desire was expressed for Baptists and Anglicans to take every opportunity to confess publicly together their common faith, so that "the world may see a united and harmonious witness".

## Creeds and confessions

19. For doctrinal standards, the canons of the Church of England point first to the scriptures and, under them, to the "Catholic creeds" and other such teaching of the fathers and councils of the ancient church as are "agreeable to the scriptures". The Church of England also regards its own historic formularies – namely the Thirty Nine Articles of Religion, the *Book of Common Prayer* (1672) and the ordering of bishops, priests and deacons – as trustworthy witness to the gospel. [34] Anglicans confess the apostolic faith in a liturgical way, preserving from the older catholic church in the West and East the recitation in worship of the Apostles' Creed and the Creed of Nicea-Constantinople. Subordinate to these authorities are various recent statements of doctrine that have been endorsed by Anglican synods and councils as being in agreement with the faith of Anglicans; these statements have often arisen out of ecumenical dialogue (for example the Chicago-Lambeth Quadrilateral of 1888). Each province in the Anglican Communion draws from the same list of authorities for the making of doctrine.

20. In modern times, Baptists have characteristically refused to bind themselves to creeds, appealing to the authority of scripture as sufficient witness to the gospel of Jesus Christ. But historically they have not been reluctant to compile "confessions" for use in teaching, for making clear the basis on which they covenant together, and for explaining their belief and practice to those outside Baptist communities. It was reported in the Latin American conversations, for example, that a Baptist confession of faith had recently been presented to the government of Chile under a change of law that gave freedom of religion to all denominations whose registration was accepted by the state. British Baptists (outside Northern Ireland) have not had a confession of faith since the 18th century, making do with a brief three-point declaration of principle. This affirms: (a) the final authority of Christ as revealed in the scriptures and the liberty of the local church to interpret the "laves" of Christ; (b) the nature of baptism, and (c) the duty of all Christian disciples to engage in mission. In this brevity, however, they are exceptional among all other Baptist groups in the modern world.

21. The distinction for Baptists between creeds and confessions is not an absolute one, and the issue seems to be more about the way that statements of faith are *used*. In Baptist confessions of the past and present the major creeds and statements of the worldwide church have in fact often been explicitly acknowledged. A confession of a group of English General Baptist churches in 1678, for instance, explicitly affirms that the Creed of Nicea and the so-called Athanasian Creed are to be "received" and "believed" and

"taught by the ministers of Christ".[35] Generally, moreover, the ordering of the early Baptist confessions follows the shape of the creeds, and their doctrinal formulations show credal influence, even to the extent of particular wording.[36] In the later 20th century the German-language Baptist confession used in Germany, Austria and Switzerland declares that it presupposes the Apostles' Creed as a common confession of Christendom,[37] and the Norwegian Baptists in their confession have affirmed "the content" of both the Apostles' and the Nicene Creed.[38] A "model" covenant service, recently produced by the Baptist Union of Great Britain for use in churches in 2001, provides in its main text the alternatives of a selection of scripture verses and the Apostles' Creed as a means of confessing the Christian faith, and includes the Nicene Creed in further resources. It is also worth recalling that at the first Baptist world congress on 12 July 1905, all the Baptists attending stood voluntarily and recited the Apostles' Creed, "as a simple acknowledgment of where we stand and what we believe".[39] The ambivalence of Baptist attitudes towards creeds, however, was demonstrated in the Caribbean round of conversations. While a participant from the Bahamas believed that the adoption of creeds as authoritative tends to give them a greater importance than the scriptures from which they are derived, and that creeds suppress individual freedom to interpret the scriptures with the aid only of the Spirit,[40] a Baptist from Jamaica reported that some Baptist churches in his country include the recitation of the Apostles' Creed in baptismal services, as a way for all to renew their baptismal vows. The point was also made by Baptist participants from the same region that the Spirit interprets scripture in the midst of the community, not only in the hearts of individuals, and the whole community of the church is wider than Baptists alone. Despite varying attitudes, we may conclude from these conversations that there is more common ground between Baptists and Anglicans in appeal to the historic creeds than is often supposed; there is certainly no disagreement about the *content* of the creeds.

22. The Baptist participants in the European phase at Norwich had no common confession of faith in use among European Baptists to offer, but one paper did record a study document of the European Baptist Federation which had gained wide consent and use. This begins with the statement, "We are part of the whole, worldwide Christian church and we confess faith in one God as Father, Son and Holy Spirit", and the following summary of beliefs was included in the note of explanation:

> Holding faith in the triune God, Baptists share basic beliefs with other Christian churches, including: God's work as Creator; the fallen nature of human beings; the perfect humanity and deity of Jesus Christ, who is God manifest in a human person; redemption through the life, atoning death and resurrection of Christ; the transforming of personal and social life by the power of the Holy Spirit; and the final fulfilment of God's purposes.[41]

The credal shape of this summary is obvious. What Baptists often overlook in such an affirmation of "basic doctrines", however, is the doctrinal centrality of the nature of ecclesiology to churches who stand in the Roman, Orthodox and "Reformed Catholic" tradition. Modern Baptists will often view the doctrine of the church (including ministry and sacraments) as something "additional" to the "fundamentals of the faith", and while acknowledging that what it means to be distinctively Baptist lies in this area, they are often surprised by the dislocation with other traditions that it seems to open up. At Yangon it was instructive to find that the Baptist Convention in Myanmar has a list of "Baptist beliefs and distinctives" which combines doctrinal and church order issues, and that they believe these not only "enhance the solidarity of Baptist churches" but also "provide us with the awareness of the spirit of ecumenism, deepening koinonia". [42] They also, we should note, affirm the ecumenical agreed statement *Baptism, Eucharist and Ministry* [43] as "a matter of our faith as well as our order".

## *Interpreting the faith*

23. Confessing the apostolic faith also includes interpreting it faithfully for the contemporary world. As an example, the African conversations mentioned Christology as "one of the most challenging areas" for the church in its doctrinal teaching in an African context. Both Anglican and Baptist representatives explained that it is easier for an African to identify Christ as mediator between humanity and the supreme God than as "the second person" in the Trinity. One Baptist theologian commented that "when African men and women pray through Jesus Christ, they are in the same mood that they were when praying through their ancestors", and another added that Christ could be seen as the "supreme ancestor" in making it possible to by-pass the hierarchies of ancestors who bridge the material and the spiritual world. An Anglican bishop pointed out that in the gospel portrayal of Jesus the African would recognize, in human terms, features of the *Inanga* ("medicine-man"). Confession of the faith in a way that is faithful to scripture and Tradition is clearly more than adoption of ancient formularies, and cannot be separated from contextualization.

24. Many times in the conversations mention was made of the tolerance and latitude of Anglicans, as a "middle way", in holding together different interpretations of scripture. There was some characterization of the Anglican ethos as that of openness and acceptance, particularly between those of catholic and evangelical convictions. Baptists too pointed out that they offered a broad umbrella for diversity, stemming from difference in context, freedom of interpretation of the scripture under the inspiration of the Spirit, and the liberty under Christ of the local church. Baptists, wrote one from the Bahamas, have "agreed to disagree" about a whole range of issues, including the role of the Holy Spirit in the church, the ministry of women, openness of church membership, and the eternal security of the believer. [44] Both Anglicans and Baptists felt that, while they needed to be sensitive to the prophetic word of dissent, boundaries for diversity were nevertheless offered by the corporate mind of the church in its gathering together, at local and at synodical or convention level.

## *Sources of authority*

25. The regional meeting in North America provided a special opportunity to sum up the approaches of Anglicans and Baptists to sources of authority in affirming the Christian faith and determining Christian practice. There was complete agreement that final authority belonged to Jesus Christ, as head of the church and as the revelation of the triune God. There was also agreement that among the sources of authority which witness to Christ and are subordinate to him, the holy scriptures – inspired by the Spirit of God – take primary place as the ultimate written standard for faith and practice. [45] Article 6 of the Thirty-Nine Articles concurs with many Baptist confessions in speaking of the "sufficiency" of the scriptures for salvation.

26. But scripture needs to be interpreted in each age, and at this point there appear differences, at least in emphasis. Anglicans place tradition and reason alongside (but secondary to) scripture, while – for the right understanding of scripture – Baptists will appeal to the illuminating work of the Spirit within the mind of the individual believer and within the corporate mind of the church meeting. While Baptists often claim that their approach amounts to affirming "scripture alone", it appears that there is actually a considerable overlap between the two approaches. "Reason" within the Anglican triad is not, suggested the Anglican participants, to be best understood as "the mind of the culture in which the church lives" (despite this definition in the *Virginia Report*, 1997), but rather as the "mind of the church" – that is, the thinking of human minds transformed by the grace of God, though always contextualized in human culture. This brings the Anglican "reason" close to the enlightened conscience of the believer and the mind of the church meeting as understood by Baptists. The Baptist participants for their part recognized that interpretation of scripture by individuals and the fellowship was inevitably shaped by the tradition of the church (see above §§7-9). In particular, the debt to the doctrinal concepts of the church fathers with regard to Trinity and Christology, as evidenced in Baptist confessions, means that it would be more accurate to regard the Baptist view of scripture as *suprema scriptura* rather than *sola scriptura*. One Baptist contributor thus noted a "growing recognition in Baptist theology that biblical authority always exists and functions in relationship to other sources of authority that inform the community's interpretation and practice of the biblical story".[46]

MISSION AND MINISTRY

*Two models of mission*

27. In the first round of conversations in Norwich, it was observed that there was a widespread perception that Baptists are more committed to evangelism than Anglicans. Similarly, a paper from the Anglican delegation in Nairobi made the comment that "obviously the Anglicans have little culture of evangelism" compared with the Baptists,[47] and curiously exactly the same comment was made by Anglicans in Yangon, adding that "Anglicans are more prone to be priests than evangelists". In Norwich this perception was given some examination, and it was thought that it was helpful to look at the situation in a different way, from the perspective of various models of *mission*. In the context of the life of the UK at least, two models of mission could be discerned, to *both* of which *both* communions are committed, but with different emphases. There is first the model of mission which sees it as inseparable from spiritual and pastoral care for those within the boundaries of the church community. Second, there is the model of mission as going out from the community to minister in a secular and non-Christian society. The practice of infant baptism, the position of the established church and the nature of the parish system leads the Church of England to see the scope of its borders as being very wide, and so to lay more emphasis on the first type of mission than Baptists do (see also below on membership). Baptist churches, viewing baptism as a commissioning of adult disciples to service in the world, tend to lay more stress on the second type, with the consequence of giving a higher profile to evangelism as proclaiming good news in Jesus Christ.

28. In the first approach, a mission-field is created within the area of the church; in the second, disciples enter a mission-field outside the church. This difference of emphasis

appears to persist elsewhere in the world outside England, despite lack of establishment. One of the Anglican participants in the West Indies commented that evangelism by Baptists seemed to be "external and visible in secular society", where Anglican evangelism was seen "as a form of pastoral care".[48] Only in the conversations in Latin America was it impossible to discern this difference; instead a distinction was drawn by both Anglicans and Baptists between evangelism as conducted by Protestants and "evangelization" by Roman Catholics. A Chilean bishop distinguished between "evangelism seeking faith response" (Protestant) and evangelism seeking the affiliation of a community to faith (Roman Catholic).[49] If Baptists tend to stress the model of a mission field outside the church, it should also be noted that they have developed ways to open up the boundaries of the Christian community to those who have no clear Christian faith as yet; it was, for example, remarked in the African conversations that at the time of crisis of death, Baptists in Kenya will perform burial rites for those who either have no church or who have been "rejected by their own churches for various reasons".[50] At the other end of life, it was pointed out in the Latin American conversations that the blessing of infants is practised throughout the area by Baptists, and used as an opportunity to bring families into the orbit of the church fellowship.

*Holistic mission*

29. It is misleading to equate these two models of mission with "social service" and "preaching the gospel" respectively; both models have a place for the whole range of mission, including various forms of service to others and the proclamation of the message of salvation. In differing circumstances the elements of proclamation and service may stand out in particular ways; in the UK, for example, the place of the Anglican church in English society tends to give it a higher profile in issues of social justice and welfare, and may give it more opportunities to enter into dialogue with the governing authorities on questions of social morality. On the other hand, the indigenization of Baptist churches throughout Europe has given them more opportunities than Anglicans to be involved in relief work in situations of economic deprivation in the former eastern Europe and the former Yugoslavia. Both communions have been recently involved in taking up the cause of immigrants and refugees in the UK. Some Baptist conventions, notably that of the Southern Baptists, want to reserve the term "missions" to proclamation of the gospel,[51] but these too are actually involved in providing a range of social services and in seeking to alleviate world hunger as a matter of Christian responsibility.

30. Given the commitment of both communions to mission which includes proclamation of the gospel and Christian social service, it is interesting that both Anglican and Baptist representatives in the African round of conversations felt that past missionaries had failed to carry through a holistic kind of mission. They believe that they have been left with a heritage which is more concerned for the individual soul than for the corporate and bodily being of persons. They see the African emphasis on the church as a "community for the promotion of life" as a distinctive quality over against their sponsoring churches: "a sense of the wholeness of the person is manifest in the African attitude to life. Just as there is no separation between the sacred and secular in communal life neither is there separation between the soul and the body."[52] An Anglican participant defined the ministry of the church as the serving of those who suffer, and the speaking a word of prophetic protest against injustice. A Baptist participant recalled that the purpose of the

All Africa Baptist Fellowship was an "evangelistic programme to win Africa for Christ", and here he was reflecting the widespread African Baptist emphasis on proclamation, discipleship and nurture in the faith; but he also stressed that this programme should include "priestly care of the environment" and a radical discipleship that "relates to issues of human development".[53] Both groups felt that they were inhibited at times by the hesitations of their Western partners in making a prophetic critique of society.

31. The same stress on the holistic nature of mission was seen in conversations in Latin America and the Caribbean, though criticism of Western missionaries only emerged explicitly in the latter. No difference could be traced between Baptists and Anglicans in either of the two areas in their view of the scope of mission; declaration of the gospel by word must be accompanied by working for social transformation and the struggle for justice. Both Anglicans and Baptists were more ready to speak openly of theologies of liberation and emancipation in the West Indies, where both were more reserved about this *terminology* in Latin America, tending to associate it with Roman Catholicism. One Brazilian Anglican remarked that members of his church saw Jesus "more as a captive than a liberator".[54] But much of the substance of liberation theology was present, even if the participants did not use such phrases as "evangelism of the poor by the poor", and "God's option for the poor" such as appeared explicitly in the presentations from the Caribbean.[55] A Baptist from Argentina insisted that evangelism was personal but never private, and that evangelism as "joyful witness to the redeeming love of God" could never be separated from social responsibility in mission. An Anglican contributor from Guatemala pointed out that Jesus' aim for us to have "life in abundance" could not be restricted to spiritual abundance, but that it had economic and social implications. Both Anglicans and Baptists spoke of participating in the mission of God rather than in human "missions". "Evangelism follows God's will, not ours" commented an Anglican, so that it "mean implementing God's vision";[56] a Baptist urged that "the churches lose effectiveness and content when they do not discover the accomplishment of the mission of God in the world and outside them". Thus, mission is nothing less than "the adoration of the self-manifestation of the triune God in history".[57] In the Caribbean conversations, an Anglican contributor drew the conclusion for worship, that in the liturgy worshippers can know the realities of mission, entering into the "drama of the salvation of the world, revisioning lives".[58]

32. The African critique of missionary theology was echoed in presentations from the Caribbean, with particular reference to the institution of slavery. One paper, analyzing that situation, found that a false dichotomy was created in missionary preaching between the body and the spirit, and that an individual appropriation of personal salvation was taught in order to prevent the creation of what was perceived as a dangerous sense of community and solidarity among slaves.[59] The present context is a traumatic period of transition, politically, culturally, economically and religiously. There is a deliberate movement from a dominant Western culture to a variety of cultural identities, including a pervasive African identity which was previously suppressed, and both Anglicans and Baptists clearly see the task of mission in that context. The context in South America is similarly one of convulsive political and socio-economic upheaval, calling for a vision of the kingdom of God and holistic mission. But the churches there also view mission in the context of a turmoil which is religious and ecclesial. Both Baptists and Anglicans are concerned about the rise of independent religious groups which are neo-charismatic, Pentecostal and even New Age. This is coincidental with the rapid and massive decline

of the primacy of the Roman Catholic Church. The new Christian groups have a pro-active approach to promoting the faith, including use of modern media and a widespread use of "cultural symbols"; neither Anglicans nor Baptists seem to be interesting in copy-ing their approaches, but realize that they cannot be entirely content with past methods. Baptists and Anglicans regard this double situation of rapid political and religious change as also calling for stronger mutual recognition between themselves (see also §88).

33. In the North American phase of conversations it was observed that churches of the various African-American Baptist conventions are far more overtly political than their white counterparts. The pastor is understood as having a particular role as a spokesper-son for social justice as well as the proclaimer of a gospel of spiritual salvation, and this sometimes involves both pastor and church explicitly in political matters.[60] Martin Luther King Jr (who was also a pastor within the American Baptist Convention) was one who stood in this tradition as an opponent of racism and advocate of non-violent social change.

### Mission and church growth

34. Both Anglicans and Baptists in Latin America affirmed that mission must have depth (maturity) as well as breadth (statistical expansion), and that the growth of the church must never be mere expansion but contribute to the growth of the kingdom of God.[61] Growth in numbers is to be sought and welcomed, as long as it is accompanied by depth of discipleship.

### Mission and dialogue

35. While need for dialogue with other faiths was mentioned in the African round of talks, particularly with regard to Muslims, it was a much more marked feature of the con-versations in Asia. It was stressed that such dialogue should be marked by (a) sensitiv-ity, respect and courtesy, with a genuine listening to the other; (b) the aim of being able to *tell* our own Christian story better as a result of dialogue; and (c) the aim of *under-standing* our own story better for ourselves through listening to others. It was thought that relations and theological conversations between the Christian churches should pro-vide a model and incentive for wider dialogue beyond the churches. In general, issues of holistic mission and interfaith dialogue were not perceived to divide Anglicans and Bap-tists in either Asia or Africa. With regard to the holistic nature of mission, a contributor from South Africa remarked that in that area political views were "largely determined by race" rather than by denomination or theology.[62]

### Ministry and mission

36. While Baptists affirm the "priesthood of all believers", Anglicans intend the same thing by the term "the royal priesthood of all the baptized". The phrases derive from 1 Peter 2:9, "You are a royal priesthood", in a letter which is much concerned with the life of newly baptized believers. Both communions encourage all their members to use their spiritual gifts in sharing in God's mission in the world, in obedience to the "great

commission" (Matt. 28:19-20), while believing that there is still a God-given office of ministry to which only some are called. Both Anglicans and Baptists use the word "ministry" in a double sense to cover the vocations of both people and pastors, while Anglicans also use the word "priesthood" in a similar dual way. For Baptists there are different expressions of *ministry*, while "priesthood" is ascribed only to the whole body of believers; for Anglicans, there are also different expressions of priesthood among the lay and the ordained. Different vocabularies should not obscure the common underlying ground. However, the feeling was expressed in these conversations that Baptists have more practical scope to express the ministry, and hence a sharing in mission, of all the members of the church. Some Anglican participants in the African round thought that the demarcation of the ordained through Western liturgical vestments and a hierarchy of "priestly" ministry led to a passivity in church members. One African Anglican paper proposed, in a way similar to Baptist thought, that,

> Baptism is the essential opening to ministry in the church. The Christian is not baptized into a passive group of spectators, but into action, into church, and also into service. The nature of the church is a community of disciples, with the participation of all members in all things. [63]

In the light of this, Baptists drew attention to what they saw as an inherent connection between the baptism of professing disciples and the commissioning of a whole priestly people to service in the world. On the other hand, African Anglican participants stressed the value of having received the heritage of an ordained ministry marked by the name "priest", closely connected with the administration of the sacraments as well as the word ("a sacramental ministry" was a phrase often used), and which they saw as a means of enabling and equipping the ministry of all the faithful. As a matter of fact, it appeared that the weight of evangelism undertaken by both communions, whether in Europe, Asia or Africa, was carried by the non-ordained. In Africa, for instance, Anglicans commented that new congregations were largely founded by evangelists, catechists and "sub-deacons".

*Mission and liberty*

37. Baptists and Anglicans alike regard liberty as a consequence of mission. But it has appeared as a Baptist emphasis to want to safeguard freedom *within* the very process of evangelism. As a Baptist from Argentina put it: "The legitimacy of evangelism must be maintained, because everybody has the freedom to confess freely his/her faith, and the freedom to incorporate himself/herself into any religious group, even after being a member of another one." [64] In that round of conversations, attention was given to the issue of proselytism as a misuse of freedom, from which both Anglicans and Baptists wished to distance themselves. While it was stated that this was only occasionally an issue at present between Anglicans and Baptists in Latin America, it was perceived as a potential problem that could become more weighty. The formulation offered by a WCC publication on common witness was quoted, that proselytism is the act of encouraging someone to change their church allegiance by methods that "contradict the spirit of Christian love, violate the freedom of the human person and diminish trust in the Christian witness of the church"; such means may involve manipulation, violence, coercion or ridiculing of others. [65] The question was raised whether this is not too comfortable a definition; rather than the issue being one of illegitimate method, proselytism might be seen as any kind of encouragement to change denominational membership, where what was

needed was simply encouragement to turn to the love and mercy of God. What was desirable, it was suggested, was "proselytism towards God", and towards the kingdom of God, rather than towards any particular denomination of the church.[66] It was clear that while disavowing *encouragement* to change church membership, Baptists would still want to emphasize, however, the freedom of the person concerned to choose his or her own church-home for Christian life and witness after experiencing a new or renewed faith.

38. Such a defence of freedom of conscience is rooted deeply within historic Baptist aversion to any connection between church and state which gives territorial privileges to a particular church, or which allows the state to interfere in the inner life of the church, or which prevents the church from exercising a prophetic voice in society. In most parts of the world this has taken the form of urging a constitutional "separation of church and state", though a flexible view of this theory has been taken by some Baptists, such as in England. In the Latin American round, in a strongly Roman Catholic context, Baptists thought it important to record that there had been Baptist influence on the enshrinement of separation between church and state within the Brazilian constitution.[67] Traditionally, Southern Baptists of the USA have been amongst the strongest advocates of the separation of church and state, but one Baptist contributor explained that they have recently interpreted this to mean that the state should take positive steps to "make room" for the church to proclaim the gospel and to exert its influence in the process of making of law on social issues;[68] one high-profile issue has been its advocacy of the legalizing of Christian prayer in state schools. Another Baptist contributor suggested that there has been a shift from emphasizing one clause in the first amendment of the US constitution, that prohibiting the "establishment of religion", to another clause allowing the "free exercise of religion". States may then be encouraged to make laws which allow for a "freedom of exercise" in a way that some might think "establishes" the majority (evangelical/Baptistic) view.[69] It remains to be seen what effect this change will have on the character of Baptist churches and on society.

39. While Anglicanism has been traditionally associated with the establishment of the church within the structures of the state, the basic Anglican view is one of a necessary *relationship* between church and state, preventing a privatization of the gospel and ensuring the influence of Christian values throughout society. This relationship can take different forms in different situations, ranging from the establishment in law of the Church of England in England to the willingness of a church to register with the appropriate government department in countries where this is required.

Baptism and the Process of Initiation

40. In any conversations between Anglicans and Baptists the question of baptism will present something of an impasse. On the one hand, Baptists find it impossible to treat as equivalent acts the baptism of young infants and the baptism of disciples who can confess their own faith, and so they find difficulties with the ecumenical notion of a "common baptism". On the other hand, Anglicans find it to be scandalous, and a real breach of fellowship in the universal church, if a Baptist congregation baptizes as a believer someone who has previously been baptized as an infant. Both communions agree that baptism is unrepeatable, and yet draw altogether different conclusions from this affirmation. Where Christian baptism is regarded *only* as the baptism of a disciple

able to confess faith for himself or herself, then baptism of someone baptized as an infant will not be considered to be rebaptism.

*Grace and faith in baptism*

41. One step towards mutual understanding would be to abandon a certain "typecasting" that sometimes happens, in which Baptists are represented as only interested in the confession of *faith* made in the baptism of believers – or more accurately, of disciples – and Anglicans are represented as only interested in the *grace of* God manifested in the baptism of infants. In *both* kinds of baptism, those who practise them can perceive elements of divine grace *and* human faith as being mingled there. The baptism of the believer, in most Baptist thought, offers a rendezvous between the disciple who comes in trusting faith, and the triune God who graciously transforms the life of the believer and endows him or her with spiritual gifts for service. This is also the case where Anglicans practise the baptism of adults who have come to a personal faith (as long as they have not previously been baptized as an infant). Those Baptists who think of baptism as essentially an obedient profession of faith will, of course, add that this faith is itself the gift of a gracious God. In Anglican thought about the baptism of an infant, while the prevenient grace of God is poured out in this act, there is also the offering of human faith by the parents and by the community which surrounds the child with its love and prayers. The Baptist problem with regarding infant baptism as "baptism", in the fullest sense, must be seen in this context of both grace and faith. It is not only that the nature of the faith present does not include the personal trust of the child; there also seems, to Baptists, to be some limit on the effect of the grace of God, as it appears to them that the baptism of an infant cannot include endowment with *charismata* for active service, and much of the New Testament language of change and regeneration also seems difficult to apply at such a young age.

*A process of initiation*

42. Another step towards a better understanding of each other's position on baptism might be to recognize that the "beginning" of the Christian life – or initiation – is not so much a single event, but a process or a journey which may extend over a considerable time. Divine grace and human faith, in their many and different aspects, are woven together during this "pilgrim's progress".[70] In line with this, the conversations at Norwich affirmed that "understanding initiation as a 'process' has been widely accepted as a helpful approach". While the whole of the Christian life is a journey of growing into Christ, there is a first stage to this journey that is aptly called a beginning. During the course of the conversations, the suggestion has gained ground that baptism, whether of infants or disciples, certainly plays a key part in this story of "beginning" but is by no means the *whole of* the story. In seeking for greater understanding between churches, it was urged that comparison should be made not simply between the ways in which baptism is practised as a single event, but between varying shapes of the *whole journey of* initiation.[71] This journey will include, as well as baptism, the working of the grace of God that prepares the human heart, early nurture within the community, the responsible "yes" of faith by the individual, a sharing for the first time with other Christians in the

Lord's supper, and the commissioning of the disciple for service. Thus, the question that arises is not whether the two communions can affirm a "common baptism"; these conversations did not have that aim. The question is how far each communion might be able to recognize that members of the other have made the same journey, wherever the place of baptism is located within it.

43. Discussion of baptism in the African round of conversations showed a strong identification between the rite and initiation into the corporate life and relationships of the community, while placing this point of entry and responsibility at two different stages of human growth. For those practising infant baptism, the Christian rite corresponds to the "naming" ritual in traditional African religion, when the young child is first inducted into the community and "becomes a human being" through receiving a name. Baptists see the act of infant blessing (sometimes called "dedication") as fulfilling this essential function, and regard baptism as an equivalent to the African act of initiation into adult life within the community at the time of puberty. Both communions find resonance with African views of the life-giving aspects of water, and see the act of baptism as a rite of renewal. Life is renewed for the whole community at birth and at the transition into adult responsibilities. Of course, when adults are baptized in Anglican churches, it is the latter kind of initiation and renewal that is in mind, as among Baptists. This African concept of continually renewed membership of the community might provide some support for a theology of a "journey of initiation", though it seems that as yet this idea has not been considered in ecumenical theology in Africa.

*Confirmation and initiation*

44. It will enlarge the common ground between Baptists and Anglicans if Anglicans clearly regard the laying-on of hands in confirmation (however ambiguous the history and development of this rite may be) as *part of initiation*. It will help Baptists if Anglicans do not regard the "beginning" of Christian life as being *complete* until there is this occasion for public profession of faith, and for receiving spiritual gifts for service in the world. It was recognized at Norwich that it is more difficult to recognize each other's journey into faith where stress is laid on baptism alone as "complete sacramental initiation",[72] and where confirmation is accordingly diminished in significance and understood simply as an occasion for the renewal of baptismal vows. While this trend was seen to be quite strong in the Church of England, it was notable that representatives of the Scottish Episcopal Church and the Church of Ireland regarded confirmation as the key place where those who had been baptized in infancy could make their own personal profession of faith, and that this should normally precede participation in the eucharist. Anglican representatives at Norwich thought that it was possible to speak of baptism as being complete (i.e. not being defective), while insisting that *initiation* was not completed by baptism alone. It was suggested that, while baptized but not yet confirmed infants need not be excluded from the eucharist, this should not be taken to imply that initiation *had been completed* even by participating in the eucharist for the first time, if confirmation had not yet taken place.[73]

45. In the Asian phase of conversations there was an even stronger assertion that, confirmation was essential to full initiation as a Christian disciple, parallel to the baptism of believers among Baptist congregations. The view of several Asian participants, and par-

ticularly those from the Church of North India and from Myanmar, was that the mutual life and mission of the churches that had been achieved would not have been possible without the place that confirmation had played within it. The example was cited of the shape of church unity within the Church of North India, where there is a parallel acceptance of two patterns of Christian nurture and initiation: (a) infant dedication (or blessing) followed by baptism as a believer with confirmation, and (b) infant baptism followed by later confirmation as a believer. The Baptist declaration of principle within the constitution of the CNI was quoted here, that "profession of faith is required of those baptized in infancy before admission to membership in full standing in the church, thereby acknowledging the nature of the church as a fellowship".[74] A bishop of the CNI present also stressed that "those who desire infant baptism for their children can have them baptized and, when they are grown enough to make a personal confession of faith and commitment to Christ, they are confirmed as full communicant members".[75] Problems of fellowship will naturally arise within this parallel process of nurture if only one group of children within a single congregation, those who have been baptized, are admitted to the Lord's supper, a situation that occurs in some Local Ecumenical Partnerships in the UK. In the CNI it seems that this problem does not arise since, in all congregations, confirmation precedes communion, and this is also the majority practice in Asian Anglican churches. In Korea, however, baptized children can be admitted to eucharist before confirmation.

46. In African churches, the traditional importance of initiation into adulthood (see above) has not led to an emphasis on confirmation among Anglicans. Indeed, unlike the Asian scene, the decline of confirmation elsewhere in Anglican churches appears to be reflected in African Anglicanism. Two reasons suggest themselves. First, there is widespread adult baptism in a situation of large church growth. Second, the strong view of life in community means that when an infant is named/baptized, many of the aspects that the West attributes to an "age of responsibility" are already assigned to the child vicariously (e.g. the responsibility to bury one's parents). This does mean, however, that there is generally an insistence that children will only be baptized when their parents are believers and already members of the community of faith; baptism, affirmed one Anglican participant, is "about corporate commitment".[76] The growing practice of admission of baptized children to communion before confirmation also usually applies only to children of believing parents.

47. By contrast, the Province of the West Indies follows classic Anglican practice in formally requiring confirmation for sharing in the eucharist, according to its canon law (though it still offers eucharistic hospitality to baptized and communicant members of other denominations). Canon 30 in fact requires that every priest "shall diligently seek out persons whom he shall think meet to be confirmed". This seems to be supported by a "confirmation culture" where the whole local church community gathers for the visit of the bishop; perhaps here there is a combination of factors that make confirmation so significant – the making of a personal link between the believer and the bishop as his or her pastor, as well as laying-on of hands for spiritual gifts. In fact, the only exception to the importance of confirmation in the West Indies seems to be Haiti, where there is strong emphasis on baptism, which is regarded as the key moment for receiving the Spirit rather than confirmation.

48. An increasing number of Baptist churches also practise the laying-on of hands after baptism,[77] following a custom which was common among General Baptists in England

in earlier years. One Baptist participant in the North American conversations pointed out that this ought to be kept in mind in discussing the place of confirmation.[78] Like confirmation this provides an explicit opportunity for the commissioning of the disciple for service in the world – although this is already implied in the baptism of a believer – and for equipping with spiritual gifts to meet the task. Whether practised by Anglicans or Baptists, the act thus also draws attention to the association between baptism in water and baptism in the Holy Spirit. Baptists, like Anglicans, can regard this act of laying-on hands as part of the journey of beginning in the Christian life.

*Open membership among Baptists*

49. If there is a challenge to Anglicans to develop a new theology for confirmation in new circumstances, a challenge to Baptists is whether some positive theological place could be given to the baptism of young infants within a larger process of initiation. For those wishing to do so, this would imply, as a first step, a church polity of "open membership" where intending members are not required to be baptized as believers. In the European phase of conversations, it was reported that most Baptist churches belonging to the Baptist Union of Great Britain are "open"; only 17 percent of Baptist churches require believers' baptism for people to be any kind of member; 51 percent of churches admit to full membership without requiring believers' baptism, and another 24 percent admit to an "associate membership" without it. Elsewhere in Europe some form of "associate membership" is widespread; "open membership" is less usual, but 40 percent of Baptist churches in Denmark practise it, as do some churches in Scotland, Germany, Sweden, Lithuania, Estonia and Georgia,[79] together with 90 percent of Baptist churches in Italy with regard to those baptized as infants in Protestant churches.

50. In the Asian phase of the conversations, it was reported that open membership is universal among Baptist churches in Myanmar and in all Baptist churches which are members of the Church of North India. Though there are no full statistics for the remainder of the 53 member bodies of the Asian Baptist Fellowship, the BWA regional secretary spoke about a new emergence of open membership among churches of the North East Christian Council in India, and offered his impression that there is widespread hospitality offered to members of other denominations in Baptist churches throughout Asia, regardless of the mode of baptism; exceptional among these is Sri Lanka, where all of the churches are open membership. Closed membership is still common in large conventions which are based on the missionary activity of Southern Baptists, in Singapore, the Philippines and Hong Kong; these were unfortunately not represented at the conversations, although an invitation had been sent to the Philippines. The Baptist representative from Korea reported that while baptism as a believer by immersion was necessary for leadership in the church, it was not usually required for church membership. In Latin America, the representative group of Baptists gathered for conversation knew of no open membership churches at all.[80] In the West Indies, by contrast, there are many open membership churches in Jamaica, but only a few elsewhere. In North America, open membership churches are common among the American Baptist Churches of the USA (about 30 percent), and very rare (about 1 percent) among churches of the Southern Baptist Convention. Open membership is similarly rare among African-American Baptist churches in the USA. Open membership numbers in Australia vary from 4 percent in Queensland

to 20 percent in the states of New South Wales, Victoria and South Australia, while it is found in 50 percent of churches in New Zealand. The picture, then, is a mixed one, and statistics are incomplete, but it would be safe to conclude that overall there is a sizeable majority of Baptist churches worldwide which have closed membership.

51. Where open membership is practised among Baptist churches this does not, however, usually mean that a person cannot be baptized as a believer when he or she has previously received baptism as an infant. A Baptist church meeting finds it very difficult to refuse people who, after careful counselling, continue to insist from an instructed conscience that such a step is part of their path of discipleship. Nor does open membership mean in itself that a positive theological view is being taken of infant baptism; it may simply mean that, in a desire to be hospitable to other Christians, a profession of personal faith and an evident Christian life-style are considered to be the essential elements for membership (see further §§83-85). There are exceptions to this rule, however: some Baptist churches in Denmark, for example, require for admission to membership either baptism as a believer or a transfer from a church where the person has been baptized as an infant, thus implicitly giving some recognition to infant baptism where it has been followed by personal faith. Despite open membership, it would be very rare for a Baptist union or convention (outside the unique church unity scheme of the CNI) to issue a direct request to its member churches to decline from baptizing as a believer someone already baptized as an infant. Such a request would not only be unenforceable in practice; it might also be thought to infringe the freedom of conscience of the individual, and to infringe the freedom of a local church to discern the mind of Christ for itself.

52. Here the partnership between Baptists and Anglicans in the Myanmar Christian Council offers a striking development which deserves reflecting upon. In responding to the request of the document *Baptism, Eucharist and Ministry* to refrain from any actions that might be regarded as repeating baptism, the Myanmar Baptist Convention pointed out that the real difficulty lay with new members who "themselves request to be given a second baptism", rather than with what the churches themselves required.[81] At the conversations in Yangon, the MBC then described how it had embarked on a process of "conscientization" among the churches, using *BEM* as a study guide, to enable Baptist church members to understand the place of baptism in infant-baptist churches. The result was an agreement at the level of the Myanmar Council of Churches to refrain from what could be understood by others as a "second baptism", and Baptist ministers are encouraged to carry out this policy. While there must remain some uncertainty about how far this request is actualized at a local level, both the Baptists and the Anglicans of Myanmar affirmed that the existence of the agreement made possible the extraordinarily close cooperation enjoyed in that country between Baptists and Anglicans. It is worth recording also that the response of the Myanmar Baptist Convention to the entire BEM document included the following words:

> We do not respond simply because it is expected of us. We respond because of our commitment to unity and the ongoing mission of the whole church in the whole world.[82]

MEMBERSHIP OF THE CHURCH

*Different ways of belonging*

53. Anglicans and Baptists accept from the apostle Paul that there is the closest association between baptism and becoming a member of the body of Christ, which is the church (1 Cor. 12:13). Baptists will, however, understand this affirmation as referring to the baptism of a disciple able to confess his or her own faith. In some ecumenical situations, such as that of the Church of North India, an adjustment has been made to accommodate the whole process of initiation, by reserving the notion of "*full* membership", or "*full communicant* membership" for the stage of confirmation. By contrast, at Norwich the Anglican participants made clear that they could not accept the theological concept that infant baptism only offered a "partial membership" in the body of Christ, which had to be followed by a "full membership" later on. However, if initiation is to be understood as a "journey" rather than a single point, this calls in turn for some re-thinking of the concept of membership. This seems necessary for Anglicans when literally millions of people in a country (say, the UK) have reached the first stage of baptism but never proceeded any further into an active sharing in the life of a church. In what sense are these people members of the body of Christ? A similar situation can also obtain, of course, when people have been baptized as believers but no longer seem to have an active faith. But a larger issue, perhaps, for Baptists is the status of the many believing children within their churches: are these "members of the body", when they are certainly "in Christ" through their own faith, but have not yet been baptized, and may not be commissioned as disciples through baptism for a number of years?

54. It was suggested from the Baptist side that a way forward here is not along the lines of partial and full membership, but through *different ways of being* a member, or different ways of "belonging" within the body, according to the stage of the journey of faith which has been reached. This approach was echoed in the Latin American round of conversations when Anglicans took the view that infants at baptism become part of "the body of Christ, but when confirmed as believers they "take responsibility and leadership" in the church. A distinctive feature of membership on the African scene is the belief that this membership persists across the generations and beyond death, joining the living and the dead together in "a great cloud of witnesses" (Heb. 12:1).

*Membership local and universal*

55. A further issue about membership is whether this has any meaning other than the membership of the one universal (catholic) church. Because of its historic claim to be the continuing catholic church in England, serving the whole of the nation and having a responsibility for every person in a parish, the Church of England resists the idea of "membership" of a local congregation. According to this way of thinking, through baptism someone becomes a member of the body of Christ universal, and this is – in theological terms – the only membership there can be. For practical purposes, one can be a "member of the electoral roll" of a particular parish church, but this is regarded as a means of church government rather than a theological category. Membership of a single congregation is also less meaningful since the "local church" is, according to the Anglican understanding of the church, the diocese or the extended congregation of the bishop.

56. By contrast, Baptists think of local church membership as a covenantal relationship between disciples "gathered together" into a community in one place, normally entered by baptism. It was emphasized at Norwich that this must not be taken to mean that Baptists do not feel a responsibility to serve everyone in the society around them. Nor is local membership the whole meaning of church membership; the local covenant is a visible expression in one particular place of membership of the church universal, the great company of all those whose lives have been regenerated through the grace of God in Christ. Outside the Church of England, it is noticeable that an Anglican church takes on much more the aspect of a "gathered community", and this was especially clear in conversations in the Asian context. An Anglican representative from Korea mentioned that, although the diocese was divided into parishes, this made little sense as a unit for ministry in the Korean context. A representative from Hong Kong was more supportive of the parish system, but the situation may well change with a less British environment and a new Chinese ethos. An Anglican representative from Melbourne, Australia, could still see a use for some form of parish system, but thought it needed to be reformed and "loosened up".

57. The witness of the churches in Asia was that the Christian churches together are tending to form a common sub-culture or counter-culture over against the dominant culture of the country, and this is bound to give the churches the feel of a "gathered community". Differences in their own structure are often much less important than their difference from the dominant culture around. In Myanmar, for instance, in a largely Buddhist culture, Baptist ministers share a common identity with Anglican clergy as Christian ministers, sometimes identified by the same dress in church; they try to live as much as possible of a common life together, including sharing in the Lord's supper, as a witness to the surrounding society. The convergence of the act of believers' baptism with the rite of confirmation may also be due to the need to have a unified Christian act of commitment which corresponds to some "rite of passage" in the majority culture, such as the customary Theravada Buddhist initiation of all young Buddhist males for a temporary monastic experience. The point was made, however, from representatives of several Asian countries, that the dominant culture concerned (whether Hindu, Buddhist or Muslim) was not strictly the same as the dominant religion of the area; the "way of life" was connected with the tenets of a particular religion, but was not exactly identical with its doctrines and practices.

58. Another reason for less difference in the view of church membership between Anglicans and Baptists outside England (see §§53-54) is the identity of denomination with ethnic group, arising from the old "comity" arrangements of the missionary societies. Where to be a Naga Christian in northern India, for example, means being Baptist for 80 percent of the Christian population – itself 95 percent of the whole population – there is bound to be an overlap between the boundaries of church and society which has some affinity in practice to the Anglican church in England.

*"Autonomy" and interdependence*

59. In Africa, both Anglicans and Baptists appealed to the idea of a "covenant community", finding resonance with African tradition in Old Testament ideas of covenant, and this again tends to foster the sense of a gathered community. The close-knit sense of

membership of a particular community may, however, lead to the elevation of local community over a more universal kind of fellowship; Baptists noted that there was a strong view of the autonomy of the local church in Africa, and Anglicans noted problems that sometimes arose from claims to autonomy by the separate dioceses and their bishops within a province.

60. The "autonomy" of the local church was frequently mentioned in the conversations as a basic Baptist tenet reinforcing the importance of membership in a local church; it was just as frequently challenged by other Baptists present who pointed to the interdependency of churches in many areas of life. A paper from a Baptist in the West Indies began by stating that "local autonomy is at the heart of Baptist life", but soon noted the key part played by the convention in such matters as ordination and ownership of property, concluding that "our experience has been that some [local Baptist pastors] use this issue as a tool of convenience".[83] A Baptist contributor in the Latin American conversations referred to a concept of "*independent interdependency* among local churches and also among pastoral leadership".[84] Baptists in fact have never held to autonomy in the literal sense of "self-rule", but have instead held to direct dependence of the local church on the *rule of Christ*. Nothing can be imposed upon a local church meeting by other churches or assemblies of churches because members have the freedom and the responsibility to find the mind of Christ who rules in the congregation (see Matt. 18:15-20). They share in the threefold office of Christ as Prophet, Priest and King, and so have the liberty to discern his kingly role. But on the other hand, local churches have gladly affirmed that they often need the counsel and insight of other Christian congregations to find the mind of Christ. Because the local congregation makes the body of Christ visible in one place, it is under the direct authority of Christ and cannot be dictated to by human agencies; but just because its aim is to find the mind of Christ it will seek fellowship, guidance and counsel from as much of *the whole body of Christ* as it can relate to. It will associate and unite with others, not only for the sharing of resources for mission,[85] but because Christ is calling it to covenant with others. Baptist churches have therefore always lived together in spiritual interdependence with each other in associations, and their members regard themselves as having membership in the universal church of the redeemed, not just in a local congregation.

61. In practice, on the ground, the situation in a Baptist congregation may not appear very different from an Anglican one, where decisions taken at synodical level need to be *received* at the more local level. The local unit (whether parish or diocese) is obliged to follow synodical decisions in certain areas, but it will have been represented on the wider body on which the decisions were taken, and finally a policy will be applied in a way that meets the needs of the particular situation. A representative from ECUSA pointed out that winning the "consent of the faithful" may mean that a decision is yielded to, resisted or adapted in subtle ways in the parish.[86] Moreover, the principle of "subsidiarity" is strongly embedded in all decision-making, whereby "activities should be carried out at the lowest level at which they can be effectively undertaken".[87] A task force that recently reviewed jurisdiction in the Anglican Church of Canada with regard to doctrine and discipline stated a variation of this principle, affirming that the power to decide a matter "should rest at the diocesan level unless the 'mind of the church' deems it to belong at another level".[88] If a diocese is regarded as the "local church" then this is quite close to a Baptist polity. Thus, Anglicans and Baptists alike desire to see the rule of Christ (what might be called "Christonomy") worked out in *both* the local church and in the

assembling of churches together, but they deal with the balance – and sometimes tensions – between these levels in somewhat different ways. It is worth also remarking that at the level of world communion, the Anglican Consultative Council of the Anglican Communion is at present a body for consultation and fellowship in a remarkably similar way to the council of the Baptist World Alliance. In addition, however, the BWA has the mandate to bring as many church members as possible together in communion in congress every five years.

THE EUCHARIST OR LORD'S SUPPER

*The Lord's supper and spiritual nourishment*

62.  In these conversations, only one paper was formally presented on the nature of the Lord's supper, and that was by a Baptist from Jamaica. But from the conversation generated on that occasion, and from later discussion in the North American phase, there seems to be much less variation between Baptist and Anglican understanding of the Lord's supper or eucharist than is often assumed. Rather, one might say that there is a similar range of variation within each communion. Baptists and Anglicans stress, to varying degrees, elements of *anamnesis* (remembrance as "making the past present"), *eucharisteia* (thanksgiving), *koinonia* (communion and fellowship), anticipation of the future kingdom and meeting with Christ at his table. Anglicans go on to emphasize the grace imparted by God through the sacrament. This is not without some counterpart in Baptist thinking, and it is wrong to regard Baptists in general as having an extreme Zwinglian view of "mere memorial" (indeed, it is doubtful whether Zwingli held such a view himself); many have followed Calvin in his understanding of a "spiritual nourishment" offered through the supper, and in finding a special opportunity provided there for sharing in the benefits of the death of Christ. Like other Reformed groups, Baptists have refused to locate the presence of the Christ in the elements in any restrictive way, finding the presence of the crucified and risen Christ in the whole event of the meal and in the gathered congregation. They have also declined to identify any change in the bread and wine other than a change in significance in the special use to which the elements are being put. All this is well summarized in the Baptist contribution to which reference has been made, and from which the following is a helpful extract:

> Baptist churches in the Caribbean affirm the eucharist as *anamnesis* of Christ... A strong focus is placed on the past, but this is accompanied by a strong recognition of the immeasurable benefits of Christ's unrepeatable sacrifice at Calvary for those participating in the holy communion. To this extent, the matter of the presence of Christ at the Lord's supper is deemed to be real. After wails of grief follows the confession of sin... [and then] shouts of joy accompany the participation in the communion. These pious shouts bespeak a clear sense of the nearness of the one who gave his all for the sake of our salvation.[89]

In the North American phase, a Southern Baptist representative commented that, although his tradition places emphasis on remembrance in the sense of memorialism, "there is a rising sense among younger Southern Baptists that the Lord's supper should be understood in a Calvinistic sense as a spiritual communion with the risen Christ and his body".[90]

*Sacrament and ordinance*

63. While Baptists in England in the 17th and 18th centuries used the words "sacrament" and "ordinance" interchangeably, reaction against the Oxford Movement in the 19th century led to a favouring of the term "ordinance" by many (but not all) Baptists. It is now almost universal on the continent of Europe and in the USA. The term "ordinance" is used positively to affirm the institution of the supper by the Lord himself, and negatively to deny any change in the *substance* of the elements. It should, however, not be taken to mean a denial of the presence of Christ *in any manner* in the meal, nor as simply equivalent to a "bare memorialist" view. The Jamaican writer of the paper referred to above rightly comments that "the tradition of type-casting churches as sacramental and non-sacramental has negatively affected the question of the real presence of Christ at the Lord's supper". Differences between Anglicans and Baptists have been described in exactly this simplistic way. The group gathered for the North American phase wanted to stress that a recognition that the manner of the presence of Christ is not definable by any theory is common ground between Anglicans and Baptists.

64. Anglicans generally regard the elements of bread and wine as both "expressive" signs (portraying the death of Christ) and "effective" signs (conveying the grace of God which springs from the sacrifice of Christ). The emphasis often heard among Baptists that the elements are "only a symbol" should not be taken to mean "only a visual aid". Those who use this language may mean by it what Anglicans often indicate by speaking of an effective sign; but Baptists are making clear that it is *God* who creates the effect *through* the sign. One more quotation from the Jamaican Baptist paper is apposite: "Caribbean Baptists sometimes put it like this – 'Something happens to us whenever we partake of the Lord's supper'… they experience the gracious hand of God upon their lives, forgiving their sins, offering them nourishment for the pilgrimage of the Christian life, and drawing them into ever deeper communion with the Trinity… ordinance is understood to have sacramental significance."[91]

65. Anglicans are accustomed to speak of the Lord's supper or holy communion as "a sacrifice of praise and thanksgiving". While this is not a familiar expression among Baptists, when they hear it they are likely to be comfortable with this use of a scriptural phrase. The term "eucharistic sacrifice" sometimes used by Anglicans may sound more alarming to Baptists, but it should be remembered that "eucharist" here simply means "thanksgiving". In both communions there has been a renewal of theologies of creation in recent years, and the idea that the prayer of thanksgiving sums up "the sacrifice of praise" of all created things has found a place in both Anglican and Baptist liturgies and is reflected in the setting before God of the elements of bread and wine. Within the movement of the service, both Anglicans and Baptists re-dedicate themselves to the Lord "as a living sacrifice" (Rom. 12:1) in and through the once-for-all sacrifice of Christ on the cross. Like Baptist thought, Anglican theology emphasizes that this sacrifice cannot be repeated; Anglicans may, however, lay more stress on the way that the elements portray or represent the sacrifice of Christ, and they have recently found it helpful to think of being "drawn into the movement of his self-offering" in the eucharist.

*Presidency at the supper*

66. For the first two centuries of their life in England, Baptists generally insisted that only the ordained minister could preside at the communion table. This was partly

because the pastor had been set aside for this ministry by the church meeting, and partly because the pastor had been ordained by other pastors who represented the wider fellowship of churches. A change came in the 19th century, when it became widely accepted that other church members could be called and appointed by the church meeting to preside in case of need. It is incorrect then to regard the historic Baptist view as being that "anyone can preside at the table", and to link this view with the "priesthood of all believers". Only those may preside who are recognized by the church meeting as having been called by Christ to do so, and those are *usually*, as a matter of "good church order", those already called by Christ to be pastors. The possibility in principle of a non-ordained member presiding on occasion does differentiate Baptists from Anglicans, for whom episcopal ordination as priest is the requirement, without any exceptions. For Baptists, the commission from Christ, through the Spirit, is the key. However, an Anglican representative from Chile also offered the view that, for pastoral reasons, a lay-person should be able to preside at communion when no priest was available (a view which has also been espoused by some Roman Catholic liberation theologians); moves had apparently been made in this direction within Chile, but had been halted by the province in deference to the wider Anglican Communion.[92] In the conversations in both Latin America and the Caribbean it was noted that, despite a professed "anti-clericalism", Baptist church members in fact wanted the pastor to preside. This is in fact thoroughly in line with Baptist tradition, and any surprise only comes from the fact that regular practice within free evangelical churches of presidency by those other than the pastor has gradually seeped into Baptist practice too.

*Eucharistic hospitality*

67. Without any recorded exception, Anglican churches offer hospitality at the communion table to baptized Christians who would normally share in communion in their own churches. Some complaint was heard at the Latin American conversations that there was not the same openness of the table in Baptist churches. Baptists responded that this was admittedly the case in the past, but that the situation had changed and "most" Baptist churches in Latin America now have an open table, including in Brazil where this was a recent development (though here it seems to be restricted to fellow Protestant believers). The open table, it was reported, is almost universal in the West Indies. This in fact is the prevailing practice among Baptist conventions and unions affiliated to the Baptist World Alliance, though exceptions include Southern Baptists who generally open the table only to other Baptists.

68. Typical explanations offered by those Baptist churches which offer an open table despite closed membership would be that the table belongs to the Lord and not to the church, and that the table is the visible sign of the spiritual unity of all Christian people despite other divisions. Indeed, Baptist understanding of the Lord's supper has always given a central place to the fellowship of believers with each other around the Lord's table. Baptists believe that they can know the mind of Christ in church meeting because, joined in covenant relationship, they are his body. This embodiment of Christ in the church will also be expressed in the celebration of the Lord's supper; the congregation *as* the body of Christ breaks bread which represents the body of Christ. There is an overlap here with recent Anglican thinking that it is the whole congregation that celebrates the eucharist with the priest as the president of the assembly. The wider context is the

Anglican understanding that the church is identified by the administration of the sacraments (eucharist and baptism) together with the preaching of the word. With regard to the aspect of "fellowship" of members with one another in the supper or eucharist, the most obvious difference is probably not in theology at all, but in the manner of reception of the bread and wine. Baptists sit together in fellowship "around the table" by remaining in their seats and being served by the deacons. Anglicans come forward and kneel at the altar rail to be served; while this emphasizes the nature of the elements as "gifts of God for the people of God", it can also be a communal act which expresses mutual fellowship as people kneel together. The physical difference between sitting and coming to kneel at the rail may be felt as the most evident difference between Anglican and Baptist services by many participants.

## EPISCOPE OR OVERSIGHT

*Three dimensions of* episcope

69. In the Norwich conversations, Anglican participants returned to the wording of the Chicago-Lambeth Quadrilateral of 1888, which proposed four principles as the basis for visible unity between the churches. Alongside holy scripture, the Apostles' and Nicene Creeds and the two sacraments of baptism and eucharist, it placed "the historic episcopate, locally adapted... to the varying need of the nations and people called by God..." In the Yangon conversations, the presentation made by the Anglican church in Myanmar similarly highlighted the Chicago-Lambeth Quadrilateral, regarding it as "a point of identity for much of the Anglican Communion".[93] It also featured centrally in a presentation on the meaning of authority from the Anglican Church of Canada.[94] In the 1888 statement, and in recent ecumenical conversations, Anglican churches have stressed that the episcopal office – while not being of the very essence of the church – plays a vital part in maintaining the health of the church, as having a "representative nature in focusing the koinonia of the church in time and space".[95] In accord with a widespread understanding among churches today, Anglicanism defines *episcope* (oversight) as having three dimensions: communal (exercised by the church corporately, especially in synod), personal (embodied in a single person in an area) and collegial (as exercised by bishops in communion with each other and with presbyters). None *of* these dimensions exists on its own, and the three are interdependent.

70. In Norwich, Baptists replied that they also have always recognized these three dimensions of *episcope* within and among the churches.[96] However, in the first place the basic personal ministry of oversight is given to the minister or pastor in the *local* church, whom many early Baptists called either "elder" (*presbuteros*) or "bishop" (*episcopos*) without distinction. Oversight in the local community flows to and fro between the personal and the communal, since the responsibility of "watching over" the church belongs both to all the members gathered in church meeting and to the pastor. This is grounded in the theological principle of the primary rule of *Christ in* the congregation. Baptists do, however, also recognize *episcope* at an interchurch level. Oversight is exercised communally by a regional association of churches, which in assembly seeks the mind of Christ for the life and mission of the member churches, while having no power to *impose* decisions on the local church meeting. Oversight flows freely between the communal and the personal here too, as personal oversight is exercised by various kinds of senior

ministers who are linked either with the association or with the convention/union at state or national level.

## *Two offices or three orders of ministry?*

71. Anglicanism places the personal ministry of *episcope* within the context of a three-fold order of ministry. In the words of the preface to the ordinal (1662), it affirms that "from the apostles' time there have been these orders of ministers in Christ's church; bishops, priests and deacons". In Baptist practice, there are variations on a basically twofold office. In British Baptist life, "regional ministers" (previously called "general superintendents") are appointed to minister among the churches in regional areas. In Baptist unions elsewhere in Europe which are smaller in size, this oversight role may be undertaken by officers of the whole union or convention; in some Eastern European Baptist unions (for example, Latvia, Moldova and Georgia), these pastors are explicitly designated as "bishops". In a different situation, the title "bishop" may also be held in some African-American churches. Such interchurch ministry is certainly understood to be episcopal, in the sense of being a form of pastoral oversight, but in nearly all places it is not understood as creating a third order of ministry beyond the twofold office of deacons and pastors (one exception appears in the Georgian Baptist convention).[97] Rather, this ministry is seen as an extension of the episcopal ministry of the local pastor, and appointment of such senior ministers is made by the churches together in assembly, just as a local church meeting sets aside its own *episcopos*.

72. The theological principle here is that first the church gathers in fellowship (koinonia), and this calls for oversight (*episcope*) to guide and maintain it; there is no sense that the office of oversight, however it is expressed, *creates* the fellowship and unity of the church. As a Baptist contribution in Santiago put it, "Baptists in Latin America do not accept that the episcopal role is the safeguard of the unity of the church, because real unity rests in Christ himself not in a human office."[98] It should be noted, however, that an Anglican bishop from Chile agreed that while the presence of the bishop was *a help* towards unity, no bishop on his own constituted the unity of the church.[99]

## *Local "adaptation" of episcope*

73. In Norwich, the question was raised as to what the phrase "locally adapted" in the 1888 statement might mean in practice with regard to the episcopate, and how open the Church of England might be to a re-shaping of the *episcope*. One answer was given in the North American phase, when representatives of the Episcopal Church of the USA (ECUSA) described their adaptation of the role of bishop in a context where there was an existing pre-Revolution tradition of strong involvement by the laity in congregational government of the church. Here the principle of the parish "vestry", a council elected by members of the church, was extended into a wider sphere. Thus the parish vestry calls the rector, though with the approval of the bishop. At the diocesan level, standing committees which comprise elected lay and ordained members share the oversight of the diocese with the bishop.[100] One bishop of ECUSA who participated in the conversations remarked that "there is very little a bishop can do on his or her own".

74. In the meeting in Yangon, the model of unity in the Church of North India (CNI) was cited as another possible example of adaptation, as the CNI declares in its constitution that "the church is not committed to any one particular theological interpretation of episcopacy". A bishop of the CNI with a Baptist background stressed that the CNI defines the episcopate as being both "historic and constitutional". The "constitutional" aspect means that in all decisions the bishop has to win the consent, not only of fellow bishops, but of the church council which he serves. This evidently blends personal and communal *episcope* (and so gives a new meaning to collegiality) in a way which builds upon both the Anglican and Baptist tradition, without exactly duplicating either. Here the degree of sharing in oversight between bishop and council seems to exceed even the cooperation between bishop and standing committees in the ECUSA model. The bishop expressed the situation in this way:

> As president of his diocesan council... [the bishop] has obviously a great deal of influence. If he has earned the trust of his people, there is a great deal of freedom available to him to take initiatives. But in all matters he must carry his council with him... Pastoral authority is not a coercive authority. It is based on a leader's servant spirit, which must manifest the compassion of Christ. [101]

75. It was significant that, in the formation of the CNI, the uniting Baptist churches in their declaration of intent took note that the proposed episcopate would make "reasonable provision for all believers to share in seeking the mind of Christ in the affairs of the church as far as they are able". The Baptist churches also affirmed that they were acting "in exercise of the liberty that they have always claimed... to interpret and administer the laws of Christ". [102] This reflects in a new context the general Baptist understanding of the liberty of the local church; it seems that the Baptists of North India were claiming a freedom to work out the implications of the "Lordship of Christ in his church" in new forms of *episcope*. It must be added, however, that not all Baptist churches in the existing Council of Baptist Churches in North India agreed with them, and most did not join the new CNI.

76. The African round of consultation suggested another way of understanding the relation between personal and communal *episcope*, based in traditional understanding of the relation between leader and community rather than a Western concept of individualism. The Anglican representatives conceded that the bishop appears as a strongly authoritative figure, and recognized the Baptist suspicion of a hierarchy which (in their view) disempowers the congregation. [103] This impression has been reinforced by the taking of traditional chieftaincy titles by some bishops in Nigeria. However, the rooting of leadership in community means that the bishop is expected to represent and to voice the consensus of the people. This kind of representation does not fit in neatly to Western democratic traditions of majority voting, but still requires a deep immersion into the life of the people and sensitivity to their concerns. In the Latin American conversations, an Anglican complaint was heard that the model for a bishop is North American, and contains a large element of the administrator. The result is the "loneliness of the bishop".

*A sign of apostolicity?*

77. Whatever the structures of consultation and consent with which *episcope is* surrounded, the Anglican understanding of *episcope* as a historic sign of apostolic continu-

ity means that those ordained to parish ministry (presbyters and deacons) must be ordained by the bishop. While there are some Baptist unions (in Eastern Europe, for example) in which the union or convention president *must* be involved in laying-on of hands, the presiding of such a regional minister is usually regarded as "good order" rather than essential. Baptists, however, more generally require the gathering of other churches and their ministers to offer their consent for ordination, since the local minister represents the wider church of Christ to the local community. Such seeking of the guidance of the Holy Spirit shows again an integration of personal and communal *episcope*. The presentation of the Baptist Convention of Myanmar laid stress on their tradition of an "ordination council" consisting of about seven neighbouring churches and ministers (common among many Baptists in the USA and in Canada); indeed, it lamented that this tradition was being ignored by some places at present, due to the influence of new church movements that it clearly regarded as non-Baptistic.[104] There is a kind of extension of the "ordination council" in the state Baptist unions affiliated with the Baptist Union of Australia, where ministers are ordained at an assembly of the state union, or at least at a service arranged or approved by the union.

78. In summary, Baptists and Anglicans are agreed that "apostolicity" consists in the succession of the *faith*, as it is received and passed on, through the whole *community* of the people of God. Both Anglicans and Baptists understand that God has given a variety of means for preserving and interpreting the apostolic faith, which will include the minister in a single congregation and regional ministries. But among these means, Anglicanism finds one particular office – the regional bishop – to be a sign and safeguard of the apostolic tradition in a way which is indispensable for the well-being of the life of the church.

THE MEANING OF RECOGNITION

*Stages towards recognition?*

79. One aim of these conversations between Baptists and Anglicans has been to look for ways "to increase our fellowship and common witness to the gospel". This does not, of course, imply any intention to move towards a unity of churches, other than to deepen our already existing spiritual unity with each other; but it does raise the question as to whether, and in what sense, we can "recognize" each other as true churches of Jesus Christ. This kind of mutual recognition will seem to be more important for some Baptists and Anglicans than for others, and it will seem more urgent in some circumstances than others. For some who read this report it will not appear to be a question at all, while for those participating in the conversations from the areas of the world we visited it seemed that the task of mission would be helped by greater public affirmation of each other. We need to be sensitive to different needs *within* our communions in this matter, as much as *between* the communions. These conversations are not intended to commit any unions, conventions or provinces to steps that they do not wish to take at this time, although we hope that all will find some challenge in the questions that arise.

80. At the meeting in Europe, the delegates from the Church of England proposed an approach "in stages" to the question of recognition of each other as Christian churches. At the first level, local churches share fellowship in practical ways in worship and mission, and so informally recognize the reality of Christian life and ministry in each other.

This could be called recognition in the sense of "*seeing each other as*" Christian communities, but it is not recognition in the sense of "approval" or "validation". It was clear at Norwich that the Anglican participants regarded Local Ecumenical Partnerships in the UK as an extension of this first stage of "seeing as", and that the agreement of churches to walk together as pilgrims in an interchurch process or to form national councils of churches was the taking of this stage to a more corporate level. The second stage is official recognition, where each church formally affirms the other as a "true church belonging to the one, holy, catholic and apostolic church", and states that in the other church the word of God is authentically preached, the sacraments are truly celebrated and the ministry is truly given by God. [105] The Anglican delegation at Norwich made clear that this stage requires at least an *intention* to move towards fuller visible unity in due time. There can, however, at this second stage still be issues on which agreement has not yet been reached – such as lay presidency at the eucharist, or forms of oversight which do not fully correspond to the Anglican episcopacy. The third stage is "full communion" (sometimes just called "communion"), marked by a common celebration of the sacraments, a common ministry and common structures for mutual consultation and shared decision-making.

81. If these three stages are clearly separated out in this way, then the present conversations between the BWA and the Anglican Communion have their place only within the first stage. This indeed has been the view taken by the Anglican representatives on the continuation committee. These discussions are not of the kind that can result in the second stage of "formal recognition", though they can prepare for further conversations that might have this result. A staged approach was reflected in the resolution of the Lambeth Conference (1998) which committed Anglicans to the present conversations, and which welcomed the idea that "an initial core group... could meet Anglicans and Baptists in different regions for a first quinquennium, with a view to the identification of issues for study in an international forum in a second quinquennium". [106] As noted in the introduction to this report, the present quinquennium has, nevertheless, been marked by serious theological discussion which has been welcomed by the representatives of both communions.

*An overlap of stages?*

82. It must be said that Baptists approach the issue of recognition a little differently from the "staged" approach. Although it is probably only a small minority of Baptists throughout the world who are committed to a search for "visible unity" (stage 3), most Baptists will find it difficult to separate out the first two stages of "recognition" quite so sharply. They find a constant overlap between them, which becomes more and more blurred as churches live and work together at a local level. "Seeing each other as" Christian communities leads for Baptists naturally into a public affirmation of the other as a truly apostolic church and to an acceptance of the validity of ministry within that church. For Baptists on the UK scene, for example, participating in the interchurch process of "Churches Together" implies a recognition of each other as part of the one, holy, catholic and apostolic church. In the Asian phase of the BWA Anglican conversations these two stages also tended to merge into one another. In the context of a dominant non-Christian culture, such as Theravada Buddhism in South and Southeast Asia, churches are more ready to recognize the integrity of the orders of ministry among each other (rather as a military

chaplain from one denomination might serve all Protestant Christian believers in time of conflict). In both Latin America and the West Indies, there was some ambivalence towards recognition of Baptist ministry by Anglicans; on the one hand, there was a distinct sense of the necessity for episcopal ordination as part of Anglican identity, while on the other hand there was some impatience with denominational divisions which it was felt had been brought to their countries by missionaries in a colonial situation, and which it should be possible to get beyond. The blurring between "stages of recognition" is less marked, however, where Baptists insist that unity is "only spiritual" without implications for the concrete life of the church, as would be the case – among others – with the Southern Baptists of the USA.

### Limits in recognition: ministry and baptism

83. Each of the communions in conversation feels that the other falls short in one area of recognition in particular – for Anglicans it is the refusal of most Baptists to recognize their baptism as infants, and for Baptists it is the reluctance of many Anglicans to recognize their ordained ministry. It has emerged in these conversations that the Anglican church is in fact in the process of a "paradigm shift" in its recognition of the ministry of those who have not been ordained through an episcopal succession, and this seems to be reflected in the ambivalence towards Baptist ministerial orders mentioned in the previous paragraph. At the "second stage" of recognition it is certainly possible now to recognize the authenticity of the ministry in word and sacrament of those who have not been episcopally ordained, and who serve in churches where there are not (or not yet) bishops in the sense of the Anglican threefold order. Their ministry can be recognized as being a genuine call from God and a means of feeding the life of the people of God. Recognition of genuineness does not, however, mean an "interchangeability" of ministry, in which a minister of a non-episcopal church could simply be substituted for an Anglican priest. This awaits fuller communion. While episcopacy is *a sign* of apostolic succession, and is not of the essence of the church, interchangeability would require an agreement concerning oversight, and this would involve being in canonical relationship to a bishop.

84. Now, within this perspective, it seems that in many situations the same practical recognition of the genuineness of Christian ministry can be extended to churches which are still at the "first" stage of recognition, which includes Baptists. Just as Christian communities can be "seen as" places where the church of Christ is present, so ministry *can* be "seen as" really happening there. In this Anglican view, an ordained minister of another church has a genuine ministry within that church and within the universal church, and people (including Anglicans in appropriate circumstances) can receive genuine pastoral care and sacramental nourishment from that ministry, while it is not of course a ministry within the Anglican church. Baptists will feel that this marks an advance in mutual understanding and partnership in the gospel. Moreover, it appears that in at least two situations where Baptist and Anglican churches are in fellowship with each other and other Christian churches, in the group of Covenanted Churches in Wales and in the South African Council of Churches, a more formal recognition of the validity of ordained ministry among Baptists has been declared by the Anglican participants. This seems to be the kind of recognition of authenticity (though not of course interchangeability) of ministry which would normally belong to the "second stage" of recognition. However, where

there is no formal acknowledgment of the other as a true church of Jesus Christ, it seems that there will be ambiguities about even a practical recognition of ministry, and this must be felt by Baptists as a limit on the possibilities of fellowship and shared mission.

85. For their part, however, most Baptists do not notice any incongruity in their willingness to recognize another Christian community as a true church of Christ, affirming its ministry and its celebration of the Lord's supper, while at the same time declining to recognize its *baptism*. Some Baptists will recognize others as being members of a true church, although they have only been baptized as infants, while still insisting that they should be baptized as a confessing disciple before admission to their own church ("closed membership"). Others practise "open membership" and do not insist on what other Christians may regard as a re-baptism, though they find it difficult to refuse baptism to any who sincerely desire it, and might even (in some pastoral circumstances) encourage that desire. But in all these cases the acceptance of another church can be *regardless* of the kind of baptism practised there. A typical Baptist explanation for this position would be that true baptism is indeed the baptism of a confessing believer, and that this is the "one baptism" referred to in Ephesians 4:5, but that other Christian communities can still be recognized as true churches because they exhibit in their lives the one Spirit, one body, one hope, and one faith which God grants (Eph. 4:3-8).

86. Some Baptists will offer a doctrinal justification for this separation of baptism from church membership, along the lines that faith alone is required for the gathering of a church and that baptism is not a "church ordinance" but a matter of personal obedience to Christ. Other Baptists feel that there is an inconsistency here, since they agree with the Reformers that a true church is one where "the word of God is rightly preached and the sacraments rightly administered"; but they are prepared to live with this anomaly on the grounds of giving to others the right of freedom of conscience, of respecting the obedience of others to the commands of Christ, *and* of recognizing that "God has accepted them" (Rom. 14:3). A third group of Baptists will try to resolve the inconsistency by recognizing the baptism of infants as a form of baptism which is derived from the norm of believers' baptism, and which is valid when it is part of a whole process of initiation which includes the faith of the individual believer. In one of these three ways, all of which have been expressed by various participants in these conversations, Baptists can recognize as "church" a Christian community which baptizes infants; they also think it to be part of their Baptist ethos to give one another the freedom to differ among themselves about this issue.

87. Anglicans, however, will insist without exception on baptism as entrance to the Christian church, and – despite Baptist protestations – will feel that they are being "unchurched" if their baptism is not recognized. This itself makes difficult the *formal* recognition of Baptist churches. It is compounded because Anglicans take the Reformation view that one of the marks of a true church is that the sacraments should be "rightly administered". Anglicans will, of course, gladly recognize a baptism which has taken place in a Baptist church with the use of the triune name of God and water, as long as it is not – in their view – a rebaptism. But the practice of baptizing as a believer someone previously baptized as an infant cannot be regarded by them as a proper administration of the sacraments, since baptism by its nature (as entrance into the church, and participation in the once-for-all act of salvation by Christ) is unrepeatable. In face of this dilemma, the writers of this report suggest that the image of initiation as a journey (see

above §42) may increase understanding of other's position, although it seems that it cannot at this stage resolve the differences in conviction.

*Failures in recognition*

88. The African round of conversations disclosed less joint fellowship and activity between Baptists and Anglicans than happens in the UK and in many parts of Asia, although there was a more cooperative situation in East Africa and overall there was a great deal of common ground in the Africanization of theology. In the conversations between Baptists and Anglicans in Latin America, identity seemed almost interchangeable, with a shared concern for evangelism that put differences about baptism and ministry into the shade; but this commonality, discovered in conversation, was by no means reflected in existing cooperation which was limited. In Brazil, Anglicans are often regarded by Baptists as a branch of Roman Catholicism, or at least non-Protestant, and contact between the two groups is virtually non-existent. The situation in the West Indies is patchy; in the Bahamas, for instance, while Baptist and Anglican ministers "know each other as friends", and many Anglicans will speak of their roots in both Anglican and Baptist sectors, there is little joint activity among the congregations; by contrast, there are strong ecumenical relations in Jamaica, and there is an obvious influence on the churches which comes from the ecumenical theological training at United Theological College, Kingston.

89. In the African round there was a perception among Anglicans, particularly in South Africa, that recognition was hindered by different approaches to scripture between the two communions. However, while Baptists were often thought to adopt a more literalist interpretation than Anglicans, the conversations themselves showed that there was a similar approach to scripture as "sacred story" among both groups. One Anglican comment was that there was more acceptance and partnership at the local than regional level, marked by celebration in funerals, weddings and festivals shared together in the "extended family". A Baptist from Zimbabwe felt that in his country and others (Malawi, Uganda, Kenya and Zambia were also named at different times) the mission agencies still exercised a great deal of influence in inhibiting ecumenical relations which the churches were more anxious to pursue, and that this was blocking joint action in mission.

*The desire for mutual recognition*

90. In all places where conversations were held, there was a strong desire expressed by the participants for increased recognition of each other as partners in the faith, to be expressed in life and work together. The term "ecumenical" was thought to be a hindrance among Baptists in some places, and especially in Latin America, but the reality it signified was thought desirable without exception. As well as an inner motivation for unity, the context was seen to exert a pressure for greater sharing, in different ways. In Asia, as already observed, there is the incentive of being surrounded by a dominant non-Christian culture. In Latin America the need for Baptist-Anglican cooperation is heightened by the distressing fragmentation in Christian witness brought about by new independent churches, using television evangelism and appealing to a prosperity gospel; in this situation, as one Baptist put it, "the pastoral ministry of the church is challenged to

work for a true unity of the church". [107] In the West Indies, a Baptist participant stressed that mutual recognition by Christians would be a means towards finding a basis for Caribbean unity at a regional level. In the face of a lack of a common body of historical and cultural traditions, due to the activity of multiple colonial powers, the church can and must be part of the process towards social, political and economic unity. [108]

## 4. Questions and challenges

The following questions are directed to churches and individuals who read this report, both Anglicans and Baptists. They are posed in the light of the experience of the conversations throughout the world, and so the questions are listed under the headings which correspond to those in the account above, and references are added to particular paragraphs which may give a helpful background. Some of the questions are intended simply to aid further exploration of the themes of the report. Some, however, are also intended to be challenges to the understanding that Anglicans and Baptists might have of each other, and to offer suggestions for further action.

1. THE IMPORTANCE OF CONTINUITY

- Can Baptists understand why Anglicans value being part of a continuous story of the church through history since the time of the apostles? Can Anglicans understand why Baptists think it essential for their story to connect directly with the experience of the disciples in the New Testament? (3-9)
- Is it possible that a Baptist emphasis on being directly linked to "the New Testament church" might lead to individualism and a kind of self-sufficiency, neglecting the reality of the church through time and across the world? Is it possible that an Anglican emphasis on being part of the "catholic church" through the ages might lead to a rejection or marginalizing of those who do not think of themselves as standing in this tradition?
- In what ways might Baptists and Anglicans see their stories as having run in parallel, in the purposes of God, since the Reformation of the church? Might this especially apply to the place of the two traditions (establishment and dissent) in the life of Britain? (4)
- What difference does it make to a sense of continuity when a Christian community values the cultural heritage of its own society or ethnic group, and sees God as having been at work within it? (10-14) In this situation, in what new ways might both Anglicans and Baptists have to tell their stories?

2. CONFESSING THE FAITH

- Anglicans and Baptists in these conversations affirmed that the "supreme authority in faith and practice" is Jesus Christ himself. (25) Do the implications of this principle need to be worked out more thoroughly in current disputes within both communions?

- Can Baptists recognize how much their reading of scripture is in fact shaped by the historic creeds of the Christian church? Would it be better to talk of "scripture as primary" rather than "scripture alone"? (26) Is there really a difference between a creed and a confession? (20-22)
- Can Anglicans ask what they mean by "reason" in the famous triad "scripture-Tradition-reason", in view of comments made about this in the conversations? (26) Can Anglicans ask themselves whether they always make Tradition and the use of reason secondary to the authority of scripture?
- Can Anglicans recognize the essence of the ecumenical creeds in the prayers, hymns and preaching of a church which does not normally use the actual creeds in its liturgy? Can Baptists who do not normally say creeds make special occasions when they *can* be used (e.g., covenant renewal services)? How can Baptists answer the Anglican anxiety that without a creed there would be no clear standard or basis of faith?
- How far – if at all – do differences between Anglicans and Baptists in their practice of ministry, oversight and baptism reflect differences in the understanding of the apostolic faith itself?
- What occasions might there be for making clear publicly that Anglicans and Baptists confess the same faith in Christ and proclaim the same Christian gospel?

3. MISSION AND MINISTRY

- Does the distinction suggested in the report between two models of mission – inside and outside the borders of the church (27-29) – help to clarify different approaches to mission sometimes taken by Anglicans and Baptists?
- Are Anglicans still working with the stereotype that Baptists only have a pastoral concern for their own members, while Anglicans care for all the members of society? Are Baptists still working with the stereotype that Anglicans think there is no need to proclaim the gospel to those who have been baptized as infants?
- Can Anglicans and Baptists in the West face the criticism from those in the South and the East that missionary preaching in the past failed to have a "holistic" view of the human being? Are Western Christians aware that churches in the South and East think that their prophetic and servant ministries are often inhibited by the altitudes and expectations of their partners in Western churches? (30-32)
- What is meant by the "priesthood of all believers", or "the royal priesthood of the people of God", and how does this relate to involvement in mission? In what ways is the practice of believers' baptism helpful in fostering this link? What is implied by calling a Christian minister a "priest" in different cultures, and how does this relate to the task of mission? (36)
- Does the present situation of rapid political and social change call for stronger mutual recognition between Baptists and Anglicans for the sake of the mission of God? If so, what forms might this take locally? (32)
- Do Anglicans understand how the passion for religious liberty can influence some forms of Baptist evangelism? (37-38). Do Baptists understand why Anglicans have tended to view the relationship between church and state more positively than Baptists? (39) How is it possible to observe the line between freedom to evangelize and proselytism? (37)

### 4. BAPTISM AND THE PROCESS OF INITIATION

- Are Anglicans still working with the stereotype that Baptists regard baptism simply as a profession of faith, with no room for the activity of God's grace? Are Baptists still working with the stereotype that Anglicans regard baptism simply an instance of the prevenient grace of God, with no room for the exercise of faith? (41)

- Do Baptists understand the pain caused to Anglicans when people already baptized as infants are baptized as believers, thereby seeming to deny the validity of their own baptism and church membership? Do Anglicans understand the pain caused to Baptists, previously baptized as infants in another church, who are now asked to forgo a baptism which they understand to be a step of obedience to Christ – especially when their infant baptism led to no effective contact with the church community?

- Can Baptists and Anglicans agree that initiation – or the beginning of the Christian life – is not a single point but a process or journey within which baptism plays a part, and that the whole process includes a personal profession of faith? Can they see ways in which their own practice of baptism implies this? (42)

- In the light of the understanding of initiation given above, can Baptists understand the place that Anglicans give to infant baptism within the journey with which the Christian life begins? Might this also help Baptists in thinking through the theological reasons for the presentation (or blessing, or "dedication") of infants?

- Anglicans will reject the practice of what they consider to be "re-baptism", while Baptists will be unhappy with the practice (where it happens) of baptizing infants whose parents have no continuing contact with the church. Should these circumstances be allowed to disturb a partnership in mission between Anglicans and Baptists? (cf. 51)

- What are the theological reasons for the Baptist practice of "open membership" where it exists? Is it enough to base "open membership" simply on the valuing of a profession of faith over all forms of baptism? Might recognizing a place for infant baptism in the whole "journey of initiation" help to develop further Baptist thinking in this area? (49-52)

- How might the understanding of initiation as a process help Anglicans in thinking through the theological reasons for the practice of confirmation, or restoring it to its former importance? (44-45) Has any new thinking been done about confirmation to meet new ecumenical and cultural situations?

### 5. MEMBERSHIP OF THE CHURCH

- How should a local church be defined and identified? Does the fact that Anglicans see the whole diocese as a "local church" help to bring Baptists and Anglicans closer together in their view of the nature of the church? (55) Do we have to re-think the meaning of "local church" in a social context in which communities are now fluid, and in which "networks" of relationship may be more important than a geographical locality?

- How much do Baptist church members understand themselves to be members of the church universal, and does this give them a vision of the mission of God beyond their own locality? (56) Do Anglicans give sufficient attention to "finding the mind of Christ" amongst the members in the local congregation?

- For Baptists, what is the difference between the secular word "autonomy" and the biblical idea that each congregation has "liberty" under the rule of Christ to order its life? (60) For Anglicans, can the process of "receiving" synodical decisions by the local congregation be made more vital than it sometimes is? (61)

- Outside the parochial system of the Church of England, is there any real difference between Baptist and Anglican concepts of "membership" of the church? If the church is understood as a "gathered church", how does this relate to the rest of society? (55-57)

- How is membership in the church related to baptism? Do any Baptists think that it is possible to be baptized and not be a "member" of the church? Do Anglicans think that young infants are members in the same sense as confessing disciples?

- How does being a "member of the body of Christ" relate to membership of a local church or single congregation? If you are Baptist, do you think that believing children, before they are baptized, are members of the body of Christ? If you are Anglican, do you think that all those who are baptized as infants remain members of the body of Christ, even if there is no contact at all with the church afterwards? (53-54) Does an understanding of initiation as a process, or journey, help to answer these questions?

- Is it possible in your region to share baptism and confirmation services between Anglicans and Baptists?

6. THE EUCHARIST OR LORD'S SUPPER

- How can we understand the "presence" of Christ in the eucharist or Lord's supper? Are there as many differences of understanding *within* Anglican and Baptist life as *between* Anglicans and Baptists? Should any differences of understanding prevent us from sharing in the Lord's table together? (62-65)

- In the light of these conversations, should any Baptists continue to have a "closed table", restricted only to those who have been baptized as believers? Were the participants in these conversations right to suppose that Anglicans everywhere offer eucharistic hospitality to those who are baptized in any trinitarian church? If not, why not? (67-68)

- Can Anglicans affirm that Christ can graciously come to nourish his people with his life in a Baptist communion service, presided over by an ordained Baptist minister? Can they affirm this if a lay pastor presides at the table? (66) Should any Baptists feel inhibited from sharing in an Anglican communion because the person presiding is called a "priest" and wears liturgical garments?

- Why do Anglican parishes differ in their views as to whether baptized children, before confirmation, can receive holy communion? In a Baptist church, can it ever be the practice for believing children to receive bread and wine before they are baptized? Can you place your answers in the context of understanding Christian initiation as a journey?

- What implications might a sharing in holy communion between Anglicans and Baptists have for other areas of church life?

7. *EPISCOPE* OR OVERSIGHT

- Can Anglicans and Baptists discern the same reality of *episcope* (pastoral oversight and responsibility) in each other's churches, despite differences in church structures? In particular, can Anglicans find the reality of *episcope* in Baptist churches even though there is no bishop in the Anglican understanding of this office?
- Can Baptists understand why Anglicans value highly the ministry of bishops as a sign of historical continuity between the church of the apostles and the mission of the church today? (69,78) Can Anglicans understand why Baptists want to insist that the basic ministry of oversight is that of the minister in the local congregation? (70)
- What do Baptists mean by the title "bishop" in conventions where such offices have been appointed? In what ways is the Baptist trans-local or interchurch ministry (called variously "regional minister", "executive minister" or "association/convention president") like an Anglican bishop, and how is it different? (71-72)
- Is it possible to regularize the act of ordination among Baptists, so that a minister with an interchurch ministry of oversight always presides? (77) What would be the theological reasons for this?
- In the conversations it was noted that there was a kind of "flow" of oversight backwards and forwards between the communal and the personal. (70) How is this the same in Anglican and Baptist structures, and how does it differ?
- Somewhat different models of episcopacy from those in Europe are offered by the Church of North India (which includes former Baptists) and the Episcopal churches of the USA; moreover, African concepts of leadership may point towards aspects of oversight unfamiliar in the West. (73-76) What other "local adaptations" of episcopacy are evident already, or may be possible? Would any adaptation be acceptable to Baptists at present?

8. THE MEANING OF RECOGNITION

- In the light of these conversations, are Baptists and Anglicans everywhere able to "see" the presence of the one church of Jesus Christ in each other's churches? How much can be built on this first step of "seeing" what is apostolic within each other's lives? (79-81) In what ways might it be publicly expressed? Is it desirable to move on to more formal recognition? (81)
- Should Baptists admit an inconsistency when they recognize Anglican churches as true, apostolic churches of Christ, while at the same time they give no place within the purposes of God to the baptism of infants in those churches? (85-87) If so, how should this inconsistency be resolved? Do answers to the questions about baptism, above, give any help answering *this* question?
- Can Anglicans see ordained Baptist ministers as exercising an authentic ministry of word and sacrament which is being used by the Holy Spirit to nourish and build up the church of Christ? (83-84)
- How far are Baptists and Anglicans able to see each other's churches as truly sharing in the apostolic mission? What might be the consequences for the way that evangelism and church-planting is carried out when they see each other in this way?

*[Section 5, Part Two, consists of stories of Anglican-Baptist partnership around the world, and is not included here]*

## 6. Conclusion to the Report: "sharing in the apostolic mission"

This report began by remarking that these conversations throughout the world have not fitted into the usual pattern of ecumenical conversations. While not "formal talks" on the way to visible union, in their range and content they have been more than simply "getting to know you" exercises. They have also made a thorough effort at contextualization of the issues discussed, through drawing on many regional participants. The account of the conversations has shown another way they have broken an accepted pattern, and made something of an experiment. The participants have taken seriously the "first stages" of conversation, rather than seeing these as necessary preliminaries ("talks about talks") to be hastened through as quickly as possible. Formal recognition, in the sense of mutual recognition between Baptist unions or conventions and Anglican provinces is not in prospect at the moment, since accepted procedures have not yet been embarked upon; but, given this situation, the conversations have stretched the possibilities that lie within informal and practical acceptance of each other at this time. This has been, in the words of one objective of the talks, to "increase our fellowship and common witness to the gospel" (objective 4).

The participants have thus tested out the potential within what might be called "*seeing the presence of the one church of Jesus Christ in each other's churches*", which involves "*seeing each other as*" standing within the apostolic Tradition, preaching the apostolic gospel and sharing in the apostolic mission. They have concluded that much can be built upon this approach. The final section of the report ("The Meaning of Recognition") does explore an unfolding process through which the two communions might seek an increasing sense of mutual recognition in the future, if this is desired, but it also registers what is possible within an existing unity in Christ here and now.

As far as confessing the apostolic faith is concerned, those engaged in these conversations were satisfied that Baptists and Anglicans share "one faith", and that there is every reason to share together in God's mission to the world. Despite the fact that one communion is episcopal and synodical in nature, and the other is congregational and associational, the conversations show that there is also a greater closeness than might have been expected in the understanding of such matters as the ministry of oversight and the relation of the local congregation to the universal church. Despite considerable differences of emphasis in some places, the participants found that each communion was committed to a full range of mission and evangelism, from proclamation of the good news of Christ to practical care for the individual, the society and creation. The Western members of the group, however, accepted the judgment of those from the South and East that this holistic view of the gospel had, tragically, not always been communicated by missionary enterprises in the past, whether by Baptists or Anglicans.

While there was a good deal of convergence on the meaning and benefits of the eucharist or Lord's supper, considerable differences about baptism remain, and especially about the practice that Anglicans deprecate as "rebaptism". These have not been resolved, but the members of the conversations think that a first step is better mutual understanding of each other's perspective, which might be achieved by seeing baptism as part of a larger process of initiation, or one stage on a journey of beginning in the Christian life.

The next phase in these conversations will, it is hoped, happen among the many congregations of Baptists and Anglicans dispersed throughout the world, who are encouraged to address the questions and challenges provided in the report. In particular, it is hoped that those who participated in the conversations at the regional level (see Appendix A) will respond to this invitation. The nature of the "continuing forum at the world level" envisaged by the Lambeth Conference will be largely shaped by responses received. The questions might simply be used as a basis for discussion of the report by study groups in churches and theological colleges, but it is hoped that responses will also be sent to the offices of either the Baptist World Alliance or the Anglican Communion. These can be addressed, through the respective offices, to either of the co-chairmen of the continuation committee.

In each of the regional meetings the wish was expressed for increased recognition of the historical and theological integrity that underlies each of these world communions, Baptist and Anglican. There was also a strong desire for what had been achieved in the meetings to be extended into more occasions for shared worship and working together. Each meeting ended, as does this report, with a sense of gratitude to God for each other's story.

## Appendix A: Participants in the International Conversations

THE CONTINUATION COMMITTEE

Rev. Dr Paul S. Fiddes (Baptist, Co-chairman, England)*
Dr Bruce Matthews (Anglican, Co-chairman, Canada)*

*Director of Ecumenical Affairs, Anglican Consultative Council (Co-secretary)*
Rev. Canon David Hamid (2000-2002)
Rt Rev. John Baycroft (2003)
Rev. Canon Gregory Cameron (2003-2005)*

*Director of Study and Research, Baptist World Alliance (Co-secretary)*
Rev. L. Anthony Cupit*

Rev. Prebendary Dr Paul Avis (Anglican, England)*
Most Rev. Samuel San Si Htay (Anglican: 2000-2001, Myanmar)
Rev. Canon Alyson Mary Barnett-Cowan (Anglican: 2002-2003, Canada)
Chancellor Rubie Nottage (Anglican: 2003-2005, Bahamas)*

Rev. Dr Ken Manley (Baptist, Australia)*
Rev. Dr Timothy George (Baptist: 2000-2001, USA)
Rev. Dr Malcolm B. Yarnell (Baptist: 2002-2004, USA)

1. EUROPE: NORWICH, ENGLAND, 21-25 SEPTEMBER 2000

*Anglican:*
Rev. Dr Timothy Bradshaw (England)
Dr Martin Davie (England)
Mr Charles Gore (Scotland)

---

* Those responsible for the final text of the report.

Rev. Susan Huyton (Wales)
Mr Dermot O'Callaghan (Ireland)
Rev. Andrew Sully (Wales)

*Baptist:*
Rev. Gethin Abraham-Williams (Wales)
Rev. Myra Blyth (England)
Rev. Dr Christopher J. Ellis (England)
Rev. Anna Maffei (Italy)
Rev. Dr Kenneth Roxburgh (Scotland)
Rev. Dr Karl Heinz Walter (Germany)

2.  ASIA AND OCEANIA: YANGON, MYANMAR, 18-21 JANUARY 2001

*Anglican:*
Rev. Andrew Chan (Hong Kong, People's Republic of China)
Rev. Simon Biben Htoo (Myanmar)
Rev. Andrew Zaw Lwin (Myanmar)
Rev. David Powys (Australia)
Rev. Dr Jeremiah Guen Seok Yang (Republic of Korea)

*Church of North India (Anglican Communion):*
Rt Rev. S.R. Cutting (Agra)
Rt Rev. Dr Dhirendra Kumar Sahu (Eastern Himalaya)

*Baptist:*
Mrs Young Shim Chang (Republic of Korea)
Rev. Dr Simon Pau Khan En (Myanmar)
Rev. Jill Manton (Australia)
Rev. Dr J. Maung Lat (Myanmar)
Rev. P. Bonny Resu (India)
Dr Anna May Say Pa (Myanmar)

3.  AFRICA: NAIROBI, KENYA, 24-27 JANUARY 2002

*Anglican:*
Rev. Dr Victor R. Atta-Baffoe (Ghana)
Rt Rev. Dr Nolbert Kunonga (Zimbabwe)
Rev. Matava Musyimi (Kenya)
Rev. Hannington Mutebi (Uganda)
Rev. Chalton Ochola (Kenya)
Rt Rev. Nicholas Dikeriehi Okoh (Nigeria)
Rev. Linda Schwartz (South Africa)

*Baptist:*
Rev. Dr Frank Adams (Ghana)
Rev. Chamunorwa H. Chiromo (Zimbabwe)

Dr Louise Kretzschmar (South Africa)
Rev. Dr Douglas W. Waruta (Kenya)

4. THE SOUTHERN CONE: SANTIAGO, CHILE, 22-24 JANUARY 2003

*Anglican:*
Carlos Enrique Lainfiesta (Central America)
Jerson Darif Palhano (Brazil)
Mrs Ione Walbaum (Chile)
Rt Rev. Héctor Zavala (Chile)

*Baptist:*
Mrs Rachel Contreras (Chile)
Alberto Prokopchuk (Argentina)
Mrs Amparo de Medina (Colombia)
Tomas Mackey (Argentina)
Zaqueu Moreira de Oliveira (Brazil)
Josué Fonseca (Chile)

5. THE CARIBBEAN: NASSAU, BAHAMAS, 26-28 JANUARY 2003

*Anglican:*
Ven. Ranfurly Brown (Bahamas)
Rev. Bumet Cherisol (Haiti)
Very Rev. Knolly Clarke (Trinidad and Tobago)
Most Rev. Drexel W. Gomez (Bahamas)
Rt Rev. Sehon Goodridge (Windward Isles)
Dr Monrelle Williams (Barbados)

*Baptist:*
Rev. Dr Cawley Bolt (Jamaica)
Rev. Dr Neville Callam (Jamaica)
Rev. Peter Pinder (Bahamas)
Mrs Beth Stewart (Bahamas)
Rev. Dr William Thompson (Bahamas)

6. NORTH AMERICA: WOLFVILLE, NOVA SCOTIA, CANADA, 10-13 SEPTEMBER 2003

*Anglican:*
Rev. Canon Alyson Mary Barnett-Cowan (Canada)
Dr Howard Loewan (USA)
Rev. Canon Saundra Richardson (USA)
Chancellor Ronald Stevenson (Canada)
Rt Rev. Douglas Theuner (USA)
Rev. Dr David Wheeler (Baptist, representing ECUSA)

*Baptist:*
Rev. Dr William Brackney (USA)
Rev. Dr Curtis Freeman (USA)
Rev. Dr Steve Harmon (USA)
Mrs Audrey Morikawa (Canada)
Rev. Alan Stanford (USA)
Rev. Dr Andrew MacRae (Canada)

NOTES

1   Lambeth 1998, Section IV, *Called to Be One*, Harrisonburg, Morehouse, 1999, Resolution IV.15, p.45.

2   In Anglican ecclesiology, the local church is understood, strictly speaking, as being constituted at the diocesan level. A church, in this understanding, is the gathering of the people of God around their bishop. However, classically and more pragmatically, Anglicanism has tended to use the national level as the definitive level of church organization. In this, it was probably influenced both by Orthodox ecclesiological polity, and by the constraints of Reformation realpolitik.

3   The Church of Ireland was united with the Church of England between 1800 and 1869.

4   Timothy Bradshaw, "Some Distinctive Features of the Church of England", p.1. [Unless otherwise noted, the papers cited are from the regional consultations that contributed to this report.]

5   Martin Davie, "The Church of England Story", p.1.

6   Thra Wilfred Saw Aung Hla Tun, Samuel Mahn Si Htay and others, "A Brief Outline of Anglican History in Myanmar and the Contact between the Anglican Church and the Baptist Church in Myanmar", p.1.

7   *Ibid.*, p.2.

8   Andrew Chan, "An Overview of Anglican Life in Asia", p 1.

9   Héctor Zavala, "Identidad Anglicana", pp.1-2.

10   "The Myanmar Baptist Convention", by Baptist participants in the conversations in Yangon, p.4.

11   William H. Brackney, "Baptists and Continuity", p.2.

12   *Ibid.*, pp.3, 8-9.

13   Zaqueu Moreira de Oliveria, "The Baptists: Historical Versions of Their Origin", p.5.

14   *Ibid.*, p.5.

15   *Ibid.*, p.l; Brackney, "Baptist Continuity", pp.8-9.

16   Monrelle Williams, "Anglican Identity: Expressing and Confessing the Christian Faith in Worship, Teaching and Evangelism", pp.2-3.

17   *Ibid.*, pp.6-7.

18   Victor Atta-Baffoe, "Mission and Ministry in the African Church", p.5.

19   Similar affirmations of African traditional culture and the importance of African traditional religion were made in the (undocumented) papers by two Baptists – Douglas Waruta (Kenya) and Frank Adams (Ghana).

20   Williams, "Anglican Identity", pp.4-5.

21   Rubie M. Nottage, "Anglican Life in the Caribbean", pp.2-5.

22   *Ibid.*,p.7.

23   Sehon Goodridge, "Colonialisation, Liberation and the Mission of the Church in the Caribbean: An Anglican View", pp.1-3.

24   Cawley Bolt, "Colonialism, Liberation and the Mission of the Church in the Caribbean: A Baptist View", pp.6,8. See also Goodridge, "Colonialisation", pp.9-10.

25   Bolt, "Colonialism", pp.7,10; Peter Pinder, "Baptist Life in the Caribbean", p.3.

26   Martin E. Marty, "Baptistification Takes Over", *Christianity Today*, 1983.

27   Thomas Ferguson, "Anglican Life and Continuity in North America", p.2.

28   *Ibid.*, p.5.

29   Malcolm B. Yarnell, "From Christological Ecclesiology to Functional Ecclesiasticism: Developments in Southern Baptist Understandings of the Nature and Role of the Churches", p.5.

[30] *Ibid.*, p.7.

[31] David L. Wheeler, "Keeping the Faith, Keeping Together: Common Challenges for Baptists and Anglicans", pp.4-7.

[32] Jill Manton, "Baptist Ecclesiology in the Australian Context", p.1.

[33] De Oliveira, orally; but also see his paper "The Baptists", pp.6-7.

[34] Canons A5 and C15 of the Church of England.

[35] *Orthodox Creed*, art. 38, in W.L. Lumpkin, *Baptist Confessions of Faith*, Philadelphia, Judson, 1959, pp.326-27.

[36] Steven R. Harmon, "Baptist Understandings of Authority, with Special Reference to Baptists in North America", pp.1-2; similarly, Brackney, "Baptists and Continuity", p.3.

[37] G. Keith Parker, *Baptists in Europe: History and Confessions of Faith*, Nashville TN, Broadman, 1982, p.57. So also the Baptist Union of Finland, *ibid.*, p.111.

[38] Parker, *Baptists in Europe*, p.111.

[39] *First Baptist World Congress: London, July 11-19, 1905*, London, Baptist Union, 1905, pp.19-21. The words quoted were those of Alexander Maclaren, in leading the assembly. In commemoration of this event, and to urge the recitation of either the Apostles' Creed or the Creed of Nicea-Constantinople at the Centenary Congress in 2005, a document was issued in 2004 entitled "Confessing the Faith", co-written by four Baptist professors of theology (Curtis W. Freeman, Steven R. Harmon, Elizabeth Newman, Philip E. Thompson) and signed by a wide range of Baptist educators throughout the world (see *Baptist Standard Website*, July 2004).

[40] William Thompson, "How to Express and Confess the Christian Faith in Worship and Evangelism", pp.3-5.

[41] Fiddes, "A Particular Faith? Distinctive Features of Christian Faith and Practice held by Baptist Christians in Europe", pp.6-7; the document is called "What are Baptists? On the Way to Expressing Baptist Identity in a Changing Europe", European Baptist Federation, 1993.

[42] "The Myanmar Baptist Convention", pp.4-5.

[43] *Baptism, Eucharist and Ministry*, Faith and Order Paper 111, Geneva, WCC, 1982.

[44] Pinder, "Baptist Life in the Caribbean", p.3; cf. Thompson, pp.3-5.

[45] Ronald C. Stevenson, "An Anglican Understanding of Authority", p.5; Harmon, "Baptist Understandings of Authority", pp.2-3.

[46] Harmon, "Baptist Understandings of Authority", p.6.

[47] Chalton S. Ochola, "Issues Arising in Local Anglican-Baptist Relations: An Anglican View from Kenya", p.8.

[48] Nottage, "Anglican Life in the Caribbean", p.7.

[49] Héctor Zavala, in an oral presentation.

[50] *Ibid.*

[51] So Yarnell, "From Christological Ecclesiology to Functional Ecclesiasticism", p.13.

[52] Atta-Baffoe, "Mission and Ministry in the African Church", p.6.

[53] Frank Adams, "Overview of Baptist Life in Africa", oral presentation.

[54] Jerson Zarif Palhano, oral contribution.

[55] Goodridge, "Colonialisation", p.10; Bolt, "Colonialism", p.10

[56] R.P. Carlos E. Lainfiesta, "Evangelismo, Proselitismo y Misión en America Latina", p.6.

[57] Mackey, "Evangelism, Proselytism and Mission", pp.8,9.

[58] Goodridge, "Colonisation", p.7.

[59] Bolt, "Colonialism", p.6.

[60] Stanford, "An Overview of Baptists in North America", p.11.

[61] Josué Fonseca, "The Ministry of Pastoral Oversight", p.4; Mackey, "Evangelism, Proselytism and Mission", p.4; Lainfiesta, "Evangelismo", pp.3-4.

[62] Louise Kretzschmar, "Baptist-Anglican Interaction in South Africa", Nairobi, 2002, p.2.

[63] Atta-Baffoe, "Mission and Ministry in the African Church", p.8.

[64] Mackey, "Evangelism, Proselytism and Mission", p.6.

[65] *Ibid.*, p.8, quoting *Towards Common Witness*, Geneva, WCC, 1980, pp.24-25.

[66] Lainfiesta, "Evangelismo, Proselitismo y Misión", p.7.

[67] De Oliveira, "The Baptists", section VI.

[68] Yarnell, "From Christological Ecclesiology to Functional Ecclesiasticism", p.14.

69 So Steve Harmon, written communication.

70 This phrase was made famous by John Bunyan, a Baptist writer, through his book of that title (1678); he applied it to the whole of the Christian life.

71 Fiddes, "A Particular Faith?", pp.26-28.

72 See "The Toronto Statement", Recommendation (c), in David R. Holeton ed., *Christian Initiation in the Anglican Communion: The Toronto Statement "Walk in Newness of Life"*, the findings of the fourth international Anglican liturgical consultation, Toronto, 1991, Grove Worship Series no. 118, Bramcote, UK, Grove Books, 1991.

73 This approach seems to be accepted by the recent *An Anglican-Methodist Covenant* (London, Methodist Publ. House and Church House Publ., 2001), which states that "in our churches baptism is generally seen as the essential first stage of a process of Christian initiation that includes confirmation and participation in communion" (§122, p.40). Again, "confirmation is regarded by both our churches as a means of grace within the total process of Christian initiation" (§126, p.41), and "baptism (in the context of full Christian initiation) lies at the root of all Christian ministry" (§143, p.145).

74 S.R. Cutting, "Union between the Anglicans and the Baptists in the Church of North India", p.2.

75 *Ibid.*, p.1.

76 Nolbert Kunonga, "Christian Initiation. Practical and Pastoral Implications facing Anglicans", undocumented paper, Nairobi, 2002.

77 See, for example, Baptist Union of Great Britain, *Patterns and Prayers for Christian Worship: A Guidebook for Worship Leaders*, Oxford, Oxford UP, 1991, pp. 102-104.

78 So Steve Harmon, in a written communication.

79 A survey undertaken by the department of study and research of the Baptist World Alliance, 2003-2004, showed that in Lithuania 30 percent of churches were open membership, in Scotland 27 percent, in Estonia 4 percent, and in Georgia 2 percent.

80 This situation was subsequently confirmed by survey (see footnote 76), except that the Baptist Convention of Bolivia reported a 2 percent open membership.

81 Response of the Burma Baptist Convention, in Max Thurian ed., *Churches Respond to BEM: Official Responses to the "Baptism, Eucharist and Ministry" Text*, 6 vols, Geneva, WCC, 1986-88, vol. IV, p.186. Altogether, nine Baptist unions or conventions responded to BEM.

82 *Ibid.*, p.185.

83 Pinder, "Baptist Life in the Caribbean", p.1.

84 Fonseca, "Ministry of Patoral Oversight", p.3.

85 Amparo de Medina (Columbia), "Identidad Bautista en América Latína", p.11, remarked that it is evangelism that holds Baptists together in unity.

86 Saundra Richardson in discussion of Stevenson's paper.

87 See Stevenson, "An Anglican Understanding of Authority", p.11.

88 *Ibid.*, p.11.

89 Neville Callum, "Eucharistic Theology", p 4.

90 Yarnell, "From Christological Ecclesiology to Functional Ecclesiasticism", p.12.

91 Callum, "Eucharistic Theology", p.5.

92 Bishop Héctor Zavala, verbally.

93 Thra Wilfred Saw Aung Hla Tun and others, "A Brief Outline of the Anglican History in Myanmar", p 4.

94 Stevenson, "An Anglican Understanding of Authority", p.2.

95 *Anglican-Methodist Covenant*, 2001, p.52.

96 Fiddes, "A Particular Faith?", pp.30-31.

97 An exception appears in the Baptist Convention of Georgia, where unusually the language of a threefold ministry is used.

98 Fonseca, "Ministry of Pastoral Oversight", p.3.

99 Bishop Héctor Zavala, Chile, oral contribution.

100 Ferguson, "Anglican Life and Continuity in North America", pp.5-6.

101 Dhirendra Kumar Sahu, "Episcopacy in the Church of North India", pp.5-6.

102 Baptist Declaration of Principle, in *The Constitution of the Church of North India*, Delhi, ISPCK, 2001, p.15.

103 Ochola, "Local Anglican-Baptist Relations in Kenya", Nairobi, 2002, p.4.

104 "The Myanmar Baptist Convention", p 6.
105 For a recent example, see *An Anglican-Methodist Covenant*, 2001.
106 Lambeth 1998, Section IV, *Called to Be One*, Resolution IV.14, p.45.
107 Fonseca, "Ministry of Pastoral Oversight", p 7.
108 Bolt, "Colonialism", p.5.

# 35. Growth in Communion

## Anglican-Lutheran International Working Group

### Porto Alegre, Brazil, 2002

## I. INTRODUCTION

1. Anglicans and Lutherans began formal conversations at the world level in 1970. While Anglicans and Lutherans had no history of mutual condemnation or recrimination, difficulties in union negotiations involving Lutherans and Anglicans, especially in Asia and Africa in the 1950s and 1960s, indicated the need for such conversations. That first dialogue resulted in the *Pullach Report* of 1972, which surveyed the range of issues affecting Anglican-Lutheran relations. While discovering extensive agreement, the dialogue also discovered significant differences over apostolicity and episcopal ministry. The report urged both closer cooperation and continuing dialogue.

2. The Anglican Consultative Council and the Lutheran World Federation convened a joint working group in 1975 to review responses to the *Pullach Report* and to chart further work. The group suggested that regional dialogues be pursued in Europe, Africa and North America. Dialogue took place in the first and third of these regions over the next eight years.

3. A new joint working group was convened in 1983. Their *Cold Ash Report* surveyed the state of Lutheran-Anglican relations and explored the concept of "full communion" (cf. section III.B) as a description of the life together sought in Anglican-Lutheran ecumenical efforts. They also called for the creation of an Anglican-Lutheran International Continuation Committee (ALICC), with a mandate to foster dialogue at the worldwide level and to help make the results of the various national and regional Anglican-Lutheran dialogues contribute to progress elsewhere.

4. Between 1986 and 1996, ALICC (later renamed the Anglican-Lutheran International Commission) sponsored consultations on *episcope* and the episcopate, leading to the *Niagara Report* (1988), and on the diaconate, leading to the *Hanover Report* (1996). It also sponsored a series of conferences to further Anglican-Lutheran relations in Eastern and Southern Africa. Its work contributed significantly to the breakthroughs in Anglican-Lutheran relations that have recently occurred in Northern Europe (the Porvoo common statement), the USA ("Called to Common Mission"), and Canada (the Waterloo declaration).

5. Following the 1997 assembly of the Lutheran World Federation and the 1998 Lambeth Conference, the present Anglican-Lutheran international working group was appointed. It met for the first time in February 2000. Its terms of reference are:

a)  to monitor the developments and progress in Anglican-Lutheran relations in the various regions of the world and, where appropriate, encourage steps towards the goal of visible unity;

b)  to review the characteristics and theological rationales of current regional and national dialogues and agreements, particularly with reference to the concept of unity and to the understanding of apostolicity and episcopal ministry; this review would include an evaluation of their consistency and coherence with each other and with Anglican-Lutheran international agreed statements and would take note of issues of wider ecumenical compatibility;

c)  to explore the implications of regional developments for deepening and extending the global relationships between the Anglican and Lutheran communions;

d)  to propose forms of closer contact and cooperation between the international instruments of both communions, in specific projects and programmes and in addressing practical issues;

e)  to advise whether an Anglican Lutheran international commission should be appointed and to recommend the issues that require further dialogue.

Over three meetings (Virginia, USA, 2000; Skálholt, Iceland, 2001; Porto Alegre, Brazil, 2002), the international working group has pursued its work under these terms of reference. This report gives a picture of the present state of Anglican-Lutheran relations, analyzes issues raised by the present relations between us, and recommends future action.

## II. REVIEW OF PROGRESS

### A.  General factors

*a) Practical steps*

6. The *Niagara Report* sets out four practical steps by which Anglicans and Lutherans can realize full communion.

*Step 1*: Regional or national churches recognize each other as sharing the same faith and hence as being a "true church of the gospel".

*Step 2*: Create provisional structures to express the degree of unity so far achieved and promote further growth. Examples of how to further growth included among other things: eucharistic sharing, regular meetings of church leaders, invitation to speak at each other's synods, creating common agencies, joint theological education and mission programmes, limited interchange of ministers, and the twinning of congregations.

*Step 3*: The exploration of changing particular practices with respect to *episcope* and the full recognition of ministries.

*Step 4*: Public declaration and celebration of full communion, after which "joint consecration and installation of bishops and ordinations of new ministers should be possible".

### b) Common witness and action

7. As the various regions began their mutual dialogues (some having begun long before Niagara), other issues emerged as important. Niagara concentrated on the issue of *episcope* in relation to the mission of the church because ALICC had asked it to do so, but regions quickly identified other areas of concern. Picking up the theme of mission from Niagara, some churches shifted the focus more towards common witness and action in the world than on issues of ministry per se, although ministry questions have historically been the most neuralgic between the two communions.

### c) Contexts

8. Because Lutherans and Anglicans have approached unity on a regional or national basis, the context of their conversations has influenced the style, content and outcome of agreements. The differing patterns of exercising *episcope* among the Lutheran churches have meant that in some places mutual recognition of ordained ministries is easier than in others. The churches which are signatories to both the Meissen and Reuilly agreements in Europe include Anglican churches on the one hand and Lutheran, United and Reformed churches on the other. The pressing needs of mission have made some churches more interested in getting on with common projects than in addressing questions of order. The differences in demographics and geography have also played a role: for the state churches of Europe, it is possible to imagine one episcopal ministry in each place, but for the churches outside Europe, overlapping jurisdictions will be a reality for the foreseeable future.

## B. Regional agreements

9. The various regional agreements, where agreements have been entered into or where churches are engaged in active dialogue, will be examined with respect to eight factors:

a)  context;

b)  origin of the dialogue;

c)  agreement in faith and ecclesial recognition (step 1);

d)  current state of development (steps 2-4);

e)  commitment to common mission;

f)  definition of proximate and ultimate goals;

g)  particular issues arising from the context;

h)  mutual accountability within the agreements.

Issues of possible anomalies raised by the regional agreements, the particular terminology with respect to the goal of unity and matters of coherence with other dialogues and within the two world communions are addressed later in the report.

10. In the analysis which will follow in Section III, our report focuses in greater depth on the most mature agreements: the Meissen agreement (Church of England and the German Evangelical churches, 1988), the Porvoo common statement (the British and Irish Anglican churches and the Nordic and Baltic Lutheran churches in the Nordic and Baltic nations, 1992), the Reuilly common statement (the British and Irish Anglican churches and the Lutheran and Reformed Church in France, 1997), "Called to Common Mission" (ELCA and ECUSA, 1999), the Waterloo declaration (the Anglican Church of Canada and the Evangelical Lutheran Church in Canada, 1999), and Covenanting for Mutual Recognition and Reconciliation (Anglicans and Lutherans in Australia; draft proposal of September 1999). In addition we took note of earlier documentation dealing with eucharistic sharing in North America, prior to the present agreements (agreement on interim eucharistic sharing 1982).

## A) AFRICA

### Context

11. In Africa there are around 36.7 million Anglicans and 10.6 million Lutherans. Anglicans and Lutherans find themselves together in places where Anglican and Lutheran missions coincide. Thus there is cooperation between Anglicans and Lutherans in Malawi, Namibia, Zimbabwe, Tanzania and South Africa. The goal of a pan-African agreement is challenged by the geography of a vast continent, the differing histories, and the cost of gathering people.

### Origin of dialogue

12. Formal dialogue was encouraged by ALIC, beginning with an African Anglican/Lutheran consultation on ecclesiology in Harare in 1992. Most recently, the All Africa Anglican Lutheran Commission was established, which held its first meeting in Nairobi in April 2001.

### Agreement in faith/ecclesial recognition

13. "Both Anglicans and Lutherans belong to the one, holy, catholic and apostolic church, which we confess in the Nicene Creed." Although the Nairobi report states agreement in faith, there has not been a formal commitment to mutual ecclesial recognition (step 1 of Niagara).

### Steps to communion (steps 2 to 4 in Niagara)

14. The commission proposes that:

a) in countries where Anglican-Lutheran cooperation is already experienced this should be intensified and nurtured towards official relationships of communion;

b) in countries where Anglicans and Lutherans coexist but where there are no bilateral relationships between the two churches, immediate contact be encouraged between the appropriate authorities at the national level to consider ways of cooperation;

c) in both these cases, the following steps be taken by the churches involved:

  i) to undertake education at grassroots level to bring about knowledge and understanding of each church as to history, liturgy, doctrine, church order and polity; to exchange visits, extend mutual invitations to each other's synods, hold discussions, and engage in other forms of getting to know each other;

  ii) to plan and carry out together joint theological education, lay training, women's and children's programmes as a way of deepening cooperation between the two churches;

  iii) to take formal action in these matters at provincial/synodical level as soon as the time is right.

Some of these projects are envisaged in step 2 of Niagara, but there is not yet a call to formalize eucharistic sharing which in many cases already occurs informally.

*Commitment to common mission*

15. Mission for the sake of the healing of the world, and for justice, is the context of the conversations in Africa.

> The tough realities that impact on the daily life of the churches have been central in these discussions. Anglicans and Lutherans in Africa are convinced that it is in taking these realities into account in a common, ecumenical way, that the churches will be strengthened, both in service and in witness to Christian unity. (Nairobi §4)

*Definition of proximate and ultimate goals*

16. *Proximate goals*:

> The vision which guides our deliberation is that of a united African church with an African identity, in which Anglicans and Lutherans are in full communion and visible unity with one another. We look forward to a unique liturgical unity so that we may worship God as one church. We hope for a spirit of generosity, which will accommodate our cultural and regional differences, so that we can celebrate our God-given diversity. We commit ourselves to the proclamation and teaching of the gospel as our primary task. We hope to foster ecumenical fellowship throughout all levels of our churches and to be steadfast in the tasks of evangelism, mission and social activism as imperatives of the gospel of our Lord and Saviour, Jesus Christ. (Report of the interim committee of the African Anglican-Lutheran consultation, Harare, 1999)

17. *Ultimate goal*:

> As there is essentially only one ecumenical movement, an issue at stake in this bilateral dialogue is not only how this particular dialogue can contribute to a closer communion between the churches involved, but also how it can serve the wider cause of Christian unity. The question must be kept alive, therefore, how the positive developments taking place between Anglicans and Lutherans in Africa can contribute to Christian unity in Africa and indeed in the world at large. (Nairobi §5)

### *Particular issues arising from the context*

18. The chief commitment is to mutual cooperation and action to meet the pressing social needs of African society. To this end, education about one another's churches is essential. Doctrinal questions, and questions of order, have not emerged at this point as central to the relationship.

### *Mutual accountability within the agreements*

19. A commission has been established for all of Africa, which will stimulate action between the churches at the national level. At this stage, cooperation is being encouraged in education, theological education, visits, invitations to each other's synods, and pastoral work. It is premature to speak of mutual accountability.

B) AUSTRALIA

### *Context*

20. In Australia there are around 94,000 Lutherans and 4 million Anglicans.

### *Origin of dialogue*

21. Dialogue between the Anglican Church of Australia and the Lutheran Church in Australia began in 1972 and has produced combined statements on the eucharist and on ministry, agreed statements on baptism and on *episcope* and unity, as well as information and guidance regarding Anglican-Lutheran marriages. Some practical cooperation is already in place, from consultation at the heads of churches level to local pastoral arrangements for eucharistic hospitality in special circumstances.

### *Agreement in faith/ecclesial recognition*

22. These churches identify the following areas in which they believe and practise a shared faith: the Bible, God's will and commandment, the gospel, the creeds, liturgical worship, the church, baptism, the Lord's supper (eucharist), membership in the church, pastoral office and ordained ministry, orders of ministry and the episcopal office, a

common hope and mission. Their agreements are set out in appendix 1 of "Common Ground". The covenant, if adopted, would declare, "We recognize each other as churches that, despite our failings, stand in the continuity of apostolic faith and ministry" (step 1 of Niagara).

*Steps towards communion (steps 2 to 4 of Niagara)*

23. In January 2001 the Anglican-Lutheran dialogue in Australia published "Common Ground: Covenanting for Mutual Recognition and Reconciliation". It is "a plan for the future on the basis of common confession and practice. It is not a declaration of church union but a solemn pledge to walk together towards that goal." No formal decision has been made by the churches involved to date.

24. Under this covenant each church would be able to invite and welcome the members of the other church in a particular locality to share in holy communion and to receive pastoral care according to need (step 2 of Niagara). Particular local agreements are to be negotiated at the level of the diocese and district, and are to be made on the following basis:

a) joint public profession, by participating congregations, of the catholic faith as contained in the Nicene Creed;

b) an undertaking to respect the distinctive traditions enshrined in the Augsburg Confession and the *Book of Common Prayer* with the Thirty-nine Articles of Religion;

c) joint commissioning of clergy by the local Anglican bishop and Lutheran president.

*Commitment to common mission*

25. "A common hope and mission" is identified as one of the areas of shared faith believed and practised ("Common Ground" §3.1). This is articulated in appendix 2 §19:

> We are called to work now for the furtherance of justice, to seek peace and to care for the created world, and to live responsibly in all areas of life. The obligations of the kingdom are to govern our life in the church and our concern for the world.

In the covenant, the churches would "pledge to work together to develop joint participation in mission and witness" (§4.1).

*Definition of proximate and ultimate goals*

26. *Proximate goals*: The document has been presented to the churches in the hope that they

> can affirm the stated agreement in faith and practice as a sufficient basis for negotiating a national covenant for eucharistic hospitality and a recognition of each church's ministry. This agreement would first be implemented at the local level for the pastoral care of our members. (Foreword to "Common Ground")

27. *Ultimate goal*: The final goal has so far been described as "a concordat for full communion and reconciliation of ministries" (Foreword to "Common Ground").

*Particular issues arising from the context*

28. There are different emphases in the two churches in Australia on matters of confession, ministry and *episcope*. The "Common Ground" statement is a theological document, which provides a basis for further work. It appears to be the basis for negotiating a national covenant, rather than a covenant itself.

*Mutual accountability within the agreement*

29. The document in circulation for study is the basis for the preparation of a covenant between the churches. It is premature to speak of mutual accountability.

C) BRAZIL

*Context*

30. In Brazil there are around 714,000 Lutherans and 103,021 Anglicans. Brazilian Lutherans and Anglicans are both participants in minority churches in a predominantly Roman Catholic country. They have been active participants alongside other churches for many years in the Conselho Nacional das Igrejas Cristãs (CONIC, National Council of Christian Churches).

*Origin of dialogue*

31. The national Anglican-Lutheran committee met from 1984 to 1991. They measured their common stance by the *Niagara Report* of 1987. Steps are presently being taken to reactivate the dialogue.

*Agreement in faith/ecclesial recognition*

32. The two churches accept the authority of the canonical scriptures of the Old and New Testament and... read both liturgically during the ecclesiastical calendar". They

> accept the creeds of the ancient church... and confess the same basic trinitarian and christological doctrine, for which these creeds are testimony. So, we believe that Jesus of Nazareth is true God and true man and that God is authentically identified as the Father, Son and Holy Spirit. (Declaration of the National Anglican-Lutheran Committee)

There does not appear at this point to be a call for the churches to recognize each other as churches of the gospel.

*Steps towards communion (steps 2 to 4 of Niagara)*

33. The committee made a "declaration" in 1991 which identifies agreement on common faith, similar orders of liturgy, baptism, eucharist, the gospel, justification, the church, the mission of the church, baptismal and ordained ministry, the episcopate, and hope for the kingdom of God. No formal decision has been made by either church involved. A programme of joint theological education for Lutherans and Anglicans is to begin next year.

*Commitment to common mission*

34. "This is not only a doctrinal dialogue, but a human dialogue about action on issues. The people of Brazil are not interested in asking for confessions of faith, but about how Christians live the faith. The call is to act for transformation of society."

*Definition of proximate and ultimate goals*

35. At this point, there is no definition of either proximate or ultimate goals.

*Particular issues arising from the context*

36. As the dialogue is in a preliminary stage of development particular issues which will need to be addressed have not yet been identified.

*Mutual accountability within the agreement*

37. The relationship is in an early stage of development. The commitment is to work together in mission, service and education.

D) CANADA

*Context*

38. Lutheran churches in Canada emerged from many different settlements from all the European countries with Lutheran identities. They operated with different ecclesiologies, depending on the tradition of the country of origin, and the influence of Pietist movements. After a century of smaller mergers, the Evangelical Lutheran Church in Canada was formed in 1986. As part of the merger agreement, the five synods and the national church installed persons in oversight with the title of bishop. There are approximately 200,000 Lutherans in the ELCIC. The Lutheran Church, Canada, about one third the size of the ELCIC, is affiliated with the Lutheran Church-Missouri Synod in the USA and is not party to ecumenical agreements.

39. The Anglican Church of Canada has about 3 million adherents according to census identification, but is closer to 800,000 in terms of active members. The difference in size,

and geographical distribution of Anglicans and Lutherans, have been factors in the relationship. For example, the province of Newfoundland and Labrador, in which 18 percent of Anglicans live, has no Lutheran congregations, while on the prairies, both Lutherans and Anglicans are fairly evenly matched in numbers, albeit in small, scattered and diminishing communities.

## Origin of dialogue

40. Inspired by activity in the US, dialogue in Canada began in 1983. The first set of meetings (Canadian Lutheran-Anglican dialogue I) issued in a report and recommendations which included agreed statements on justification, the eucharist, apostolicity, and the ordained ministry and called for an interim sharing of the eucharist. This agreement was entered into in 1989.

## Agreement in faith/ecclesial recognition

41. On the basis of the theological work of CLAD I, the two churches "acknowledge that both our churches share in the common confession of the apostolic faith" (step 1 of Niagara).

## Steps towards communion (steps 2 to 4 of Niagara)

42. CLAD II engaged in a major study of the *Niagara Report*, called for the removing of any impediments for members to be received into each other's church, encouraged local congregations to take on joint actions in mission and service, made provision for clergy to serve in each other's churches in special situations, and called for the preparation of a proposal for full communion (step 2 of Niagara).

43. The Waterloo declaration was prepared by a joint working group. Waterloo makes a series of acknowledgments and affirmations leading to the recognition and interchangeability of ordained ministries, and a series of commitments to live out the reality of full communion (step 3 of Niagara). In July 2001 it was overwhelmingly approved by the governing bodies of both churches, and on 8 July 2001 the churches entered full communion by the signing of Waterloo at a joint eucharist (step 4 of Niagara).

## Commitment to common mission

44. Waterloo §1 begins with a reference to John 17, where Jesus prayed for unity "so that the world may believe". "Christians have begun to see the fulfilment of Jesus' words as they unite in action to address the needs of local and global communities." Commitments 5 and 6 of Waterloo call for the establishment of "appropriate forms of collegial and conciliar consultation on significant matters of faith and order, mission and service" and "regular consultation and collaboration among members of our churches at all levels to promote the formulation and adoption of covenants for common work in mission and ministry, and to facilitate learning and exchange of ideas and information on theological, pastoral, and mission matters".

*Definition of proximate and ultimate goals*

45. *Proximate*: Full communion is described as

> a relationship between two distinct churches or communions in which each maintains its own autonomy while recognizing the catholicity and apostolicity of the other, and believing the other to hold the essentials of the Christian faith. In such a relationship communicant members of each church would be able freely to communicate at the altar of the other and there would be freedom of ordained ministers to officiate sacramentally in either church. Specifically in our context we understand this to include transferability of members; mutual recognition and interchangeability of ministries; freedom to use each other's liturgies; freedom to participate in each other's ordinations and installations of clergy, including bishops; and structures for consultation to express, strengthen and enable our common life, witness, and service, to the glory of God and the salvation of the world.

46. *Ultimate*: Commitment 9 of Waterloo pledges the churches "to continue to work together for the full visible unity of the whole church of God".

*Particular issues arising from the context*

47. The main issue on which Waterloo focused was episcopal ministry and finding common ground in understanding the relationship of *episcope* and the apostolicity of the church. There were particular ways in which this issue had been treated in Canada which made it possible for a broader interpretation of the phrase "episcopally ordained" to be applied within the parameters of Anglican canon law, thus eliminating any canonical requirement for the re-ordination of ordained Lutheran ministers.

*Mutual accountability within the agreement*

48. Commitment 5 of Waterloo commits the churches "to establish appropriate forms of collegial and conciliar consultation on significant matters of faith and order, mission and service". Commitment 6 is "to encourage regular consultation and collaboration among members of our churches at all levels, to promote the formulation and adoption of covenants for common work in mission and ministry, and to facilitate learning and exchange of ideas and information on theological, pastoral, and mission matters". Commitment 7 is "to hold joint meetings of national, regional and local decision-making bodies wherever practicable". Commitment 8 establishes "a joint commission to nurture our growth in communion, to coordinate the implementation of this declaration, and report to the decision-making bodies of both our churches".

E) EUROPE

49. The home territory of both Lutheran and Anglican churches, Europe has three different agreements among them. Churches signatory to the Porvoo agreement "value… the sign of the historic episcopal succession" (Porvoo, §57). The churches signatory to

Meissen and Reuilly do not share a common view of the episcopate, and the agreements are further complicated by the presence in these dialogues of Reformed and United churches.

50.  The Anglican jurisdictions involved in dialogue with Lutherans in Europe are as follows:

–   the Church of England (Porvoo, Meissen and Reuilly): 43 dioceses in England and 1 in mainland Europe; 27 million members;

–   the Scottish Episcopal Church (Porvoo, Reuilly): 7 Dioceses; 53,000 members;

–   the Church of Ireland (Porvoo, Reuilly): 12 dioceses in Northern Ireland and the Republic of Ireland; 376,000 members;

–   the Church in Wales (Porvoo, Reuilly): 6 dioceses; 90,300 members.

51.  The Lutheran churches which have been involved in dialogue with Anglicans in Europe are as follows:

–   the Evangelical Lutheran Church of Finland (Porvoo): 8 dioceses; 4,600,118 members;

–   the Evangelical-Lutheran Church of Iceland (Porvoo): 1 diocese with 2 suffragan sees; 247,245 members;

–   the Church of Norway (Porvoo): 11 dioceses; 3,800,000 members;

–   the Church of Sweden (Porvoo): 13 dioceses; 7,399,915 members;

–   the Estonian Evangelical-Lutheran Church (Porvoo): 1 diocese; 200,000 members;

–   the Evangelical-Lutheran Church of Lithuania (Porvoo): 1 diocese; 30,000 members;

–   the Evangelical Church in Germany (Meissen): a communion of 24 member churches, most Landeskirchen or territorial churches, some are Lutheran, some Reformed and some United): 26.8 million members;

–   the Church of the Augsburg Confession of Alsace and Lorraine (Reuilly): 7 inspectorates; 195,000 members;

–   the Evangelical Lutheran Church of France (Reuilly): 2 inspectorates; 40,000 members.

52.  The Evangelical-Lutheran Church in Denmark and the Evangelical-Lutheran Church of Latvia both participated in the Porvoo conversations but have not as yet signed the agreement. The Reuilly agreement includes two Reformed churches: the Reformed Church in France and the Reformed Church of Alsace and Lorraine.

53.  In Europe there is a major shift from the time of the Reformation when it was assumed that virtually all Christians (apart from Dissenters) were members of the state church towards a new pluralist context which is both multifaith and secular. Anglicans and Lutherans do not share the same territory to any large extent, but there are overlapping jurisdictions. Anglicans have congregations in the Nordic and Baltic countries, and Lutherans – some signatory to agreements and some not – have congregations in Britain and Ireland.

54.  Further complicating the situation is the existence of several overlapping Anglican jurisdictions – ECUSA and the Church of England both have parishes in Europe, while the Spanish Reformed Episcopal Church and the Lusitanian Church, both member churches of the Anglican Communion, are now also signatories to Porvoo. There is discussion of a "communion of Porvoo churches" which is composed of member churches of two other communions – the Anglican Communion and the Lutheran World Federa-

tion. At the same time, there is a commitment to bring about one episcopal pattern for Europe, and talks are proceeding among the participants and the Old Catholic churches.

*Origin of dialogue*

55. *Meissen*: Dialogue was initiated in 1983, the fifth centenary of the birth of Martin Luther. At public celebrations, the archbishop of Canterbury proposed that closer relations be established between the Church of England and the Evangelical churches in both German republics (GDR and FRG). Formal dialogue began in 1987 and concluded with the Meissen common statement in 1988.

56. *Porvoo*: A series of theological conversations took place from 1909-51 between Anglicans and Lutherans in the Nordic and Baltic region. These led to various interim agreements in the 1930s and 1950s. New conversations were held between 1989-92 on the joint initiative of the archbishops of Canterbury and Uppsala. The aim was to move forward from the previous existing piecemeal agreements (step 2 of Niagara), to resolve long-standing difficulties about episcopacy and succession, and on the basis of a sufficient consensus on the faith, sacramental life and ministry, to establish communion (step 4 of Niagara) and share a common mission.

57. *Reuilly*: The Lutheran and Reformed churches in France were excited by the possibilities modelled in Meissen. The different circumstances of the churches in France made it difficult for them to simply sign on to Meissen, and a separate dialogue was called for in 1989. Thus in 1992, a dialogue was initiated between the British and Irish Anglican churches and the French Lutheran and Reformed churches.

*Agreement in faith/ecclesial recognition*

58. *Meissen*: Building on the *Niagara Report*, chapter 3, the Meissen common statement makes ten common statements of agreed faith: on the scriptures, the creeds and Christology, the liturgy, baptism, eucharist, justification, the church, mission, *episcope*, and hope for the kingdom of God. This was largely taken from the *Niagara Report*.

59. The declaration, on the basis of this shared faith, "acknowledges one another's churches as churches belonging to the one holy and apostolic church of Jesus Christ and truly participating in the apostolic mission of the whole people of God" (step 1 of Niagara).

60. *Porvoo*: The Porvoo common statement makes statements on the same ten topics as Meissen, although in a slightly rearranged and expanded form. On the basis of this agreement, the Porvoo declaration makes the same statement of recognition as Meissen (step 1 of Niagara).

61. *Reuilly*: The Reuilly common statement makes statements on the same ten topics as Meissen, in the same order as Porvoo, but somewhat changed in wording. On the basis of this agreement, the Reuilly declaration, made on 3 July 2001, makes the same statement of recognition as Meissen (step 1 of Niagara). Some sections are enhanced from Meissen: "The apostolicity of the church and ministry" (section VI) and "Wider ecumenical commitment" (section IX.B.)

*Steps towards communion (steps 2 to 4 of Niagara)*

62. *Meissen*: The agreement was approved in 1991 by the general synod of the Church of England, by the responsible bodies of the federation of the Evangelical churches and its member churches and by the EKD and its member churches. (By the time of the signing of the agreement, Germany had been reunited.) The stage which was reached was stage 2 of Niagara, involving the establishment of provisional structures and the commitment to common life and mission. In terms of mutual recognition of ministry Meissen encouraged the ordained ministers of the churches, in accordance with their rules, "to share in the celebration of the eucharist in a way which advances beyond mutual eucharistic hospitality but which falls short of the full interchangeability of ministers" (Meissen 17.B.vi).

63. *Porvoo*: This agreement, built on earlier dialogues, applied the insights of Niagara, and anchored doctrinal discussions firmly in the mission context of Northern Europe. It broke new ground by spelling out a deeper understanding of apostolicity, of the episcopal office and of historic succession as "sign". Significantly the Porvoo declaration included an acknowledgment "that the episcopal office is valued and maintained in all our churches...", as well as commitments "to welcome persons episcopally ordained in any of our churches... without re-ordination" and "to invite one another's bishops normally to participate in the laying-on of hands at the ordination of bishops..." (Porvoo, §58.a.vi and b.v and vi). This agreement (step 4 of Niagara) was synodically approved by the British and Irish Anglican churches and by most of the Nordic and Baltic Lutheran churches (not Denmark and Latvia). It was celebrated and formally signed in 1996 at Trondheim, Tallinn and London.

64. *Reuilly*: In 1999 the dialogue was concluded and in 2001 the agreement was signed and celebrated, first in Canterbury then in Paris. Again, like Meissen, the stage reached was stage 2 of Niagara, involving agreement

> to share a common life in mission and service, praying for and with one another and working towards the sharing of spiritual and human resources; to welcome one another's members to each other's worship and to receive pastoral ministrations; to welcome one another's members into the congregational life of each other's churches.

While Reuilly encourages shared worship, the nature of the participation of ordained ministers in each other's worship "still falls short of the full interchangeability of ministers" (Reuilly, §46.b.iv).

*Commitment to common mission*

65. *Meissen*: "We commit ourselves to share a common life and mission" (17B). In the acknowledgment of each other as churches it is asserted that they truly participate "in the apostolic mission of the whole people of God" (17.A.i).

66. *Porvoo*: This report was published under the title "Together in Mission and Ministry" and has a major section on "our common mission today" (§§10-13), concluding "our churches are called together to proclaim a duty of service to the wider world and to the societies in which they are set" (13). In its portrait of a church living in the light of the gospel, Porvoo notes that "it is a church with a mission to all in every race and

nation..." and "it is a church which manifests through its visible communion the healing and uniting power of God amidst the divisions of humankind". "It is a church in which the bonds of communion are strong enough to enable it to bear effective witness in the world,... and to share its goods with those in need" (20). In the declaration itself, Porvoo picks up the theme of Meissen 17.a.i (58.a.i) and makes a commitment "to establish forms of oversight so that our churches may regularly consult one another on significant matters of faith and order, life and work" (58.b.viii).

67. *Reuilly*: "The church exists for the glory of God and to serve, in obedience to the mission of Christ, the reconciliation of humankind and all creation. Therefore the church is sent into the world as a sign, instrument and foretaste of a reality which comes from beyond history – the kingdom, or reign of God" (18). The commitments section begins with a commitment to share a common life and mission, seeking appropriate ways to do this (46.b.i).

## Definition of proximate and ultimate goals

68. *Porvoo*: *proximate goals*: "The aim of these conversations was to move forward from our existing piecemeal agreements towards the goal of visible unity" (Porvoo, §6). Such a level of communion is described as entailing "agreement in faith together with the common celebration of the sacraments, supported by a united ministry and forms of collegial and conciliar consultation in matters of faith, life and witness" (Porvoo, §28).

69. *Ultimate goal*: "Set before the church is the vision of unity as the goal of all creation (Eph. 1) when the whole world will be reconciled to God (2 Cor. 5) (Porvoo, §27). This agreement is seen as a step towards the visible unity which all churches committed to the ecumenical movement seek to manifest" (Porvoo, §60).

70. *Meissen*: *proximate goals*: The churches in the Meissen agreement are committed "to strive for the 'full, visible unity' of the body of Christ on earth" while recognizing that the characteristics of that unity will become clearer as the churches grow together.

> That full, visible unity must include: a common confession of the apostolic faith in word and life... the sharing of one baptism, the celebration of one eucharist and the service of a reconciled, common ministry... bonds of communion which enable the church at every level to guard and interpret the apostolic faith, to take decisions, to teach authoritatively, to share goods and to bear effective witness in the world. The bonds of communion will possess personal, collegial and communal aspects. (Meissen, §§7,8)

71. *Ultimate goal*: "Our growing together is part of a wider movement towards unity within the one ecumenical movement" (Meissen, §13).

72. *Reuilly*: *proximate goals*: The Reuilly agreement brings the churches to a stage along the way to full visible unity. It is described as "mutual recognition" which for Lutheran and Reformed churches "entails full communion, which includes full interchangeability of ministries". Anglicans see this stage as a recognition or acknowledgment which leads to a further stage as "the reconciliation of churches and ministries" (Reuilly, §27).

73. *Ultimate goal*: The goal of full visible unity described in Reuilly is reminiscent of Meissen. It includes:

> A common proclamation and hearing of the gospel, a common confession of the apostolic faith in word and action… The sharing of one baptism, the celebrating of one eucharist and the service of a common ministry (including the exercise of ministry of oversight, *episcope*)… Bonds of communion which enable the church at every level to guard and interpret the apostolic faith, to take decisions, to teach authoritatively, to share goods and to bear effective witness in the world. The bonds of communion will possess personal, collegial and communal aspects. (Reuilly, §23)

There is explicit recognition of "wider ecumenical commitment" which involves deepening relationships within and between our three world communions and supporting efforts towards closer communion between Anglican, Lutheran and Reformed churches in Europe and in those parts of the world where good relations between our church families exist (Reuilly, §39).

*Particular issues arising from the context*

74. *Porvoo*: All the participating churches were episcopally ordered, although not all the bishops, up to now, were in historic succession. The tiny minority of clergy not episcopally ordained are not covered by the agreement.

75. *Meissen*: The theological conferences have given further attention to disagreement about the nature of the historic episcopate, which has not yet been resolved. The possibility of establishing local ecumenical projects in Germany is seen as a fruitful way forward.

76. *Reuilly*: Despite the high degree of theological agreement on the understanding of ministry and ordination, there is work yet to be done on the issue of historic episcopal succession, the understanding of the threefold nature of the one ministry, eucharistic presidency, women in ministry of oversight and the process of formally uniting the ministries (Reuilly, §43).

*Mutual accountability within the agreements*

77. The Porvoo contact group was set up in 1996 to foster implementation of the Porvoo agreement. It holds annual meetings and sponsors a theological conference. The Porvoo panel in England encourages and monitors the development of active Porvoo links by parishes, dioceses and central bodies.

78. The Meissen commission, established in 1991, oversees the implementation of that agreement. It also holds a theological conference and sponsors parish links and visits.

79. A contact group will be established for Reuilly and they may hold joint theological conferences with Meissen counterparts.

F) USA

*Context*

80. The Episcopal Church in the United States of America (ECUSA) and the Evangelical Lutheran Church in America (ELCA) are churches contiguous with each other within the USA. There are some exceptions to this national contextualization, e.g. the ECUSA includes an extra-national province comprised of Mexico, Central America, Ecuador, Columbia, Venezuela, Haiti, and the Dominican Republic; the ELCA similarly includes the Bahamas beyond the borders of the USA.

81. Demographically, the ELCA has a membership of 5.1 million, just under twice the size of the ECUSA with 2.5 million, though Episcopalians are more evenly distributed throughout the country, while Lutherans feature in areas of heavy concentration and relative sparsity. In terms of mission both churches face the same problems and opportunities within American culture and its regional variations.

82. The ELCA came into constitutional being in 1988 as a merger of the ALC, LCA, and AELC which was both a welcome development and one which provided its own set of issues to the common ecumenical engagement.

*Origin of dialogue*

83. Official dialogue was authorized in 1969 between the ECUSA and churches of the Lutheran Council in the USA (ELCA predecessor bodies, and the Lutheran Church, Missouri Synod). Lutheran-Episcopal dialogue I concluded its work in 1972 and submitted a positive report to the churches which was received without result largely due to the press of issues internal (but at the same time somewhat common, e.g. ordination of women, liturgical renewal, civil rights, etc.) to the churches.

*Agreement in faith/ecclesial recognition*

84. A second series of LED was initiated in 1977 and the work of the dialogue submitted to national governing bodies of the churches in 1982 as a report and recommendations. As a result, with the exception of the LCMS, the churches accepted each other's baptism without exception, mutually recognized each other specifically as churches, and, more specifically, as churches where the gospel was rightly preached and the sacraments rightly administered.

*Steps towards communion (steps 2 to 4 of Niagara)*

85. On this basis a relationship of "interim sharing of the eucharist" was established among ECUSA, on the one hand, and the American Lutheran Church (ALC), the Lutheran Church in America (LCA), and AELC, on the other hand. These churches also authorized a third series of LED (to begin in 1983) to consider other questions that remained to be resolved before full communion could be established between the traditions. LED III was specifically charged with further explication of the "implications of

the gospel" and the "ordering of ministry (bishops, priests and deacons) within the total context of apostolicity".

86. Two official publications resulted from LED III: *Implications of the Gospel* (1988) and *Towards Full Communion and Concordat of Agreement* (1991). The latter part of the second document contains the actual proposal for full communion to be initiated and specified the actions that would be necessary to both churches. In brief, the ECUSA agreed to suspend the operation of its "Preface to the Ordinal" in the *Book of Common Prayer* in order immediately to realize the interchangeability of ELCA and ECUSA presbyters while the ELCA agreed to accept ECUSA clergy without requiring subscription to the Augsburg confession. Mutual future participation in the consecration/installation of new bishops as part of the plan envisioned ultimate reconciliation of the churches respective episcopates.

87. After a six-year's process of reception by both churches under the auspices of a joint coordinating committee, the *Concordat of Agreement* came to a vote in 1997 at the national governing bodies of both the ELCA and ECUSA meeting within two weeks of each other. It was overwhelmingly passed by ECUSA's general convention and failed of a required two-thirds majority by only six votes in ELCA's churchwide assembly. Subsequently, at ELCA initiative, a small team of theologians and ecclesial leaders appointed by presiding bishops of both churches met to formulate a revision of the Concordat that was designated "Called to Common Mission". Following a reception process by both churches this document brought a revised proposal for full communion before both churches in the summer of 1999 (ELCA) and 2000 (ECUSA). Having passed both churches' highest governing bodies, a relationship of full communion was celebrated at the national cathedral in Washington DC on the feast of the Epiphany 2001 and regionally in following weeks and months.

## Commitment to common mission

88. For CCM, unity and mission stand together at the heart of the church's life. In the final paragraph, for example, the agreement notes that "entering full communion... will bring new opportunities and levels of shared evangelism, witness and service". It then relates the mission of the church to "the mission of the Son in obedience to the Father through the power and presence of the Holy Spirit" (§29).

## Definition of proximate and ultimate goals

89. The LED series had presumed that the goal of the dialogue was full communion as defined by agreement in the faith, sharing of worship and especially the sacraments, mutual ecclesial recognition, and interchangeability of ministries. The Concordat and CCM both relied upon the description of full communion in the *Cold Ash Report* to define the full communion being sought. This description was in line with the official ecumenical policies of the two churches. No distinction was made between proximate and ultimate goals. CCM (§§14,29) explicitly notes the communion is to be grown into and so the relation is open to deepening as the two churches experience the possibilities and potential limitations of their new relation.

*Particular issues arising from the context*

90. The wish to reconcile a continuing minority of Lutheran opposition to CCM led the ELCA churchwide assembly in 2001, at the unanimous urging of the ELCA conference of bishops, to unilaterally decide to provide a process whereby synodical bishops might permit exceptions "in unusual circumstances" to the rule that a bishop preside at all ordinations. This action was immediately addressed by the presiding bishop of the Episcopal Church as materially damaging to CCM and most unfortunate in its unilateral nature. At the time of the writing of this report, no such exceptions to the rule of episcopal presidency at ordinations have been made. The round of ordinations in the summer of 2002 will be a test of the effects of this provision.

91. More positively, there are instances of ECUSA clergy serving Lutheran congregations and vice-versa under the authorizations required by the agreement. There are also joint congregations and joint projects in theological education.

92. Other issues revolve around establishing effective means at all levels of church life for mutual consultation not only to meet potentially divisive problems, but for the promotion of the means of common life and mission throughout the churches.

*Mutual accountability in the agreement*

93. The principal provision for mutual accountability in the relationship of full communion established between the ECUSA and the ELCA is found in §23 of "Called to Common Mission". By this provision both churches authorized the establishment of a joint commission "fully accountable to the decision-making bodies of the two churches". It is envisioned that this joint commission will not only be consultative, but also, through its "work with the appropriate boards, committees, commissions and staff", advise the churches regarding common decision-making "in fundamental matters that the churches may face together in the future". The authorization of this body simply enacts the definition of full communion that CCM proclaims at the outset, namely, that such full communion "includes the establishment of locally and nationally recognized organs of regular consultation and communication…" (CCM, §2) Other aspects of mutual accountability relate to the manner over time whereby the episcopates of both churches may be reconciled through conjoint participation in the ordination of bishops (CCM, §12) and whereby the office and ministry of bishop can be mutually subjected to periodic review for "evaluation, adaptation, improvement, and continual reform in the service of the gospel" (CCM, §17).

G) OTHER REFLECTIONS

94. Information was received from some regions where contact between Anglicans and Lutherans is at a very preliminary stage. The state of development is summarized below

*India*

95. Lutherans in India are in dialogue with Anglicans who are not independent, but who form part of ecumenical church expressions (Church of North India, Church of South India). CNI and CSI are also part of a joint council, along with the Mar Thoma Church. Both Lutherans and Methodists wanted to be part of this wider dialogue. In order to be members of the joint council, churches must be in full communion with each other. Hence, the name of the council has been changed to "Communion of Churches in India", and constitutional amendments have been made which will allow other churches to join this fellowship. The existence of the ecumenical churches in India for common mission creates a unique context. It would appear that Lutherans (and Methodists) are being invited into a relationship, which has itself been formed over many years of dialogue and sense of common mission. The proximate goal appears to be "full communion". There is no definition of an ultimate goal. At present there is no common statement of the faith involving Lutherans and Anglicans in India.

*Japan*

96. There are five Lutheran bodies in Japan, which have agreements among each other that require mutual affirmation of new actions by any one of them. This can make theological dialogue difficult. However, there are regular meetings between the Nippon Sei Ko Kei (the Anglican Communion in Japan) and the Evangelical Lutheran Church in Japan, and there is a desire for dialogue between them. There is no documentation available at present.

*Middle East*

97. In the 19th century a joint bishopric in Jerusalem was established which was later discontinued. The complexities of the political and social situation in the Middle East make it difficult to have theological dialogue. Both Anglicans and Lutherans are active participants in the Middle East Council of Churches, and share a common approach to their region. There was an attempt in the 1970s to bring Anglicans and Lutherans together. Concelebration at the eucharist by both bishops has occurred. Some clergy have served in interim ministry in each other's churches. Joint services are held in Advent and Lent, and pulpit exchanges take place. At present no work has been done towards a common statement on the faith, nor the definition of proximate or ultimate goals.

*Hong Kong, Malaysia, Papua New Guinea, Southeast Asia*

98. In addition requests for information were sent to churches in Hong Kong, Malaysia, Papua New Guinea and Southeast Asia. Hong Kong was the only one to reply, and it indicated that although there is ecumenical cooperation between Lutherans and Anglicans in the Hong Kong Christian Council, there are no particular bilateral agreements or dialogues.

# III. EVALUATION OF CONSISTENCY AND COHERENCE IN THE DIALOGUES

99.  The variety of recent national and regional Anglican-Lutheran dialogues and agreements has produced a rich, but potentially confusing network of relations. In line with its terms of reference, the international working group has examined two questions raised by this situation. First, are the various relations theologically consistent in their use of foundational documents, their concepts of unity, and their understanding of apostolicity and episcopal ministry? This question is addressed in this section with respect to Meissen, Porvoo, Reuilly, CCM, Waterloo and Covenanting for Mutual Recognition and Reconciliation. Second, what ecclesiological issues are raised by the imperfect character of this web of relations, in which churches, each in communion with some third church, are not in communion with each other? This question is addressed in section V.

## A.  Foundational documents

100.  Among the "issues remaining to be addressed" in the various Anglican-Lutheran regional dialogues, the 1998 Lambeth Conference included "the status of our foundational documents" (Lambeth Conference 1998, 248). The meaning of "foundational documents" is not elaborated, but can be taken to refer to post-biblical texts, other than the shared ancient creeds, which each tradition appeals to as normative within its life. For Lutherans, confessionally important texts are gathered into the *Book of Concord*. Among the Lutheran churches, the Augsburg confession and the Small Catechism occupy a central role. Anglicans have no clearly defined collection of texts, but the *Book of Common Prayer*, in its various national editions, including its ordinal and catechism, and the Thirty-Nine Articles have at various times played a normative role in Anglican faith and practice.

101.  Various Lutheran-Anglican dialogues have noted that Lutherans and Anglicans appeal to such foundational documents in different ways. The 1972 *Pullach Report* of the first international Anglican-Lutheran dialogue noted that for Lutherans "the confessions of the Reformation still occupy officially a prominent place in theological thinking and training, in catechetical teaching, and in the constitutions of the individual Lutheran churches and at the ordination of pastors" (§29). While the Anglican Thirty-Nine Articles are "universally recognized as expressing a significant phase in a formative period of Anglican thought and life", "the significance attached to them today in Anglican circles varies between Anglican churches and between groups within Anglican churches". The *Book of Common Prayer*, however, "has for a long time served as a confessional document in a liturgical setting" (§30). Other dialogues have made similar observations (US 1988 Implications, §69; Canada 1986 Report and Recommendation, Appendix 1, §6-7).

102.  No dialogue has seen this difference between Lutherans and Anglicans as a significant obstacle to communion. The *Pullach Report* stated that "since confessional formularies are not a mark of the church, their significance lies in their expression of the living confession to the living Lord. Different approaches to the authority of these formularies

are possible between communions so long as they share a living confession which is a faithful response to the living word of God as proclaimed in holy scripture" (§31).

103. Although they are not extensively quoted in the regional texts, the foundational documents of the two traditions were examined thoroughly in the dialogues. References to them in the European Porvoo, Meissen, and Reuilly common statements are few. The most extensive appeal to and discussion of foundational documents occur in the US texts (see below, §109).

104. When they are appealed to the foundational documents play two, seemingly opposite roles in the agreements. On the one hand, they are used as evidence of the common faith shared by the two traditions. On the other, they are cited to establish the specific positions of each tradition in distinction from the other. This twofold use is not contradictory. The foundational documents of each tradition seek both to assert the one faith of the one church and to testify to the particular understanding and appropriation of that one faith within its own tradition.

105. First, the foundational documents of both traditions are claimed as testimonies to a common profession of the one faith of the entire church. Porvoo cites the explicit affirmations of classical dogma in the Reformation era formularies of the two traditions. In its listing of "the principal beliefs and practices that we have in common" (§32), it states (d):

> We accept the faith of the church through the ages set forth in the Niceno-Constantinopolitan and Apostles' Creeds and confess the basic trinitarian and christological dogmas to which these creeds testify.... This faith is explicitly confirmed both in the Thirty-Nine Articles of Religion [reference to article VIII] and in the Augsburg Confession [reference to articles I and III].

The Australian 2001 "Common Ground" statement repeats this sentence verbatim, but without the references to particular passages (§11). The Canadian Waterloo declaration (2001, Acknowledgments, 2, Commentary) and the US 1999 "Called to Common Mission" (§4) cite the various foundational texts in general as witnesses to "the essentials of the one catholic and apostolic faith" (CCM) or to "the faith of the Catholic Church" (Waterloo).

106. The French-British Isles Reuilly common statement follows this pattern, but, since the Lutherans are joined in this dialogue by Reformed churches, relevant Reformed confessions are noted. Reuilly, §31b, closely resembles Porvoo, §32d, but instead of citing specific passages in only two confessions, it more generally states, "This faith of the church through the ages [i.e., the christological and trinitarian faith of the creeds] is borne witness to in the historic formularies of our churches." In a footnote, it then lists these, adding, however, that "these confessional statements were produced in different circumstances and do not play an identical role in the life of the churches".

107. The German-English Meissen common statement is similar, but subtly different. In Meissen, the Lutherans are joined by the United and Reformed member churches of the Evangelical Church in Germany, and so the Reformed Heidelberg Catechism is added to its fund of formularies. It treats the formularies of the traditions, however, not as witnesses to the common faith of the church catholic, but rather as signs of a common "Reformation inheritance expressed in the Thirty-Nine Articles of Religion, the *Book of Common Prayer* and the Ordinal, and the Augsburg confession and the Heidelberg catechism" (§9).

108. Second, but less often, the foundational documents of the two traditions are cited to elaborate the specific position of one or the other tradition on some particular question. The foundational documents are not treated as witnesses to what the traditions have in common, but to what makes each distinctive. For the Australian "Common Ground" statement, "Anglicans are identified by acceptance, as 'agreeable to the word of God', of the *Book of Common Prayer* of 1662 and the Articles of Religion (with the Homilies)" (§2.4), while Lutherans are identified by adherence to the confessional writings contained in the *Book of Concord* of 1580, "because they are true expositions of scripture" (§2.5). The European Porvoo, Meissen and Reuilly statements and the Canadian Waterloo declaration make no use of specific foundational documents to elaborate the specific identities of the two traditions.

109. The US dialogue makes by far the greatest use of foundational documents to elaborate the differences between the two traditions, especially on the question of episcopacy. The US dialogue appended to its full communion proposal an explanatory text, the length and detail of which is much greater than the common statements that introduced the Meissen, Porvoo and Reuilly declarations. Its chapter on "The Lutheran churches and Episcopal Ministry" included a section on "The Lutheran Confessional Heritage" (§§37-47). Normative conclusions for present Lutheran practice are drawn directly from the confessions: "churches which accept the doctrinal authority of the Book of Concord... are committed in principle to a preference for 'the ecclesiastical and canonical polity' with its 'various ranks of the ecclesiastical hierarchy'" [Apol. 14] (§44). The parallel chapter on "the episcopal church and the ministry of the historic episcopate", although it contains a section entitled "The Prayer Book Teaching on the Episcopate" (§69), does not derive such normative conclusions directly from particular texts, but rather draws upon the range of Anglican history to portray Anglican attitudes. The specific attitudes to episcopacy portrayed on the basis of the documents of the two traditions are then used to argue that each tradition should be open to the proposal that follows. Alone among these statements, the US agreement commits each church "to encourage its people to study each other's basic documents" (§4).

110. Two conclusions may be drawn from this survey. First, there is no indication that the different ways that Anglicans and Lutherans appeal to and utilize the specific foundational documents of their traditions pose any difficulty for Anglican-Lutheran relations. Neither explicitly nor implicitly has this difference played any role in Anglican-Lutheran separation. Second, the differences among the dialogues in the way they appeal to foundational documents are not significant. All find in these documents a witness to the faith shared by Anglicans and Lutherans. The extensive and unique discussion of foundational documents by the US dialogue represents a decision on its part that such a discussion would demonstrate in its context the faithfulness of its full communion proposal to the norms of each tradition. The full communion proposal advanced, however, is consistent with that offered by such other proposals as Waterloo and Porvoo.

## B. Describing the goal of unity

111. All the agreements affirm a commitment to the goal of visible unity, even if this goal is sometimes described in the various texts using different terminology. Generally, the divergences which exist between the statements from Anglican-Lutheran dialogues

should not be seen as results of varying concepts of unity, but rather as signs that these texts reflect different historical and ecclesiastical contexts and different stages on our mutual journey towards the goal of visible unity.

112. The texts agree in their picture of the goal being sought in Anglican-Lutheran relations. Even where the texts use different terms – "full communion", "full visible unity" – we note that they describe a similar reality. Nevertheless, ecumenical terminology continues to evolve. Thus, in some texts a term refers to the goal of the particular dialogue process. For others the same term may refer to the ultimate goal of the ecumenical journey. We find that Meissen speaks of the goal of EKD-Church of England relations as "full visible unity". Waterloo understands "full communion" between Anglicans and Lutherans as the goal of the agreement, but helpfully contextualizes this goal within the wider goal of the ultimate full visible unity of the whole church of God. CCM sees the result of its dialogue as "full communion" but does not speculate about any further goal beyond this particular dialogue. The Porvoo agreement does not use the terms "full communion" or "full visible unity" but speaks simply of "communion". "...the unity to which we are summoned has already begun to be manifested in the church. It demands fuller visible embodiment in structured form, so that the church may be seen to be, through the Holy Spirit, the one body of Christ and the sign, instrument and foretaste of the kingdom (Porvoo, §22).

113. The similarity in these descriptions of the goal stems from a common development of the Cold Ash statement (1983) of the Anglican-Lutheran joint working group:

> By full communion we here understand a relationship between two distinct churches or communions. Each maintains its own autonomy and recognizes the catholicity and apostolicity of the other, and each believes the other to hold the essentials of the Christian faith:
>
> a)  subject to such safeguards as ecclesial discipline may properly require, members of one body may receive the sacraments of the other;
>
> b)  subject to local invitation, bishops of one church may take part in the consecration of the bishops of the other, thus acknowledging the duty of mutual care and concern;
>
> c)  subject to church regulation, a bishop, pastor/priest or deacon of one ecclesial body may exercise liturgical functions in a congregation of the other body if invited to do so and also, when requested, pastoral care of the other's members;
>
> d)  it is also a necessary addition and complement that there should be recognized organs of regular consultation and communication, including episcopal collegiality, to express and strengthen the fellowship and enable common witness, life and service.
>
> Full communion carries implications which go beyond sharing the same eucharist. The eucharist is a common meal, and to share in it together has implications for a sharing of life and of a common concern for the mission of the church. To be in full communion implies a community of life, an exchange and a commitment to one another in respect of major decisions on questions of faith, order and morals. It implies, where churches are in the same geographical area, common worship, study, witness, evangelism, and promotion of justice, peace and love. It may lead to a uniting of ecclesial bodies if they are, or come to be, immediately adjacent in the same geographical area This should not imply the suppressing of ethnic, cultural or ecclesial characteristics or traditions which may in fact be maintained and developed by diverse institutions within one communion. (Cold Ash §25,27)

114. The six texts examined by ALIWG reflect a basic compatibility in terms of the description of the goal of unity. Nevertheless, they represent different stages on our journey and grow out of churches in different contexts, with different shared histories, and to some extent, with different participants in the dialogue. Reuilly and Meissen, for instance, are trilateral dialogues with input from Reformed and United as well as Lutheran and Anglican churches. Particularly in those texts which are still working towards "full communion" (Reuilly, Meissen and "Common Ground") churches still find themselves struggling with episcopacy and its relation to communion.

115. Three of the current texts bring the churches involved into a relationship, which from an Anglican perspective is largely indistinguishable, canonically, from that between churches within the Anglican Communion. These agreements have resolved the issue of episcopacy and its relation to communion and contain agreements on the office of bishop and the historic episcopal succession. In these texts, which establish full communion between the churches involved, full communion is re-described, but in language still reminiscent of Cold Ash. Thus CCM states the following:

> We therefore understand full communion to be a relation between distinct churches in which each recognizes the other as a catholic and apostolic church holding the essentials of the Christian faith. Within this new relation, churches become interdependent while remaining autonomous. Full communion includes the establishment locally and nationally of recognized organs of regular consultation and communication, including episcopal collegiality, to express and strengthen the fellowship and enable common witness, life and service. Diversity is preserved, but this diversity is not static. Neither church seeks to remake the other in its own image, but each is open to the gifts of the other as it seeks to be faithful to Christ and his mission. They are together committed to a visible unity in the church's mission to proclaim the word and administer the sacraments. (CCM §2)

116. The Porvoo common statement asserts:

> Such a level of communion has a variety of inter-related aspects. It entails agreement in faith together with the common celebration of the sacraments, supported by a united ministry and forms of collegial and conciliar consultation in matters of faith, life and witness. These expressions of communion may need to be embodied in the law and regulations of the church. For the fullness of communion all these visible aspects of the life of the church require to be permeated by a profound spiritual communion, a growing together in a common mind, mutual concern and a care for unity (Phil. 2:2). (Porvoo, §28)

117. The Waterloo declaration uses the following extensive definition of full communion:

> Full communion is understood as a relationship between two distinct churches or communions in which each maintains its own autonomy while recognizing the catholicity and apostolicity of the other, and believing the other to hold the essentials of the Christian faith. In such a relationship, communicant members of each church would be able freely to communicate at the altar of the other, and there would be freedom of ordained ministers to officiate sacramentally in either church. Specifically, in our context, we understand this to include transferability of members; mutual recognition and interchangeability of ministries; freedom to use each other's liturgies; freedom to participate in each other's ordinations and installations of clergy, including bishops; and structures for consultation to express, strengthen, and enable our common life, witness, and service, to the glory of God and the salvation of the world. (Waterloo, §7)

118. In the Reuilly statement we detect a possible discrepancy. In the joint statement, the dialogue partners say they "are totally committed to strive for the 'full visible unity' of the body of Christ on earth" (Reuilly, §22). Elsewhere, however, the Lutheran and Reformed participants expressed their conviction that "mutual recognition already expresses and signifies the unity of the church. Mutual recognition for them entails full communion, which includes full interchangeability of ministries" (Reuilly, §27). While Reuilly may contain this potential inconsistency, nevertheless, this text, like the other five we examined, moves beyond the narrow description of the goal as "pulpit and altar fellowship" and understands unity to include the visible expression of the unity of the church for the credibility of its mission in the world.

119. Because communion is a common life in Christ and the Spirit into which churches grow, defining the moment at which the goal of full communion is reached may be difficult. Theological differences can also contribute to this difficulty, when churches place differing emphases on certain elements in their common life. Thus, the ELCA and the ECUSA, in CCM §14, agree that full communion "begins" with the adoption of the agreement. The ECUSA adds, however, that full communion is its view will not be fully realized until there is "a shared ministry of bishops in the historic episcopate," i.e., until all ELCA bishops have been consecrated in historic succession.

120. Despite some variations, all our dialogue texts see unity as a dynamic reality. Thus, there is a commitment to further growth in unity – between the dialogue partners as well as in a larger ecumenical perspective. This entails an obligation to make our communion ever more visible. Such visibility should be seen as a sign and a witness to a world that clearly lacks but desperately needs unity.

121. As noted in section II A above, our dialogue texts consistently, but in varying ways, emphasize the church's mission as the context and the goal of unity. Unity, in other words, is not merely a means employed to achieve the end of mission. The unity of the church and faithfulness to its apostolic mission of self-offering and witness to the kingdom of God belong together as two sides of the same reality. Since the consultation in Niagara, which described the apostolicity of the church as the mission of self-offering for the life of the world, Anglicans and Lutherans have together recognized the call to serve the mission of God's suffering and vulnerable love as an expression of "Christ's way of being in the world" (§23). Our agreements speak concretely of mission as concerned with the healing of the world and justice; transforming society; addressing the needs of local and global communities; and sharing evangelism, witness and service. The unity of the church thus bears witness, in the words of Porvoo, to "the healing and uniting power of God amidst the divisions of humankind" (§20).

## C. Apostolicity and episcopal ministry

122. Just as the *Cold Ash Report* was significant in shaping the conversations around the theme of full communion, the *Niagara Report* was significant for all the regional dialogues in laying out Anglican and Lutheran agreement and divergence on *episcope* and episcopacy. Indeed, the most significant aspect of the reception of Niagara has been the incorporation of its insights on episcopacy and *episcope* into the regional agreements.

123. The *Niagara Report* has been particularly important as the regional dialogues addressed issues of episcopacy and succession within the total apostolicity of the church (Niagara was itself influenced by BEM and prior Lutheran-Roman Catholic dialogue on the ministry).

> Apostolic succession in the episcopal office does not consist primarily in an unbroken chain of those ordaining to those ordained, but in a succession in the presiding ministry of a church, which stands in the continuity of apostolic faith and which is overseen by the bishop in order to keep it in the communion of the catholic and apostolic church. (Niagara, §53, cf. BEM Ministry §38, LRCJC, The Ministry in the Church, §62).

124. Just as in the understanding of full communion, the type of agreement reached on *episcope* and episcopacy was influenced by different historical, geographical and cultural contexts. For example, in the United States of America, Canada and Australia relations are between churches in the same country with members of both traditions frequently living in close proximity. In Europe relations are primarily between Anglicans and Lutherans separated in different countries. Additionally, in the United States of America, the Lutheran church involved, the ELCA, was itself the result of a recent merger of three distinct Lutheran churches with a diversity of traditions regarding the episcopate. In Canada, an uneven geographic overlap of Lutherans and Anglicans and a discrepancy in the size of the two churches involved affected the character of the agreement.

125. Among the agreements examined by the ALIWG, the same two categories emerged with regard to the treatment of episcopacy and succession as emerged with regard to the treatment of the goal of unity. Those which have come to an agreement about full communion have each found ways, slightly different, but all drawing on Niagara, to recognize each other's expression of episcopal ministry as a sign of continuity and unity in apostolic faith. Those texts which are still working towards "full communion" (Reuilly, Meissen and "Common Ground") have not reached consensus on episcopal ministry and succession.

126. The Meissen statement records this disagreement, reflected in the *Pullach Report* (1973), concerning the historical Anglican position and the historical Lutheran position on episcopacy and succession, and does not try to bring them together:

> Lutheran, Reformed and United churches, though being increasingly prepared to appreciate episcopal succession "as a sign of the apostolicity of the life of the whole church", hold that this particular form of *episcope* should not become a necessary condition for "full, visible unity". The Anglican understanding of full, visible unity includes the historic episcopate and full interchangeability of ministers. "Yet even this remaining difference, when seen in the light of our agreements and convergences, cannot be regarded as a hindrance to closer fellowship between our churches." (Meissen, §16)

127. The Reuilly statement similarly makes an honest statement of the two positions that cannot be reconciled at present.

Anglicans believe that the historic episcopate is a sign of the apostolicity of the whole church. The ordination of a bishop in historic succession (that is, in intended continuity with the apostles themselves) is a sign of God's promise to be with the church, and also the way the church communicates its care for continuity in the whole of its faith, life and mission, and renews its intention and determination to manifest the permanent characteristics of the church of the apostles. Anglicans hold that the full visible unity of the church includes the historic episcopal succession.

Lutherans and Reformed also believe that their ministries are in apostolic succession. In their ordination rites they emphasize the continuity of the church and its ministry. They can recognize in the historic episcopal succession a sign of the apostolicity of the church. They do not, however, consider it a necessary condition for full visible unity (Reuilly, §37,38).

128. The "Common Ground" statement from Australia is at a more preliminary stage than any of the other agreements. Although unable at present to find a way of mutually recognizing the ministries of Anglicans and Lutherans, nevertheless it is able to affirm "that the historic pattern of ministry, in which the bishop exercises a regional ministry of oversight with presbyters exercising a local ministry, can continue to serve the unity and apostolicity of the church in every age and place" and that "the episcopal office in succession as one sign of the church's intention to ensure the continuity of the church in apostolic life and witness" ("Common Ground", app. 1, §18). The Lutheran church is challenged to receive this by accepting "the episcopal office as a sign of the apostolicity and catholicity of the church" and affirming "the value of the historic episcopate within the orderly succession of the ministry of Christ through the ages, without implying the episcopal office is necessary for salvation or that it guarantees, by itself, the orthodoxy of the church's faith" ("Common Ground", app. 2, §24.2). Anglicans are challenged to "recognize the intention of the Lutheran church to be nothing other than apostolic and truly catholic in its faith and practice" ("Common Ground", app. 2, §24.3).

129. On the other hand, the Porvoo common statement is able to affirm that:

> Faithfulness to the apostolic calling of the whole church is carried by more than one means of continuity. Therefore a church which has preserved the sign of historic episcopal succession is free to acknowledge an authentic episcopal ministry in a church which has preserved continuity in the episcopal office by an occasional priestly/presbyteral ordination at the time of the Reformation. Similarly, a church, which has preserved continuity through such a succession, is free to enter a relationship of mutual participation in episcopal ordinations with a church which has retained the historical episcopal succession, and to embrace this sign, without denying its past apostolic continuity. (Porvoo, §52)

130. In Canada, each of the churches was able to respond clearly to Niagara and incorporate its insights. Thus, the Anglican Church of Canada agreed to view "the historic episcopate in the context of apostolicity articulated in *Baptism, Eucharist and Ministry*", (Waterloo, §8), and the ELCIC agreed "to take the constitutional steps necessary to understand the installation of bishops as ordination" (Waterloo, §9).

131. In CCM, the ELCA and ECUSA are able to assert that they "value and maintain a ministry of *episcope* as one of the ways, in the context of ordained ministries and of the whole people of God, in which the apostolic succession of the church is visibly expressed and personally symbolised in fidelity to the gospel through the ages" (CCM §12).

132. Despite these agreements being at different stages and in different contexts and therefore having different questions to resolve, nevertheless we see a consensus emerging and a general compatibility.

133. Increasingly Lutherans around the world are prepared to appreciate the significance of the episcopate in apostolic succession as a sign and servant of the apostolic continuity and unity of the church. The agreements show a growing readiness to become part of this succession by inviting Anglican and Lutheran bishops who belong to churches that share in the historical episcopal succession to actively participate in the ordinations or installations of Lutheran bishops in churches which have not so shared. Lutherans are free to take up the historic episcopal succession when (1) this integration of Lutheran bishops into historic episcopal succession occurs after mutual recognition of churches and ministries and declaration of church fellowship/full communion have been expressed, (2) this integration does not imply an adverse judgment on the Lutheran ministries in the past nor an increase of their ecclesiastical power in the future, (3) there is the continuing liberty for different interpretations of the office of bishop and its ecumenical significance.

134. On the Anglican side, the following three features are understood to be crucial: (1) an awareness that the threefold ministry should not be seen as the only theologically possible ministerial form, but rather comes through as the structure which benefits the mission and service of the church in the best way; (2) a realization that the church's apostolicity can be kept up also in times when some of its signs have been lost; (3) an understanding of the historic episcopate as "a sign, though not a guarantee" without reducing this sign to a mere "optional extra" in the life of the church.

135. A feature which is evident to a greater or lesser extent in the agreements, which ALIWG observes as offering a constructive approach to the thorny issue of episcopal succession and apostolicity, is an approach where the different signs of apostolicity are seen less as juridical requirements than as gifts which the churches share within the framework of community. According to Porvoo:

> To the degree to which our ministries have been separated, all our churches have lacked something of that fullness which God desires for his people (Eph. 1:23 and 3:17-19). By moving together, and by being served by a reconciled and mutually recognized episcopal ministry, our churches will be both more faithful to their calling and also more conscious of their need for renewal. By the sharing of our life and ministries in closer visible unity, we shall be strengthened for the continuation of Christ's mission in the world. (Porvoo, §54)

This approach is evident or implicit in the reports we have examined, a factor which contributes significantly to the reality that Anglican-Lutheran dialogue remains among the most constructive dialogues in the ecumenical scene today.

## IV. DIVERSITIES, BEARABLE ANOMALIES AND POTENTIALLY CHURCH-DIVIDING ISSUES

### A. The issue identified

136. Anglicans and Lutherans affirm that in Christ's body there exists a variety of charisms and that the church seeks to use them faithfully, both for the building up of the

body "until all of us come to the unity of the faith and of the knowledge of the Son of God, to maturity to the measure of the full stature of Christ" and "to equip the saints for the work of ministry" (Eph. 4:12-13). From the first meeting at Virginia Theological Seminary in 2000 the members of the ALIWG have stressed, in monitoring the ongoing development of relations between churches of our two communions, the important distinctions between: genuine and beneficial diversity; anomalies, bearable and unbearable; and issues which threaten unity or further divide churches. The purpose of ecumenical dialogue is not to seek a uniformity in Christian expression. It is essential, however, to seek assurance that diversity is a genuine expression of the life of Christ and the kingdom. Thus, the ALIWG has come to review differences between churches in communion in the light of the following categories:

a) legitimate diversity on secondary or non-essential matters;

b) bearable anomalies;

c) potentially church-dividing issues.

## B. Diversity in the body of Christ

137. The report of the 1998 Lambeth Conference reminded us that our communion is grounded in the trinitarian life of God. This is to understand something of fundamental significance in the search for deeper unity among Christians: that at the centre of the communion of the church is life with the Father, through Christ, in the Spirit. The church, in her unity, will therefore rejoice in and celebrate the richness of diverse gifts of the Holy Spirit, which are given so that the gospel can be lived out in the specificity of cultural and historical contexts. Thus, within the church of Christ, there are differences from place to place and from local community to local community which, arising from particular cultural and historical contexts, place the accent on different aspects of the one faith. Such complementary insights into that one faith equip the church to carry out the mission of Christ in a particular place, and enrich the totality of Christian witness.

138. Within each communion, there are diverse traditions of theological method and of spirituality and liturgy. Such diversity is understood to be a desirable dimension of the catholicity of the church, where judged to be genuine expressions of a faith held in common. Anglicans and Lutherans can enjoy such a diversity within the body of Christ. A sufficient agreement in faith does not require us "to accept every doctrinal formulation characteristic of our distinctive traditions" (PCS, §33). This is similar to the diversity, which was agreed to be acceptable between Anglican and Old Catholic churches, according to the Bonn agreement of 1931.

## C. Bearable anomalies

139. The 1998 Lambeth Conference further noted (p.260) that "in moving towards visible unity we recognize that temporary anomalies are likely to arise". This issue was explored in the section IV report entitled "Called to Be One" and was pinpointed in the following resolution of the whole conference:

[This conference] recognizes that the process of moving towards full, visible unity may entail temporary anomalies, and believes that some anomalies may be bearable when there is an agreed goal of visible unity, but that there should always be an impetus towards their resolution and, thus, towards the removal of the principal anomaly of disunity. (Resolution IV.1.c)

140. Similarly, the 1991 LWF review of their bilateral dialogues (Communio and Dialogue: Compatibility – Convergence – Consensus) addressed the issues raised by a church being in communion with two churches which are not in communion with one another. While noting the "inherently anomalous" character of such a situation, it also noted that "as ecumenical progress is made in a tentative, stepwise fashion, such anomalies cannot be avoided". It emphasized the practical questions that arise from this situation. How does a church live up to its responsibilities to the differing churches with which it is in communion?

141. Variance and even a certain inconsistency in faith and order among Christians can be tolerated, temporarily, when our communities, attentive to the high priestly prayer of Christ, are committed to manifest their unity in him, and thus seek to remove all which may hinder the building up of the one body. Such bearable anomalies are understood to be a provisional untidiness, which has good prospect of resolution in view of an agreed goal of visible unity.

### D. Potentially church-dividing issues

142. In one of the eucharistic prayers shared by many Anglicans and Lutherans, there is a prayer for the church that God might "guard its unity and preserve it in peace". It is clear that the unity and peace of the church are somehow constantly vulnerable. Indeed, the ALIWG has signalled at its meetings the possibility that there might be issues arising within each communion that could potentially disrupt existing relations between churches of both communions (as well as between churches of the same communion). An anomaly may be unbearable if it threatens to disrupt the measure of unity already achieved, impede the development of closer fellowship or indeed cause further division. It follows that such divisions within and between churches are a hindrance to the church's mission of reconciliation in the world, and as such are an affront to its very nature. In other words, they are limitations of communion.

143. Some divisions arise within and between churches when they, in their life, witness and teaching, come to uphold distinctions that keep them apart from others rather than uphold their common faith and common calling. Sensitivity and generosity of spirit is required in such situations where different pastoral approaches, details of church order and teaching are understood by members of one church to be faithful and appropriate responses to gospel witness in a particular time and place. Where such divisions hinder relations of communion, dialogue is necessary to determine whether the distinctions are within the one tradition received from the apostles and are perhaps complementary aspects of one truth and therefore have their place within the life of the whole church.

144. The difficulty is that when differences, whether by anomaly in practice or by developments which depart from the gospel or from apostolic Tradition, result in ecclesial separation. It then becomes difficult for joint judgment and discernment to take place, and

the sin of division can be perpetuated and the church's mission and witness weakened. For this reason Anglicans and Lutherans are not content to live with anomalies that may be unbearable, and which could more permanently threaten closer sacramental and ecclesial communion.


## E. The task and context of discernment

145. Within each communion mechanisms are evolving which can assist with the task of discernment of legitimate diversity, bearable anomaly and potentially church-dividing issues which arise in ecumenical dialogue. Which issues fall into which of the above categories, and what are the boundaries between categories? It is precisely these questions that require discernment.

146. The Anglican Communion, following the Lambeth conference of 1998, set up the Inter-Anglican Standing Commission on Ecumenical Relations (IASCER) and specifically charged this new body with a task of discernment in this area:

> to give particular attention to anomalies which arise in the context of ecumenical proposals with a view to discerning those anomalies which may be bearable in the light of progress towards an agreed goal of visible unity, and to suggest ways for resolving them. (Resolution IV.3.b.iv)

147. Within the Lutheran World Federation, since 1993, there has been an acknowledgment of the desirability for member churches to seek the counsel and advice of other member churches when seeking to enter a new relation of communion with an ecumenical partner, with a view to enhancing the fellowship and avoid inadvertently creating new barriers within the Lutheran communion. The standing committee on ecumenical affairs of the LWF, although not specifically mandated in this area, has the competence to take part in this discernment, if so desired.

148. The ALIWG understands it has a role in assisting the churches of both communions to discern jointly the criteria, which may help to distinguish between bearable and unbearable anomalies on the way to greater unity as well as issues arising within each communion that might disrupt existing relations.

149. Three basic criteria provide a context for assessing how far the differences between Anglicans and Lutherans, as seen in particular agreements, are legitimate or anomalous:

a) The articulation of a common vision of the goal of visible unity.

b) The extent to which unity in diversity is understood to be much more than mere concession to theological pluralism, but something of fundamental ecclesial importance that is grounded in the Holy Trinity (see PCS, §23). This is akin to the "comprehensiveness" Anglicans prize within the Anglican Communion, which is set within the context of the Chicago-Lambeth Quadrilateral. Although originally a brief, shorthand expression of the features necessary for visible unity, the Quadrilateral is increasingly helping Anglicans to understand their own unity and identity. Similarly, we see the Lutheran emphasis on the diversity permitted in "human rites and ceremonies", providing there is agreement in the proclamation of the gospel and the administration of the sacraments (*CA*, 7). Clearly, diversity is not without limits (see *The Official Report of the Lambeth Conference 1998*, pp.227-28 on "living with difference").

c) The extent to which Anglicans and Lutherans express sufficient agreement in faith which would not require them "to accept every doctrinal formulation characteristic of our distinctive traditions" (see PCS, §33).

## F. Some comments on actual issues

150. This working group did not attempt to construct a comprehensive list of issues which have arisen, or which may arise in the context of Anglican-Lutheran dialogue. There were, however, three main areas referred to it by the communions for study:

a) the status of foundational documents;

b) the articulation of the goal of unity;

c) the historic succession of bishops as sign of the apostolicity of the church.

In a previous section of this report the working group has concluded that any anomalies in the expression and formulation of agreement in these areas have been understood to be bearable, indeed with a clear consensus emerging.

151. In addition to these major areas, we suggest that some other issues of difference may be seen to be expressions of legitimate diversity which have been observed in different times and places throughout the whole church:

a) the minister of confirmation;

b) the admission of children to holy communion before confirmation;

c) the relations between church and state and between church and nation.

152. Certain differences in ordained ministry may be understood by some to be anomalies, which are bearable in the light of basic agreement on the nature of the ordained ministry in the church. Many others, however, see these as anomalies which may be temporarily bearable but nevertheless ought to be addressed with some urgency, as different approaches in these particulars raise questions as to the real meaning of recognition and reconciliation of ministries:

a) the meaning of reconciliation of threefold and non-threefold ministries;

b) the ordained diaconate and non-ordained diaconal ministries;

c) the tenure and jurisdiction of bishops.

153. Some differences cause strains within each communion as well as between churches of the two communions. They are potentially or presently church-dividing and require ongoing dialogue. Some different emphases and practices related to the ordained ministry among Anglican and Lutheran churches are at present barriers to the development of fuller relations between Anglicans and Lutherans in certain places, or risk impairing the relation of communion already established:

a) the ordination or non-ordination of women as deacons, priests / pastors and bishops;

b) the acceptability of historical episcopal succession in the service of the apostolicity of the church;

c) the delegation of ordination by bishops;

d) lay presidency of the eucharist.

154. In addition there are developments currently being discussed in parts of both communions in the area of church teaching and practice concerning moral life. Examples of such issues are:

a) issues related to the beginning and end of life;

b) the ordination of non-celibate homosexuals and the blessing of same-sex unions.

These issues might in some cases have a divisive effect among provinces/churches from each communion seeking mutual relations. Regarding these issues, the two world communions might consult and learn from each other about substantive as well as procedural aspects.

## G. Conclusions

155. Legitimate diversity, temporary anomalies and potentially church-dividing issues are simple ways to categorize differences among Anglicans and Lutherans and between churches of the same ecclesial family. Diversity does not lead to division where it is a necessary feature of the church's catholicity. Temporary anomalies occur in the stages along the way to the church's full visible unity, but mechanisms to discuss and address such anomalies are desirable between churches that are in a relation of communion. Potentially church-dividing issues between Anglicans and Lutherans may be referred to a commission that is competent to address the theological issues involved, with a view to seeking deeper agreement in these areas.

## V. THE IMPERFECT WEB OF COMMUNION

### A. Introduction

156. When an Anglican church and a Lutheran church enter a new relation of full communion, is the Anglican church involved also in a new relation with the other Lutheran churches with which this Lutheran church is in communion? Is the Lutheran church involved in a new relation with the other Anglican churches with which the Anglican church involved is in communion? If other Anglican or Lutheran churches wish to do so, could they attach themselves to the new relation? If so, how? These questions are the occasion for the discussion of what we have called the "transitivity" of communion.

### B. Transitivity and communion

*Instruments of decision-making*

157. The issue is rooted in the way our two traditions make decisions. In each case, although our churches understand themselves to be parts of a worldwide communion of

Anglican or Lutheran churches, binding decision-making on ecumenical matters occurs at the level of national churches (or, in the Anglican Communion, provinces). This structure of decision-making is in accord with the ecclesiology of a communion of interdependent churches. This structure of decision-making leaves us with the questions, however, both of the immediate impact of these decisions on the ecumenical relations of the other churches in the respective communions and of the possibility that such decisions might be easily extended to other churches of the communion. The question is thus raised by our similar organization as national churches within worldwide communions. For an outline of the present organs of accountability and decision-making in both communions, see appendix II.

*Transitivity: definition*

158. We have found the concept of transitivity, borrowed from mathematics and logic, helpful in addressing this problem. In logic and mathematics, a transitive relation is any relation x for which if a and b stand in relation x and if b and c stand in relation x, then a and c stand in relation x also. For example, if Jane and Allison are sisters and if Allison and Sarah are sisters, then Jane and Sarah must be sisters also. Friendship, however, is not transitive. That Mary and Ann are friends and Ann and Fred are friends does not necessarily imply that Mary and Fred are friends. My brother's brother must also be my brother, but my friend's friend is not necessarily my friend.

159. There are good theological reasons to think that communion between churches should be transitive, i.e., that if two churches are in communion, they ought in principle to both be in communion with all churches with which either is in communion. All communion is communion within Christ's one body, which cannot be divided. If communion is the realization of a common life in Christ, then how can one church truly realize a common life in Christ with two churches who themselves refuse such a common life with each other? Both a 1991 consultation of Lutherans involved in international ecumenical dialogues and the 1998 Lambeth Conference used the word "anomalous" to describe situations where relations of communion are not transitive.

*Organizational reasons for intransitivity*

160. Within our present structures of decision-making, relations of communion established by new ecumenical agreements cannot be automatically transitive. If they were so, then a pair of Anglican and Lutheran churches would each be able to bring the other into communion with all the churches of their own world family without the consent of these other churches. The consequence would be to delay any new ecumenical relation until it had been approved by all churches with which any of the involved churches share communion. Such a requirement would lead to ecumenical paralysis.

161. In addition, many ecumenical texts and proposals are rightly contextual in nature. The new relation depends both upon agreements formulated in line with the specific theological and ecclesiastical realities of the churches involved and upon the shared history of these churches. Beyond this context, the agreement may take on a different character.

162. Action simply at the level of the entire Anglican or Lutheran world communions would not solve the problem. On the one hand, neither communion appears ready to grant the necessary authority to its world organs to make such a decision. On the other hand, churches in both communions share communion with churches outside either communion (e.g., Lutheran communion with United and Reformed churches and Anglican communion with the Old Catholic churches of the Union of Utrecht, the Iglesia Filipina Independiente and the Mar Thoma Syrian Church of Malabar). Even if communion-wide action were possible, it would not remove the anomaly that our communion with one another is not transitive with such churches. The working group attempted to take some account of existing relations of communion, in this case between Anglicans and Old Catholics, by inviting an Old Catholic observer to participate fully in the discussions, which led to the production of this report.

163. An additional complication arises through the definition of the Anglican Communion as communion with the see of Canterbury. Thus any regional agreement of full communion with the Church of England raises questions about the relation of those churches with Anglican churches in communion with the see of Canterbury. The bishops of these churches were described at the Lambeth Conference in 1998 as "bishops in communion", even though other Anglican provinces have not had the opportunity of agreeing to the relationships. Some differentiation of the regional and global roles of the archbishop of Canterbury might alleviate this anomaly.

*Theological reasons for intransitivity*

164. Most Lutheran-Anglican full communion agreements have involved theological and ecclesiastical actions by both partners: actions by the Anglican churches to recognize ordained ministries usually seen previously as non-episcopal, and actions by Lutheran churches to take on the sign of episcopal succession. Such actions, though not preconditions of the agreements, are integral parts of the new relations. Other Anglican and Lutheran churches could participate in these new relations only if they are willing to take the same or similar actions. Such actions cannot be forced upon them or be presumed. The individual churches would need to take the required action.

*Intransitivity as anomaly: the thorn in the side*

165. The intransitivity of our ecumenical relations remains, however, anomalous. It is a presence even within our steps towards unity of the larger context of disunity, reminding us that true unity perhaps cannot be achieved in just one bilateral relation. The transitivity problem is the thorn in the side of any bilateral relation, keeping us "from being too elated" (2 Cor. 12:7). It is the sign, the intrusive mark, within any relation of communion of the larger reality of non-communion that forms its context. It reminds us that the ecumenical goal must be the full, visible unity of all in each place. Nevertheless, the anomaly caused by intransitive relations of communion is less serious than the principal anomaly of division. Partial movements towards the ultimate goal of full, visible unity must not be condemned simply because they are partial.

## C.  Patterns of further development

166. Even if the anomaly of intransitive relations of communion between individual churches in our two communions cannot be simply eliminated, creative thought needs to be given to how these particular relations of communion might more easily be extended to a wider range of churches in our communions. We now have an increasing number of such relationships. If new relations can be modelled on these, the possibility of such relations at least coming to be transitive among themselves (i.e., all Lutheran and Anglican churches which have committed themselves to theologically and structurally similar relations might be in communion with one another) would be increased.

167. Might it be possible for some decision-making body within a communion to formulate guidelines indicating what sort of agreement would be widely acceptable within the communion? For example, would an Anglican or LWF body be able to specify what sorts of contents would need to be found in a Lutheran-Anglican agreement if that agreement were likely to find wide affirmation throughout the Anglican or Lutheran communion? Such guidelines could have no juridical authority, but if they came to be widely affirmed, they would indicate that a particular relation is apt to be affirmed by others churches of the communion if the guidelines are met. Such guidelines might even indicate a recommendation that certain relations should be affirmed as far as possible by the other churches of the communion and indicate possible means by which this might be done. The question of authority and its structures are under serious discussion within both of our communions. The problem of the intransitivity of our present ecumenical relations may be an area in which creative thinking could contribute not just to our ecumenical life, but also to the internal lives of our two communions. We draw attention to recommendations 4 and 5 below as examples of the application of guidelines, which the authorities of the communions may care to consider.

# VI.  MUTUAL ACCOUNTABILITY AND COMMON LIFE

## A.  Mutual accountability in the regional agreements

168. All the agreements which are in a mature state of development have made provision for a contact group or continuation committee to oversee the implication of the agreements. These report to the respective authorities of the churches involved. The different agreements have kept in contact through the agency of this working group, and it is recommended below that such contact be made more formal and regular through its successor body, ALIC.

## B.  Common life and action between the Anglican and the Lutheran communions

169. The fact that several Anglican and Lutheran churches have entered into binding relations of communion, coupled with the fact that all the churches of the Anglican and

Lutheran communions respectively maintain communion among themselves, represents a call to the Anglican Communion and the LWF to explore how their life might develop in ways representing rapprochement on the global level, expressed through common actions and programmes.

### a)  An Anglican-Lutheran International Commission (ALIC)

170.  The working group finds that Anglican-Lutheran relations around the world are developing to such an extent that the establishment of an Anglican-Lutheran International Commission needs to be considered. The mandate of such a commission, consisting of church leaders, representatives of governing bodies and staff, could include:

a)  to monitor the continued development of Anglican-Lutheran relations around the world;

b)  to consider issues of compatibility regarding further Anglican-Lutheran developments;

c)  to promote joint study projects of issues relevant to Anglican-Lutheran relations;

d)  to explore possibilities of common actions and declarations;

e)  to discuss ways to promote the role and contribution of the CWCs in the wider ecumenical movement;

f)  to participate, together with the central staffs of the two communions, in the initiation of meetings of the top leadership of the two communions, particularly as pertains to agenda items and their preparation

### b)  Joint staff meetings

171.  The working group welcomes the establishment of joint staff meetings between the ACC secretary general and the LWF general secretary and their assisting staff. A proposal in this regard was set forth by the working group in the course of its work. First meetings of preliminary kind were held in 2001 in connection with the celebrations of "Called to Common Mission" in the USA and of the Waterloo declaration in Canada. The first full joint staff meeting took place in Geneva in January 2002.

172.  The purpose of joint staff meetings would be similar to that of equivalent meetings involving the Anglican Communion and the LWF respectively in their relationship to other ecumenical partners, and would have a directly operational character. Among the areas where joint action would be relevant, the following can be mentioned:

a)  general information-sharing;

b)  programme coordination in areas of common concern;

c)  common, specific consideration of the way in which programmes of the two communions contribute to the goal of Christian unity;

d)  discussion of specific Anglican and Lutheran ecumenical initiatives and processes in other relations and contexts beyond their bilateral relationship;

e)  preparation of items to be presented to ALIC and appropriate implementation of agreements reached in the framework of this commission.

## VII.  COMMUNION OF ALL THE CHURCHES

173.  Lutheran-Anglican relations do not exist in isolation, but are one aspect of the wider movement towards the visible unity of the church among all who follow Christ. As Porvoo (§60) states, "We do not regard our move to closer communion as an end in itself, but as part of the pursuit of a wider unity" (cf. Reuilly, §48; Waterloo, conclusion/commentary). Anglicans and Lutherans are thus in their relations to one another accountable to their other ecumenical partners and to the church universal. A criterion of any truly ecumenical development is that it contributes to and not hinder the wider quest for unity.

174.  Anglicans and Lutherans tend to focus on the local and national church and sometimes need to be reminded of the universal church and its mission. Our ecumenical efforts need to be aware of and contribute to the tasks of the worldwide church. Again to quote Porvoo: "Together with [other churches] we are ready to be used by God as instruments of his saving and reconciling purpose for all humanity and creation" (§61). Our regional agreements commit us to continue to work together for the full visible unity of the whole church.

175.  Anglican-Lutheran discussions and agreements have taken place in the context of the larger ecumenical movement and have profited from its results. The *Niagara Report* in particular manifests its dependence on a range of earlier work, citing BEM (§§3,17,19,20), the international Lutheran-Roman Catholic dialogue (§§3,45,53,91,94), the Anglican-Roman Catholic International Commission (§§42,52), and the international Anglican-Reformed dialogue (§70). The recent breakthroughs in Lutheran-Anglican agreements on episcopacy can be seen as specific responses to the proposal in the Ministry section of BEM for a reconciliation of ministries with and without particular forms of episcopal succession.

176.  As Anglicans and Lutherans have received from other dialogues, so they offer their results for the potential enrichment of other discussions. CCM is most explicit in this regard, offering itself "for serious consideration among the churches of the Reformation and among the Orthodox and Roman Catholic churches" (§24).

177.  As the discussion above of transitivity and the imperfect web of communion shows, however, the inter-relation of various bilateral relations and the interweaving of bilateral and multilateral relations is complex. The Canadian and US agreements (Waterloo, §D9, Commentary; CCM, §25) explicitly note that the existing relations of the signatory Anglican and Lutheran churches with other churches will continue. The situation in continental Europe is especially complex, where the Anglican churches of the British Isles have entered into interim agreements with Lutheran churches acting in partnership with Reformed and United churches. The coexistence of multiple bilateral relations calls both for careful theological reflection on the compatibility of such relations and for creative institutional action that will make this multiplicity fruitful for the pursuit of wider unity. Work on these issues has already begun (ecclesiology consultation, Riverdale, 1993; Leuenberg, Meissen and Porvoo consultation, Liebfrauenberg, 1995).

178.  While the present situation of partially overlapping networks of communion is theologically anomalous, it also keeps both of our traditions alive to our accountability to the wider church and provides an opportunity for the insights and experiences of one

bilateral relation to enter and affect another. The lack of organizational and theological tidiness perhaps can prevent us from becoming closed to the disturbing work of the Spirit and keep us open to new partnerships.

## VIII. THE ULTIMATE GOAL OF UNITY

179. From its beginnings, the ecumenical movement has debated the nature of the unity we seek. This debate has also taken place within our two traditions. Nevertheless, each of our traditions has been able to affirm generally similar pictures of the ultimate ecumenical goal. In 1984, the Budapest assembly of the Lutheran World Federation adopted a comprehensive statement on "The Unity We Seek." Such a unity will be

> a communion in the common and, at the same time, multiform confession of one and the same apostolic faith. It is a communion in holy baptism and in the eucharistic meal, a communion in which the ministries exercised are recognized by all as expressions of the ministry instituted by Christ in his church… It is a committed fellowship, able to make common decisions and to act in common.

The portrait of visible unity begun by the 1998 Lambeth Conference (§§229-233) is strikingly similar. Differences do exist between typically Lutheran and typically Anglican perceptions of the final ecumenical goal (e.g., Anglicans are often more opposed to the continuing existence of parallel jurisdictions than are many Lutherans). Such differences have not hindered Anglicans and Lutherans, however, from moving together towards that goal. As such progress is made, we come to a clearer perception both of the elements of that goal and of the difficulty of describing it in advance of its attainment.

180. Neither Anglicans nor Lutherans have employed a consistent vocabulary to describe or to refer to this final ecumenical goal (cf. above, section III.B). Recent texts show a common tendency to use the phrase "full, visible unity" (or "full visible unity") to refer to such a goal (see Meissen, §7; Reuilly, §22). Waterloo explicitly distinguishes the communion it establishes from the "full visible unity of the whole church" (§D.9) towards which the two churches pledged to work. While a more consistent ecumenical terminology would be desirable, past attempts to devise a common vocabulary (such as that of the 1952 Lund Faith and Order conference) have not become widely accepted. Perhaps our understanding of such a final goal is necessarily too imprecise and too open to revision as we progress towards it to allow the development of a clear and agreed terminology.

181. Lutherans and Anglicans in official dialogue during the past three decades have attempted to keep the nature of the unity we seek clearly in mind. Specific dialogues as well the progress of other conversations in the larger ecumenical context have, however, given Anglicans and Lutherans occasional cause to restate the fundamental shape of and motivation for ecclesial unity.

182. Thus, in concert with others in the ecumenical movement, we have maintained constant reference to the classical locus of ecumenical motivation in John 17:20-22. At the same time, due to the very progress of dialogue, the nature of the unity we seek has come under scrutiny and re-evaluation. The goal of unity, for instance, is presently seen, not so much as an agenda to be achieved, but as a divine reality to be received, appropriated, and exhibited by the churches. This may be taken to be an exegesis of Jesus' prayer

> I do not pray for these only, but also for those who believe in me through their word, that they may all be one; even as you Father, are in me, and I in you, that they also may be in us...

In this case, ecclesial unity is taken to be a deep and continuing sacramental expression of life together in the triune God. Such ecumenism is much more, then, than simply meeting minimum standards for mutuality, removal of ecclesiastical obstacles, or the overcoming of previous difficulties between or among traditions.

183. In the reflected light of such a life together, reconciled churches may indeed be able better to engage the mission of the gospel with confidence that the hope of this fundamental ecumenical imperative can be sustained, namely, that the mission may be credible in the world to the extent that such unity is received, appropriated, and exhibited in the church. There is, in other words, no lessening of the purpose of unity "so that the world may believe that you have sent me", but it is the reality of the divine life ecumenically lived out that informs mission.

184. The conclusion of this passage confirms the point: "The glory that you have given me I have given to them, that they may be one even as we are one." Yet there is also here an eschatological dimension which energizes the life and mission of the churches and beckons them beyond particular realizations of communion with one another. And precisely here is the present challenge for the future: (a) how can the ultimate goal of unity be described in such a way that present bilateral achievements between Lutherans and Anglicans forward rather than hinder future prospects; and (b) what wider connections or multilateral networks of mutuality might provide ways forward?

## IX. SUMMARY AND RECOMMENDATIONS

185. As ALIWG reaches the end of its short-term mandate, it offers to its parent bodies the present report and recommendations. We believe that the task of monitoring Anglican-Lutheran relations carried out by the Anglican-Lutheran International Commission (ALIC) during 1986-96 and by ALIWG during 2000-2002 needs to continue. In the light of its experience the working group has come to the view that a new, more long-range joint commission needs to be set up. A recommendation to this effect is presented below (point 7, cf. section VI.B).

186. The following brief summary is presented of the work carried out by the Anglican-Lutheran International Working Group, arranged according to the points in its terms of reference. Added at each point are the relevant recommendations made by the working group.

## 1. Developments and Progress in the Regions

187. The working group was asked to monitor developments and progress in Anglican-Lutheran relations in the various regions of the world and, where appropriate, encourage steps towards the goal of visible unity.

188. The working group has considered available information on Anglican-Lutheran relations in Africa, Australia, Brazil, Canada, Europe, India, Japan, the Middle East and the USA. Requests were made for information from other places as well, but this did not result in a broader picture. The report provides assessments of the various developments and relations considered, taking into account the four practical steps suggested by the *Niagara Report* for realizing full communion: mutual recognition as churches, provisional structures of unity, possible changes of practices, and declaration of full communion.

189. Since the mid-1990s significant Anglican-Lutheran relations have developed in different parts of the world, most of them drawing on results achieved by the international Anglican-Lutheran dialogue. These relations continue to develop further in common life and mission and also towards more formal patterns of communion, sometimes under the guidance of specially established coordinating committees. However, communication among the regions regarding these developments remains uneven and uncoordinated.

190. In some parts of the world, there can be valuable ecumenical cooperation between Anglicans and Lutherans, even without substantial initiatives to establish formal church relations. Through its report, the working group draws attention to the ecumenical significance of formal agreements of communion relations with a view to the goal of visible unity.

*Recommendation 1*

191. We recommend that those responsible for Anglican-Lutheran contact groups or continuation bodies should be requested to keep the appropriate offices of the Anglican Communion and the Lutheran World Federation informed of their meetings and activities and to send them copies of documents which may be of interest to other regions. The working group also recommends that the appropriate bodies of the Anglican Communion and the Lutheran World Federation encourage Anglican-Lutheran church relations in areas where such relations have not yet been substantially developed.

## 2. Consistency and Coherence of the Regional Agreements

192. The working group was asked to review the characteristics and theological rationales of current regional and national dialogues and agreements, particularly with reference to the concept of unity and to the understanding of apostolicity and episcopal ministry. This review would include an evaluation of their consistency and coherence with each other and with Anglican-Lutheran international agreed statements and would take note of issues of wider ecumenical compatibility.

193. The report provides an evaluation of the consistency and coherence of the different agreements reached on the basis of their foundational documents. Special focus is

given to the descriptions in these documents of the goal of unity and the understanding and practices related to apostolicity and the episcopal ministry. The differing patterns of exercising *episcope* among the Lutheran churches have meant that in some areas mutual recognition of ordained ministries is easier than in others. The observation is made that Anglicans and Lutherans approach unity on a regional and national basis, and that the contexts of their conversations influence the style, content and outcome of the agreements. Certain agreements are found to represent relations of church communion, whereas others represent various significant degrees of fellowship on the way towards communion. The report also discusses the presence within the various Anglican-Lutheran church relations of legitimate forms of diversity, of bearable anomalies and of issues that could possibly have a church-dividing effect.

194. The report provides an evaluation of the consistency and coherence among the various formal agreements involving Anglicans and Lutherans according to two aspects. The question is raised whether the various agreements are consistent in their use of foundational documents and concepts of unity, as well as other aspects (specified in the report, section II.B). Such a consistency is found to be present, taking into account the different stages the agreements represent. ALIWG considers this task as having been completed. The report also considers the ecclesiological issues raised by the existing complex web of bilateral ecumenical relationships involving churches of various Christian world communions.

*Recommendation 2*

195. The working group recommends that the appropriate bodies of the Anglican Communion and the Lutheran World Federation, at the level of the two communions, receive this report's evaluation of the compatibility of the documents examined and welcome the achievements of the Anglican-Lutheran regional agreements.

3. IMPLICATIONS FOR GLOBAL ANGLICAN-LUTHERAN RELATIONS

196. The working group was asked to explore the implications of regional developments for deepening and extending the global relationships between the Anglican and Lutheran communions.

197. Two main perspectives, developed separately in the report, are important for understanding the implications of national and regional Anglican-Lutheran developments for the global relationship between the two world communions.

198. First, the report describes how the two world bodies understand themselves as Christian world communions. Although the historical and ecclesial differences between the two traditions are not insignificant, the international Anglican-Lutheran dialogue has shown that the two communions have important similarities in their doctrine as well as in their confessional and ecumenical self-understandings. An important common characteristic is that both communions see themselves as belonging to, and part of, the one, holy, catholic and apostolic church. National and regional communion agreements are entered into with a clear understanding of this wider, common ecclesial frame of reference.

199. Second, the report discusses in some detail whether bilateral agreements that have been reached between Anglican and Lutheran churches can be considered to apply to other churches in the same communions or to churches of other communions with which the relevant Anglican and Lutheran churches are also, or could be, in church fellowship. The report terms this issue "transitivity". In popular speech, it concerns "whether your friends are my friends also". The report maintains that bilateral ecumenical agreements that have been reached formally at national or regional level do not automatically extend to other church relations in which the parties find themselves, either within or beyond their own communion. In this perspective, the agreements reached do not per se have formal ecumenical implications more broadly, either within or between the Anglican and Lutheran communions globally. The working group did, however, note certain ambiguities arising from communion with the see of Canterbury (see §163 above).

200. The ecumenical relations entered into by individual provinces/member churches are connected to, and influence, the character and self-understanding of the respective world communions. Important aspects of these agreements relate to the ways of overcoming our traditional difficulties with mutual recognition of episcopal ministries. Such formal agreements make a valuable contribution to the search for the full visible unity of the church. The ecumenical fruits that these agreements represent need to be recognized and appreciated at global level with regard to the self-understanding and the mutual relationship of the two communions, as well as the broader ecumenical movement.

*Recommendation 3*

201. The working group recommends that the appropriate bodies of the Anglican Communion and the Lutheran World Federation welcome the Anglican-Lutheran agreements which have resulted in relations of communion in various regions; and take them into account in the development of their self-understanding as Christian world communions which are moving towards the full visible unity of the church.

4. INTERCHANGEABILITY OF ORDAINED MINISTERS

202. Regional agreements do not automatically extend to other Anglican and Lutheran provinces/churches. Nevertheless, the working group sees here an ecumenical possibility. In regions where agreements have been signed that include the mutual interchangeability of ordained ministers, the provinces/churches could take actions to extend that interchangeability to ordained ministers from other regions where similar agreements have been signed.

*Recommendation 4*

203. The working group recommends that the Anglican Communion and the Lutheran World Federation encourage Anglican and Lutheran provinces/churches which have signed agreements that include the mutual interchangeability of ordained ministers to take action at the synodical level to extend that interchangeability to ordained ministers

from other regions which have also signed agreements, applying the terms of the relevant agreements appropriately, subject to the canonical provisions of their own churches.

5. HOSPITALITY TOWARDS INDIVIDUALS

204. Even though regional agreements do not automatically extend to other Anglican and Lutheran provinces/churches, the working group sees that there could be a basis, in the light of the regional agreements that have been achieved, and that the working group has found to be compatible, for such provinces/churches that have not yet entered into a formal agreement, nevertheless to extend sacramental and pastoral hospitality to individual members and ordained ministers from other Anglican/Lutheran churches. The global movement of laity and clergy among our churches makes this a growing need. Such hospitality might also include invitations to visiting clergy to exercise ministerial functions subject to local permission.

*Recommendation 5*

205. In the light of the regional agreements that have been achieved, which the working group has found to be compatible, the working group recommends that provinces/churches that have not yet entered into a formal agreement, should consider extending sacramental and pastoral hospitality to individual lay members and ordained ministers from other Anglican/Lutheran churches. Such hospitality might also include invitations to visiting clergy to exercise ministerial functions subject to local permission. The working group recommends the appropriate bodies of the Anglican Communion and the Lutheran World Federation to consider this possibility.

6. FURTHER CONTACT AND COOPERATION

206. The working group was asked to propose forms of closer contact and cooperation between the international instruments of both communions, in specific projects and programmes and in addressing practical issues.

207. The working group has discussed various possible instruments of contact and cooperation between the communions at the international level. It welcomes first of all the fact that the practice of holding annual joint staff meetings, which the working group considered at its first meeting, has already been put into effect at the level of the secretary general (Anglican Communion) and the general secretary (Lutheran World Federation) and relevant staff persons from both sides. In addition, the working group sees possibilities for contact and cooperation in certain specific areas described in the recommendation below.

*Recommendation 6*

208. The working group recommends that contact and cooperation between the Anglican Communion and the Lutheran World Federation at the worldwide level be furthered by the following instruments:

209. *Programmatic cooperation:* Relevant offices and agencies of the two communions should develop ways of sharing tasks and resources in such areas as: worship and liturgy, Christian education, gender issues, human rights and international affairs, and diaconal services.

210. *Theological education and research:* Increased ecumenical awareness, knowledge and understanding can be fostered among students by encouraging church-related centres of learning and research to prioritize ecumenical cooperation whenever possible in different disciplines. Helpful initiatives might include offering credit for ecumenical training, ecumenical exchanges of faculty and students, and networking among Anglican and Lutheran seminaries in the area of theological and ecumenical research.

211. *Consultations:* In the past, occasional consultations on specific issues have proved fruitful, e.g. the Niagara consultation in 1987 on "Episcope in Relation to the Mission of the Church", the Harare consultation in 1992 on African issues and the West Wickham consultation in 1995 on the renewed diaconate. We recommend that from time to time further consultations should be held on central issues of common concern, preferably in different parts of the world.

212. *Ordination candidates and ordained ministers:* We recommend that, where Anglican-Lutheran agreements have been reached, the theological formation of ordination candidates should include study of the other tradition's identity, practices and foundational documents. Any ordained minister who intends to serve within the other tradition should receive training as to the customs and practices of that tradition.

213. *Meetings of church leaders:* Such meetings could possibly take place every three years, and should include church leaders, together with theologians, from various regions of the world, also including such regions where formal Anglican-Lutheran relations are not yet established. Such meetings could find it useful to focus on topics that have also been dealt with in consultations.

214. *Mutual visits and common action by church leaders:* Mutual visits of Anglican and Lutheran church leaders at global or regional levels should be encouraged. Joint visits by such leaders to public authorities and other churches should also be encouraged.

7. FUTURE

215. The working group was asked to advise whether an Anglican-Lutheran International Commission should be appointed and to recommend the issues that require further dialogue.

216. In view of the solid theological progress already made, the working group believes that, whilst a commission for theological dialogue is not required at the present time, a more permanent body is needed to maintain the focus and momentum of global Anglican-Lutheran relations.

*Recommendation 7*

217. The working group recommends that a new Anglican-Lutheran International Commission (ALIC) should be set up. It should be appointed for four years at a time by the

appropriate bodies of the Anglican Communion and the Lutheran World Federation. The commission should consist of church leaders and theologians. Persons who have not had a long history with Anglican-Lutheran relations should be included along with persons experienced in this area. Its composition should enable proper communication between the Anglican-Lutheran contact groups or continuation bodies related to the agreements achieved in different regions, with a view to broad information sharing and possible coordination of initiatives. The mandate of the commission should include:

a) monitoring and stimulating the continued development of Anglican-Lutheran relations around the world;

b) consideration of ways to promote the role and contribution of the Christian world communions in the wider ecumenical movement; and

c) facilitating the implementation of those recommendations by this working group that the appropriate bodies of the Anglican Communion and the Lutheran World Federation approve.

### Appendix I:  Members of the Anglican-Lutheran International Working Group

*Lutheran members*

Rt Rev. Ambrose Moyo (Co-chair), Bulawayo, Zimbabwe

Dr Kirsten Busch Nielsen, Copenhagen, Denmark

Rev. Dr Hartmut Hövelmann, Munich, Germany

Prof. Dr Michael Root, Columbus, Ohio, USA

Prof. Dr Mickey Mattox (Consultant), Institute for Ecumenical Research, Strasbourg, France

Prof. Dr Ola Tjørhom (Consultant), Stavanger, Norway

Rev. Sven Oppegaard (Co-secretary), Lutheran World Federation

*Anglican members*

Rt Rev. Dr David Tustin (Co-chair), Brigg, North Lincs, England

Rt Rev. Dr Sebastian Bakare, Mutare, Zimbabwe

Rev. Canon Alyson Barnett-Cowan, Toronto, Ontario, Canada

Rt Rev. Orlando Santos de Oliveira, Porto Alegre, Brazil

Rev. Dr William H. Petersen (Consultant), Columbus, Ohio, USA

Prof. Dr Gunther Esser (Observer), Bonn, Germany

Rev. Canon David Hamid (Co-secretary), Anglican Consultative Council, London, England

## Appendix II:  Structures of the Communions and Their Instruments for Consultation and Decision-making

### A.  *The LWF as a communion*

218.  Before the second world war Lutheran churches held gatherings of a consultative nature in the Lutheran world convention. The need for a stronger LWF emerged in the aftermath of the war, in order to provide coordinated church relief for refugees in Europe and promote reconciliation among the Lutheran churches.

219.  The ecclesial profile of the LWF as a global organization has undergone a significant development since its establishment in 1947. The decisions taken by the seventh assembly in Budapest (1984) stand out as particularly significant in this regard. After a broad consultative process over several years, a decision was made that membership in the LWF involved being in pulpit and altar fellowship with all the other member churches. At the same time it was made clear that the Lutheran communion of churches does not see itself independently of, but as an expression of the wider fellowship of the universal Christian church.

220.  In its statement on the self-understanding and task of the LWF the seventh assembly stated:

> This Lutheran communion of churches finds its visible expression in pulpit and altar fellowship, in common witness and service, in the joint fulfilment of the missionary task and in openness to ecumenical cooperation, dialogue and community. The Lutheran churches of the world consider their communion as an expression of the one, holy, catholic and apostolic church. Thus, they are committed to work for the manifestation of the unity of the church given in Jesus Christ.
>
> The LWF is an expression and instrument of this communion. It assists it to become more and more a conciliar, mutually committed communion by furthering consultation and exchange among its member churches and other churches of the Lutheran tradition as well as by furthering mutual participation in each other's joys, sufferings, and struggles. (LWF Report 19/29, §176)

221.  As a consequence of the decisions of the seventh assembly, the eighth assembly in Curitiba (1990) adopted a change in the LWF constitution describing the Federation as a communion of churches. Since Budapest and Curitiba, ecumenical theology has intensified its focus on the understanding of the church as communion or koinonia. In many ways, the developments and actions taken by the LWF in 1984 and 1990 point ahead to some of the current developments of the ecumenical movement.

222.  The governing bodies of the LWF are the assembly, meeting as a rule every six years, and the council, meeting once a year. These two bodies have the authority to make decisions that are binding for the communion that is the LWF.

223.  In addition to decisions of structural and programmatic nature, the governing bodies have also taken some decisions pertaining to church discipline and doctrine.

224.  In 1977 the sixth assembly in Dar-es-Salaam decided that the practice of racial discrimination in the church brought into question the *status confessionis* of the churches involved. On that basis, the eighth assembly suspended the membership of two member

churches in South Africa. This membership has since been restored, after changes introduced.

225. In 1999 the LWF and the Roman Catholic Church signed jointly the Joint Declaration on the Doctrine of Justification, expressing that there is a consensus in basic truths regarding justification and that the 16th-century mutual condemnations concerning justification do not apply to the teaching by the two partners as expressed in the joint declaration.

226. The member churches of the LWF remain autonomous. Decisions by the LWF council or assembly apply to the common life of the world communion as such. Decisions that have impact on the common life of the communion can only be reached if there is a firm basis for the decisions among the member churches. The churches which did not vote in favour of the Joint Declaration on the Doctrine of Justification, or who voted against it, remain members of a communion that nevertheless has only one official position on the issue, expressed in the council decisions of 1998 and 1999.

227. The LWF regards the development of its communion as a contribution to the one ecumenical movement. The building of fellowship among individual churches living in various regions of the world is a complex process. The Christian world communions can contribute to this among its own member churches in ways that differ from, or lie beyond, the possibilities of other ecumenical instruments. This is an important factor to consider, in the context of the World Council of Churches as well as by the various Christian world communions, as the communions move closer to each other in bilateral and multilateral relations.

## B. Instruments of the Anglican Communion – their development and authority

228. The 1930 Lambeth Conference in resolution 49 agreed a helpful description of the nature of the Anglican Communion:

The Anglican Communion is a fellowship, within the one holy, catholic and apostolic church, of those duly constituted dioceses, provinces or regional churches in communion with the see of Canterbury, which have the following characteristics in common:

a) they uphold and propagate the catholic and apostolic faith and order as they are generally set forth in the *Book of Common Prayer* as authorized in their several churches;

b) they are particular or national churches, and, as such, promote within each of their territories a national expression of Christian faith, life and worship;

c) they are bound together not by a central legislative and executive authority, but by mutual loyalty sustained through the common counsel of the bishops in conference.

229. Today, there are over 70 million Anglicans in 38 provinces and 8 extra-provincial churches worldwide. As Anglicanism spread beyond the shores of Great Britain and Ireland, as a result of British colonization, provinces were formed, each with its own episcopal and synodical structures for maintaining the life of the church. Today, the various independent Anglican churches are governed by synods which recognize bishops' authority in some form as crucial and distinct, but which include not only presbyteral representation, but also lay representation. Each province too has developed some form of primatial office in the role of archbishop or presiding bishop.

230. In the development of the Anglican Communion to this time, there is no legislative authority above the provincial level. Nevertheless, while each province maintains the legal and juridical right to govern its way of life, in practice, there has been an implicit understanding of belonging together and being interdependent within a worldwide communion. Today Anglicans recognize four "worldwide instruments of communion" or structures of unity in the Communion: the Lambeth Conference, the primates meeting, the Anglican Consultative Council and the archbishop of Canterbury. The first three of these instruments are meetings or councils, and are all recent in origin, relatively speaking. The office of archbishop of Canterbury is the only instrument with a history longer than 150 years.

231. The first Lambeth Conference took place, at Lambeth Palace, the London seat of the archbishop of Canterbury, in 1867 and was called to address an issue which threatened to divide the Communion. It is unlikely that the 76 bishops who gathered at that time understood that such gatherings of bishops would become a regular feature of Anglican life. Today, the Lambeth Conference is a gathering of all the diocesan bishops of the Communion, and takes place every ten years. The most recent conferences included suffragan and assistant bishops as well, either a representative number, or all who are active, as was the case in 1998 when close to 800 bishops in total gathered at the university of Kent in Canterbury. The Lambeth Conference, although not a legislative body, does pass resolutions which provide an interesting and representative snapshot of the mind of the Communion on the issues of the day, every decade or so. It seeks to be a way to strengthen the unity of the Communion, but through the experience of the entire college of bishops taking counsel together, in the context of prayer and discussion, for the good of the whole church. At times, provinces have taken resolutions passed at Lambeth Conferences to their own synods for a binding resolution, but this is not an automatic process.

232. The Anglican Consultative Council (ACC) came into being out of a resolution of the 1968 Lambeth Conference. It was set up to share information, advise on inter-Anglican relations (division and formation of provinces), agree policies in world mission, and to foster collaboration and maintain dialogues and relations with other Christian churches. It is the only body in global Anglicanism that has a constitution and legal standing. It meets every three years in different parts of the Communion and has a standing committee, which meets annually. Every province is assigned from 1 to 3 members depending on its population. As the Council is made up of bishops, other clergy and laity, some might say that the ACC is the "synodical" instrument of global Anglicanism, inasmuch as the whole people of God are represented. Again, as with the Lambeth Conference, the decisions of ACC are not binding on provinces unless action is taken at the provincial level to make them so.

233. The first primates meeting was held in 1979 following a proposal by the Lambeth Conference the year before. The meetings are supposed to be for "mutual counsel and pastoral care" (see "The Virginia Report" in *The Official Report of the Lambeth Conference 1998*, p.61). It has met about every two years, although in recent years the tendency is towards annual meetings, at the specific request of the archbishop of Canterbury. In practice, the primates meeting, as a meeting of bishops, does provide for a way for the global episcopate of the Anglican Communion to be consulted, in a limited, but somewhat representative way, between Lambeth conferences. It is thus a useful instrument for individual primates to test out regional concerns within the wider church. The primates

meeting does not pass resolutions, but seeks to communicate pastoral messages to the churches by letter or statement.

234. These three instruments of the Communion are presided over by the archbishop of Canterbury, either in an honorary capacity (in the case of the ACC which elects its own chairman), or in an active convening and presiding role, in the case of the Lambeth Conference and the primates meetings. The archbishop of Canterbury is the link, which interweaves all the other instruments, besides the Anglican Communion secretariat, which staffs them. Thus the primacy of honour which the archbishop of Canterbury holds within the college of Anglican bishops is enhanced by his visible role in gathering and presiding over the other instruments. To be an Anglican it is necessary to be in communion with him, although churches in communion with the see of Canterbury are not necessarily Anglican.

235. The instruments of Anglican unity are still developing. Reports and resolutions pose some sharp questions about the inter-relatedness of the current instruments and their authority. At various levels in the Communion study is ongoing about how the structures of communion at a world level can become more effective tools to strengthen the Communion and guard its unity.

# 36. Theological Conversations
## Baptist World Alliance-Mennonite World Conference

### Amsterdam, Netherlands, 1989-1992

## Preface

The four years of theological conversations in which Mennonites and Baptists engaged from 1989 to 1992 were historic not only for the event but also for the process. We found that from many different avenues of Christian service and a wide expanse of geography, we easily became brothers and sisters in Christ.

For many years both Mennonites and Baptists at the international levels had engaged in ecumenical dialogue with numerous other denominations. Baptists have held dialogues with Roman Catholics, Lutherans, and various segments of the Reformed tradition. Likewise, Mennonites have discussed issues of theological and practical concern with Lutherans and the Reformed churches. It was fitting then that we should join in a truly Free-church conversation ourselves.

The plan for a meeting of representatives from the Baptist World Alliance and the Mennonite World Conference was jointly nurtured by Noel Vase and Paul Kraybill. Both had a history of deep appreciation for the other's tradition. From this beginning teams were chosen to represent broadly our constituencies.

The purpose of our getting together was stated as follows:

> to engage in theological conversations exploring each other's history, theology and faith; to engage in a common search for greater mutual understanding in the hope that we may find new areas of common agreement.

Some have asked whether the goal is to seek a merger of these two denominations. The answer is NO; the purpose is rather to get to know each other better, to deepen our fellowship in the body of Christ and to explore whether there are some common projects in which we can cooperate.

Our first meeting was held at Eastern College in St David's, Pennsylvania, an American Baptist-related institution. There we focused upon our individual backgrounds as members of the two teams; Paul Kraybill and Noel Vase presented papers on the denominational heritages of Mennonites and Baptists worldwide, and we carefully laid out our agenda for the next four years, based upon critical questions we identified in small groups.

To introduce ourselves to each other, we were each asked to say in one or two words what we think is the most important Mennonite or Baptist value. The Mennonites said: community, mutual aid, discipline, service, love, peace, justice, global church, discipleship, suffering. The Baptists said: religious liberty, freedom (of conscience/of interpretation), soul liberty, believers' baptism, autonomy of the local church, witness, evangelism, separation of church and state, believers' church.

The second session of our conversations was held at Associated Mennonite Biblical Seminaries in Elkhart, Indiana, a Mennonite institution. There we interacted with papers on the Dutch connection between the groups, biblical interpretation, individualism-community relationships, Christian service, the social gospel and the African-American influence upon Baptists. We also visited Menno-Hof, a centre of Mennonite interpretation.

The location of our third meeting was McMaster Divinity College in Hamilton, Ontario, a Canadian Baptist-related institution. At McMaster we focused our attention on the nature of the church, worship, the ordinances/sacraments and evangelism. We also began to note areas of convergence and divergence between Baptists and Mennonites.

Our fourth and final session was held in Amsterdam, Netherlands, at the Singelkerk, a 17th-century Mennonite congregation to which John Smyth and Thomas Helwys and the earliest Baptists had definite connections. Overlooking the historic canals, we reviewed our previous work and completed the task of preparing the final draft of our joint report. In the evenings we rediscovered the places and routes of our religious ancestors in ancient churches, alleyways and archives.

Our final report defines the areas of discussion points which we share in common, and those positions where we differ. Often we wrestled with definitions of the same realities. Many times we re-discovered that our views of scripture, the church and Christian service were very close. And we also realized that our divergent paths from the 17th century have left us in differing places of emphasis. We made no attempt to conduct primary research into our topics of interest, for the literature of both traditions is vast. Instead, we attempted to present our denominations faithfully and listen to each other in an attempt to understand better our commonalities and areas for growth in relationships.

All of us on both teams realized after our first session that personal bonds were being created across confessions. This was deepened after the tragic loss of Dr Heather M. Vose from our midst in 1990, and after travelling and rooming together in differing contexts. Not unlike Hans de Ries, John Smyth and Thomas Helwys almost four centuries ago, we discovered a true sense of brotherhood and community in sharing our stories. We unanimously agree that this was an unusual theological conversation, in that we were able to experience for ourselves the values which we had previously discovered in the pages of history and literature.

At the beginning of our conversations, it was observed that the original theological conversations between Baptists and Mennonites had ceased amicably about 1630. Basically, our ancestors just stopped writing to each other! We were pleased to have begun anew that historic conversation.

Ross T. Bender
Chair for the Mennonite team

William H. Brackney
Chair for the Baptist team

# Introduction

HISTORICAL SUMMARY OF THE THEOLOGICAL CONVERSATIONS 1989-92

As part of an ongoing series of conversations with other world Christian denominational groups, the Baptist World Alliance (BWA) invited the Mennonite World Conference (MWC) to engage in theological conversation. Both the BWA and the MWC had previously been in dialogue with the Reformed churches, but this new conversation was unique in exploring commonalities in history and Free-church tradition as well as discussing faith and practice. The purpose, as stated at a meeting of BWA and MWC leaders in McLean, Virginia, 25 August 1988, was to "engage in a common search for greater mutual understanding in the hope that we may find new areas of common agreement". Each body appointed a team of five persons plus a chair and a staff facilitator; these eleven men and three women, from Australia, Canada, France, Netherlands and the United States, were primarily teachers and scholars. In four annual meetings, hosted alternately by the Baptists and the Mennonites from 1989 to 1992, they presented papers on significant issues from the authority of scriptures to baptism and the Lord's supper, from individualism versus community to the church in the world. At each meeting the participants celebrated their groups' original contacts in 1608, and also experienced warm "family reunion" fellowship, with discoveries of many cherished practices and theological emphases held in common.

The conversations made no attempt to cover the many topics of systematic theology. Baptists and Mennonites share the great affirmations of orthodox Christian faith, but because both groups are congregationally organized and both are non-credal, the shades of theological difference within the two world bodies are likely to be as significant as the differences between Baptists and Mennonites. Topics chosen for examination were in general those that distinguish Baptists and Mennonites from other Christian traditions or that distinguish Baptists and Mennonites from each other. The following report is limited by the fact that it was written by a group composed primarily of Caucasians from North America, who particularly explored the history and foundational documents of the two groups, and whose direct knowledge of the church of Africa, Asia and Latin America is limited.

The final meeting in Amsterdam, in August 1992, prepared the following report for the members of the Mennonite World Conference and the Baptist World Alliance. Each section alternates Baptist and Mennonite statements and ends with a list of convergences and divergences between the two groups as observed in the four dialogue sessions. The lists are not exhaustive, and the points identified as divergences tend to be relative differences in emphasis rather than mutually exclusive positions.

These comparisons are not designed to express relative value judgments of the two groups: instead they are attempts to focus issues about which continuing dialogue may be productive. The members of the dialogue teams learned much from each other as brothers and sisters in Christ. The recommendations in the final section of the report express their conviction that other Baptist and Mennonite individuals, congregations and associations should discover or rediscover each other in dialogue, cooperation and Christian fellowship at many levels.

*Origins*

Mennonites derive from the Anabaptist movement which began in Zurich, Switzerland, in 1525, as a radical split from the Reformed movement and then emerged semi-independently in several locations in Germany and Holland, growing rapidly despite severe persecution from both Protestant and Catholic churches. The major Anabaptist groups emphasized the believers' church, whose members (1) were baptized as adults, (2) committed themselves to searching the scriptures in disciplined groups, and (3) literally followed Christ's teachings of non-resistance (with refusal of military service), sharing goods, the refusal to swear oaths (including oaths of allegiance to the state), and the great commission to evangelize. After the 1540s, Anabaptists were increasingly known by the name of their Dutch leader Menno Simons. By the end of the 16th century, Mennonites experienced toleration in the Netherlands, but persecution and hardship elsewhere led to continuing migrations.

The Baptists emerged in a small band of Puritan/Separatist dissenters from the Church of England, who emigrated to the Netherlands in 1607 under the leadership of John Smyth. In Amsterdam, where Smyth re-baptized himself and some thirty followers, they sojourned with the Waterlander Mennonites and many ultimately joined them. However, a minority under the leadership of Thomas Helwys returned to England in 1612 to preserve their English identity and more Baptists and the Amsterdam Mennonites continued their contacts until about 1630, although they differed on issues such as war and oath-taking. The Particular Baptists, who emerged in the 1640s in London with a strong Calvinist theology and conviction about immersion, sought their own contact in 1640 with the Dutch Rhynsburgers (which included Mennonites), who baptized by immersion. It was the Particular Baptists who ultimately flourished and spread to North America and other continents.

*Developments*

Dutch Mennonites experienced a "golden age" of peace and prosperity in the 17th and 18th centuries. Under continuing persecution, Swiss Anabaptists, including the Amish, fled to Germany and France, and then mostly to North America. Many Mennonites of Dutch background had migrated to drain the swamps of the Vistula River delta near Danzig, then after the 1780s to open new farm lands in the Ukraine, and then in the 19th and 20th centuries to settle in North and South America, always in search of military exemption and freedom for their religious community. Hardship and persecution led Mennonites to keep themselves in German-speaking communities, practising mutual aid, simplicity and non-resistance. Mission efforts were renewed in the 19th century, at first among the Dutch and Russian Mennonites, who were influenced by Baptists and various German Pietist groups. By 1900 North American Mennonites learned from other Protestants to organize vigorously for education and overseas mission, but local evangelism generally was weak. The fundamentalist-modernist controversy created tensions before world war II. After the war, the most dynamic trends have been (1) the development of peace-and-justice concerns among North American and European Mennonites and of worldwide service programmes under Mennonite Central Committee; and (2) the emergence and rapid expansion of Mennonite churches in Africa, Asia and Latin America. The number of baptized Mennonites on these three continents will soon exceed the number of Mennonites in North America and Europe. Total world membership of Mennonites is about 900,000.

Baptists emigrated as individuals and later congregations to the British colonies in North America, beginning in the 1630s. In New England, the maritime provinces, and the middle states, associations developed and churches were planted along the moving frontier. In the South, Baptists thrived in an unusual way among both Caucasians and African American populations, with the resulting Southern (predominantly Caucasian) and National Baptist (predominantly African-American) Conventions being the largest bodies of Baptists in the world. In the United States, Baptists became keen advocates of evangelism, home mission work and religious liberty, the latter issue most often expressed in the doctrine of separation of church and state.

From the United States and Great Britain in the late 18th and early 19th centuries, Baptists launched major efforts in world mission. Unions or conventions of Baptist churches exist in virtually every country, with large communities of Baptists in Myanmar, India, Brazil, Nigeria, Zaire, Korea, Russia and the Ukraine. Baptists over the years have been active in benevolent enterprises such as Bible translation and distribution, education, cross-cultural services and refugee resettlement.

Theological confessionalism among Baptists arose in the 19th and 20th centuries in North America and Britain. New Baptist groups with strict confessional boundaries added variety to the original streams of the denomination; many of these groups do not participate in national and international bodies of fellowship. In the 1990s, Baptists number over 38 million (baptized) members worldwide.

*Contemporary intersections*

The Baptists considerably influenced the origin and development of the Mennonite Brethren in Russia in 1860; the question of their Mennonite or Baptist identity was often hotly debated. Currently, in what was the USSR and in Germany, many former Mennonites identify themselves as Baptists. In North America, where both groups are fragmented, the Mennonite Brethren have had the closest relationship to Baptists. Mennonites have attended Baptist seminaries, served as missionaries under Baptist agencies, and joined Baptist churches. There has often been cooperation between local Baptist and Mennonite congregations and between Baptist and Mennonite mission agencies overseas, for example in India. Helpful exchanges have occurred at believers' church conferences, like those in Canada and the United States in the 1980s. In social services, Baptists have cooperated with Mennonites, for example, in the World Food Bank in Canada and in various projects of the Mennonite Central Committee. Baptists and Mennonites have therefore continued to show a high regard for each other in matters of faith and practice.

Mennonites and Baptists today are increasingly aware of the points of intersection in their history, even though they have each developed in unique ways. Baptists are less conscious of their 17th-century roots than Mennonites. Mennonites in North America, Europe, and in the communities that have migrated from these continents, have maintained strong ethnic and cultural identities and have not been very successful in local evangelism. Baptists through evangelism have grown spectacularly in North America among African-American, Caucasian and other ethnic groups. Today there is a genuine desire among many Mennonites and Baptists to learn from each other's strengths so that together they can achieve a greater measure of faithfulness to the gospel.

## The believers' church

Baptists and Mennonites together affirm the great common core of Christian faith, in our worship of God, our proclamation that Jesus is Lord, and our earnest searching of the scriptures, guided by the Holy Spirit. The 1989-92 theological conversations focused less on these issues than on matters related to our identity as believers' churches. These were organized under three headings: (1) the nature and role of authority in the Christian life, (2) the nature of the church, and (3) the mission of the church in the world. Each of them can be discussed in greater depth in the future to illuminate both our shared convictions and our differences. Underlying these church-related issues, however, are certain differences of emphasis in interpreting our common faith, for example, the meaning and implications of Jesus' death on the cross, that Baptists and Mennonites need to probe and share in further conversations.

## Authority

Mennonites and Baptists both stem from the larger Reformation movement of the 16th and 17th centuries which defined the locus of authority in opposition to the concepts of authority which had developed in the Roman Catholic Church. The Reformers strongly rejected the authority of the pope and of church tradition and strongly asserted the authority of scripture (*sola scriptura*) and the priesthood of all believers. What appeared to be a relatively simple choice between two competing sources of authority has proved over the centuries to be a much more complex issue. It continues to be a matter of serious debate and repeated fragmentation in many church traditions.

MENNONITE PERSPECTIVES ON AUTHORITY

Anabaptists in the 16th century have often criticized the mainline Protestants for not putting into practice what they confess concerning the scriptures. Obedience to the written word of scripture has been regarded as the true test of faith for Mennonites. Believers are called to mutual discernment and admonition as it relates to life. Anabaptists in the 16th century were much more concerned about discipleship (orthopraxy) than about right belief (orthodoxy). The fact that they and their descendants have not produced major systematic and philosophical-theological treatises is more than a matter of circumstance. Although persecution and martyrdom in the early years prevented many of their leaders from writing extensively on doctrinal issues, the writings that exist show much more concern about questions of ethics and community. Anabaptists did not generally reject the historic creeds of the Christian church, but neither did they elevate them to the position that the creeds held in other traditions. Although Mennonite denominations today have confessions of faith, they are reluctant to use them in a very prescriptive manner and are quite open to revising them.

Another important issue for the Anabaptists was the relationship between the Old Testament and the New Testament. Whereas the view of the mainline Protestants is sometimes characterized as a "flat book" approach, the Anabaptists emphasized the priority of the New Testament over the Old Testament. Furthermore, in other traditions the writings of Paul and the gospel of John are cited frequently, especially in relation to conversion and justification, whereas Mennonites often elevate the synoptic gospels, and particularly the Sermon on the Mount, above the rest of the New Testament.

The Anabaptists were especially concerned about the authority and example of the life of Jesus. Jesus was seen as the central expression of God's revelation to humankind. Although the divinity of Jesus was strongly affirmed by most, Jesus' human nature received much more attention by most Anabaptists. Even Jesus' suffering and death were seen as a model for Christians. Among the Dutch Anabaptists, however, a unique Christology emerged which emphasized the divinity of Jesus in a particular manner. This resulted in an intense struggle for the purity of the church to reflect the perfect divinity of Christ.

The church, or *Gemeinde*, was clearly another locus of authority for the Anabaptists. Matthew 18:15-17 has been called the basis of church government among the Anabaptists. The authority of popes, priests and scholars was rejected in favour of a more radical concept of mutual admonition and the priesthood of believers was more important than the training of an individual or his appointment by the temporal authorities.

Finally, some Anabaptists pointed in a new way to the authority of the Spirit. For them, the written or outer word alone was dead; the inner word was the voice of the Spirit. Although Mennonites have not on the whole been characterized by a unique emphasis on the Spirit, considerable attention has been given to the function of the Spirit in community rather than on the personal gifts of the Spirit.

Anabaptists of the 16th century and Mennonites in later centuries have often departed from such idealized versions of Anabaptism. Some have been extremely literalistic and legalistic; some have experienced the tyranny of individuals over communities to enforce conformity; still others have experienced the extreme pressures of conformity to the community and its traditions. In the 16th and 19th centuries some were caught in a web of apocalyptic extremism and millenarianism which focused on selected portions of both the Old Testament and the New Testament.

Mennonites also have been influenced greatly by modern intellectual and scientific developments. The advent of modern science (especially Darwinism) and modern methods of biblical interpretation affected Baptists earlier and more profoundly than Mennonites, but Mennonites in Europe and North America have also had to deal with these influences. Some have retreated from these modern influences and have sought refuge in small rural communities where the authority of their traditions and the authority of their leaders has brought a measure of security. Others have been influenced by revivalism, dispensationalism, fundamentalism, or even by modernism at the other end of the spectrum. Mennonite fundamentalism has often taken a unique shape, concentrating on plain dress and rejection of modern technology. As many Mennonites have become urbanized, Mennonite concepts of the authority of community have come under severe stress.

Mennonites today range widely in their interpretation of the scriptures and the role of the community. Some are preoccupied with concerns about the nature of inspiration (inerrancy, infallibility, etc.) while others are more concerned about the relationship of Christology to ethics and mission. Some Mennonite theologies make the case that Anabaptism really represents a third way which is neither Catholic nor Protestant. To confess "Jesus is Lord" is to express the authority of Jesus in terms of a new life-style of servanthood and suffering love. Jesus is the model and the power for a transformed world order. The atonement is regarded as more than substitutionary. The vertical dimension of reconciliation with God is balanced by a concern for the horizontal dimension of reconciliation with fellow human beings.

Despite Mennonite concerns about community as the locus of authority and the focus of salvation, there has been serious breakdown in the experience of this reality. Ironically, discipleship and community have often become creeds rather than visible realities. The ultimate test of Mennonite conceptions of authority remains the commitment to a life which results in new communities of love and service.

BAPTIST PERSPECTIVES ON AUTHORITY

The problem of authority has always been a controversial issue in the life of the church and, like the Mennonites, Baptists struggle with questions of its nature, forms and function. Baptists understand authority as the right and power to command obedience in the context of responsible freedom.

But this statement needs explanation. The word responsible underlines the fact that relationship is the essential medium in which authority functions: no relationship, no answerability. The term right indicates a claim that is just, that is a capacity to create a sense of obligation. Where authority is real, one ought to obey. Power indicates the ability to assert and maintain a just claim. Obedience expresses recognition of right and power in terms of appropriate behaviour. The term freedom gathers up the ideas of relationship, justice and answerability which distinguish authority from coercion.

Among Baptists, religious authority centres in the person of Christ. Thoroughly trinitarian, Baptists affirm in all matters of faith and practice the Lordship of Christ (Phil. 2:9-11). Baptists have stated this clearly: we revere and obey the Lord Jesus Christ our God and Saviour, the sole and absolute authority as revealed in the scripture and present in the church.

Christ's person binds all humanity to God transfiguring the Creator-creature relationship with a new moral dimension. Christ's work unites power and right with love so that his command is never arbitrary. He approaches his church with the words, "You call me Master and Lord, and you are right, for so I am" (John 13:13). The claim is made against the background of self-giving service and love in which He locates his authority. To this the church can give only one response: "Jesus Christ is Lord."

Scripture is also an important source of authority for Baptists. Because Jesus Christ is Lord, his attitude to scripture is paramount, and also quite clear. Through scripture He expresses his will which is to be heard and obeyed as finally authoritative. Baptists therefore have no difficulty in embracing the Reformation dictum of *sola scriptura*: in contrast to many Reformation churches, Baptists do not accord any official authority to creeds. Scripture is viewed as having the last word. Thus, love for and assiduous use of the Bible in daily life is often an identifying mark of Baptists, which makes authority not only doctrinal but experiential – that is, related to life. Although more attention is given to the New Testament (Heb. 1:1-2), the authority of the Old Testament is acknowledged (2 Tim. 3:16-17).

Reverence for scripture also demands recognition of the authority of the Holy Spirit, who inspired it. Word and Spirit belong together. One without the other is a distortion of truth, and the bond between them is seen by Baptists as key to the functional authority of Christ in his church.

The fourth and final emphasis among Baptists is the church's role as a vehicle of authority. The presence of Christ makes the "gathered community" unique: a society within which God's authority is transmitted and expressed by the Spirit through scripture. Such a high view of the church must not be understood in an exclusive sense. Authority may be expressed through appointed offices but is not confined to them. Among Baptists, the mind of Christ is sought through the prayerful submission of the individual to the community which seeks the will of the Spirit through scripture. The commanding impulse is personal but never private. Liberty of conscience, a vital plan in Baptist doctrine, is never meant to imply privatized religion.

What are the ideal forms of authority? What are the tests by which Baptists both recognize and exercise authority? Christ's pattern of holiness, self-giving ministry, power and love is the litmus. Moral persuasion rather than legal or institutional demands compels the obedience of Baptists. The absence of love and holiness and self-giving quickly produces centrifugal tendencies.

To understand Baptists requires a clear view of the function of authority in Baptist life and how it relates to freedom. Freedom is essential in Baptist thought, but often it is in tension with obedience. For that reason the notion that freedom and obedience are both elements of authority is vital. The New Testament presumes their reconciliation by proclaiming them in a paradoxical fashion. Paul is equally ready to call himself a *doulos* (slave of Christ) and at the same time extol his freedom in Christ (Gal. 1:10 with 5:1). But what is experientially true for the individual is not so easily grasped in the interpersonal relationships of a congregation. Freedom is often the first casualty of social cohesion.

In common with much of modern society generally, Baptists face prejudice against authority caused by individualism, preoccupation with freedom, the difficulty of relating liberty and obedience, and a general reaction to authoritarianism. To illustrate: liberty of conscience is sometimes misconstrued as freedom from the church rather than freedom in the church. And a secular democratic approach to the congregational principle produces the doctrine of "the voice of the people is the voice of God" which is clearly not a New Testament basis for authority.

If people are to do their duty, they must be free in order for the moral response to be genuine. Members of John Smyth's first congregation in Gainsborough glimpsed this truth in the covenant "to walk as the Lord's free people". Among Baptists, submission to spiritual authority is, ideally at any rate, the voluntary and free response of obedience to the compulsion of love. The fusion of freedom and obedience produces a cohesive moral power which marks the church as a society which is *sui generis*.

CONVERGENCES AND DIVERGENCES ON AUTHORITY

*Convergences*

1. Baptists and Mennonites affirm:
   a) the scripture as God's written word, while emphasizing the New Testament as the guide for faith and life;
   b) the ultimate authority of the Christ of scripture;
   c) the Holy Spirit as the one who gives life to scripture and is the continuing presence of Christ in his people;
   d) "the gathered congregation" as primary locus of discernment and decision-making.
2. Baptists and Mennonites are non-credal.
3. Baptists and Mennonites have felt the impact of modern scientific and intellectual developments which have created tensions and fragmentation.

*Divergences*

1. Mennonites have tended to appeal to the Jesus of the Synoptics and particularly the Sermon on the Mount whereas Baptists have tended to appeal to Johannine and Pauline sources.
2. Baptists tend to emphasize "orthodoxy" (right belief as related to scripture and confessions of faith) whereas Mennonites tend to emphasize "orthopraxy" (right practice as faithful discipleship).
3. Baptists are concerned about "soul freedom" and individual accountability before God whereas Mennonites are concerned about accountability to God through community.

## Church

Christian debates concerning the nature of the church have focused on various issues through the centuries. In the 4th/5th century, Augustine articulate a concept which strongly asserted the invisibility of the true church based on his concept of election and predestination. This resulted in a territorially defined church in which church and state were closely allied in seeking to create a *corpus christianum*. Although this point of view continued to be held into the modern era by many Christians, increasingly in the West churches became disestablished or separated from the state. The "Free churches" and "believers' churches", including both the Baptists and the Mennonites, were significant forces in bringing about such changes. However, many other issues were of vital concern to these churches – questions concerning the nature of church government and the autonomy of the local church, the nature of the sacraments, the role of church discipline, the nature of worship, and the nature of Christian community. While there is diversity on all of these issues within both the Baptist and Mennonite traditions, there are elements which they tend to hold in common and which distinguish them from other church traditions. Other teachings and practices tend to distinguish Baptists and Mennonites from each other.

MENNONITE PERSPECTIVES ON THE CHURCH

When Mennonites set out to describe the nature of the church, they turn to two major sources: the New Testament and 16th-century Anabaptism. From the New Testament they draw on three images in particular; the people of God (1 Pet. 2:9-10); the body of Christ (Eph. 4:15-16); and the community of the Holy Spirit (1 Cor. 12).

From the 16th-century Anabaptists comes the description of the church as a believers' church, a body of believers who enter the church by baptism upon their voluntary confession of faith. It is not an institution but a fellowship of truly converted believers in Christ, committed to following him in full obedience as Lord. Although there was diversity among Anabaptists who emerged in different places, those groups that survived past the 1560s were those that were peaceful, missionary, willing to suffer, and sought to shape their lives together according to the New Testament church. Menno Simons, who gave organizational shape and doctrinal clarity to the Anabaptist movement in the Netherlands, listed six marks of the true church: (1) unadulterated pure doctrine; (2) scriptural use of baptism and the Lord's supper; (3) obedience to the word of God; (4) unfeigned brotherly love; (5) candid confession of God and Christ; (6) persecution for the sake of the word of the Lord.

According to the historic confessions of the faith, Mennonite understandings of the nature of the church induce the following particular emphases.

First, church membership is based on a voluntary confession of faith followed by believers' baptism as the point of entrance into church membership. True repentance and faith is to be demonstrated by a life of purity and obedience to Jesus Christ, obeying his teachings and following his example.

Contemporary Mennonites practise believers' baptism, some by sprinkling or pouring, some by immersion. In North America the age of baptism has tended to shift from early adulthood to adolescence or sometimes even to childhood (age six and upward). While most Mennonite congregations require believers' baptism for prospective members who have been baptized as infants, some congregations in recent decades have simply accepted their letters of transfer from other denominations upon evidence that the candidates have been walking with the Lord as adult believers. Occasionally a person who has been converted outside any congregation requests baptism without joining a congregation, but Mennonites generally refuse to separate baptism from church membership.

Secondly, Mennonites follow a congregational polity rather than an episcopal or presbyterian polity. From the beginning Anabaptists and Mennonites have been strongly congregational. Yet none would deny that the local congregation needs the fellowship, counsel, and support of the wider church in order to be faithful. There were synodal tendencies in the 16th- and 17th-century meetings of church leaders to discuss faith and practice and to prepare confessional statements. Organization into district and national conferences began in the 19th century and is typical today except in some Old Order groups. However, individual congregations may have different degrees of relationship to the district conferences and the denomination. Although Mennonites often cooperate with congregations of other denominations or with ministerial councils on the local level, they have been very cautious about larger ecumenical groups, and cooperation with other denominational bodies has tended to be on specific projects.

A common pattern of ministry in the 19th century was for local congregations to call and ordain from among their own members deacons, preachers, and supervising bishops or leaders, who might oversee groups of congregations. This pattern has not been widely adopted by mission churches, and increasingly in Europe and North America, the pattern has been a single trained, salaried and mobile pastor cooperating with an elected board of deacons or elders. No human being – pastor, bishop or moderator – is considered to be the head of the church. All stand under the authority of Jesus Christ, who is the head of the body.

Thirdly, the issue of church discipline has been of crucial importance to Mennonites. Historically, Mennonites have tried to follow Matthew 18:15-22, with its stages of counsel, confrontation, reconciliation and forgiveness or, finally, separation in dealing with members who were not living lives worthy of the Lord. Even in the 16th century there were differences of opinion on excommunication and the ban. In recent decades individualism has eroded the practice of church discipline. The principle of accountability to the community in maintaining a life-style that is faithful to Christ is now more often called discipling than disciplining, and the preferred methods are teaching, counsel and spiritual formation.

Traditionally, an important element of discipleship for Anabaptists and Mennonites has been the life of simplicity. This has served as a distinctive sign of rejecting worldly fashions, ostentation, and among some groups even modern technology. Among contemporary Mennonites, simple living is most often seen as a means of conserving the earth's resources and of economic sharing.

Contemporary emphasis is less on congregational discipline than on congregational fellowship and mutual support. Gatherings for worship and Bible study are warm social occasions, supplemented by fellowship meals and a variety of activities for all ages. Additional fellowship is experienced as part of district and denominational conference gatherings.

Fourthly, suffering for the sake of Christ has been a frequent experience of Mennonites and has often been understood as an integral aspect of their understanding of the church. Anabaptists and Mennonites have seen suffering and persecution as the cross commanded by Jesus: "If any want to become my followers, let them deny themselves and take up their cross and follow me" (Mark 8:24). The martyrdom of many Anabaptists and their faithfulness under persecution continues to be a powerful influence on present-day Mennonite identity, as evidenced by the continued use of the *Martyrs Mirror* stories.

Although most Mennonites today do not suffer for their faith in Christ, they often teach that in loving one's enemies one chooses to absorb suffering rather than to inflict it or even to assert one's own rights aggressively. Particularly in wartime, Mennonites' historic non-resistant stance has led to difficulties with governments which lack provision for conscientious objectors and has evoked hostility from neighbours. Mennonites of the former USSR frequently suffered persecution, and more recently Mennonites in China, Central America and Ethiopia have undergone severe suffering. At the same time, these churches have experienced phenomenal growth, underscoring again that the martyr church is both a suffering and a witnessing church.

Finally, the nature and understanding of worship including the faithful observance of the ordinances as commanded by Jesus Christ is also distinctive among Mennonites. Mennonite worship is usually neither liturgical (emphasizing the glory and transcendence of God) nor charismatic (emphasizing the presence of the Holy Spirit). Mennonite worship focuses most distinctly on Jesus Christ as Lord. The reading and preaching of the written word are central to the worship, and they testify to Jesus as the incarnate Word. Earnestness about following Christ rather than exuberant joy characterizes the mood and ethos of a traditional Mennonite service, although the style of worship varies from one congregation or culture to another. Congregational singing is a beautiful, meaningful, and emotional part of Mennonite worship, and prayer is an essential element of the worship. A freewill offering is also a typical way for a congregation to express a response to God in worship. Both the worship service itself and the meeting house are typically characterized by simplicity, with sparing use of visual symbols and rejection of ostentation. The number of women pastors and church leaders is rapidly increasing in North America, Europe and in some other parts of the world.

From the beginning Anabaptists and Mennonites have spoken of baptism and the Lord's supper as signs and symbols of the grace of God rather than sacramental channels or re-enactments of that grace. As a person responds in faith and obedience to God's free offer of grace and forgiveness, God's grace becomes effective in that person's life. The believer then gives public witness to that inner reality by requesting believers' baptism.

With respect to the Lord's supper, the foundational documents of the Anabaptist-Mennonite tradition offer three ways of expressing its meaning: (1) The bread and wine are signs pointing to the broken body and shed blood of Christ who died for our sins. (2) The Lord's supper is a memorial meal to remind us of what Christ has done for us in his suffering and death. (3) The Lord's supper is a union and communion with Christ and with the members of his body. Therefore most Mennonite groups practise open communion, inviting all professing believers to share the Lord's supper. Contemporary Mennonite meditations on the Lord's supper sometimes also call Christ's followers to a willingness to be broken and poured out for others as Christ gave his life for us.

BAPTIST PERSPECTIVES ON THE CHURCH

Emerging in England at the beginning of the 17th century, Baptists were indebted to Puritans, Separatists and Anabaptists as they defined their view of the church. Arguably more dependent upon English writers, Baptists started with the proposition that "the true church is composed of true believers". This early understanding of General Baptists reflects their antagonism to parish system, prayer books and hierarchies. Baptists preferred to apply the term "church" to congregations rather than to structures or organizations.

Later Calvinistic Baptists also emphasized the particularity of local congregations. Such bodies, called into being by God's Spirit, "have all the means to their salvation", and as the first London confession put it in 1644, "all power and authority… in any way needful". In the dynamic, then, of small, intimate congregations, the true church took shape.

Baptists of all persuasions have stressed the concept of a voluntary church. This means that one enters the fellowship by a voluntary commitment to follow Jesus Christ as Saviour and Lord, and that new members covenant with each other to "walk in the ways of Christ as revealed in scripture". The congregation, moreover, voluntarily makes decisions about its own life and relationships with other Christians. Important to early Baptists was the principle that offerings in support of church and ministry were to be completely voluntary.

Important in the Baptist concept of a "voluntary church" are the covenant and confession of faith. The Baptist use of covenants modified the Separatist form: following the experience of believers' baptism, members of the fellowship voluntarily created covenants. These agreements stated membership expectations between members and benefits enjoyed by God's people from God's faithfulness. The written covenant helped to build a bond among members and gave shape to the body politic of the church. In contrast, confessions of faith were created first by individuals, later by congregations, to be theological statements of consensus, modified from time to time within congregations. Standard covenant and confessional forms gradually emerged among many Baptist congregations and later associational bodies, some with anachronistic elements. In the 20th century, many Baptist bodies have used confessions of faith as doctrinal standards for theological clarity and as bases for fellowship.

Since the late 19th century, Baptists have also used the word "autonomy" and "interdependence" to describe their doctrine of the church. By autonomy, Baptists mean the authority under Christ to make all decisions at the congregational level, without interference from other ecclesiastical or civil authorities. Because this emphasis has too often led to schism and isolationism, mainstream Baptists have also taught and practised interdependence. This has been realized in the shape of associations, conventions, unions, societies and other ecumenical bodies to advance the cause of Christ. For most Baptists, the terms "autonomy" and "interdependence" are used in dynamic tension.

The task of the church is also inherent in the Baptist doctrine of the church. Local congregations are to receive new members and nurture them in faith and godliness. The church is to be an evangelizing community, always witnessing to the love and reconciliation of God in Christ. Finally, the church has a direct responsibility to be a worshipping community. This includes prayer, stewardship, proclamation of the word, exhortation, singing, and celebration of the ordinances/sacraments.

Baptist worship has been characterized by a wide variety of forms and practices. Many congregations in the British and North American cultures follow less formal patterns in which the sermon is a high priority. Choirs, hymns and gospel songs bring additional life to the principal weekly worship service. In the African-American Baptist tradition, emphasis is placed upon musical expression and personal, vivid response to prayer, exhortation and preaching. Among many Baptist groups, a primary focus is evangelism. Thus, an invitation to Christian discipleship follows an evangelistic sermon. A minority of Baptists prefer more formal worship where modifications of the Anglican, Lutheran and Reformed patterns are practised. The ordinances provide important punctuation in the worship life of Baptists, regardless of the sub-category or cultural context.

Baptists approach baptism and the Lord's supper in the theological contexts of the 17th century. Early on, there was a debate about whether these rites were sacramental or important teachings of Christ. Many followed the examples of John Calvin and Huldrych Zwingli, in teaching that both were sacramental, though perhaps not fully "sacraments". In order to distinguish themselves from other English churches and to restore a simple New Testament understanding, most Baptist congregations adopted the terminology of "ordinance". Generally, the ordinances are two, but in North America footwashing, anointing with oil and the laying-on of hands have also at times been considered ordinances.

Baptism replaced the covenant as a sign of the church for Baptists. Baptism pointed to a common experience rather than mere intellectual assent, and it was required of all true and able believers at the time of entry in the church. By the mid-17th century, after conferring with a Dutch Rhynsburger congregation which included Mennonites, English Baptists adopted believers' baptism by immersion as the common mode. Immersion portrayed not only obedience to Christ, but a dying and rising with Christ (Rom. 6:1-4). Thus it was a powerful witness for new believers and a renewal experience for existing members. Baptists do expect that members will want to follow Christ in the ordinance of believers' baptism by immersion, and they have written more on the topic than any other subject.

For most Baptists, the Lord's supper is a periodic re-enactment of the last supper in the Pauline tradition of scripture. It is a "memorial feast" open to all true believers, particularly those who are members of the celebrating congregation. Open communion, or the allowance of persons who are not members of the congregation or those who profess faith through a another denominational tradition, has become increasingly widespread in the last few decades. Generally, Baptists use simple bread and grape juice for the elements, in which the stress is upon the broken body and shed blood of Christ for the remission of sins. Much debate occurred in the North American context over the use of fermented wine or grape juice, illustrating a cultural impact upon theological issues.

CONVERGENCES AND DIVERGENCES ON THE CHURCH

*Convergences*

1. Baptists and Mennonites affirm:
   a) the believers' church as a free church, a voluntary body of believers baptized upon confession of faith;
   b) the local congregation (i.e., a gathered community) as the primary expression of the church;
   c) the interdependence of congregations in associations and conferences;
   d) a cautious concern for cooperative Christianity beyond denominational boundaries;
   e) the importance of a strong and warm community life.

2. Baptists and Mennonites practise believers' baptism which is regarded as the sign and symbol of a person's response in faith and obedience to God's free offer of grace and forgiveness in Christ. Baptism is expected of believers and is generally viewed as entry into church membership and a commitment to follow Christ.

3. Baptists and Mennonites celebrate the Lord's supper primarily as a sign and symbol of Jesus' suffering and death and as an experience of union with Christ and one another, to be shared by professing believers.

4. Baptists and Mennonites practise a simple worship style with the focus on Jesus Christ as Lord. The sermon is a central feature together with prayer, scripture and congregational singing.

*Divergences*

1. Historically Baptists have tended to understand Christ's death as a vicarious, substitutionary atonement for sin, whereas Mennonites have tended to emphasize Christ's death as a demonstration of God's suffering love, reconciling the world to himself.

2. Baptists emphasize personal salvation whereas Mennonites emphasize commitment to follow Christ in life.

3. Baptists view immersion as the proper mode of baptism to represent the believers' identification with the death, burial and resurrection of Christ. Mennonites practise several modes of baptism.

4. Mennonites often see suffering as a mark of the true church whereas Baptists do not.

5. Mennonites have been more concerned about issues of church discipline than Baptists have been.

## The mission of the church in the world

The people of faith have always struggled with the questions of how they as a people called by God are to relate to the larger world – its environment, its people, its social institutions. This task has been especially high on the list of concerns of the people known as Baptists and Mennonites. Both communities understand that in important ways to be Christian is to be called out and to be different. The kind of relationships between the church and the world that these two traditions have fostered demonstrate much about their understanding of the nature of God's sovereignty, the nature of Christ's life and ministry, and understanding of human nature, and the nature of sin and human need. In this portion of our conversation, much is revealed about how Mennonites and Baptists understand themselves and some critical points which we share and points at which we differ.

MENNONITE PERSPECTIVES ON THE MISSION OF THE CHURCH IN THE WORLD

*Mission*

Together with other Christians, Mennonites confess that Jesus Christ is the sole means of salvation and the norm for faith and life in all cultures. They also affirm that witness for Jesus Christ in both word and deed is an essential dimension of the church's life and its reason for being. For Mennonites, the mission of the church includes both the commission to make disciples "teaching them all that I have commanded you" and ministries of compassion and service.

Many early Anabaptists and Mennonites were aggressively missionary and witnessed boldly regardless of the consequences, which were very severe as the *Martyrs Mirror* attests so vividly. Many persons were added to the church. Menno Simons became a fugitive in danger of his life during his entire ministry as he went about preaching, baptizing and building up the church. Persecution took its toll and the Mennonites became more withdrawn as they sought to survive.

In the past century, however, Mennonites have been caught up in the modern missionary movement. In the early decades of the 19th century, Mennonites in the Netherlands and Russia who had been influenced by the Pietist tradition were the first Mennonites to support the modern mission movement. In both the Netherlands and Russia, Mennonites supported the Baptist foreign mission endeavours before sending out their own missionaries or establishing their own mission programmes. In 1847, the Dutch organized the Mennonite Association for the Spread of the Gospel in the Dutch colonies, which was preceded by the Dutch section of the (English) Baptist Missionary Society (1821-47), which also consisted mostly of Mennonites. The Dutch organization was supported significantly by Russian and German Mennonites. When they established their own mission programmes, the Dutch went first to Java in Indonesia. The General Conference Mennonites in America began extensive work among the American Indians following 1880. The General Conference Mennonites, the Mennonite church, and the Mennonite Brethren church all began their foreign mission programmes in India in 1899 in response to famine conditions.

An important feature of the Mennonite mission today is the work of the Mennonite Central Committee, a North American organization begun in 1920 to help their fellow religionists who were suffering in the Soviet Union. It developed into a relief service agency which sends volunteers to many parts of both North America and the rest of the world to feed the hungry, clothe the naked, and bind up wounds in the name of Christ. In recent years two new emphases have emerged in response to a growing sensitivity to the causes of the human misery to which MWC has ministered. They are development and concern for justice for the oppressed.

Initially, Mennonites in the modern period did not have a strategy for mission. They borrowed their approach to mission from Protestant programmes. In more recent years the MCC has frequently opened the way into new areas for mission. The service base of these projects has aided in the contextualization of these missions, in giving recognition to the cultural, historical and socio-political position of the people among whom the witness takes place. Contextualization has been applied to structures, worship and ritual, as well as a theology which centres on the incarnation of Jesus Christ. At the same time, Mennonites have emphasized simplicity of life, both as a distinctive mark of discipleship (including non-conformity in the face of affluence or waste) and as a mean of conserving the earth's resources and of economic sharing.

The mission approach of Mennonites has been particularly well adapted to serving non-Western Christian groups that have already accepted the Christian message – together with an emphasis on peace – but who desire assistance with Bible study and who wish to understand more adequately the relationship of faith to daily life.

## Peace

Mennonites are one of the historic peace churches and most Mennonites view peace and non-resistance as a fundamental dimension of the gospel. Mennonites' understanding of peace is based on their reading of the New Testament, and particularly of Matthew 5:38-48 in the Sermon on the Mount. Here Jesus tells his followers not to resist the one who is evil, but rather to turn the other cheek, to go the second mile, and to love their enemies. Earlier in the chapter He says, "Blessed are the peace-makers" and calls them children of God.

Mennonite confessions have been remarkably consistent in including an article on peace. Practice has been far less uniform. Several major migrations were directly related to reluctance to participate in military service: from Prussia to Russia ca. 1790 to 1820; to Canada and the United States from Alsace between 1830 and 1870; and from Russia following 1870. Mennonites remaining in Europe following these migrations often accepted participation in compulsory military service, although an alternative service programme existed in Russia for a time. In Canada and the United States young Mennonite men were generally granted the status of conscientious objectors, fulfilling the obligation to the state by payment of fines or alternative service.

Voluntary service and relief programmes have provided opportunities for serving humankind, especially following world war I (France, the Middle East, Russia) and world war II (primarily Europe), and currently in the third world. PAX, one of the alternative service options included in the I-W programme which functioned from 1952 to 1973 in the US, made it possible for many conscientious objectors to render their service abroad. In recent years a number of European countries have legally recognized conscientious objectors and have instituted alternative service programmes.

A significant number of Mennonite men have chosen various forms of military service. A survey in the 1980s indicates that 69 percent of young men in North America said they would take the position of conscientious objection if drafted.

Mennonite peace literature prior to world war II was minimal. In 1944 the publication of Guy F. Hershberger's *War, Peace, and Nonresistance* presented the biblical rationale for peace. It considered both Old and New Testament foundations. The book was widely accepted by North American Mennonite groups. Since that time a vast amount of Mennonite literature has been published on peace and justice concerns. From 1950 to 1980, as Mennonites became significantly acculturated, peace often became a focus of identity. The theological base has been expanded with further reflection on the meaning and implications of the Lordship of Christ, the Christian witness to the state and socio-political responsibility, together with an emphasis on "shalom" and peace- and justice-making. This includes a new concern for reconciliation that embraces all of creation because the violence against creation is of the same order as the violence in human society.

## Politics

Mennonites affirm the Lordship of Jesus Christ over all creation and human life; they also affirm the separation of the church from the political order and, hence, the freedom of the church from the dominion of the state. Mennonites have generally viewed participation in the political order with scepticism.

The first Anabaptist confession or positional statement, formulated at Schleitheim on the German-Swiss border in 1527, takes a strong position concerning separation from the world, and contains a lengthy article on the sword. Its main thrust is that a Christian may not serve as a magistrate. The argument is based on the example and teaching of Jesus and is taken directly from the gospels. Menno Simons, leader of the Dutch Anabaptists, took a less stringent position on participation in government. In fact, Mennonites of Swiss and Dutch origins have differed more significantly in their relation to the political order than in any other expression of their faith. In the 20th century, Mennonites have become increasingly aware of social issues, and of the need and the possibilities of changing unjust social structures.

Mennonites of Swiss origin continue to adhere to a remarkable degree to the early Swiss position of not holding political office. Mennonites and Amish, however, early voted in political elections in Pennsylvania, particularly before 1750. As early as the French and Indian war they also sent petitions to the government of Pennsylvania. In the 20th century several persons have served in political office on the state level. More frequently, persons hold township-level offices where the use of force is not required.

Mennonites originating in the Dutch stream, on the other hand, have actively participated in government office-holding. Mennonites in the Netherlands early experienced toleration and participated somewhat in political affairs. In Russia, Mennonites were responsible for the political structures governing their communities, and in time those structures intermingled somewhat with those of the Russian government. Several also became representatives in the *Duma*, the Russian parliament. In the United States and Canada, the Mennonite Brethren Church discouraged active political participation for its members until about 1950.

Members of the General Conference Mennonite Church have been the most active politically. Recently Mennonites have held various governmental offices in the five western provinces of Canada and have also been members of parliament in Ottawa.

In the 1950s and 1960s, the appropriateness of a Christian witness to the state became the subject of international discussion between Mennonites and mainline Christians, primarily in Europe, but also in America. Political activism on the part of American Mennonites has been significant, especially since the establishment of an office in Washington DC in 1968. An MCC office has also been established in Ottawa. Many of these concerns expressed to government have grown out of social injustices witnessed in countries where Mennonites have engaged in relief work. Frequently these injustices were perceived to be associated with US foreign policy. In connection with this issue, it must also be said that Mennonites in general tend to reject national patriotic concerns to the extent that they are regarded as nationalistic.

BAPTIST PERSPECTIVES ON THE MISSION OF THE CHURCH IN THE WORLD

Although there have been a few exceptions, Baptists generally have defined a primary task of the church as evangelism and missions. The numerical and geographical expansion of the church has been the primary standard by which the vitality and authenticity of any Christian group has been measured. Prominent among Baptists and, indeed, evident to the entire church and world have been Baptist leaders in missions and evangelism such as William Carey, Anne and Adoniram Judson, Lottie Moon and Billy Graham.

This emphasis on missions and evangelism has led to the establishment of systems and structures to accomplish these purposes. Often the mission board and evangelism department of a Baptist convention or union will receive the majority of the attention and support from the churches. These mission efforts frequently have been the most unifying element in Baptist life. Considerable attention is given to techniques and procedures that are designed to achieve the greatest results. Missionaries and evangelists are carefully trained in programmes of outreach. Often these programmes are very structured and detailed in spelling out the steps to be taken in achieving the greatest positive response to the mission efforts. All of these features demonstrate the centrality of missions and evangelism among Baptists.

There have been and continue to be differences among Baptists regarding their understanding of different dimensions of the mission effort. For example, various motives for doing missions receive differing emphases among Baptists. Some respond to the commandment of the great commission to go and proclaim the gospel to all corners of the world. Others are driven by the power of their own Christian experience to share with others the hope and joy that they have found in Christ. Still others are drawn primarily by the tragic dimensions of the human condition to go and be servants to those in need. Of course these different motives need not be mutually exclusive but usually one of them will be dominant.

There are differences in styles of missions among various Baptists. Within the modern missions movement there have been some mission efforts that make a sharp distinction between the "sending" churches and the "receiving" churches. In these mission efforts the "sending" churches exercise a careful control over the programmes and personnel of the mission effort. Care is taken that missionaries not lose their cultural identity and become too closely identified with the culture of the mission field.

A contrasting style has tended to encourage the development of indigenous churches that incarnate the Christian faith into the cultural body of the mission field. Here the emphasis is on the development of indigenous leadership within the church and on phasing out the leadership role of the missionary. Indeed this approach to mission tries to eliminate the distinction between the "sending" and the "receiving" churches and to establish a relationship in which churches from different cultures learn from each other.

Also, there have been different understandings of the substance of the mission effort. One approach has put emphasis upon meeting the spiritual needs of the lost. The primary purpose of missions is to bring the lost to a sense of their sins and an understanding of God's forgiving love that redeems them from sin. This approach usually emphasizes the personal and individual nature of the religious experience.

Others have focused upon a broader range of human needs and understand a broader range of divine acts in meeting those needs. The Christian experience is not only forgiveness but also, most importantly, regeneration and sanctification in which the total life is transformed. The mission effort challenges the social injustices that oppress people. Christ is understood as the suffering servant who identifies with the outcast of the world and comes to meet their social, economic and physical needs as well as their spiritual needs.

A belief in a righteous (i.e., moral) God whose kingdom or reign extends into all areas of human experience has led Baptists to define broadly the task of the church. Walter Rauschenbusch has influenced Baptists to understand more fully the social implications of the gospel. A variety of social service institutions have been established to meet this wide range of human needs. Some examples of such institutions include orphanages, hospitals, counselling centres, homeless shelters, soup kitchens and schools.

In addition to such service organizations, many Baptist unions and conventions have established agencies to provide leadership for the churches and their members in analyzing and responding to major social problems. Attention has been given to sexual behaviour and family life. The importance of the family as a God-ordained institution has been stressed and recommendations have been made as to how the family can be protected from many of the threats to its stability. In recent years much attention has been given to the expanding role of women within the family, the church, the other social institutions.

In considering economic issues Baptists have focused on the Christian doctrine of vocation and its meaning for the work life in all professions and occupations. Much attention and activity has been committed to the problems of hunger and poverty, both domestically and globally. This task has focused attention on different economic structures and systems and upon the disparity of wealth that exists in today's world.

Baptists have struggled with the sins of racism and ethnic conflict. The attempt has been to understand the importance of ethnic identity and to avoid those forms of pride and discrimination that deny God's equal love for all of the human family and to eliminate social patterns that oppress people and deny them complete access to the blessings of a full life.

In recent years the advances in medical technology have shifted attention to such issues as abortion, euthanasia, reproductive technology and the justice of various systems of health-care distribution. There has not been widespread agreement among Baptists on a number of these ethical issues in health care.

A wide variety of positions on Christian involvement in the political process can be found in Baptist history and contemporary life. Some have sought to withdraw as much as possible from the political process. This abandonment of politics usually has grown out of an experience of persecution in which the state has become a mortal enemy or out of an eschatalogical expectation that views the orders of this world as under the dominion of Satan.

A second position of some Baptists involves cautious and limited political involvement. The church must maintain its integrity and not become indebted to or under the control of the state. Religious liberty for all and the separation of church and state are stressed in this tradition.

A third position calls for a wider range of efforts by the church to work with and through the state to transform society. While carefully avoiding any merger of church and state in which either would be under the essential control of the other, these Baptists advocate an active role of the church in the political process whenever possible.

A fourth position, referred to historically as the theocratic view, sees the government under the sovereignty of God and, therefore, properly directed by Christians to enforce God's will on earth.

Unlike Mennonites, the issue of peace has not been a defining issue for Baptists. Like many other Christian traditions there have been those who have advocated non-violence as the proper social strategy for Christians. In recent Baptist life this position has been advocated by Martin Luther King Jr. and by several Baptist peace fellowships in different regions of the world.

Most Baptists can be identified with the just-war tradition which accepts the tragic necessity of the use of force to maintain order within a sinful world. Baptists generally have been active in supporting their governments by serving in the military as combatants and chaplains or working in defence industries. There are also examples of Baptists who, under the influence of nationalistic fervour, have moved into essentially a holy war mode and promoted warfare as a divine cause.

CONVERGENCES AND DIVERGENCES ON THE MISSION OF THE CHURCH IN THE WORLD

*Convergences*

1. Baptists and Mennonites affirm:
   a) the Lordship of Christ over creation and human life;
   b) Jesus Christ as the sole means of salvation and the norm for faith and life in all cultures;
   c) witness for Jesus Christ in both word and deed as an essential dimension of the church's life;
   d) that the church must be free, i.e. neither the church nor the state is to dominate the other (separation of church and state).
2. Both Baptists and Mennonites have strong overseas missions programmes resulting in vigorous indigenous churches in many nations.

*Divergences*

1. Baptist identity is shaped more by concern for proclamation, whereas Mennonite identity is shaped more by service.
2. Mennonites are one of the historic peace churches and most Mennonites see peace and non-resistance as a fundamental aspect of the gospel, whereas Baptists generally identify with the just-war tradition.
3. Baptists generally affirm participation in the political order, whereas Mennonites tend to view it with scepticism.
4. Whereas Baptists are often sympathetic to national patriotic concerns, Mennonites tend to reject those concerns as nationalistic.
5. Mennonites often have viewed suffering as a mark of faithfulness.

6.  Mennonites have emphasized simplicity of life, both as a distinctive mark of rejecting worldly fashions and as a means of conserving the earth's resources and of economic sharing.

*Recommendations*

1) that the BWA and MWC invite each other to participate regularly through official representatives at their world congresses and, as appropriate, at their general council meetings;

2) that the leaders and staff of the BWA and MWC regularly seek each other's advice and support on matters of mutual concern;

3) that the BWA and MWC encourage member bodies within the same country to exchange official representatives at their national meetings or assemblies;

4) that the BWA and MWC encourage several member bodies to convene (Perhaps through mission agencies or educational institutions) a Baptist-Mennonite consultation on the "mission and peace witness of the church" (or "peace evangelism");

5) that the BWA and MWC encourage several member bodies to convene a Baptist-Mennonite consultation on themes of just war, responsible use of coercive power, non-violent resistance and biblical pacifism;

6) that the BWA and MWC encourage cooperation in mission, service, and peace and justice projects at all levels;

7) that the BWA and MWC encourage exchanges at various levels, including cross-congregational fellowship, pulpit exchanges, academic exchanges of both students and faculty, and national and international youth conferences;

8) that the BWA and MWC encourage continued research into the 1608-40 period of Baptist-Mennonite intersection with a view of mutual sharing a publication;

9) that the BWA and MWC review Baptist-Mennonite relationships by 1999;

10) that this report be distributed as widely as possible among the member churches of the BWA and MWC;

11) that upon approval of these recommendations by the general councils of the BWA and of the MWC, the general secretaries of both global bodies meet to discuss and plan implementation of these recommendations.

# 37. Called to Communion and Common Witness

## Joint Working Group between the Lutheran World Federation and the World Alliance of Reformed Churches (1999-2001)

### Geneva, October 2001

## Introduction

1. Twelve years ago, a joint commission of the Lutheran World Federation and the World Alliance of Reformed Churches called on all Lutheran and Reformed churches throughout the world to "declare communion with one another" (§79) and to "make their unity more real and visible for their members as well as for the world" (§85). It also urged the Lutheran World Federation and the World Alliance of Reformed Churches to collaborate in their work wherever possible.[1]

2. Much has happened during the last decade. In many parts of the world, Lutheran and Reformed churches have, indeed, established binding forms of communion. Although progress is uneven, bonds between the two families have become stronger. At the international level cooperation between the LWF and WARC has significantly advanced.

3. Recognizing the new situation, the decision was taken in 1999 to establish a joint working group with the mandate:

a) to review the present state of Lutheran-Reformed relations on the regional and international level;

b) to assess the implications of regional developments for the global relationship;

c) to examine ways in which the governing bodies of the two communions might fruitfully cooperate;

d) to identify other possible forms of practical cooperation; and

e) to consider whether it would be helpful to begin a new full round of international Lutheran-Reformed dialogue.

4. The joint working group has sought to respond to this mandate. It has met three times: in November 1999 in Geneva, in November 2000 in Campinas, Brazil, and in October 2001 again in Geneva.

5. The group's mandate was expanded in 2000 when the United churches in Germany asked the two general secretaries for discussion about how they might develop their relationship with the LWF and WARC. These churches combine Lutheran and Reformed traditions, but are not at present members of either world organization. Prior to the third meeting of the group, a consultation was held in Geneva with representatives of these churches and other churches uniting Lutheran and Reformed traditions from the Czech

Republic, Madagascar, the Netherlands, Russia and Zambia. The lively discussion stimulated us to make a new assessment of how these German churches might be included in the growing collaboration between the LWF and WARC and our relationships with United churches in other regions.

## I. Lutheran-Reformed developments in recent years

6. During the past decade many significant developments have taken place. Since the publication of the report *Toward Church Fellowship* in 1990,[2] Lutheran and Reformed churches in different parts of the world have pursued dialogues and have in several cases officially declared church communion. We begin our report with a summary survey of these developments.

### 1. DEVELOPING COMMUNION AT REGIONAL LEVEL

#### a. United States: the formula of agreement

7. In 1997, after thirty-five years of dialogue, a formula of agreement was formally adopted by the national assemblies of the Presbyterian Church (USA), the Reformed Church in America, the United Church of Christ and the Evangelical Lutheran Church in America. This was the first full communion agreement entered into by a Lutheran church in the USA. The ecumenical approach characterizing this agreement was first articulated in *Marburg Revisited* (1963), the report of the first dialogue between Lutheran and Reformed churches in the United States. The lead concept governing the formula of agreement is that of "complementarity", calling both for "mutual affirmation" of areas of common understanding and for "mutual admonition" where different emphases still prevail. No longer are the traditions of Reformation churches considered to be church-dividing. Complementarity allows for the reconciling of "their diverse witness to the saving grace of God that is bestowed in Jesus Christ, the Lord of the church". This understanding urged the churches to bear a common mission in the context of the American culture. Competition has been replaced by a common and cooperative spirit in proclaiming the gospel of God's saving grace in Jesus Christ. The agreement is being implemented through the work of a joint coordinating committee in areas such as the exchange of pastors, the training of global missionaries and the planning for theological consultations. Other areas of collaboration among the programme boards of the churches are also emerging.

#### b. Indonesia: towards a United church

8. The Communion of Churches in Indonesia (PGI) includes 79 churches: 11 Lutheran, 50 Reformed, 1 Methodist, and 17 Evangelical and Pentecostal churches, with a total membership of 13 million. In 1950 a council of churches was established to express and to further a movement towards one church in Indonesia. A more decisive step was taken

in 1984 with the establishment of the PGI based on a consensus set out in the "Five Documents of Unity". In March 2000, the 13th general assembly of the PGI adopted a revised version of these documents, in the hope of moving closer to the long-stated goal of a United church in Indonesia (Gereja Kristen yang Esa di Indonesia). The assembly agreed on four areas of common work. Some Lutheran and Reformed churches feel that the basis for uniting has not yet been sufficiently established. It is hoped, nonetheless, that the 14th general assembly in 2005 will agree on further moves towards manifesting the unity of the Indonesian churches.

*c. New developments in the Leuenberg fellowship*

9. In the past decade, the communion among Lutheran, Reformed and United churches in Europe based on the Leuenberg agreement (1973) has been consolidated, strengthened and expanded. Two further assemblies of the signatory churches have been held – 1994 in Vienna and 2001 in Belfast. The theological conversations have led to the publication of a number of significant statements clarifying remaining differences or responding to new challenges. Of particular importance is the statement "The Church of Jesus Christ", which was adopted by the Vienna assembly. Additional churches have formally accepted the agreement, among them the Evangelical Church in Germany (1998), the Evangelical Lutheran Church in Russia (1999), the Church of Norway (2000) and the Evangelical Lutheran Church in Denmark (2001). In 1994 representatives of the Evangelical Methodist Church in Europe signed a declaration endorsing the Leuenberg agreement. In 1997 five Evangelical Methodist churches joined the fellowship and are now actively involved in its work.[3]

*d. Further developments at national level*

10. In several countries, Lutheran and Reformed churches are united. Examples are the Church of the River Plate (Argentina), the Church of Lippe (Germany), the Evangelical Church of the Czech Brethren (Czech Republic), and the Ethiopian Evangelical Church Mekane Yesu (Ethiopia). Reformed and Lutheran churches in the Netherlands – in a journey that is not yet complete – are engaged in a unification process called "Together on the Way". In a large number of countries, Lutheran and Reformed churches include within their life and membership, to varying degrees, elements of the other tradition. The Church of Lippe belongs to both the LWF and WARC. Since 1989 two more churches – the Evangelical Church of the River Plate, Argentina, and the Ethiopian Evangelical Church Mekane Yesu, Ethiopia – have applied for simultaneous membership in both bodies.

11. A new development has taken place with regard to the United churches in Germany. They represent almost half of German Protestantism. Resulting from historical developments in the 19th century, they combine Lutheran and Reformed traditions and seek to witness as United churches to the heritage of the Reformation. At the national level they act through the Evangelical Church of the Union and/or the Arnoldshain conference. Through the Leuenberg agreement they have declared communion with Lutheran and Reformed churches throughout Europe. At the international level they have traditionally stressed their ecumenical commitment through the World Council of Churches. They

have at the same time maintained close partner relations with many member churches of the LWF or WARC or both. In recent years, there has been a growing desire among these United churches to find appropriate ways to be associated with the two world bodies and share in their common life and work (for more details cf. appendix 2).

12. In various parts of the world Lutheran and Reformed churches are actively engaged in dialogue. Conversations between the Church of Sweden (Lutheran) and the Mission Covenant Church of Sweden (Reformed) centre on baptismal practice and seek to deepen mutual understanding and cooperation. The joint council of the Church of North India, the Church of South India and the Mar Thoma Church is engaged in dialogue with the Evangelical Lutheran Church in India and the Methodist Church in India.[4] They hope for closer working cooperation and possibly a communion agreement.

## 2. OTHER PATTERNS OF RELATIONSHIP

13. In many contexts, ecumenical challenges arise from Lutheran and Reformed churches' pastoral engagement in the local context and from their national or regional historical and geographical situations, which often tend to shape distinctive practices. A few examples may illustrate this.

14. At an encounter with church leaders, preceding our meeting in Campinas, Brazil, in 2000, the working group learned about the diversities that exist between the Lutheran and the Reformed churches. But it also learned about several joint initiatives in the areas of diaconal and developmental work (Ecumenical Coordination of Service, CESE) and theological education (especially in the framework of the Brazilian Association of Protestant Theological Schools, ASTE). Collaboration in theological work, already existing together with other churches at the level of a single ecumenical board of graduate studies for two major institutes, has a potential to bring together churches which, also for geographical reasons, do not know enough about each other. The Evangelical Church of Lutheran Confession (IECLB) in Brazil and the United Presbyterian Church of Brazil are both members of the National Council of Christian Churches. The IECLB and most of the Presbyterian and Reformed churches work together in the Latin American Council of Churches (for more details cf. appendix 2).

15. In Venezuela, the Presbyterian church has been in contact with the Evangelical Lutheran church for about fifteen years, first through the Student Christian Movement, then through the Latin American Council of Churches (CLAI), and for about five years through the World Day of Prayer. About three years ago, the two churches began conversations about developing a joint programme of theological education and have already initiated a joint programme of adult theological education for non-ordained ministries. They are now developing a new ecumenical institute of higher studies which will serve them both in the areas of lay education, seminary education, and eventually university-level education. Another example is found in El Salvador, where the small Reformed church is educating its pastors at the new Lutheran university.

16. In other countries and regions of the world, there are councils or working committees in place that coordinate the work of Lutheran and Reformed churches. In Hungary, for example, there exists a joint Reformed-Lutheran committee, which brings together leadership of both churches for informal meetings at least twice a year. They exchange

information and plan common strategy for the future. They agree in many practical tasks of the churches and on common representation for ecumenical and national events. In the Middle East, Reformed and Lutheran churches cooperate closely within the Fellowship of Middle East Evangelical Churches. They also, together with the Anglicans, form one "family" of churches in the Middle East Council of Churches. Joint seminars, pastors' retreats, youth retreats, and educational endeavours are common.

### 3. Lutheran and Reformed Agreements with Third Parties

17. Lutheran and Reformed churches are committed to ecumenical dialogue with other Christian traditions. In recent years conversations have led in several countries to new agreements and even declarations of communion with third parties. These developments are significant in that they show that Lutherans and the Reformed are able to act together in ecumenical partnership.

### a. The Meissen agreement

18. The Meissen agreement is the result of dialogue between the Church of England, the Federation of the Evangelical Churches in the German Democratic Republic and the Evangelical Church in Germany (EKD), which began officially in February 1987 and was concluded in March 1988. It built on previous developments, such as twinning relationships between cities (e.g., Coventry and Dresden) after 1945, theological conversations since 1964, and the reports of the Anglican-Lutheran European commission (1982), the International Anglican-Lutheran joint working group (1983), the Anglican-Reformed international commission (1984) and the Faith and Order document *Baptism, Eucharist and Ministry* (1982).

19. The text of the agreement deals with (i) the church as sign, instrument and foretaste of the kingdom of God; (ii) the church as koinonia; (iii) growth towards full, visible unity; (iv) communion already shared; (v) communion in faith, and (vi) mutual acknowledgment and next steps. The signatory churches acknowledge one another as true churches belonging to the one, holy, catholic and apostolic church of Jesus Christ and truly participating in the apostolic mission of the whole people of God. The agreement was approved in 1991 by the general synod of the Church of England, the responsible bodies of the Federation of the Evangelical Churches in the GDR and its member churches, and the EKD and its member churches.

### b. The Reuilly common statement

20. In 1999 the British and Irish Anglican churches and the French Lutheran and Reformed churches issued the Reuilly statement, "Called to Witness and Service". It was signed by the churches in 2001. The dialogue leading to the Meissen agreement produced a lively interest among French Reformed and Lutheran churches and a desire to take steps towards closer fellowship with the Anglican churches across the Channel. It was considered important to work in continuity with the Meissen agreement, and also with

the Porvoo common statement between the British and Irish Anglican churches and Nordic and Baltic Lutheran churches. The outline of the agreement is similar to that of the Meissen agreement, but there are separate sections on the apostolicity of the church and ministry and on wider ecumenical commitment. The mutual acknowledgments and commitments are also similar to those of the Meissen declaration. Both Meissen and Reuilly commit the signatory churches to work for the goal of full visible unity of the church, and both already allow for a much higher degree of fellowship between them. Since no agreement was reached on the historic episcopate, the statement does not allow for the interchangeability of ministries.

### c. Churches Uniting in Christ

21. Inaugurated in January 2002 and involving nine US churches, Churches Uniting in Christ (CUIC) is the successor to the forty-year-old Consultation on Church Union (COCU). The consultation envisioned a new church that would be "truly catholic and truly reformed", and had its origins in a proposal made by the Presbyterian leader, Eugene Carson Blake, in a sermon preached at Grace Episcopal Cathedral, San Francisco, in December 1960.

22. The Presbyterian Church (USA) and the United Church of Christ are full participants in CUIC, alongside the African Methodist Episcopal Church, the African Methodist Episcopal Zion Church, the Christian Church (Disciples of Christ), the Christian Methodist Episcopal Church, the Episcopal Church, the International Council of Community Churches, and the United Methodist Church. The Evangelical Lutheran Church in America has agreed to become a "partner in mission and dialogue" with the CUIC churches, although the ELCA assembly resolution stops short of full membership.

23. CUIC churches explicitly recognize each other as authentic expressions of the one church of Jesus Christ, having in common faith in one God, commitment to Jesus Christ as Saviour and as the incarnate and risen Lord, faithfulness to scripture, commitment to faithful participation in the two sacraments baptism and eucharist, and grateful acceptance of the ministry which the Holy Spirit has manifestly given to the churches. As with the Meissen and Reuilly agreements, however, episcopacy remains a sticking point and ministries are not yet interchangeable, although eucharistic sharing is encouraged.

24. CUIC churches include three predominantly African-American churches, thus challenging the colour barrier that has so divided churches in the United States. They see challenging racism as being at the core of their common engagement in mission: "There can be no authentic Christian community in CUIC if, by their unquestioning acceptance of unjust gains granted by an unjust system, white members of the community continue their tacit complicity in this unjust social order that denies the fullness of life to black members of the community."

### 4. THE WIDER CONTEXT OF LUTHERAN AND REFORMED INTERCONFESSIONAL DIALOGUES

25. Lutheran-Reformed church fellowship serves a larger ecumenical goal, the communion of the one church of Jesus Christ, and must be viewed in the context of the worldwide ecumenical movement. In recent decades Lutherans and the Reformed have

engaged in many bilateral dialogues (cf. appendix 4). These dialogues, and the changes in church relationships that result from them, are part of the wider setting in which Lutheran-Reformed relationships are developing. They demonstrate the necessity for Lutheran-Reformed bilateral relations to take into account the commitments that each family of churches has been making to others. They also show the necessity for both the Lutheran and Reformed churches to make plain to ecumenical partners the commitments they have made to each other.

## II. Developing visible structures of communion

26. As this survey shows, many Lutheran and Reformed churches have already declared communion, and this movement continues. This confirms us in the view that there is no need for a new international dialogue on the classical differences which in the past kept Lutheran and Reformed churches apart. The challenge to the two world bodies today is not to discuss whether communion is possible but to help churches in our families to move towards declarations of communion, to advance in communion, and to celebrate unity as God's gift to us all. A new set of tasks needs to be faced: to encourage churches that are in altar and pulpit fellowship to deepen their relationship, to invite churches that are not yet in altar and pulpit fellowship to move towards it, and to consider ways in which, at the world level, the two communions may intensify their common life and witness.

27. We are aware, however, that Lutheran and Reformed churches are guided in their life and witness by different ecclesiological emphases. In order to advance towards more visible forms of shared life and common witness, these need to be taken into account and addressed together.

### 1. *SATIS EST*

28. There is a common conviction that a fundamental doctrinal agreement in the preaching of the gospel and a common understanding and praxis of the sacraments are sufficient for declaring communion. Basically, as the *Confessio Augustana* explicitly states, nothing more is required (*satis est*). In his *Institutes* Calvin expressed the same conviction (IV.1.9). This principle must not be misused, however, to neglect the need for structural expressions of the unity of the church. To be experienced and recognized, communion must become visible. There are, on both sides and sometimes across the boundaries of the two traditions, different approaches to this issue. Often, the view is held that declaring communion does not call for any further steps. We believe that mutual recognition implies a commitment to work together towards greater visibility. Lutherans and the Reformed need therefore to engage in a common reflection on the appropriate forms of the visible unity of the church. These forms may differ from place to place. But to secure mutual accountability and common witness common structural frameworks are required.

## 2. PROCLAMATION AND COMMUNION

29. Both Lutherans and the Reformed give priority to the proclamation of the gospel – the gift of God's liberating grace. As Christians we are compelled to witness to God's reconciliation in Christ. Clearly, this witness presupposes that believers are reconciled with one another. Lutherans and the Reformed differ in spelling out the relationship between proclamation and the need for koinonia. The Reformed place strong emphasis on confessing the gospel faithfully in today's world. In the past decades, many Reformed churches have engaged in formulating contemporary confessions of faith. They have given less attention to "maintaining the bonds of unity" with the result that many splits have occurred in their midst. Lutheran churches have pursued more consistently the building-up of communion in and among the Lutheran churches, although the history of the Lutheran churches around the world also shows many examples of splits and persistent tensions. These two emphases on proclamation and koinonia are by no means mutually exclusive. But as we engage in a process of implementation, the difference needs to be addressed. The two approaches may prove to be mutually enriching.

## 3. COMMUNION AND COMMITMENT TO JUSTICE

30. On both sides there is a strong concern to communicate the gospel to the world. The gift of communion is realized not only in formal declarations, but in reconciliation, in sharing of gifts, and in common service. Communion implies a call for mutual recognition and a commitment to justice. It is significant that both Lutherans and the Reformed have declared *status confessionis* with regard to racial discrimination and in particular apartheid. Spiritual discourse neglecting the dimension of justice in practice is misleading. While churches in the North often concentrate on declaring communion for the sake of common mission, churches in the South often begin by taking common steps in life and mission and move on the basis of this experience to new forms of communion. We consider these two approaches to be complementary. We see a need for the churches in the North to acquire increased understanding and appreciation of how ecumenism develops in the South.

## 4. LOCAL – UNIVERSAL

31. Communion in Christ must find expression at all levels of the church's life. Lutherans and the Reformed have given different expressions to communion at the universal level. The WARC provides for its member churches a theological and ethical forum and an instrument for mutual aid and public witness, especially through work for Christian unity and justice in the world and inclusiveness in church life. The LWF defines itself explicitly as a communion of churches and has declared altar and pulpit fellowship a binding condition for membership. Its member churches share the same confession and see in the LWF an instrument for their common commitment at the universal level. As the two world bodies engage in common witness and sustained collaboration at the international level, this difference needs to be addressed.

5. DIVERSE BILATERAL ECUMENICAL COMMITMENTS

32. The difference also affects the choices of partners in the ecumenical movement (cf. §25 and appendix 4). While both the LWF and the WARC have conducted bilateral conversations, the LWF has given more attention to the process of reception of their findings. It has developed a stronger sensitivity with regard to the binding character of bilateral dialogues. The two families also relate to different partners. While the WARC has reached statements of mutual recognition with Methodists and the Churches of Christ (Disciples), Lutheran churches have established communion with Anglican churches. What is the place of the particular relationship between Lutherans and the Reformed within this wider ecumenical context? Implementation of the gift of communion needs to be seen as a service to the wider ecumenical scene.

6. OVERSIGHT *(EPISCOPE)*

33. In this context, inevitably the issue of oversight arises. Many Lutheran churches have maintained or introduced episcopal structures and are prepared to develop further their understanding of episcopacy and apostolic succession. Reformed churches are generally reluctant to adopt episcopacy as a possible structure of church order. They affirm the need of oversight (*episcope*) exercised through a collegial ministry. On both sides, synods remain the main form of church governance. Both sides agree that a particular form of *episcope* cannot be a condition for communion. As Lutherans and the Reformed consider the appropriate structures of unity, they need to engage in a discussion on the nature and appropriate exercise of *episcope*.

7. THE WORLD COUNCIL OF CHURCHES

34. Both sides affirm the oneness of the ecumenical movement and support every effort to secure the coherence of ecumenical initiatives. In expressing their support of the World Council of Churches (WCC), the LWF and the WARC have taken slightly different lines. The WARC has consistently sought to give priority to the life and witness of the WCC. It avoided duplicating programmes and invited its member churches to act directly through the WCC. While many Lutheran churches were among the founders of the WCC and have remained active members, the LWF has to a larger extent than the WARC sought to contribute to the wider ecumenical movement also through its common life and witness as a federation and as a communion. The role of the two families in the ecumenical movement and in particular in the WCC requires fresh exploration. How can they best contribute to the integrity of the WCC? How can they represent together in constructive ways the voices of the Reformation within the ecumenical movement and promote together the wider ecumenical cause?

### III. Present state of collaboration between the Lutheran World Federation and the World Alliance of Reformed Churches

35. Both our world bodies have changed importantly in recent decades. They have grown in size, and the balance in their membership has shifted towards the churches of the South. Each of them has taken significant decisions which have redefined the character of its life. For example, the 1977 LWF declaration and the 1982 WARC declaration of *status confessionis* in relation to apartheid showed the capacity of their member churches to make a common and binding commitment. This capacity is being further tested in the current debates about economic injustice and ecological destruction. The 1984 declaration of altar and pulpit fellowship in the LWF and the 1990 constitution defining the LWF as a communion deeply affect the way in which its member churches relate to each other. The LWF continues to explore the significance and further development of these decisions.

36. Collaboration between the LWF and the WARC has considerably increased during the last decades and there is on both sides the definite wish to join forces in as many areas of life and witness as possible.

1. CONTACT AND COOPERATION AT THE LEVEL OF THE SECRETARIATS IN GENEVA

37. The location of both the WARC and the LWF secretariats in the Ecumenical Centre in Geneva contributes substantially to contact and collaboration between the two organizations. Cooperation is furthered by regular joint staff meetings chaired alternately by the two general secretaries and including senior executives from both sides. In these meetings discussion and coordination takes place with regard to projects and programmes where there is joint involvement. The pattern of programmatic collaboration characteristically connects to several of the main areas of activity within the two organizations, such as mission, theology, ecumenism and human rights. Direct contact and cooperation between members of staff in connected areas are maintained in a variety of ways throughout the year.

38. Some of the cooperation between the two secretariats also takes place jointly with the WCC. The three general secretaries hold regular coordination meetings, together with the general secretary of the Conference of European Churches. At the present time (2001-2002), the three organizations meet monthly in a joint staff group with the particular purpose of discussing and expanding areas of cooperation. A report from this staff group will be presented in late spring 2002. In addition, the three secretariats cooperate in the house committee of the Ecumenical Centre as well as in the coordination of various in-house activities.

2. JOINT STUDIES AND CONSULTATIONS

39. The WARC and the LWF have participated jointly in several consultations and programmes set up either by themselves or by others. The following common efforts may serve as illustrations.

*a. Economic injustice and ecological destruction*

40. At its 23rd general council (Debrecen, 1997), the WARC launched a study and action process to gain clarity on the question in what way and to what extent the economic injustice and ecological destruction resulting from the present economic order constitute a *status confessionis* for the churches. The project, first known under the title *processus confessionis* (a process of confession) and now as covenanting for justice in the economy and the earth, met with a wide response both within and beyond WARC member churches. The LWF is engaged in similar initiatives, but focused on the implications of what it means to be a communion in the face of economic globalization. The two families have initiated conversations on themes related to these studies. The LWF and the WARC bring different but related strategies to these matters. Hopefully, these will be further developed in relation to the LWF assembly in 2003 and the WARC general council in 2004. Collaborative efforts will at the same time shed new light on the relationship between confessions and confessing and may lead to a deeper common understanding of the relevance of inherited confessions for the churches' witness today.

*b. Church structures in times of global transformations*

41. Following a WARC study in 1993 on "The Challenge of Emerging Ecclesiologies to Church Renewal" and a three-year LWF study on "Communion, Community, Society" (1997-2000), the two organizations have jointly sponsored an exploratory meeting in February 2001 and a consultation in February 2002 on "Church Structures in Times of Global Transformations". The two consultations aim at understanding ongoing structural changes taking place in Reformation churches, both in the light of the changing role played by religion in contemporary societies and in the light of church priorities related to the understanding of the gospel message in different historical, cultural and ecclesial contexts.

*c. Indulgences*

42. Prompted by Reformed and Lutheran reactions to the papal bull *Incarnationis Mysterium* (1998) and the way in which the celebration in Rome of the jubilee year 2000 was prepared and interpreted, the Pontifical Council for Promoting Christian Unity invited the LWF and the WARC to a consultation in Rome in February 2001 to discuss historical and systematic aspects of the Roman Catholic practice of indulgence. Papers and responses were presented by all three sides and discussed. No report was adopted, but a communiqué was issued (cf. appendix 1). Publications in English and German of the papers presented are being prepared.

*d. The Joint Declaration on the Doctrine of Justification in a wider ecumenical*
   *framework*

43. The significance of the Joint Declaration on the Doctrine of Justification (1999) in a wider ecumenical framework was the topic for a consultation ("Unity in Faith") in November 2001. The LWF and the Pontifical Council for Promoting Christian Unity had

jointly invited the WARC and the World Methodist Council to discuss how the Reformed and Methodists, in particular, might be associated with the agreements reached and formulated in the joint declaration. A communiqué and a report were adopted by this consultation (cf. appendix 3).

### 3. HUMAN RIGHTS

44. The WARC and the LWF, together with the WCC, work together closely on human rights. During the annual session of the UN Commission on Human Rights, joint statements are made on certain questions. On the occasion of the 50th anniversary of the Universal Declaration of Human Rights, the LWF and the WARC, together with the WCC, published liturgical material on selected human-rights issues. More substantial cooperation took place in revising the document adopted by WARC in 1976 on the theological basis of human rights. The LWF as well as the WCC accompanied the WARC process, particularly by taking part in a consultation held in 1997. This process is not yet finished, and cooperation between the two organizations in this area continues.

### 4. OTHER AREAS OF COLLABORATION

45. In many other areas regular exchange takes place. This applies in particular to mission work, and issues related to women and to youth. The preparation of the assemblies in 2003 and 2004 provide an opportunity to consult one another on various aspects of the programme, in particular the preparation of Bible studies and worship materials.

## IV. LWF-WARC relations: new steps in deepening communion

46. Our discussion has persuaded us that there is need for the WARC and the LWF to take concrete actions that can further stimulate processes to develop and transform our common life.

### 1. DECLARING MUTUAL COMMITMENT

47. Lutherans and the Reformed have come a long way together. The time has come for our highest governing bodies to make a joint declaration on the importance that they attach to the further development of Lutheran-Reformed relationships. The joint working group recommends that the general secretaries take the steps necessary to prepare a declaration to be presented to the LWF council and the WARC executive committee and thereafter to the LWF assembly and the WARC general council.

2. The role of the two world bodies in promoting national and regional
   relationships

48.  The path towards closer fellowship may differ greatly from one part of the world to another. While recognizing that only individual churches have the authority to establish church fellowship with other churches, the WARC and the LWF should play an active role in enabling and deepening communion relations between Reformed and Lutheran churches in different areas. They have an important task in communicating and interpreting regional and national agreements and their theological foundations to the whole of our two church families. In all of this, the two world bodies should be aware that all ecumenical agreements have a contextual character and cannot simply be duplicated elsewhere. Sharing of experiences across regional and national boundaries may, however, stimulate developments in other churches, showing them that obstacles to communion can be overcome and giving them the confidence to take their own steps forward.

49.  We see a specific opportunity for an initiative by the world bodies to support the Lutheran and Reformed churches in Indonesia as they move towards a united church.

3. Study project on "Structures of Communion"

50.  We recommend to the LWF and WARC to initiate a study process on structures of communion. Its mandate would consist in exploring the theological issues listed in Part II and providing clearer perspectives on the diversity and complementarity of different ecclesiological options and emphases. The aim of the study process would be to assist Lutheran and Reformed churches as they move towards new forms of communion. Particular attention needs to be given to the diversity of contexts (cf. §§26-34).

4. The history of Lutheran-Reformed relationships since the Reformation

51.  To build relations of communion it is important to deepen the awareness of the separate histories of Lutheran and Reformed churches. The history of Lutheran-Reformed relationships has not yet been sufficiently explored. How did the two streams of the Reformation become distinct at the time of the Reformation? How did they relate to other streams that took shape at the time? How did they evolve throughout the centuries since the Reformation? How did they interact and affect one another? Clearly, many misconceptions and sensitivities have their root in historical developments and events. A deliberate common attempt to present the history for Lutheran and Reformed readers could contribute significantly to a deeper mutual understanding. We propose that the LWF and the WARC approach a university or an institute to organize such a study, covering the Reformation period and the time since the Reformation and focusing on the particular periods which have determined – both positively and negatively – relationships.

5. THE ROLE OF UNITED CHURCHES IN THE LWF AND THE WARC

52. The presence within our memberships of United churches combining Lutheran and Reformed traditions reminds us that, even at the world level, the Lutheran and Reformed traditions are intertwined. Neither of our world communions is purely Lutheran or Reformed. We value the presence within our membership of United churches, and we affirm that we need to reflect together on the significance of their membership, their special contributions and special needs. We are grateful to the United churches for the conversations which took place at their initiative.

53. Constitutionally, there are no obstacles to the United churches in Germany entering into membership in the two world bodies, and we would see definite value in their doing so. In the meantime, we encourage the two world bodies to involve these churches in as many ways as possible in their ongoing work (for more details, cf. appendix 4).

6. COLLABORATION AT THE LEVEL OF GOVERNING BODIES

54. After years of collaboration at the staff level and in working groups, it is time to involve the governing bodies more directly.

*a)  The LWF council and the WARC executive committee*

55. We propose that the opportunity be created for the LWF council and the WARC executive committee to meet and clarify issues that they both face. Exchanges at this level could in our view help to strengthen and broaden the common witness of the world bodies. They would need to be carefully prepared in common. A first step could be parallel meetings of the WARC executive committee and the LWF council where blocks of time would be reserved for a common agenda. It will not be possible to hold such a parallel meeting before the LWF assembly in 2003 and the WARC general council in 2004. We propose that the LWF and WARC begin now to schedule and prepare such a meeting for 2005 or 2006.

*b.  Common assemblies*

56. The WARC general council in Debrecen (1997) proposed that common assemblies of the WARC and the LWF, together with the WCC, should be explored. This idea has been followed up to a certain extent by an LWF-WCC staff group (1999-2000), in which the WARC was an observer, which presented its report in spring 2000. At the present time, the issue is again being discussed in the new LWF-WARC-WCC staff group (2001-2002) which will present its report in spring 2002. The matter is also being discussed within the LWF and will be an item at the LWF council in 2002. It seems clear that the upcoming assemblies of the three world bodies will all have the same distinct formats as until now. However, there is the possibility that some decisions will be made that could open the way for joint or coordinated assemblies in the future.

57. For the LWF assembly and the WARC general council in 2003 and 2004, similar themes have been chosen, and each world body has welcomed a representative of the other tradition as a member of its assembly planning committee. A longer-term objective is to hold joint or parallel assemblies. A common theme would enable joint preparation of study materials. Preparation of a joint worship book would involve our world bodies in further study of our traditions of worship, a task that we have long considered important. Joint discussion in such world meetings would lead to elements of a common mandate in the period following them.

## 7. A Lutheran-Reformed joint commission

58. This joint working group has had a three-year mandate, and its work now comes to an end. As we look back at Lutheran-Reformed relationships at the world level during the last decades, we realize that there have been several working groups which have made valuable recommendations, but mechanisms to implement these ideas have been lacking and progress has, in consequence, been impeded. We recommend that in order to further the growing relationships between our two families, a joint commission with a more than temporary mandate be created. This commission should have the mandate to monitor the implementation of the decisions taken by the governing bodies regarding the recommendations of this report.

59. The mandate of the Lutheran-Reformed joint commission should be reviewed at regular intervals.

## V. Summary of recommendations

We recommend that the general secretaries of the LWF and the WARC:

1. Take the steps necessary to prepare a declaration of mutual commitment to be presented to the LWF council and the WARC executive committee and thereafter to the LWF assembly and the WARC general council.
2. We recommend that the LWF and the WARC:
   a) encourage and assist churches in regions where Lutheran-Reformed agreements do not yet exist to enter into dialogue with a view to establishing communion;
   b) help in interpreting national and regional Lutheran-Reformed agreements to the whole constituency, so that all may profit from the experience of all in finding ways forward that are contextually appropriate;
   c) examine the implications for their own life and work of these national and regional experiences;
   d) reflect on the specific needs and contributions of United churches within their fellowships; and
   e) explore ways in which the United churches in Germany may be further involved in their work.

3. Establish a joint international study project on structures of church communion with the mandate to reflect on the diversity and complementarity of ecclesiological approaches within our two confessional families, so as to assist Lutheran and Reformed churches as they move towards new forms of communion.

4. Endorse the proposal to develop a common history of the relations between Lutheran and Reformed churches.

5. Identify distinctive areas of Lutheran-Reformed joint study and action on which they may work together; and cooperate closely within the World Council of Churches on their common ecumenical agenda.

6. Prepare the next LWF assembly (Winnipeg, 2003) and WARC general council (Accra, 2004) in ways that encourage the formation of a mandate for common Lutheran-Reformed work in the period that follows.

7. Schedule parallel meetings of the LWF council and the WARC executive committee in 2005 or 2006, with careful joint preparation beforehand.

8. Make possible holding the following assembly and general council at the same time and in the same place, with common preparation and the greatest possible degree of common programme.

9. Create a joint commission with a mandate to monitor the implementation of the decisions taken by their governing bodies regarding the recommendations of this report.

## Members of the Lutheran-Reformed joint working group

*Lutheran members*

Rt Rev. Guy Edmiston, Co-chair, Bishop Emeritus of the Lower Susquehanna Synod, Evangelical Lutheran Church in America
Rev. Fui-Yung Chong, Basel Christian Church of Malaysia
Prof. Dr Luis Henrique Dreher, Evangelical Church of the Lutheran Confession in Brazil
Superintendent Dieter Lorenz, Church of Lippe [Lutheran Section], Germany

Consultant
Prof. Dr André Birmelé, Institute for Ecumenical Research, Strasbourg, France

Staff
Rev. Sven Oppegaard, Lutheran World Federation, Geneva, Switzerland

*Reformed members*

Prof. Dr Jane Dempsey Douglass, Co-chair, USA
Dr Karel Phil Erari, West Papua, Indonesia
Dr Hermann Schaefer, Germany

Consultant
Dr Lukas Vischer, Geneva, Switzerland

Staff

Rev. Dr Odair Pedroso Mateus, World Alliance of Reformed Churches, Geneva, Switzerland

Rev. Páraic Réamonn, World Alliance of Reformed Churches, Geneva, Switzerland

## Appendix 1: Ecumenical Consultation on Indulgences

For the first time since the Reformation, Catholics, Lutherans and Reformed held an ecumenical theological consultation on the theme of indulgences. The meeting, involving the Pontifical Council for Promoting Christian Unity (PCPCU) the Lutheran World Federation (LWF) and the World Alliance of Reformed Churches (WARC), took place in Rome, 9 and 10 February 2001, upon invitation by the PCPCU.

The purpose was to clarify historical, theological and pastoral issues related to indulgences in order to come to a better understanding of each other's traditions. It did not aim at an agreement on indulgences – an issue on which there have been long-standing differences between the Roman Catholic Church and the churches of the Reformation.

The consultation took place in a positive atmosphere which lent itself to honest and constructive discussion. There were common prayers at the beginning of each day and at the end of the consultation. Two presentations described the Roman Catholic understanding of indulgences. Prof. Gerhard L. Mueller (Munich, Germany), addressed the "Historical Aspects of the Indulgence". Prof. Jared Wicks, SJ (Rome, Italy), gave a systematic presentation entitled "Towards Understanding Indulgences: Vetera et Nova". On the Lutheran and Reformed side the following responses were given: Prof. Michael Root, Lutheran (Columbus OH, USA), gave an analysis of "The Jubilee Indulgence and the Joint Declaration on the Doctrine of Justification". Prof. Ellen Babinsky, Reformed (Austin TX, USA), presented "A Reformed View of Indulgences". Prof. Theodor Dieter, Lutheran (Strasbourg, France), gave a response to Prof. Mueller's paper. Prof. George Sabra, Reformed (Beirut, Lebanon), responded to Prof. Wicks's paper.

Bishop Walter Kasper, secretary of the PCPCU, Rev. Dr Ishmael Noko, general secretary of the LWF, and Rev. Dr Setri Nyomi, general secretary of the WARC, each took turns chairing the meeting. His Eminence Edward Idris Cardinal Cassidy, president of the PCPCU, took part in several sessions of the consultation.

Other participants included, on the Catholic side, Prof. Barbara Hallensleben (Fribourg, Switzerland), Prof. John M. McDermott, SJ (Columbus OH, USA), Msgr John Radano and Rev. Matthias Türk (PCPCU staff, Rome, Italy); on the Lutheran side Archbishop K.G. Hammar (Uppsala, Sweden), Dr Pirjo Työrinoja (Helsinki, Finland) and Rev. Sven Oppegaard (LWF staff, Geneva, Switzerland); on the Reformed side Dr Alan Falconer (Geneva, Switzerland), Dr Fulvio Ferrario (Milan, Italy) and Dr Odair Pedroso Mateus (WARC staff, Geneva, Switzerland).

It is intended that the papers from this consultation will be published as a contribution to further discussion in the churches.

Rome, 10 February 2001

## Appendix 2:   United Churches in Their Relationship to the LWF and the WARC

Representatives of Lutheran, Reformed and United churches combining both traditions came together in Geneva 11-14 October 2001, in the first week of the war against Afghanistan. The air raids on that country, already devastated by twenty years of conflict, together with the criminal attacks in the USA which prompted them, brought home to us the importance of our working together, as churches of the Reformation, in witnessing to the gospel and serving a broken world.

We met at the invitation of the general secretaries of the Lutheran World Federation (LWF) and the World Alliance of Reformed Churches (WARC). Our group of almost thirty people from many regions of the world included invited representatives of United churches in Germany, the Czech Republic, Madagascar, the Netherlands and Zambia (see "the experience of United churches" below.)

We have shared information, experience and ecumenical passion; clarified misunderstandings; and explored together the significance of United and Uniting churches in our two fellowships and how the United churches in Germany might appropriately relate to them. Recent developments at all levels have created a new context for our discussions and have led to a new desire for common witness and practical collaboration.

Approximately fifty United or Uniting churches cross the boundaries of the existing Christian world communions; of this fifty, almost half combine Lutheran and Reformed traditions. Some are members of the LWF or the WARC, others are members of both (the Church of Lippe, the Ethiopian Evangelical Church Mekane Yesus, and the Evangelical Church of the River Plate). At its meeting in Bangalore in 2000, hosted by the Karnataka central diocese of the Church of South India, itself a United church combining Reformed and other traditions, the WARC executive committee "strongly affirmed" the participation of United and Uniting churches in the Alliance.

THE EXPERIENCE OF THE UNITED CHURCHES REPRESENTED

*Germany*

These churches combine Lutheran and Reformed traditions. Some belong to the Evangelical Church of the Union, all of them to the Arnoldshain conference. They go back to a movement to unite the different confessions of the Reformation at the beginning of the 19th century. They have kept a clear constitutional relationship to the historic Lutheran and Reformed confessions, and are keenly interested in how their confession is to be actualized today. Therefore the theological declaration of Barmen (1934) plays an important role in their life. Of the 24 regional churches (Landeskirchen) in Germany, 12 are United.

Like other United and Uniting churches, they participate enthusiastically in the ecumenical movement. At the international level, they have traditionally expressed their ecumenical commitment through the World Council of Churches and the group of United and Uniting churches, which meets in consultation from time to time.

In recent years, the United churches in Germany have turned their attention to their relationship to the LWF and WARC:

a) At the international level, the German United churches express the desire for a platform on which they may meet their partner churches, most of whom already belong to the LWF and WARC.

b) Recent developments, such as the Joint Declaration on the Doctrine of Justification, raise the question of how churches that share a common heritage in the Reformation and its teachings can speak with a common voice on matters that concern them all.

*Czech Republic*

The Evangelical Church of Czech Brethren traces its origins to reforming movements in the 14th and 15th centuries and above all to the struggle of Jan Hus (1370-1415). An important development was the creation in 1457 of the Unitas Fratrum (the unity of the brethren).

In 1620, the Protestant faith was proscribed throughout the Austro-Hungarian empire. By 1781, when Joseph II issued an edict of toleration, only 100,000 Protestants remained in the Czech lands. They were not allowed to organize themselves in continuity with their indigenous Czech tradition, but were obliged to register as either Lutheran or Reformed.

Following the first world war, the state of Czechoslovakia was created and the larger Reformed and the smaller Lutheran church decided to reject their artificial separation and recover their authentic history by uniting as the Evangelical Church of Czech Brethren. This church has played a leading role in the discussions on the "first" and "second" Reformations and in developing a wider understanding of what it means to be Reformed.

*Madagascar*

The Church of Jesus Christ in Madagascar was formed in 1968 during the celebration of the 150th anniversary of the arrival of Protestant missions: it is a union of three strands (the Church of Christ in Madagascar, which grew out of the work of the London Missionary Society; the Evangelical Church in Madagascar, the result of French missionary efforts; and the Malagasy Friends' Church, created by Quaker mission).

In 1980, it founded the National Council of Christian Churches in Madagascar, together with the Lutheran, Anglican and Roman Catholic churches: a particular concern was to unify Christian language and to agree on a common Malagasy version of the name of Jesus Christ: Jesoa Kristy. The church is active in the fields of evangelism, education and development. In 1991, it played an active role in the fall of the second republic and in developing the constitution of the third republic.

The small Malagasy Protestant Church (FPMA) in France, which was set up by students in 1959, has dual membership in the LWF and WARC.

*Netherlands*

In 1973, the two largest Reformed churches – the Netherlands Reformed Church and the Reformed Churches in the Netherlands – held their first joint synod. Later they joined with the Evangelical-Lutheran Church in the Kingdom of the Netherlands in a tripartite project of union, *Samen op weg* (Together on the way). This project heightened the awareness in the churches of their historical and confessional roots; at the same time, it made it clear that confessional loyalty did not require them to remain separate. A union scheme was adopted in 1997, and the three churches are already united administratively.

*Zambia*

The United Church of Zambia, with a million members, is the largest Protestant church in Zambia. In 1965, less than three months after independence, it brought together into a single union four Reformed and Methodist churches: the Church of Central Africa in Rhodesia (itself a union of the Church of Scotland and the London Missionary Society churches with the Union Church of the Copperbelt), the congregations of the Copperbelt Free Church Council, the Church of Barotseland, and the Methodist Church.

The UCZ sees itself as showing that unity in diversity is possible and fulfilling in a small way the prayer of Jesus in John 17. But it also understands itself contextually: it is proud of its contribution in the struggle for independence in southern Africa and in building a peaceful nation out of a diverse tribal society. "We are called to be one Zambia, one church." Evangelization remains the main goal of the church.

THE LWF AND THE WARC

Cooperation between the two world communions goes back as far as the 1950s and springs from the recognition that, although they are separate organizations, they have much in common. It has had an erratic history, as we must admit, but in the last decade it has been greatly intensified.

The 1989 report of the joint commission of the LWF and the WARC, *Toward Church Fellowship*, concluded that "nothing stands in the way of church fellowship" between churches of the Lutheran and Reformed traditions. It called on member churches of both organizations to establish full pulpit and table fellowship and to grow in unity through new steps in church life and mission together. At the international level, it called on the LWF and WARC to work together wherever possible.

From 1993, the LWF and the WARC began to collaborate in different programmes. A further impetus came from the 25th anniversary of the Leuenberg agreement and the new formula of agreement between one Lutheran and three Reformed churches in the USA. In March 1999, senior staff of the two organizations began to meet at regular six-monthly intervals to deepen their cooperation.

A joint working group was appointed by the general secretary of the LWF and the executive committee of the Alliance with a three-year mandate (1999-2001) to review Lutheran-Reformed relations on the regional and international levels. The group has focused on taking forward the positive results of previous dialogues. It sees its task as accompanying and promoting the implementation of their recommendations, furthering and making visible the growing communion among member churches, and calling for specific initiatives of cooperation between the two international bodies.

In this consultation, we were pleased to learn of the extent to which the LWF and the WARC are already cooperating and of their vision of their life together in the years immediately to come.

In addition to the senior staff meetings mentioned above, the general secretaries of the two organizations meet regularly in the Ecumenical Centre. There is reciprocal involvement in work on mission. The two bodies are co-sponsors of the "Prague" dialogue on the "first" and "second" Reformations. The WARC will share in discussions, initiated by the LWF and the Vatican, on the follow-up to the Joint Declaration on the Doctrine of Justification. The LWF programme on church structures in times of global transformation has become a common project. The WARC process on economic injustice and ecological destruction has attracted regular LWF involvement; inversely, the WARC has been involved in the emerging LWF programme in this area. A WARC study on the theological imperatives for human rights has widened to embrace the LWF. The two bodies have worked together on peace and conflict-resolution in Africa. The LWF and and WARC are founding sponsors of the ecumenical news agency *Ecumenical News International*. There are regular joint discussions and coordination in relation to the United Nations and human rights. The two organizations have long worked together in the area of partnership of women and men and are cooperating in developing a gender training manual. The list is growing, and reflects a growing conviction that it is better to do things together and that, when they are done together, they are done better – a conviction that springs from the common sense that, despite their obvious differences in history and profile, the LWF and the WARC have in common that they are fellowships of churches of the Reformation.

The two organizations are coordinating their preparations for the LWF general assembly in 2003 and the WARC general council in 2004, and envisage a joint meeting of the LWF council and the WARC executive committee in 2005 or 2006. The WARC already in 1997 envisaged a joint meeting, or parallel meetings, of the two supreme governing bodies; it proved impossible to realize this vision immediately, but proposals on this point will be brought for decision to the two meetings in 2003 and 2004.

In all these ways, the commitment of the LWF and WARC to be together and to work together deepens and intensifies.

The United churches in Germany have a strong desire to find appropriate ways to share in this common life and work. Both fellowships understand and welcome this desire.

Both communions make provision for membership by United churches and many United churches have been welcomed into membership of one or other or both. For both fellowships, the presence in these churches is a living reminder of what they already know: that their relationship to the confessional heritage is complex and that confessional loyalty is not to be confused with confessionalism.

WE ARE ALL HEIRS OF THE REFORMATION

Our self-understandings as Lutheran, United or Reformed make us ecumenical and exclude all sectarianism. We find our identity in the gospel of Jesus Christ proclaimed by the universal church.

Within this one worldwide church, we recognize the Lutheran, Reformed and United churches combining both traditions as a natural grouping, with a common heritage in the Reformation of the 16th century. Because of that heritage, this group of churches is often referred to as churches of the Reformation (*Reformatorische Kirchen*): the term is not exclusive, since there are other churches that also claim a link to the Reformation.

We do not privilege this grouping over others: in the ecumenical house, there are many mansions, and all of us are bound in wider sets of ecumenical relationships. But as churches of the Reformation we affirm that we can and should face the future together. Around this table, in all our difference and distinctiveness, we recognize ourselves in one other. We belong together.

We echo the words of *Toward Church Fellowship* (§78):

> We believe that unity, diversity and harmony are all God's gifts to the church. Therefore diversity must not obscure unity, nor concern for unity deny diversity. Together we serve one Lord, through whom alone we have access by the one Spirit to the Father.

ACTUALIZING OUR CONFESSION

We value our confessional heritages, but we are not imprisoned by them. Our confessional traditions are precious resources as we study the scriptures and strive to interpret the will of God for our times. To us, as in every Christian generation, Jesus of Nazareth poses the question, "Who do you say that I am?" As we seek to answer responsibly, we actualize our confession.

In recent times, we have seen examples of this actualizing in the theological declaration of Barmen; the debates over weapons of mass destruction; the struggle against apartheid reflected in the *status confessionis* declarations of the two communions and in the confession of Belhar; the question of the church and the Jewish people; the conciliar process on justice, peace and the integrity of creation; the campaigns for the cancellation of international debt; and the current programmes on economic justice and ecological destruction. These efforts, in which we have all shared, mark our common desire to witness to a timeless Saviour: a Christ who speaks to the world yesterday, today and tomorrow.

THE WAY FORWARD

What can be done to deepen understanding between churches of the Reformation, to dispel old prejudices, and to respond together in concrete witness and action to the challenges of God's world? Specifically, what steps can be taken at the international level and how can the United churches in Germany be involved?

We discussed this question in three aspects:

*1. Engagement of the German United churches*

We can envisage many ways in which the German United churches could share in the work of the LWF and WARC, for example:

a)  reception of and response to dialogue results and other completed work;

b)  participation in programmes, dialogues or projects;

c)  observer or consultant status in consultations or meetings of governing bodies.

The LWF and the WARC are open to such possibilities. They would warmly welcome, for example, involvement by the United churches in ongoing work on economic globalization.

*2. Structures of cooperation*

The current Lutheran-Reformed joint working group has a time-limited mandate, but a joint commission to further cooperation and deepen relationships between the two world bodies may well be needed for the longer term. This commission, supported by the necessary staff, should also further relations with the United churches. During our brainstorming, some participants raised the question of whether a common desk would be helpful towards these goals.

*3. Membership in the world bodies*

It would be possible for some or all of the German United churches to enter into membership of one or both Christian world communions. It was suggested that such membership, especially if it were dual membership, would help in shaping from within the future of the two bodies. It was also suggested that the question may be premature: the German United churches are currently engaged in a fundamental restructuring of their own relationships, in which it is likely that the Arnoldshain conference and the Evangelical Church of the Union will be replaced by a single but open structure. It may be that the question of membership in the two Christian world communions would be best raised in the course of that restructuring or when it is complete.

Our conversations here in Geneva will be taken up, on the side of the two world bodies, by the Lutheran-Reformed joint working group, which will report to the WARC executive committee and through the general secretary of the LWF to its council; and on the side of the German United churches, within the Arnoldshain conference and the Evangelical Church of the Union. The reorganization of the United churches in Germany and the meetings of the LWF general assembly in 2003 and the WARC general council in 2004 provide a larger time-frame for our discussions.

None of us came to this consultation with a blueprint for our future life together. We go away knowing that we have not yet arrived at complete clarity on the way forward; but we are clear that this way must be a common way. We shall stay together. We walk by faith, and we find our way in small and fumbling steps; but we put our trust in the leading of the Holy Spirit.

We commend these reflections to the Lutheran-Reformed joint working group and the governing bodies of the two Christian world communions, and to the leading bodies of the Arnoldshain conference and the Evangelical Church of the Union and their member churches.

### Appendix 3:  Unity in Faith

THE JOINT DECLARATION ON THE DOCTRINE OF JUSTIFICATION
IN A WIDER ECUMENICAL CONTEXT – REPORT

Columbus, Ohio, 27-30 November 2001

In 1999, the Lutheran World Federation and the Roman Catholic Church signed the Joint Declaration on the Doctrine of Justification (JDDJ). Such an agreement was bound to have repercussions for all the churches which have been in dialogue with the signatory churches. In the case of Methodists and Reformed, these dialogues have included the very subject of justification and the results encourage an exploration of ways in which the joint declaration might be more widely affirmed. To begin this process, a consultation was held in Columbus, Ohio, 27-30 November 2001, with the participation of theologians and some church leaders from the Roman Catholic Church, the Lutheran World Federation, the World Methodist Council and the World Alliance of Reformed Churches.

The consultation identified theological and procedural issues involved in the possible association of the Methodist and Reformed families of churches with the joint declaration. The importance of doctrinal agreements for the development of official church relations was recognized especially for those churches that have been involved in church-dividing doctrinal condemnations.

It was agreed to propose that the consultative process be continued. Given the different characters of the World Alliance of Reformed Churches and the World Methodist Council, two distinct but inter-related processes are proposed to the four partners:

1. In light of the appreciation already formally expressed by the executive committee of the World Methodist Council in favour of the JDDJ, the Methodist understanding of justification and its relationship to the JDDJ should be theologically explained and substantiated. To facilitate this, a small commission should be established representing the WMC, the LWF and the PCPCU. In this commission, the Methodist understanding of and relationship to the agreements reached in the JDDJ would be discussed with a view to producing an official text that the WMC might, in accordance with its own procedures, present to the LWF and the Roman Catholic Church for possible endorsement by these two parties. It would be appropriate that an observer from the WARC participate in this process.

2. In light of the strong commitment of the Reformed tradition since the Reformation to the doctrine of justification and its connections with individual and social life, the Reformed participants would be agreeable to the establishment of a quadrilateral study commission, wherein their perspective could contribute to the understanding

of the doctrine of justification. For Methodists, such a commission would be a welcome opportunity to process some of the wider issues relevant to justification. For Lutherans and Roman Catholics such a commission could be one way in which to pursue further, and ecumenically, some of the issues that are identified in JDDJ 43 and the official common statement. It would be appropriate to invite the Faith and Order commission of the World Council of Churches to be represented with an advisory status in such a commission. As part of the commission's work, the Reformed participants would continue to explore the question of whether and how they might express support for the agreements set forth in the JDDJ. Any recommendations agreed by these participants would be discussed in the commission and forwarded to the WARC executive committee for consideration.

It is the conviction of us all that the attainment of agreement in the doctrine of justification is an important step forward towards the goal of church unity and necessary for the credibility of our common witness before the world.

Columbus, 30 November 2001

## Appendix 4:
## The Wider Context of Lutheran and Reformed Interconfessional Dialogues

The following overview does not include Lutheran-Reformed dialogues and agreements at international, regional and national levels, nor those cases (Meissen, Reuilly, Churches Uniting in Christ) in which Lutherans and Reformed have together entered into dialogues and agreements with others, since these are described extensively in the report itself.

A. INTERNATIONAL[5]

*1. African Instituted dialogue*

Dialogue between the WARC and the Organization of African Instituted Churches began in 1998 and will conclude in 2002. The 1999 Kigali statement identified historical, cultural and ecclesial challenges facing Christian churches in Africa and proposed concrete responses.

*2. Anglican dialogue*

The LWF began dialogue with the Anglican Communion in 1970, WARC in 1978: several reports have been published. The Anglican-Reformed dialogue report, "God's Reign and Our Unity" (1984), is noteworthy for describing the unity and mission of the church within the perspective of the kingdom of God. An Anglican-Lutheran international working group began work in 2000 on various aspects of Anglican-Lutheran relations today and is expected to report in summer 2002.

### 3. Baptist conversations and dialogue

WARC began dialogue with the Baptist World Alliance in 1974, reporting in 1977. Mutual challenges and warnings were issued within the context of common rejoicing "in our membership of the one church of Jesus Christ". Conversations between the Baptist World Alliance and the LWF took place between 1986 and 1989 and addressed, among other matters, Lutheran condemnations of the Anabaptists in the 16th century.

### 4. Churches of Christ (Disciples)

The WARC engaged in dialogue with the Disciples' Ecumenical Consultative Council from 1984 to 1987. The dialogue report called on churches in the two traditions, which are historically close, to say whether or not they could accept the declaration that "the Disciples of Christ recognize and accept each other as visible expressions of the one church of Christ"; acceptance of this declaration "presses us beyond our divided histories towards a common ecumenical future".

### 5. Mennonite dialogue

The WARC entered into dialogue with the Mennonite World Conference in 1984. The 1986 report addresses the condemnation of the Anabaptists in Reformed confessional documents and calls for dialogue at the local level.

### 6. Methodist dialogue

Dialogue between the LWF and the World Methodist Council (1977-84) resulted in the 1984 report, "The Church, Community of Grace", recommending steps towards closer fellowship between Lutheran and Methodist churches. Dialogue between the WARC and the World Methodist Council (1985-87) attempted a joint statement of faith and concluded that the classic doctrinal differences were not impediments to unity; the dialogue report asked member churches to consider the implications of this observation.

### 7. Oriental Orthodox dialogue

Dialogue between the WARC and the Oriental Orthodox churches (1992-2001) led to an agreed statement on Christology (1994) and a final report identifying convergences and divergences on a range of theological issues.

### 8. Orthodox dialogue

Dialogue between the LWF and the Orthodox church from 1981 led to joint statements on divine revelation, scripture and Tradition, and the canon and inspiration of holy scripture; in 1999, a new phase of this dialogue was begun on word and sacraments (*mysteria*) in the life of the church. Dialogue between the WARC and the Orthodox from 1988 resulted in agreed statements on the Trinity (1992) and Christology (1994); currently under discussion are aspects of the church.

## 9. Pentecostal dialogue

WARC-Pentecostal dialogue (1996-2001) focused on spirituality and contemporary challenges, the role of the Bible in both families, the role of the Holy Spirit in proclamation and praxis, and the key issue of charismata.

## 10. Prague consultations

These multilateral conversations seek a more inclusive understanding of the Reformation movement. They began in 1986 in Prague and initially involved only churches or movements with roots in the "first" or radical Reformations: Brethren, Czech Brethren, Hussites, Hutterian Brethren, Mennonites, Moravians, Quakers and Waldensians. From 1994, the meetings moved to Geneva and then Strasbourg and were organized by the WARC, the LWF and the Mennonite World Conference; they were also attended by Baptists, Methodists and a representative of the Pontifical Council for Promoting Christian Unity.

## 11. Roman Catholic

The LWF began dialogue with the Roman Catholic Church in 1965, the WARC in 1970. The Reformed-Roman Catholic dialogue report, "Towards a Common Understanding of the Church" (1990), called for a "reconciliation of memories"; dialogue continues on the topic of church and kingdom. In the Joint Declaration on the Doctrine of Justification (1999), the LWF and the Roman Catholic Church established a differentiated consensus in basic truths regarding justification and declared that the mutual condemnations from the time of the Reformation do not apply to the teaching presented in the declaration.

## 12. Seventh-day Adventist conversations and dialogue

The report of Adventist-Lutheran conversations (1994-98) deals with justification by faith, scripture and authority in the church, and eschatology, and presents several recommendations to the churches on both sides. A dialogue between the WARC and the Seventh-day Adventist church in 2001 noted that "the Reformed and the Adventists have frequently misunderstood one another"; it focused on challenges to Christian mission today, particularly economic injustice, environmental destruction, HIV/AIDS, prejudice in many forms, and violence against women and children.

### B. NATIONAL OR REGIONAL

At national or regional levels, dialogue involving Lutherans and/or Reformed has resulted in binding forms of church communion, for example:
- in Canada, the Waterloo agreement (2000) is a communion agreement between the Anglican Church of Canada and the Evangelical Lutheran Church in Canada;

– the Porvoo common statement (1996) is a communion agreement between Nordic and Baltic Lutheran churches and the Anglican churches of Britain and Ireland;
– formal declarations of communion have been made between the Methodists and the Evangelical Church in Germany (EKD), the Church of Norway and the Church of Sweden;
– in Italy, Waldensians and Methodists are practically united in one church, the Waldensian Evangelical Church; they have also reached agreement with the Italian Baptists on mutual recognition of baptism;
– in the USA, "Following Our Shepherd to Full Communion" (1999) is a communion agreement between the Evangelical Lutheran Church in America (ELCA) and the Moravian Church in America; and "Called to Common Mission" (2000) is a communion agreement between the ELCA and the Episcopal Church, USA.

NOTES

[1]   *Toward Church Fellowship*, report of the joint commission of the LWF and WARC, Geneva, 1990; *Auf dem Weg zur Kirchengemeinschaft*, Bericht der Gemeinsamen Kommission des LWB und des RWB, Genf, 1990.

[2]   In its 1990 report the joint commission of the LWF and WARC gave a detailed survey of the state of relationships at that time, cf. *Toward Church Fellowship*, §§ 27-50.

[3]   These are: the Methodist Church (Central Conference, Germany); the Methodist Church (Central Conference Central and Southern Europe), the Methodist Church (Central Conference, Northern Europe), the Methodist Church in Great Britain, and the Methodist Church in Ireland.

[4]   The Church of North India and the Church of South India are both United churches with Reformed roots and both are members of the WARC.

[5]   The dialogues are listed alphabetically by dialogue partner. Most of the dialogue reports are to be found in *Growth in Agreement I* and *Growth in Agreement II*.

# 38. Word and Spirit, Church and World
## International Pentecostal-Reformed Dialogue 1996-2000

### Sao Paulo, Brazil, 2000

## Introduction

This is a report from the participants of an international dialogue (1996-2000) between the World Alliance of Reformed Churches (WARC) and leaders from some classical Pentecostal churches. It had its beginnings in the 22nd WARC general council (Seoul, 1989), which proposed exploration of the possibility of organizing an international dialogue with Pentecostal churches. This was made possible through the contacts made in 1993 between the general secretary of the World Alliance of Reformed Churches, Milan Opocensky, and professor of church history and ecumenics at Fuller Theological Seminary, Cecil M. Robeck, Jr, a Pentecostal minister. Over the next two years, they exchanged correspondence and talked with one another about the possibility that such a dialogue might be held. They attempted to discern both the need for such a conversation, and the potential outcomes that might result. Finally, they agreed to bring together a small group of scholars who could explore the potential for such a dialogue with them.

In 1995, Dr Opocensky received encouragement from the WARC executive committee to pursue an exploratory meeting with the Pentecostals. Dr Opocensky appointed Dr Henry Wilson of the WARC staff to facilitate the discussion from the WARC side. Dr Robeck acted in that capacity for the Pentecostals. They convened a small exploratory committee at Mattersey Hall in Mattersey, England, from 8 to 9 July 1995.[1] The committee determined that a dialogue between WARC and Pentecostals might serve several useful purposes. They noted that those who are disciples of Jesus Christ are all members of the one church. They were concerned, however, that this reality receive attention not merely at an abstract theological or ideological level, but also at the practical level where the churches of the Reformed tradition and the churches of the Pentecostal movement touch the lives of one another directly.

The committee noted that in many places around the world, members of the Pentecostal and Reformed communities are uncomfortable with one another. Sometimes they are openly antagonistic towards one another. In a few places such as South Korea, Brazil and South Africa, tensions between the Reformed and Pentecostal communities were clearly evident and often painful for both parties. The committee was concerned that there was no identifiable, formal way for these communities to relate to each other. These facts seemed to indicate that conversation between the various parties involved was not only advisable, it was essential.

The exploratory committee believed that some of these tensions were the result of the state of ignorance that these communities often manifested towards one another. Other tensions seemed to emerge as a direct result of honest theological disagreement. Some of these issues were rooted deeply in the history of one group or the other, while other issues were the result of more recent claims. Still other tensions could be attributed to certain contemporary practices in which one group or the other was engaged. In some places in the world these practices yielded public charges of unfair competition, proselytism, fanaticism or dead religion. The committee believed that this state of affairs was not only unhealthy for Christians to endure, but that it communicated the wrong message to the world. If the gospel of reconciliation seemed to lack the power necessary to help Christians to resolve differences between themselves, how could it be trusted to bring reconciliation between human beings and their God?

As a result of these considerations, the committee concluded that an international dialogue between representatives of these traditions would go far to help both groups gain a greater understanding of one another, to explore their common concerns, and to confront their differences. They established three limited goals by which the dialogue could begin. First, they hoped that such a dialogue would increase mutual understanding and respect between the churches of the Reformed and Pentecostal traditions. Second, they asked that the dialogue seek ways to identify areas of theological agreement, disagreement and convergence so that both communities might be mutually strengthened. Third, they suggested that those who would engage in the dialogue would help these two communities by exploring various possibilities for common witness. They also hoped that by entering into the life of these local communities the dialogue might be an encouragement to Christians who were embattled, or who were looking for new ways to validate their message of reconciliation before the world.

The next step was more difficult. Since members of the Pentecostal community and members of the Reformed community did not already have close relations, the exploratory committee looked for ways by which to enter such a dialogue. There is no international Pentecostal group that is equivalent to the World Alliance of Reformed Churches. Thus, there was no formal organizational source willing or able to provide support or direction for the Pentecostal participants. While this fact held the potential for some imbalance in the process, the committee believed that it was better to begin the conversation than not. This would be a new experience for many of the participants. The committee struggled with what topics should be addressed and with what methodologies of exploration they would recommend.

The committee recommended that the dialogue begin with a tentative discussion of contemporary understandings of spirituality as it is viewed and practised in these respective communities. To aid the dialogue in understanding spirituality, not only theologically but also as experienced practically, the committee recommended that the dialogue be hosted in alternate years by each of the traditions. They further recommended that the dialogue include, as part of its ongoing life, opportunities for worship in each of the traditions. It was agreed that the members of the subsequent dialogue teams would engage in acts of common prayer and Bible study on a daily basis, but further, that they would enter into the parish life of the local community of the team that acted as host. This tradition of common worship and witness has proven to be one of the most significant tools for helping both teams understand one another.

The first official meeting of the international Reformed-Pentecostal dialogue was finally convened in Torre Pellice, Italy, from 15 to 20 May 1996. The Waldensian Church served as the dialogue's host. Abival Pires da Silveira and Cecil M. Robeck, Jr, were asked to serve as co-chairs. The dialogue included delegates from the Pentecostal and Reformed traditions who literally came from throughout the world. The theme for the opening discussion was "Spirituality and the Challenges of Today". Papers were offered by members of both teams in the following three areas: "Spirituality and interpretation of scripture", "Spirituality and justice" and "Spirituality and ecumenism".[2] Each of these papers provided insight into the similarities and differences between the traditions, but as the members of the dialogue felt their way into the lives of each other, they began to recognize two things. First, it was too much to ask for the members of the dialogue to do justice to all the material that was presented in these papers in the time allotted. Second, various members of the teams lacked an adequate understanding of the other tradition, and therefore often lacked a language by which the two could communicate. They decided that they would seek fewer papers at their next meeting and spend more time exploring the ideas that were presented.

The dialogue held its second meeting in Chicago, Illinois, USA, from 11 to 15 May 1997. While the Pentecostal team hosted this meeting, McCormick Theological Seminary provided the facilities. The theme was "The Role and Place of the Holy Spirit in the Church". Three papers were presented at this meeting. One was presented on "The relation of the Holy Spirit to the Bible"; the other two explored the role of the Holy Spirit in proclamation and the place of charismatic manifestations within the church.[3] While both groups found commonality in God's revelation of Jesus Christ as scripture bore witness to it, they struggled to understand the implications of ongoing revelation for faith and practice. They recognized the sovereign role of the Spirit in the bestowal of gifts upon the faith community as it seeks to address the diverse needs that arise in the church, society and the world. Both teams began to note that they had much in common, but they took note of the fact that they differed on some important issues as well. While the number of papers they had solicited for this round of discussions was half that solicited during the first round, they concluded that they needed to solicit even fewer papers for the third round.

The dialogue seemed to find its rhythm when it met in Kappel-am-Albis, Switzerland, from 14 to 19 May 1998. It provided a unique opportunity for participants to hear from Prof. Walter J. Hollenweger, a former Pentecostal pastor of the Swiss Pentecostal Mission, now a minister in the Swiss Reformed Church, and to meet with the host of the dialogue, president of the cantonal Reformed Church of Zürich, Rev. Ruedi Reich. In the absence of Rev. Abival Pires da Silveira, Rev. Salvatore Ricciardi acted as the Reformed co-chair for this session. The dialogue studied two papers on a single topic, one from each team. The topic was "The Holy Spirit and Mission in Eschatological Perspective".[4]

It became apparent within that context that the dialogue would be significantly aided if there were greater continuity of the members of the dialogue through the years. While those providing leadership to the dialogue had hoped to include people for whom an international encounter would be an experience of personal growth, the lack of understanding of global Christianity by some participants continued to be a handicap to the project. Similarly, it had been hoped that the dialogue would be composed of people at a variety of educational levels from within the respective traditions. This also proved to be a handicap in the sense that the group continued to lack a common language and methodology by which to pursue their assigned tasks. At the close of this third session, then, the leaders determined to bring teams to the table that embodied greater parity.

From 14 to 20 May 1999, the dialogue discussed "The Holy Spirit, Charisma, and the Kingdom of God" in Seoul, Korea.[5] The Rev. David Yonggi Cho and Yoido Full Gospel Church served as the hosts of the dialogue this year. From this point on, the members of the dialogue felt that the teams that could best facilitate their common task were finally in place. Furthermore, the venue provided members of the dialogue with a first-hand opportunity to observe members from both the Reformed and Pentecostal communities where tensions were known to exist. While the primary discussion at the table focused on the topic at hand, what took place at the times of common worship, in the visits to local churches, and at other specified times proved to be significant to the hopes expressed by the exploratory committee. Local guests from both communities were invited to sit in and observe some of the discussions. At times, members of the local Christian press as well as the secular press were invited to observe particular sessions. On several occasions, members of the dialogue offered press interviews that allowed them opportunity to talk about the hopes of the dialogue and address some of the concerns that were present in the Presbyterian and Pentecostal communities in Seoul. These limited encounters proved to be highly successful in building bridges between the communities at that time.

The first five-year round of discussions between WARC and Pentecostals concluded with a meeting in São Paulo, Brazil, from 20 to 24 May 2000. The Independent Presbyterian Church of Brazil and the First Independent Presbyterian Church of São Paulo jointly hosted the dialogue. During this session, Milan Opocensky served as chair for the Reformed team. The papers that had been presented in each of the previous four years, agreed accounts from these meetings, and a working draft that was largely derived from these accounts became the materials from which members of both teams drew while preparing this report. Work was undertaken in plenary sessions and in four groups, each working on one of the four major sections of the body of this report. Specialists were invited to work on the language of the text and to provide the introduction. One day was taken for the two traditions to meet in caucus in order to clarify their concerns. In the end, the report was submitted to the plenary for final approval.

This process, upon which both teams agreed, allowed for the recognition of new insights and information that could only be seen at the end of the discussion. Each year had a way of providing parts to the total discussion, but they begged for integration. The members of both teams, therefore, believe that the following statements fairly represent not only their personal concerns, but the concerns of those they sought to represent in this ongoing discussion.

## I. Spirit and word

*The Spirit and the word in the context of the Trinity*

Together, the members of the Pentecostal and the Reformed teams agree that we stand in communion with the Nicene-Constantinopolitan Creed in our belief that the Holy Spirit is the Lord and Giver of life and, together with the Father and the Son, is to be worshipped and glorified. We also believe that the Father and the Son and the Spirit send the church into the world. We regard the older conception of the contrast between the Reformed and Pentecostal families as consisting of a difference in emphasis between the word (Reformed) and the Spirit (Pentecostal) to be in need of correction. Both the Reformed and Pentecostal traditions consider Jesus Christ to be the criterion for the work of the Holy Spirit.

Pentecostals are aware that some have viewed the Pentecostal movement as overly concerned with the Holy Spirit. Though Pentecostals draw attention to the work of the Spirit, they do not generally detach this work from a trinitarian understanding of God's activity. Pentecostals, in general, tend to agree together that God's work and our worshipful response have a certain trinitarian structure (involving the Father through the Son in the power of the Spirit). Most Pentecostals accept a trinitarian understanding of the Godhead, although a wing of the Pentecostal movement affirms only the oneness of God.[6] If there is a centre to the Pentecostal message, it is the person and work of Jesus Christ. From the beginning of the Pentecostal movement, its central message has referred to Jesus Christ as Saviour, Sanctifier, Spirit Baptizer, Healer, and Coming King. In fact, Pentecostal practice strives to conform to the biblical injunction that the yardstick of Christ must judge those things ascribed to the Holy Spirit.

In the context of the Holy Trinity, Reformed churches have affirmed the christological criterion for the Spirit's work but they have also paid special attention to the work of the triune God in creation. The world is a good work of the triune God who called it into existence through the Word by the Spirit and continues to sustain it. In spite of sin and rebellion, the earth remains the "theatre of the glory of God". There is, as a consequence of this focus on the earth giving glory to God its Creator, an openness in the Reformed tradition to the work of the Spirit in creation and culture. We must fulfil our vocation in this world, over which Jesus Christ is Lord and which by the Spirit will be renewed and brought to its final consummation.

*The Spirit and the Word in creation and culture*

We agree that God has revealed Godself decisively in Jesus Christ, the one in whom the fullness of the Godhead dwells. God's Son is the eternal Word of God, who became flesh (cf John 1:14; Heb. 1:1-2 and Col. 2:3,9). In addition, God has revealed Godself through the scriptures; and scripture, as the word of God, is not to be isolated from the agency of the Holy Spirit.

We agree that the Holy Spirit is present and active, not only in the Christian church, but also in human history and in various cultures. The work of the Spirit is broader than we think. Nevertheless, we believe that every culture, as well as our own churches, is in need of being re-shaped by the Holy Spirit in accordance with the revelation in Jesus Christ as witnessed to in scripture. We believe that Jesus Christ, the one in whom the fullness of God dwells, is the perfect icon of God, the decisive self-revelation to human beings (Heb. 1).

With a focus on preaching and experiencing the ministry of Jesus Christ, Pentecostals have generally emphasized the work of the Spirit in culture as a preparation for the ministry of Christ through the church in the world. The corresponding emphasis has been on the sinfulness and needs of a "world without Christ". More recently, some Pentecostals have begun to reflect on the role of the Spirit in creation and culture to reveal God and to accomplish God's just and holy will, but not to the extent of believing that there is saving grace outside of the ministry of the gospel. Jesus Christ is "the way, the truth and the life". On the other hand, without diminishing the unique role of Jesus Christ in God's saving plan, the Reformed tradition has regarded the role of the Spirit in culture more expansively and positively than solely as a preparation for the ministry of the gospel.

*Spirit, proclamation and spiritual discernment*

Together, we stress the mutual bond of the word and the Spirit. Through the Holy Spirit, the Bible speaks the word of God. The indispensable action of the Spirit makes the text into a living and life-giving testimony to Jesus Christ, transforming the lives of people, for scripture is not a dead text. This confession involves more than an articulation of a biblical truth, or an expression of doctrine. It communicates how we understand, relate to and engage the Bible in everyday life. The Bible nourishes the people of God and enables them to discern the spirits.

Pentecostals and most Reformed Christians believe that Jesus Christ is "the way, the truth and the life" and, therefore, that no one can come to the Father except through the Son (John 14:6). The Holy Spirit convinces people of sin, righteousness and judgment (John 16:8-11), leading towards a personal response to the divine invitation to seek him and to find him (Acts 17:27). Both traditions acknowledge that the Holy Spirit is at work among all peoples, including peoples of other faiths, preparing them to receive the proclaimed word (Ps. 139; Acts 14:15-17). There is, therefore, a common challenge for believers from both traditions to learn together the ways in which the Spirit of God teaches the church to utilize various cultural elements in the service of God and the proclamation of the word of God.

Pentecostals affirm that Christians must continue to work for Jesus Christ through the empowerment of the Holy Spirit. By proclaiming the gospel, healing the sick, and confronting demonic powers, Pentecostals seek to be involved in a vibrant proclamation of the gospel, accompanied often by manifestations of the power of God. Healing is probably the most common manifestation of God's power among Pentecostal churches worldwide. Healings (including exorcisms) manifest the presence, compassion and power of God.

For Pentecostals, the anointing of the Spirit makes proclamation an event and an encounter between people and God. A Spirit-empowered proclamation of the scriptural message thus holds an important place in Pentecostal worship services. But the communication of God's will and action in Pentecostal services is not confined to the event of proclamation. There are multiple gifts of the Holy Spirit at work in Pentecostal worship to channel God's presence and to communicate God's will. The locus of discernment tends to be distributed in many Pentecostal churches among the entire congregation, so that whether gathered in worship or dispersed in society, all members are called to exercise their gifts in ministry. In various times and places, some Pentecostals have even reported that the Spirit worked so dramatically through multiple, extraordinary gifts in a particular church service, that the preached word of God was not given as it usually is. There is a tendency in many Pentecostal congregations to decentralize the communication of God's word and to encourage ordinary believers to speak for God alongside the preaching ministry of the ordained minister.

Reciprocity is established between word, Spirit and community so that the Spirit enlivens the word, the word provides a context for the Spirit's work, and the community lives out the Spirit's directions. Pentecostals place priority on the "leading of the Spirit" both individually and corporately.

While Pentecostals employ different methods and approaches to interpret the Bible, central to their interpretation is the conviction that the word of God speaks to today's world. Pentecostals strive to hear what the word of God has to say to them and their era as they live in restored and ongoing continuity with the mighty acts of God recorded in the Bible. For Pentecostals, the Bible is a story; they read their lives into that story and that story into their lives. They stress returning to the experiences of God to which scripture bears witness, but also moving forth into the world to witness to the deeds of God multiplied through them in new contexts. Essential to hearing the word, therefore, is the spiritual openness and fitness of the interpreter. The gap between the Bible and the contemporary world, which is emphasized among Pentecostals, is not historical but spiritual.

Pentecostals generally advocate a disciplined study of the Bible that employs methods that do not alienate the reader from the text or cast doubt on the miraculous nature of God's deeds, whether in biblical times or now. For this reason, they have often been wary of historical-critical methods of interpreting the Bible. Some also follow the fundamentalist defences of the inerrancy of scripture and strive to enter the modernistic struggle over the proper use of historical method in interpreting the Bible. Others are trying, instead, to explore post-modern interpretations of the Bible in order to transcend the limits of historical investigation in encountering the meaning of scripture. But Pentecostals normally emphasize that the Bible speaks and transforms lives only through the work of the Holy Spirit.

While Pentecostals originally came from diverse denominational backgrounds, they sought to go beyond what they had commonly experienced as "dead forms and creeds" to a "living, practical Christianity". Thus, the revelation of God through the preaching of the Bible was aided, not by conscious devotion to past denominational traditions, but to various signs and wonders of the Spirit indicating the last days, one of the important ones being prophecy. It is a Pentecostal conviction that the Spirit of God can speak through ordinary Christians in various ways that are consistent with the biblical message (1 Cor. 12-14). Ideally, these inspired words aid the preached word in making the will of God revealed in scripture dynamic and relevant to particular needs in the church. As the Acts of the Apostles shows, the church is to be directed today by the Spirit prophetically. "Let those who have an ear to hear, hear what the Spirit is saying to the churches" (Rev. 1-3).

The Bible is essential to Reformed faith and life. People entering a Reformed church normally find a Bible on the communion table or the pulpit. That the Bible is open indicates that God wants to speak. The word of God wants to answer questions that people may carry in their hearts. The word also wants to put a vital question to those who enter the church. Keeping an open Bible in the church is a symbolic act, which affirms that the Bible is central in Reformed experience and worship. The decisive moment in the worship service is, indeed, the reading and preaching of the word. The entire liturgy is structured to keep preaching of the word at the centre. However, the Bible is not an end in itself, for both scripture and preaching point to the living Word, Jesus Christ.

Reformed churches understand that the word of God is addressed to the whole people of God. Thus, congregations emphasize teaching, studying, discussing and learning the scriptures so that the community of faith and all its members may hear the word of God in its fullness.

In previous centuries, Reformed theologians usually said that all signs and wonders were confined to the apostolic age. Increasingly, theologians, pastors and church members see that this opinion finds no ground in the scriptures. However, a careful reading of Paul's letters leads Reformed Christians to the conviction that it would be wrong to concentrate attention on the so-called supernatural gifts, such as glossolalia and healing. In the Pauline lists of spiritual gifts, the more common gifts, such as leading, organizing and teaching, are mentioned in juxtaposition with the more spectacular gifts. In fact, we cannot sharply differentiate "supernatural gifts" from "natural" gifts. What we see as "natural" can be seen as a miracle, whether in nature, personal experience, or the history of humankind. This is evident in the "miracles" of the growing concern for the equality of women and men, the abolition of apartheid, and the struggle for the abolition of weapons of mass destruction. In these events and efforts, we may see the Spirit working in our day for the healing of the world.

Reformed people acknowledge that the word of God comes to them through the faithfulness of those who have preserved and proclaimed it, giving witness in ministry and mission throughout the centuries. The apostle Paul underscores the importance of tradition when he gives instruction concerning foundational elements of the Christian message, such as the resurrection of Jesus Christ (1 Cor. 15:3) and the Lord's supper (1 Cor. 11:23). Because the word has reached us over a long span of time, it should be approached through any means of interpretation that will make its message intelligible. One of these means, though not the only one, is the historical-critical method. No interpretative method may take the place of the word itself. While exegetical work helps the church discern meaning in scriptures, it is only by the Holy Spirit that the scriptures become the living word of God for the church.

The word of God addresses not only the church or individuals, but also the entire world, which God has deeply loved (John 3:16). This is why proclaiming the word and living in obedience to the word is central to the Reformed tradition, enabling the church to oppose all oppressive situations in the name of God. Such opposition is normally termed the "prophetic" task of the church, but it cannot be taken for granted that any proclamation is "prophetic". In any case, the prophetic word is first addressed to the church and so the first task of the church is to listen to the prophets and then – faithfully and humbly – to make the meaning of God's word clear to the present generation. The word proclaimed by the church may become prophetic only when and where it pleases God, and it is only "after the fact" that a proclamation by a church may be considered prophetic.

Pentecostal and Reformed Christians conclude that the Bible is the word of God in its witness to Jesus Christ through the work of the Holy Spirit. They tend to have different expectations concerning the role of the Spirit in culture and the significance of extraordinary gifts of the Spirit in manifesting the power of God in the proclamation of the gospel. Thus, we affirm the Bible as the word of God, an instrument of the Spirit to proclaim the grace of Jesus Christ to all people. The word of God inscripturated in the Bible becomes the living Word that speaks by the action of the Spirit of God, because the Spirit, who speaks through the Bible, is the same Spirit who was present in the formation of the scriptures. This role of the Bible as an instrument of the Spirit may not be understood in an exclusive way, however, for the Spirit cannot be confined to the text of the Bible. We of the Pentecostal and the Reformed traditions may understand the prophetic task of the church somewhat differently, but we agree that the Spirit of God continues to speak in and through the church in a way consistent with the biblical message.

## II. The Holy Spirit and the church

The teams of Pentecostal and Reformed theologians share the following affirmations about the Holy Spirit and the church.

- The church is the creature of the word and Spirit.
- The church is the community of the Holy Spirit's leading.
- The church is the community of the Spirit's gifts.
- The church is in but not of the world.

In each of these areas of common conviction, Reformed and Pentecostal emphases are often different. These differences are sometimes complementary, sometimes divergent. In all cases, however, ongoing dialogue helps to clarify complementarities and divergences, as well as suggest ways of deepening the ongoing conversations between us.

### *The church is the creature of the word and Spirit*

Reformed and Pentecostal Christians share the firm conviction that the church is God's creation. The church is a people called by the word and shaped by the Spirit, all to the glory of God. The gracious action of God precedes all human forms, communities and institutions. In speaking of the church, we stress the mutual connection of word and Spirit, and the church as creature of the word and Spirit called upon to respond to God's grace by worship in spirit and in truth. However, Pentecostal and Reformed Christians may use different language to express this common conviction.

Reformed Christians tend to use the language of "covenant" to describe the initiative of God and the formation of God's people. The covenant is the expression of God's gracious action in Christ to reconcile us to Godself, and to one another. Reformed understanding of the church is based on both the promises and the commandments of God. The deepest intention of the covenant is the reconciled life, for reconciliation in Jesus Christ is the basis and motive for life according to the will of God through the power of the Spirit. The shape of the covenant is expressed in the two great commandments – love of God and love of neighbour. Reformed Christians tend to identify the faithful church as that community where the word of God is rightly preached and heard, and where the sacraments are celebrated according to Christ's institution. Reformed Christians thus affirm that we receive the gospel of Christ through the living community of faith, which is sustained and nurtured though the word of God, as the Holy Spirit seals the word in us.

Pentecostals tend to use the language of "the outpouring of the Spirit" to describe the initiative of God and the formation of the church as the body of Christ. They tend to identify the faithful church as the community where Jesus Christ is lifted up, the word of God is preached and obeyed, and where the Spirit's gifts are manifested in the lives of believers. The Spirit sovereignly bestows charisms upon the community and its members. These gifts of the Spirit manifest themselves in a variety of ways so that the role of the word and the function of the Spirit are contextualized within the community. Each Pentecostal community, formed by the outpouring of the Spirit and shaped by the Spirit's gifts, discerns what the Spirit is saying to the church through the word and is thereby shaped by the Spirit in conformity to the word.

From the covenant it follows that Reformed Christians nurture an awareness of living in congregations, whereas Pentecostal Christians tend to focus more upon the life of the local assembly as it gathers together in the name of Jesus Christ in the power of the Holy Spirit.

The common affirmation that the church is the creature of the word and Spirit can lead us into fruitful conversations regarding the ways the word is given space among us and the ways the Spirit moves among us. Both Pentecostal and Reformed Christians understand worship as the church's primary response to God's grace. Furthermore, both understand that it is the Spirit who enables faithful worship by the community. Yet the two communities of faith express the Spirit's presence and action differently. Much more conversation should occur on the concrete reality of worship. Deeper dialogue concerning the role of sacraments or ordinances, and the place of the Holy Spirit's gifts, may lead to mutual enrichment.

*The church is the community of the Holy Spirit's leading*

Both Pentecostal and Reformed Christians recognize the Spirit's leadership in the church as the church confesses its faith, gathers as a community of worship, grows in edification and fellowship, and responds to its mission in the world. In these and other ways the church is facilitated by the Spirit's guidance in the process of spiritual discernment.

Reformed communities affirm that the Spirit leads the church as a community in ongoing confession of Christian faith. Reformed people have always been confession-making people, exercising their God-given freedom and obligation to confess the faith in each time and place. From the earliest beginnings of the Reformation through the 20th century, Reformed communities have formulated creeds and confessions that express the lived faith of concrete communities. The churches acknowledge the ongoing guidance of the Spirit to lead the community of faith into the truth and to make the gospel intelligible and relevant to specific places and times. This ongoing reformulation of confessions is based on fidelity to the scriptures – the word of God that bears witness to the incarnate Word of God.

Reformed churches strive to reach consensus through mutual discernment of word and Spirit. Yet we confess that we are imperfect hearers of the word who may resist the Spirit's leading. As a community of redeemed sinners, we remain sinners nonetheless. "Let anyone who has an ear listen to what the Spirit is saying to the churches."

While some Pentecostals have enacted confessions or statements of faith written in formal propositions, frequently they manifest their beliefs through expressions of personal testimony made in daily life and worship. Pentecostals explicitly affirm that it is the Spirit who both leads and enables them to worship God. They attempt to be sensitive to the movement of the Holy Spirit because they believe that the Spirit leads them into all truth and points them towards Jesus Christ.

Reformed worship is the place where the gathered community confesses common faith. In creeds and confessions from the early church, the Reformation period and contemporary settings, the worshipping assembly gives voice to the beliefs that bind individual believers together in common faith, life and witness.

Ideally, spiritual discernment plays an essential role in Pentecostalism. The practice of Pentecostal spirituality collectively prepares congregations, ministries and denominations to discern God's will in concrete situations. Functioning within many dimensions of the church as community, the discernment dynamic relies upon the Spirit's assistance and leadership for an authentication of communal prayer. This is manifested in a collective inner witness that is consistent with scripture. Prayerful deliberations or conversations enable the local church to arrive at consensus about its response to an issue or situation. Included in the communal discernment is the interaction between Pentecostals and society.

Social changes and developments sometimes awaken a Christian group to the need to wrestle with an issue. Coupled with communal discernment is personal discernment by each member. Each person participates in the discernment, ascertaining her or his judgment on the emerging or established consensus. Pivotal in personal discernment is the role of conscience. While the term is rarely used among Pentecostals, it is often implied. In the personal discernment of individual Pentecostals, the conscience is shaped, in part, by their spirituality.

The Pentecostal expectation is that the exercise of discernment is distributed throughout the entire congregation. Whether gathered in worship or dispersed in society, all are called to exercise their gifts in ministry. All individuals are accountable to the group and any individual may challenge the group as to who has "the mind of the Spirit". Discernment, then, requires active participation by all the members of the community. They listen for the Spirit to speak through the word communicated by preaching, teaching, testimony and action. They are encouraged to bring their Bibles to meetings and to read them for themselves. They weigh the value of the proclamation they hear by reference to scripture as well as "promptings" of the Spirit and prayerful reflection.

### *The church is the community of the Spirit's gifts*

Although the gifts of the Spirit are often associated with Pentecostal churches, Reformed churches also acknowledge that the church is established and maintained by the gracious presence of the Spirit who gives gifts to the people of God. Pentecostal and Reformed ways of speaking about and also receiving the gifts vary, yet both affirm that the Holy Spirit's charisms are constitutive of ecclesial life.

Pentecostals affirm that spiritual gifts enhance the faith of believers, deepen their fellowship with God, edify the church, and empower mission in the world. Pentecostals love and respect the word of God, so they expect God's Spirit to reveal his power through manifestations of grace. These manifestations of spiritual gifts are signs that God is with God's people. Spiritual gifts such as healing, prophesying, casting out demons, speaking in tongues, and other charisms enrich the lives of persons and the life of the community of faith.

The participants in this dialogue affirm that the gifts of God to the church are real, the Holy Spirit is the giver of gifts to the church, and the gifts are given to the church to work together for the common good. Reformed as well as many Pentecostal churches acknowledge that their understanding of the Spirit's gifts is broader than the classic list of spiritual gifts in 1 Corinthians 12:8-10. Furthermore, consideration of the Spirit's gifts is shaped by the overarching theme found in 1 Corinthians 12:4-7:

> Now there are varieties of gifts, but the same Spirit, and there are varieties of service, but the same Lord; and there are varieties of activities, but it is the same God who activates all of them in everyone. To each is given a manifestation of the Spirit for the common good.

Reformed Christians affirm that the Spirit's gifts are experienced in the congregational life of Reformed churches. Every congregation can point to numerous instances where, in official and unofficial ways, words and acts have led congregations in faithfulness. Wherever in the church acts of reconciliation are initiated, words of the good news of Christ are proclaimed, gestures of consolation are shared, injustices addressed, or prayers for healing and wholeness are uttered, the Holy Spirit is at work among the people of God. Yet representatives of Reformed churches confess that their churches are sometimes too casual in seeking and receiving the Spirit's gifts. Reformed Christians must proclaim forcefully that it is God who gives the gifts, and not we ourselves.

As we, the Reformed and Pentecostal participants in this dialogue, have reflected on the biblical texts and the life of the church, we have been convinced that no single gift or set of gifts is normative for every believer, every congregation or every church in every time or place. We share the conviction that gifts are not permanent possessions of believers or congregations, for the Spirit gives various gifts at different places as those gifts are needed.

We also agree that no biblical listing of gifts is a template to be laid over the entire church. On the one hand, we recognize that many Pentecostals limit the gifts of the Holy Spirit to those mentioned in 1 Corinthians 12:8-10. They do not value the charismatic nature of those mentioned elsewhere in the Bible (cf. 1 Cor. 12:27-30; Rom. 12:3-8; Eph. 4:11; 1 Pet. 4:10-11). On the other hand, many Reformed Christians recognize the theoretical possibility that the gifts mentioned in 1 Corinthians 12:8-10 might somewhere be appropriately exercised, but normally they do not encourage or even sanction them to be exercised in their own services. In addition, there are those in both traditions who value one gift over the contribution of another, or who seem to limit the Holy Spirit's sovereign distribution of gifts.

These things being said, it is important to note that most Pentecostals affirm the fact that the gift of tongues is not expected to be given to all Christians. Many of them do argue, however, that the ability for Christians to speak in tongues enjoys a privileged position. They contend that the Pentecostal experience enjoyed by the 120 in Acts 2, an experience in which they spoke in other tongues as the Spirit gave them utterance, is ultimately available to all who believe (Acts 2:38-39). In this sense, many Pentecostals distinguish between speaking in tongues as a gift of the Holy Spirit (not available to all) and speaking in tongues as sign or evidence (potentially available to all) that one has been baptized with the Holy Spirit (Acts 1:8, 2:1-4).

It is our common conclusion that these Reformed and Pentecostal positions are ultimately no less than concessions to the reality of our separated existence as Christian churches. We believe that those who embrace these positions, or elevate their status by giving voice to them in doctrinal or political statements, must be challenged to recognize their limitations. They need to be asked to broaden their understanding of the gifts which the Holy Spirit desires to give to the church. Only in so doing can they enter fully into the life of the church as the body of Christ. Only in so doing can they participate in what it means to be a priesthood of all believers. Only in so doing can they experience the fullness of what Joel prophesied, and Peter proclaimed on the day of Pentecost, that God's Spirit would be poured out on all flesh, thereby equipping them to participate in God's work in the world.

Reformed Christians affirm that God calls men and women and endows them with different gifts to exercise various forms of ministry in order to equip the whole people of God for mission in the world. Reformed churches express this conviction by affirming that all are commissioned to ministry by their baptism. The classic understanding of "priesthood of all believers" leads Reformed churches to encourage all Christians to participate fully in the life and ministry of the church. Some Reformed churches embody the ministry of the whole people of God by not confining ordained office to the ministry of word and sacrament. These churches ordain persons as elders and deacons to be full partners with ministers in the service of the church. Other churches commission members to such ministries of the church as caring for the poor and the marginalized, teaching Sunday school, leading youth ministries, furthering women's ministries, and more. Thus, the gifts given to individual members are recognized and encouraged.

### The church is in but not of the world

Both teams in this dialogue affirm that since the church is meant to be an instrument for the transformation of the world, "it is in the world, but not of the world". The church as the community of believers should be a "model", making evident – even in an inadequate way – what the future kingdom will be. Just as unity in the faith is manifested on the local level through the reciprocal love of the members of the congregation, similarly the unity of the Spirit already granted to us by God is manifested in the relations between congregations, groups, churches and denominations on the regional, national and global levels.

The church works in fidelity with the word and Spirit to live out the message and will of God. The members of the community offer themselves up as the eyes, ears, mouths and hands, which allow the Spirit and the word to address needs that arise in the church or the world.

From time to time, Reformed churches have been involved in prophetic acts to alter oppressive situations in society. Sometimes, Reformed churches have been part of oppressive structures. Thus, the church's life must be informed by the sustained study and application of scripture to various situations and social systems, and also by active engagement in the various aspects of society as the church bears witness to the reign of God.

Pentecostals focus more on individuals than on structures, viewing persons as individuals. When a person is in need, Pentecostals will often attend to the immediate need, without always analyzing the systemic issues that might give rise to the situation. As they probe more deeply, they uncover systemic issues that produce or aggravate the pastoral issue being addressed. Some Pentecostals, then, confront systemic issues out of strong pastoral concerns about an individual or a group of people. While Pentecostals have frequently been stereotypically portrayed as passive and "other-worldly", programmes of personal renewal at grassroots levels have had far-reaching implications for social transformation.

## III. The Holy Spirit and mission

*Holy Spirit and* missio Dei

The relation between the Holy Spirit and mission clarifies the issue of who determines mission and how mission is best carried out in each context. Is mission primarily the work of the church or does the church participate in the mission initiated by God?

When we say we are involved in *missio Dei* it is a correction of the notion that the mission in which Christians are involved is only the mission of the church. The church is a sign of the reign of God that has been inaugurated by Jesus Christ. While it has been called into this privilege, it does not claim to limit God's reign and sovereignty in all God's creation. We see that mission has its source and authority in the triune God. The biblical foundation points to the imperative for us to witness to all people in word and deed (Matt. 28:18-20; Luke 24:46-47; John 20:21-23; Acts 1:8).

We affirm that the Holy Spirit empowers women and men for mission in God's world. In the Reformed community it is not usual to define this empowerment as the baptism with the Holy Spirit. The empowerment as a gift is implied in the grace given to the members of the communities. In recent times, however, it has been recognized that bestowal of grace has a goal: that Christians may become co-workers of God in Jesus Christ (1 Cor. 3:9). Therefore, some have proposed the concept of "vocation" as an element with specific significance beside justification and sanctification.

In the experience of Acts 2, Pentecostals are convinced that they have a mandate for mission before the return of the Lord. They see that mandate as rooted in the eschatological significance of the prophecy in Joel 2:28-30. Most Pentecostals believe that baptism in the Holy Spirit is for the empowerment of believers to be effective witnesses of the gospel to the ends of the earth (Acts 1:8). This empowerment includes divine calling, equipping, commissioning, and the continuing presence of the Holy Spirit throughout mission.

Together, we affirm that *missio Dei* has implications for the ways we view culture and religions. We believe that the sovereign God is present in all societies and cultures. We believe that the Spirit of Christ goes ahead of the church to prepare the ground for the reception of the gospel.

*Holy Spirit and culture*

Pentecostals and Reformed believers are both challenged to learn together the ways in which the Spirit of God teaches the church to utilize various cultural elements and how these elements can be put into the service of God, in accordance with the biblical revelation.

The Holy Spirit is present and active in human history and culture as a whole as well as in the Christian church. However, every culture has to be transformed and reshaped by the Holy Spirit, in accordance with the revelation of Jesus Christ as witnessed to in scripture.

Pentecostals emphasize the work of the Spirit in support of the missionary outreach of the church in the world. Their conviction is that human culture stands in alienation from God and God's truth. The ministry of the gospel is meant to liberate people from captivity to that which is godless in culture. They further believe that godlessness in culture degrades human dignity and occasions social oppression. The ministry of the gospel implies first the salvation of humanity, but also the enhancement of human dignity and liberation.

Pentecostals and Reformed people believe that cultures are elements within God's creation and so embody many positive elements despite the existence of sin. The relationship between the gospel and culture is dialogical; no one operates in a cultural vacuum. Therefore, witness to the gospel should be embodied in culture. Our mission efforts demonstrate that we have not always paid due attention to issues of culture.

Whether there are salvific elements in other religions, however, is currently being debated by individual theologians within the Reformed family. While Pentecostals and many Reformed find it impossible to accept the idea that salvation might be found outside Jesus Christ, some Reformed agree with the ecumenical observation made at the world conference on mission and evangelism in San Antonio, Texas, USA, in 1989, that "we cannot point to any other way of salvation than Jesus Christ, at the same time, we cannot set limits to the saving power of God"[7] (cf. Acts 17:28).

On the whole, Pentecostals do not acknowledge the presence of salvific elements in non-Christian religions because they view this as contrary to the teaching of the Bible. The church is called to discern the spirits through the charism of the Holy Spirit informed by the word of God (1 Cor. 12:10, 14:29; cf. 1 Thess. 5:19-21; 1 John 4:2-3). Pentecostals, like many of the early Christians, are sensitive to the elements in other religions that oppose biblical teaching. They are, therefore, encouraged to received the guidance of the Holy Spirit.

### The multifaceted mission

Within an eschatological perspective, the mission of the church is to witness to the truth that the kingdom of God, which yet awaits full consummation in the future, has already broken into the present age in Jesus Christ. The ministry of Jesus Christ, therefore, continues in the world by the power of the Spirit working through the eschatological people of God. The integrity of mission is bound up in a commitment to multi-dimensional mission. Those dimensions include, but are not limited to, proclamation of the gospel (Matt. 28:19-20; Acts 1:8), fellowship (2 Cor. 5:17-20), service to the world (Matt. 25:34-36), worship, and justice (Acts 2:42-47).

### Service to the world

The grace of the Holy Spirit, given to us by Jesus Christ through the proclamation of the reign of God, prompts us to serve and participate in the mission of God in the world. This mission includes both proclamation and social engagement, which cannot be separated. Mission is concerned with the righteousness of our horizontal relationship with our neighbours and nature, as well as the vertical relationship with God.

We recognize that the understanding of mission varies with the social location of the given situation. The Holy Spirit empowers and leads us to work for the structural transformation of society as well as the individual transformation of ourselves without committing the church to a specific political ideology. This transformation is an ongoing process and realization of the prayer for the coming of the kingdom of God.

## IV. Spirit and kingdom

*Working definition of the kingdom*

The kingdom of God is apocalyptic and prophetic, both present gift and future hope. The kingdom of God is the broad theological term that represents God's sovereign, gracious and transformative reign of righteousness and truth in the face of, but also beyond the forces of evil and sin. The kingdom cannot be identified strictly with earthly rule, although God reigns and acts in history. Neither can the kingdom be identified strictly with the church, although the church and all creation exist in the eschatological hope of the fulfilment of the kingdom.

*Spirit, kingdom and eschatology*

Eschatology has often been confined to a theology of the last things, related to the consummation of the kingdom of God. For Reformed and Pentecostal churches, eschatology is not only a theology of the last things as the concluding part of our doctrinal system, but also an overall perspective of our theology and life. Although the kingdom of God has already come in Jesus Christ through the power of the Spirit, it is yet to be fulfilled in the future with the return of Christ. Until then, God rules in the world in the power of the Spirit, who grants a foretaste of the fulfilled kingdom (2 Cor. 1:22, 5:5; Eph. 1:7-14). God calls us to proclaim and participate in the kingdom of God.

Reformed and Pentecostal churches agree that the church is birthed by the Spirit and serves as an instrument of the kingdom that Jesus Christ proclaimed and inaugurated. The church is called to serve the kingdom, rather than be self-serving or an end in itself. The Spirit's role in ushering in the kingdom relates to its presence in the church

Both Reformed and Pentecostals also agree that the gospel that is at the heart of the church's mission, therefore, is not only directed to individual life in the Spirit and to hope for life after death, but is also future-oriented and directed to the resurrection of the dead and the new heavens and the new earth. Christian hope is not just individual and heaven bound, but is social and cosmic (Rom. 8) and directed towards the kingdom-to-come at Christ's return.

Thus, for Pentecostal and Reformed Christians to hold eschatology as a context for understanding mission means that the ultimate demands of God's eternal kingdom continue to confront Christians and the churches with the challenge of obedience. Our experience of God's Spirit as an experience of "eternity" in time must be viewed in relation to the horizon of God's ultimate future for humanity and all of creation, which is yet to be fulfilled. The victory of Christ over sin and death and the presence of God's Holy Spirit urge us towards courage and hope in our obedience to God's missionary call. But since the kingdom of God has not yet come in fullness, we confront trials and weakness with patience. We experience the dynamic tension between the "now" and the "not yet" of the fulfilment of God's kingdom in the world by engaging in patient action and active patience. Our actions and our prayers yearn patiently but fervently for God's will to be done on earth as it is in heaven.

Reformed churches affirm the second coming of Christ. Yet we are aware that God's time is different from ours. Thus, every form of prediction of the end time is excluded. The final victory of Christ gives ultimate significance to life in this world as God's time breaks into our time. Life in Christ is eschatological life.

The Reformed churches know that Christ will come as judge, but stress that the judge is none other than the Saviour. Judgment is not confined to the future, for judgment of sin and death happens in our time as well. The motive and attitude of our mission should always be love and compassion, reflecting the grace of the Lord Jesus Christ, the love of God, and the communion of the Holy Spirit.

Pentecostalism was born in a milieu of growing disillusionment with 19th-century theological optimism concerning the coming of the millennial reign of Christ. This post-millennial theology, in Britain and North America at least, was being displaced in some circles by a pre-millennial eschatology, which focused on the return of Jesus to rapture the church. It was the personal return of Christ to bring the kingdom, rather than the return of Christ to receive the kingdom which was already to have been established on earth. This eschatology has shaped Pentecostal missions since that time. It implies a focus on mission as evangelism.

Pentecostals believe that Christians move relentlessly towards that ultimate fulfilment of God's kingdom through prayer and battle against the forces of evil. Meanwhile, this tension between the "now" and the "not yet" of Christian hope grows ever more intense as the Spirit of God is poured out in ever-greater abundance in the direction of final fulfilment at Christ's return.

From their inception, Pentecostals have held to a firm belief that the return of Christ was close at hand. Early Pentecostals zealously proclaimed the message of the gospel to the whole world, in light of the return of Christ. Scripture passages such as John 16:12-16, Matthew 25:31-46, 1 Thessalonians 4:13-17 and 2 Peter 3:8-9 continue to fuel the missionary zeal of Pentecostals. The Holy Spirit's work in inspiring Pentecostals to missionary activity, service and giving is in anticipation of the kingdom of God. The eschatological urgency that Pentecostals feel, therefore, should not be thought of only as the hope for the return of Christ, but a firm realization that there remains a responsibility to humanity of providing for the needs of people, such as shelter, education, food and medical concerns.

Generally, Pentecostal mission cares for the total person. Indeed, prayer for healing and ministry to the personal needs of people such as food and education have always been present in Pentecostal missions. It does suggest, however, that Pentecostal missions have not always challenged social or structural issues prophetically. There are at least two reasons for this. The first is that the social location of Pentecostals was, on the whole, marginal to society and Pentecostals had limited access to the power centres of the social establishment. Second, those structures were viewed as part of the system, which Jesus' coming would replace by the righteous reign of God.

### Spirit, kingdom, creation

The relationship of creation to the Spirit and the kingdom is a pivotal eschatological theme for many churches, both Reformed and Pentecostal. The topic challenges restricting the signs of God's reign to human history. Creation as a topic within Spirit and kingdom introduces the cosmos as an object of God's engagement.

For Reformed and Pentecostal churches, the Holy Spirit is integrally involved in creation. Both recognize the Spirit's role at the beginning of creation as well as acknowledge the Spirit's role in the sustaining and renewing of creation. For Reformed churches and some Pentecostal churches, the expectation of the kingdom includes the restoration and renewal of the cosmos.

In Pentecostal worship, sighs too deep for words are given expression. These are often understood as speaking in tongues (Rom. 8:26), offered in anticipation of the kingdom of God yet to come in fullness. Such a yearning for the kingdom implies a desire for the salvation of the lost and the redemption of the entire creation. Examples of their concern for creation are demonstrated through Pentecostals' prayer for rain, especially during droughts, or their prayer for a bounteous harvest. All creation benefits from this concern, and they believe that without God's blessing, creation itself will not be sustained.

For the Reformed churches, the expectation of the coming of our Saviour does not exclude but includes the expectation of the kingdom. The fulfilled kingdom is not just the collection of all believers, but shalom for the totality of creation. It represents the restoration and renewal of the cosmos. Churches of the Reformed tradition strive to be faithful to the creation because God remains faithful to it. Human beings are part of the cosmos, and so together with the whole creation are invited to participate in the celebration of life.

### Spirit, kingdom, world

The location of the world within the topic of Spirit and kingdom is central to identifying the boundaries of the arena in which the Spirit and kingdom intersect in history. Key questions are: Is the work of the Spirit confined to the church? Does the kingdom engage the world? Is the world an arena of the Spirit or the kingdom?

Reformed churches acknowledge that all Christians, as stewards of the rich gifts of God, are called to act in responsible faith towards all creation. Therefore, we are called to proclaim, both in word and deed, the will of God concerning personal and social injustices, economic exploitation and ecological destruction. Moreover, Reformed churches affirm that the Holy Spirit guides the faithful to work for both personal and structural transformation of society, thus participating in the ongoing process and realization of the prayer for the coming of the kingdom of God.

Pentecostals differ on how they view the role of the Holy Spirit in sustaining, reforming or transforming human society. Some Pentecostals interpret reality dualistically. They understand that a state of warfare exists between the people of God and "the world". They believe that the Holy Spirit is the one who will triumph over the "principalities and powers and spiritual wickedness in high places". How that warfare is defined varies from those who interpret the warfare in moral terms, to those who employ the term "spiritual warfare" in describing the battle between the godly and ungodly powers. Pentecostals who employ moral terms identify the role of the Spirit as one who restrains evil in the world. Others identify the role of the Spirit as one who invites Christians to engage in the reforming and transforming of society. This perspective also recognizes the role of the Holy Spirit in reproving the human society in terms of righteousness.

Some Pentecostals around the world engage the political arena from the underside. Many are in countries where there is no political space for them to engage the political order directly. Their social locations shape their understanding of the Holy Spirit. However, among these are those who respond differently from the majority. They create alternative societies modelling resolutions to social issues within their ecclesial structures. The issues they address include, but are not limited to such evils as racism, classism, materialism and sexism.


**Conclusions**

Several clear benefits have emerged as a direct result of this dialogue. One of the obvious fruits enjoyed so far has been the friendships that have been established across denominational lines and the lines of our various traditions. These friendships have expanded beyond the realm of everyday life into the recesses of our common spiritualities and our ecclesial experiences. Genuine ecumenism begins when Christians find each other and learn to enter into the lives of one another.

A second obvious benefit of the dialogue to date has been the individual studies that have been offered in the form of papers presented. Some of these have found their way into publication, thereby challenging those who cannot participate at the limited space a dialogue table allows. In addition, press reports from the meeting have been published in a number of papers and journals, expanding the awareness of this dialogue in a number of ecclesial and scholarly communities. They have found their way into classrooms and are contributing to the ecumenical formation of the next generation of pastors and teachers in both communities.

Third, the dialogue has been able to give and to receive from Christians in each of the regions in which it has convened its meetings. It has delved into the lives of Christians who live, sometimes in difficult situations, whether they be members of a minority community in the Italian Alps, an African-American congregation in the USA, an affluent Reformed community in Switzerland, a Pentecostal congregation separated from family members in Korea by an artificial boundary, or a Reformed community in a large Brazilian city, teeming with both hope and despair.

Finally, the dialogue had helped its participants realize the critical necessity for ongoing contact between these two vital Christian traditions. With the completion of this report, the participants in this dialogue wish to encourage others in their respective communities to join in this mutual exploration.

**Appendix**

Portions of this document were developed over the period of five years from 1996 to 2000. While many people during each of these years made substantive contributions that led to this document, only those who were present at the meeting in São Paulo, Brazil, in May 2000 had a part in the final drafting and editing of this document. They are indicated with an asterisk (*). Those who chaired the meetings are indicated with a (c), while those who served as staff from the WARC office are indicated with an (s). Those who presented papers are indicated with a (P) following the year in which they made their presentation. Those who attended the meetings as observers, are indicated with an (o). Those regular participants who were part of the original exploratory committee are noted with attendance in 1995.

*Pentecostal participants*

*Daniel Albrecht, Scotts Valley CA, USA, 1996 P, 1997, 1998, 2000
Miguel Alvarez, Honduras/Philippines, o 1999
Arto Antturi, Helsinki, Finland, 1996
*Anthea Butler, Los Angeles CA, USA, 1996 P, 1997, 1998, 2000
*David Daniels, Chicago IL, USA, 1996, 1997, 1998, 1999, 2000
Harold Hunter, Oklahoma City OK, USA, 1996, 1997, 1998, 1999
Richard Israel, San Jose CA, USA, 1995, 1996 P, 1997, 1998, 1999
*Veli-Matti Kärkkäinen, Jyväskylä, Finland, 1997, 1998, 1999, 2000
Byron Klaus, Costa Mesa CA, USA, 1998 P
*Julie [Jungjia] Ma, Baguio City, Philippines, 1997 P, 1998, 1999, 2000
*Wonsuk Ma, Baguio City, Philippines, 1997 P, 1998, 1999, 2000
*Frank Macchia, Costa Mesa CA, USA, 1995, 1996, 1997, 1998, 1999 P, 2000
*Jean-Daniel Plüss, Zürich, Switzerland, 1995, 1996, 1997, 1998, 1999, 2000
*c Cecil M Robeck, Jr, Pasadena CA, USA, 1995, 1996, 1997, 1998, 1999, 2000

*Reformed participants*

Solomon DL Alagodi, Balmatta, Mangalore, India, 1996
Aldo Comba, Torre Pellice, Italy, 1996 P
Hugh Davidson, Scotland, 1995
*Paul A Haidostian, Chouran, Beirut, Lebanon, 1999, 2000
*Marsha Snulligan Haney, Atlanta GA, USA, 1997, 1998, 1999, 2000
*Yohan Hyun, Seoul, Korea, 1997, 1998, 1999 P, 2000
Moses Jayakumar, Bangalore, India, 1998
*Gesine von Kloeden, Bad Salzuflen, Germany, 1999, 2000
Margaret M McKay, England, 1995
*Cephas Omenyo, Legon, Accra, Ghana, 1996 P, 1997 P, 1998, 1999, 2000
Jana Opocenská, Geneva, Switzerland, 1999

\*Milan Opocensky, Geneva, Switzerland, 1998, 1999, c 2000
\*s Odair Pedroso Mateus, São Paulo, Brazil/Geneva, Switzerland, 2000
\*Nils E Norén, Vétlanda, Sweden, 1999, 2000
\*Aureo R Oliveira, Fortaleza, CE, Brazil, 1999, 2000
Claudio Pasquet, Luserna San Giovanni, Italy, o 1996
Silas Pinto, Brazil [Wheaton IL, USA], 1997
\*Abival Pires da Silveira, São Paulo, SP, Brazil, c 1996 P, c 1997, c 1999, 2000
\*Salvatore Ricciardi, Milan, Italy, 1995, 1996, 1997, c 1998, 2000
Silvia Rostagno, Ladispoli, Italy, 1996
Sydney Sebastian Salins, Balmatta, Mangalore, India, 1997
\*Joseph D Small, Louisville KY, USA, 1999, 2000
\*Jan Veenhof, Gunten, Switzerland, 1996, 1997 P, 1998, 1999, 2000
s Henry Wilson, Geneva, Switzerland, 1996 P, 1997, 1998

NOTES

1   Those present at the Mattersey conference included Hugh Davidson, Margaret M McKay, Salvatore Ricciardi and Henry Wilson for the Reformed churches, and Richard Israel, Frank Macchia, Jean-Daniel Plüss and Cecil M Robeck, Jr, for the Pentecostals.

2   The presentations made in 1996 included Aldo Comba, "Spirituality and ecumenism: Reformed", Abival Pires da Silveira, "Spirituality and justice", and Henry Wilson, "Spirituality and interpretation of scripture", for the Reformed team; and Daniel Albrecht, "Spirituality and ecumenism: Pentecostal", Anthea Butler, "Facets of Pentecostal spirituality and justice", and Richard Israel, "Pentecostal spirituality and the use of scripture", for the Pentecostals. Edited versions of the papers by Anthea D Butler and Richard D Israel have since been published in Hubert van Beek ed., *Consultation with Pentecostals in the Americas: San Jose, Costa Rica, 4-8 June 1996*, Geneva, WCC, 1996, pp.28-55. Daniel Albrecht's paper was published under the title, "Pentecostal spirituality: ecumenical potential and challenge", in the *Cyberjournal for Pentecostal Charismatic Research* [www.pctii.org/cyberj/cyber2.html] #2 (July 1997).

3   In 1997, Wonsuk and Julie Ma collaborated on "'An immanent encounter with the transcendental': Proclamation and manifestation in Pentecostal worship", while Jan Veenhof wrote on the subject of "Orthodoxy and Fundamentalism" with a "Short note on prophecy", and Cephas Omenyo addressed "The role of the Spirit in proclamation and manifestations of the charismata within the church" on behalf of the Reformed team.

4   In 1998, Byron Klaus delivered "The Holy Spirit and mission in eschatological perspective: A Pentecostal viewpoint", while Cephas Omenyo delivered the Reformed paper titled "The Holy Spirit and mission in eschatological perspective".

5   In 1999, Yohan Hyun presented "The Holy Spirit, charism and the kingdom of God from the Reformed perspective", while Frank D Macchia addressed "The struggle for the Spirit in the church: The gifts of the Spirit and the kingdom of God in Pentecostal perspective". Subsequent to the 1999 meeting in Seoul, these papers were published as Yohan Hyun and Frank Macchia, *Spirit's Gifts – God's Reign*, Theology & Worship Occasional Paper no. 11, Louisville KY, Presbyterian Church [USA], Office of Theology and Worship, 1999, 66pp.

6   This dialogue has not included any representatives from this wing of the larger Pentecostal movement. These Pentecostals are sometimes known as "Apostolics", "Oneness", or "Jesus' Name" Pentecostals. They baptize according to Acts 2:38, and tend to embrace a modalist understanding of God.

7   "Reports of the Sections: Section I: Turning to the Living God", in the *International Review of Mission* LXXVIII, nos 311-12, July/October 1989, p.351.

Part D

# 39. Joint Working Group between the Roman Catholic Church and the World Council of Churches

# Eighth Report
# 1999-2005

## Geneva-Rome, 2005

**Foreword**

We have been privileged to moderate the Joint Working Group during its eighth mandate. The fruits of its work are the substance of this report.

Though not itself a council, the Joint Working Group has acted as an instrument of the World Council of Churches and the Roman Catholic Church (Pontifical Council for Promoting Christian Unity) in promoting the ecumenical movement. Its study entitled "Inspired by the Same Vision" has addressed conciliar developments throughout the world and the impetus given by Catholic participation in national and regional councils of churches. It also speaks from experience in addressing the nature and purpose of ecumenical dialogue, the privileged modality of interchurch engagement.

Not forgetful of the goal of the ecumenical movement it has, at the insistence of its parent bodies, examined in depth the ecclesiological and ecumenical implications of a common baptism, and recommends to churches a study of its findings. In baptism and the profession of (baptismal) faith the journey of the Christian and all Christian faith communities begins, a journey which has a common goal in and through Christ Jesus our Lord. To bear united witness to his gospel provokes our ecumenical efforts; our as yet unfinished study on Christian anthropology will cast light on human nature as shaped by grace on which such efforts must be based. This is a study which we believe must continue.

We thank the officers of our respective mandating bodies – the World Council of Churches and the Pontifical Council for Promoting Christian Unity – and all the members of our plenary meetings for their generous commitment to the cause of church unity, and recommend to our readers the study of our report.

*Rt Rev. Dr Jonas Jonson*
*Bishop of Stängnäs, Sweden*

*Most Rev. Mario Conti*
*Archbishop of Glasgow, UK*

Co-moderators of the Joint Working Group

# I. INTRODUCTION

The Joint Working Group (JWG) appreciates the importance of the mandate it has received from the Roman Catholic Church and the World Council of Churches to assist in carrying out the ecumenical mission of the churches. In seeking to fulfil our mandate in the period 1999-2005 we are increasingly convinced of the priority that needs to be given to efforts to grow towards the unity that Christ wills for his church.

The year 2004 is the 40th anniversary of the Decree on Ecumenism of the Second Vatican Council (*Unitatis Redintegratio*) and 2005 that of the foundation of the JWG. It is proposed that these anniversaries be marked by a joint consultation between the RCC and the WCC. The JWG also looks forward to the assembly of the WCC in Porto Alegre Brazil, 14-23 February 2006, on the theme "God, in Your Grace, Transform the World".

In the period of our mandate the Group held five plenary meetings: in Antelias (Lebanon 2000), Dromantine (Northern Ireland 2001), Stjärnholm (Sweden 2002), Bari (Italy 2003) and Chania/Crete (Greece 2004). In expressing thanks to those who hosted the meetings, the Group wishes to acknowledge the hospitality of the local churches that shared their lives, their struggles, their traditions and their ecumenical experiences with us.

The period 1999-2005 began in the anticipation of the Jubilee of the year 2000 and the hopes awakened by the celebrations of two millennia of Christian history. Many of those hopes are bearing fruit, but the period has also been marked by difficult and tragic situations for the world and by new challenges for the churches.

This report outlines the activities of the JWG during these years and includes three completed study documents, as well as some themes pursued and issues addressed.

Among the most valuable aspects of our work has been the Christian fellowship we have experienced, the sharing that has been possible of information from every part of the world, and the growth in communion and understanding that has taken place among us.

# II. RELATIONSHIPS 1999-2005

## 1. Significant moments: bilateral visits, leadership meetings

During the period under review, there have been several significant moments in the bilateral relations between the World Council of Churches and the Pontifical Council for Promoting Christian Unity. Bishop Walter Kasper, then secretary of the PCPCU, paid his first official visit to the WCC (31 January-1 February 2000). The purpose of the visit was threefold:

– to get to know the WCC and its programmes;
– to meet the staff leadership group and other members of the WCC staff; and
– to evaluate the state of the relations between the two partners.

One session with the PCPCU delegation focused on three aspects:

1) a review of plans for the JWG plenary foreseen that year in May;

2) the participation of the RCC in WCC programmes without being a member of the WCC (except in Faith and Order, and Mission and Evangelism) and participation or full membership in councils of churches at local and regional level;

3) the changing ecumenical configuration whereby churches find themselves in a new situation with Pentecostals and Evangelicals being among the fastest growing communities and yet the large majority of them still outside the WCC and the ecumenical movement.

There was consensus in this free discussion that there was a need to assess the impact of the changing situation on the ecumenical movement. In this context, several questions emerged for further reflection and discussion by both sides:

1) Could the WCC and the RCC think of a consultation where all possible partners would come together and exchange their ideas on the changing shape of the ecumenical movement?

2) What role would Christian world communions (CWCs) play in such a consultation?

3) What kind of an agenda would be discussed at such a consultation?

The second significant moment in the relations between the two partners was the leadership meeting that took place on 31 May 2000 in Antelias, Lebanon, on the occasion of the JWG plenary, 25-31 May 2000, hosted by Catholicos Aram I. Present at the meeting were, from the WCC, Catholicos Aram I (moderator of the WCC central committee), Rev. Dr Konrad Raiser (WCC general secretary) and Bishop Jonas Jonson (co-moderator of the JWG); from the RCC, Cardinal Edward Cassidy (president of the PCPCU), Bishop Walter Kasper (then secretary of the PCPCU) and Bishop Mario Conti (co-moderator of the JWG). The meeting was also attended by staff members on both sides.

The issues discussed on this occasion included the following: a brief evaluation of the JWG plenary in Antelias; information on future priorities of the JWG and methodology; a sharing of ideas on WCC-RCC collaboration through Faith and Order; WCC-RCC collaboration on mission and evangelism; and issues of collaboration in the coming years.

The second leadership meeting also took place in Antelias, Lebanon, on 4 March 2004, hosted by Catholicos Aram I, on the occasion of the meeting of the JWG executive 4-7 March 2004. The leadership meeting was convened following the election of the new WCC general secretary, Rev. Dr Samuel Kobia. The meeting took place in three phases. Catholicos Aram I met with Cardinal Walter Kasper, they were then joined by Dr Samuel Kobia and Bishop Brian Farrell, and finally the leadership group met with all members of the JWG executive.

The agenda discussed at this leadership meeting included issues such as: the possibility of RCC membership in the WCC under the category of "churches in association with the WCC"; mutual invitation to one another's major events; proper procedures for communication between departments of the WCC and the Roman Curia; and the mandate of the JWG. Attention was drawn to the fact that the JWG would be celebrating its 40th anniversary in 2005. The leadership meeting accepted a proposal that on the occasion of that anniversary, the two partners could convene a consultation that would evaluate the relationship between the RCC and the WCC.

During this period, the WCC received Bishop Marc Ouellet (then secretary of the PCPCU) on his first official visit to the WCC on 25 October 2001. A similar visit by Bishop Brian Farrell (secretary of the PCPCU) took place on 1 April 2003. Both visits were mutually arranged for the purpose of getting to know the WCC, its programmes and staff, as well as some of the issues in which the two partners are engaged.

The PCPCU received the staff team of Mission and Evangelism on its visit to Rome, 19-24 October 2001. The programme, organized by the PCPCU, involved participation in the general audience of Pope John Paul II, and contacts with the offices of the Roman Curia that have relationship with programmes of CWME, the faculty of missiology at the Urbaniana Pontifical University, the Union of Superiors General (women religious) and the Sedos Centre for Documentation.

From 4 to 7 December 2003, a delegation of 12 persons representing various offices of the Roman Curia, some faculties of theology, religious men and women and the Centre for Documentation, visited the WCC at the invitation of the staff working on the programme on Mission and Evangelism. The purpose of the visit was mainly to receive information from the WCC on the conference on world mission and evangelism, to be held in Athens 9-16 May 2005 under the theme "Come, Holy Spirit, Heal and Reconcile!". Besides an introduction to the WCC for the delegation, some of whom were visiting the WCC for the first time, the programme included an exposure to the theme of the conference and concluded with a morning of prayerful retreat in the style of *lectio divina*. In connection with the CWME conference in Athens, the PCPCU has already received an invitation from the WCC to send a delegation.

## 2. Celebration of the Jubilee 2000

In its seventh report (1998), the JWG highlighted the ecumenical potential of the celebration of the Jubilee Year 2000. The preparation required continuous dialogue with ecumenical partners through the "Ecumenical Commission of the Central Committee of the Great Jubilee". Besides other ecumenical partners, the WCC was represented on this commission by a fraternal delegate (Mr Georges Lemopoulos, deputy general secretary) 1996-99. Three WCC delegates (Bishop Jonas Jonson, Rev. Dr Alan Falconer, director of Faith and Order, and Ms Teny Pirri-Simonian, co-secretary of the JWG) were among the 23 fraternal delegates that attended the opening of the Holy Door by Pope John Paul II, at the Basilica of St Paul Outside the Walls on 18 January 2000. It was the first time in history that such a Jubilee liturgical event took place in an ecumenical service.

Another Jubilee event at which a fraternal delegate represented the WCC was the "Ecumenical Commemoration of Witnesses to the Faith in the Twentieth Century", on 7 May 2000 at the Colosseum in Rome. Pope John Paul II reflected on this event earlier when he said, "The greatest homage which all the churches can give to Christ on the threshold of the third millennium will be to manifest the fruits of faith, hope and charity present in men and women of many different tongues and races who have followed Christ" (*Tertio Millennio Adveniente* [TMA], 37).

A third important event during the Jubilee year was the celebration entitled "Ecumenical Witness as the Third Millennium Begins". Pope John Paul II led this ecumenical celebration of the word on 25 January 2001, at the Basilica of St Paul Outside the Walls, together with representatives of other churches, Christian world communions and the WCC, represented by Bishop Jonas Jonson (co-moderator, JWG) and Rev. Dr Alan

Falconer (director of Faith and Order). As described by Pope John Paul II, the purpose of the celebration was to demonstrate the determination of Christians to embark upon the new millennium in a spirit of reconciliation, providing an atmosphere of heartfelt prayer that the Holy Spirit may grant the gift of visible unity to Christ's followers (cf. presentation for the Week of Prayer for Christian Unity Celebration at St Paul's Outside the Walls, 25 January 2001).

The calendar of the Jubilee of the Catholic Church included a "prayer vigil in response to the appeal of the patriarch of Constantinople" on the evening of 5 August 2000. In this event the Catholic Church accepted the 1996 appeal of the Ecumenical Patriarch Bartholomew I that all Christians promote a common spirit of doxology and invocation on the eve of the Solemn Feast of the Transfiguration of Our Lord.

Throughout the Jubilee year representatives of other churches were invited to send fraternal delegates to other events such as a jubilee event for journalists, a meeting of university teachers and the World Congress of Catholic Laity. The ecumenical patriarch organized an international Orthodox youth assembly in Istanbul, Turkey, in June 2000, at which a delegation of ten young Catholics, representing various youth organizations, took part. At the World Youth Day in August 2000, ecumenical prayers were organized every evening. Important ecumenical events also took place at local levels. It is worth remembering, for example, the common celebration of all the churches present in the Holy Land and Jerusalem.

### 3. Assisi World Day of Prayer for Peace

Threats to peace and justice in the world have continued and in many ways intensified during the period of the JWG mandate. Pope John Paul II convened the Assisi World Day of Prayer for Peace on 24 January 2002, mainly in response to the build-up of tensions following the tragic events of 11 September 2001. The pope invited the leaders of various churches, representatives of Christian world communions and the WCC, as well as leaders of other world religions, to a day of prayer for peace in Assisi. Catholic bishops from different regions of the world participated in the event. The WCC was represented by the Rev. Dr Konrad Raiser who read the first of ten commitments to peace.

The Day of Prayer for Peace of 24 January 2002, like the two previous ones in Assisi, was both ecumenical and inter-religious, and thus only the opening of the event and its conclusion were done together, leaving a moment of prayer for each religious group to pray in a different place according to its own faith, language, tradition, and with full respect for others. What bound together all participants in Assisi was the certainty that peace is a gift of God, for each person is called to be a peace-maker. The event was all the more interesting due to the fact that it included a pilgrimage by train, carrying the pope and all specially invited delegates to Assisi and back together.

### 4. The one ecumenical movement: questions of "reconfiguration"

From 1991 to 1998 the WCC concentrated its attention on a reflection process entitled "Towards a Common Understanding and Vision of the WCC" (CUV). The RCC offered a substantial contribution that was taken into consideration when drafting the policy statement which ensued. The process known as "the reconfiguration of the one ecumenical movement" has been one of two direct results of the policy document, also entitled "Towards a Common Understanding and Vision of the WCC". The first one was the exploration of a global Christian forum (see point 6) to address the issue of widening the fellowship of churches to include Evangelical, Pentecostal and Independent churches, as well as the Roman Catholic Church, and the other churches and organizations which have traditionally been part of the ecumenical movement. The second result was the Special Commission on Orthodox Participation in the WCC (see point 5), which dealt mainly with issues internal to the fellowship of the member churches of the WCC and became the place for a sustained reflection on models for a possible restructuring of the Council itself.

Discussions about a possible new reconfiguration of the ecumenical movement have started in meetings between various ecumenical partners such as the regional ecumenical organizations (REOs), national councils of churches (NCCs), Christian world communions (CWCs) and ecumenical agencies. The general secretary of the WCC brought the matter to the attention of the central committee and the decision was taken to initiate a process of consultation in order to address the question of how relationships can be strengthened between existing ecumenical actors.

A first meeting took place in Antelias, Lebanon, 12-17 November 2003, with the participation of a staff member of the PCPCU. A report entitled "From Antelias with Love" was issued and sent to WCC member churches, the PCPCU and other ecumenical partners for discussion and response. It suggested some next steps and affirmed the need for the WCC to "consult with other churches who are part of the ecumenical movement, such as the Roman Catholic Church" and to "encourage their participation in discussions of reconfiguration". A second meeting was held at the end of 2004. There are some conceptual difficulties which need to be considered in this process. Thus it is proposed to continue the exploration of a "reconfiguration" within a general perspective on "the one ecumenical movement in the 21st century".

## 5. Special Commission on Orthodox Participation in the WCC

The Special Commission on Orthodox Participation in the WCC was inaugurated at the WCC's eighth assembly in Harare, Zimbabwe, in 1998, because of serious concerns about aspects of the functioning of the WCC expressed among Orthodox churches. Furthermore, the assembly noted that other churches and ecclesial families had concerns similar to those expressed by the Orthodox. The Special Commission has been unique in WCC history in being composed of an equal number of representatives from Orthodox churches and from the other member churches of the WCC.

The commission fulfilled its twofold task: "to study and analyze the whole spectrum of issues related to Orthodox participation in the WCC" and "to make proposals [to the WCC central committee] concerning the necessary changes in structure, style and ethos of the Council". Its report was presented to the central committee in 2002, making concrete proposals in five areas: (1) membership, including the creation of a new possible place for "churches in association with the fellowship of the WCC"; (2) consensus decision-making; (3) ecclesiology; (4) ethical and social matters; and (5) common prayer. A steering committee was set up and mandated to continue work in these areas until the ninth assembly of the WCC, when a final report will be presented. Some of the constitutional and institutional changes proposed by the commission which will have to be considered by the assembly include: (1) the addition of theological criteria to the "criteria of membership"; (2) churches becoming members of the fellowship after a probation period; and (3) new rules of debate, according to the consensus method. The statement on ecclesiology prepared by Faith and Order for the next assembly has largely covered the ecclesiological concerns expressed by the Special Commission.

The Joint Working Group received regular reports on the work of the Special Commission as the RCC is interested in relationships with Orthodox churches, on the one hand, and in institutional developments in the WCC, on the other.

## 6. Global Christian forum

In the context of the exploration in the 1990s of a "Common Understanding and Vision of the WCC" (see JWG seventh report, III A.5), the general secretary, Rev. Dr Konrad Raiser, raised the question of whether there was need for an "ad hoc ecumenical forum of Christian churches and ecumenical organizations" in which various partners could come together in a new way, with the WCC being one participant among them. It would also include those Evangelicals and Pentecostals whose communities are growing and have not been involved in the organized ecumenical movement.

During 1997-98, the WCC invited the PCPCU to explore the feasibility of this idea with representatives of other churches and ecumenical organizations. The PCPCU accepted the invitation, with the following understanding: that priority should be given first to settling the reorganization of the WCC outlined in the CUV policy statement; that the forum should be a channel for strengthening the goal of visible unity which is stated in the constitution of the WCC, even if this goal was not expressly stated in the purposes of the proposed forum; and that it should meet a need not being met by any existing organization. The PCPCU expressed the hope that a proposed forum could serve as an occasion to draw into the one ecumenical movement those many Christians who presently seem to steer clear of the ecumenical movement in its more organized forms.

A first consultation was convened by the WCC in August 1998. Noting the diversity of efforts to advance Christian unity, the participants felt a forum was possible because of the unity already given in Christ and was *called for* because of our common faith in a reconciling God. A preliminary proposal was drawn up and a continuation committee was appointed with the task to explore the idea further. From the beginning a PCPCU staff person has taken part in the committee. To underline that this is a common search and not a project of the WCC or any other organization or church, the committee is considered autonomous.

The first step taken by the continuation committee was to test the proposal with those who thus far had not been so involved in the organized forms of the ecumenical movement. Thus some twenty leaders from Evangelical and Pentecostal churches responded to an invitation to a meeting which was held in September 2000 at Fuller Theological Seminary, Pasadena, USA. The group responded positively to the idea, which they named a "global Christian forum". They agreed that the forum should focus on the mission of the church and that the purpose should be to foster common witness.

The positive response from the preliminary testing of the idea encouraged the continuation committee to organize a further event in June 2002, also at Fuller Theological Seminary. Some sixty participants from Orthodox, Catholic, Protestant, Anglican, Evangelical, Pentecostal, Holiness and African Instituted churches and from international Christian organizations were brought together. It was the first time that such a broadly representative group of all the main traditions of Christianity in the world today met to discuss the forum proposal. The meeting affirmed the proposal and formulated a provisional purpose statement. It affirmed that the forum should hold together mission and unity, and underlined the value of the process of bringing Christians and churches together. It also expanded the continuation committee. Afterwards, a plan was devised covering the years 2004-2007.

## 7. *Koinonia*: central to the ecumenical movement

During the period under review, 1999-2005, both the WCC and the PCPCU focused attention on the question of the unity of the church expressed as *communio/koinonia* and on the nature of the fellowship of churches in the WCC within the one ecumenical movement. Catholicos Aram I, in his report as moderator of the WCC central committee in 1999, dealt with the issue of the fellowship of churches in the context of the WCC eighth assembly in Harare and the study process on "A Common Understanding and Vision of the WCC", which "sought not only to clarify a vision for the WCC, but also to elucidate the nature of the fellowship of churches in the WCC".

At the WCC central committee of August-September 1999, the moderator underlined the centrality of ecclesiology in speaking about both the WCC fellowship of churches and the ecumenical movement in general. The report of the central committee described fellowship in terms of mutuality: mutual vision, mutual respect, mutual love, mutual understanding, mutual correction, mutual challenge and mutual accountability. From the principle of mutuality, the report underlined the specific identity of the WCC that creates a sense of togetherness among member churches: a fellowship of churches with an inclusive vision, open to sharing the drama of a broken world. The fellowship of churches has a vocation to reach out beyond its borders in a situation of globalization marked by increasing interdependence and growing pluralism. The report thus called for collaboration with regional and national councils of churches in a spirit of mutual respect and trust. It also urged the Council to develop this vision of a fellowship that is open to all churches, beyond present institutional boundaries, leading them together towards the full and visible unity of the church.

The PCPCU from 2001 onwards considered not only the present state of the journey of churches towards Christian unity, but also the need to clarify a vision of ecumenism from the RCC perspective.

At its plenary of November 2001, Cardinal Walter Kasper, the president of the PCPCU, spoke of communion as the guiding concept of Catholic ecumenical theology. In his address he noted that in the bilateral dialogues in which the Catholic Church has been engaged over 35 years the central concept is that of *communio*. It is indeed the key concept for all bilateral and multilateral dialogues. The theological foundations of this concept of *communio* can be traced to the New Testament where, for example, in the Acts of the Apostles, the early church in Jerusalem constituted a *koinonia* in the breaking of bread and in prayer (Acts 2:44, 4:33). *Koinonia* is also a central theme in the Johannine and Pauline epistles. The Cardinal also observed that the Second Vatican Council adopted this *communio* ecclesiology (*LG* 3, 7, 11, 23, 26; *UR* 2) that contains both a vertical sacramental view and a horizontal communal perspective. The Second Vatican Council considers ecclesial *communio* to be based on, and prefigured in the trinitarian *communion* of Father, Son and Holy Spirit (*LG* 4; *UR* 2), a model of *communio* that is constitutive of the church. The president of the PCPCU observed that even though we may speak of a far-reaching ecumenical convergence on the concept of communion, it was clear that a firm ecumenical consensus was still far away, given the different ecclesiologies that are still operative among dialogue partners.

## III. COLLABORATION BETWEEN THE RCC AND THE WCC

The JWG oversees and seeks to foster not only ad hoc relationships which allow the RCC and the WCC to address together specific issues of mutual concern, but also to encourage the establishment of institutional links between programmes and teams of the WCC and the Vatican whereby the partners can formally collaborate in the wide range of issues being addressed by both.

### 1. Faith and Order

Even though the RCC is not a member of the WCC, it is fully represented with 12 members, drawn from different regions of the world, on the commission on Faith and Order.

Since the Harare assembly in 1998, major studies of the Faith and Order commission have focused on: the nature and purpose of the church; baptism; ecumenical hermeneutics; theological anthropology; ethnic identity, national identity and the search for unity; worship; and (since 2002) theological reflection on peace. The secretariat has also been involved in supporting United-Uniting churches, at their request, through a biannual survey of church union negotiations and through the organization of a conference in Driebergen in 2002 for these churches. It has also responded to the request of the conference of secretaries of Christian world communions to bring together those involved in bilateral dialogues in the bilateral forum to consider issues of common concern. The last of these took place in 2001. The secretariat published a collection of all international bilateral dialogues 1982-98 – *Growth in Agreement II* (Faith and Order paper 187, 2000).

The work on ecclesiology has involved a number of facets. The commission has been engaged in re-drafting the nature and purpose of the church in light of some 45 responses from churches, councils of churches and theological institutes. A major contribution was submitted by a group of Roman Catholic theologians convened by Cardinal Kasper, president of PCPCU, while another came from the archdiocese of Toronto. Moreover, a series of consultations have been held on ecclesiology and mission, co-sponsored with the commission on World Mission and Evangelism: "Does the Church Have a Sacramental Nature?", "Authority and Authoritative Teaching", and "Ministry and Ordination in the Community of Women and Men and the Church". The papers and reports from these consultations are in process of publication. The commission has also been invited to prepare a statement on ecclesiology: "The Church: Local and Universal, One and Diverse" for the WCC's ninth assembly.

During this period, the secretariat has been involved in a number of collaborative ventures, leading to the presentation to central committee and subsequent publication of a statement "A Church of All and for All" with the Ecumenical Disability Advocates Network, and a discussion paper with Mission and Evangelism and Inter-religious Dialogue teams on "A Theology of Religious Plurality".

## 2. Mission and Evangelism

The PCPCU continues to support and facilitate collaboration with the work of the WCC staff team responsible for mission and evangelism, as well as for health and healing, community and justice, and education and ecumenical formation. This is demonstrated significantly through the continued appointment of a full-time Roman Catholic consultant to work with the WCC staff team in these programme areas. During this mandate of the JWG, the person holding this appointment has been Sister Elizabeth Moran of the Missionary Sisters of Saint Columban.

During this mandate of the JWG there have been changes in personnel and organizational structure in the WCC staffing of this work. The Roman Catholic consultant was asked by the WCC to play a key part in the reorganization, and with the full support and approval of the PCPCU undertook the role of interim coordinator of the staff team during this period of realignment, which led to a new team on Mission and Ecumenical Formation. This interim assignment bears witness to the maturity of the partnership between the WCC and the RCC, in that the WCC could invite a consultant from a non-WCC member church to undertake such a key role, and that the RCC could commit itself to sharing its gifts and expertise in such a way with a partner organization.

Some additional appointments of Catholics to WCC bodies have brought a new dimension to the spectrum of cooperation and liaison between the WCC and the RCC. The new by-laws of the commission on World Mission and Evangelism (CWME) provide for the presence of three Roman Catholic members. The PCPCU has appointed three full members of the 30-person commission that advises the Geneva staff on mission concerns. There is also provision for the presence of one Roman Catholic member in the advisory body for Education and Ecumenical Formation and the PCPCU has appointed a religious sister.

A warm invitation has been offered by the WCC to the RCC to participate in the next world mission conference planned for May 2005 in Athens. An equally warm response from the PCPCU has led to a series of meetings to cooperate in preparing this important meeting. The conference theme is "Come, Holy Spirit, Heal and Reconcile!" Such joint preparation is enhancing collaboration between the WCC and the RCC in this significant global gathering that will focus on healing and reconciliation in our world.

Access to resources in the field of mission continues to be facilitated through visits and consultations between the WCC staff and the offices of the Secretary for Education and Documentation Service (SEDOS), the Union of Women's Religious Institutes (UISG) and the Union of Men's Religious Institutes (USG), as well as with several dicasteries of the Roman Curia. WCC representatives have been routinely invited to conferences and meetings organized by the RCC in Rome. Particularly noteworthy was the visit of Geneva staff to Rome in October 2001, which included attendance at the Wednesday public audience with Pope John Paul II, followed by a personal meeting with the Holy Father. In November 2002 the coordinator of the WCC team on Mission, Evangelism and Ecumenical Formation (Rev. Dr Carlos Ham), accompanied by the Roman Catholic consultant (Sr Elizabeth Moran), visited the offices of the Congregation for the Evangelization of Peoples and had a fruitful exchange of information with Archbishop Robert Sarah, secretary of the Congregation, and members of the staff.

Collaboration has been ongoing in the field of health and healing. A particular area of growing dialogue and collaboration is seen in the relations between the WCC and the Pontifical Council for Health Pastoral Care. WCC staff members have been welcomed as participants in the annual international conference organized by the Pontifical Council for Health Pastoral Care. There has been cooperation between the WCC and the RCC in shared work at the World Health Organization and during the world health assembly. On both regional and global levels, the WCC and the Catholic Church have collaborated in the development of the Ecumenical Pharmaceutical Network. Particular note must be made of the cooperation in the event of the major inter-religious consultation "Strategies to Increase Access to HIV/AIDS Prevention, Care and Treatment through Closer Cooperation between Faith-based Organizations and International Organizations" in Nairobi (7-10 May 2003), jointly convened by the WCC, Caritas International and the World Conference on Religion and Peace, and hosted by the All Africa Conference of Churches. This conference laid the ground for new partnerships between faith-based organizations, UN organizations, and internationally operating organizations. These partnerships are intended to assist development of new international initiatives to increase access to prevention, care and treatment for HIV/AIDS.

## 3. Ecumenical formation

The JWG has over the years expressed concern for ecumenical formation and education as fundamental to the search for the unity of the church. In the last mandate, the JWG published a study document entitled "Ecumenical Formation: Ecumenical Reflections and Suggestions". During the present mandate, the JWG has continuously encouraged efforts of ongoing ecumenical formation at the WCC Ecumenical Institute of Bossey, the WCC programme on Education and Ecumenical Formation (EEF) and the WCC programme on Ecumenical Theological Education (ETE).

## 3.1. *Ecumenical Institute of Bossey*

In its commitment to the work of ecumenical formation at Bossey, the PCPCU appoints a full-time Catholic professor on the staff of the Institute. Currently Father Gosbert Byamungu occupies that post and accompanies the students each year in their visit to Rome. The PCPCU is also represented on the Bossey board by one of its staff in the capacity of observer. In 2003, Bossey and the PCPCU co-sponsored a major seminar on the "Nature and Purpose of the Ecumenical Movement" at which a paper by Cardinal Walter Kasper with the same title was read on his behalf by a member of the PCPCU. In 2003, Bossey invited Msgr Frank Dewane of the Pontifical Council for Justice and Peace to give a lecture on issues of justice and peace.

The JWG encourages collaboration between the WCC and the RCC on several aspects of the work of the Ecumenical Institute of Bossey. In the first place, the PCPCU, through its committee for cultural collaboration, offers two full scholarships each year to Bossey for two Orthodox students. Secondly, the PCPCU organizes and sponsors the annual visit to Rome by the students and staff of the Institute. The purpose of the one-week programme in Rome is mainly to offer an opportunity to the students to get to know the Catholic Church from the perspective of its highest offices in order to overcome stereotypes and allow each to get to know the other better. Thus the programme includes an audience with the Holy Father, visits to various offices of the Roman Curia, encounters with representatives of men's and women's religious orders and with Catholic lay movements with ecumenical participation such as the Focolare movement and the St Egidio community. Other aspects of the programme include visits to some faculties of theology and guided tours to important places of Christian history. In recent years, some Catholic students have also participated in the Bossey programme.

The PCPCU considers the role of Bossey in ecumenical formation and education of church leaders as an important contribution to the journey towards Christian unity. The publication by Bossey of "Fifty Years of Ecumenical Formation at the Ecumenical Institute of Bossey: 1952-2002" bears witness to its important contribution over the years.

## 3.2. *Education and Ecumenical Formation (EEF)*

The WCC also has a programme on Education and Ecumenical Formation (EEF) geared to help member churches of the WCC. The PCPCU collaborates in that programme by appointing a Catholic consultant as an observer to the EEF working group.

## 3.3. *Ecumenical Theological Education (ETE)*

Over the years, the WCC programme on Ecumenical Theological Education (ETE) has worked closely with the RCC directly and indirectly. Father Fred Bliss, a professor of ecumenism at the St Thomas Aquinas Pontifical University in Rome, has been appointed by the PCPCU as consultant to the ETE working group. The PCPCU has suggested Catholic experts for meetings of ETE. The interactive study process on theological education and ministerial formation in Africa in 2001-2002 culminated with a conference in Johannesburg, South Africa, in September 2002, on the theme "The Journey of Hope in Africa Continued". On that occasion the PCPCU proposed both Catholic theological educators and others active in the ecumenical movement in Africa, especially in theological associations, to attend the conference.

## 3.4. *WCC youth internship programme*

The WCC youth internship programme provides ecumenical learning to young people between 18 and 30 years, seeking to equip them for deeper involvement in the ecumenical movement, and to aid networking among ecumenical youth movements. The networking has been strengthened since 2001, with study visits to Rome included in the yearly programme. Groups of interns have visited Rome in 2001, 2002 and 2004.

The main objectives of the study visits to Rome are to familiarize the interns with the cooperation between the RCC and the WCC and to equip them to strengthen ecumenical relations with the RCC in their countries.

With the support of the JWG, preparations for the visits begin with orientation by WCC staff with explanations of current relations between the WCC and the RCC. The PCPCU organizes and hosts the programme in Rome. Whenever feasible these visits have been scheduled around the meeting of the executive group of the JWG. This has also allowed the interns to attend some of those sessions and learn directly from the work of the JWG.

The programme organized by the PCPCU normally includes, besides participating in the general audience of the Holy Father, visits to a number of Roman Curia offices, Catholic movements such as the Focolare and the St Egidio community as well as the Centro Pro Unione. In addition the group has had guided tours of historical places related to the Christian tradition. The programme has also included a visit to the faculty of theology of the Waldensian church, a WCC member church in Italy.

Each part of the programme has included a time for presentation followed by time for questions and comments. In addition to all the knowledge and information shared, the spiritual life of the Catholic Church, as experienced in the meetings together with the aforementioned lay movements, has been very much appreciated by the interns. Some of them have followed up on the contacts made in Rome by getting to know local Focolare and St Egidio communities in their home countries after the end of their internships. All interns have highlighted the study visits to Rome as a remarkable learning experience which broadens and deepens their understanding of the RCC. The visits to Rome have also provided the interns with an opportunity to strengthen the bonds of friendship and care within their own community. Participation by additional Roman Catholic interns would be welcomed.

## 4. Inter-religious dialogue

Continuing exchange and cooperation have for a long time characterized the relationship between staff of the Pontifical Council for Interreligious Dialogue (PCID) and the WCC Office on Interreligious Relations and Dialogue (IRRD). This positive relationship has also been characteristic of the time between the eighth and ninth assemblies of the WCC. Yearly joint staff meetings alternating between the Vatican and Geneva have generally involved the entire staff, providing an opportunity for mutual information and exchange as well as for evaluation of ongoing projects and planning for upcoming projects. These staff meetings, unique in the relationship between the WCC and the Vatican, offer a possibility to reflect together on issues of common concern and where possible address them through common projects.

Staff members from the PCID and the IRRD are regularly invited to attend and contribute to meetings organized by the other office, e.g. the PCID assembly, the IRRD dialogue advisory group, as well as other consultations.

*Highlights include the following:*

1. Since 11 September 2001, inter-religious initiatives at the local, national and international levels have mushroomed and there is a need to keep abreast of developments as well as to engage in mutual consultation on inter-religious relations. The joint meetings enable staff to respond better to initiatives and to provide a foundation for a common approach or policy.

2. Throughout the period 1999-2005 there has been a mutual exchange on relations with Muslim organizations and an ongoing assessment of the status of Christian-Muslim relations.

3. The PCID and the IRRD have been reflecting on how to relate to the worsening situation between Christians and Hindus in India where concerns have been expressed by Hindus regarding proselytism, and where anti-conversion laws are in place in some Indian states. Given the sensitivities of perceiving an initiative by the PCID-IRRD as undue interference, plans are evolving to address conversion as a general issue in inter-religious relations and dialogue.

4. Building upon the common study project on inter-religious prayer in the mid-1990s (cf. special issues of *Pro Dialogo* and *Current Dialogue*), preparations are under way to address together emerging theological questions evolving in relation to inter-religious prayer.

5. A common initiative was launched to focus on the contributions of Africa to the religious and spiritual heritage in the world. This project is an attempt to provide space for various aspects of African religiosity and culture to be explored as a constructive and resourceful contribution to a world of religious plurality. This focus should not only give visibility to problems in Africa but also to the many and deeply spiritual contributions provided by the manifold expressions of religion on the continent and in the African diaspora. The project has so far seen three meetings: in Enugu, Nigeria (January 2001); Dakar, Senegal (December 2002); and Addis Ababa, Ethiopia (September 2004). These meetings brought together representatives of Christianity in Africa, representatives of Islam, and followers of African Traditional Religion, as well as representatives of some of the various religious communities of Africa in the diaspora. The theme focused on the family as a source of values and spirituality. A concluding publication of the findings is available.

## 5. Bilateral and multilateral dialogue

The importance of multilateral dialogue has been effectively illustrated by the fact that the Faith and Order convergence text *Baptism, Eucharist and Ministry* (BEM) has contributed significantly in various ways to reconciliation and/or new relationships between separated churches. The RCC cooperates with the WCC in multilateral dialogue as a full member of the Faith and Order commission, and by participating in Faith and Order's broad range of studies. When Cardinal Kasper met with Catholicos Aram I and the Rev. Dr Samuel Kobia at Antelias in 2004, he emphasized the importance of this work as a priority for the continuing collaboration of the RCC with the WCC.

Bilateral dialogues are important because they permit two Christian churches or communions to face together issues directly related to the particular division they have experienced with each other. Many WCC member churches such as the Orthodox or Oriental Orthodox churches are engaged in bilateral dialogue with the Roman Catholic Church. Others are involved in these dialogues or consultations on the national level, and especially on the international level through their Christian world communion, including Lutherans, Anglicans, Methodists, Reformed, Disciples of Christ, Mennonites, Baptists and Pentecostals. The 1999 signing of the Joint Declaration on the Doctrine of Justification by the Roman Catholic Church and the Lutheran World Federation was a particular achievement in which Lutheran member churches of the WCC took part.

The secretary of the PCPCU and officials of the WCC participate in the annual meetings of the conference of secretaries of the Christian world communions (CWCs). This informal body has periodically sponsored a forum on bilateral dialogues to monitor developments in bilateral dialogues and foster the coherence between bilateral and multilateral dialogue within the one ecumenical movement. The CWCs ask Faith and Order to convene this bilateral forum on its behalf. The eighth forum's theme was "The Implications of Regional Bilateral Agreements for the International Dialogues of Christian World Communions" (2001). One aspect of its report illustrated briefly the way in which the results of both bilateral and multilateral dialogue are being received through formal agreements instituting changed relationships. The report also noted the difficulty of reception of the results of bilateral dialogues because of asymmetrical structures for reception, while at the same time noting that some communions have developed structures precisely to further reception processes.

## 6. Week of Prayer for Christian Unity

Since 1966 the WCC Faith and Order commission and the PCPCU have collaborated annually in preparing the materials used ecumenically during the Week of Prayer for Christian Unity, and on other occasions. This long-standing cooperative project between the RCC and the WCC offers each year materials for prayer and biblical reflection on the theme of Christian unity. Both parties believe that such prayer and reflection is the very basis of the search for Christian unity.

Faith and Order and the PCPCU continued this close collaboration on the Week of Prayer for Christian Unity during the period of the present mandate of the JWG. The parties alternate in identifying a local ecumenical group to produce a draft set of materials, and in making arrangements for the international preparatory meeting at which these local draft texts are revised for international distribution. Several of the themes from recent years have found a special echo among the churches and communities: for example the 2004 theme of peace, with material produced by local ecumenical partners in Aleppo, Syria.

In a series of meetings, starting from an intensive brainstorming at Los Rubios, Spain, in 2001, the preparatory group has reflected on the process of the Week of Prayer materials from initial preparation to production and use. The central concern continues to be the relation between a local group responsible for the initial draft material and the international preparatory group whose role is to advise and revise.

With the Week of Prayer materials for 2005, an important advance is noted: the WCC Faith and Order commission and the PCPCU have moved beyond joint preparation and parallel publication to formal *joint publication* of the materials, now in a common format.

Topics of the Weeks of Prayer for 2000-2005 and the location of the initial preparatory group are as follows:

2000: Blessed be God who has blessed us in Christ (Eph. 1:3-14), preparatory material, Middle East Council of Churches; meeting at La Verna, Italy

2001: I am the Way, and the Truth, and the Life (John 14:1-6), preparatory material, Romania; meeting at Vulcan, Romania

2002: For with you is the fountain of life (Ps. 36:5-9), preparatory material, Concilium Conferentiarum Episcoporum Europae and the Conference of European Churches; meeting near Augsburg, Germany

2003: We have this treasure in clay jars (2 Cor. 4:4-18), preparatory material from Argentina; meeting at Los Rubios, Spain

2004: My peace I give to you (John 14:23-31), preparatory material from Aleppo; meeting in Palermo, Italy

2005: Christ, the one foundation of the church (1 Cor. 3:1-23), preparatory material and meeting, Slovak Republic

## IV. COLLABORATION THROUGH THE JWG

### 1. Character and nature of the JWG

The JWG was set up in May 1965 by mutual agreement between the WCC and the RCC as an instrument of collaboration between the two partners. Its purpose, described in 1966, was "to explore possibilities of dialogue and collaboration, to study problems jointly, and to report to the competent authorities of either side". In the seventh report, the JWG was described as a consultative forum that "has no authority in itself but reports to its parent bodies – the WCC assembly and the central committee, and the PCPCU". Thus the JWG has an advisory function and serves as an instrument for promoting cooperation between the RCC and the WCC. The JWG receives its mandate every seven years from its parent bodies – the WCC assembly and the PCPCU. At the end of each mandate, the JWG prepares and submits to its parent bodies a detailed report on its activities. This report is examined by the parent bodies who offer their observations and approval and give further guidelines for the next mandate.

During this term, each parent body appointed 17 members to the JWG, selected from different regions of the world, with varied pastoral and ecumenical experiences. The JWG meets in plenary once a year led by two co-moderators. The co-moderators, the co-secretaries and two corresponding staff persons form an executive that meets twice a year. The executive oversees the work of the JWG between its plenaries and prepares the agenda and materials for them.

As stated in the seventh report, the JWG "initiates, evaluates and sustains forms of collaboration between the WCC and the RCC, especially between the various organs and programmes of the WCC and the RCC". The structure and style of the JWG is meant to be flexible and adaptable to the changing needs and priorities of the JWG agenda. The JWG thus sets up sub-commissions to study specific topics on its agenda. Some topics may require the participation of experts from outside the group who may contribute to the ongoing study. The JWG has among its tasks the function of initiating and helping to keep alive the discussion, in the member churches of the WCC and the RCC, of issues facing the ecumenical movement. It also assesses the current trends in the ecumenical movement with a view to offering recommendations to its parent bodies.

*A. Assessment*

Reviewing its work 1999-2005, the JWG recognizes that its performance has been stronger in some respects than others.

In response to the 1966 mandate "to stimulate the search for visible unity" (cf. appendix A of this report [not included here]), there has been an emphasis on the discussion and the development of texts on issues of theological and pastoral concern and on learning from the experience of local churches.

It might be good for the next JWG to give more attention to the task of "initiating evaluating and sustaining forms of cooperation between the WCC and the RCC". It may also be fruitful to pay greater attention to "ad hoc initiatives". The JWG recognizes with satisfaction that new forms of collaboration have developed during the years of its mandate, and that there is now a stronger commitment for this kind of exchange.

The new JWG might also consider how it could more effectively fulfil the mandate of "being a challenge to the parent bodies by proposing new steps and programmes".

*B. Suggestions*

With the experience of these years, the JWG offers the following comments.

The importance of ecumenical spirituality needs to be reflected in the way the JWG operates. Its meetings might, for instance, begin with a day of recollection or retreat. Although during this period we have valued the opportunity to share one another's liturgies, we believe that the new JWG could further develop the possibilities for sharing the riches of our spiritual traditions.

There is need for a clear and comprehensive orientation for JWG members at the beginning of each new term. It would be essential if new members were well briefed on the mandate and the history of the JWG since 1965.

It is important that the parent bodies try to ensure that those appointed as members appreciate the importance of consistent attendance, not least to maintain regional balance.

The "reception" of the JWG's efforts needs to be enhanced. With and beyond the reporting required by the two parent bodies, initiatives are required to make the JWG's work accessible to the churches more widely, more speedily and in a more user-friendly form. One possibility is that study guides might be developed, for example, for use in connection with the documents on baptism and dialogue.

One of the JWG's functions is to "facilitate the exchange of information about the progress of the ecumenical movement, especially at the local level" (1975 guidelines). This has been very fruitfully achieved among the members themselves, but we believe that the task of making the fruits of this work known needs more attention.

The link between the JWG and NCCs and REOs could be developed. In addressing issues related to the proclamation of the gospel in the varied cultural context of today, these links could be particularly valuable.

The work of the JWG is, first and foremost, a journey of faith. Worship has been central to its life. There have been many contacts with local churches, ranging from a church-sponsored orphanage in Lebanon to a migrant community in Sweden to courageous efforts at peace-building in Northern Ireland. Through it all, relationships have deepened, and trust has grown.

## 2. Joint Working Group study documents

The JWG has produced three significant studies during this mandate, which are commended for use in a wide variety of contexts.

### 2.1. *Ecclesiological and Ecumenical Implications of a Common Baptism (Appendix C – here document 41)*

The gradual development within the modern ecumenical movement of a common understanding of baptism is one of the basic factors that have enabled long separated Christians to speak today of sharing a real though imperfect communion. Both multilateral (e.g., BEM) and bilateral dialogues have contributed to theological convergence and/or agreement on baptism.

The purpose of the JWG study document on the ecclesiological and ecumenical implications of a common baptism is to assist the churches to recognize what has been accomplished, and to build on it. The document therefore reviews important aspects of the growing convergence on baptism, noting the still-remaining differences. The text illustrates the ecumenical impact of what has been achieved by showing examples of the way common perspectives on baptism have helped foster changed relationships, in some cases full communion, between churches long separated.

Both the ecclesiological and the ecumenical implications of the growing common understanding of baptism highlighted in the study are important if further steps towards visible unity are to be taken. Ecclesiological implications, noted at the end of each of the document's first five sections, refer to issues uncovered in that section which also must be considered in dialogue in order to work towards a common understanding of the church. Ecumenical implications listed together in section six refer to pastoral or practical steps that might be taken now within the churches in order to receive and to build on the growing common understanding of baptism.

The JWG hopes that this study document will be used by the churches in various educational settings in order to deepen the appreciation that, even though the goal of visible unity has not yet been achieved, through a common baptism separated Christians already share deep bonds of communion.

The study proceeded in the following way. Initial material for reflection was presented to the JWG executive in January 2000, which included a summary of implications of baptism gleaned from many responses to BEM (Msgr John Radano) and an overview of current Faith and Order work on baptism (Rev. Dr Alan Falconer). These two members were asked to coordinate the project. The JWG plenary in May 2000 developed five main areas which became the focus of discussion for the study. Drafting meetings took place in 2001 and 2002 (Geneva), February 2003 (Rome) and September 2003 (Geneva). Work in progress on the study was presented each year for discussion at annual JWG meetings. Participating in various drafting sessions were Dr Eugene Brand, Rev. Dr Thomas Best, Fr Gosbert Byamungu, the Rev. Dr Alan Falconer, Dr Mark Heim, Prof. Nicholas Lossky, Dr Thomas Pott, Msgr John Radano, Dr Teresa Rossi and Dr Liam Walsh. Dr Teresa Rossi did additional research on media presentations on baptism for the project, and Dr William Henn contributed suggestions for improving certain aspects of an advanced draft of the text. Bishop David Hamid reviewed the advanced text for editorial clarity and consistency. The study was adopted by the JWG plenary in Chania, in May 2004.

## 2.2. *Nature and Purpose of Ecumenical Dialogue (Appendix D – here document 42)*

When the JWG between the RCC and the WCC was formed in 1965, it began its work by reflecting on the nature of ecumenical dialogue. The report, published in 1967, has served as a useful framework for ecumenical dialogues for some thirty years.

Since that time, relations between Christian communions and churches have grown and developed. The dialogues have helped to shatter stereotypes and dispel misunderstandings, and have led to changed relationships between churches on the way to visible unity. In this period of thirty years, there has developed a culture of dialogue.

However, there has also developed a renewed confessionalism. Difficulties in processes of reception have also led to division within confessional traditions participating in dialogues. Are issues of ethics and culture, which have not necessarily been the subject of dialogue, now becoming the sources of division within and between churches?

It was therefore felt appropriate that the JWG explore again the nature and practice of dialogue in the light of the experiences of thirty years, and of the new challenges and opportunities for dialogue at the beginning of the third millennium.

To initiate the process, two presentations were made on this topic at the beginning of this mandate of the JWG by then Bishop Walter Kasper and the Rev. Dr Konrad Raiser (published in *The Ecumenical Review*, 52, 3, 2000).

The document draws on: extensive discussions from meetings of the JWG plenary in Beirut (2000) and Dromantine (2001), both regions where community tension exists and where processes of dialogue have been developed; the papers of Cardinal Kasper and the

Rev. Dr Raiser; the 1967 document; and subsequent published reflections from a number of theologians engaged in processes of dialogue.

The statement points to the development of the culture of dialogue, examines different approaches and notes the impact of the dialogues in creating new relationships between churches and communities. In the light of thirty years' experience of dialogues involving the Catholic Church, it explores anew the theological basis of dialogue, elicits a number of principles of dialogue, and develops some theses on the spirituality and practice of ecumenical dialogue. Attention is paid to the question of "reception", and reflection is given on the difficulties and positive experiences of such reception processes. The document concludes with some challenges posed to dialogue in the 21st century and underlines how the culture of dialogue is an essential expression of the nature of Christian living and is a key element of the common pilgrimage of churches as they seek to be faithful to the prayer that all may be one... so that the world may believe (John 17:21).

The study proceeded in the following way. After the presentations on dialogue by then Bishop Walter Kasper and the Rev. Dr Konrad Raiser, the first plenary developed a series of issues to be considered in a study document on dialogue. A small drafting group consisting of Eden Grace, Dr Susan Wood, Msgr Felix Machado, Msgr John Radano and Rev. Dr Alan Falconer met in Cartigny, Switzerland (February 2003), and produced an initial draft. After discussions in the plenary in Bari, the text was further developed through e-mail correspondence and at a one-day drafting session in September 2003 (the Rev. Dr Alan Falconer, Msgr John Radano, Rev. Dr Thomas Best). After further discussion at the JWG executive meeting in November 2004, Bishop David Hamid was asked to review the text for editorial consistency. The study document was adopted by the JWG plenary at Chania, Crete, in May 2004.

### 2.3. *"Inspired by the Same Vision": Roman Catholic participation in national and regional councils of churches (Appendix E – here document 40)*

Because the JWG is responsible for overseeing and fostering relationships between the RCC and the WCC, it is fitting that this body present an overview of the nature, extent and quality of participation by the Catholic Church in councils of churches and regional ecumenical organizations around the world. This is not the first time the JWG has conducted such a review, but contexts continue to evolve. The number of Roman Catholic bodies participating in councils of churches continues to increase. And so, as the study document "Inspired by the Same Vision" states, "After more than forty years of experience, the JWG is asking some basic questions about Roman Catholic involvement in national and regional councils of churches and other ecumenical instruments. What works well? What is not working well? Why?" That is the purpose of this study.

The document recognizes that in many regions of the world councils of churches are a primary means whereby relationships among churches are nurtured and advanced. All involved will admit that the path is not always smooth. The study attempts to look forthrightly at problems and challenges that inhibit participation by the Catholic Church, in an effort to stimulate constructive reflection on ways through difficulties. To the degree that "all in each place" have representatives at the ecumenical table, the quest for full visible Christian unity is enhanced.

Specific recommendations are offered at the conclusion of the document, proposing that "representatives of NCCs, REOs and episcopal conferences in places where the Roman Catholic Church is not in membership... should consider the document 'Inspired by the Same Vision' and reflect on the experience others have gleaned regarding Catholic participation". Governing bodies of councils of churches and Catholic bishops conferences in every setting are urged to read and reflect on the document, and to do so together. In addition, the PCPCU and the WCC should sponsor a new international consultation to bring together representatives of NCCs, REOs and episcopal conferences, especially from places where the Roman Catholic Church is not in membership.

The text is divided into eight sections: a statement of purpose, definition and history of Roman Catholic participation, evolving attitudes towards membership, the value and benefits of membership, issues and concerns, questions to consider, concluding observations and recommendations.

The text concludes with the words, "We pray that the document will strengthen appreciation for, understanding of, and participation in councils of churches."

The study proceeded in the following way. A JWG sub-committee, co-chaired by the Rev. Thomas Michel, SJ, and the Rev. Dr Diane C. Kessler, worked steadily on this project beginning with the second meeting in Dromantine, Northern Ireland (2001). The other members were Rev. David Gill, Rev. Prof. Viorel Ionita, Sr Joan McGuire, OP, and Bishop Paul Nabil Sayah, with the assistance of Msgr John Mutiso-Mbinda and Ms Teny Pirri-Simonian, respectively of the PCPCU and WCC staff. The drafting group customarily met for two days prior to sessions of the full JWG, held a drafting session in Rome in March 2003, and worked during the year sharing drafts via email. The topic was discussed in plenary sessions of the JWG in 2001-2003, and was considered by the JWG executive committee.

In August 2002, Rev. Dr Kessler presented the early stages of the draft at a meeting of the general secretaries of national councils of churches at Bossey in Celigny, Switzerland, and invited their participation in a study-and-response process. A number of councils requested copies of the draft for consideration, and several responded with recommendations. Councils that requested the draft and/or offered responses included those from Austria, Britain and Ireland, France, India, Norway, Slovak Republic, Sudan, Swaziland, Sweden, Switzerland and Tanzania. The Protestant Federation of France undertook the translation of the draft text into French. A gathering of state council of churches executives in the United States discussed the topic in one of their annual meetings and offered input into the study. The input provided by these and other bodies significantly enhanced the quality of the study. The study document was adopted by the JWG plenary at Chania, Crete, in May 2004.

## 3. Issues studied by the JWG

### 3.1. Theological anthropology

The proposed study on theological anthropology emerged from discussion at the JWG meeting in Antelias, Lebanon, in May 2000. This area of common interest has become increasingly urgent due to a range of issues affecting the understanding and protection of the human person posed, for example, by bio-ethics, human sexuality and violence.

During the period 2000-2004 a number of sessions were held to discuss those issues. Papers were presented at the Dromantine and Bari plenaries by Bishop Marc Ouellet, Prof. Nicholas Lossky, Archbishop Jozef Zycinski, Bishop Donal Murray and Dr Teresa Rossi. The topics explored were biblical anthropology, theological anthropology, the concept of *imago Dei*, particularly in the writings of Pope John Paul II.

A small group was formed to begin the process of drafting a study document, but due to change of staff personnel the group was not able to meet and the JWG executive recommended that discussion of the question should continue but that substantive work be taken up by the 2006-13 JWG, who could use the papers and reports submitted to the present JWG as a basis for their discussion.

## 3.2. Interchurch marriages

The issue of interchurch marriages has been on the agenda of the JWG at different periods of its mandate. For instance, from 2 to 4 October 1989 in Geneva the JWG held a consultation on interchurch marriage to "assess the difficulties and opportunities of interchurch marriages".

During the current mandate of the JWG, discussion on this issue began at the first meeting plenary in Antelias, Lebanon, in 2000, and from the start the JWG took account of its previous work. It acknowledged that this is still an important and urgent matter before the churches and recognized that many look to the JWG to contribute to the churches' response to this pastoral concern. The following steps were proposed as a service that the JWG might offer to the RCC and to member churches of the WCC who are continuing to work on the questions and problems associated with interchurch marriages:

- to identify the available materials on interchurch marriages; (Association of Interchurch Families)
- to study these materials to assess which factors are specific to the life of the churches, and which are more likely based on cultural considerations; (Association of Interchurch Families)
- to identify initiatives that may be helpfully shared across the churches.

It is with considerable disappointment that, due to a sheer limit of time and staff resources, this JWG was not able to act upon the recommendations from its first plenary meeting.

The JWG is acutely aware that the *theological* issues involved in interchurch marriage are extremely complex. Beyond the pastoral concerns lie far-reaching ecclesiological implications for the churches as well as challenges to the varied understandings of the sacramentality of marriage. Despite the limitations of time and resources, the JWG was committed to listen sensitively to current reflection in the churches on this pastoral issue, the source of considerable hurt and pain for many Christians. It recognized the particular wisdom and experience that the Interchurch Families Association can offer in this area. Consequently, in Dromantine in 2001, four presentations were made to the plenary:

- ecumenical and ecclesiological implications of interchurch marriages, by Dr Ruth Reardon (Association of Interchurch Families);

- proposed ways to move forward, by the Rev. Canon Martin Reardon (Association of Interchurch Families);
- comments on the *Ecumenical Directory*, by Bishop Donal Murray;
- a summary of the 1996 agreement on interchurch marriages between Catholic and Orthodox patriarchs in the Middle East, by Archbishop Paul Sayah.

The third plenary in Stjärnholm in 2002 devoted a session to the issue of interchurch marriages. Three papers were presented reflecting three distinct Christian traditions: Bishop Marc Ouellet spoke of the "Sacrament of Matrimony according to the Catechism of the Catholic Church", Rev. Prof. Viorel Ionita presented an Orthodox perspective, and Rev. David Gill spoke from the point of view of a church of the Reformation. The ensuing discussion revealed that there may be possibilities of convergence on matters of grace and sacrament and the JWG recognized that the issue of interchurch marriage was not unrelated to the implications of the recognition of common baptism.

The difficult theological issues notwithstanding, the JWG continued to underline the need to remind the member churches of the WCC and the RCC of their pastoral responsibilities towards couples in interchurch marriages.

## 4. Areas of shared concern regarding social issues

### 4.1. Social thought and action

Even though social thought and action have been on the JWG agenda from the beginning, it has been difficult in the term of this mandate to find adequate ways to collaborate in this area. Among the reasons are the different nature of the partners, one a church, the other a council of churches, and their different approaches to dealing with social questions. The JWG study document "The Ecumenical Dialogue on Moral Issues: Potential Sources of Common Witness or of Division" remains a useful resource for confronting moral issues.

However, because of the locations in which it has met, the JWG has been able to explore issues of peace and reconciliation. At its first plenary in Antelias, in post-civil war Lebanon, meetings with representatives of local churches afforded opportunities to reflect not only on the character of ecumenical relations there, but also on experiences of dealing with violence, conflict, and the possibilities of reconciliation.

In the second plenary, in Dromantine, Northern Ireland, there were discussions of the conflicts that had taken place in Northern Ireland. Papers were presented by Dr David Stevens of the Irish Council of Churches, Rev. Dr Alan Falconer, and Bishop Anthony Farquhar, Catholic Auxiliary Bishop of Down and Connor. The recommendations of the working party on sectarianism were presented and the Irish School of Ecumenics' project on reconciliation was described. A visit to Belfast provided opportunities to come to a deeper understanding, not only of the conflicts, but also of the efforts at reconciliation that were taking place. The members saw, for example, the efforts of the Anglican and Roman Catholic cathedrals to build bridges between the two peoples in conflict.

## 4.2.  Decade to Overcome Violence (2001-10) (DOV)

Cooperation on the DOV began with contacts around the topic of small arms followed by an invitation from the WCC to the Pontifical Council for Justice and Peace to have a staff member serve on the DOV reference committee. Another opportunity for joint work between the DOV staff at the WCC and the Pontifical Council for Justice and Peace arose within the framework of an international coalition for the UN Decade for a Culture of Peace and Nonviolence for the Children of the World, based in Paris, France. The coalition was founded in the summer of 2003 and both the DOV coordination office and the PCJP are observing members of the international committee.

The DOV coordination office has made efforts to publicize on the DOV website organizations, events, resources and stories from within the RCC, so as to make visible the fact that the DOV initiative reaches far beyond the formal WCC membership. Dioceses, local parishes and interchurch joint efforts are given visibility. In some countries national justice and peace commissions are part of the ecumenical DOV effort. For example, the DOV study guide *Why Violence? Why Not Peace?* was translated into French in Belgium by a group under Catholic leadership.

The third plenary in Stjärnholm was able to consider rich input from three events. These included the "Ten Points of Commitment to Peace" proclaimed at an ecumenical and inter-religious gathering of religious leaders in Assisi, 24 January 2002, at the invitation of Pope John Paul II; the Brussels Declaration of 20 December 2001 from the meeting organized by Ecumenical Patriarch Bartholomew; and the statement of an interfaith meeting organized by the Archbishop of Canterbury in Alexandria, Egypt, in January 2002. The JWG executive at its meeting in March 2003 suggested that the JWG might consider publishing these three statements, with introductions, as a contribution to the DOV.

The same plenary heard a presentation, "Global Peace, Global Conflict, and Human Responsibility" by Prof. Peter Wallensteen of Uppsala university. Dr Teresa Rossi presented a 90-page printed report produced by a seminar which she conducted on the DOV at the St Thomas Aquinas Pontifical University in Rome during the 2003 spring semester, the first seminar in a long-term programme she has introduced on DOV. The report has also been presented at the PCPCU and sent to the WCC offices.

Concerning the war in Iraq, the WCC organized a prayer service for peace on the day the bombardment began. The WCC, with the assistance of Archbishop Diarmuid Martin, then the permanent representative of the Holy See to the UN bodies in Geneva, and former member of the JWG, invited representatives of religious communities in the city and the diplomatic corps in Geneva to take part in the service.

There is much room for increased cooperation with both the Vatican and Catholic constituencies within the framework of the DOV.

## 4.3.  Other contacts between RCC/WCC

### 4.3.1. REFUGEES AND MIGRATION

Cordial relations have developed between the Pontifical Council for the Pastoral Care of Migrants and Itinerant Peoples and the WCC staff working on this same area. WCC representatives participated in the fifth world congress for the pastoral care of migrants and refugees, held in Rome, 17-22 November 2003. In 2001, His Eminence Cardinal Stephen Fumio Hamao and Rev. Fr Michael Blum (president and under-secretary of the Pontifical Council) visited WCC staff in Geneva to discuss ways of working together more collaboratively. The Rev. Fr Frans Thoolen of the Pontifical Council staff participated in meetings of United Nations High Commissioner for Refugees (UNHCR) governing bodies, often serving as the representative of the Holy See in these meetings. The possibility of strengthening collaboration in the area of programme is limited by staff capacity.

Cooperation between Roman Catholic organizations and the WCC has been particularly strong in the area of refugees and migration. Since the Harare assembly, cooperation between WCC and Caritas International, the International Catholic Migration Commission (ICMC) and the Jesuit Refugee Service (JRS) has continued. The ICMC and the JRS both have representatives in Geneva and WCC staff work closely with them on a number of advocacy initiatives, particularly related to the work of the UNHCR. This cooperation is often expressed through participation in NGO networks, particularly the International Council of Voluntary Agencies. In addition, there is mutual consultation, sharing of information from respective networks, and discussion of common priorities. The WCC and Caritas International are members of the 9-member steering committee for humanitarian response. Caritas and WCC networks share similar concerns and complement each other's awareness of the importance of working through local and national organizations. Caritas International also has close relations with Action by Churches Together (ACT) and is invited to participate in the annual meetings of the ACT emergency committee.

### 4.3.2. DIAKONIA AND DEVELOPMENT

Archbishop Paul Josef Cordes, president of the Pontifical Council Cor Unum which undertakes charitable work, visited Geneva and the WCC in 2002. He had conversations with the Council leadership and staff working in areas of common interest with Cor Unum. Following this visit, the WCC director of the churches' commission on international affairs strengthened the relationship with the WCC by representing the WCC in the Cor Unum plenary assembly in 2003, where he was a keynote speaker.

### 5. Topical issues: the documents *Dominus Iesus* and *Ecclesia de Eucharistia*

During the period of the present mandate of the JWG, the WCC members of JWG held discussions with the Roman Catholic partners on two documents, namely, the instruction *Dominus Iesus* (published in 2000) and the 2003 encyclical on the eucharist, *Ecclesia de Eucharistia*. Both documents have important ecumenical implications and therefore needed to be discussed. For that reason, following their publication, the JWG played a valuable role as a forum where a frank discussion of the documents could take place. This process of dialogue was useful for clarifying some of the misunderstandings about the purpose of issuing such documents on the part of the RCC. The very fact that the

RCC is open to listening to the reactions of the WCC representatives is in itself an important sign of its commitment to ecumenical dialogue.

At the JWG plenary of May 2001, some members of the JWG shared reactions received from WCC member churches on the document *Dominus Iesus*. The WCC made use of this spirit of dialogue and openness to continue the discussion of this document through a subsequent exchange of communication with the PCPCU.

## V. PROSPECTS FOR THE FUTURE (2006-2013)

### Revisiting the mandate

As the JWG approaches the end of this working period, the members are deeply convinced that "there continues to be a need for a forum enabling the RCC and the WCC to evaluate together the development of the ecumenical movement". The JWG has amply proven that it is a necessary, vital instrument for the growth of ecumenical relations and the facilitating of a joint Christian response to the needs of the people of our time. But the members also see reasons for revisiting the mandate originally given in 1966 and modified in 1975, and for giving further attention to the composition and working style of the JWG.

The members agree that the JWG, as a consultative forum, is truly capable of inspiring, directing and sustaining dialogue between the RCC and the WCC regarding issues of concern to the ecumenical movement, and of facilitating collaboration between the various organs and programmes of the WCC and the RCC. But it is clear that we live in a changing world, marked by the destabilizing effect of globalization on peoples' lives and cultures, that the ecumenical horizon is undergoing rapid change, and that the churches, within themselves and in their service to the human family, face new and demanding challenges which call for ever greater commitment to the search for visible unity and common witness.

The members of the JWG have bonded well during the period of their engagement and common toil. They have reached a level of mutual understanding and trust that has allowed them to examine the issues before them with objectivity and critical discernment. They now set before the parent bodies areas of common concern which need further attention on the part of the next JWG. They have a sense that the JWG has the potential to achieve even greater results, and that consultations between the RCC and the WCC on the JWG's way forward should stress the original aim of the group as primarily that of "discovering and assessing promising new possibilities for ecumenical development", and in "proposing new steps and programmes" as a challenge to the parent bodies (cf. guidelines for the future of the JWG, *Breaking Barriers: Nairobi 1975*, David M. Paton ed., 1975, pp. 276-78).

## Recommendations from the Joint Working Group to the RCC and the WCC

The following areas of common concern require particular attention, either because of their potential to strengthen relations between the churches and between Christians at all levels, or because they are perceived as continuing sources of pain or reasons of scandal between divided Christians.

1.  Among the first, we point to a clear convergence between all the members of the JWG regarding the need to promote a return to the spiritual roots of ecumenism. Crucial at the beginning of the ecumenical movement was the spiritual ecumenism that inspired the Week of Prayer for Christian Unity, the commission on Mission and Evangelism, and the Faith and Order commission. At the November 2003 plenary assembly of the PCPCU, Cardinal Kasper stated:

> When we speak of ecumenical spirituality, we do not use this word – which is unfortunately overused – to mean a spirituality that is vague, weak, merely sentimental, irrational and sub-jective, that does not take into account the objective doctrine of the church, or even ignores it. On the contrary, we mean the teaching of scripture, of the living tradition of the church, and of the outcomes of ecumenical dialogues that have been personally and totally assimilated, are infused with life and in contact with life. Mere ecumenical activism is destined to exhaust itself; merely academic debate among experts, no matter how important it may be, eludes the "normal" faithful and touches only the margin of their hearts and lives. We can only expand the ecumenical movement by deepening it.

At the general assembly of the All Africa Conference of Churches, Yaoundé, Cameroon, in November 2003, Rev. Dr Samuel Kobia, general secretary-designate of the World Council of Churches, said:

> From baptism to communal sharing of meals and reception of the spirit, the memory of Christ's suffering, death and resurrection becomes a reality in anticipation of another reality. The past in our minds is memory. Human beings cannot create, or even imagine, anything that is entirely new. But in the eucharistic meal something new always happens. Christ, in whose suffering our suffering as a community of faith is embodied, creates a new community. Once incorporated into the body one is expected to live by the mind of Christ in order to function fully and bring health to the life of the body. Activity within the body of Christ produces a new group identity and world-view. And by extension we can claim this ecclesiology as part of our ecumenism/ecumenical spirit...

> It is vitally important that we bring theology back to the people, and craft new themes of spir-ituality that are congenial to our unique experience and place in the world. We must re-empha-size the need for spirituality as the basis for the work we do in the world. That way we avoid being tantalized by the trappings of prestige that come with power even when such power is derived from a moral imperative...

> If we have the courage and tenacity of our forebears, who stood firmly like a rock against the lashes of slavery, we shall find a way to do in our times what they did for theirs and be awak-ened someday by the hope to a new dream come true.

What is needed is a renewed ecumenical spirituality based on the riches of our respec-tive traditions, centred on continual conversion to Christ, able to intensify at the spiritual level relations between the ecumenical partners. We must be convinced that only by enriching one another spiritually, through common prayer and other forms of spiritual sharing, will it be possible for Christians successfully to tackle the important questions before us in dealing with one another and with the world around us. A return to the spiritual roots of ecumenism must be an aspect of any reflection on the renewal of the ecumenical movement itself.

2. We likewise agree that greater effort is needed in the field of ecumenical formation. Both parent bodies need to be concerned about Christians and clergy who need ecumenical formation. A new generation of Christians is sometimes unaware of the way things were and how much things have changed in the decades since the founding of the WCC and since the Second Vatican Council. In this respect much is being done, but we advocate an effort to improve the coordination of such formation through a more effective sharing of information and resources, and by providing greater opportunities for participation in each other's life. We especially recommend that the JWG keep before the churches the importance of offering young people opportunities to be exposed to traditions other than their own, especially in shared programmes of formation, mission and service. We also recommend the valuable study by the last JWG on ecumenical formation (cf. *Seventh Report of the JWG*, 1998, pp.57-59).

3. Among the areas of concern that are already having serious consequences for the churches and for ecumenical relations we point to the continuing, pressing, possibly church-dividing difficulties encountered in giving common witness in the field of personal and social moral issues. Society is becoming more confused and fragmented in its understanding of what it means to be truly human. Consequently, all churches are being called to respond to society's profound questioning in important matters of bio-ethics, human, civil and religious rights, issues of peace, social justice, healing of memories, human sexuality and reproduction. We believe that the JWG should, as a matter of urgency and in cooperation with Faith and Order and in consultation with other bodies, seek ways to develop the already-begun joint exploration of the philosophical and theological foundations of Christian anthropology. The 1991-98 JWG offered a valuable document in 1996: "The Ecumenical Dialogue on Moral Issues: Potential Sources of Common Witness or of Divisions". This 1998-2005 JWG has followed the topic closely (cf. *Seventh Report*, 1998, appendix B, p.31) and strongly recommends that it be carried forward into the next mandated period.

4. Other new challenges to Christians demand a response. Inter-religious dialogue has become an urgent necessity and Christians have to engage in this together. Religious pluralism and, in some places, the increasing absence of God in cultural life are challenging Christians to "give an account of the hope that is in [them]" (1 Pet. 3:15) and to live out together [their] common calling to mission. The spread of modern technology and the power of the media to form people's opinion and even their perception of reality calls for Christians to be responsibly critical towards the ensuing style of interpersonal, family and social relationships, and to be more effective in using the positive opportunities that these instruments offer. The prevalence of injustice, different forms of violence and the fear induced by international terrorism are directly opposed to the respect for human dignity that is at the heart of the Christian message. These are among the issues which can fruitfully be examined by the next JWG, as it seeks ways to improve and intensify cooperation between the churches.

We recommend therefore that in preparing the next JWG the parent bodies stress those parts of the original mandate that have perhaps been less to the forefront and which, nevertheless, are especially indicative of what is now needed. The JWG should be alert to identifying and proposing fresh forms of collaboration between the WCC and the RCC. The members should be asked to commit more effort to interpreting the major streams of ecumenical thought at the general and local levels, without undertaking study processes which are or could be carried out by other bodies.

In response to the changing needs of the ecumenical task, the JWG might fruitfully reflect on how its work can be related more closely to the context and praxis in different local situations around the world. Like flexibility and adaptability to the changing circumstances of the mission entrusted by Christ to his disciples (cf. Matt. 28:19) these are also essential qualities of the ecumenical cooperation which are also required of the JWG itself.

The task of the JWG is in fact to facilitate the advent of a time when the RCC and the WCC member churches can meet in genuine koinonia and can therefore give convincing witness to the world of the transforming message of the gospel of Jesus Christ. We entrust the work of the past seven years to the Triune God and pray that the Holy Spirit "will bring to completion the work he has begun in us" (cf. Phil. 1:6).

## MEMBERS OF THE JOINT WORKING GROUP 1999-2006

### Representatives of the Roman Catholic Church

Most Rev. Mario CONTI
*Co-moderator JWG*
Archbishop of Glasgow
Glasgow, UK

Most Rev. Walter KASPER
*1999-2001*
Secretary
Pontifical Council
for Promoting Christian Unity
Vatican City

Most Rev. Marc OUELLET
*2001-2003*
Secretary
Pontifical Council
for Promoting Christian Unity
Vatican City

Most Rev. Brian FARRELL
*since 2003*
Secretary
Pontifical Council
for Promoting Christian Unity
Vatican City

Most Rev. Giampaolo CREPALDI
*since 2001*
Pontifical Council for
Justice and Peace
Vatican City

Most Rev. Michael FITZGERALD
*1999-2002*
Pontifical Council
for Interreligious Dialogue
Vatican City

Most Rev. Diarmuid MARTIN
*1999-2001*
Pontifical Council
for Justice and Peace
Vatican City

Most Rev. Donal B. MURRAY
Bishop of Limerick
Limerick, Ireland

Most Rev. Donald J. REECE
Bishop of St John's Basseterre
St John's, Antigua, West Indies

Most Rev. Paul Nabil SAYAH
Archbishop of Haifa
and the Holy Land (Maronite)
Jerusalem

Most Rev. Buti J. TLHAGALE, OMI
Archbishop of the Diocese
of Johannesburg
Doornfontein, South Africa

Most Rev. Józef M. ZYCINSKI
Archbishop of Lublin
Lublin, Poland

Rev. Dr Remi HOECKMAN
*1999-2001*
Pontifical Council for
Promoting Christian Unity
Vatican City

Rev. Monsignor
Felix A. MACHADO
*since 2002*
Pontifical Council for
Interreligious Dialogue
Vatican City

Sister Joan McGUIRE, OP
Ecumenical Officer
Archdiocese of Chicago
Chicago IL, USA

Sister Celine MONTEIRO, FMM
Franciscan Missionaries of Mary
Generalate, Rome
Rome, Italy

Sister Elizabeth MORAN, MSSC
World Council of Churches
Mission and Ecumenical Formation
Geneva, Switzerland

Rev. Monsignor
John MUTISO-MBINDA
*Co-Secretary JWG*
Pontifical Council
for Promoting Christian Unity
Vatican City

Rev. Monsignor
John A. RADANO
Pontifical Council
for Promoting Christian Unity
Vatican City

Dr Teresa Francesca ROSSI
Centro Pro Unione
Roma, Italy

Sister Theresa SEOW, FdCC
St Anthony's Canossian Convent
Singapore

Ms Denise SULLIVAN
*1999-2000 (passed away)*
Catholic Bishop's Committee
for Ecumenical and Interfaith Relations
Mawson ACT 2607, Australia

Rev. Father
Juan USMA GÓMEZ
*since 2001*
Pontifical Council
for Promoting Christian Unity
Vatican City

Rev. Father
Thomas MICHEL, SJ
Consultant since 2001
Secretary for Interreligious Dialogue
Jesuit Curia
Rome, Italy

*Administrative staff*

Dr Paola FABRIZI
Pontifical Council for
Promoting Christian Unity
Vatican City

**Representatives of the World Council of Churches**

Bishop Dr Jonas JONSON
Church of Sweden (Lutheran)
*Co-moderator JWG*
Bishop of Strängnäs
Strängnäs, Sweden

Prof. Dr Oscar CORVÁLAN-VÁSQUEZ
Pentecostal Church of Chile
Talca, Chile

Rt Rev. Bishop H. Mvume DANDALA
Methodist Church of South Africa
General Secretary
All Africa Conference of Churches
Nairobi, Kenya

His Grace Metropolitan
Philipos Mar EUSEBIUS
Malankara Orthodox Syrian Church
St Basil Aramana
Kerala, India

His Eminence Metropolitan Prof. Dr
GENNADIOS OF SASSIMA
Ecumenical Patriarchate
of Constantinople
Istanbul, Turkey

Rev. David GILL
Uniting Church in Australia
Kowloon
Hong Kong SAR, China

Rt Rev. David HAMID
Anglican Consultative Council
Suffragan Bishop in Europe
Westminster, London, UK

Rev. Prof. Viorel IONITA
Romanian Orthodox Church
Study Secretary
Conference of European Churches
Geneva, Switzerland

Dr Musimbi KANYORO
Lutheran
General Secretary
World Young Women's
Christian Association
Geneva, Switzerland

Ms Ülle KEEL
Estonian Evangelical Lutheran Church
Tallinn, Estonia

Rev. Dr Diane C. KESSLER
United Church of Christ, USA
Executive Director
Massachusetts Council of Churches
Boston, USA

Prof. Nicholas LOSSKY
Russian Orthodox Church
Paris, France

Rev. Valamotu PALU
Free Wesleyan Church of Tonga
General Secretary
Pacific Conference of Churches
Suva, Fiji

Rev. Dr Alan FALCONER
Director, Faith and Order
World Council of Churches
Geneva, Switzerland

Mr Georges LEMOPOULOS
Deputy General Secretary
World Council of Churches
Geneva, Switzerland

Ms Teny PIRRI-SIMONIAN
*Co-Secretary JWG*
Church and Ecumenical Relations
World Council of Churches
Geneva, Switzerland

*Administrative staff*
Ms Luzia WEHRLE
Administrative Assistant
Church and Ecumenical Relations
World Council of Churches
Geneva, Switzerland

# 40. "Inspired by the Same Vision": Roman Catholic Participation in National and Regional Councils of Churches

## Joint Working Group

### Kolympari – Chania, Crete, Greece, 6-13 May 2004

## I. The purpose of this document [1]

"The member churches of the World Council of Churches and the Roman Catholic Church are *inspired by the same vision* of God's plan to unite all things in Christ" (Common Understanding and Vision 4.11). One means of moving towards this vision has been membership and participation in councils of churches. After more than forty years of experience, the Joint Working Group is asking some basic questions about Catholic involvement in national and regional councils of churches and other ecumenical instruments. What works well? What is not working well? Why?

Many councils of churches are struggling with a variety of issues that, in some cases, also are vexing their member churches, such as trying to clarify anew purpose and direction, seeking to capture the imagination of new generations, and finding the financial resources needed to meet the expectations of members and the demands of common ministry. These issues have been considered in other contexts, and some references are listed at the conclusion of this text.

Because specific questions about Roman Catholic participation are being raised in the conciliar context, this document will examine some systemic issues that councils of churches are facing. Some of these are inherent in the very nature of councils. Some are new problems in a world that has changed significantly since councils first were formed. This is the contemporary environment in which we are shining a lens on particular questions.

When the Roman Catholic Church is a member of a national council of churches (NCC) or regional ecumenical organization (REO), what were the circumstances that facilitated membership? If concerns have surfaced, what are they? How are they being addressed? If signs of growth have resulted, what are they? How have they been nurtured? How has Catholic membership affected relationships among all the member churches?

When the Roman Catholic Church is not a member of an NCC/REO, what are some of the reasons? If concerns are cited, what are they? Have other ways, short of membership, been used to encourage participation? How has Catholic ecclesiology affected issues of participation and membership in councils? Has the possibility of participation by the Roman Catholic Church discouraged involvement by another church, and if so, for what reasons?

This study addresses one aspect of a multi-faceted ecumenical scene, and it is part of a series of periodic reflections about the nature and purpose of councils of churches. It was prepared by the Joint Working Group, the post-Vatican II instrument created to enhance relationships between the Roman Catholic Church and the World Council of Churches, in consultation with the leaders of NCCs and REOs, who offered valuable suggestions. We pray that it will strengthen appreciation for, understanding of, and participation in councils of churches.

## II. Councils of churches and regional ecumenical organizations

When churches come together to form a council of churches, they consider the theological basis that becomes their organizing principle. Some of these bases have been trinitarian (e.g. all churches who subscribe to the baptismal formula of "Father, Son, and Holy Spirit") or christological (e.g. all churches which claim "Jesus Christ as Lord and Saviour"). Either implicit or explicit in this basis is a definition of their purpose in coming together through the council, and of the marks of membership. These bases, which vary somewhat, become the framework in which churches choose to apply for membership.

The ultimate aim of churches in the ecumenical movement is full visible Christian unity. Councils of churches are a privileged instrument by which churches can move towards this goal as they witness to a real, though incomplete unity in their service of the mission of the church.

At the same time, this study needs a working definition for councils of churches. One such definition has been given by a document produced by the Massachusetts Council of Churches:

> A council of churches is an institutional expression of the ecumenical movement, in which representatives of separated and autonomous Christian churches within a given area covenant together to become an enduring fellowship for making visible and effective the unity and mission of the church (*Odyssey Towards Unity*, p.30).

Sometimes membership in a council or conference includes not only churches, but also other ecumenical organizations. In these cases, the ecumenical body may use another name, such as "Christian Council", but the precise nature of membership is not necessarily self-evident from the organizational title alone.

1. ROMAN CATHOLIC PARTICIPATION IN NCCs: THE CURRENT SCENE

The participation of the Roman Catholic Church in national councils of churches is a phenomenon that has grown consistently since the Second Vatican Council. At the time of the Council, the Roman Catholic Church did not take part in any national council of churches, but at the present time, of approximately 120 national councils of churches, the Roman Catholic Church is a full member in 70.

The continents and regions where the Roman Catholic Church has membership in an NCC reflect a broad geographical spectrum. Europe, Africa, Oceania and the Caribbean make up the bulk of the regions in which the Roman Catholic Church is fully represented in national councils of churches. Elsewhere, the Roman Catholic Church is a member in some countries of Asia, Latin America and North America.

In several countries, partial or restricted membership has been achieved. In some countries, such as Zimbabwe and the Slovak Republic, the Roman Catholic Church enjoys observer or consultant status in the NCC. Elsewhere, as in the USA and in many Asian countries, the Roman Catholic Church, although still lacking any structural connection with other Christian churches through councils, has ongoing working relationships between the Catholic episcopal conference and the national council of churches. In the United States, for example, the Office of Ecumenical and Inter-religious Affairs of the US Conference of Catholic Bishops is a member of the Faith and Order commission of the National Council of the Churches of Christ in the USA. In Chile, Argentina and Ecuador, "ecumenical fraternities" exist among church leaders. While not councils of churches, these fraternities serve as instruments of community.

Moreover, in many countries where the Roman Catholic Church is not a member of the NCC, Catholic dioceses are represented in the local or statewide councils of churches. For example, in Caracas, Venezuela, there is a council of the historical churches of which the Roman Catholic Church is a member. A less formal ecumenical association of churches, with Roman Catholic participation, exists in Mexico City. In the USA, of 41 state councils of churches, Catholic dioceses are members in at least thirteen state councils and participate as observers (variously defined) in at least six others.

Membership in 70 national councils does not show the full extent of Catholic participation. In 12 countries of the Middle East where there are no NCCs, the Roman Catholic Church is a full and active member of the regional body, the Middle East Council of Churches. At the fifth plenary assembly of the MECC in 1990, seven distinct churches in communion with Rome joined the MECC, forming the Catholic family of churches, along with the Orthodox, Oriental Orthodox and Evangelical families.

2. CATHOLIC PARTICIPATION IN REOS: THE CURRENT SCENE

Of the seven REOs associated with the World Council of Churches, the Roman Catholic Church is a member of three: the Caribbean Conference of Churches (CaCC), the Pacific Conference of Churches (PCC), and the Middle East Council of Churches (MECC). In 1973, after a process of consultation and prayer begun in 1969, the Caribbean Conference of Churches was formed, with the Roman Catholic Church as a founding member. This was the first instance after the Second Vatican Council where the Roman Catholic Church entered into the process of founding a new regional ecumenical organization. The Pacific Conference of Churches was formed in 1966 and the Roman Catholic Church became a full member in 1976.

Participation of the Roman Catholic Church in a regional conference does not imply that the Catholic Church in every nation of that region also is a member of its respective national council. For example, although the Roman Catholic Church in some dioceses is a member of the regional Caribbean Conference of Churches, the Catholic Church in Haiti, Puerto Rico, Cuba and the Dominican Republic is neither a member of the CaCC nor of its respective national council of churches.

In regions where the Roman Catholic Church is not a member of the regional ecumenical organization, a good working relationship often exists between the REO and the continental association of Catholic episcopal conferences. In Europe, for example, a year after the Council of Bishops' Conferences in Europe (CCEE) was founded in 1971, the Conference of European Churches (CEC) established, in cooperation with the CCEE, a joint committee to promote collaboration. The two European bodies, the CEC and CCEE, following the encounters at Basel 1989 and at Graz 1997, in April 2001 signed a *Charta Oecumenica*, "Guidelines for CEC/CCEE Cooperation", which continues to have positive ripple effects in countries throughout the region.

In Asia, the Federation of Asian Bishops Conferences (FABC) and the Christian Conference of Asia (CCA) have intensified efforts at greater coordination and cooperation on common projects. Most recently, the two associations have undertaken cooperative projects on ecumenical formation, peace studies and inter-religious dialogue. Despite Pope John Paul II's appeals that the Roman Catholic Church in Asian countries should consider joining, where pastorally feasible, in ecumenical association with other churches, the churches in Asia have been relatively slow in responding. Only in Australia and Taiwan is the Roman Catholic Church a full member of the national council of churches. In Malaysia, the Catholic Church is not a member of the NCC, but takes part in the more inclusive association of the Christian Federation of Malaysia. It is perhaps because of this reluctance that the pope specifically urged, in his post-synodal exhortation *Ecclesia in Asia* of December 1999, that "the national episcopal conferences in Asia invite other Christian churches to join in a process of prayer and consultation in order to explore the possibilities of new ecumenical structures and associations to promote Christian unity" (§30).

The Australian experience is worth noting here. The Australian Council of Churches, formed in 1946, had Protestant, Anglican and eventually Orthodox membership. The Roman Catholic Church was not a member, nor were several Protestant churches. In 1988, the AuCC members extended an invitation to churches that were not part of the AuCC to work together towards creating a new structure that might more effectively express ecumenical relationships and serve the ecumenical movement in Australia. A planning group tried out ideas on prospective member churches and finally proposed that the AuCC make way for a National Council of Churches in Australia (NCCA) with a rewritten constitution, revamped programme emphases, new decision-making processes and a more inclusive self-understanding. In 1994, the new NCCA came into being with 14 member churches: Eastern and Oriental Orthodox, Catholic and Protestant. The process has served as a catalyst for all the member churches to renew and deepen their ecumenical commitment.

Early relations between the Latin American REO, Consejo Latinoamericano de Iglesias (CLAI, Latin American Council of Churches), and the Consejo Episcopal Latinoamericano (CELAM, Latin American Episcopal Conference) were limited and often strained.

Since 1995, however, the two organizations have reinitiated relations and have undertaken meetings, mutual visits, and a common project on the study of Pentecostal Christianity. The two organizations now are considering a proposal to form a permanent joint working group. In some countries of the region, such as Costa Rica, the churches are engaged in discussions that, it is hoped, will lead to an inclusive ecumenical association.

There are no projects in common between the 150-member All Africa Conference of Churches (AACC) and the Symposium of Episcopal Conferences of Africa and Madagascar (SECAM). However, the two organizations regularly extend invitations to each other to attend their plenary assemblies as observers.

### III. Evolving attitude of the Roman Catholic Church to membership in NCCs

The Roman Catholic Church came late to the ecumenical movement. This is partially due to an attitude that ecumenism would constitute a compromise with error, partly because Catholics in the early part of the 20th century were hoping that other churches would "return" to the "fullness" of Christian faith which was to be found in the Catholic tradition. The turning point came with the 1964 Second Vatican Council Decree on Ecumenism, often referred to by its Latin title *Unitatis Redintegratio* (*UR*). Although the Decree on Ecumenism did not refer explicitly to councils of churches, the document laid the theological foundations for Catholic participation in such councils by recognizing the ecclesial character of other churches, repeatedly referring to them as "churches and ecclesial communities". Moreover, the Decree on Ecumenism shifts the focus on Christian unity for Catholics from an ecumenism of a return to Rome as the centre of the church to one in which Christ is seen "as the source and centre of ecclesiastical communion" (*UR* 20).

At the time of the Second Vatican Council, the Roman Catholic Church was not a member of any national council of churches, and the document *Unitatis Redintegratio* included no explicit encouragement to seek membership in NCCs. However, in a dramatic development in 1971, only seven years after the Decree on Ecumenism was promulgated, the Roman Catholic Church had joined the national council of churches in 11 countries. The number increased to 19 by 1975, to 33 by 1986, to 41 by 1993, to 70 in 2003 (or 82, if one includes the nations of the Middle East Council of Churches).

1. The 1975 document, Ecumenical Collaboration

Before 1975, Catholic participation in NCCs was approved by the Holy See on a case-by-case basis, but no overall guidelines for participation had been published. The first explicit treatment came in 1975 in a document issued by the Pontifical Council for Promoting Christian Unity entitled *Ecumenical Collaboration at the Regional, National, and Local Levels* (*EC*). By then, the Roman Catholic Church was a member of the NCC in 19 countries.

This document is important for two reasons: (1) it elaborated the principles on which Catholic participation in councils of churches is based, and (2) it formed the basis of the position taken in the official 1993 *Guidelines*, which often simply restates the 1975 document. At the same time, the 1975 document must be understood in the context of an evolving attitude towards councils. Some elements regarding the nature and scope of ecumenical organizations as understood in *Ecumenical Collaboration* were subsequently modified in later documents.

Chapter 5 of the document, entitled "Considerations Concerning Council Membership", takes up the theological motivations for joining in ecumenical association with other Christian churches, as well as the practical difficulties to be kept in mind. The document holds that "since the Second Vatican Council's recognition of the ecclesial character of other Christian communities, the church has frequently called upon Catholics to cooperate not only with other Christians as individuals, but also with other churches and ecclesial communities as such" (5a). This association with other churches as churches, states the document, should not be seen as a purely pragmatic cooperation on matters of social and human concern, but should go beyond that to the more essential form of cooperation in the area of a common Christian witness of faith.

Membership in a council of churches implies "recognition of the council of churches as an instrument, among others, both for expressing the unity already existing among the churches and also of advancing towards a greater unity and a more effective Christian witness" (5b). Catholics and other Christians must not see their participation in councils of churches as the final goal of ecumenical activity, as though full Christian unity were to be achieved simply by joining a council of churches. Prayer and worship in common, cooperation in biblical translation and coordination of liturgical texts, joint statements on moral questions, and common responses to social issues of justice and peace are also steps towards unity and can be undertaken also in those regions where the Roman Catholic Church does not belong to a national or regional council, but such paths to unity can be facilitated and encouraged by Catholic participation in the council of churches.

This does not diminish the value of councils of churches, but rather underlines their importance in helping the churches to seek the fullness of unity that Christ desired among his disciples. As the document later concludes: "Among the many forms of ecumenical cooperation, councils of churches and Christian councils are not the only form, but they are certainly one of the more important" (6g). They play "an important role in ecumenical relations" and hence are to be taken seriously by all the churches.

The document seeks to relieve some of the theological disquiet that some Catholics might feel about joining a council of churches. Joining a council in which the Roman Catholic Church would find itself on equal footing with other bodies does "not diminish its faith about its uniqueness" (5b). The document cites the well-known statement of Vatican II that the unique church of Christ subsists in the Catholic Church (*Lumen Gentium* 8), and this uniqueness is not compromised by the church taking part, on equal footing with other churches, in a council at the national or regional level. Similar questions about the implications of membership in councils have been raised by other churches. These questions were addressed by the central committee of the World Council of Churches in Toronto in 1950, which stated that membership in a council of churches does not necessarily imply "that each church must regard the other member churches as churches in the true and full sense".

The document underlines that councils of churches are not churches; nor do they have the responsibility of churches to engage in conversations leading to full unity. As the document saw it in 1975, the scope of councils of churches is mainly in the practical realm, rather than in the dogmatic, a perspective that has since continued to evolve. In saying this, the Holy See does not forbid councils of churches to study together questions of "faith and order", and the document later notes that "it is normal that councils should want to discuss and reflect upon the doctrinal bases of the practical projects they undertake" (6h). Such discussions, it states, have "a deep importance in stimulating member churches to a deeper understanding of the demands of unity willed by Christ and to facing deadlocks in a new way" (5c). Nevertheless, it "is not the task of a council to take the initiative in promoting formal doctrinal conversations between churches. These belong to the immediate and bilateral contacts between the churches." Thus, in joining a council of churches, Catholics need not fear that they will be drawn into technical dogmatic discussions that they may not consider appropriate in this context.

The document regards the proper domain of councils of churches as principally that of practical collaboration, giving particular attention to social problems such as housing, health, relief, etc. (5e, ii). At times, the councils will feel called to make public statements on matters of common concern in areas of peace, social justice, human development, public welfare, and personal morality or social ethics. These may vary from broad statements of position to specific stands on concrete questions. They might examine a subject and point out its social and ethical ramifications, and they often will identify various approaches to treat problems. Even though such statements reflect the theological positions of the churches, they are not to be "considered as official utterances" (5d, i) made in the name of the churches.

In fact, as the document notes, the problematic nature of issuing joint statements is one that the member churches of a council must constantly keep in mind. It has given rise to much debate, tension and hard feelings in a number of councils and on rare occasions has led one or another member church to withdraw from a council. This does not mean that in councils, churches never should make public statements. They should realize, however, that full consensus is very difficult to achieve and that sincere respect must be granted to minority views (5d, iii). All this is to say that in a council of churches the integrity of each member church constantly must be considered, its individual positions honoured, and polarization avoided.

The document notes that when bishops conferences decide to join an NCC, they should not settle for superficial participation but should fully involve their local church. It is not enough simply to send delegates, but participation in a council should be integrated into the pastoral life and planning of Catholic dioceses. When the Roman Catholic Church joins a council, this must be accompanied by "constant ecumenical education of Catholics concerning the implications of such participation" (51).

In its "Pastoral and Practical Reflections for Local Ecumenical Action" in chapter 6 of *EC*, the Pontifical Council makes two further important points. First, each council of churches is unique and must be designed according to the needs in each nation. Churches should not simply adopt models that were found to be successful elsewhere (6a). Instead, after reflecting together on the needs and challenges of the churches in their region, they should create their own specific ecumenical relationship. The Holy See thus envisions a great deal of freedom for the churches in each region to form a council which accurately reflects the actual ecumenical relationships "on the ground" and enables the churches to express their unity in realistic service to society.

Second, as valuable as councils of churches are as instruments to express the unity which exists among Christians and to work towards fuller and deeper unity, the creation of new structures never can replace "the collaboration of Christians in prayer, reflection and action, based on common baptism and on a faith which on many essential points is also common" (6c). In other words, if the search for Christian unity is solely focused on structures, procedures and bureaucracy, the unity which councils seek to achieve will be minimal and the renewal which councils of churches can help their member churches bring to the whole Christian community will not be very profound. The deeper communion that should characterize Christian unity can only come from Christians' praying together, reflecting on the word of God in scripture together, thinking through social problems together, and actually working together in various aspects of the churches' life.

The aforementioned 1975 document on *Ecumenical Collaboration* was the first official instruction given by the Holy See on the question of Catholic membership in national and regional councils of churches. It noted with satisfaction that the Roman Catholic Church in many countries had decided to join NCCs or to create new ecumenical associations in which the Roman Catholic Church would take part. It pointed out possible problems that could arise and how many of the divisive issues could be foreseen and crises avoided. The document reassured Catholics throughout the world that joining a council of churches can be an important step towards working for Christian unity, expressing the unity which already exists due to our common baptism, and renewing the churches in their commitment to serve God in Christ and, in doing so, to be of service to a world reconciled to God.

Because of the increasing number of countries and regions where the Roman Catholic Church was participating in councils of churches, the Pontifical Council for Promoting Christian Unity and the World Council of Churches, within the framework of the Joint Working Group, convened three consultations (1971, 1986, 1993) to reflect on issues connected with national councils of churches.

In a message to the 1993 consultation, held in Hong Kong, Cardinal Edward Cassidy, then president of the Pontifical Council for Promoting Christian Unity, stressed a key aspect of the function of NCCs in the ecumenical search for unity. "National councils of churches", he stated, "as servants of unity play an important role in providing opportunities for strengthening the spirit of mutual understanding among member churches." The cardinal emphasized the human dimension, the value of councils to foster personal growth in commitment to Christian unity. He affirmed that in the NCCs, Christians of various churches come to know one another personally, discover a shared Christian commitment through common action, enrich one another by the distinctive elements of Christian life which their particular traditions have preserved and emphasized, and rediscover concretely their common faith in God by praying together in the name of Our Lord Jesus Christ.

## 2. THE 1993 "ECUMENICAL DIRECTORY"

In the same year as the Hong Kong consultation, the Pontifical Council for Promoting Christian Unity issued its revised guidelines for Christian ecumenism, entitled the *Directory for the Application of Principles and Norms on Ecumenism*. The 1993 Guidelines, as the document is popularly known, replaced the temporary *Ecumenical Directory* that had been called for by the Second Vatican Council and subsequently published in 1967 and 1970. The 1993 *Directory* treats questions of Catholic participation in councils of churches in paragraphs 166-71.

Many of the instructions contained in the 1993 *Directory* repeat those already given in the 1975 document on *Ecumenical Collaboration*, but on some key points, the *Directory* goes farther than the earlier document. This is particularly the case in welcoming, for the first time, Catholic participation in councils. The *EC* document treated the phenomenon of Catholic churches joining NCCs and REOs as a de facto reality in the ecumenical movement, calling councils an "important instrument" in the search for Christian unity. The *Directory* goes beyond this to welcome positively this phenomenon in church life as something to be desired (167).

The *Directory* distinguishes (166) between a "council of churches, composed of churches and responsible to the member churches", and a "Christian council", composed of churches as well as other Christian groups and organizations, such as Bible societies or YMCAs. This distinction reflects a tendency in some regions to form more inclusive Christian councils whose members not only would be churches but also other forms of Christian association. This development recognizes that in the effort to build Christian unity, other Christian groups and organizations often play a leading role.

The *Directory* does not recommend one form of association over the other, but leaves that decision to the authorities of local churches. These authorities, states the *Directory*, "will generally be the synod of Eastern Catholic churches or the episcopal conference (except where there is only one diocese in a nation)" (168). In preparing to make this decision, the Eastern synods or episcopal conferences "should be in touch with the Pontifical Council for Promoting Christian Unity". The *Directory's* careful phraseology underlines that the authority for joining councils rests with the local bishops through their synod or episcopal conference while, as in all matters affecting the universal church, the local churches should always communicate and consult with the Pontifical Council. What is involved is not a matter of "asking permission from Rome" but of acting in communion with the worldwide Roman Catholic Church.

The *Directory* notes various considerations that must accompany the decision to take part in a council of churches or Christian council. Local and national socio-political realities must be considered. Participation in the life of the council must not blur Catholic self-understanding as to its uniqueness and specific identity (169). In other words, there must be doctrinal clarity, especially in the area of ecclesiology, and ecumenical education should be provided for church members. In ecumenical dialogue, the Roman Catholic Church can propose its ecclesiology to other member churches, but should respect their proper ecclesiological self-understanding. At the same time, the Roman Catholic Church expects that its own theology of the nature of the church will be understood and respected by its partners.

The *Directory* repeats the view of the 1975 document that councils of churches and Christian councils do not contain within or among themselves the beginning of a new church that could replace the communion that now exists in the Roman Catholic Church. They must not proclaim themselves churches "nor claim an authority which would permit them to confer a ministry of word or sacrament". In fact, the concern that councils of churches not be regarded as a new "super-church" had already been a constant preoccupation of member churches since the first councils of churches appeared a century ago. The formation of councils among churches still divided from one another is but one instrument aimed at Christian unity, and it must be clearly distinguished from the effort to achieve structural and sacramental unity in the creation of united churches.

The *Directory* notes matters to be considered before the Roman Catholic Church either decides to join an existing NCC or to take part in the creation of a new association. Such considerations include the system of representation, voting rights, decision-making processes, manner of making public statements, and the degree of authority attributed to common statements (169.) Finally, the *Directory* repeats the counsel given in the 1975 document. Joining a council is a serious responsibility that should not be taken lightly. Membership implies responsibilities that are not fulfilled simply by becoming a member only in name. "The Catholic Church should be represented by well-qualified and committed persons" who are sincerely convinced of the importance of actively pursuing Christian unity and who are clearly aware of the limits to which they can commit the church without referring to the authorities who appointed them.

The increased acceptance and encouragement for Catholic participation in councils of churches by the Holy See since the time of the Second Vatican Council is evidence of a positive experience in observing the fruits of such ecumenical involvement. Most recently, in the 1995 document on ecumenical formation of Christians entitled *The Ecumenical Dimension in the Formation of Those Engaged in Pastoral Work*, the Pontifical Council for Promoting Christian Unity lists information about councils of churches as one of the "important pastoral and practical matters which should not be omitted from ecumenical formation, especially that of seminarians".

The emerging participation of the Roman Catholic Church in national and regional ecumenical organizations would not be complete without reference to the 1995 encyclical *Ut Unum Sint* ("That They May All Be One"), which strongly reaffirmed the commitment of the Roman Catholic Church to work actively for Christian unity. Although the encyclical did not refer explicitly to NCCs and REOs, the pope affirmed that

> the relationships which the members of the Catholic Church have established with other Christians since the Council have enabled us to discover what God is bringing about in the members of other churches and ecclesial communities. This direct contact, at a variety of levels, with pastors and with the members of these communities has made us aware of the witness which other Christians bear to God and to Christ. A vast new field has thus opened up for the whole ecumenical experience, which at the same time is the great challenge of our time. (*UUS* 48)

### 3. CONCLUDING COMMENTS ABOUT THE HISTORICAL SURVEY

Tracing the historical background of Catholic participation in national and regional councils of churches shows a progressive awareness in the Roman Catholic Church, beginning at the time of the Second Vatican Council, of the value of taking part in such associations. The Roman Catholic Church has come to see participation in NCCs and REOs as an important step in pursuing the Spirit-driven goal of Christian unity. Councils of churches are not the goal in the ecumenical search for the full unity, but they are an effective tool for following the Spirit's guidance towards full unity. The late Canadian theologian and ecumenist, Fr Jean-Marie Tillard, OP, sums up this grace-filled instrumentality of councils of churches as follows:

> A council of churches makes a "loving dialogue" possible. By breaking the isolation and bringing about knowledge of each other, ecumenical encounter slowly erodes distrust, prejudices and traditional hatreds. While each church begins by hoping to impose its own views and confessional ambitions on the others, we find that among the members something gradually comes into being which triumphs over the interests and claims of each group. In learning to love one another, in the knowledge that diversities exist and in respect for them, we gradually learn the unity that God wants.

## IV. Value and benefits of membership

### 1. WHAT CAN FACILITATE PARTICIPATION AND MEMBERSHIP

When a church joins a council, it brings along not only its rich heritage, but some painful memories as well. The original fear, apprehension or suspicion does not automatically disappear. A relatively long integration process may be needed to purify memories and develop trust, enabling the new member church to perceive itself and to be perceived by others as belonging comfortably to the council.

The process of integration is facilitated by instilling a feeling of respect for the integrity of the new member church. The church needs to feel confident that membership in the council, while causing it to change, will not force unsolicited alterations in its identity. This sense of reassurance is liable to generate deeper commitment to the common agenda of the members of the council and to encourage greater openness and participation on the part of the new member church. Such a feeling of security will allow the richness of yet another tradition to be shared. Both deep theological reflection and a clear understanding of ecumenical spirituality are vital factors in the process of journeying towards the visible unity of the church.

The success of this process also is fostered by the ability of the council members to listen. It hinges on their openness, their readiness to accept and value differences, their ability to be truly inclusive. Such an attitude is bound to lead to greater sharing in the decision-making process, always taking into consideration minority views. When making decisions, no matter how insignificant they may appear, it is always preferable to aim at consensus rather than to risk alienating member churches who may have different perspectives.

The way the council is formed and the manner in which churches are represented can make a difference in how member churches perceive their role in the decision-making mechanism. For example, if the member churches are represented according to their numerical importance some may feel that their vote will not make a difference. As a result they may feel alienated from the decision-making process. Such feelings are bound to influence negatively their sense of belonging to the council.

If the representation is made, however, according to other criteria, such as the "families of churches", where each family is equally represented, independently of numbers of faithful, no member church will feel at a disadvantage when it comes to influencing decisions. Moreover, the family model may enable the member churches within a family to grow into closer relationships and cooperation with each other. In addition, this model may facilitate the entrance of a church as part of a family when it would be uncomfortable in joining a council that did not have a family structure.

When a new member feels accepted, integrated, valued and represented in the decision-making process, a deeper feeling of belonging can grow. Each member feels more ready to participate in common projects both at the level of leadership and at the grassroots, where the rapprochement remains the ultimate objective of the ecumenical journey.

Becoming part of a council of churches may enhance a church's renewal, rescue it from isolation, strengthen its awareness of the common calling, increase the effectiveness of its service, and encourage ecumenical initiatives by its people locally.

Flexibility in council structures facilitates participation and membership. For example, each member should feel free to engage in bilateral dialogue outside the structure of the council, while remaining part of it.

The factors named above are practical. They point to aspects of healthy dialogue – a subject that is being explored by a separate study on dialogue conducted by the Joint Working Group. More important, however, are the spiritual and theological motivations of member churches. By joining an ecumenical association, each member demonstrates a willingness to allow the Spirit to witness to the existing unity of the church and an intention to cooperate to further its visible unity.

## 2. WHAT CAN HELP MEMBER CHURCHES LIVE OUT STATED AIMS

Like any institution, councils of churches derive their strength partly from the quality of the people involved. The contribution of each member church depends a great deal on the capacity of its representatives – on their ecumenical formation and commitment. The ecumenical movement is a journey of the whole community and not of an elite that represents it.

Official representatives to councils should be in close contact with the leaders and people of the churches they represent. Unless the heads of churches are informed about the process and encourage it, their participation could cause internal divisions and discourage communication with the people in the pews.

When people join together through any association it makes a significant difference to the general atmosphere if people get along well and enjoy working together – hence, the importance of the development of a spirit of fellowship. An attitude of trust and readiness for true dialogue are vital starting points for the realization of the stated objectives of the council. Unless members trust each other they cannot easily be committed to the same aims, especially when the commitment involves deep theological convictions. And unless the aims are based on such acknowledged theological convictions, the partners in a council will not be able to get far in the realization of their goals in their ecumenical journey.

Thus, members should have a common mission in their journey towards unity. Ecumenical progress is thwarted by those who have hidden agendas, seek personal benefits, or entertain human ambitions. Such an approach goes counter to common witness.

In conclusion, participants in ecumenical work cannot make progress unless the persons involved succeed in creating healthy human relationships among themselves and a deep relationship with God. Differences should not be hidden. Ecumenical progress cannot be promoted by avoiding real issues or seeking easy solutions to vexing problems. The ecumenical journey is always a journey of mending relationships, of healing the wounds of division and reconciling memories in order to seek together unity in Jesus Christ through the enlightenment of the Holy Spirit.

Witnessing to the visible unity of the church starts with prayerful journeying together towards an encounter with God, towards a deeper transformation in order to manifest God's presence in the world through the church. In praying together, Christians encounter the triune God who brings about the gradual transformation of the community into a true family of Christ's disciples. This process is enhanced through a deep encounter among the various members of the council in which they discover each other's wealth of tradition and special spiritual experience. Listening to the Spirit speaking to the churches helps dissipate prejudice – at times, even hatred. It produces greater trust and leads to growth. This is perhaps the most eloquent witness of a Council to the visible unity of the church.

### 3. WHAT SHOULD BE CELEBRATED

Ecumenical awakening is one of the most important developments in the history of the church during the 19th and the 20th centuries. Some Christians began to be aware of the value of cooperation among the churches. Protestants were the first to take steps towards creating ecumenical organizations intended to overcome divisions among Christians. In 1910, the international missionary conference at Edinburgh marked the beginning of the modern ecumenical movement, and from this the churches together continued to cooperate in mission through the International Missionary Council to bring churches together to explore divisive theological issues through Faith and Order, and to engage in reflection and action on political, social and economic matters through Life and Work. In 1920 the Ecumenical Patriarchate issued an encyclical entitled "Unto the Churches of Christ Everywhere", inviting Christians to create a fellowship of churches. In the same year the bishops of the Anglican Communion issued an "Appeal to All Christian People" to manifest unity by "gathering into fellowship all who profess and call themselves Christians, within whose visible unity all the treasures of faith and order, bequeathed as a heritage by the past to the present, shall be possessed in common, and made serviceable to the whole body of Christ". The rapid development of ecumenical associations, notably the creation of the World Council of Churches in 1948, underlines the importance the churches have ascribed to working for the full visible unity of the church. In 1900 there were no national councils of churches, but by the year 2000 the number had grown to 103.

Since the Second Vatican Council the Roman Catholic Church has joined a large number of ecumenical associations. This rapprochement, along with the engagement in bilateral dialogue with a wide range of churches and ecclesial communions in both East and West, has led to the signing of christological agreements with some of the Oriental churches. Dialogue with the Lutherans recently produced significant progress shown in the Joint

Declaration on the Doctrine of Justification. The efforts of the Anglican-Roman Catholic Commission (ARCIC) have led to the publication of *The Gift of Authority*. Although not a joint declaration, this document offers valuable insights for the future directions of the ecumenical movement.

With councils of churches as their principal instruments, the churches are building relationships with each other through which they are:

- growing in mutual respect, understanding and trust;
- dissipating many prejudices through learning to pray in each other's words, singing each other's songs, reading scripture through each other's eyes;
- offering service in Christ's name to those who are in need, locally and far away;
- giving common witness to the gospel and working together for human dignity;
- listening to and learning through each other's insights into matters of faith and life over which they have been divided;
- holding Christ's people together, even when the world's pressures would tear them apart (CUV, 3.9).

Relationship-building affects all those involved. One church encountering another may find that it wants to reflect afresh on its own identity, its own thinking, its own Christian commitment to unity. Ecumenical ties bring many benefits, some quite unexpected.

## V.  Some issues and concerns

### 1.  WHAT'S IN A NAME?

Names can matter. A name says something about how the churches perceive their life together. When a Catholic bishops conference joins a national council of churches, a name change may dramatize that the churches are making a fresh beginning together. The new name may symbolize new intentions and new reality – an awareness that the culture of the council will be transformed as new churches live into new relationships through the council. Thus, names are important, but context, history and vision will determine the choice in a given place.

Most call themselves *councils* of churches. Some call themselves conferences of churches. Others have adopted names like *churches together or Christian fellowships*. In fact, the vast majority of national ecumenical bodies with Catholic membership use the phrase "council of churches" in their name. The phrase "Christian council" sometimes, though not always, indicates that other ecumenical organizations (e.g., Bible societies, Church Women United, YMCA and YWCA) also may be members.

The Roman Catholic Church's relationship to national and regional councils of churches may take one of several forms: full membership, observer status, ongoing collaboration, occasional cooperation. Although some concerns are felt more acutely when Roman Catholic Churches are involved, other churches and ecclesial communities may experience, to varying degrees, the same problems. Councils within a country (state, province, city) may have similar experiences. Thus, awareness of and attention to these concerns may enable greater and better participation in a council, not only by the Roman Catholic Church but also by the other churches.

2. ISSUES OF AUTHORITY

In national settings, the conference of Catholic bishops has the authority to make the decision about joining a national council of churches. In a diocesan setting, the bishop makes the decision. The attitude towards councils of churches taken by an individual bishop or bishops conference can either encourage or inhibit participation in a council and the movement towards membership. Just as in any church, a few ecumenically committed bishops can stimulate action by the whole bishops conference. Furthermore, positive ecumenical experiences in the diocesan context may predispose bishops to consider membership in a national council. In Australia, for example, Catholic membership in some state councils of churches preceded consideration of participation by the Australian Catholic bishops conference. Membership in the National Council of Churches in Australia in turn stimulated other Catholic bishops to lead their dioceses into state councils of churches. The positive process was circular and expansive.

Once a Catholic conference becomes a member of a council of churches, entering fully into the life of the ecumenical body, the relationships cannot be reversed lightly, without serious provocation. On rare occasions, such situations do arise. In 1998, the Catholic bishops conference in New Zealand withdrew from membership in the Conference of Churches in Aotearoa-New Zealand (CCANZ) after it became apparent that the method of representation did not afford the bishops the degree of necessary comfort with policies and practices of the new structure. The new body had set out to be a different type of council, seeing itself as a forum for various kinds of interest groups and causes as well as for the member churches who were financing it. From the outset some predicted that there would be difficulties for Catholic members. The Lutheran church in New Zealand experienced similar problems and withdrew from membership in the Conference in 1994.

Since the withdrawal of the Lutheran and Roman Catholic churches, religious leaders (especially Anglican, Presbyterian and Catholic) have made considerable effort to develop greater trust and to seek ways of working together even if their experience in CCANZ was not satisfactory. The Anglican and Roman Catholic bishops have met regularly for over a decade. They have expressed the sadness felt by many about CCANZ. Recently, CCANZ decided to conclude its organization, primarily because the remaining number of member churches is so small. At the same time, the possibility of a new body is being explored. This would give Catholics, Lutherans and Baptists (who had not joined CCANZ) a way back into a new ecumenical entity. As of this writing, plans for a new, inclusive council are scheduled to be unveiled by September 2004, when CCANZ will meet for its final annual forum.

This leads to the examination of another aspect of authority when churches are members of a council of churches. Who actually can speak for the churches at the ecumenical table? With what weight? The variations in ecclesiological self-understanding among churches sometimes are baffling to members, since all churches may be puzzled by polities and structures of authority that differ from their own. In the Catholic context the bishops need to trust that the concerns and policies of their church are reflected by the Catholic representatives, respected by other member churches and by the professional staff of a council of churches. In fact, this is true for leaders of other churches, as well.

Concerns have emerged about who, when, and on what basis the churches may speak together through a national council of churches. Members of the World Council of Churches faced these concerns early on and, in the 1950 Toronto statement clarified the limits of Council authority. Fr Yves Congar and other Catholic theologians were consulted prior to the drafting of the Toronto text.

To the degree that councils of churches and their professional leaders have honoured the policies articulated in Toronto, they have quelled fears that a council could become a "super-church", acting apart from or above its members. The WCC constitution addresses issues of authority as follows:

> The World Council shall offer counsel and provide opportunity for united action in matters of common interest.
>
> It may take action on behalf of constituent churches only in such matters as one or more of them may commit to it and only on behalf of such churches.
>
> The World Council shall not legislate for the churches nor act for them in any manner except as indicated above or as may hereafter be specified by the constituent churches.

Recognizing the complexities involved in issues of authority does not necessarily solve problems, but an awareness of the dynamics may help. In the final analysis, many issues of authority depend on styles of leadership and modes of working together. When the style is relational, even when hard issues surface where tensions are high, people can rely on the human connections they have developed to consult together to seek the will of Christ.

### 3. PROPER PREPARATION FOR MEMBERSHIP

Experience has shown that by paying careful attention at the outset to issues of representation and decision-making processes, councils can minimize the problems in these areas that could arise later on. Serious preparation for membership in a council is an important factor leading to the successful functioning of all councils, both those with and without Catholic membership. For example, both the Canadian and Brazilian Catholic conferences of bishops were engaged for over a dozen years before they became full members of their national councils.

The Canadian Catholic Conference of Bishops joined an already established council, the Canadian Council of Churches, as full members in 1997 after a lengthy process that began in the 1970s when the two organizations worked together on social justice issues. In 1984, the Catholic Church applied for associate membership. The Conference of Bishops became an associate in 1986 with the intention of becoming a full member in 1997. The differences between the two types of membership were technical, i.e., not holding the office of president or general secretary, and not voting on constitutional issues.

The Canadian Catholic Conference of Bishops and the Canadian Council of Churches saw full membership as a concrete expression of greater commitment to the ecumenical movement. The inclusion of the Roman Catholic Church also brought an increased French dimension into what had been a largely English-speaking council. Before becoming full members, the Canadian Catholic Conference made a serious review of the constitution and by-laws of the council. The council resolved the concern about the organization being perceived as a "super-church" by frequently expressing itself as a forum "in which churches meet as churches to decide together on common agenda". Particular attention was given to making public statements and to identifying the authority those public statements would have.

The Brazilian council of churches began to take shape in the enthusiastic atmosphere following the Second Vatican Council when Catholics joined with other Christian leaders to form a council. The leaders met in Rio de Janeiro and in other major cities. These ecumenical efforts throughout the country resulted in the formation of the Brazilian National Council of Churches in 1982. The membership includes the Lutheran, Evangelical, Episcopal, Methodist, United Presbyterian, Syrian Orthodox, Catholic and Christian Reformed churches.

4. FORMS OF REPRESENTATION, MODELS OF MEMBERSHIP

In countries where Roman Catholics form the majority of Christians, one of the arguments often given to explain the lack of Catholic membership in councils is that, by becoming "one church among others", the Roman Catholic Church would be conceding identity and leadership to a group of small churches. On the other hand, numerically small churches in such nations and regions also may be hesitant to welcome membership of the Roman Catholic Church, which they feel would dominate the council by its very size and social presence.

Such apprehensions could explain, for example, the absence of Catholic membership in church councils in much of Latin America and areas of Mediterranean Europe where Roman Catholics are predominant. Another factor affecting membership is that historically some councils of churches in predominantly Catholic contexts were established by minority churches precisely in order to help and support each other. In such situations, the prospects for Catholic membership may be difficult to accept for both the majority and minority churches.

Another model has been adopted by churches in Great Britain and Ireland – the churches together model. It is based on the model of "consensus". No action is taken unless and until there is agreement. The churches no longer delegate tasks to outside bodies, but each church takes responsibility in conjunction with other churches. This model very often includes as a full member the Roman Catholic Church (e.g. CTBI, ACTS, CTE in the United Kingdom). Often, in this model, there is a dual pattern of meetings of church leaders and a wider assembly of church representatives to pursue the agenda, and to provide an opportunity for mutual accountability.

Although these are real concerns, some councils, including those in regions with Catholic majorities such as Austria, Madagascar and Hungary, have found creative solutions which permit the various member churches to feel adequately represented. Several models of representation have been tried, and no single model can be said to be superior to others. It cannot be presumed that a solution that has worked well in one council can for that reason be applied successfully elsewhere. In whatever form of representation devised, the main consideration always must be to ensure that all member churches are satisfied that their voices will be heard and that their views can find a proper forum, and that no church feels that its concerns will be ignored or over-ridden by the others.

Concerns of representation are not limited to Catholic participation. It is a perennial challenge for all church councils to find a structure that both adequately reflects ecumenical relationships and provides an arena for free discussion and interaction. In virtually every nation and region, the complexion of membership varies greatly. A church that represents the vast majority of Christians in that region can be uneasy if it feels that small churches will have the ability to push through legislation and projects on a "one church, one vote" basis. Conversely, small churches often will not feel comfortable in a structure that permits one or two large churches to dominate the council and force their will on other members.

On these bases, various councils have sought to devise systems of representation according to their particular needs and relationships. For example, the Uruguay Council of Christian Churches, with eight member churches (Anglican, Armenian, Catholic, Evangelical, Lutheran, Methodist, Pentecostal and Salvation Army) has adopted a direct form of representation, with no adjustments made for church size.

By contrast, in the Canadian Council of Churches, representation of the 18 members reflects church size: three representatives from large churches, two from mid-sized, and one from small churches. Membership size of churches also determines Brazilian representation in that council's decision-making structures. The Brazilian council also rotates the presidency among leaders from different churches.

Representation based on "families of churches" rather than the size of church membership is used in other countries and regions with Catholic participation. The council of churches in France (CECEF), perhaps one of the few formed through the initiative of the Roman Catholic Church, has three co-presidents and three co-secretaries (one each from the Catholic episcopal conference, from the Protestant federation, from the assembly of Orthodox bishops). Its 16 member churches are composed of two Armenian Apostolic, five Catholic, three Orthodox, and five Protestant representatives, and an Anglican observer.

The Swedish Christian council, newly reconstituted in 1993, is based on four families, despite the fact that the Evangelical Lutheran Church of Sweden enrolls over 80 percent of the Christian population of the country. The families are the Lutheran, Orthodox, Catholic, and Free-church families.

The family model also is followed by the Middle East Council of Churches, which is made up of four families: Catholic, Eastern Orthodox, Evangelical and Oriental Orthodox churches. In this context, the family model ensures that each of the major ecclesial traditions can feel that its position in the council will be taken seriously, that factors which make some churches historically and theologically "closer" to others will be recognized within the council structure, and that no single church or group of churches will be able to dominate leadership and decision-making processes.

The family model also has its drawbacks. Churches within a family may hold different positions on various issues. Concentrating on family relationships at the expense of building broader ecumenical relations can result in introversion and self-isolation. At times, the "family" can be an artificial construct, bringing together churches into families in which they are not comfortable. Moreover, some churches may not fit well into any given family, or there might be internal disagreement among church members about the family to which they belong. A church might see itself in one family, but not be regarded as such by others in that family. The family system on occasion even can result in a church being denied membership in the council. For example, one of the factors which has thus far prevented the Assyrian Church of the East from being accepted as a member of the Middle East Council of Churches is the lack of agreement over the family to which the church should belong.

Christian charity and the desire for fairness demand that all member churches be willing to give up some measure of autonomous decision-making and independent action for the sake of common voice and endeavour. Moreover, any form of representation only will work well when the churches have a measure of trust that other members are not seeking to manipulate council structures for their own purposes. It has been the experience of some councils that the prayerful deliberations that lead to determining the type of representation to be followed have been a valuable educational exercise and one that has occasioned greater fellowship and understanding.

## 5. DECISION-MAKING

Initially, most councils used the parliamentary, majority vote method for making decisions. More recently, many councils are employing methods that use discernment and consensus as being more compatible with the goal of promoting communion among their members. A common understanding of consensus is the achievement of a decision acceptable to all members. In some cases this agreement may be unanimous. More often, the consensus involves a decision that members can accept without objection. If councils cannot reach a consensus, other actions that may be taken are to record the various opinions, to postpone the decision or to refer the issue for study rather than for action. The understanding and practice of consensus must be agreed upon and accepted by all members. It is important, therefore, to have written protocols and to follow them.

Acceptance of consensus formation as the main pattern of decision-making does not imply that recourse must never be taken to parliamentary-style voting. Some issues (e.g., disbursement of funds, the appointment of officials) simply cannot be achieved by consensus.

Some councils are moving towards a more sophisticated understanding of consensus that might be expressed by the term "differentiated agreement". Derived from the experience of bilateral dialogues, differentiated agreement indicates a consensus on basic truths, although differences of language, theological elaboration and emphasis might remain. In a differentiated agreement, each church formulates the agreed-upon statement according to its own categories and understanding of its theological import.

A consensus style of decision-making often does not enable a council to make a prophetic statement in a timely manner. Some councils refer matters to individual member churches for separate actions. Other councils develop principles on particular issues on which the churches agree. Responses then can be made flowing from these principles. Potentially divisive and strongly prophetic positions only should arise from a profound spirit of prayer. A prayerful, discerning attitude and process may enable either a consensus to be reached or a respectful acceptance by the church that is unable to act on a particular issue.

6. PUBLIC STATEMENTS

Perhaps the factor that causes the greatest reluctance for churches that are considering membership in church councils concerns apprehension about public statements. Churches fear that their name will be used against their will to endorse causes with which their church is not in agreement or to protest issues on which they feel the churches should maintain a prudent silence. They may have heard of previous instances where churches were embarrassed by the actions of a majority of member churches, committees or general secretaries whose positions were announced publicly without prior consultation or full agreement of all member churches.

Differences in ecclesiology lie at the root of some difficulties in making public statements. Some churches at the local or national level may state their position on matters of importance without consulting other bodies. Catholic positions are to be in agreement with the magisterial teaching of the universal church and to reflect the position of their national bishops conferences. For the Orthodox, statements must be in accord with Orthodox theology.

In some cases, such as on questions of abortion or homosexuality, the problem is theological; some churches are concerned lest they appear to take positions contrary to the wider community's understanding of the Christian faith. In other cases, the churches may be concerned about the political implications of public positions, particularly in instances where government policy is criticized. In the case of many controversial issues, such as the death penalty, support or condemnation of war, or reproductive technology, opinion within the individual churches itself may be divided, with various interpretations of Christian teaching put forth by segments of the local community. A public statement on which many church members agree may be hotly contested by others.

There is no easy answer to the question of public statements, and disputes over the issue sometimes have led churches to withdraw from membership when no acceptable solution can be found. Most churches agree that there are times when the Christian conscience is united on an issue that, therefore, must be stated clearly in a public way. In fact sometimes a church's collective conscience will demand that it take a prophetic stance on controversial issues that run contrary to public opinion. Extensive ongoing consultation can minimize the possibility of conflict, dissension and hard feelings.

Councils must resist the culture of the instant statement, despite the pressures to the contrary. On the one hand, in today's fast-paced world, with instant modes of communication and a demanding news media, the insistence by member churches on full consultation and consensus may mean that the churches' voice on major ethical issues will be muted. On the other hand, members of councils have found that taking adequate time to deliberate may be frustrating, but it also can result in statements that are more clear and thoughtful. When there is open, continuous communication between council officials and the leaders of member churches, questions about which issues are likely to raise controversy or to be divisive become second nature to the conciliar staff.

Most councils issue statements only when they have achieved unanimity. If unanimous agreement is not possible, the statement may not be issued in the name of the council, because the council speaks not for itself but for every church that is a member. In such situations, it always must be clarified whether council officials speak as members of the council or as the official representatives or heads of their churches. Those who support the action may sign in the name of their church, while the minority may indicate their objections and their reasons for not signing the statement.

It also is important to honour a reluctance of members to make conflicts public unless external factors, such as media scrutiny, force the situation. Therefore, councils may need a common understanding of a procedure for relating to the media. For example, if one leader receives a call that could be contentious, prior agreement on the need for consultation before any public statements are made provides a level of trust and confidence among members.

## 7. FINANCES

Because councils of churches are their members, this fact should be reflected in a fair and equitable distribution of the costs entailed by membership. As churches, themselves, are challenged economically, these challenges are felt keenly in the budgets of councils of churches.

When councils of churches are especially dependent on outside funding, they find themselves being constrained by the expectations of funding agents who try to determine the programme of the council, regardless of the needs and perspectives of the member churches within a country.

When the Roman Catholic Church considers becoming a member of an NCC or REO, questions of and fears about cost inevitably arise (as they do for any potential member). When the Roman Catholic Church is predominant in size, members and budget, questions arise about how to work out an equitable resolution to financial responsibilities. The issue is not insurmountable, nor should it be used as a convenient excuse for avoiding the membership question, but it needs to be acknowledged forthrightly.

## 8. ECUMENICAL FORMATION

Although much has been accomplished by the churches in describing "the nature of the unity we seek", not all share this vision to the same extent. Even in the midst of these ambiguities, however, all churches have a crying need to foster ecumenical formation among religious leaders, teachers, clergy and laity. Many are talking about the need for ecumenical formation. How to translate perceived need into effective action is a vexing challenge – one that councils of churches must face as they seek to juggle the sometimes conflicting demands of inclusivity, expertise and historical memory.

Attentiveness to ecumenical formation is especially important for those who are asked to serve as official representatives in ecumenical contexts such as councils of churches. The Holy See has urged that Catholic representatives have adequate ecumenical education and experience in order to express well the Catholic position, and to be aware of the history and methodology of the ecumenical movement.

All churches face the challenge of finding systemic ways to promote ecumenical formation for religious leaders, clergy, pastoral workers, and laity. The Pontifical Council for Promoting Christian Unity addressed this issue in its text, *The Ecumenical Dimension in the Formation of Those Engaged in Pastoral Work.* Seminary education is an obvious place to look for it. Ecumenical consortia of seminaries and theological faculties also could be the locus for ecumenical education.

A variety of institutes provide formation. Some of these include the Ecumenical Institute at Bossey (Switzerland), the Irish School of Ecumenics (Dublin), the Tantur Institute (Jerusalem), St Thomas University (Rome and Bari) and the Centro Pro Unione (Rome). Some councils of churches also have offered formal study. For example, the Christian Conference of Asia has offered courses of ecumenical formation for more than 25 years.

What has been lacking thus far, however, are adequate structures for monitoring and accountability of the ecumenical mandate *within* churches. Thus, we pose some questions:

- What processes are in place to encourage regular reporting back to the churches by their ecumenical official representatives?
- What mechanisms might be created to encourage the teaching of ecumenics by ecumenical teams? For example, when courses on the history, theory and practice of ecumenism are offered, are they planned, promoted, supported and taught in cooperation with ecumenical partners?
- When church leaders meet internally, do they make time to consider the ecumenical implications of their actions? Do they consider the significance of ecumenical texts for their churches?
- When churches reconsider previous positions in the process of theological development, do they make efforts to share the process and its outcome with other churches?
- In what ways can the churches better recognize, encourage and support those who have proposed fresh ecumenical initiatives?

### 9. ALTERNATIVES TO FULL PARTICIPATION

The ultimate aim of churches in the ecumenical movement is full, visible Christian unity. Councils of churches are a privileged instrument by which churches can move towards this goal. Thus all churches are encouraged to enter into prayerful reflection through which the Holy Spirit might lead them into membership in a council of churches as a step along the way towards full, visible unity.

For a variety of reasons, membership may not seem possible or advisable at a particular time in a given context. When this is the case, some alternatives may be considered. These include the following.

*Ongoing structured cooperation:* For example, the Christian Conference of Asia and the Federation of Asian Bishops Conferences have an agreed policy of reciprocal invitations to participate in each other's activities, have a joint ecumenical planning committee, and hold joint staff meetings that lead to the common planning and execution of projects. In the United States, the ecumenical and inter-religious affairs committee of the US Conference of Catholic Bishops is a member of the Faith and Order commission of the National Council of the Churches of Christ in the USA, although it is not a member of the NCCC. In Europe, the Conference of European Churches and the CCEE have been working together for a long time on a structured basis on various ecumenical projects, most recently in promoting the Charta Oecumenica.

*Occasional cooperation on specific projects:* An example might be taken from Sweden, where the Swedish Council of Churches worked together with the Roman Catholic Church in Sweden to prepare for the visit of the pope in 1989, at a time when the Catholic Church was still not a member. Inspired by the friendships formed and the cooperation achieved on that occasion, the Roman Catholic Church asked to be a founding member in the reorganized Swedish Christian Council.

*Observer status:* Some years ago, the CCEE nominated two permanent observers on the Conference of European Churches commission on churches in dialogue. The Anglican church has observer status in the Council of Christian Churches in France, as does the Roman Catholic Church in the Zimbabwe Council of Churches.

*Shared participation in ecumenical gatherings beyond one's own nation:* At the second ecumenical European assembly in Graz, Austria, in 1997, some representatives of Orthodox, Greek Catholic and Protestant churches from Romania worked together ecumenically for the first time.

10. BILATERAL DIALOGUES AND RELATIONSHIPS

Some councils have experienced a lessening of physical presence and financial support from council members who give priority to bilateral dialogues, common agreements or mergers. All these relevant venues are means of promoting the one ecumenical movement and can best be viewed as complementary rather than competing.

The numerous Catholic international bilateral forums focus on specific doctrinal issues that continue to divide the churches. Some national bilateral dialogues have provided significant theological and biblical resources for these international dialogues. Also, bilateral dialogues have allowed Catholics to have formal conversations with Evangelicals.

Some churches are moving towards fuller communion through specific bilateral or multilateral agreements. Also, some churches are developing closer relations with their worldwide community. Such movements necessarily involve the participating churches in intensive dialogue on a wide range of theological, ecclesial and other issues. When integrated into councils, these insights can be powerful means of deepening theological discussion and renewal to promote Christian unity. They also can provide for fresh opportunities and insights when viewed from the multilateral context that a council affords.

Since whatever occurs between two churches affects all churches in the ecumenical movement, churches engaged in bilateral dialogues should seek wherever possible to include observers from other churches in their dialogues. They also should encourage all participants to make detailed reports to the broader ecumenical community.

## VI. Some questions to consider

Beyond issues explored elsewhere in this document, the possibility of the Roman Catholic Church becoming part of an existing ecumenical body confronts all concerned, the council's member churches no less than the prospective newcomer, with searching questions. For churches that are already members, the challenge is not only the organizational one of accommodating one more delegation around the ecumenical table, but also presents other questions:

- Are they willing to examine critically what previously may have been a Protestant conciliar culture, and to alter that culture when Catholics become members?
- Are they sufficiently aware of Catholic documents and teachings about ecumenism?
- Do they appreciate the variety of ecclesiological assumptions that will be around the expanding table and the ways these differences will impact their ecumenical deliberations?

Catholic bishops conferences, too, may find some assumptions challenged:

- Are their members sensitive to the significantly different history of ecumenism as it has been experienced by Orthodox churches and churches of the Reformation?
- Can they deal positively with a Protestant approach to ecumenism that sometimes may seem practically oriented, cooperatively driven and less interested in addressing doctrinal differences between the churches?

And for each church involved even more fundamental questions arise:

- Is its approach to the prospect of a more inclusive council driven by self-centred considerations, a "what's in it for us?" approach – or by the gospel imperative?
- Is the church prepared to be enriched by the gifts that each church brings to the ecumenical table?
- How can we, through our participation in the council of churches, further the mission of the church of Jesus Christ?

## VII. Concluding observations

At one level a council of churches is a structure, with all the accoutrements that go with structures – memberships, constitutions, decision-making procedures, policies, programmes, budgets and, probably, staff. Structure matters. As shown above, a well-functioning council of churches can do much to further the quest for Christian unity. Functioning badly, it may slow or even obstruct the quest.

But at a deeper, more important level, a council is a set of *relationships* between still-divided churches. Under God, they are the principal actors in the ecumenical movement. A council is not primarily an organization, or staff, or programmes. It is the *member churches*, in their shared commitment to God and to one another, attempting to respond together to the pressure of their common calling.

Such ties between churches find expression in many ways, not least in the relationships between the people who lead and represent them. Hence the emphasis in these pages is on the importance of fostering mutual understanding, respect, forbearance, trust. Hence the emphasis, too, is on making decisions in ways that will strengthen such relationships and foreshadow the reconciliation for which the churches yearn. Relationship-building, for any council of churches, always takes priority over the adoption of policies, the running of programmes, the administering of an institution. At least, it should. Ecumenical structures, like others, are tempted at times to a certain introversion. If finances are inadequate, for example, or policies are contentious, a focus on organizational problems is likely to distract attention from the very movement such structures were created to foster.

Likewise, even the best council loses something vital when a pioneering generation passes, to be succeeded by church leaders and representatives who inherit commitments over which others had to struggle. Like baptismal or marriage vows, the ecumenical promises churches make to each other, and to God, would benefit from continuous renewal in the Holy Spirit.

Increased Catholic participation in NCCs and REOs may provide a stimulus for just such renewed commitment by churches already involved in councils, no less than by those considering membership. It comes as a reminder, yet again, that the gospel of reconciliation requires a visibly reconciled faith community, so that the churches dare not rest content with the status quo. Above all, it comes as a sign of hope, a reminder that God in Christ and the Holy Spirit has not abandoned his people to their divisions and does not cease to lead them forward on their pilgrimage towards unity.

## VIII. Recommendations

This document suggests many initiatives that usefully might be taken by churches, episcopal conferences, NCCs and REOs. Two further recommendations, however, might stimulate the World Council of Churches and the Holy See to encourage Roman Catholic participation in ecumenical structures.

1. *Distribution of "Inspired by the Same Vision"*. Its arguments deserve to be weighed by churches in each country and region and, if found persuasive, acted upon. Responses should be noted, so that "Inspired by the Same Vision" serves to stimulate discussion, not end it.

*Recommendation:*

*That the Pontifical Council for Promoting Christian Unity and the World Council of Churches send this document to all NCCs, REOs, Eastern Catholic synods and Catholic episcopal conferences for study and comment, with the recommendation and encouragement that in those countries and regions where the Roman Catholic Church is not presently a member of the NCC or REO, a joint committee composed of members of the NCC, REO and bishops conference be formed which would have the responsibility to translate the document and distribute it to all NCC member churches and all Catholic bishops; and where appropriate, that they initiate a joint process of consultation among representatives of the NCC and bishops conference to examine the possibility of Catholic membership in an existing NCC or the formation of a new inclusive ecumenical body.*

2. *Further consultation:* The Pontifical Council for Promoting Christian Unity and the World Council of Churches have sponsored three useful consultations on issues connected with NCCs – in 1971, 1986 and 1993. This report provides a timely occasion for another gathering. There is need for a new international consultation to bring together representatives of NCCs, REOs and episcopal conferences, especially from places where the Roman Catholic Church is not in membership.

*Recommendation:*

*That the World Council of Churches and the Pontifical Council for Promoting Christian Unity be asked to co-sponsor a consultation of representatives of NCCs, REOs and episcopal conferences from places where the Roman Catholic Church is not in membership. The consultation should consider the document "Inspired by the Same Vision" and reflect on the experience others have gleaned regarding Catholic participation.*

## IX. Appendices

A. A SHORT BIBLIOGRAPHY

1. Thomas F. Best, "Councils of Churches: Local, National, Regional", http://www.wcc-coe.org/wcc/what/ecumenical/cc_e.html
2. World Council of Churches, "Church and Ecumenical Organizations", http://www.wcc-coe.org/wcc/links/church.html
3. Huibert van Beek, "Councils of Churches – a Discussion Starter", http://www.wcc-coe.org/wcc/who/damascus_06_e.html
4. Pontifical Council for Promoting Christian Unity, *Ecumenical Collaboration at the Regional, National, and Local Levels* (Vatican City, 1975).
5. Pontifical Council for Promoting Christian Unity, *The Ecumenical Dimension in the Formation of Those Engaged in Pastoral Work*, Vatican, 1995, §29. http://www.vatican.va/roman_curia/pontifical_councils/chrstuni/documents/
6. "Directory for the Application of Principles and Norms on Ecumenism", http://www.vatican.va/roman_curia/ pontifical_councils/chrstuni/documents/
7. Diane Kessler and Michael Kinnamon, *Councils of Churches and the Ecumenical Vision*, WCC Publications, 2000.
8. Jean-Marie Tillard, OP, "The Mission of the Councils of Churches", *The Ecumenical Review*, 45, 3, July 1993.
9. *Odyssey towards Unity: Foundations and Functions of Ecumenism and Conciliarism*, by Committee on Purposes and Goals of Ecumenism, Massachusetts Council of Churches, Boston MA, Mass. Council of Churches, Oct. 1977.
10. Thomas Michel, "Participation of the Roman Catholic Church in National Councils of Churches: An Historical Survey", *Jeevadhara* (Kottayam), July 2000.
11. *Charta Oecumenica*, Guidelines for the Growing Cooperation among the Churches in Europe, Geneva/St Gallen, 2001.

B. NCCs AND REOs WITH CATHOLIC MEMBERSHIP

*Regional Ecumenical Organizations*
    Caribbean Conference of Churches
    Middle East Conference of Churches
    Pacific Conference of Churches

*National Councils of Churches/Christian Councils*

*Africa: 14*
> Botswana (Botswana Christian Council)
> Congo (Ecumenical Council of Christian Churches of Congo)
> Gambia (Christian Council of The Gambia)
> Lesotho (Christian Council of Lesotho)
> Liberia (Liberian Council of Churches)
> Madagascar (Council of Christian Churches in Madagascar)
> Namibia (Council of Churches in Namibia)
> Nigeria (Christian Council of Nigeria)
> Sierra Leone (Council of Churches in Sierra Leone)
> South Africa (South African Council of Churches)
> Sudan (Sudan Council of Churches)
> Swaziland (Council of Swaziland Churches)
> Uganda (Uganda Joint Christian Council)
> Zimbabwe (Zimbabwe Council of Churches), RC observer

*Asia: 3*
> Australia (National Council of Churches in Australia)
> Malaysia (Christian Federation of Malaysia)
> Taiwan (National Council of Churches of Taiwan)

*Caribbean: 12*
> Antigua (Antigua Christian Council)
> Aruba (Aruba Council of Churches)
> Bahamas (Bahamas Christian Council)
> Barbados (Barbados Christian Council)
> Belize (Belize Christian Council)
> Curacao (Curacao Council of Churches)
> Dominica (Dominica Christian Council)
> Jamaica (Jamaica Council of Churches)
> Montserrat (Montserrat Christian Council)
> St Kitts/Nevis (St Kitts Christian Council)
> St Vincent (St Vincent and the Grenadines Christian Council)
> Trinidad and Tobago (Christian Council of Trinidad and Tobago)

*Europe: 25*
> Austria (Council of Churches in Austria)
> Belgium (Meeting of Christian Churches in Belgium)
> Britain and Ireland (Churches Together in Britain and Ireland)
> Croatia (Ecumenical Coordinating Committee of Churches in Croatia)
> Czech Republic (Ecumenical Council of Churches in the Czech Republic), RC associate
> Denmark (National Council of Churches in Denmark)
> England (Churches Together in England)
> Estonia (Estonian Council of Churches)
> Finland (Finnish Ecumenical Council)
> France (Protestant Federation of France)
> Germany (Council of Christian Churches in Germany)

Hungary (Ecumenical Council of Churches in Hungary)
Ireland (Irish Council of Churches), RC observer
Ireland (Irish Inter-Church Meeting)
Isle of Man (Churches Together in Man)
Lithuania (National Council of Churches in Lithuania)
Malta (Malta Ecumenical Council)
Norway (Christian Council of Norway)
Netherlands (Council of Churches in the Netherlands)
Scotland (Action of Churches Together in Scotland)
Slovak Republic (Ecumenical Council of Churches in the Slovak Republic),
   RC observer
Slovenia (Council of Christian Churches in Slovenia)
Sweden (Christian Council of Sweden)
Switzerland (Council of Christian Churches in Switzerland)
Wales (Cytun – Churches Together in Wales)

*North America: 1*
Canada (Canadian Council of Churches)

*Oceania: 10*
American Samoa (National Council of Churches in American Samoa)
Cook Islands (Religious Advisory Council of the Cook Islands)
Fiji (Fiji Council of Churches)
Kiribati (Kiribati National Council of Churches)
Marshall Islands (Marshall Islands National Council of Churches of Christ)
Papua New Guinea (Papua New Guinea Council of Churches)
Samoa (Samoa Council of Churches)
Solomon Islands (Solomon Islands Christian Association)
Tonga (Tonga National Council of Churches)
Vanuatu (Vanuatu Christian Council)

*South America: 5*
Argentina (Argentine Federation of Evangelical Churches)
Brazil (National Council of Christian Churches in Brazil)
Guyana (Guyana Council of Churches)
Surinam (Committee of Christian Churches – Surinam)
Uruguay (Federation of Evangelical Churches in Uruguay)

NOTE

1  This document sometimes uses the term "Catholic Church" in preference to "Roman Catholic Church." In
   some regional and national ecumenical organizations, it is the wider "Catholic" family that is represented;
   this situation may be reflected in the constitutions of some national and regional councils of churches with
   use of the term "Catholic."

# 41. Ecclesiological and Ecumenical Implications of a Common Baptism

## Joint Working Group

Kolympari – Chania, Crete, Greece, 6-13 May 2004

## Introduction

1. In baptism one is brought into the saving mysteries of the reconciliation of humanity with God through Jesus Christ. Baptism creates a unique relationship to Christ because it is a participation in his life, death and resurrection. (cf. *Baptism, Eucharist and Ministry* [BEM], 1982, B3).

2. "Through Baptism, Christians are brought into union with Christ, with each other and with the church of every time and place" (B6), the community which is formed by the healing grace of Christ. Many persons experience the sorrows and anguish of broken social relations and broken family life, with all the devastating impact that brokenness can have on those concerned. The world itself shows signs of fractured human relationships: structures of alienation and division contradict that unity which God intends for all peoples and creation (Col. 1:15). But baptism is the joyful act of welcome into a new and caring community of the faithful bound together in Jesus Christ – a community which transcends the very divisions evident in society. Life in Christ brought about by baptism is a healing balm for individuals and community alike, in a broken and sinful world.

3. While divided churches themselves contradict God's reconciliation in Christ, one of the great achievements of the modern ecumenical movement has been to show that, as Pope John Paul II has stated, "the universal brotherhood of Christians has become a firm ecumenical conviction... [and this]... is rooted in recognition of the oneness of baptism..." (*Ut Unum Sint* 42). It is because of baptism and our allegiance to Christ that we can call one another Christians. Indeed on the basis of a common recognition of baptism into Christ, some churches have been enabled to enter new relationships of communion. Such recognition is not simply a statement of how an individual's baptism is regarded, "it constitutes an ecclesiological statement" (*ibid.*). Individual members of churches should not be considered apart from the whole community of faith that gave them birth and in which they are nourished and exercise Christian discipleship. This study therefore seeks to explore the ecclesiological and ecumenical implications of a common recognition of baptism.

4.  In undertaking the study the Joint Working Group has drawn on the insights of international bilateral and multilateral discussions on baptism and on official responses to BEM. It has also taken into account a survey of agreements on the recognition of baptism undertaken by the Pontifical Council for Promoting Christian Unity and continuing work on baptism being conducted by the Faith and Order commission of the WCC.

BAPTISM IN THE MODERN ECUMENICAL MOVEMENT

5.  In the modern ecumenical movement, the gradual acknowledgment of a common understanding of baptism has been one of the most basic reasons enabling long separated Christians to speak now of sharing a real though incomplete communion. According to the Faith and Order convergence text *Baptism, Eucharist and Ministry*, which has gained wide acceptance among Christians of various traditions, "Through baptism, Christians are brought into union with Christ, with each other, and with the church of every time and place. Our common baptism, which unites us to Christ in faith, is thus a basic bond of unity. The union with Christ which we share through baptism has important implications for Christian unity" (B6). According to the Second Vatican Council, by the sacrament of baptism one "becomes truly incorporated into the crucified and glorified Christ... Baptism, therefore, constitutes a sacramental bond of unity linking all who have been reborn by means of it" (*Unitatis Redintegratio* [*UR*] 22 1964).

6.  On the other hand, Faith and Order's evaluation of the official responses to BEM 1990 noted areas where further study should be undertaken on baptism. A comparison of some of the specific responses to BEM indicate that there are still important issues that need to be resolved in dialogue among the churches before we can speak of a genuinely common understanding of baptism. Furthermore, some new problems are emerging which need to be addressed lest the convergence/consensus achieved be somehow diminished (see §108 below).

A MORE RECENT ECUMENICAL CHALLENGE:

7.  In addition, another significant ecumenical challenge arises from among the fastest growing and largest Christian communities today, Pentecostals and Evangelicals, many of whom have not been directly involved in the modern ecumenical movement. A particular challenge that they bring is that many of these Christians do not see baptism itself as the point of entry into the body of Christ, but rather as an intimately related consequence of that entry.[1] The growth of communities with this viewpoint presents a new ecumenical challenge for today and the future.

THE PRESENT STUDY

8.  Despite these various challenges, the creation of a new relationship among separated Christians has been an ecumenical achievement. The purpose of this study is to help the churches to build on this accomplishment and, in particular, on the contribution made to

the unity of Christians by the growing acknowledgment of a common baptism. This text reviews some fundamental aspects of the degree of the current ecumenical convergences and consensus on baptism while also pointing to differences still remaining. Thus, one can speak of a "common" baptism in a legitimate, though qualified, sense. On the one hand, the degree of common understanding of baptism which has been achieved ecumenically has already been a building block for unity and has already helped to create new relationships and foster reconciliation between separated Christians. On the other hand, further ecumenical work on baptism is still needed to resolve continuing difficulties if further progress is to be made.

9. This study points also to some of the implications, ecclesiological and ecumenical, of a common baptism for the goal of unity which we seek.[2] *Ecclesiological implications* refer to issues relating to the doctrine of the church and thus inter-related with baptism. They concern those remaining theological divergences among Christians which now more urgently need to be resolved, or to which more ecumenical attention must now be given in order to take further steps towards a common understanding of the church and the healing of divisions among Christians. These will be noted in each specific section. *Ecumenical implications* refer to those practical, pastoral steps that might be taken now to implement the growing common understanding of baptism. They are steps based on the degree of communion Christians already share, and therefore may also have an ecclesial character – steps that can help separated Christians to grow together. These are listed in the section 6 at the end.

10. This is a study document meant to enable discussion. It is the hope of the Joint Working Group that this study will be used in educational contexts in which ecumenical matters are explored. It is hoped that this study can assist and encourage the Catholic Church and the member churches of the WCC to open a discussion on ecclesial and ecumenical implications of the recognition of a common baptism and to take appropriate steps to manifest a greater degree of communion.

## 1. Growing ecumenical convergence on baptism

11. From the beginning of the modern ecumenical movement baptism has been claimed as a common bond for Christians and has been the subject of intensive conversation among the churches. In this section and in the pages that follow some of the basic convergences on baptism achieved in dialogue are recalled. The differences that still remain are presented as well in order to indicate the further work that needs to be done.

COMMON PERSPECTIVES ON BAPTISM

12. Through shared study churches have discovered common perspectives on baptism relating to (a) its foundational place in the church, (b) the primary aspects of its meaning, and (c) the pattern or *ordo* of elements in the process of baptismal initiation. They have also made notable steps in bringing closer the views of baptism as sacrament and baptism as *ordinance*.

13. The ecumenical convergence and agreements on baptism found in BEM mark an important step forward in the ecumenical movement. Many of the official responses from member churches of the World Council of Churches found much to praise in the baptism section of BEM. The response of the Catholic Church to that baptism section (*Churches Respond to BEM*, vol. 6, WCC, 1988, pp. 9-16) was largely affirmative, finding "much we can agree with", while, as many other responses, raising issues in need of further study. Important clarifications on baptism have been made in bilateral dialogues as well.

14. Ecumenical study has enabled separated Christians to appreciate together the *priority of the liturgical act of baptism*. In faithful obedience to the great commission from the risen Christ (Matt. 28:19-20, "Go therefore and make disciples of all nations, baptizing them in the name of the Father and of the Son and of the Holy Spirit, and teaching them everything I have commanded you"), the church's practice of baptism responds to the apostolic calling to preach the gospel and make disciples. From the beginning, baptism was part of the mission of the apostolic church and its practice was part of the constitution of the church. Before there was an established canon of the New Testament scriptures and while the ecclesial structure was still developing, baptism was a constitutive element of Christian life. As an act of repentance, forgiveness, profession, incorporation and eschatological hope, the observance of baptism recapitulates and embodies the reality of the church, which continually lives out these same relations with God through Christ in its worship, sacraments, teaching, *koinonia* and service. As a specific rite, baptism anchors a wider complex of steps in the initiation, growth and identity of individual believers within the body of Christ. But baptism is not only an event for individuals and a bond of unity among Christians. As such, it is also one expression and icon of the church's very nature.

15. Despite variations in baptismal practice that existed within an undivided church (as for instance variations in the local baptismal creeds that were used), ecumenical dialogue has enabled separated Christians to identify the shared pattern of the early church *as a common heritage* for the divided churches today, being the foundation of the understanding and practice of baptism in each Christian communion. In that common heritage "baptism is administered with water in the name of the Father, the Son and the Holy Spirit" (B17). "In baptism a profession of faith is given according to the trinitarian content of the faith of the community (*regula fidei*)." This "baptismal confession joins the faith of the baptized to the common faith of the church through the ages" (*Confessing the One Faith*, introduction, 15).

16. "The New Testament scriptures and the liturgy of the church unfold the meaning of baptism in various images which express the riches of Christ and the gifts of his salvation" (B 2). Reflecting this heritage, *Baptism, Eucharist and Ministry* (B3-7) identifies five major sets of images: (a) participation in Christ's death and resurrection; (b) conversion, pardoning and cleansing; (c) gift of the Spirit; (d) incorporation into the body of Christ; and (e) sign of the kingdom. While ecumenical convergence can be claimed on these points, the need for further work can be illustrated by looking at point (d). While BEM states that "our common baptism… is a basic bond of unity" (B6) and that baptism is "incorporation into the body of Christ" (B comm. 14b), there are different views relating to that incorporation which reflect unresolved differences in ecclesiology. Thus, many would agree that incorporation in the church is through baptism, but some responses to BEM indicate that full incorporation into the church, the body of Christ, implies not just baptism, but rather a larger process of Christian initiation of which bap-

tism is a part. The reality of new life in Jesus Christ and rebirth in the Holy Spirit is described in BEM with a wide variety of spiritual images. Christian traditions have differed in the weight they give to these images in understanding baptism. The churches can all be enriched by learning from each other in order to grasp the breadth of the meaning of baptism.

17. Many of the convergences in these areas are reflected in results of bilateral dialogues which also point to areas where further discussion is needed. To give two examples, the Anglican-Reformed International Commission report "God's Reign and Our Unity" (1984 §§47-61) reflects BEM's convergences. But differences appear when the text discusses the related question of membership. Reformed churches have tended to define it "primarily as membership in a local congregation", while Anglicans, "by practice of episcopal confirmation, have emphasized membership in the wider church". The report states that these emphases "are complementary rather than contradictory", but "require further exploration by our churches" (§57). The international Catholic-Orthodox dialogue reflects BEM's convergences in its list of seven points of agreement ("Faith, Sacraments and the Unity of the Church", 1987, §49). However, the latter also includes important areas of agreement between Orthodox and Catholics which are not as explicitly stated in BEM, e.g., the "necessity of baptism for salvation", and as an effect of baptism, the "liberation from original sin" (*ibid.*).

18. In current ecumenical discussion three dimensions of the common pattern of baptism are noted – three distinct ways to understand the scope of this pattern. First of all, in the most basic sense, baptism refers to the liturgical water rite and the pattern for its celebration. Second, baptism may also refer to a wider pattern of Christian initiation, one that includes several components in addition to the specific liturgical rite of baptism. In a third sense, we may see that baptism points towards ongoing formation and responsible discipleship, where the pattern of our baptismal calling is worked out over a whole life. With the first perspective in view, we could say that baptism is one of the elements that make up the life of the church. With the third perspective in view, we could say that the baptismal pattern marks the entire life of believers in the church.

19. "Baptism is related not only to momentary experience, but to life-long growth into Christ" (B 9). In the early church this was expressed in the emergence of complex patterns of Christian nurture which included instruction in the faith before and after baptism, as well as an extended series of liturgical celebrations marking the journey in a growing faith. These aspects were focused in the water rite of baptism and admission to the eucharistic table. In its broadest sense the ordo (or pattern) of baptism includes formation in faith, baptism in water, and participation in the life of the community. In different Christian traditions the order and expression of these aspects varies.

20. The ecumenical and ecclesial consequences of agreement about baptism vary greatly, depending upon which dimension of this common pattern is in view. The churches have a high degree of agreement about the fundamental components of the liturgical water rite and its necessity. As the pattern is expanded, the specific agreement among the churches diminishes. For example, there are fewer disputes about recognition of baptism centred on whether the rite has been performed with water in the name of Father, Son and Holy Spirit, than relate to the place of the rite in this larger pattern of initiation or formation.

SACRAMENT AND ORDINANCE

21. Many churches use the term sacrament to express their understanding of what the common pattern or ordo of baptism is. Some churches are uncomfortable with the notion of sacrament and they prefer to speak of baptism as an ordinance. A brief look at the history of these two terms may help to identify the issue and suggest that it may not be as divisive as is sometimes thought.

22. When the Greek fathers used the word *musterion* to describe baptism, and when the Latins translated this by *mysterium or sacramentum* they wanted to say that, in the celebration of baptism, the saving work of God in Christ is realized by the power of the Holy Spirit. In the Latin church *sacramentum* (from which comes our modern word sacrament) came to be a generic term applied to baptism and eucharist, as well as to some other rites of the church. A sacrament was understood to be a symbolic action, made up of words and actions which held within it and manifested the divine reality (*res*) realized once for all in the death and resurrection of Christ for our salvation. This notion of sacrament was very carefully analyzed in Scholastic theology. Some elements of the analysis, however, lent themselves to misunderstanding, especially when they were associated with forms of liturgical practice that seemed to encourage belief in a quasi-mechanical view of sacramental efficacy, as if sacraments dispensed grace in an automatic way.

23. The word "ordinance" stresses that certain acts within the worship and liturgy of the church are performed in obedience to the specific command and example of Christ in scripture. Those who use the term "sacraments" usually also regard them as ordinances in this sense. Historically, some Christian groups adopted "ordinance" language in the Reformation era because of arguments over whether certain liturgical acts were actually instituted by Christ in scripture and because of their rejection of certain theological views about the working of God's grace which they believed were involved in the definition of "sacraments". Some churches which use only the word "ordinance" regard acts such as baptism and the Lord's supper as signs of a reality that has already been actualized and which is even now effective by faith in the life of the believer and the congregation. Some who use only the word "ordinance" would in fact give this a "sacramental" meaning, consistent with the explanation of sacraments in churches that use the term. Those who characterize baptism as an ordinance wish to safeguard an understanding of its root in scripture, its confessional character as witness to Christ, and the initiative of God, active to stir faith and conversion in the believer prior to baptism. This view has often wrongly been construed as denying that God is active in the event of baptism or that God's grace is received in baptism; in fact, it is an attempt to affirm the faithful act of discipleship through participation in baptism, the centrality of Christ to the act of baptism and the breadth of God's grace already active in our lives prior to, as well as in, baptism.

24. This divergent language is in some cases based on misunderstanding, but in other instances on disagreement which remains, even after clarification. Nevertheless, most traditions can agree that the realities in the church's life called sacraments or ordinances bring Christians to the central mysteries of life in Christ. Most would affirm of ordinances/sacraments both that they are expressive of divine realities, representing that which is already true, and also that they are instrumental in that God uses them to bring about a new reality. The two approaches represent different starting points in considering the interdependence of faith as an ongoing process and faith as a decisive event. At other points in this document further areas of convergence are explored, for instance in the discussion of the relation of baptism and faith in section 3 [of B in BEM].

THE ECUMENICAL IMPACT OF THE GROWING CONVERGENCE ON BAPTISM

25. While there is not yet a complete agreement on baptism among separated Christians, the growing convergence that has been achieved thus far can be counted among the important achievements of the modern ecumenical movement. As the following examples illustrate, this growing convergence has already been able to serve the cause of reconciliation, fostering unity between different churches in different ways. This is one sense in which the growing consensus on baptism even now has ecclesiological implications.

26. Ecumenical agreements bringing some churches into new relationships, in some cases even into full communion, include mutual understanding of baptism as part of their theological basis. The Leuenberg agreement (1973) between Lutheran and Reformed churches in Europe includes, as part of "The Common Understanding of the Gospel" needed for church fellowship among them, a basic consensus regarding baptism (§14), even though the agreement indicates that the question of "baptismal practice" needs further study (§39). The nine member churches of the Churches Uniting in Christ (2001) in the United States have included in their theological consensus the convergences and agreements on baptism found in *Baptism, Eucharist and Ministry*.

27. In several ecumenical advances which have taken place involving the Catholic Church with Christian world communions which include member churches of the WCC, a common understanding of baptism has been crucial. In their common declaration at Canterbury in 1982, Pope John Paul II and Archbishop of Canterbury Dr Robert Runcie stated that "the bond of our common baptism into Christ" led their predecessors to inaugurate the international dialogue between the Anglican Communion and the Catholic Church. The same two leaders in their common declaration in Rome in 1989 stated that the "certain yet incomplete communion we already share" is grounded in sharing together important areas of faith including "our common baptism into Christ".

28. The Joint Declaration on the Doctrine of Justification (JDDJ), officially signed by the Catholic Church and the Lutheran World Federation (1999), expresses an agreement on basic truths of the doctrine of justification. It is historic in stating that the teaching of the Lutheran churches and the Catholic Church presented in the declaration are not subject to the condemnations of the other's teaching found respectively in the council of Trent and in the Lutheran confessions in the 16th century. The JDDJ's explication of justification comes in seven core areas, in two of which baptism is central. In §25 we read, "We confess together that sinners are justified by faith in the saving action of God in Christ. By the action of the Holy Spirit in baptism, they are granted the gift of salvation, which lays the basis for the whole Christian life." And in §28, "We confess together that in baptism the Holy Spirit unites one with Christ, justifies and truly renews the person."

29. In several joint declarations between the pope and patriarchs of Oriental Orthodox churches, reflecting resolution of long-standing problems, agreement on baptism has also been an important factor. For example, the joint declaration between Pope John Paul II and Syrian Orthodox Patriarch Mar Ignatius Zakka I Iwas (1984) expresses agreement on Christology in a way which virtually resolves for them the christological conflicts arising from the doctrinal formulations of the council of Chalcedon (451). The agreement also describes common perspectives today on baptism, eucharist and other sacraments, and a common understanding of sacraments which they hold together "in one and the same succession of apostolic ministry" (§7). This allows them to authorize collaboration in pastoral care in situations where their faithful find access to a priest of their own

church "materially or morally impossible". Nonetheless, at the same time, they say that their churches cannot celebrate the holy eucharist together since that supposes a complete identity of faith, including a common understanding of God's will for the church, which does not yet exist between them.

ECCLESIOLOGICAL IMPLICATIONS

30. Many other examples could be cited that illustrate the impact of the growing convergence on baptism. But what has been said thus far in this first section suggests several *ecclesiological implications* of a common baptism. *First*, a common baptism is among those factors which have enabled, even inspired, some long separated churches to enter into new relationships with one another. Some of these are significant new relationships, but not of full communion. Others are relationships of full communion, or, as in the case of those participating in the Leuenberg Agreement, of pulpit and altar fellowship.

31. *Second*, those Christian communities which agree that baptism means incorporation into the body of Christ, the church, and who agree that the church is one, should belong to one and the same community. If there is one church of Jesus Christ and if baptism is entrance into it, then all those who are baptized are bound to one another in Christ and should be in full communion with one another. There should not be a division among ecclesial communities; baptism should impel Christians to work for the elimination of divisions.

32. It also follows that even if there is agreement on a common understanding of baptism, churches nonetheless differ concerning what they require for achieving full communion with those from whom they are separated. This is because they have divergent understandings of the nature of the church. Thus, a *third* ecclesiological implication of a common understanding of baptism, from what has been described above, is the urgency within the ecumenical movement of working towards a common understanding of the nature of the church. This is important so that, as new relationships take shape among some churches, the agreements that bind them together will include perspectives on the nature of the church which would be open to reconciliation with other churches in the future as the ecumenical movement progresses.

33. *Fourth*, since baptism is foundational for the nature of the church, then it is one of the prerequisites for full communion. If a particular Christian community does not celebrate baptism, then its members are without one of the important elements which make for communion with all other baptized Christians. The level of communion between such a community and the communities who celebrate baptism is significantly impaired.

## 2. Baptism and initiation into the life of faith

34. When the gospel is preached and the call to conversion is heard, a process of incorporation into life in Christ is set in motion in the one who is called to salvation (Acts 2:37-42). While the process continues throughout life until the Christian is definitively

incorporated into Christ at the parousia, its earthly course is marked by certain decisive moments, in which significant stages of life in Christ are first realized and manifested. These moments taken together can be called Christian initiation. They are moments of faith and conversion, of ritual celebration and of entry into the life of the church. Baptism is at the heart of the process, both as decisive moment and as model of the entire process.

35. The churches are united in confessing that "there is one Lord, one faith, one baptism" (Eph. 4:5). United in the one Lord, they affirm that faith and baptism belong together. They can agree that faith calls for baptism, and that the rite of baptism expresses the faith of the church of Christ and of the person baptized. Baptism expresses faith in the gracious gift of God that justifies sinners; it celebrates the realization of that gift in a new member of the church. This faith is handed on in the church, in its life and teaching, and is appropriated as the faith of the church by the person baptized.

THE RITES OF CHRISTIAN INITIATION

36. Christian initiation is effected in a complex interplay of faith and conversion, of ritual celebration, of teaching and spiritual formation, of practice and of mission. While there are differences between churches in the way the relationship between these elements is understood, there is widespread agreement that the water-rite of baptism is at the heart of initiation.

37. "Baptism is administered with water in the name of the Father, the Son and the Holy Spirit" (B17). The baptismal rite has taken different forms in the history of the church's life. While churches have their individual normative practices, they often recognize other forms as constituting a true baptism. On the one hand, total or partial immersion of the candidate in water seems to be the form best grounded in the Tradition, and to be acceptable to most churches. Many recognize as true a baptism that is done by the pouring of water on the person, particularly on the head. On the other hand various churches doubt whether a sprinkling with water is a sufficient sacramental sign. More ecumenically problematic is the practice of some churches, noted by BEM, that have a rite of initiation that does not use water but is nevertheless called baptism (comm. 21c). Most difficult to reconcile with the understanding of most Christians concerning baptism and the church are the procedures for initiation into Christian faith and life of some Christian communities that lack any specific rite resembling baptism and even deliberately exclude baptism.

38. In many churches chrismation/confirmation and first reception of the eucharist are associated with baptism as rites of initiation. While there are differences in the way the relationship between these three rites is understood and practised in the churches, and their bearing on Christian life is not always experienced in the same way, it is generally accepted that they give expression and reality to different aspects of a single process of initiation. Baptism is intrinsically related to the other two rites, in so far as it calls forth the gift of the eschatological Spirit and brings one into communion in the body of Christ; they, for their part, are grounded in baptism and draw meaning from it.

39. Some churches do not practise chrismation/confirmation, and others who do so allow reception of the eucharist before chrismation/confirmation. While these practices

are problematical for other churches they do not call into question the fundamental orientation of baptism to eucharist and its role as precondition for receiving the eucharist to which the whole Christian Tradition bears witness.

40. The sacrament of baptism is, in the first meaning of the term, a distinctive water-rite that occurs once in a life-time and cannot be repeated. The ongoing gift of growth in faith and the continual dying and rising in Christ that this entails is truly a living out of the once-for-all encounter of faith with Christ that is given and modelled in the rite of baptism. In this sense Christian life can be understood as a "life-long baptism", lasting until final oneness with Christ is attained.

BAPTISM AND FAITH

41. Baptism as rite, and as a daily dying and rising with Christ, is inseparable from faith. God, who calls persons by name (Isa. 43:1; cf. Acts 9:4), is the source of faith. Even the freedom to respond in faith is God's gracious gift. Faith begins in persons when God sows in them the seed of simple trust. By the witness of the Holy Spirit they grow up into Christ, in whom the fullness of God dwells (Col. 1:19). It is not on the basis of their own understanding or ability that human beings can receive God's gift, but only through the grace of our Lord Jesus Christ (Rom. 3:24; 1 Cor. 1:26ff.). Nothing can be claimed for baptism that would interfere with the utter gratuitousness of the gift of God received in faith.

42. Faith is the response of the believer to the gospel of salvation in Jesus Christ, preached in and by the community of those who already believe in him and praise the glory of his name. Drawn into that faith, the new believer gradually makes his/her own the words in which the gospel of salvation is expressed. These are primarily the words of the scriptures, and particularly the confessions of faith that they contain. They are also those symbols of faith, those distillations of the gospel, that the churches have recognized as expressions of the faith and authorized for use in worship and teaching. It is these words of faith, crystallized in the trinitarian formula "in the name of the Father and of the Son and of the Holy Spirit", that give form and meaning to the water rite of baptism and that in the early church led to it being called sacrament of faith.

43. Thus baptism situates the faith of the Christian within the living faith of the church and so contributes to the growth of his or her faith. "As Christians mature, they grow up into the fullness of the faith confessed, celebrated and witnessed to by the Christian community, both locally and worldwide... in the faith professed by the whole church throughout the ages... The 'we believe' of the Christian community and the 'I believe' of personal commitment become one" (second Faith and Order consultation on baptism at Faverges, 2001, 48).

44. The trinitarian faith confessed in the baptismal creed and the baptismal washing performed by the church in the name of the Father, Son and Holy Spirit are indissolubly united in the liturgy of holy baptism. In the creed the church testifies to its faith in the triune God, and incorporates those baptized into God's holy people. This connection between the baptismal formula and the believing church is at the core of the process of Christian initiation. In this sense baptism is always understood to be believer's baptism.

45. The faith confessed in baptism is the faith that binds believers and their churches together. In early centuries Christian communities shared their baptismal creeds as a basis of unity. Later, councils expressed the same faith in more extensive formulations. The heart of the faith expressed in the most universally acknowledged creeds used today – the Nicene-Constantinopolitan and the Apostles' Creeds – is the faith in the triune God, Father, Son and Holy Spirit. And "the profession of faith occurs also in those churches which do not formally use the words of the Nicene Creed, when baptismal confession uses other formulas authorized by the church" (*Confessing the One Faith*, introduction, §15).

46. Churches that share faith in the Trinity and fully recognize one another's baptism may, nevertheless, break communion with each other due to differences about other matters of faith or questions of order. In this case the communion which is the fruit of faith and baptism is impeded. There are churches which consider that a disagreement in faith that is sufficiently serious to be communion-breaking between them and another church makes them unable to admit baptized members of that church to full participation in the eucharist, the normal fulfillment of baptism. Many other churches, however, consider that, even in the absence of full ecclesial communion, churches should admit members of other churches, whose baptism they recognize and trinitarian faith they share, to full participation in the eucharist.

## ADULT BAPTISM AND THE BAPTISM OF INFANTS

47. Most churches can share the broad understanding of the relation between faith and baptism that has been described above. But differences remain which lead to problems for the mutual recognition of baptism. The differences are not very apparent when the baptism being considered is that of an adult. Two facts provide a unifying point of reference for churches regarding the manner and meaning of the baptism of adults. First, biblical descriptions of the pattern of initiation normally refer to adults. Second, major classical liturgies of baptism were initially intended for adults. Such baptisms, celebrated according to the present-day rituals and disciplines of almost all churches, are normally the baptism of actual believers, and can be recognized as such. But when baptism is administered to a child who is not yet capable of making a personal profession of faith, the interpretation of the scriptural and traditional material on baptism can differ. For some churches the scriptures only authorize the baptizing of those who make a personal act of conversion and a personal confession of faith. For others the scriptures provide no compelling reason for refusing baptism to children not yet capable of such personal decisions, when they are presented by those who are responsible for them and are entrusted by them to the church for their formation and instruction. Furthermore, descriptions in Acts of the baptism of whole households must be taken carefully into account. And, even though classical baptismal liturgies were designed for adults, a very early and extensive description of such a liturgy, the *Apostolic Tradition* of Hippolytus (c.215), explicitly includes the initiation of children who cannot answer for themselves (XX, 4).

48. It must be recognized with BEM that "the necessity of faith for the reception of the salvation embodied and set forth in baptism is acknowledged by the churches. Personal commitment is necessary for responsible membership in the body of Christ" (B8).

"While the possibility that infant baptism was also practised in the apostolic age cannot be excluded, baptism upon personal profession of faith is the most clearly attested pattern in the New Testament documents" (B11). The churches recognize the paradigmatic and normative quality of the baptism of adult believers, illustrated in the New Testament and practised by all churches, as the most explicit sign of the character of baptism. However, as BEM goes on to note, "In the course of history, the practice of baptism has developed in a variety of forms. Some churches baptize infants brought by parents or guardians who are ready, in and with the church, to bring up the children in the Christian faith. Other churches practise exclusively the baptism of believers who are able to make a personal confession of faith. Some of these churches encourage infants or children to be presented and blessed in a service which usually involves thanksgiving for the gift of the child and also the commitment of the mother and father to Christian parenthood" (B11).

49.  It has to be noted here that the development of infant baptism is rooted in the history of the early church and was never intended to be a departure from the pattern of initiation that we have identified and that is ordained in the New Testament texts on baptism. Children were baptized because God's call to salvation seemed to bear on them no less than on adults. Age could be no barrier to the gift of God in Christ and the Spirit. In the celebration of baptism the rite was always associated with faith and with life in the community of believers. In infants, faith took the form of the living faith of the church that gathered the child to itself in baptism. The faith of the church was understood to be now present in this new member in the form of the faith-nurture that was henceforth enfolding it. Faith was understood to be an already-present grace that would enable the child to grow up to the point of being able to make a personal confession of faith and personally ratify the grace of conversion that had been given in baptism. The ground of this conviction was the understanding that the grace of Christ has taken hold of all the children of Adam and can free them from sin once they are brought into contact with him through the preaching and sacraments of the church. It is only and always this grace that generates the human response that is inherent to faith. It can be already at work in the nurture through which children are being brought to the point of being able to make personal choices.

50.  Churches that practise only the baptism of adult believers are no less caring for children than the churches that baptize them. They also welcome children for instruction, care and blessing within the community. They mark the commitment of Christian parents and their ecclesial community (and in some cases of specific sponsors as well) to nurture a newborn child in the faith, within the life of the church. Even though the welcome is not enacted through baptism it looks towards baptism as its horizon. For people so welcomed into the church in childhood, baptism in adult age can be the personal expression of the climax of a journey of conversion and faith, which is one of the principle ways in which the scriptures speak of it. Furthermore, the ecumenical convergence being reached about the sacramental status of baptism can now enable churches that baptize only those who can make a personal act of faith to see the baptism they administer as also embodying the grace of Christ and the gift of the Spirit that brings about the personal faith and conversion that is expressed in the celebration.

51.  In the Latin tradition infant baptism received strong support in the theology of Augustine and his reaction against Pelagian views. This view gave expression to the fear of exposing infants to the danger of dying without being rescued from [original] sin by

the saving work of Christ, as well as to the positive advantages of initiation into life in Christ and his church that baptism brings. A restored theology of baptism and a critical re-evaluation of certain explanations of the consequences of original sin for children would give increased weight to the christological and ecclesiological reality of baptism. These churches also recognize that there are risks of mishandling the gifts of God in baptizing children. The promises of Christian nurture given by parents and sponsors may not be kept and the sacrament may be profaned. In fact, these churches have, theoretically if not always in practice, required that baptism be delayed until the child is old enough to speak for him/herself when there is not a reasonable guarantee that the child will be nurtured in the faith. While these concerns, which must surely be intensified in our post-Christian world, do not amount to identifying with the position of churches that practise only believer's baptism, they certainly indicate a belief that the full pattern of Christian initiation must be respected. In this they affirm something that can serve as an important ground for recognition of baptism between them and churches that practise only believer's baptism.

52. We have proposed that the pattern of baptismal initiation has three elements: formation in faith, baptism in water, and participation in the life of the community. These three elements are present in the rite of water baptism itself for every church, though not in the same way. Likewise all three elements are present in the life-long process of Christian discipleship, with its continual formation in faith, recollection of baptismal grace and promise, and deepening participation in the life of the church. If we ask about the relation of faith to baptism in reference to the water rite alone, the differences among the churches remain substantial. When we compare instead the wider pattern of baptismal initiation and formation in Christ, more extensive convergence emerges. It is a convergence that is compatible with and even enriched by the fact that different traditions emphasize one or other element of the pattern and put them together in different ways.

53. The convergence is grounded on the fact that churches recognize a paradigmatic and normative quality of baptism performed upon personal profession of faith, illustrated in the New Testament and practised by all churches, as the most explicit sign of the character of baptism. Those traditions that practise only this form of baptism in their pattern of initiation maintain a living witness to the reality of baptism the churches affirm together, and express powerfully the shared conviction that baptism is inherently oriented to personal conversion. Those traditions that practise infant baptism as part of their pattern of initiation maintain a living witness to the initiating call and grace from God that the churches agree enable human response, and express powerfully the shared convictions that infants and children are nurtured and received within the community of Christ's church prior to any explicit confession.

54. It is being suggested that each church, even as it retains its own baptismal tradition, recognize in others the one baptism into Jesus Christ by affirming the similarity of wider patterns of initiation and formation in Christ present in every community. This is the convergence foreseen in *Baptism, Eucharist and Ministry*: "Churches are increasingly recognizing one another's baptism as the one baptism into Christ, when Jesus Christ has been confessed as Lord by the candidate or, in the case of infant baptism, when confession has been made by the church (parents, guardians, godparents and congregation) and affirmed later by personal faith and commitment" (B15). Those churches that practise only believer's baptism could recognize the one baptism in other traditions within their full patterns of Christian initiation, which include personal affirmation of faith. Those

churches that normally practise infant baptism could recognize the one baptism within the full pattern of Christian initiation in "believer's churches", even where identical forms of chrismation or confirmation were lacking.

55. Recognition that the one baptism of Christ is present within another tradition's full pattern of Christian initiation can also reinforce another key affirmation in *Baptism, Eucharist and Ministry*: "Baptism is an unrepeatable act. Any practice which might be interpreted as 're-baptism' must be avoided" (B13).

ECCLESIOLOGICAL IMPLICATIONS

56. There is an intimate relationship between baptism and faith. This, and the fact that the various churches in their baptismal practice have the intent to baptize into the universal body of Christ (cf. §42), but in fact baptize into communities separated from one another, often because of serious differences in their understanding of aspects of Christian faith, suggests the following. *An ecclesiological implication of the emerging convergence on baptism is that this development makes more urgent the achievement, by separated Christians, of a common understanding of the apostolic faith which the church proclaims and in light of which a person is baptized.*

57. Concerning the disagreement about baptizing infants, those on both sides agree that baptism is related to personal faith. One position holds that personal faith is a condition for being baptized, and the other that personal faith is required of the person baptized as soon as it becomes possible. But a significant difference between the two positions concerns the role taken by the church, as suggested in statements above explaining infant baptism: "In infants, faith took the form of the living faith of the church that gathered the child to itself in baptism" (§49); faith was understood as "an already-present grace that would enable the child to grow up...able to make its personal confession of faith and personally ratify the grace of conversion... given in baptism...," a conviction based on the understanding "... that the grace of Christ has taken hold of all the children of Adam and can free them from sin once they are brought into contact with him through the preaching and sacraments of the church" (§49). *The ecclesiological implication which follows is that among the basic issues which need to be resolved in order to overcome the divergence on infant baptism are the questions of the nature and purpose of the church and its role in the economy of salvation.*

### 3. Baptism and incorporation into the church

58. Both the rite of baptism, as well as the life-long process of growing into Christ which it initiates, take place within a particular (local) church community. Its members and ministers preach the gospel, invite, instruct and ritually prepare its catechumens, celebrate the sacramental rites of initiation, register the act and take responsibility for the ongoing Christian formation and sacramental completion of those baptized in it. Such a baptizing community believes that the one, holy, catholic and apostolic church of Christ is realized in itself. Thus the baptism it celebrates is the gift of the Spirit that incorpo-

rates the baptized, at one and the same time, into its own community life and into the body of Christ that is his church. The communion which this local church has with other churches expresses and embodies the oneness of Christians that is given in the body of Christ. The eucharist, as the sacrament of the body and blood of Christ given for the salvation of all, brings the communion given in baptism to its sacramental fullness.

59.  All churches agree that the incorporation into Christ that is inaugurated in baptism is intended to be, as gift of Christ in the Spirit to the glory of God the Father, complete and full incorporation. Correspondingly, baptism expresses the intention to admit the baptized person into the universal communion of the church of Christ. Christian communities do not baptize into themselves as isolated units but as churches that believe the body of Christ is present and available in their own ecclesial reality. The desire for communion in the body of Christ inherent in baptism compels the baptized to reach out to other ecclesial communities that practise the same pattern of baptism and confess the same apostolic faith.

60.  When the communities that baptize are in full communion with each other – as when they already belong to the same ecclesial family – communion between their members is sacramentally and institutionally completed and its spiritual fruitfulness is correspondingly enhanced. The baptized together share the same eucharist, in which communion is fully expressed and nourished. They live together with the same faith, and the same institutional bonds of mission, ministry and service.

61.  When there are obstacles to full communion among different communities, baptism still provides a degree of communion that is real, if imperfect. The baptized can recognize in the baptismal faith and practice of those others a belief in and desire for the oneness of Christians in the body of Christ that corresponds to their own. They can recognize in one another's baptism a visible and institutional expression of the unity in Christ into which the members of each church believe they have been baptized and find in that an expression and nourishment of their desire for the ecclesial fullness of that unity.

62.  Nor do the difficulties that some churches have about recognizing the full sacramental reality of baptism celebrated in churches not in full communion with themselves – difficulties that have to be recognized and respected – deprive baptism of all significance for communion. The position of the Orthodox is a case in point. There is a complication when a non-Orthodox wishes to join the Orthodox church, as baptism, chrismation/confirmation and the eucharist are considered to be *one* sacrament of initiation. As a result, practices vary. Baptism is used if the postulant is deemed not to be baptized in the name of the Holy Trinity (e.g. Unitarians). Chrismation is performed in the case of absence of confirmation, or in the case of a different conception of confirmation. But in the case, for instance, of a Roman Catholic, the reception should be performed through confession and communion, recognizing and respecting the holy orders and the full sacramentality of the Roman Catholic Church. This, for example, is the *official* attitude of the church of Russia among others. However, among the Orthodox, a difficulty arises from the fact that there exists a difference between Orthodox theology which recognizes baptism in the name of the Holy Trinity, and the practice of some Orthodox communities – not churches – e.g. Mount Athos, that rebaptize non-Orthodox Christians (Mount Athos is part of the church of Constantinople which follows Orthodox theology as described above).

63. Some churches do not admit to eucharistic communion all those whose baptism they recognize. But according to Roman Catholic theology, the desire (*votum*) for the eucharist is given in every true baptism, and the reality (*res*) of grace – union with Christ – is acknowledged to exist because of baptism even when access to eucharistic communion is denied or restricted (see also §§92-95 below).

CONFIRMATION AND OTHER SACRAMENTS

64. The relation of baptism and other sacraments, especially confirmation, needs further discussion. The convergence text BEM (B14) states, "In God's work of salvation, the paschal mystery of Christ's death and resurrection is inseparably linked with the pentecostal gift of the Holy Spirit. Similarly, participation in Christ's death and resurrection is inseparably linked with the receiving of the Spirit. Baptism in its full meaning signifies and effects both."

65. But the differences might be outlined in this way. In some churches confirmation has its origins in a post-baptismal episcopal anointing or imposition of hands in early Christianity – an event which, in the course of history in the West, became separated in time from the baptismal ritual [in the East, chrismation/confirmation, being delegated to the priest by the bishop, is part of the baptismal ceremony]. In other churches, particularly Reformation churches, confirmation means a more mature profession of faith by adolescents. Thus for certain traditions confirmation is a sacramental part of the baptismal action (even if performed years later). For most traditions confirmation is understood as "completing" baptism. For some traditions, however, confirmation is a distinctive sacramental rite understood not as "completing" a person's earlier baptism – that is viewed as complete in and of itself – but as an act by a person, now "mature", that publicly witnesses to and affirms it (cf. Faith and Order consultation, Faverges, October 2001, no. 26).

66. Christians differ, then, in their understanding as to where the sign of the gift of the Spirit is to be found. Different actions have become associated with the giving of the Spirit. For some it is the water rite itself. For others, it is the anointing with chrism and/or the imposition of hands, which many churches call confirmation. For still others it is all three, as they see the Spirit operative throughout the rite. All agree that Christian baptism is in water and the Holy Spirit. But the place and role of confirmation within the practice of Christian initiation needs further clarification among the churches.

ECCLESIOLOGICAL IMPLICATIONS

67. This discussion on "baptism and incorporation into the church" suggests several ecclesiological implications. *First, the implication of the common belief that baptism is incorporation into the body of Christ, the church, is that the rite of baptism is an effective sign which really accomplishes something in the life of the person who receives it.*

68. But, despite this common belief just mentioned, there are also different convictions among Christians governing the way they understand various theological aspects of baptism, or the sacramental aspect of incorporation, or indeed the sacraments themselves. For some, incorporation into the church comes through the sacraments of initiation which include baptism, confirmation and eucharist. For others, the celebration of the sacrament of baptism alone suffices for incorporation into the body of Christ. For still others, it is a profession of faith in Jesus Christ which brings one into the church, and baptism is a sign of acknowledgment that this has taken place. *In light of these differences, a second ecclesiological implication from the discussion of this aspect of the emerging convergence on baptism is the need to develop common ecumenical perspectives on the sacraments, and especially on the relationship of sacraments to the church.*

69. Also, there are different evaluations of the nature of confirmation and its status as a sacrament. *A third implication follows, namely that it would be valuable for disagreeing communities to dialogue about the precise question of whether this difference concerning confirmation reflects any ecclesiological disagreement.*

## 4. Baptism and continual growth in Christ

70. As previously pointed out, one of the dimensions of the common pattern of baptism is the "ongoing formation and responsible discipleship where the pattern of our baptismal calling is worked out over a whole life" (see above 18). Whatever the age of the person, in fact, baptism marks the beginning of a new life in Christ and in the church, and this life is characterized by growth. The Christian life, based on and nourished by faith, involves becoming more and more what God promises and creates in baptism. Life in Christ is life in the Holy Spirit who guides and empowers us to fulfil our baptismal vocation which is to participate in the *missio Dei*, being realized in the ongoing history of salvation.

GROWTH IN CHRIST

71. Christian life is not characterized only by growth. Rather, the baptismal participation in Christ's death and resurrection includes, also, the need for daily repentance and forgiveness. Life in Christ therefore involves a readiness to forgive just as we have been forgiven, thus opening the baptized to attitudes and behaviours that shape a new ethical orientation. According to BEM: "... those baptized are pardoned, cleansed and sanctified by Christ, and are given as part of their baptismal experience a new ethical orientation under the guidance of the Holy Spirit" (B4).

72. This perspective emphasizes the awareness that baptism is an ever-present reality to be continually lived out. The baptized are drawn to become more and more "living stones... a chosen race, a royal priesthood, a holy nation, God's own people... [to] proclaim the mighty acts of him who called you out of darkness into his marvellous light" (1 Pet. 2:5,9). These are aspects of life in Christ that Christians share and can witness to together.

73. In their ecumenical efforts to respond to God's call to unity, churches are rediscovering together the ecclesial aspect to this new ethical orientation: baptism is administered by a community of faith that itself lives by God's forgiveness, which is a gift and a calling. Therefore, fundamental to ecumenical effort is the awareness of the relationship between forgiveness and a spirit of conversion, which implies a readiness to confess the sins of one against the other and to be open to the Spirit's gift of *metanoia*. This opens the churches also to the awareness of the need for a healing of memories between them, and to reconciliation. This commitment to *koinonia* flows from the new life in Christ received in baptism and it has Christ himself as pattern. The fifth world conference on Faith and Order reminded us of what *koinonia* means at both the individual and the collective level and of the relationship of *koinonia* to the very core of the baptismal process of Christian formation (Santiago report, 1993, section I, 20).

74. Recognizing baptism as a bond of unity strengthens the Christian sense of mission and witness and the call to engage together in the common work of the baptized and believing people of God. Johannes Cardinal Willebrands, then president of the Secretariat for Promoting Christian Unity, wrote about the relation of this bond of unity to mission in 1980:

> By the very fact of baptism each and every Christian is consecrated to the Trinity and called to bear witness to Christ in this baptismal profession of faith in the central Christian truths. There is one baptism and all Christians share, to a greater or lesser extent, a common baptismal profession of faith. This communion based on baptism and the profession of baptismal faith renders a common witness theologically possible. But since this communion in faith is not complete, such common witness is inevitably limited in its scope. One of the main motives that leads us to seek for unity is the need for all Christians to be able to give a truly and completely common witness to the whole Christian faith. (Cardinal Willebrands, Letter to Episcopal Conference, 22 May 1980, *Information Service*, 43, 1980, II, p.64)

75. Conversion, forgiveness and repentance, such fundamental parts of the biblical heritage, are ethical claims as well. The daily calling to a change of heart and mind (metanoia) deepens our faithfulness as Christians. It is a calling to become who we are in Christ. Forgiveness, a gift and a calling, and repentance are signified by the water rite that links the aspect of cleansing and the aspect of life.

76. The last statement opens the perspective that the liturgical life of the church expresses the patterns linking the various aspects of Christian relationship established in baptism: praising God, hearing God's life-giving and prophetic word, participating together with brothers and sisters in the eucharistic meal, interceding for all people in their need, and being sent out to proclaim and to make Christ present in and for the world. The incorporation in Christ, which takes place through baptism, gives rise to a koinonia in the church's kerygma, *leiturgia, diakonia and martyria*. These aspects of the church call both for individual and community efforts and witness.

THE CALL TO HOLINESS

77. For all the baptized, growth in Christ implies a call and an empowering to holiness realized by the Spirit: "You shall be holy, for I am holy" (1 Pet. 1:16; cf. also Lev. 11:44,

20:7). BEM reminds us of this universal call to holiness when it says that baptism initiates the reality of a new life given in the midst of the present world, gives participation in the community of the Holy Spirit, and is a sign of the kingdom of God and of the life of the world to come. "Through the gifts of faith, hope and love, baptism has a dynamic which embraces the whole of life, extends to all nations, and anticipates the day when every tongue will confess that Jesus Christ is Lord to the glory of God the Father" (B7).

78. The call to holiness is for all the faithful, and for all it has an eschatological dimension, since all are called to God's kingdom. A distinctive way of living out the vocation to holiness is, in some traditions, constituted by the consecrated life (in monastic or other forms), which is an eschatological sign and also a way of working out the baptismal life, through a particular concern for others and for the whole creation.

ETHICAL FORMATION AS PART OF CONTINUAL GROWTH IN CHRIST

79. From what has already been said, it is clear that ethical formation is part of continual growth in the saving mysteries of Christ. "By baptism, Christians are immersed in the liberating death of Christ where their sins are buried, where the 'old Adam' is crucified with Christ, and where the power of sin is broken" (B3). No longer slaves to sin, but free, the baptized are "fully identified with the death of Christ, they are buried with him and are raised here and now to a new life in the power of the resurrection of Jesus Christ" (*ibid.*).

80. This ethical orientation springing from baptism should become "intentional" for every baptized person, as a sign of growth in Christ and as a sign of ongoing formation that shapes and models our life-style to Christ's. Such an ethical commitment is an imperative that, along with the missionary imperative, needs to be cultivated and put into practical terms. Thus the churches are required to take responsibility for the formation/education of the faithful. The Joint Working Group itself, in a previous study report concerning "Guidelines for Ecumenical Dialogue on Moral Issues", reminds the churches of the important task of "seeking to be faithful to God in Christ, to be led by the Holy Spirit, and to be a moral environment which helps all members in the formation of Christian conscience and practice". It affirms "the responsibility of every church to provide moral guidance for its members and for society at large" (JWG Seventh Report, p.41).

81. There is, therefore, a deep responsibility for baptized Christians to make their life together, in the words of Pope John Paul II, the building of "the home and the school of communion", a framework in which ethical and moral aspects are part of the building up the koinonia:

A spirituality of communion means, finally, to know how to "make room" for our brothers and sisters, bearing "each other's burdens" (Gal. 6:2) and resisting the selfish temptations which constantly beset us and provoke competition, careerism, distrust and jealousy. Let us have no illusions: unless we follow this spiritual path, external structures of communion will serve very little purpose. They would become mechanism without a soul, "masks" of communion rather than its means of expression and growth. (*Novo Millennio Ineunte*, 2001, 43)

ECCLESIOLOGICAL IMPLICATIONS

82. What has been said in this section suggests several ecclesiological implications. There is general ecumenical agreement that the unity to which Christians are called includes "a common mission witnessing to the gospel of God's grace to all people and serving the whole of creation" (WCC Canberra statement on unity, 1991, 2.1). On the basis of a common baptism separated Christians can, even now, engage in some common witness to the gospel, but still limited in scope because their communion in faith is not yet complete (cf. §68). *An ecclesiological implication of a common baptism is the need for separated Christians to work towards a common understanding of the mission of the church, and to continually resolve divergences in the understanding of faith and morals which prevent them from giving full, common witness to the gospel.*

83. There is also general agreement that the unity to which separated Christians are called is not uniformity, but a koinonia characterized by a unity in diversity rooted in a deep spirituality (cf. Canberra statement, 2.2). Agreement, therefore, that baptism involves a continual, life-long growth in Christ, and a call to holiness (cf. §§77ff.) suggests the following ecclesiological implication: *that in their search for full communion, Christians assess together and find ways of sharing for the benefit of all, those various authentic gifts found in each tradition which foster holiness and life in Christ, and contribute to the church's mission of witnessing to the truth and light of the gospel before the world. In contrast to the mutual isolation that separated Christians have experienced, a sharing of gifts with one another is a way of building up koinonia and, thus, of fostering common witness.*

84. Growth in Christ means growth in holiness, which involves turning away from sin and living the new life of the Spirit. The fact that baptism, as entrance into the church, introduces an individual along this path, or reinforces one who may have begun such a change of life before baptism, draws attention to the following ecclesiological implication. *The Christian community is a moral community of disciples, made up of members who are striving, under the power of God's grace, to live as saints after the pattern of Jesus himself, who called them to be holy as their Father in heaven is holy, and who sent the Holy Spirit to bring this journey to completion. Every Christian community should be a school of prayer and of moral training and personal growth.*

## 5. Mutual recognition of baptism

85. It is in this perspective that we turn now to the importance of continuing to seek the mutual recognition of baptism as a primary aspect of fostering bonds of unity between separated Christians. "There is one body and one Spirit, just as you were called to the one hope of your calling, one Lord, one faith, one baptism, one God and Father of all, who is above all and through all and in all" (Eph. 4:4-6).

86. Confessing what is in the scriptures, Christians in dialogue have reaffirmed that "we are one people and are called to confess and serve one Lord in each place and in all the world. The union with Christ which we share through baptism has important implications for Christian unity.... Therefore, our one baptism into Christ constitutes a call to the churches to overcome their divisions and visibly manifest their fellowship" (B6).

87. Furthermore, Christians in the ecumenical movement have committed themselves to a long and demanding process of common reflection and action in order to manifest the communion they have rediscovered and recognized through decades of ecumenical dialogue. At the fifth world conference on Faith and Order delegates, in worship, "affirmed and celebrated together the increasing mutual recognition of one another's baptism as the one baptism into Christ". "Indeed such an affirmation has become fundamental for the churches' participation in the ecumenical movement" (cited in *Becoming a Christian*, Faith and Order Paper 184, 1999, §68, p.95).

88. Mutual recognition of baptism is in itself an act of recognition of *koinonia*. It becomes a way in which separated communities manifest the degree of real communion already reached, even if incomplete. There are levels or degrees of mutual recognition reflecting the extent to which separated Christians share the apostolic faith and life. Furthermore, there are different views concerning how much of the apostolic faith needs to be shared prior to mutual recognition and, indeed, in regard to baptism, what constitutes the fullness of the apostolic faith related to it. For example, there would be general agreement that the apostolic faith is represented when baptism is performed with adequate water in the name of the Father, Son and Holy Spirit. But some would add that to express the apostolic faith completely and faithfully the minister of baptism must be an ordained priest. Others would say that while the minister of baptism must normally be an ordained priest or deacon, in the case of an emergency an "extraordinary" minister can perform a valid baptism. Views held on such issues reflect ecclesiological convictions and might determine for some whether or not mutual recognition of baptism is possible.

THE NEED TO DEFINE TERMS

89. While the conditions allowing mutual recognition increase, there are also problems raised and issues that need further reflection and clarification. Among these is the question of terminology. What is the relationship between recognition and acknowledgment, and the relationship between recognition and reception? Continuing theological reflection and the application of such reflection is urgently needed. Therefore, the JWG is called to survey and seek clarity on these issues. Such an investigation has been already initiated by the Pontifical Council for Promoting Christian Unity through the survey/questionnaire to the episcopal conferences, as well as by Faith and Order through the survey on liturgical rites.

RECOGNITION AND APOSTOLICITY

90. As indicated above, among the issues raised with regard to recognition/reception is the fundamental question of apostolicity. In fact, recognition implies not only a synchronic aspect concerning the relationship among confessions today, but also a diachronic aspect, regarding the relationship with the apostolic heritage handed on over the centuries (cf. Faith and Order consultation on baptism, Faverges, 9).

91. The recognition of the apostolicity of the rite and ordo of baptism is a step towards the full recognition of the apostolicity of the churches in a wider and more profound sense: the full recognition of the same apostolic faith, sacramental order and mission. Full recognition of apostolicity, therefore, involves more than the recognition of baptism. As the world conference on Faith and Order at Santiago de Compostela stated,

> The church seeks to be a community, being faithful as disciples of Christ, living in continuity with the apostolic community established by a baptism inseparable from faith and metanoia, called to a common life in Christ, manifested and sustained by the Lord's supper under the care of a ministry at the same time personal and communal and having as its mission the proclamation in word and witness of the gospel. (Santiago report, p.231)

And as the Decree on Ecumenism stated:

> Baptism therefore constitutes a sacramental bond of unity linking all who have been reborn by means of it. But baptism, of itself, is only a beginning, a point of departure, for it is wholly directed towards the acquiring of fullness of life in Christ. Baptism is thus oriented towards a complete profession of faith, a complete incorporation into the system of salvation such as Christ himself willed it to be, and finally, towards a complete participation in eucharistic communion. (UR, n.22)

Those initiated through baptism continue in an ongoing process of conformity to Christ, both in the dynamics of their individual lives and in those of ecclesial life.

92. In the present stage of the ecumenical movement, separated churches, reflecting unresolved theological issues among them, approach various issues from different ecclesiological perspectives even when there is a common recognition of baptism. An example concerns the relationship of baptism to the eucharist. With regard to the question of what is required for participation in the eucharist, different positions are taken.

93. The churches of the Reformation affirm that the eucharist is a moment of full communion, expressing and enhancing *koinonia*. It is the spiritual basis on which churches live out their baptismal koinonia and express more fully their common confession, worship, witness and service. Furthermore, the churches of the Reformation place primary emphasis on the fact that it is Jesus Christ who invites his disciples to share in the meal. They therefore extend the Lord's hospitality, welcoming to his table all those who love Jesus Christ, have received baptism as a sign of belonging to his body, and have a sufficient understanding of the meaning of the eucharist and its implications. Among many churches of the Reformation the full communion expressed in the eucharist is already experienced in all areas of their faith and life, as reflected in numerous "full communion" or "full mutual recognition" agreements (e.g. Leuenberg and Porvoo). In other cases the full communion expressed in the eucharist is not yet, or incompletely, experienced in all areas of their faith and life. Many such churches have entered into agreements which affirm and celebrate the right of their members, when worshipping in one another's churches, to receive the Lord's hospitality at his table (e.g. the Consultation on Church Union [now Churches Uniting in Christ] in the United States). Such formal, theologically grounded agreements enable these churches to express the baptismal and eucharistic communion which is already theirs in Christ, even as they work to extend this to all areas of their faith and life.

94. The position of the Catholic Church concerning participation in the eucharist takes into account the close relationship of Christ to the church, and of the foundational role of the eucharist in the church. The Second Vatican Council is speaking especially of the eucharist when it describes the liturgy as "the summit towards which the activity of the church is directed; at the same time it is the fount from which all her power flows" (*Sacrosanctum Concilium*, 10). According to the *Directory for the Application of Principles and Norms on Ecumenism* (1993, no. 129), a sacrament is "an act of Christ and of the church through the Spirit" and its celebration in a concrete community is a sign of the reality of its unity in faith, worship and community life. Since sacraments are sources of the unity of the Christian community, of spiritual life, and are the means of building them up, eucharistic communion therefore "is inseparably linked to full ecclesial communion and its visible expression" (*ibid.*).

At the same time the Catholic Church teaches that by baptism members of other churches and ecclesial communities are brought into a real, even if imperfect, communion with the Catholic Church. Baptism constitutes a sacramental bond of unity among all who through it are reborn, and "is wholly directed towards the acquiring of fullness of life in Christ". The eucharist is for the baptized a spiritual food which enables them to live the life of Christ and to be incorporated more profoundly in him and share more intensely in the mystery of Christ (cf. *ibid.*).

In light of these two basic principles, which must always be taken into account together, the *Directory* states, "that in general the Catholic Church permits access to its eucharistic communion... only those who share its oneness in faith, worship and ecclesial life" (*ibid.*). For the same reasons, "it also recognizes that in certain circumstances, by way of exception, and under certain conditions", access to the eucharist "may be permitted, or even commended, for Christians of other churches and ecclesial communities" (*ibid.*). According to the *Directory*, this involves a "grave and pressing need" as usually determined by general norms established by the bishop (no. 130). Among the conditions referred to above is that the person who requests the sacrament "manifest Catholic faith in this sacrament and be properly disposed" (no. 131).

Thus, in this view, mutual recognition of baptism, in itself, is not sufficient for eucharistic communion because the latter is linked to full ecclesial communion in faith and life, and its visible expression.

95. The Orthodox church also places a very strong emphasis on eucharistic sharing as the *final* visible sign of full communion. Such sharing particularly implies confession of one apostolic faith which, though it may be expressed in different *terms*, must necessarily be the same. One of the impediments resides precisely in the necessary verification of this identity in the confession of the same faith. As eucharistic sharing is the expression of full communion, the Orthodox do not practise "eucharistic hospitality" (except in very special cases in which the minister responsible for the eucharist, bishop or priest, pastorally deems it necessary to make an exception; this is an example of *oikonomia*). As far as recognition/reception of baptism is concerned, it must be remembered that in the Orthodox perspective, baptism-chrismation/confirmation-eucharist are one sacrament of initiation.

96. Taking into account these different views of the relationship of baptism to eucharistic sharing, it is important nonetheless that separated Christians give appropriate concrete expression to the common bonds that they share in baptism, so that this relation-

ship is more than one of mere politeness. An important development in recent decades is found in the growing number of invitations to one another to participate in specific, even if limited, ways in major events in each other's churches. For example, the Catholic Church has invited ecumenical partners to participate as fraternal delegates in the assemblies of the synod of bishops in Rome. They are invited to address the assembly and to take part in small group discussions, even though they do not have a vote. It has become normal, too, for other Christian world communions to invite ecumenical partners to their assemblies. On the basis of the common bonds that we share in baptism we have thus begun, though still divided, to enter again into one another's ecclesial life. In order to deepen our relationships, could we not find more such opportunities? Above all, there are many opportunities that can be found for praying for one another, and praying with one another. The annual week of prayer for Christian unity has become an occasion of ecumenical prayer virtually structured into the schedules of all Christian communities, and the opportunities that it offers should not be lost. The week reminds us that prayer for unity is the most important ecumenical activity. It reminds us that our ecumenical journey must be continually supported by prayer throughout the year, and that our ecumenical efforts to pray together are an important way of praising God and begging God's forgiveness for our divisions.

97.  From what has just been said, it is clear that even when there is a mutual recognition of baptism, separated churches have different convictions concerning how this relates to other aspects of Christian life. While there are different ecclesiologies at work, there is also the awareness, at the heart of ecumenical dialogue, that each Christian community, in its life, teaching and practice, has gifts to be discovered and shared. Within the ecumenical movement therefore, churches are constantly called to a "fresh interpretation" of their life, teaching and practice, taking guidance – from this exchange of gifts – for their "worship, educational, ethical and spiritual life and witness" (BEM introduction).

ECCLESIOLOGICAL IMPLICATIONS

98.  According to the Canberra statement on unity, "the goal of the search for full communion is realized when all the churches are able to recognize in one another the one, holy, catholic and apostolic church in its fullness" (2.1). As seen above, the mutual recognition of baptism implies an acknowledgment of the apostolicity of each other's baptism, but in itself is only a step towards full recognition of the apostolicity of the church involved. *Therefore an ecclesiological implication of the efforts of separated churches to formulate and express mutual recognition of baptism is that when this is accomplished it provides a (or another) substantial basis from which to seek further recognition of apostolicity in one another, and impels those churches towards seeking to express together a shared understanding of the apostolic heritage, of the one, holy, catholic and apostolic church in its fullness.*

## 6.  Ecumenical implications

99.  The growing convergence on baptism, and the acknowledgment that through a valid baptism Christians are brought into a real though imperfect communion, has a number

of ecumenical implications, suggesting steps that might be taken now to deepen ecumenical relationships. Some of these are the following.

100. (1)  Years of dialogue have brought us to the present acknowledgment of a significant convergence on baptism. The churches have the continuing responsibility to foster knowledge of this achievement among their constituencies, and of the fact that this convergence is a major reason why, today, Christians can acknowledge that, though still separated, they share a real though imperfect communion.

101. (2)  As stated above (ch. 2, §55) a key affirmation in BEM is that "Baptism is an unrepeatable act. Any practice which might be interpreted as 're-baptism' must be avoided." It is therefore desirable for the churches to seek a common affirmation that it is illegitimate as well as unnecessary to perform baptism to mark re-dedication to Christ, return to the church after a break in communion, or the reception of special charisms or spiritual gifts. At the same time, reaffirmation and remembrance of one's baptism, in acts that may include elements or "echoes" from the baptismal rite itself, is a proper aspect of Christian worship and spirituality (as when in a baptismal liturgy those present are asked to remember and explicitly affirm their own baptismal confession).

102. (3)  Baptism has been a part of the mission and the constitution of the church from earliest times, even before the canon of scripture was established. Recalling this helps us recognize anew the fundamental importance of baptism in the life of the church. The growing ecumenical convergence on baptism has been one of the important achievements of the modern ecumenical movement, and a major factor in fostering new relationships between separated Christians. For these reasons, the importance of baptism in fostering ecumenical reconciliation should be given more visibility in the continuing ecumenical movement, as an important common factor on which to build. It is recommended therefore that, in the formation of ecumenical instruments or structures which are intended to foster unity among participating churches, such as councils of churches, or similar instruments, reference to baptism should be included in the theological basis of such instruments. In the case of those ecumenical instruments already existing and which do not have baptism as part of their theological basis, on occasions when their constitutions or by-laws are being reviewed, consideration might be given to including baptism as part of the theological basis (cf. ch. 1).

103. (4)  In order that the growing convergence on baptism be reflected in local church life, it is recommended that dialogue concerning the significance and valid celebration of baptism take place between authorities of the Catholic Church at the diocesan or episcopal conference level, with the corresponding authorities of WCC member churches in those areas. Thus it should be possible to arrive at common statements through which they express mutual recognition of baptism as well as procedures for considering cases in which doubt may arise as to the validity of a particular baptism (cf. *Directory*, §94). Consideration might be given to developing common baptismal certificates for use by churches in the same region (cf. ch. 1).

104. (5)  All Christians who have received the one baptism into Christ's one body have also received a radical calling from God to communion with all the baptized. The growing ecumenical convergence on baptism, with its insights into our shared pattern of baptismal initiation, despite the real variations in practice, offers us new opportunities to act on that calling, and in some ways to undertake common witness together. Out of the conviction that the Holy Spirit draws us towards visible *koinonia*, the churches should seek

occasions to express and deepen the existing level of oneness in a common baptism through concrete signs of unity, such as: sending and receiving representatives to be present or take part in each other's baptismal celebrations, praying regularly in our worship for the candidates for baptism and the newly baptized in all the churches, sharing together in aspects of the catechumenate (preparation for baptism) or catechesis (instruction of the newly baptized), reclaiming major Christian festivals such as Easter, Pentecost, Epiphany as common times for the celebration of baptism in our churches.

105. (6) Christians of one communion often still live with bitter memories concerning other Christians, stemming from conflicts of centuries ago which led to divisions which have still not been overcome. These memories are among the primary reasons which make full reconciliation among separated Christians difficult. Since their links to one another in baptism should bring "a wider awareness of the need for healing and reconciliation of memories" (see ch. 4, §73), this should be an impetus to separated Christian communions to take steps towards the healing of memories, as one aspect towards their further reconciliation.

106. (7) One key to ecumenical progress is renewal within each church (cf. *Unitatis Redintegratio* 6). Ecumenical dialogue on baptism implies that consideration be given to internal renewal as well (cf. BEM preface, question 3). The growing ecumenical convergence on baptism should be another reason that proper pastoral practices concerning baptism within each church focus continually on central matters of faith. For example, in those communities in which godparents play a role in baptism, the criteria for choosing godparents for the one to be baptized should relate primarily to the strong faith of the prospective godparent, and not simply to social or family reasons. Not only would this benefit the one to be baptized, but it would also be an acknowledgment of the close relation between baptism and faith which is one of the basic areas of the emerging ecumenical convergence (cf. ch. 2).

107. (8) All Christians need to give attention to the ongoing communications revolution of today, unprecedented in scope. The mass media can have a forceful and lasting impact on shaping culture, including influencing the way that religious matters are presented to the public. An ecumenical opportunity is offered for Christians to cooperate to the extent possible, and for the sake of the gospel, to see that Christian life and values are presented correctly in the media. The growing convergence on baptism is a reason for Christians to cooperate in presenting to the media information concerning baptism which focuses on the religious dimensions of this sacrament/ordinance. These efforts can help to avoid the creation of a gap between the profound spiritual meaning and significance of baptism as understood by Christians, on the one hand, and impressions of baptism which have appeared in the media, showing baptism as merely a social event, or simply stressing some cultural matters relating to baptism, on the other. Such cooperation would be a way of giving common witness to the gospel.

108. (9) The growing ecumenical convergence on baptism also calls for reflection on other contemporary cultural challenges which, if not faced together by the churches, could have a negative impact on ecumenical relationships. One such challenge is that of inculturation. Some cultures may have a more poetic or doxological way of expressing realities; others use predominately rational forms of expression. In either case, aspects of a particular culture must be brought into the baptismal rite in a way which enhances,

rather than diminishes, the normative meaning and symbolism of baptism as rebirth into Christ.

109. (10) Through the ecumenical movement, separated Christians have come to acknowledge a significant degree of *koinonia*. In light of this we ask churches not to allow practices to develop which threaten the unity they now share in respect of the ordo, theology and administration of baptism (cf. implication 4, §103 above). One example is the replacement of the traditional trinitarian baptismal formula (Father, Son, Holy Spirit) with alternative wording. Another example is the admission of persons to the eucharist before baptism (cf. ch. 1 and 2).

110. (11) Churches which share in this growing ecumenical convergence are called to dialogue with churches which are ecumenically engaged, but understand and practise baptism differently, or do not practise it at all. These include (a) churches which baptize "in the name of Jesus" rather than with the traditional trinitarian formula, but with water; (b) churches which baptize with the traditional trinitarian formula, but without water; and (c) churches in which entry into the Christian community is effected without baptismal rites. Such dialogue might well focus on the understanding of the Holy Spirit and its role in bringing persons to faith and into the church, and in the believer's life-long growth into Christ.

**Conclusion**

111. Baptism is incorporation into the life, death and resurrection of Christ, and therefore is fundamental for Christian life. That it is central for Christian mission is evident from the fact that Our Lord instructed his disciples to "go therefore and make disciples of all nations, baptizing them in the name of the Father and of the Son and of the Holy Spirit..." (Matt. 28:19). As we have explored baptism in this study we have realized more deeply the great gift that baptism is.

112. It is therefore with gratitude to God that we count the growing ecumenical convergence on baptism as one of the important achievements of the modern ecumenical movement. The degree of common understanding of baptism realized thus far has already helped to foster significant new relationships between Christian churches. The *ecumenical implications* listed just above, in part six of this study document, are intended to suggest ways in which the convergences achieved on baptism can be consolidated and received into the life of the churches so that further steps forward towards unity can be built on solid foundations. The *ecclesiological implications* mentioned in each of the other sections indicate that the convergences on baptism relate to other issues to which attention must be given in continuing dialogue if further steps towards visible unity are to be taken.

113. It is hoped that this study document, by illustrating the extent of mutual agreement on baptism discovered thus far, will enable Christians to respond together, to the extent possible now, to the Lord's commission to "go therefore and make disciples of all nations...," and to invite those who have not heard the gospel before to life in Christ through baptism.

A NOTE ON PROCESS:

Initial material presented for reflection to the JWG executive in January 2000 included a summary of implications of baptism derived from many responses to BEM (John Radano) and an overview of current Faith and Order work on baptism (Alan Falconer). The two were asked to coordinate the project. After the JWG plenary in May 2000 developed five main areas which became the focus of discussion for the study, drafting meetings took place in 2001 and 2002 (Geneva), February 2003 (Rome), and September 2003 (Geneva). Work in progress on the study was presented each year for discussion at annual JWG meetings. Participating in drafting sessions were Eugene Brand (2001, 2002), Thomas Best (2001, 2002, September 2003), Gosbert Byamungu (2001), Alan Falconer (2001, 2002, September 2003), Mark Heim (2001, 2002, February 2003), Nicholas Lossky (February 2003), Thomas Pott, osb (2002, February 2003), John Radano (2001, 2002, February and September 2003), Teresa Francesca Rossi (2002, February 2003), Liam Walsh op (2002, February 2003). Drafting was also done through correspondence between February and September 2003 by Heim, Lossky, Radano, Rossi, Walsh. Teresa Rossi did additional research on media presentations on baptism for the project, and William Henn contributed suggestions for improving certain aspects of an advanced draft of the text. David Hamid reviewed the advanced text for editorial clarity and consistency. The study document was approved at the JWG plenary meeting in Crete, in May 2004.

NOTES

[1]   In one dialogue report, Pentecostals said that they "do not see the unity between Christians as being based in a common water baptism, mainly because they believe that the New Testament does not base it on baptism. Instead the foundation of unity is a common faith and experience of Jesus Christ as Lord and Saviour through the Holy Spirit" (Perspectives on Koinonia, report of the third phase of the international Pentecostal-Catholic dialogue, 1990 §55). Concerning Evangelicals see for example "The Evangelical-Roman Catholic Dialogue on Mission, 1977-1984", in *Growth in Agreement II*, p. 422.

[2]   The most recent ecumenical description of the unity that is being sought is the Canberra statement, "The Unity of the Church As Koinonia: Gift and Calling", approved by the World Council of Churches assembly at Canberra, Australia, 1991. This will be referred to at several points.

# 42. The Nature and Purpose of Ecumenical Dialogue

## Joint Working Group

### Kolympari – Chania, Crete, Greece, 6-13 May 2004

## Introduction

DIALOGUE: A GIFT TO THE CHURCHES

1. Since the establishment of the contemporary ecumenical movement in the 20th century a "culture of dialogue" has emerged. Throughout the first half of the century, the philosophical, cultural and theological presuppositions for such a culture were elaborated. Such a culture has led to new relationships between communities and societies. However there has also emerged a counter-culture, fuelled by fundamentalism, new experiences of vulnerability, new political realities such as the ending of the cold war and the bringing into relationship peoples with very different visions and goals, and the impact of globalization which has led to increased awareness of ethnic and national identities. This has been manifested further in the destabilization of institutions and value systems and a questioning of authority. Dialogue has become a *sine qua non* for nations churches and cultures. For the Christian churches, dialogue is an imperative arising from the gospel, which thus presents a counter-challenge to those who would adopt exclusivist positions.

2. This document charts the impact of the culture of dialogue on the churches, offers a theological reflection on the nature of dialogue, and suggests a spirituality which can guide Christians and their communities in their approach to one another. It is an attempt on the basis of experience gained since 1967 to encourage the churches to continue their ecumenical dialogue with commitment and perseverance.

3. The Joint Working Group between the Roman Catholic Church and the World Council of Churches was formed in 1965. It began its work by reflecting on the nature of dialogue. In 1967, it published a report entitled "Ecumenical Dialogue", which has served since then as a useful reference. The experience of the multilateral dialogues of Faith and Order since 1927 and of church union negotiations, such as those in South India, provided insights for the Joint Working Group as it undertook its task.

The year 1967 did not mark the beginning of ecumenical dialogues, but due to the active participation of the Roman Catholic Church after the Second Vatican Council, ecumenical dialogues received a new energy and scope. They soon developed into a key instrument for ecumenical progress.

4. Almost forty years have passed. The Joint Working Group again presents a study document on "The Nature and Purpose of Ecumenical Dialogue". Organized dialogues have taken place at local, national and international levels involving all major churches and confessional communions. Substantial achievements have been reached and the participating bodies have clarified positions, and consensus has emerged on important matters of division and remaining obstacles to unity have been identified. In the meantime, the context of dialogue has changed, the reflection on dialogue has continued and the urgency of seeking visible unity through honest and persistent dialogue seeking truth with love has increased.

5. Since 1967 relations between different churches, Christian world communions and Christian families have grown and developed as a result of dialogue. Dialogue has encouraged churches to understand one other, and has helped to shatter stereotypes, break down historic barriers and encourage new and more positive relationships. Some examples include:

– the 1965 common declaration of Pope Paul VI and the Ecumenical Patriarch Athenagoras I which removed from the memory and midst of the church the sentences of excommunication mutually pronounced in 1054;

– the christological agreement between the Roman Catholic Church and the Assyrian Church of the East (1994);

– the Joint Declaration on the Doctrine of Justification signed by the Lutheran World Federation and the Catholic Church in 1999, which states that the condemnations of each other's view of justification pronounced during the Reformation period in the Lutheran confessions and the Council of Trent do not apply today, insofar as they hold the understanding of that doctrine found in the Joint Declaration.

These are significant stages on the path towards mutual recognition, communion and the visible unity of the church.

6. The results of international dialogues have fostered a number of new church relationships. The Faith and Order statement, *Baptism, Eucharist and Ministry* (BEM 1982), and bilateral dialogues combined to lay the foundations for the Meissen, Porvoo, and "Called to Common Mission" agreements between Anglicans and Lutherans in different parts of the world. The bilateral agreement between Orthodox and Oriental Orthodox churches has facilitated reconciliation between these church families. The theological dialogue of the Anglican-Roman Catholic International Commission (ARCIC) has led to the establishment of a new commission to foster growth in communion between these churches, through the reception of the agreements and the development of strategies for strengthening the fellowship (IARCCUM – International Anglican-Roman Catholic Commission for Unity and Mission).

7. Dialogues have also helped to challenge and change attitudes in communities living in tense situations.

8. Insights from the dialogues have led different churches towards renewal and change in their life, teaching and patterns of worship. For example, BEM has encouraged more frequent celebrations of the sacrament of the Lord's supper in some communities, and influenced revision of their liturgy itself.

9. Since 1967 it is clear that a culture of dialogue has emerged among some churches which influences every aspect of Christian living. It is evident in projects of collaboration as members of different communities seek to address the needs of those who are marginalized in our world. It is also seen in a variety of discussion groups involving members of different communities. It is an attitude of openness to other communities and their members.

10. His Holiness Pope John Paul II has called this culture "the dialogue of conversion" where, together, Christians and communities seek forgiveness for sins against unity and live into the space where Christ, the source of the church's unity, can effectively act, with all the power of the Spirit (*Ut Unum Sint*, 34, 35). While the attitude of dialogue is to be evident in every aspect of Christian living, engagement in international and bilateral dialogues is a very specific form of dialogue.

TWO APPROACHES TO DIALOGUE

11. Since 1967 two distinct approaches to this specific form of ecumenical dialogue have been evident, each with its own character and each addressing different, but related, aspects of the quest for full communion.

12. The bilateral dialogues between officially appointed representatives of two Christian world communions or church families seek to overcome historical difficulties between these communities. Attention is paid to the history and classic texts which define those communities, and to the current issues, past and present, which have inhibited relations between them and which hinder movement towards communion. These dialogues normally identify that which is held in common, clarify differences, seek solutions and encourage collaboration where possible.

13. The multilateral dialogues operate in a wider framework, with officially appointed representatives of churches seeking to draw on the wisdom of all Christian traditions to investigate a theological issue. This has enabled distinctions to be made on issues over which Christians have been divided (e.g. between *episcope* and episcopacy), offering bilateral dialogues new approaches to historical difficulties. Christians have been reminded that multilateral and bilateral dialogue takes place within the context of the mission of the church and as such are in the service of the unity of the church "so that the world might believe…" (John 17:21). Multilateral dialogue has also emphasized that non-doctrinal factors are important for understanding doctrinal divisions; such divisions have occurred for a multiplicity of reasons – political, cultural, social, economic, and racial as well as doctrinal – and these factors also need to be addressed in processes of reconciling and healing memories.

14. Both multilateral and bilateral dialogues are essential for the dialogical process. At best there is a continuing interaction between them, with each drawing on insights gained in the other. All dialogue will be subject to the historical and cultural context which influences the relations between different communities.

15. While churches have embraced a culture of dialogue and it is possible to chart a number of achievements arising from the engagement in formal ecumenical conversations, new factors have emerged in the thirty-six years since the publication of "Ecumenical Dialogue" which signify a new context in which such dialogue takes place.

16. While dialogue has led to increased sensitivity and ecumenical commitment among ecclesial traditions, a renewed allegiance to confessional identity has also developed, leading possibly to exclusivist confessionalism. There has often been a reluctance to change in the light of the results of dialogue. Sometimes this has been caused by the difficulty of achieving wider consensus within the different churches. Difficulties in reception have sometimes led to division *within* confessions, since it is increasingly clear that no church or confessional tradition is a homogeneous entity. In some cases, reception has been made more difficult as divisions within and between some churches have emerged on cultural and ethical issues – matters rarely the subject of the dialogues themselves. For some churches the issues being addressed in the international bilateral and multilateral dialogues are perceived as remote from their existential concerns. After over thirty years of theological dialogue and despite significant agreements during this period, not all issues required to lead to unity between churches have been resolved. The process of reconciliation has been slow. For some, and for different reasons, this has put in question the value of undertaking such theological dialogues.

17. Yet it is clear in every part of the world that the gospel of reconciliation cannot be proclaimed credibly by churches which are themselves not reconciled with each other. Divided churches are a counter-witness to the gospel.

18. What can be learned from the experience of dialogue about the nature of ecumenical dialogue itself? The new context suggests that a re-examination of ecumenical dialogue is needed, lifting up the insights of "Ecumenical Dialogue" from 1967, reflecting on over three decades of multilateral and bilateral dialogue activity, and considering challenges which have arisen.

## The nature and purpose of ecumenical dialogue

19. Ecumenical dialogue is pursued in response to Our Lord's prayer for his disciples "that they may all be one so that the world may believe" (John 17:21). It is essentially a conversation, a speaking and a listening between partners. Each speaks from his or her context and ecclesial perspective. Dialogic speech seeks to communicate that experience and perspective to the other, and to receive the same from the other in order to enter into their experience and see the world through the other's eyes, as it were. The aim of dialogue is that each understands the partner in a deep way. It is a spiritual experience in understanding the other, a listening and speaking to one another in love.

20. Dialogue entails walking with the other; pilgrimage is an apt metaphor for dialogue. Dialogue represents a word – neither the first nor the last – on a common journey, marking a moment between the "already" of our past histories and the "not yet" of our future. It images the disciples' conversation on the road to Emmaus, recounting the wonders the

Lord has worked during a journey culminating in the recognition of the Lord in the breaking of bread at a common table.

21. Dialogue is more than an exchange of ideas. It is a "mutual gift exchange". It is a process through which together we seek to transcend divisions by clarification of past misunderstandings through historical studies, or bypass obstacles by discovering new language or categories. And more: it involves being receptive to the ethos of the other, and those aspects of Christian tradition preserved in the heritage of the other. Different church traditions have often given preference to certain biblical texts and traditions over others. In the process of dialogue, we are invited to reappropriate these and thus witness to the richness of the gospel in its integrity.

22. An important focus of dialogue involves mutual exploration of the meaning of the apostolic faith. At the same time dialogues are conducted within the context of the living faith of communities in particular times and places; thus they should always reflect contextual experience. They do not simply focus on systems or formulae of belief but on how these are lived out by the communities involved in the dialogue. This is particularly true with regard to national dialogues. While context is also an essential consideration in international dialogue, in this case, no particular local context can dominate, and the total, often complex, self-understanding of a Christian world communion is taken into consideration.

23. Furthermore, there is another difference in regard to context. It stems from the very different understandings found among the Christian world communions concerning the relationship between the local and universal expressions of the church. This in turn has an influence on the impact of contextual experience within the whole. Thus, for many, final authority (and therefore an aspect of independence to one degree or another) rests in each member church of a world communion (e.g., in churches stemming from the Reformation). In another case (e.g. the Catholic Church), bonds of communion of a theological, canonical and spiritual nature govern the relationships between the particular churches and the universal church. The very understanding of a particular or local church involves its being in communion with every other local church and with the church of Rome. Thus there is a continual mutual influence between the particular and universal expressions of the church. While particular and universal expressions of the church are interdependent, priority is given to the unity of the whole.

24. Dialogue addresses the divisions of the past, examining them through scholarship, seeking to state what the dialogue partners can say together about the faith today. Dialogue seeks to discern the evangelical character of the present faith, life and worship of the partner. Thus dialogue has a descriptive character.

THEOLOGICAL FOUNDATIONS OF DIALOGUE

25. Ecumenical dialogue reflects analogically the inner life of the triune God and the revelation of his love. The Father communicates himself through his Word, his Son who, in turn, responds to the Father in the power of the Spirit – a communion of life. In the fullness of time, God spoke to us through his Son (cf. Heb 1:1-2); God's Word became flesh and dwelt among us (John 1:14).

26. The exchange between the Father and the Son in the power of the Spirit establishes the mutual interdependence of the three persons of the triune God. In God's self-communication to God's people, God invites us to receive his word and respond in love. Thus we enter through a participation in God's gracious activity and the imperative of Christian obedience into communion with God who is communion – Father, Son and Holy Spirit. In emulating this dialogical pattern of speaking and listening, of revealing ourselves and receiving the other, we leave our illusion of self-sufficiency and isolation and enter a relationship of communion.

27. The very nature of human existence also emphasizes that we do not live or exist without each other."We not only have encounter, we are encounter. The other is not the limit of myself; the other is part of and an enrichment of my own existence. Dialogue thus belongs to the reality of human existence. Identity is dialogical" (H.E. Cardinal Kasper).

PRESUPPOSITIONS OF DIALOGUE

28. Ecumenical dialogue presupposes our common incorporation in Christ, through faith and baptism and the action of the Holy Spirit and we recognize in one another faith communities seeking oneness in Christ (see the JWG statement, "Ecclesiological and Ecumenical Implications of a Common Baptism", 2004). Within ecumenical dialogue we meet not as strangers but as co-dwellers within the household of God, as Christians who through our communion with the triune God already experience "a real, though imperfect communion" (*Unitatis Redintegratio*, 3).

29. Thus ecumenical dialogue presupposes engagement in prayer. It assumes a cruciform pattern, at the intersection of our "vertical" relationship with God and our "horizontal" communion with one another. In this we also imitate Christ's self-giving and vulnerability. We turn from our self-absorption and self-interests to the experience of the other, assuming the vulnerability of allowing ourselves to be known by the other and of allowing ourselves to see another's Christian pattern of life, witness, and worship through their eyes. Within this reciprocal exchange we allow ourselves to experience a fusion of horizons, enabling us to heal our divisions, strengthen our common witness, and engage in the shared mission of furthering God's reign.

THE PURPOSE OF ECUMENICAL DIALOGUE

30. The goal of ecumenical dialogue as expressed in the Canberra statement "The Unity of the Church as Koinonia: Gift and Calling" is that of the ecumenical movement itself:

> The unity of the church to which we are called is a *koinonia* given and expressed in the common confession of the apostolic faith; a common sacramental life entered by the one baptism and celebrated together in one eucharistic fellowship; a common life in which members and ministries are mutually recognized and reconciled; and a common mission witnessing to the gospel of God's grace to all people and serving the whole of creation. The goal of the

search for full communion is realized when all the churches are able to recognize in one another the one, holy, catholic and apostolic church in its fullness. This full communion will be expressed on the local and the universal levels through conciliar forms of life and action. In such communion churches are bound in all aspects of their life together at all levels in confessing the one faith and engaging in worship and witness, deliberation and action. (2.1)

31. Dialogue aims not only at agreement on doctrine, but also at the healing of memories through repentance and mutual forgiveness. It may also be an avenue for exploring those activities we can pursue together, in order to undertake together everything that we are not obliged to do separately, as was expressed in the statement of the Faith and Order conference at Lund in 1952.

32. Christian unity is a gift of the Holy Spirit, not a human achievement. Dialogue prepares for that gift, prays for it, and celebrates it once received.

33. Ecumenical dialogue is ecclesial; the participants come as representatives of their ecclesial traditions, seeking to represent their tradition while exploring the divine mysteries with representatives of other traditions (cf. *Directory for the Application of Principles and Norms on Ecumenism*, 176).

34. Dialogue assumes an equality of the participants, as partners working together for Christian unity. It exhibits reciprocity, so that partners are not expected to adopt "our" structures for dialogue (cf. *Ut Unum Sint*, 27).

35. As dialogue proceeds, it is important to be conscious of the "hierarchy of truths" where not everything is presented at the same level of integration with the essential doctrines of the Christian faith (cf. *Directory, supra*, 176).

36. Doctrinal formulations of the faith are culturally and historically conditioned. One and the same faith can be expressed in different language at different times, reflecting new insights and organic developments. The awareness of this has proved to be a liberating experience in dialogues and has helped to create possibilities for the development of new understandings and relationships. The process of discerning a consensus in faith, must take into account different approaches, emphases, and language respecting the diversity and the limits to diversity within and among the dialogue partners.

## The spirituality and practice of ecumenical dialogue

37. Since Christian life is itself dialogical (cf. §§23-24 *supra*) ecumenical dialogue is a way of being, of living the Christian life. Although it has specific features, it presupposes a broad spirituality of openness to the other in light of the imperative of Christian unity, directed by the Holy Spirit. Dialogue is a process of discernment, and as such requires patience, since ecumenical progress may be slow. Humility is required in order to be

open to receiving truth from another. Commitment in love is also required, to search together to manifest that unity willed by our Lord. Thus we may include the following considerations about a spirituality for dialogue.

38. Communities engaging in dialogue commit themselves to a shared journey. While conducted by just a few persons on each side, a dialogue aims to assist those communions involved to move step by step towards unity by working to ensure that each partner understands to the degree possible how the life and witness of the other can be beneficial for all. When this aspect of dialogue is neglected, dialogue results will seem remote from the experience of the church and may not be received into its life and transform relationships. Furthermore, when this aspect of dialogue is neglected, the ecumenical endeavour itself becomes an excuse for maintaining the status *quo ante*. Thus ecumenical dialogue implies new spiritual obligations not only for individual participants, but also for the communities as a whole.

39. A willingness to change through dialogue requires seeing the other differently, changing our patterns of thinking, speaking and acting towards the other. Since Christian unity is realized through God's power, not our own, dialogue is also a process of conversion, of discernment, of being attentive to God's impulse. It opens us up for judgment and renewal. Thus in seeking openness to transformed and reconciled relationships, we explore processes of healing and forgiveness.

40. Dialogue with Christians from whom we are divided requires examining how our identity has been constructed in opposition to the other, i.e. how we have identified ourselves by what we are not. To overcome polemical constructions of identity requires new efforts to articulate identity in more positive ways, distinguishing between confessional identity as a sign of fidelity to faith, and confessionalism as an ideology constructed in enmity to the other. This entails a spiritual as well as a theological preparation for ecumenical dialogue. Through understanding mutual hurts and expressing and receiving forgiveness we move from fear of one another to bearing one another's burdens, to being called to suffer together. Commitment to dialogue requires, at the least, a review of how our church educates its members about the dialogue partner(s).

41. Preparation for dialogue includes recovering theological resources for the development and refinement of doctrine within our own tradition. This requires a willingness to be challenged by, and to learn from, others. As encounter deepens, we find ourselves incorporating theological reflection from the partner's tradition(s) into our *own* life, embracing the other's thoughts and words as our own.

42. Our common commitment to Christian unity requires not only prayers for one another but a life of common prayer.

**Practice**

43. Each dialogue is unique and must take into account the factors drawing these partners into this dialogue at this time. Here the following points may be relevant.

*Configurations of dialogue partners*

44. The configuration of partners will necessarily affect the practice of each dialogue. To agree the goals and methods for the dialogue, whether bilateral or multilateral, it is critical to understanding who the partners are, the origin of their divisions, and/or the way these Christian communities have related to each other in the past.

45. Each partner has a particular understanding of the history of the divisions. One or both may have neuralgic memories of power and victimization stemming from the actions of representatives of the other community in dialogue. There may be considerable asymmetries between partners (e.g. of size, ecclesial self-understanding, ability to speak on behalf of the larger ecclesial community, majority or minority status). Dialogue must consider such asymmetries, with each partner understanding the other's entry point. Many dialogue partners are also engaged in other dialogues, both bilateral and multilateral. Dialogues should be inter-related, and influence one another.

TOPICS AND AGENDA ITEMS FOR DIALOGUE

46. Dialogue aiming at Christian unity demands more than cooperation on non-divisive matters. We bring to ecumenical dialogue all that falls outside the Lund principle which asks "whether they [churches] should not act together in all matters except those in which deep differences of conviction compel them to act separately". Where conscience has, thus far, forbidden unity, we engage in dialogue precisely to clarify and overcome these past and present deep differences of conviction.

47. The subjects for dialogue are drawn from the partners' past and present relationship. In discerning topics to pursue we might ask: "Where, in our relationship as dialogue partners, is the gospel at stake? What prevents us from fully recognizing one another?" Context will influence the choice of dialogue topics; yet these topics will be all the more relevant if understood within the wider spectrum of the basic, historic Christian divisions.

48. The choice of topics should be informed by history. Although each generation must reappropriate what has come before, we should not forget that we are contributing to a journey which began before us and will continue after us.

49. Topics may include not only formulations of doctrine, but also ways of doing theology and using sources of faith. Methodologies may themselves become the subject of dialogue. Choosing points of departure requires discernment of what is ripe for discussion. It may be important to begin by examining what *unites* the partners; the most divisive questions may need to be set aside until a shared experience of trust makes it possible to tackle them. But dialogue between divided churches cannot postpone indefinitely an examination of the issues at the crux of their division.

50. Dialogues that have matured through considerable agreement on areas of conflict may be drawn on to further constructive engagement on particular issues.

## Methodologies

DIVERSE CONTEXTS AND APPROACHES

51. Since different dialogue topics call for different methodologies, we cannot speak of *one* way of approaching dialogue. Each partner will be more comfortable with some methods than others. We should not assume that certain ways of engaging one another should be favoured over others.

52. The experience of ecumenical dialogue in the 20th century has shown how important it is to examine the historical and socio-economic factors affecting doctrinal issues. Situating doctrinal formulations in their historical context can free us to express the same faith in new ways today. This methodology that resulted in the Joint Declaration on the Doctrine of Justification modelled a hermeneutic which may be fruitful elsewhere.

53. The work on hermeneutics by the Faith and Order commission (*A Treasure in Earthen Vessels*, Faith and Order Paper 182, 1998) draws attention to how we "read" our own story as a community, and how we find points of convergence with the stories of others. A "hermeneutics of coherence" suggests sympathetic awareness of the faith and witness of others, as complementary to our own. A "hermeneutics of confidence" suggests that mutual reception and recognition is possible through the Holy Spirit's gifts to the Christian community. A "hermeneutics of suspicion" suggests the question, "Whose interests are being served by this particular reading?" Because dialogue serves the cause of the one gospel of Jesus Christ, each mode of "reading" can lead us together into greater understanding of the truth.

54. Dialogue is not negotiation towards a "lowest common denominator", but a search for new entry-points in order to discover the way forward together. Sometimes dialogues confront issues which gave rise to mutual condemnations in the past. Here it can help to clarify what the actual position of each side was at that time and how each sought, through their position, to preserve the integrity of the gospel in a particular context. Perhaps the demands of the gospel today enable the partners to find common ground.

55. Not all doctrinal conflicts can be easily resolved. Therefore a careful consideration of the positions – how far they are complementary, and where and how they diverge – can be very useful in furthering the churches' growth in ecumenical relationships.

PARTICIPANTS AND COMPETENCIES

56. A variety of competencies are required in ecumenical dialogue today. Those with historical and doctrinal expertise are necessary; but so are those bringing other forms of expertise, such as liturgists, ethicists, missiologists, and those with pastoral oversight responsibilities. The broader a church's participation in a dialogue, the more applicable will be its findings for the life of the church as a whole. Different churches have different understandings of how an individual "represents" the church in a dialogue, but all participants should be aware that they stand within the discipline of their tradition and are accountable to it.

57. As "Ecumenical Dialogue" advises, it is often appropriate to include observers in the dialogue, to recognize and encourage the wider ecumenical implications of the work.

**The reception of ecumenical dialogues**

58. If the agreements reached through ecumenical dialogue are to have an impact on the life and witness of the churches and lead to a new stage of communion, then careful attention needs to be paid to processes for receiving the agreements so that the whole community might be involved in the process of discernment.

THE MEANING OF RECEPTION

59. "Reception" is the process by which the churches make their own the results of all their encounters with one other, and in a particular way the convergences and agreements reached on issues over which they have historically been divided. As the report of the sixth forum on bilateral dialogues notes:

> Reception is an integral part of the movement towards that full communion which is realized when "all the churches are able to recognise in one another the one, holy, catholic and apostolic church in its fullness. [Canberra statement]

Thus reception is far more than the official responses to the dialogue results, although official responses are essential. However, even though they are not concerned with the full range of interchurch relations, the results of international theological dialogues are a crucial aspect of reception, as specific attempts to overcome what divides churches and impedes the expression of unity willed by our Lord.

INSTRUMENTS OF RECEPTION

60. Churches have developed appropriate modes and instruments for receiving the results of bilateral and multilateral international dialogues. The structures and processes of decision-making that determine the "mind" of a church or community of churches reflect each church or communion's self-understanding and polity and their particular approach.

DIFFICULTIES IN RECEPTION

61. Churches have encountered difficulties in the process of reception in part because of different modes and processes of reception.

62. Issues of consistency have emerged. When a church community is involved in several dialogues with partners from different ecclesial traditions, the presentation of its self-understanding must be consistent with what is said to all the partners, and the results achieved in one dialogue must be coherent with those achieved in the others. Some Christian world communions (the Anglican Communion, the World Alliance of Reformed Churches, the Lutheran World Federation) have developed structures to test this.

63. Issues of perceived relevance have emerged. Are the subjects of ecumenical dialogue largely those on the agenda of European and North American churches, even if the doctrinal divisions in question were transported throughout the world through missionary activity?

64. How do international dialogues relate to pastoral and theological priorities of the local churches? If the issues addressed are not existential questions faced by the churches, reception becomes difficult. New ways are needed to help churches see that disunity contradicts the gospel of reconciliation. How can the results of international dialogues engage the churches existentially in their different contexts? Many factors inhibiting the reception of dialogues are non-doctrinal. Where majority and minority tensions are evident, processes of forgiveness, healing and reconciliation must proceed before, and alongside, processes of reception.

65. By their very nature, dialogues are conducted by officially appointed representatives, competent in the issues under discussion. But reception, while a process of discernment by the leadership of the churches, also involves the discernment of the whole people of God. Insensitivity to the need for education and discernment by the *whole* community has made reception difficult. "Top-down" rather than "bottom-up" language has appeared at critical points in some processes. Thus while dialogues seek communion among churches, they may lead to the formation of dissenting groups and divisions *within* churches.

POSITIVE EXPERIENCES IN RECEPTION

66. How might reception processes be conducted so as to overcome these problems? In the past thirty years several international dialogues have been widely received, leading to new expressions of church fellowship and the renewal of the churches involved. Perhaps these can provide some clues about what is essential if reception is to take place.

*A multilateral case study*

67. The multilateral dialogue leading to *Baptism, Eucharist and Ministry* offers one such example. The BEM process required time, constant dialogue with the churches, the provision of study materials, serious consideration of responses to the draft texts, translations into many languages, building upon what had been previously achieved in dialogue, and drawing on other dialogues and ecumenical initiatives.

68. This process took nearly twenty years, and indeed there had been discussion of the issues for a prior forty years. In the period 1963-82 the draft-in-process was sent three times to churches, theological colleges and ecumenical instruments for comment and reaction. The drafts were published widely, and comments taken seriously in each stage of redrafting. Many churches encouraged discussions of drafts in congregations, thus involving the whole community. Drafters also drew on international bilateral dialogues on related subjects, and on insights from the liturgical movement. The multilateral approach went behind the divisions between the churches, seeking biblical roots for

understanding the specific issues (e.g. *anamnesis*). This provided points of reference, placing historical differences in a fresh perspective.

69. Whenever it became clear that agreement on a particular issue was going to be elusive, the specific issue was addressed by a gathering of theologians (e.g. the relation between baptism of those making a personal profession of faith and infant baptism; the issue of episcopacy). From these consultations new language was found enabling agreement to be expressed.

70. Once finalized and acclaimed by the Faith and Order commission in 1982, the text was sent to the churches for response. Carefully crafted questions accompanied the document, so that the churches in a process of discernment could receive it. An accompanying commentary facilitated understanding by those not party to the discussion. A volume of theological essays encouraged discussion in theological colleges, while a collection of liturgical materials assisted churches in reflecting on the relation between their theological understanding and liturgical practice. To give a liturgical expression to the eucharistic agreement, a liturgy was developed which illustrated what the convergence enabled in respect of celebrating the sacrament. This "Lima liturgy" undoubtedly helped to popularize the BEM agreement and process.

71. BEM was translated into more than thirty languages, facilitating its reception around the world. The process was enhanced by seminars led by Faith and Order commissioners and staff. Study guides were produced in various contexts, assisting congregational and interchurch discussions of the text. The process which from the beginning engaged the churches in the actual development of the text, facilitated official responses "at the highest level of authority" when the text was completed in 1982. Some 186 responses were received and published in six volumes. This resulted in the text having an unprecedented ecumenical authority, which in turn encouraged churches to develop new relationships with each other.

72. On the basis of this convergence several churches were able to enter new relationships of communion (e.g. Lutheran and Anglican churches in Nordic and Baltic countries, Britain, Ireland, Canada, Germany, United States; Reformed and Lutherans in the United States; United/Uniting churches in South Africa…). Other churches were encouraged, through responding to the questions, to renew the frequency and liturgical content of their eucharistic celebrations. The distinctions made concerning ministry have facilitated bilateral dialogues, even in situations where these issues had become difficult to pursue.

SOME BILATERAL CASE STUDIES

73. Several international bilateral dialogues also developed mechanisms and work patterns which have fostered reception.

74. The official signing of the Joint Declaration on the Doctrine of Justification was the result of a series of events of Lutheran-Catholic cooperation. The Joint Declaration drew from results of more than thirty years of international and national dialogue. In 1991, having decided to focus more on the reception of dialogue results, the Lutheran World Federation and the Pontifical Council for Promoting Christian Unity developed a work-

ing paper entitled "Strategies for Reception: Perspectives on the Reception of Documents Emerging from the Lutheran-Catholic International Dialogue". In 1993, they established a small joint commission to draft a Joint Declaration on the Doctrine of Justification. Each side then submitted the draft to its respective internal processes of evaluation. The results of the evaluation led to a revision of the draft. At every stage each side was supported by the highest levels of authority. The final version of the joint declaration was formally accepted by both sides in 1998 and signed in 1999. The successful reception of the declaration was helped by the close collaboration between the two partners in the reception process.

75. The agreement resulting from the dialogue between Reformed churches and Mennonite churches was sealed through a visit to the battle sites at which their forces had fought in the Reformation period. The churches repented, received forgiveness for allowing the memory of these events to determine present-day relationships, and sought to initiate a new relationship. A constant interplay of agreement, comment and elucidation by the bodies sponsoring the Anglican-Roman Catholic International Commission may have facilitated the reception of its dialogue reports. A concern in several dialogues involving the World Alliance of Reformed Churches and the Roman Catholic Church was relating the theological agenda to actual Reformed-Roman Catholic relations around the world. This was an early attempt to hold together the agendas of a dialogue and of local churches.

SOME CONCLUSIONS CONCERNING RECEPTION

76. Since 1967 several factors essential to reception processes can be discerned. For dialogue results to be appropriated, the widest possible engagement with the community and their theologians is needed. This is best effected by interchange at appropriate points in the development of a text between persons engaged in dialogues and the churches concerned, with the text being developed in light of comments received.

77. The process is enhanced by sharing biblical, theological and liturgical resources which help communities understand the journey undertaken by the drafters and situate the theme both within the confessions involved and within contemporary scholarship. The text should be translated into all appropriate languages, and accompanied by study guides (written by members of the drafting group, since only they know the road travelled to reach agreement). Reception can be enhanced by appropriate symbolic gestures by the sponsoring bodies, indicating that a new stage on the journey towards fuller manifestation of communion has been reached.

78. For reception and for subsequent implementation it is important to devise instruments for cooperative oversight. In the light of agreements reached, consideration needs to be given to processes of reception which involve both communities seeking to discern together. At present many reception processes are conducted within each community separately.

79. Visits between communities foster growth in relationship. It should become natural to invite partners to significant events in the life of the church, and to encourage Christian friendships at the local level. The ecumenical movement includes a spirituality of

hospitality, of willingness to receive the other in our own place. Commitment to dialogue requires the willingness of church leaders to be examples of new openness, for example through shared symbolic acts, visits, and being present in times of joy and sorrow. All of these contacts foster mutual understanding and the reception of dialogue results.

### Challenges for dialogue in the 21st century

80. The ecumenical movement has helped Christians move from the churches' virtual isolation from one another, experienced for centuries due to 5th-, 11th-, or 16th-century divisions. By the end of the 20th century, the churches could speak of a new relationship of sharing even now a "real, though imperfect", communion. Given these achievements, what are the challenges for ecumenical dialogue in the 21st century?

81. While these achievements have been considerable, during this same period there has also been a tendency to greater fragmentation and fracture between and within churches. There are those who assert strongly that dialogue is inimical to the Christian tradition, and who wish to assert claims of absoluteness and uniqueness. Under the influence of post-modern culture authority structures and authority in all aspects of life have been called into question. This raises challenges within the churches to doctrinal statements and to structures of governance as well. Some question whether it is at all possible for any one of any group to represent a community. The treatment of ethical questions in revolutionary ways by society has increasingly influenced the way these issues appear on the agenda of the churches, where it is clear that different views and approaches are discussed across denominational and confessional lines. It is crucial that these features of contemporary church life are taken into account as the culture of dialogue is developed in this decade.

82. However, we limit ourselves to some broader perspectives which must be considered, and to some challenges to the ecumenical movement and to dialogue in particular.

THE CHALLENGE OF A CHANGING WORLD

83. The broad context in which people live today, characterized by an increasingly interdependent and inter-connected world, will continue to have an impact on Christians. In its most positive sense, this globalization expresses the aspiration of human beings to become one family. However, globalization has further divided humanity because in the present world order the forces of globalization work to the benefit of some and to the detriment of many.

84. In this context the ecumenical movement can be a seed of hope in a world that is divided economically, culturally, socially and politically. The joys and sorrows, hopes and despairs of all peoples are those of Christians as well. While respecting all human efforts to draw people together, the ecumenical movement can make its specific contribution to the unity of the human family by healing divisions among Christians. One response to globalization calls for the development of healthy mutual relationships between global and national social structures. A parallel ecumenical challenge is achieving

common perspectives on the proper relationship between universal and local expressions of the church, and between unity and diversity. By showing that dialogue can resolve persistent differences, progress made on these ecclesiological questions can have a positive impact on persons responding to globalization.

85. Thus the continuing commitment to ecumenical dialogue not only fosters reconciliation among Christians, but is also a sign of humanity's deepest aspirations to become one family.

86. Some challenges relate specifically to the ecumenical movement itself.

87. While we rejoice in the achievements of the 20th century ecumenical movement we recognize that Christian reconciliation is far from complete. Ecumenical dialogue must continue in order to resolve serious divergences concerning the apostolic faith. These hinder the achievement of visible unity among Christians, the unity necessary for mission in a broken world.

88. Second, the ecumenical movement is important for Christians everywhere. Early in the ecumenical movement most participants came from Europe and North America, though the minority from other continents made an important impact in early ecumenical meetings, asserting that the disunity of the church was a sin and a scandal. As noted above many major divisions among Christians started in Europe, with European and American missionaries taking these to other continents in the course of their activities.

89. Today, however, dialogue participants come also from Africa, Asia, Latin America, Oceania and the Caribbean – and their contributions are significant. For many the ecumenical agenda is deemed to be less appropriate and urgent than their work for the provision of the basic needs of their communities. Yet many Christians realize that perpetuating divisions undermines the credibility of the one gospel, and that many of the issues that they face are indeed issues of unity and division. This gospel speaks to people in their different cultures and languages; and healing the wounds of division requires the efforts of Christians in every part of the world. The diversity among Christians around the world should receive much more attention in ecumenical dialogues in the 21st century.

90. Third, we have become aware of a changing Christian landscape. We acknowledge that some of the fastest-growing Christian communities are Evangelical and Pentecostal. Many if not most of these are not involved with the ecumenical movement and have neither contact with the WCC nor dialogue with the Roman Catholic Church. Indeed the very words "unity" and "ecumenical" are problematic for these communities. Their major focus is on mission and they do not necessarily see this in the context of collaborating with other churches in a given region, even where these churches have been established for centuries. A challenge today is finding ways to make ecumenical dialogue more inclusive of these important Christian groups.

91. Fourth, bilateral dialogues have focused on matters needing resolution so that reconciliation between two communions can be achieved. This must continue. But it may be helpful if some dialogues give more systematic attention to the Christian heritage shared by both East and West, as a frame of reference for all. Perhaps all dialogues, even

as they address their own particular issues, could benefit by attending to this common Christian heritage.

THE CHALLENGE OF INTER-RELIGIOUS DIALOGUE

92. But although inter-religious dialogue cannot replace ecumenical dialogue, inter-religious dialogue is held among the world's religions. It seeks not to create one religion, but to enable collaboration among religions in fostering spiritual values to contribute to harmony in society, and to help to build world peace. Cooperation among Christians to promote inter-religious dialogue is necessary, even imperative, today. Recently religions have been abused in order to justify and even promote violence, or have been marginalized from efforts to build human community. Through ecumenical cooperation in inter-religious dialogue, Christians can support the world's religions in promoting harmony and peace.

93. Ecumenical dialogue and inter-religious dialogue must not be confused. While both are germane to the culture of dialogue, each has a specific aim and method. Ecumenical dialogue is held among Christians; it seeks visible Christian unity. It must continue because discord among Christians "openly contradicts the will of Christ" (*Unitatis Redintegratio*, 1) and must be overcome.

## Conclusion

94. Since the 1967 JWG statement on dialogue, churches have participated in dialogue especially over the last decades of the 20th century. Ecumenical dialogue has opened new vistas, showing that despite long centuries of separation, divided Christians share much in common. Dialogue has contributed to reconciliation. The reception of dialogue results has been instrumental in bringing Christians together in various ways.

95. Now in the 21st century ecumenical dialogue continues with the same goals, but in a new context. Dialogue is still an instrument which Christians must use in their search for visible unity, a goal which still remains to be fulfilled. Dialogue continues to be an instrument to assist in reconciliation of divided Christians. In this time before us, the results of dialogue must be continually reviewed in the churches. Ecumenical dialogue has already helped to change relationships between churches. In the new context of a more globalized world, of a world of instant communication and abundant information, the church's task of proclaiming the word of God and salvation in Christ comes into unprecedented competition with proclamations of every sort of information aimed at capturing the human heart. All the more urgent in this time of history is the common witness to the gospel by Christians who can put aside their divisions and take up common witness to the Lord, who prayed for his disciples "... that they may all be one... so that the world may believe" (John 17:21).

A NOTE ON PROCESS

After papers on dialogue were presented by Bishop Walter Kasper and Dr Konrad Raiser, the first plenary developed a series of issues to be considered in a study document on dialogue. A small drafting group consisting of Eden Grace, Dr Susan Wood, Msgr Felix Machado, Msgr John Radano, and Rev. Dr Alan Falconer, met in Cartigny, Switzerland (February 2003), and produced an initial draft. After discussions in the plenary in Bari, the text was further developed through email correspondence and at a one-day drafting session in September 2003 (Falconer, Radano, Dr Thomas Best). After further discussion at the JWG executive meeting in November 2004, Bishop David Hamid was asked to review the text for editorial consistency. The study document was adopted by the JWG plenary at Chania, Crete, in May 2004.

Part E

# 43. Called To Be the One Church

## An Invitation to the Churches to Renew their Commitment to the Search for Unity and to Deepen their Dialogue

### Ninth Assembly, World Council of Churches, Porto Alegre, Brazil, February 2006

*WCC assemblies have adopted texts offering a vision, or identifying the qualities, of "the unity we seek".[1] In line with these texts the ninth assembly in Porto Alegre has adopted this text inviting the churches to continue their journey together, as a further step towards full visible unity.*

*The purpose of this invitation to the churches is twofold: (a) to reflect what the churches, at this point on their ecumenical journey, can say together about some important aspects of the church; and (b) to invite the churches into a renewed conversation – mutually supportive, yet open and searching – about the quality and degree of their fellowship and communion, and about the issues which still divide them.[2]*

### I

1. We, the delegates to the ninth assembly of the World Council of Churches, give thanks to the triune God, Father, Son and Holy Spirit, who has brought our churches into living contact and dialogue. By God's grace we have been enabled to remain together, even when this has not been easy. Considerable efforts have been made to overcome divisions. We are "a fellowship of churches which confess the Lord Jesus Christ as God and Saviour according to the scriptures, and therefore seek to fulfil their common calling to the glory of the one God, Father, Son and Holy Spirit".[3] We reaffirm that "the primary purpose of the fellowship of churches in the World Council of Churches is to call one another to visible unity in one faith and in one eucharistic fellowship expressed in worship and in common life in Christ, through witness and service to the world, and to advance towards that unity in order that the world may believe".[4] Our continuing divisions are real wounds to the body of Christ, and God's mission in the world suffers.

2. Churches in the fellowship of the WCC remain committed to one another on the way towards *full visible unity*. This commitment is a gift from our gracious Lord. Unity is both a divine gift and calling. Our churches have affirmed that the unity for which we pray, hope and work is "a koinonia given and expressed in the common confession of the apostolic faith; a common sacramental life entered by the one baptism and celebrated

together in one eucharistic fellowship; a common life in which members and ministries are mutually recognized and reconciled; and a common mission witnessing to the gospel of God's grace to all people and serving the whole of creation".[5] Such koinonia is to be expressed in each place, and through a conciliar relationship of churches in different places. We have much work ahead of us as together we seek to understand the meaning of unity and catholicity, and the significance of baptism.

## II

3.  We confess one, holy, catholic and apostolic church as expressed in the Nicene-Constantinopolitan Creed (381). The church's oneness is an image of the unity of the triune God in the communion of the divine Persons. Holy scripture describes the Christian community as the body of Christ whose inter-related diversity is essential to its wholeness: "Now there are varieties of gifts, but the same Spirit; and there are varieties of services, but the same Lord; and there are varieties of activities, but it is the same God who activates all of them in everyone. To each is given the manifestation of the Spirit for the common good" (1 Cor. 12:4-7).[6] Thus, as the people of God, the body of Christ, and the temple of the Holy Spirit, the church is called to manifest its *oneness in rich diversity*.

4.  The church as communion of believers is created by the word of God, for it is through hearing the *proclamation of the gospel* that faith, by the action of his Holy Spirit, is awakened (Rom. 10:17). Since the good news proclaimed to awaken faith is the good news handed down by the apostles, the church created by it is *apostolic*. Built on the foundation of the apostles and prophets the church is God's household, a *holy* temple in which the Holy Spirit lives and is active. By the power of the Holy Spirit believers grow into a holy temple in the Lord (Eph. 2:21-22).[7]

5.  We affirm that the apostolic faith of the church is one, as the body of Christ is one. Yet there may legitimately be different formulations of the faith of the church. The life of the church as new life in Christ is one. Yet it is built up through different charismata and ministries. The hope of the church is *one*. Yet it is expressed in different human expectations. We acknowledge that there are different ecclesiological starting points, and a range of views on the relation of the church to the churches. Some differences express God's grace and goodness; they must be discerned in God's grace through the Holy Spirit. Other differences divide the church; these must be overcome through the Spirit's gifts of faith, hope, and love so that separation and exclusion do not have the last word. God's "plan for the fullness of time [is] to gather up all things in him" (Eph. 1:10), reconciling human divisions. God calls his people in love to discernment and renewal on the way to the fullness of koinonia.

6.  The *catholicity* of the church expresses the fullness, integrity, and totality of its life in Christ through the Holy Spirit in all times and places. This mystery is expressed in each community of baptized believers in which the apostolic faith is confessed and lived, the gospel is proclaimed, and the sacraments are celebrated. Each church is the church catholic and not simply a part of it. Each church is the church catholic, but not the whole of it. Each church fulfills its catholicity when it is in communion with the other churches. We affirm that the catholicity of the church is expressed most visibly in sharing holy communion and in a mutually recognized and reconciled ministry.

7. The relationship among churches is dynamically interactive. Each church is called to mutual giving and receiving gifts and to *mutual accountability*. Each church must become aware of all that is provisional in its life and have the courage to acknowledge this to other churches. Even today, when eucharistic sharing is not always possible, divided churches express mutual accountability and aspects of catholicity when they pray for one another, share resources, assist one another in times of need, make decisions together, work together for justice, reconciliation and peace, hold one another accountable to the discipleship inherent in baptism, and maintain dialogue in the face of differences, refusing to say "I have no need of you" (1 Cor. 12:21). Apart from one another we are impoverished.

## III

8. All who have been baptized into Christ are united with Christ in his body: "Therefore we have been buried with him by *baptism* into death, so that, just as Christ was raised from the dead by the glory of the Father, so we too might walk in newness of life" (Rom. 6:4). In baptism, the Spirit confers Christ's holiness upon Christ's members. Baptism into union with Christ calls churches to be open and honest with one another, even when doing so is difficult: "But speaking the truth in love, we must grow up in every way into him who is the head, into Christ" (Eph. 4:15). Baptism bestows upon the churches both the freedom and the responsibility to journey towards common proclamation of the word, confession of the one faith, celebration of one eucharist, and full sharing in one ministry. There are some who do not observe the rite of baptism in water but share in the spiritual experience of life in Christ.[8]

9. Our common belonging to Christ through baptism in the name of the Father and of the Son and of the Holy Spirit enables and calls churches to walk together, even when they are in disagreement. We affirm that there is one baptism, just as there is one body and one Spirit, one hope of our calling, one Lord, one faith, one God and Father of us all (cf. Eph. 4:4-6). In God's grace, baptism manifests the reality that *we belong to one another*, even though some churches are not yet able to recognize others as church in the full sense of the word. We recall the words of the Toronto Statement, in which the member churches of the WCC affirm that "the membership of the church of Christ is more inclusive than the membership of their own church body. They seek, therefore, to enter into living contact with those outside their own ranks who confess the Lordship of Christ."[9]

## IV

10. The church as the creation of God's word and Spirit is a mystery, sign and instrument of what God intends for the salvation of the world. The grace of God is expressed in the victory over sin given by Christ, and in the healing and wholeness of the human being. The kingdom of God can be perceived in a *reconciled and reconciling community* called to holiness: a community that strives to overcome the discriminations expressed in sinful social structures, and to work for the healing of divisions in its own life and for

healing and unity in the human community. The church participates in the reconciling ministry of Christ, who emptied himself, when it lives out its mission, affirming and renewing the image of God in all humanity and working alongside all those whose human dignity has been denied by economic, political and social marginalization.

11.  Mission is integral to the life of the church. The church in its mission expresses its calling to proclaim the gospel and to offer the living Christ to the whole creation. The churches find themselves living alongside people of other living faiths and ideologies. As an instrument of God, who is sovereign over the whole creation, the church is called to engage in dialogue and collaboration with them so that its mission brings about the good of all creatures and the well-being of the earth. All churches are called to struggle against sin in all its manifestations, within and around them, and to work with others to combat injustice, alleviate human suffering, overcome violence, and ensure fullness of life for all people.

## V

12.  Throughout its history the World Council of Churches has been a privileged instrument by which churches have been able to listen to one another and speak to one another, engaging issues that challenge the churches and imperil humankind. Churches in the ecumenical movement have also explored divisive questions through multilateral and bilateral dialogues. And yet churches have not always acknowledged their *mutual responsibility* to one another, and have not always recognized the need to give account to one another of their faith, life and witness, as well as to articulate the factors that keep them apart. Bearing in mind the experience of the life we already share and the achievements of multilateral and bilateral dialogues, it is now time to take concrete steps together.

13.  Therefore the ninth assembly calls upon the World Council of Churches to continue to facilitate *deep conversations* among various churches. We also invite all of our churches to engage in the hard task of giving a candid account of the relation of their own faith and order to the faith and order of other churches. Each church is asked to articulate the judgments that shape, and even qualify, its relationship to the others. The honest sharing of commonalities, divergences and differences will help all churches to pursue the things that make for peace and build up the common life.

14.  Towards the goal of full visible unity the churches are called to address recurrent matters in fresh, more pointed ways. Among the questions to be addressed continually by the churches are these:

a)  To what extent can your church discern the faithful expression of the apostolic faith in its own life, prayer and witness and in that of other churches?

b)  Where does your church perceive fidelity to Christ in the faith and life of other churches?

c)  Does your church recognize a common pattern of Christian initiation, grounded in baptism, in the life of other churches?

d)  Why does your church believe that it is necesssary, or permissable, or not possible to share the Lord's supper with those of other churches?

e) In what ways is your church able to recognize the ordered ministries of other churches?

f) To what extent can your church share the spirituality of other churches?

g) How will your church stand with other churches to contend with problems such as social and political hegemonies, persecution, oppression, poverty and violence?

h) To what extent does your church share with other churches in the apostolic mission?

i) To what extent can your church share with other churches in faith formation and theological education?

j) How fully can your church share in prayer with other churches?

In addressing these questions churches will be challenged to recognize areas for renewal in their own lives, and new opportunities to deepen relations with those of other traditions.

## VI

15. Our churches *journey together* in conversation and common action, confident that the Risen Christ will continue to disclose himself as he did in the breaking of bread at Emmaus, and that he will unveil the deeper meaning of fellowship and communion (Luke 24:13-35). Noting the progress made in the ecumenical movement, we encourage our churches to continue on this arduous yet joyous path, trusting in God the Father, Son and Holy Spirit, whose grace transforms our struggles for unity into the fruits of communion.

### Let us listen to what the Spirit is saying to the churches!

NOTES

[1]  The present Invitation to the churches was produced at the request of the central committee of the WCC (2002), in a process organized by the WCC's Faith and Order commission. A first draft was written at a meeting in Nicosia, Cyprus, in March 2004; this was revised (on the basis of extensive comments received from WCC governing bodies, the Faith and Order commission, and the steering committee of the Special Commission) at a second meeting in Nicosia in May 2005. Faith and Order extends on behalf of the WCC its appreciation to the Church of Cyprus, which graciously hosted these preparatory meetings. A final revision took place at the Faith and Order standing commission meeting in Aghios Nikolaos, Crete, in June 2005.

[2]  To assist this process, Faith and Order has produced and sent to the churches a new study document, "The Nature and Mission of the Church: A Stage on the Way to a Common Statement", Faith and Order Paper no. 198.

[3]  Basis, WCC, Constitution, I.

[4]  Purposes and Functions, WCC, Constitution, II.

[5]  "The Unity of the Church as Koinonia: Gift and Calling", Canberra statement, 2.1.

[6]  The scripture quotations contained herein are from the New Revised Standard Version of the Bible, (c) 1989, 1995 by the Division of Christian Education of the National Council of the Churches of Christ in the United States of America, and are used by permission. All rights reserved.

[7]  "The Nature and Mission of the Church", §23.

[8]  Cf. "The Unity of the Church as Koinonia: Gift and Calling", Canberra statement, 3.2.

[9]  Toronto Statement, IV.3

# Abbreviations

| | |
|---|---|
| *AA* | *Apostolicam Actuositatem*: Decree on the Apostolate of the Laity |
| AAALC | All Africa Anglican-Lutheran Commission |
| AACC | All Africa Conference of Churches |
| *AAS* | *Acta Apostolica Sedis* |
| ACC | Anglican Consultative Council |
| AELC | Association of Evangelical Lutheran Churches |
| *AG* | *Ad Gentes*: Decree on the Church's Missionary Activity |
| AIC | African Independent or Instituted Churches |
| ALC | American Lutheran Church |
| ALIC | Anglican-Lutheran International Commission |
| ALICC | Anglican-Lutheran International Continuation Committee |
| ALIWG | Anglican-Lutheran International Working Group |
| AMIC | Anglican-Methodist International Commission |
| Amsterdam | "The Amsterdam Declaration: A Charter for Evangelism in the 21st Century" |
| Apol | Apology of the Augsburg Confession (1531) |
| ARCIC | Anglican-Roman Catholic International Commission |
| ARCUSA | Anglican-Roman Catholic Dialogue in the USA |
| AuCC | Australian Council of Churches |
| | |
| B | Summons to Witness to Christ in Today's World: A Report on the Baptist-Roman Catholic International Conversations 1984-1988 |
| Balamand | "Uniatism: Method of Union of the Past, and the Present Search for Full Communion. Report of the Joint International Commission for the Theological Dialogue between the Roman Catholic Church and the Orthodox Church" (Balamand, 17-24 June 1993) |
| BC | The Book of Concord. The Confessions of the Evangelical Lutheran Church |

| | |
|---|---|
| BEM | *Baptism, Eucharist and Ministry* (Faith and Order commission, World Council of Churches, 1982) |
| *BOD* | The Book of Discipline of the United Methodist Church |
| BU | Building Unity |
| BWA | Baptist World Alliance |
| | |
| *CA* | *Confessio Augustana*: Augsburg Confession |
| CaCC | Caribbean Conference of Churches |
| CCA | Christian Conference of Asia |
| CCANZ | Conference of Churches in Aotearoa-New Zealand |
| *CCC* | Catechism of the Catholic Church |
| CCEE | Consilium Conferentiarum Episcoporum Europae |
| CCM | Called to Common Mission |
| *CD* | *Christus Dominus*: Decree on the Pastoral Office of Bishops in the Church |
| CDF | Congregation for the Doctrine of the Faith |
| CEC | Conference of European Churches |
| CECEF | Conseil d'Eglises chrétiennes en France (Council of Christian Churches in France) |
| CELAM | Latin American Episcopal Conference |
| CIC | Code of Canon Law (1983) |
| CICO | Code of Canon Law for the Eastern Churches (1991) |
| CLAD | Canadian Lutheran-Anglican Dialogue |
| CLAI | Consejo Latinoamericano de Iglesias (Latin American Council of Churches) |
| CMC | Christian Medical Commission |
| CNI | Church of North India |
| COCU | Consultation on Church Union [USA] |
| CONIC | Conselho Nacional das Igrejas Cristãs (National Council of Christian Churches [Brazil]) |
| CTBI | Churches Together in Britain and Ireland |
| CUIC | Churches Uniting in Christ [USA] |
| CUV | Towards a Common Understanding and Vision of the World Council of Churches |
| CW | "Common Witness": A Study Document of the Joint Working Group between the Roman Catholic Church and the World Council of Churches |
| CWC | Christian world communion |
| CWP | "Common Witness and Proselytism: A Study Document," *The Ecumenical Review*, 23, 1, 1971, pp.9-20 |

| | |
|---|---|
| *DH* | *Dignitatis Humanae*: Declaration on Religious Liberty |
| DHn | Denzinger, Heinrich, *Enchiridion Symbolorum Definitionum et Declarationum de Rebus Fidei et Morum*, 37th ed., hrsg. Peter Huenermann, Freiburg, i.B., Herder, 1991 |
| *Directory* | *Directory for the Application of Principles and Norms on Ecumenism* (1993) |
| DS | H. Denzinger and A. Schönmetzer, *Enchiridion Symbolorum* (33rd ed.) |
| *DV* | *Dei Verbum*: Dogmatic Constitution on Divine Revelation |
| | |
| E | See ERCDOM |
| *EC* | *Ecumenical Collaboration at the Regional, National, and Local Levels* |
| ECUSA | Episcopal Church of the United States of America |
| ELCA | Evangelical Lutheran Church in America |
| ELCIC | Evangelical Lutheran Church in Canada |
| EKD | Evangelische Kirche in Deutschland (Evangelical Church in Germany) |
| *EN* | *Evangelii Nuntiandi*: On Evangelization in the Modern World (1975) |
| ERCDOM or E | Evangelical-Roman Catholic Dialogue on Mission 1983 |
| | |
| FABC | Federation of Asian Bishops Conferences |
| FC Ep | Formula of Concord (1577), Epitome |
| FC SD | Formula of Concord (1577), Solid Declaration |
| FRG | Federal Republic of Germany |
| FU | Facing Unity |
| | |
| *GA* | *Growth in Agreement: Reports and Agreed Statements of Ecumenical Conversations on a World Level*, eds Harding Meyer and Lukas Vischer, Faith and Order Paper no. 108, Ecumenical Documents 2, New York and Geneva, Paulist and WCC, 1984 |
| *GC* | *Growing Consensus: Church Dialogues in the United States*, 1962-1991, ed. Joseph A. Burgess and Jeffrey Gros, Ecumenical Documents 5, New York, Paulist, 1995 |
| GDR | German Democratic Republic |
| *GS* | *Gaudium et Spes*: Pastoral Constitution on the Church in the Modern World |
| | |
| IARCCUM | International Anglican-Roman Catholic Commission for Unity and Mission |

| | |
|---|---|
| IASCER | Inter-Anglican Standing Commission on Ecumenical Relations |
| ICC | Irish Council of Churches |
| | |
| J | See JWG |
| JCG | Joint Consultative Group |
| JDDJ | Joint Declaration on the Doctrine of Justification, 1999 |
| JPIC | Justice, Peace and Integrity of Creation (WCC programme unit) |
| JWG or J | Joint Working Group between the Roman Catholic Church and the World Council of Churches |
| | |
| LA | Leuenberg agreement, 1973 |
| Lausanne | "Lausanne Covenant", 1974 |
| LC | Large Catechism of Martin Luther (1529) |
| LCA | Lutheran Church in America |
| LCMS | Lutheran Church – Missouri Synod |
| LCWE | Lausanne Committee on World Evangelization |
| LED | Lutheran-Episcopal Dialogue [USA] |
| *LG* | *Lumen Gentium*: Dogmatic Constitution on the Church |
| LRCJC | Lutheran-Roman Catholic Joint Commission |
| LW | Luther's Works |
| LWF | Lutheran World Federation |
| | |
| Manila | "Manila Manifesto", 1989 |
| MECC | Middle East Council of Churches |
| MWC | Mennonite World Conference |
| | |
| *NA* | *Nostra Aetate*: Declaration on the Church's Relations with Non-Christian Religions |
| NCC | national council of churches |
| NCCA | National Council of Churches in Australia |
| NRMs | New Religious Movements |
| | |
| OAIC | Organization of African Instituted Churches |
| *OE* | *Orientalium Ecclesiarum*: Decree on the Catholic Eastern Churches |
| *OL* | *Orientale Lumen*: Light of the East |
| | |
| *P* | *Evangelization, Proselytism and Common Witness* |
| PCC | Pacific Conference of Churches |
| PCCW | The Presence of Christ in the Church and World |

| | |
|---|---|
| PCFNA | Pentecostal Charismatic Fellowship of North America |
| PCID | Pontifical Council for Interreligious Dialogue |
| PCPCU | Pontifical Council for Promoting Christian Unity |
| PCR | Programme to Combat Racism (WCC) |
| PCS | Porvoo Common Statement |
| *PL* | *Patrologia Latina* |
| PNG | Papua New Guinea |
| *PO* | *Presbyterorum Ordinis*: Decree on the Life and Ministry of Priests |
| | |
| REO | regional ecumenical organization |
| *RM* | *Redemptoris Missio*: On the Permanent Validity of the Church's Missionary Mandate |
| | |
| SA | Smalcald Articles (1537) |
| Santiago | *On the Way to Fuller Koinonia: Official Report of the Fifth World Conference on Faith and Order* [Santiago de Compostela, 3-14 August 1993], eds Thomas F. Best and Günther Gassmann, Faith and Order Paper no. 166, WCC, 1994 |
| *SC* | *Sacrosanctum Concilium*: Constitution on the Sacred Liturgy |
| SECAM | Symposium of Episcopal Conferences of Africa and Madagascar |
| | |
| *UR* | *Unitatis Redintegratio*: Decree on Ecumenism |
| *UUS* | *Ut Unum Sint*: That They May Be One |
| | |
| WA | Martin Luther, *Werke*, Weimarer Ausgabe |
| WARC | World Alliance of Reformed Churches |
| WC | Ways to Community (Roman Catholic-Lutheran Commission, 1981) |
| WCC | World Council of Churches |
| WEA | World Evangelical Alliance |
| WEF | World Evangelical Fellowship (now Alliance) |
| WMC | World Methodist Council |
| WMC/RC | Joint Commission for Dialogue between the Roman Catholic Church and the World Methodist Council |
| | |
| YMCA | Young Men's Christian Association |

This printer has a green label guaranteeing environmentally-friendly printing procedures.

IMPRIMERIE
LUSSAUD
OFFSET&NUMERIQUE

L'impression et le façonnage de cet ouvrage
ont été réalisés à l'Imprimerie LUSSAUD
85200 FONTENAY-LE-COMTE

Dépôt légal 2<sup>e</sup> trimestre 2007 - n° 4390
N° d'impression : 205130